# Classical Myth and Legend
# in Renaissance Dictionaries

# Classical Myth and Legend in Renaissance Dictionaries

A STUDY OF RENAISSANCE DICTIONARIES
IN THEIR RELATION TO THE CLASSICAL LEARNING
OF CONTEMPORARY ENGLISH WRITERS

BY

DeWITT T. STARNES
and
ERNEST WILLIAM TALBERT

*CHAPEL HILL*

THE UNIVERSITY OF NORTH CAROLINA PRESS

# PREFACE

THE STUDY HERE PRESENTED WAS CONCEIVED AND BEGUN BY THE authors more than twelve years ago and has been carried on, not without interruptions, to the present stage. It is not exhaustive but it is sufficient to demonstrate the significance of contemporary dictionaries for Renaissance authors.

On the ultimate classical sources of the major writers of the English Renaissance, editors and commentators have done much scholarly work, work that has been indispensable as a basis for our own study. The value of this earlier work we would not minimize or disparage. We are convinced, however, that, to the present day, Renaissance scholars have paid too little heed to contemporary reference books which were sources of classical lore for authors and readers. We refer especially to Latin and Latin-English dictionaries, including those devoted solely to proper names as well as those treating them in special sections of the text or distributing them with other parts of speech through the alphabet. As a concise account of these lexicons is given in our first chapter, we need not dwell upon them here.

Our aim in this study is to show the immense vogue of these popular reference dictionaries (and, incidentally, of other compendiums of classical learning, such as Comes' *Mythologiae*), and to supply evidence which strongly suggests that these books were frequently consulted, even by major authors—Spenser, Ben Jonson, and Milton, for example—and that, in many instances, the dictionaries contributed definitely to the phrasing and content of the great poetry and drama of the period.

If our thesis is tenable—and we think it is well supported—then our study throws new light on the workmanship of the major writers of the English Renaissance. It shows also what knowledge of classical myth and history was common to the authors and their readers, or, if not known to the readers, easily available in the current popular reference books. General recognition of these conditions should result in simplifying and clarifying lines and passages in some of the more important writings which hitherto have called forth much learned comment but little illumination.

Although the authors of *Classical Myth and Legend* have collaborated in the book as a whole and in some individual chapters, the division of labor in general may be stated as follows. For Chapters I, III, IV, V, VII, and VIII, Mr. Starnes is largely responsible; for Chapters II and VI of the text proper and for the three Appendices, Mr. Talbert assumes responsibility.

For permission to use, in revised form, matter published earlier on Ben Jonson and the dictionaries, Mr. Talbert acknowledges the courtesy of the editors of the *Philological Quarterly, Studies in Philology,* and the University of Texas *Studies in English;* to the same journals and also the *Library Chronicle* of the University of Texas, and *Notes & Queries,* Mr. Starnes is indebted for permission to reprint with revisions matter which first appeared in those journals.

For courteous and useful services in our researches, we wish to express our gratitude to the librarians and assistants in the British Museum, the Bodleian, Cambridge University, Duke University, the University of North Carolina, the Folger Shakespeare Library, the Library of Congress, and the University of Texas Library.

To the Research Council of Duke University and to the Folger Shakespeare Library, we owe thanks for grants to defray a portion of the expenses incurred while preparing this study. For subsidies to aid in its publication, we thank the Research Council of the University of Texas and the University of North Carolina Press.

D. T. S.<br>E. W. T.

# CONTENTS

# ILLUSTRATIONS

# Classical Myth and Legend
# in Renaissance Dictionaries

CHAPTER I

# THE SINEWS OF POETRY IN RENAISSANCE

# DICTIONARIES

A S THE RENAISSANCE DICTIONARIES WHICH ARE BASIC IN THIS study are relatively rare and sparsely distributed, it seems desirable to present at once a brief account of the texts to which we constantly refer. Such a survey will reveal certain concise sources of information, with respect to history, legend, and mythology, well known to authors and readers in the sixteenth and seventeenth centuries, but little regarded by scholars of the present day.

In his Greek dictionary of the tenth century, not to go further back, Suidas[1] includes in his alphabetical list of words a considerable number of proper names—names of persons and places together with succinct biographic or geographic information on each name. With the advent of printing in the fifteenth century the lexicon of Suidas became widely known and constituted a source, especially as to proper names, for Renaissance lexicographers. John Balbus' *Catholicon*,[2] a large Latin dictionary compiled near the end of the thirteenth century, likewise contained proper names, biblical and classical, with their legends. First printed in 1460, and frequently thereafter, the *Catholicon* was one of the most influential lexicons of the fifteenth century. In 1489 Nicholas Perottus published his *Cornucopiae*,[3] a commentary on the epigrams of Martial, which in its extensive exposition of Latin terms, including proper nouns, contained the materials of a Latin dictionary with more insistence on classical authority than had appeared in Suidas or in Balbus.

The *Cornucopiae* was a major source for the *Dictionarium* (1502)[4] of Friar Ambrosius Calepine, a Latin dictionary at first and later a polyglot destined to continue its vogue for two hundred years. Calepine borrowed materials from Perottus and followed his precedent and that of Suidas and Balbus in inserting proper-name entries along with the definitions of other parts of speech. The practice of including in the general dictionary the names of places and persons, historical, legendary, and mythical, with descriptive and biographical sketches, continues in the *Thesaurus Linguae Latinae* (1531; 1543)[5] of Robert Stephanus—a thesaurus superior in its Latinity and in its adherence to classical authority to any of the texts mentioned above, and of much significance in the history of lexicography.

The dictionaries of Suidas, Balbus, Perottus, Calepine, and Stephanus, with their dispersed proper-name entries, were, then, in vogue when Sir Thomas Elyot first published his Latin-English *Dictionary* in 1538. Elyot, admittedly indebted to Suidas and Calepine and, later, to Robert Stephanus, maintains the tradition of his predecessors in including proper names in his general dictionary, increasing the number of entries in the editions of 1542 and 1545—editions published with the title *Bibliotheca Eliotae: Eliot's Library*. In the revisions of the *Bibliotheca*, 1548, 1552, 1559, Thomas Cooper further extended the entries on persons and places, and thus enhanced the historic, geographic, and mythic.

Personal and place names in the *Bibliotheca*, with their accompanying sketches, Cooper took over in his *Thesaurus Linguae Romanae & Britannicae* (1565), grouping them, however, in a separate section under the heading *Dictionarium Historicum et Poeticum propria Locorum et Personarum Vocabula*. Precedent for this arrangement he found in a type of dictionary devoted wholly to proper names; in vogue, as we shall see, from the end of the fifteenth century. Cooper's *Thesaurus*, with subsequent printings in 1573, 1578, 1584, and 1587, was the recognized authority in the schools and among scholars generally in the last quarter of the sixteenth century. The vogue and prestige of the *Thesaurus* seem to have determined for succeeding English lexicographers in the sixteenth and seventeenth centuries the arrangement of proper names in an independent section of the general dictionary.

As early as 1587 Thomas Thomas followed a similar grouping in his *Dictionarium Linguae Latinae et Anglicanae*, a dictionary which went through ten editions by 1620.[6] In the augmentation of John Rider's *Bibliotheca Scholastica* in 1606, Francis Holyoke added, besides the Latin-English division, an index of proper names, indicating by the separate title, as Cooper had done, that this was a poetic, historic, and geographic dictionary. By 1659 there were at least six subsequent editions of the Rider-Holyoke dictionaries.

After the Restoration this type of organization was continued in the large dictionaries, Latin-English and English-Latin, of Francis Gouldman (1664),[7] of Thomas Holyoke (1677), and of Adam Littleton (1678).[8] Although new entries and new materials were introduced from time to time, all these lexicographers owed much to their predecessors of the sixteenth century—to Calepine and Stephanus, and especially to the Elyot-Cooper dictionaries. In 1678, for example, Adam Littleton alludes to the myths and legends recounted in the proper-name section of his dictionary and admits that many of the stories were taken from Elyot and Cooper though somewhat amended to conform to the refined diction of his own day. Littleton asserts further that such stories were used as *dictamens* or theme topics for schoolboys. The wish of every lexicographer of the period to make his dictionary useful to schools and schoolboys, whether or not designed primarily for them, was undoubtedly a factor in the continued emphasis on proper names and the associated myths and stories. Another factor, perhaps more potent, was the competition offered by dictionaries devoted exclusively to the elucidation of proper names involving myth and legend and history and designed to be helpful to readers of classical poetry and history. In response to the demands for such aids, a lexicon historical, geographical, and poetic had evolved and had become immensely popular.

The earliest dictionary of this kind was written by Herman Torrentinus (*ca.* 1450-1520). Torrentinus—Van Beeck, in the vernacular—was a Dutch scholar who, in the 1490's, was professor of rhetoric in the college of Groningen. At Deventer, in 1498, Torrentinus first published his small Latin manual with the title

Elucidarius carminum et historiarum vel Vocabularius poeticus, continens fabulas, historias, provincias, urbes, insulas, fluvios, et montes illustres. . . .[9]

In the address to the reader, the author explains why he compiled the *Elucidarius*[10] and what authorities he had followed. His students and other friends, knowing the reputation of their teacher as a classical scholar, frequently came to him, he tells us, for explanation of allusions and for comment on the meaning of the classical Latin poems then being printed and eagerly studied. Being himself the editor of some of these poems (for example, *Commentarius in Bucolica ac Georgica Virgilii*), Torrentinus felt impelled to comply with their requests. He found, however, that various readers often sought information about the same names and al-

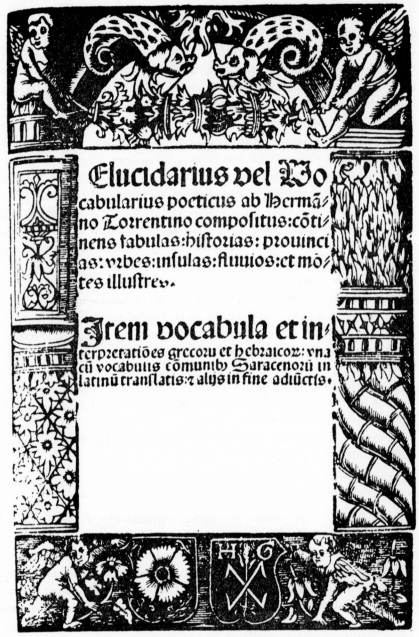

Title page of Torrentinus' *Elucidarius Poeticus,* printed at The Hague, 1514, from a copy in the University of Texas Library.

lusions, and, as a result, his explanations had frequently to be repeated. He decided therefore that it would be a service to his friends and economy of his own time to collect and publish in a small volume his comments on subjects which elicited recurrent inquiry. He explains specifically that his expositions are concerned with the names of gods and their fables, with celebrated men, with countries and islands, with cities, and with rivers, lakes, and mountains. He hopes that his book may be profitable to the studious readers of poetry and history and even of the Holy Scriptures.

To establish confidence in the authority of his work, Torrentinus assures his readers that the matter has been gathered from approved writers; to wit, Sallust, Livy, Strabo, Pliny, Justinus, Virgil, Ovid, Perottus, Tortellius; and the Greek-Latin lexicon of Ioannis Crastoni, the Carmelite.[11] It is clear, from the address to the reader, that the purpose of the *Elucidarius* is to help the less cultivated to an understanding of poetry and history by supplying in concise form information on unfamiliar classical names. A few entries from the *Elucidarius*[12] will show the author's method:

### ADONIS

Adonis was the son of King Cynaras, by his daughter Myrrha. As Adonis was a beautiful boy, he was beloved by Venus. Finally, he was killed by a boar, and yearly festivals of mourning were instituted for him. It is feigned that his blood was changed into a flower. Adonis had a temple in Byblus, a city of Phoenicia. A river near the city of Byblus is also called Adonis.

### AEOLUS

Aeolus was the son of Jupiter from Acesta, the daughter of Hippotes the Trojan, from whom he is called Hippotades. Ovidius. *Aeolon hippotaden cohibentem carcere ventos.* He ruled in Aeolia. He found out the reason for the winds and forecast storms. By the poets he is called the king and the god of the winds.

### AETNA

Aetna is a mountain of Sicily, frightful because of its perpetual fiery globes.

### DODONA

Dodona was a town of Epirus, near which was a grove of oak trees, sacred to Jove. In these, doves once gave responses.

### GENIUS

Genius was called by the ancients the god of Nature, who had the power of procreating all things. For everything born, there was said to be a genius. Some assign to each man two genii: a good and an evil one, just as theologians ascribe two angels. Genius is taken also for Nature itself. *Vt suum fraudans genium.*

## HESPERIDES

The Hesperides were the daughters of Hesperus, or as some write of Atlas, and were called Aegle, Arethusa, and Hesperethusa. They had most delightful gardens in Africa, near the city of Lixos. In these were golden apples which a wakeful dragon guarded. But Hercules, sent by Eurystheus, killed the dragon and carried away the apples. But all these things are fables.

## PARNASSUS

Parnassus is a mountain in Phocis, having two peaks, which some wrongly call Citheron and Helicon, for these are mountains themselves. Parnassus was sacred to Apollo and Bacchus. Hence the poets are said to frequent it, and the muses are called Parnassides.

## PROMETHEUS

Prometheus, son of Iapetus, fashioned images from clay. Hence they say that he made men. They feign that he ascended to heaven and with his ferule stole fire with which he gave life to an image he had made. Wherefore, Jupiter was angry and caused Prometheus to be bound to a rock on Mt. Caucasus and sent an eagle to eat away his heart.

The *Elucidarius* obviously fulfilled a need. Its popularity was immediate and long-sustained. At least eleven editions were printed in various cities on the Continent between 1498 and 1518.[13] After Torrentinus' death in 1520, the *Elucidarius* was frequently reissued with augmentations, first by Robert Stephanus[14] and then by his brother Charles. As Robert expanded the scope of the book, the original title was gradually subordinated, as indicated by the following title-page:

Dictionarium poeticum quod vulgo inscribitur Elucidarius carminum . . . Parisiis, 1530.[15]

Before 1555 the *Elucidarius* as revised by the Stephani had suffered a sea-change. This work had been so much extended in scope and so augmented by Charles Stephanus that he was justified in publishing the enlarged volume under a new title with his own name on the title-page:

Dictionarium historicum ac poeticum, omnia gentium, hominum, locorum, fluminum ac montium antiqua recentioraque, ad sacras ac prophanas historias poetarumque fabulas intelligendas necessaria, vocabula . . . Lutetiae . . . C. Stephani, 1553.

Stephanus' book, a direct offshoot of the *Elucidarius,* enjoyed even greater popularity than the original. At least nine editions, with slightly expanded title-pages, were printed in various continental cities between 1553 and 1600. The vogue continued through the seventeenth century, eleven other editions having been published by 1693,[16] some on the Continent, some in England.

After the death of Charles Stephanus in 1559, his *Dictionarium* continued to be augmented by subsequent editors whose names are not known. New entries appear, though much of the increase is found in the elaboration and enrichment of original entries, the editors drawing freely from recent geographical works such as those of Ortelius, and from sixteenth-century mythological treatises such as Comes' *Mythologiae* and Cartari's *Imagines Deorum,* so that for students and authors and readers the *Dictionarium* by 1600 had become increasingly significant. Comparison of entries above—*Adonis, Aeolus, Aetna,* for example—with the same entries in the 1595 *Dictionarium* of C. Stephanus, will show that, though these items were retained from Torrentinus, they were elaborated with important details drawn from many sources.

To recapitulate, we may say that the *Elucidarius,* first published in 1498, as a small handbook to assist students in understanding poetry and history, ran through numerous editions in the original and in translation during the sixteenth century. It acquired new life and usefulness through the augmentations by the Stephanus brothers, finally becoming the basis of Charles Stephanus' *Dictionarium.* This grandchild of Torrentinus seems to have been especially cherished by English poets and dramatists in the Renaissance. After many printings in the sixteenth and seventeenth centuries, the *Dictionarium* became at last the basis of Louis Moreri's encyclopedic *Grand Dictionnaire Historique* (Lyon, 1674).[17]

But the influence of Charles Stephanus' *Dictionarium* was not destined to end with the seventeenth century. In 1788 Lempriere compiled his *Classical Dictionary, containing A Full Account of all the proper names in Ancient Authors.* He drew heavily from a late edition—probably 1670 or 1685—of the Stephanus *Dictionarium,* as a comparison of the texts will readily reveal. And the Lempriere had a wide vogue throughout the nineteenth century.[18] In 1794 Herman Bosscha, a Dutch scholar, published at Daventry his *Bibliotheca Classica . . . quo Nomina Propria Pleraque apud Scriptores Graecos et Romanos.* Bosscha refers, in his introduction, to Lempriere's debt to Stephanus as edited by Lloyd. Though Bosscha himself may owe something to Lempriere, both compilers profited greatly by constantly consulting the Stephanus. Bosscha's Latin frequently corresponds verbatim with that of Stephanus, and Lempriere has many literal translations from the same source. This is not to imply that Stephanus was a sole source for either of the eighteenth-century compilers, but it is worth noting that the Stephanus *Dictionarium* was still a valuable reference work, and that, through Lempriere and Bosscha, is demonstrated the continuity of the work of Torrentinus and Stephanus from the end of the fifteenth century to the end of the nineteenth.

CHAPTER II

# THE DICTIONARIES AND THE SCHOOLS

O THE PRESENT AGE, SURFEITED WITH CLAIMS MADE BY A LEGION
of publishers, the connotation of the word "dictionary" may almost
obscure the soundness and the importance of the information filed
between the covers of the works of reference that have been enumerated in
the preceding chapter. Yet even a brief consideration of the material just
surveyed should go far toward dispelling such a predisposition. The
origin and purpose of Torrentinus' *Elucidarius Poeticus,* of Calepine's
*Dictionarium,* and of the genuinely studious, scholarly, and far-reaching
mutations which they underwent at the hands of the Stephanus brothers
testify to the need felt by the age for sound reference works that would
provide editor, scholar, or courtly reader with reliable materials for understanding the literary productions of the ancient world or for acquiring the
age's indispensable veneer of learning.

A brief consideration of the fortunes of Calepine will illustrate the point,
though the *Dictionarium* of the Italian monk was criticized more frequently perhaps than was any other compilation in the group with which we are
primarily concerned. Having been surpassed by the *Thesaurus* of Robert
Stephanus as a guide to the Latin tongue, the *Dictionarium* branched out
as a polyglot lexicon. By the seventeenth century it had been edited and
re-edited until it was so thoroughly overlaid with additions and accretions
that Olaus Borrichius, the learned Dane, could refer to it with contemptuous
familiarity: "Bonus ille Calepinus toties coctus et recoctus parum sapit."
Yet until the first half of the eighteenth century the *Dictionarium,* in one or
another of its editions, was generally relied upon by Latinists in Italy.[1]
Out of its re-editing in France arose Robert Stephanus' *Dictionarium sive
Thesaurus* of 1543, a compilation that appeared almost simultaneously
with Dolet's *Commentarii Linguae Latinae* (1536-8) and thereby marked

what Sandys calls "an epoch in the history of Scholarship."[2] Such a work
could never have been accomplished without the aid of many precursors
and contemporaries, and in his prefatory pages Robert Stephanus spoke of
his indebtedness to individuals and listed the classical, medieval, and
modern treatises that he had found most useful. At one point Calepine
was singled out with these words: "Pro testimoniis authorum minus lo-
cupletium, quibus saepe vsus est Calepinus, ex probatissimis exempla at-
tulimus." Although the words may imply the fact that Calepine was at
times inaccurate and that his examples sometimes could perpetrate barbar-
isms, with commendable justness Robert included his predecessor in his
list of grammatical authorities and thus Calepine appeared with Cato, Varro,
Cicero, Quintilian, Strabo, Macrobius, Servius, Priscian, Erasmus, Linacre,
and Alciatus. The fifteenth-century Italian monk also found himself in
the company of Guillaume Budé, the luminary of the new humanism to
whom Robert Stephanus felt particularly indebted. As Robert noted
twice in the pages prefatory to the *Thesaurus,* the famous scholar
had aided immeasurably in preparing the 1543 edition—an enterprise
that must have been most congenial to the author of *De Asse et
Partibus* and *De Transitu Hellenismi ad Christianismum.* Robert consequently testifies to what descriptions of the work in the previous chapter
have indicated; namely, that the erudition and the relative completeness of
Calepine's *Dictionarium* were neither negligible nor commonplace to the
Renaissance.

In England the story is not essentially different. Until the lexicographical work by Charles and Robert Stephanus and by Elyot and Cooper made
itself felt, the compilation by Calepine was pretty clearly the standard work
of reference for students of Latin. Although Luis Vives expressed dis-
satisfaction with Calepine a century before Olaus Borrichius did, the
Spaniard's references to the work as they apply to the English scene indicate that Vives considered the *Dictionarium* and the *Cornucopiae* by
Perottus to be the best available lexicons. In his plan of study for Charles
Mountjoy, one finds that the *Dictionarium* and the *Cornucopiae* lack "com-
prehensiveness, scholarliness, accuracy" but that the works by Varro,
Festus, and Marcellus are too difficult.[3] To Vives there are no satisfactory
vocabularies of the Latin tongue. Some lexicon, however, was indispensable; and Vives' condemnation of Calepine's lack of scholarliness should be
read in conjunction with his precepts (1523) for the education of the
Princess Mary. Although Mary was a woman, the plan for her training

emanated from the outstanding authority on female discipline; and as with the education of all royalty, we should expect that the material to be used would be the best available. Consequently, when Vives recommends that the Christian Princess study Christian poets, he also recommends a "Calepine for instance or Perottus, to which she may refer, being stuck on the Latin word."[4]

A similar but even more revealing indication of the attitude toward Calepine shown by the early Renaissance in England occurs in some notes made by the Oxford bookseller John Dorne three years before Vives wrote about Princess Mary's education. From Dorne's *Day-Book* we learn that during a portion of the year 1520 a Calepine was bought not infrequently when a purchaser acquired individual or collected works of ancient authors—a Latin edition of Dionysius, presumably the Areopagite; the works of Virgil, with commentary; or an edition of Cicero's *Offices,* with commentary. Dorne's best sellers were academic texts, particularly those written or compiled by Erasmus. Of the Latins prescribed for study in the academic curriculum, works of Terence, Cicero, Virgil, and Ovid, or copies of works derived from their texts, sold most frequently. The *Dictionarium,* however, had a steady sale, comparable to that maintained by Horace, Pliny, Seneca, or Sallust.[5] Similarly, as late as 1556 George Medley generously purchased for his nephew attending Saffron Walden grammar school not only "a dixionarie in Englysshe" but also a *"Colopine cum onomastico,"* that is, a copy of the *Dictionarium* that contained the "Onomasticon Latinogrecum." Indeed, Medley's nephew, Francis Willoughby, had for his private use a number of texts usually found in the libraries of grammar schools or colleges—good editions with commentaries of Terence and of Cicero's *Epistles* as well as copies of Erasmus' *Adagia* and *Copia* and of Valla's *De Elegantia Linguae Latinae.*[6]

When the *Dictionarium* was expanded into a polyglot lexicon, it of course filled a need not satisfied by the thesauri that otherwise replaced it. In 1573 the Chancellor, Lord Glammis, considered a Calepine that referred to seven languages to be a fitting gift for James VI; apparently it accorded with the Chancellor's dignity and with a hope, which might be expressed thereby, for young James's progress.[7] In the same year appears the earliest recorded purchase of a book for St. Paul's library (1572-3), a purchase that may well refer to the polyglot Calepine:

Allowed Mr. Malim for a new Lexicon or Dictionary in Latin, Greek, Hebrew,

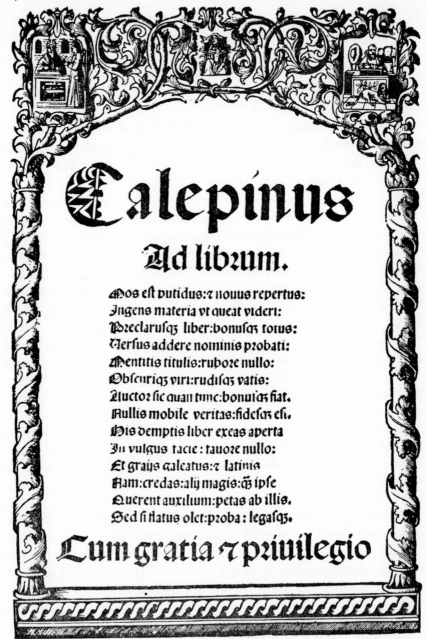

# Calepinus

## Ad librum.

Mos est putidus:z nouus repertus:
Ingens materia vt queat videri:
Præclarusqz liber:bonusqz totus:
Versus addere nominis probati:
Mentitis titulis:rubore nullo:
Obscuriqz viri:rudisqz vatis:
Auctor sic quam tunc:bonuiqz fiat.
Nullis mobile veritas:fidesqz est.
His demptis liber exeas aperta
In vulgus tacie : tauore nullo:
Et graijs galeatus:z latinis
Nam:credas:alij magis:qz ipse
Querent auxilium:petas ab illis.
Sed si flatus olet:proba : legasqz.

## Cum gratia z priuilegio

Title page of Calepine's *Dictionarium,* printed in Venice, 1509, from a copy in the University of Texas Library.

French, Spanish, and High Dutch, always to remain as an implement to the Schole, well turned and bossed, xix *s*.[8]

Whether this particular copy was lost, worn out by use, or supplemented by another edition we do not know.  At least one other *Dictionarium,* however, was bought for the same library, for in 1590-1 appears the notation that "Callipin's Dictionary" cost 1.2*s*.[9]  Two copies of the *Dictionarium* were in the library of St. Leonard's college at the turn of the century, and as late as *ca.* 1612 a professor of theology considered the common library of St. Andrew's to be the appropriate place both for a copy of Calepine and for the standard Greek lexicon by Scapula.[10]

It is not surprising, then, that the dictionary which went under the name of a fifteenth-century Italian monk was so well known by John Donne's audience that the point of one of his barbs thrown at a conventional object of satire could reside in a reference to this polyglot lexicon.  When in his third Satire, Donne attacked the traveller—"A thing . . . Stranger than seaven Antiquaries studies"—he ridiculed the vapid flattery of the creature and particularly its pretensions to learning acquired abroad.  Such a thing had "travail'd" and consequently boasts that it "speaks all tongues."

> He saith, Sir,
> I love your judgement; Whom doe you prefer,
> For the best linguist? and I seelily
> Said, that I thought Calepine's Dictionarie.
>
> (ll. 51-54)

As a number of the preceding details show, the dictionaries reached a wide and presumably studious audience.  At the very end of the fifteenth century, the zealous readers of Torrentinus were his students and his "other friends," those who also used his editions of the *Georgics,* for example, and his commentaries on that text.  As the sixteenth century progressed, the dictionaries with which we are concerned naturally found their way into the schools and thereby became one of the means whereby the solid learning and literature of the ancient world could form part of the fundamental discipline of a new generation.  Even a cursory survey of lists of books found in English libraries of the period reveals that the compilations by Elyot and Cooper, by Charles and Robert Stephanus, were considered more fundamental, more necessary for a reference, or "common," library than was the *Dictionarium* by Calepine.  The two thesauri, for example, were among the chained books that Archbishop Parker had provided for the

common use of his Norwich scholars during the years that Christopher
Marlowe held the Archbishop's Canterbury scholarship;[11] and the reason
for Parker's gift is particularly interesting in that it accords with one of
Charles Hoole's precepts published as late as 1660. When Hoole's students
had completed work in the sixth form and were ready for the university, he
would have them purchase for future use texts of the Latin and Greek
orators and poets. For those authors that "they cannot understand without
a Commentary or Scholiast," they should procure "those whereby they may
best help themselves." But for future work at the universities they should
have "ever at hand" five basic reference works, of which Robert Stephanus'
*Thesaurus* is one, the others being Suidas, Hesychius, Budé's commentaries
and the Greek thesaurus by Henry Stephanus.[12] Similarly, when in 1574
Archbishop Parker allotted six rooms to his Norwich scholars and furnished
at least three of them, he provided that "the Under-Chamber of the Tenth
Chamber on the East Side" should be their common library and procured
for them nine books, including Cooper's *Thesaurus* and Robert Stephanus'
*Thesaurus,* books that the students "must otherwise have gone out of their
Purses to provide."[13]    Indeed as late as 1612, when James gave to the
common library of St. Andrews the then definitive *Thesaurus Linguae
Graecae* by Robert Stephanus' son Henry, Queen Anne gave the equally
definitive *Thesaurus Linguae Latinae.*[14]    We have already noted the presence of a Calepine there. Undoubtedly the dictionary by Charles Stephanus
might have been found there too, as it could have been, for example, at
the Bodleian.[15]

   At the end of our period, Hoole likewise notices the usefulness of
Cooper's *Thesaurus* and also of Charles Stephanus' proper-name dictionary
when he discusses the work of the fourth and fifth forms.    The two lexicons, as well as Robert Stephanus' *Thesaurus,* he considers to be works
helpful and necessary to scholars "in performing their tasks with more ease
and benefit."    Since not all students in a grammar school, particularly the
beginners, would have as much need of some of these subsidiary texts as
would others, and since the total number of such texts would be "more than
any one will desire to buy," the lexicons by Cooper, by Charles Stephanus,
and by Robert Stephanus, along with other comparable aids to study and
good editions of the best authors, were to be "laid up in the Schoole
Library, for every Form to make use on, as they shall have occasion."[16]
In this respect, as in many others, Hoole was continuing the practice of
grammar schools in sixteenth-century England.    Indeed, twelve years be-

fore Parker furnished the nucleus of a common library for his Norwich scholars at Cambridge, he had similarly concerned himself with the common library of at least one grammar school. A notation of April 5, 1562, indicates that the Archbishop, like Hoole, desired at least some of the lexicons with which we are concerned to be available for every form. On that date Alderman Thomas Parker brought into the court of the corporation five books as gifts from the Archbishop for the Norwich grammar school, two of which were Robert Stephanus' *Thesaurus* and Elyot's *Bibliotheca* (for Cooper's *Thesaurus* had not yet appeared).[17]

Like other academic texts and aids to scholarship, dictionaries were compiled for various levels of accomplishment. Lexicons of the Latin-English type, more elementary and more manageable than Cooper's *Thesaurus,* were provided for pupils of the lower forms; but the works by Calepine, by Charles and Robert Stephanus, by Elyot, and later by Cooper, were to be available as reference works. Purchases for the library at St. Paul's, for example, accord with the practice of Schoolmaster Hoole and the actions of Archbishop Parker. In 1582-3, for the grammar school that John Milton was to attend, there was bought a "Thesaurus Ling[uae] Lat [inae] Steph[anus] in 2 vols," presumably the 1543 edition; a "Thesaurus Cowperi"; and a "Dictionarius Historicus and Poeticus [*sic*]," in all probability the lexicon of proper names by Charles Stephanus. As we have noticed, a copy of Calepine's dictionary was already there. Of these works, apparently the Cooper was used most frequently, for records have survived of the purchase of another copy in 1590-1 and yet again in 1614-5.[18]

All books in a common library received hard use, as the records of the library at the Merchant Taylors' School clearly indicate. There at Spenser's school, as at Milton's, might be found by 1599 a Cooper and presumably a Charles Stephanus ("Dictionarium poeticum. 4to"). Just as at least one Calepine may have been worn out at St. Paul's, so among other references to the Merchant Taylors' library occurs a note of 1650 concerning ten books "that are wanted in the Schoole (the old ones being through long vse) worne out." Three of the ten are a Calepine, a Cooper's *Thesaurus,* and—in all probability—a copy of the compilation by Charles Stephanus, i.e., a "Poeticum dictionarium" that cost the same amount as the "Dictionarius Historicus and Poeticus" mentioned above.[19] At St. Albans likewise, the phrase "vetus and laceratus" is attached to the 1624-6 notice of the "one remaining Cooper"; for in 1587-8 there had been at

least two Coopers in the library. It is also interesting to note that in
1597-8 one of the books given by the scholars to the common library of
St. Albans was "An historicall and poeticall Dictionary."[20] Indeed, the
continued presence of these lexicons in the school libraries of the period
indicates what we have noted before; namely, that those concerned with
perpetuating an educational program recognized the soundness and the
importance of the information filed between the covers of these dictionaries.

In view of such considerations, it is not surprising to find that the lexicons here discussed also appeared in the libraries of such diverse individuals
as Queen Mary, John Palsgrave, King James, Robert Burton, Elizabeth's
embezzling teller Richard Stonely, and Elizabeth herself.[21] Also interesting
to note is the fact that the *Elucidarius Poeticus* by Torrentinus, which was
the earliest example of a proper-name dictionary, but a work vastly inferior
to the compilations that grew out of it, appears early in the sixteenth
century as a volume in the library of one who was scholarly enough to
have read "Rodolphes logike, publikly in the vniversities"[22] and that late
in the century it was in the library of Richard Stonely and valued at the
same price as Alciati's *Emblems*. Both works in all probability were relics
of Stonely's school days, when undoubtedly he was taught a "moral virtue"
much better than the one he practiced. The history of our dictionaries,
however, does not always run from scholar to embezzler. Elyot's lexicon
and one of the early editions of Robert Stephanus' *Thesaurus* were on
John Palsgrave's desk in 1540 as he prepared his translation of the play
*Acolastus* in hopes that it would become the authoritative text for the study
of familiar Latin.[23] But later in the century another writer of plays,
Shakespeare, "pretty clearly used Cooper constantly as his Latin-English
reference dictionary," a habit that he probably formed when attending
grammar school; for a copy of Cooper had been in the common library at
Stratford-on-Avon since 1565.[24]

The way in which these dictionaries were used from the days of Robert
Stephanus to those of John Donne indicates the importance that the lexicons
may have for modern students of literature and of the humanities. Like the
treatises on schemes and tropes, like the commonplace books that ranged
from vernacular adaptations to Latin volumes by Erasmus and Nannus
Mirabellius Dominicus, the lexicons found their way into academic and
private libraries because Renaissance pedagogy emphasized continual, rep-
etitious parsing, the elucidation of proper names, a detailed analysis of

devices of ornamentation, the scanning and proving of verses, and similar exercises involved in the process of prelection, double translation, paraphrase, and imitation. Ideally such a procedure led to composition without an example. In view of the preceding details there is little need perhaps to elaborate upon the hard use given the lexicons by Renaissance schoolboys, by contemporaries of Spenser, Shakespeare, Jonson, and Milton. We should note, however, that the dictionaries would be used frequently when ancient poetry was studied and that they might be used not only by those "stuck on the Latin word," but also by those engaged in the process of paraphrase and imitation which accompanied the study of any particular author or any particular type of literature.

In his preface to the *Thesaurus* Cooper, for example, enumerates the uses of his lexicon. From its pages one may learn accent, pronunciation, and such information as the various meanings, uses, and constructions of Latin words, elegant phrases, and metaphors. As master of Magdalen College school, he knew that teachers were also anxious for their students to acquire "copy," Erasmus' *copia;* and as lexicographer, he so designed the *Thesaurus.* Consequently, according to Cooper, the student will find that the *Thesaurus* can serve also as a sort of commonplace-book, that it can be used to fill a collection designed to aid the writer in varying and amplifying his discourse with pithy sentences, impressive *exempla,* and apt phrases: "Last of all, a studious yong man, with small paines, by the helpe of thys booke may gather to himselfe good furniture both of wordes and approued phrases and fashions of speaking for any thing, that he shall eyther write or speake of, and so make vnto his vse, as it were a common place booke for such a purpose." If the student wishes to write on love or friendship, for example, he may choose two or three words—*amicus, amo, amor*—and consider the words derived from them and the phrases belonging to the same, with the result that there is nothing "partaining to that matter, but that he shall be able copiously to vtter it." To demonstrate fully how his lexicon might aid the writer would, says Cooper, be unsuitable to his preface, but "a matter of smaler vse and copie" may serve. He then chooses the subject of shooting, the words *arcus* and *sagitta,* and the phrases which go with them, and demonstrates, with a passage of some two hundred and fifty words, how young scholars "may procure this store and furniture."[25] Indeed, an examination of a few pages of the text of the *Thesaurus* will give ample proof of the variety and abundance—that is, of the copy—

which Cooper calls to his readers' attention, and which undoubtedly aided such studious pupils of his as the famous William Camden.

The commendatory verses by Cooper's colleagues, wherein the terms *copia, opes, munus* recur, also stress this useful feature of the lexicon. Typical of the group is the poem by James Calfhill, who at the time had been recently appointed Lady Margaret professor of divinity at Oxford.

> The Nymphs nursed Jove in the vale of Ida, and the reward of the nurses was a goat's horn. From this fecund horn flowed all copy, copy not lacking any benefit. If Jupiter is therefore so called from aiding the world, he who favors and aids all, he also cherishes Jupiter. Copiousness should not be lacking to anyone who nourishes those things which aid his country with richer enjoyment. Cooper, therefore, sucking the Muses, as it were, in his rich work has the exuberant horn of plenty. Here, youths with your studies draw out the rewards; here, nothing explicit that you desire is lacking. For the cornucopia of Cooper gives more richly than that of Amalthea, which was a goat's horn.[26]

Calfhill's commendatory verses are not simply a fulsome expression of Cooper's own hopes, for late in our period Thomas Hoole's testimony corroborates the assumption that studious young men might and probably did use the *Thesaurus* in accordance with the directions given by Cooper in his preface. When Hoole laid down his pedagogical precepts, many aids to scholarship not available in Cooper's day had acquired standing in the academic world. It is to Cooper, nevertheless, that Hoole would have his students of the fifth form turn if they were capable of inventing anything by themselves:

> ... and if at any time they can wittily and pithily invent any thing of their own brain; you may help them to express it in good Latine, by making use of Cooper's *Dictionary,* either *as he himself directeth in his preface,* or *Phalerius* will more fully shew you, in his *Supplementa ad Grammaticam.*[27]

The Renaissance student might also have become familiar with portions of the dictionaries in his school library, that is, with the proper-noun entries in such lexicons, when his practice in composition took the form of a *dictamen.* In such an exercise a student was expected to translate material from an "unexpected author (extempore) into good Latin" or into good Greek.[28] In 1678 Adam Littleton advised his readers that the fables and stories under his entries for proper nouns were rendered in current idiom. His reason for calling attention to such a feature of his own Latin-English lexicon is obvious, if, as he maintains, it had become customary in many schools to use stories derived from Eliot and Cooper for this material to be translated "extempore." Littleton, at any rate, writes:

The English Stories, which . . . are in many schools made use of for Dictamens, having been taken out of Eliot and Cooper, and continued in that old fashioned Language, we have here and there amended and somewhat refined by bringing them nearer to our present dress.[29]

It is interesting to note, consequently, that one type of *dictamen* included in a late seventeenth-century schedule of the curriculum at St. Paul's is described as "a story in Heathen Gods."[30]   One would like to know whether the schedule of study at St. Paul's early in the century included such an exercise, and whether the "stories" used were taken from standard reference works like Cooper's *Thesaurus*.   If so, young John Milton by such an exercise might have had engraved upon his memory the phraseology of certain entries in at least one of the dictionaries with which we are concerned.   Unfortunately, although the possibility exists, we cannot be sure that Milton performed the particular exercise designated as "a story in Heathen Gods," nor can we be sure that this particular *dictamen* represents those to which Littleton refers.   The phrase occurs in a manuscript that is dated *ca.* 1672-97, and the schedule of study there outlined represents the situation when the writer was a pupil at St. Paul's.   The testimony of Littleton and that of the unknown writer, however, do seem to corroborate each other.

Moreover, from the exercise of prelection and lesson alone, English students of the late sixteenth and early seventeenth centuries probably became thoroughly familiar with dictionary entries under both proper nouns and common words, particularly when they encountered the major Latin poets in the upper forms.   In their study of Virgil, for instance, the text was scrutinized by preparing lessons of some ten or twelve verses each. The student memorized, construed, parsed, scanned, and proved the verses; gave the tropes and figures discovered in the lesson, as well as an appropriate definition of each; noted the phrases, epithets, and other elegances; and gave "the Histories or descriptions belonging to the proper Names, and their *Etymologies*."[31]   A similar procedure, which also agrees with some of the uses of a lexicon as outlined by Cooper, had been followed when students were introduced to the *Metamorphoses*.   They were expected to repeat five or six verses by heart, to construe the passage verbatim, to parse every word grammatically, and to prove and scan each verse. In addition, Hoole writes, "Let them give you the Tropes and Figures, the Derivations and Differences of some words, and relate such Histories as the proper names will hint at, which they may peruse before hand in their Dictionarie."[32] The exercise in paraphrase or imitation that accompanied the study of Ovid was, of course, to turn a fable into English prose, then into Latin prose according to the rules of rhetoric, and occasionally students would also have an opportunity to see who could turn the fable into the most varieties of English verse.

The existence of such a program throughout the sixteenth and early seventeenth centuries explains how modern students of the Renaissance can demonstrate that the method of the schools and the information in standard texts are reflected continually in the mature literature of the period. And the appearance of any work in the academic program is a sign that its influence may be surprisingly far-reaching, once it has been used by a future literary genius, and once its contents have sunk into his memory. It is only natural to assume, moreover, that, like Palsgrave and Shakespeare, even the mature scholar and writer would continue the habit of consulting, not necessarily Cooper's Latin-English lexicon, but standard reference works to which he had already been introduced. What we know of the activity of John Milton after he had moved into "a pretty Garden house in *Petty-France* in *Westminster*" (1652) is a case in point. There he was able to continue "his own Studies and private Designs," among which was the assembling of material for a Latin thesaurus of his own. Although descriptions of this work vary, they are not necessarily contradictory. It was to be "to the emendation of that done by Stephanus" or "according to the manner of Stephanus." The material to be used, Milton "had been long since Collecting from his own Reading, and still went on with at times, even very near to his dying day."[33] Both descriptions of the work imply great familiarity with the basic Latin lexicon of the period. Such a knowledge of Robert Stephanus' *Thesaurus,* as well as the habit of collecting apt quotations from his own reading, undoubtedly stretched back to Milton's school days. Consequently in the preceding chapter and in all those following, we are concerned not with the shorter Latin-English dictionaries of the period, not with the history of any one dictionary per se, but with reflections of basic and standard reference works of the period in the literary productions of the age, with Thomas Cooper's basic Latin-English dictionary, with the fullest Latin proper-name lexicon, and with the basic Latin thesaurus—works that had as continual and as varied a body of users as did the *Dictionarium* of Calepine, a standard and massive polyglot dictionary, with which we are also concerned.

Certain aspects of such a study—those which pertain to the literary milieu of the English Renaissance—should be kept in mind by the reader of the following chapters. Much of the material found in the dictionaries here considered must have been woven into the fabric of men's thoughts when they were of school age—Spenser, Shakespeare, Jonson, Milton not excluded. Moreover, as we have indicated above, to the sixteenth and seventeenth centuries these dictionaries were not contemptible. Thus any suggestion that the learned Ben Jonson, for example, consulted works also used by grammar-school boys need not, and should not, be construed as smacking of sacrilege or perverse debunking. If it can be established as probable that the scholarly Jonson turned to one of the lexicons while composing a mature work of his own, we shall have an additional body of concrete materials whereby we can perceive more clearly than before how, throughout the literature of the period, there ran a body of knowledge, a practice, and a procedure that were basic to the literary discipline of the age and were consequently not simply in elementary school exercises but in the most finished of literary masterpieces.

An investigation of this nature, however, is perforce limited to material in the dictionaries that normally might be carried over into vernacular literature. Although the lexicons by Calepine, Cooper, and the Stephanus brothers might supply "copy" for their users, they also aided a reader immeasurably in understanding his Latin text. Thus the immature schoolboy, let alone the mature writer, might not, and probably would not, show the extent of his indebtedness to a lexicon. In his translation, imitation, phraseology, or turn of thought, he primarily would reflect his knowledge of a particular classical text—the words of Cicero, Ovid, or Seneca, rather than the words of a dictionary that helped him to understand that text. Moreover, a writer well-schooled in the discipline of the age might be expected to become increasingly less dependent upon any reference lexicon for his "copy." In such an extended translation as Palsgrave's *Acolastus* or Chapman's *Homer,* the use of Robert Stephanus' *Thesaurus* or of Scapula's Greek-Latin lexicon can be demonstrated.[34] But in the *Shepheardes Calendar,* or *The Rape of Lucrece,* or *The Masque of Augurs,* or

*Paradise Lost* the problem is vastly different.  Only a relatively few passages, for example, demonstrate Shakespeare's knowledge of entries under common words that are found in Cooper's *Thesaurus,* and then most of the passages are, to a greater or less degree, amusing parodies of pedantry.[35]  The descriptions or explanatory comments found in the lexicons under proper nouns, however, might provide a reader with distinctive information, with an account or digest of matter found in a number of classical texts, and thus with material that might be peculiar in content or form to one of the reference dictionaries discussed above.  The use of "stories" connected with proper nouns might in itself be one means of achieving a meaningful and original "copy."  In the following chapters, therefore, we are concerned with passages in the works of various authors wherein the phraseology and context of the lines in which occur geographical names and proper nouns of ancient myth and history seem to show reflections of the wording or of the arrangement of material in proper-noun entries found in certain basic lexicons of the period.

Just how widely dispersed much of this material was should be thoroughly recognized.  By the time Elizabethan literature burgeoned into its admirable growth during the Renaissance, at least one generation of schoolboys had been drilled constantly in classic myth and the "histories" of proper nouns.  Even when they first memorized their grammatical precepts, a certain knowledge of classic myth was acquired:

> Q. *Cuius generi sunt nomina Divorum?*
> A. *Masculini.*
> Q. *Quomodo dicis Latine* The God of Battaile?
> A. *Mars,* hic *Mars, Martis*[36]

As we have already noticed, more advanced students would encounter the histories of proper nouns in their master's prelections and their own lessons, particularly when they studied Latin poetry.  In assigning themes the master might draw from classic myth or legend, as Erasmus counsels.  The students would thus utilize "histories" of proper names in writing on such subjects as "Hercules gained immortality for himself by destroying monsters," "The Muses rejoice in the fountain and the grove; they shun the smoky cities of men,"[37] or in comparing Hector and Achilles.[38]  Writing a *narratio,* for example, whether poetical, historical, or civil, would involve a knowledge of such figures as Pyramus and Thisbe, Cyrus, Tomyris, and P. Clodius.  The conventional school exercises called *destructio* (or *refutatio*) and *confirmatio,* respectively attacked and defended, by a set formula, the credibility of such fables, myths, or legends as those involving Arion, Daphne, or Dido. Conventional topics for "Impersonation" were to compose, according to formulae, the words of Niobe over her dead children, Hercules speaking to Eurystheus, or Andromache lamenting the death of Hector.[39] In all of this work, both oral and written, an important part of the task was to point the moral leading to the good life, and in performing exercises other than those noted above, fables and histories were particularly apt for inculcating a virtue or disparaging a vice.[40] If any one fable received particular attention, the pupils might be encouraged to "strive (who can best) to turn the Fable into English prose, and to adorn and amplifie it with fit Epithetes, choice Phrases, acute Sentences, wittie Apophthegmes, livelie similitudes, pat examples, and Proverbial Speeches, *all agreeing to the matter of moralitie therein couched. . . ."*[41]

Of the four dictionaries concerned, even the one that was most frequently criticized was a standard work of reference in England after the first half of the sixteenth century. As we have noted, all four works appear constantly as subsidiary texts in the curriculum. They were kept, for example, in common libraries of grammar schools for the use of all forms; and they seem to have been used constantly by the students. These lexicons were perhaps most helpful for understanding or preparing "histories" of proper nouns—a task that must have been an almost daily necessity and one that might be utilized in demonstrating a pupil's "store and furniture" of good words and phrases. Naturally we may assume that the information acquired in the schools, as well as the methods there inculcated, remained with the students who became the authors of the period.

Our concentration upon the lexicons, however, is not meant to minimize the importance of other compilations which were also standard works of reference during the Renaissance, such specialized compendiums in classical mythology as Natalis Comes' *Mythologiae sive Explicationis Fabularum* . . . or Vincenzio Cartari's *Le Imagini dei Dei degli Antichi*. These works, which have been better known to modern students of the period than have the basic lexicons, also appear among the subsidiary texts in the Renaissance curriculum. A copy of Comes, for example, was in the library of Richard Stonely as well as in the library of the Merchant Taylors' school by 1599.[42] The *Mythologiae* is listed by Hoole in his discussion of the work of his fourth form, that is, when his students began to study Ovid. He groups it with the seventeenth-century mythological treatises by Bacon

and by Alexander Ross, with Sandys' translation of Ovid, and with
Antoine du Verdier's *Imagines Deorum,* the widely circulated Latin version of *Le Imagini dei Dei degli Antichi* by Vincenzio Cartari.   These
books "and the like," writes Hoole, are "fitting to be reserved for your
Scholars use in the Schoole-librarie."   Such texts in one place "will invite
them like so many bees to busie themselves sucking up matter and words
to quicken their invention and expression."[43]

   In this group of books, however, Hoole also lists Charles Stephanus'
*Dictionarium Historicum, Geographicum, Poeticum,* and the reason for its
inclusion is easily perceived in the light of the preceding chapter.   By
1600 or earlier, editors of Charles Stephanus were incorporating into the
lexicon matter from Comes and from Cartari, as well as material from
Gyraldus' *De Deis Gentium,* the third outstanding work of Renaissance
mythography.   At the same time additional geographical information
was being added to entries in the proper-name lexicon.[44]   Thus the
*Dictionarium Historicum, Geographicum, Poeticum* would in a number of
respects be the most satisfactory work of reference and the most likely
compendium for a student to consult first.   In convenient size and arranged
in alphabetical order, it would provide him with concrete information about
all sorts of names, information drawn from classical and contemporary
authors, from ancient prose and poetry, and from recent specialized
treatises.   There too he would find cited appropriate passages in the writings of ancient and modern authors, including the mythological as well as
the geographical compendiums of the Renaissance.   In a well-stocked common library, the student might then turn directly to the literature of the
ancient world or the more detailed compendiums for further information.

   For that matter, even when entries in the lexicons do not incorporate
material drawn from current scholarly compendiums, the information in
the dictionaries represents a sound nucleus of fuller discussions in the more
specialized treatises or in the longer comments provided by scholarly editions of classical authors.   This useful feature of the lexicons is illustrated
in the Appendix by a discussion of the myth of the Fates.   There the
dictionary entries are placed against information in the more specialized
treatises and against passages in the vernacular literature of the period.
The discussion clearly shows that even though the lexicons may not always
incorporate material from the Renaissance mythographers, they nevertheless
cite the basic *loci classici* and provide a kernel for various interpretations
of a myth, or sum up in a terse maxim the moral to be derived therefrom.

The dictionaries thus specify what was well known to the era, and their entries represent what Renaissance readers trained in the academic tradition of the period might be expected to know.

As an examination of the myth of the Parcae also indicates, mature authors of the Renaissance seem to have been thoroughly aware of what was probably best known to their audience. In particular, Milton's handling of the Fates in *Arcades,* Spenser's account of Merlin's advice, Spenser's and E. K.'s treatment of the Fates as *lanificae,* and Jonson's allotment of time to Clotho and Lachesis in his *Entertainment at Theobalds* make it a fair presumption that these poets knew something about the pertinent mythological entries in the lexicons. Milton, Spenser, and Jonson were also familiar in varying degrees with current specialized treatises and with the classical texts upon which those treatises might be based. But they were also men of their age. With their audience, they had probably used the reference lexicons that could be found in grammar-school libraries— lexicons that were instrumental in making certain features of ancient literature poetic commonplaces.

Although caution must be exercised in positing a writer's indebtedness to any one work, the existence of good classical texts with annotations, as well as the availability of treatises devoted entirely to such a subject as classic myth, does not preclude a writer's turning to a familiar dictionary or remembering the words of a school "history" when he refers to geographical names or to figures of ancient myth and history. The lexicons with which we are concerned were designed to elucidate matter that otherwise was scattered throughout classical texts or, at best, gathered together in glosses and commentaries on various writings of the ancient world. With their entries for all types of proper nouns, the dictionaries provided a much more complete survey of poetic materials than a writer would be likely to gather by himself or to store up in his memory—even if after a long period of time he might have planned to emend material found in one of the basic reference works. For that matter, although a proper-name entry in such subsidiary texts might not have supplied a future writer with information for his school exercises, if it were encountered in later years by a poet who was a reader of classical and contemporary texts, it might have been the inciting force which recalled classical passages to mind, which directed him to poems or to particular lines in classical texts, or which evoked other fuller elucidations of a myth or legend. Information on the Parcae, for example, could have served this purpose. We must always remember that the authors considered in the following pages were neither pedants nor pedagogues; they were writers, "poets," in the Renaissance sense of that word. They were not demonstrating for master or pupil the fact that they had mastered their texts. They took material where they found it and turned it to their purpose. If Spenser, or Shakespeare, or Milton by accident or design repeated the phraseology of a dictionary entry, if Jonson used current works of reference—lexicons among them—to find useful details, they are certainly not to be censured. They grew up in Renaissance England. For their era, the Stephanus dictionaries were of a sound classical quality; Cooper was pre-eminent among sixteenth-century English lexicographers; and Calepine was immensely popular. Use of those dictionaries was part of the academic training of the Renaissance, a training that was particularly suited for the development of poets and readers of poetry. Proper-noun entries in the lexicons by Charles and Robert Stephanus, by Calepine, and by Cooper might be expected to supply an appreciable portion of the basic information known both to the poets of the age and to their readers.

# CHAPTER III

# THE DICTIONARIES AND MINOR
# ELIZABETHAN WRITERS

O F THE POPULARITY OF THE BIOGRAPHICAL ELEMENT IN THE REN-
aissance dictionary there is much evidence. Marginal manuscript
notes in a contemporary hand concerning the sketches, found in
a 1545 Elyot in the British Museum and in copies of Cooper's *Thesaurus*
in the Folger Shakespeare Library, are but early instances of the interest
with which this matter in the dictionaries was read. More significant is
the extensive borrowing by other compilers and authors, including poets
and writers of prose fiction. In his revision of William Baldwin's *Morall
Philosophy* (*ca.* 1557), Thomas Palfreyman takes almost verbatim eighteen
of the brief biographical sketches from the *Bibliotheca Eliotae*.[1] In a book
entitled *Ptochomuseion, The Poore Mans Librarie* (1565, 1571), William
Alley (1510?-1570) borrows freely from the Elyot-Cooper biographies
and other items; and Stephen Batman, augmenter of Bartholomaeus' *De
Proprietatibus Rerum,* incurs a similarly heavy indebtedness to Cooper.[2]

### 1. George Pettie

As early as 1928, Douglas Bush pointed out the most probable ultimate
sources of George Pettie's stories in *A Petite Pallace of Pettie His Pleasure.*[3] Our study will in part supplement that of Professor Bush and will
also offer new evidence of other and more immediate source materials
borrowed by Pettie.

In the preparation of his collection, Pettie seems to have taken many
suggestions from the *Dictionarium Historicum et Poeticum* of Cooper's
*Thesaurus* (1565). In at least six of his stories[4] there is fairly definite
evidence that the *Thesaurus* is the source of Pettie's allusions or illustrations and, in some cases, of the main outlines of the myths or legends which
Pettie expands.

Of the "Tereus and Progne," the main source is, as Bush notes,[5] Ovid's *Metamorphoses* (vi, 424 ff.). Another source which furnished certain details and phrases is Gascoigne's "The Complaynt of Phylomene." Finally, the entry under *Philomela* in Cooper's *Thesaurus* seems to have made a slight contribution. A comparison of the quoted lines which follow will show that Pettie is nearer in his phrasing to Cooper than to any other source:

COOPER: But she [Philomela] being very *cunning* in *working* and *imbrodering,* did in such sort set out the *whole matter* in a garment, that any man might understand it.

OVID: (Golding's translation):
 A warpe of white upon a frame of *Thracia* she did pin,
 And weaved purple letters in betweene it, which bewraide
 The wicked deede of *Tereus.*

GASCOIGNE:
 With curious needle worke,
 A garment gan she make.
 Wherin she wrote what bale she bode. . . .

PETTIE: . . . she *wrought* and *embroidered cunningly* in cloth the *whole discourse* of her . . . careful case

As the italicised words and phrases common to Cooper and Pettie are nowhere found in the other versions, we feel certain that, in this instance, Pettie was using the language of the *Thesaurus.*

In the same story (pp. 65-66) four successive allusions—to Demophoön and Phyllis, Theseus and Ariadne, Jason and Medea, Nero and Agrippina —seem to derive from other entries in the *Thesaurus.* As an example, compare these:

COOPER: (under *Agrippina*): . . . For soone after, hir owne sonne Nero . . . (as some men supposed) abused hir carnally, hauing hir in most mortall hate, caused hir to be most cruelly slaine.

PETTIE (p. 66): He cometh of Nero his cruel kind, who carnally abused his own mother Agrippina, and then caused her to be slain.

Though the contribution of the *Thesaurus* to the "Tereus and Progne" is slight, the debt of Pettie to this source is beyond the realm of conjecture.

"Germanicus and Agrippina," the next story in Pettie's collection, owes even a greater debt to an entry in Cooper's *Thesaurus.* The original Germanicus story is recounted at rather widely separated intervals in Suetonius' *Lives* and in Tacitus' *Annals.*[6] A more succinct version— hardly more than an outline, indeed—is that in the second entry under

*Agrippina* in the *Thesaurus.* To this account, Pettie's version, as far as his basic story is concerned, corresponds in details and phraseology and also in certain divergences from Suetonius and Tacitus.

We have noted in the discussion of "Tereus and Progne" that Pettie had drawn certain phrases from the dictionary account of Agrippina, the daughter of Germanicus and mother of Nero. It is but natural that Pettie should have read the entry immediately succeeding, which is concerned with Agrippina, the wife of Germanicus and grandmother of Nero. As evidence that Pettie was familiar with this entry and therefore with Cooper's outline of the Germanicus and Agrippina story, we offer the following parallels:

COOPER: Agrippina, Mother to the sayde Agrippina [Nero's mother], was *daughter of M. Agrippa,* and wife to Germanicus, whome Tiberius, by the commaundement of Octauian, *had declared to bee his heyre apparant to the Empire* . . . .

PETTIE: For this gentleman Germanicus, frequenting the Court of Octavian, the Emperor, chanced to fix his eyes on the face of a noble gentlwoman named Agrippina, the *daughter of M. Agrippa.* . . .

Germanicus . . . becoming amorous of the Lady Agrippina . . . *getteth her to wife*: and through his valiancy winneth to be *proclaimed heir-apparent to the Empire.* (I, 72, 71)[7]

COOPER: For whose death the sayde Agrippina . . . *determined to die,* by absteining from meate. And although the *Emperour caused meate to be put into hir throte,* she would not receyue it, but in that voluntarie abstinence finally dyed.

PETTIE: Hereupon she [Agrippina] *resolved* . . . *she would end her* days by not receiving that which she should: and so defrauding herself of food . . . And when *the Emperor Octavian caused meat to be thrust in her throat,* she cast it up again . . . and so in short time died. (I, 109)

Not only are the parallels in the phrasing of Cooper and Pettie significant, but even more important is the common use of *Octavian.* Pettie, probably misreading Cooper, supposes Octavian (Augustus?) to have been emperor at the time of Germanicus' death. There is no basis for this statement in either Suetonius or Tacitus; in fact these authors do not mention Octavian. Furthermore, both Cooper and Pettie state positively that Tiberius poisoned Germanicus; neither of the classical authors makes this assertion. They suggest rather that Gnaeus Piso (impliedly an agent of Tiberius) was responsible for Germanicus' death by poison. There is not, so far as we can discover, one jot of evidence to prove that Pettie had read either the Suetonius or Tacitus. There is nothing in Pettie's story, as respects the

Germanicus legend, that Pettie could not have got from Cooper. On the contrary, Pettie's general ignorance of the earlier accounts, his mistaken assumption that Octavian was emperor, his use of Cooper's language—all point to the *Thesaurus* as the sole source.

For his story of "Amphiaraus and Eriphile," Pettie seems to have read Hyginus' *Fables* (69-73), as Bush suggests.[8] Common elements in the two accounts, not found in other versions, support this suggestion. But for this story Pettie took also certain details, including the phrasing, from two entries in the *Thesaurus*—those under *Eriphile* and *Amphiaraus*. For example, Cooper writes that "Eriphile, The wyfe of Amphiaraus . . . betrayed hir husbande for an *ouche of golde,* at the siege of Thebes." Pettie (I, 127) has Eriphile ask ". . . shall not I for great *ouches of gold* bewray my husband to the king, who meaneth by his means to preserve our city?" Pettie, following here the dictionary phrasing, takes *ouch* to mean a sum of gold, or possibly golden ornaments. But Hyginus specifies that Adrastus, the king, made and presented to Eriphile a golden necklace adorned with gems ("monile aureum ex gemmis fecit"). Also, the account in Charles Stephanus' *Dictionarium Historicum,* employs the term "aureo monile." Pettie, we think, recorded the language he had found in Cooper.

From the same source Pettie draws one other detail. Referring to Amphiaraus, Cooper writes, "And the first day that he came to Thebes, *the earth opened and swallowed him."*[9] Of the episode Pettie writes, ". . . he [Amphiaraus] *no sooner set foot in the Theban soil,* but that *the earth opened and swallowed him up."* (I, 130) The passage in Hyginus concerning the tragic end of Amphiaraus is in these words: ". . . *qui postquam apud Thebas terra est devoratus."* We doubt whether even Pettie, had he been following Hyginus, would have translated *postquam* as "no sooner" than, or *est devoratus,* as "opened and swallowed him up." His language is that of Cooper.

Hyginus' *Fables* (L-LI) have been suggested[10] as the source of Pettie's "Admetus and Alcest." This legend as related by Hyginus is very brief; and Pettie's version, aside from borrowings from Painter's *Pallace of Pleasure,*[11] and the author's own inventions in the way of letters and soliloquies, has certain important details not found in Hyginus. In Cooper's *Thesaurus* the original legend is summarized under the entry *Admetus.* And in this summary are the details which appear in Pettie and are lacking in Hyginus. According to Cooper and Pettie, for example, Apollo obtains for Admetus from the destinies the privilege of prolonging his days; and Admetus indulges in extended lamentations on the death of his wife. Hyginus makes no mention of the privilege obtained from the destinies or of the lamentations of Admetus. Both Cooper and Pettie state that Proserpina restored Alcest to her husband; Hyginus makes Hercules the restorer.

There are, also, certain correspondences in phraseology between Pettie's version and that of the *Thesaurus*. Compare the following:

COOPER: Apollo . . . *obteyned of the destenies* . . . that when the day of the death of Admetus . . . .

PETTIE: And *of the destinies of death* [Apollo] *obtained* thus much for him, that if when the time and term of his natural life drew to an end . . . . (I, 192)

PETTIE: . . . to what purpose was that which he [Apollo] *obtained of the destinies for you?* (I, 195)

COOPER: . . . Proserpina, moued with compassion, sent Alceste again out of hell vnto hir husbande.

PETTIE: And Proserpina, the goddess of hell, especially pitying the parting of this loving couple . . . put life into his wife again, and with speed sent her unto him. (I, 195)

The evidence indicates that the *Thesaurus* is a more probable source than the *Fables* for the basic story of Pettie's "Admetus and Alcest."

A few details in the "Minos and Pasiphae" seem to indicate that Pettie had read the version of the legend in Ovid's *Ars Amatoria*.[12] But, once again, Pettie's indebtedness to the *Thesaurus,* as far as the original legend is concerned, is demonstrable. Under *Pasiphae,* Cooper puts together the essentials of the Ovid story and Servius' comment in a single entry. Details from this entry, Pettie must have borrowed. Compare the following:

| COOPER | PETTIE |
|---|---|
| *Pasiphae* . . . The wife of Minos kinge of Crete, who *hauing companie with a bulle,* *brought foorth* the monster called Minotaurus, which was halfe a man, and halfe a bulle. But *Seruius writeth* that kinge Minos secretarie named Taurus, had companie with Pasiphae *in the house of one Daedalus.* She therfore *beyng after deliuered, had twoo sonnes, one like to Minos, and the other to Taurus the kinges secretary:* and that *therevpon Poetes tooke ocassion to deuise the fable* of the monster Minotaurus begotten on Pasiphae, being by Daedalus inclosed in a timber Cowe. | *Pasiphae becoming unnaturally amorous of a bull,* by means of the carpenter Dedalus, *bringeth forth a monstrous Child,* in part resembling the sire, and in part the mother. (II, 84) . . . by the opinion of one *Servius, who writeth,* that Pasiphae indeed played false with one Taurus,—which signifieth a bull —, secretary to her husband, *in the house of Daedalus, and after, being delivered, had two sons, the one like Minos, the other like Taurus, and thereupon the poets feigned the fable* aforesaid. . . . (II, 105) |

The nearness of details and phrasing in these two passages strongly suggests Pettie's debt to Cooper. This suggestion is supported by additional evidence. In reporting Servius, for example, the two authors[13] make the same mistake. Both Cooper and Pettie assert that Servius "writeth" that Pasiphae had two sons; Servius does not say so. Both write that the poets feigned the fable on the basis of the story aforesaid. Servius had no similar declaration. Similarity of phrasing, a common mistake in quoting Servius, details in common but not in the Servius constitute evidence of Pettie's borrowing from Cooper.

Although the legend of Alexis was well known in the sixteenth century and Pettie could have read it in the *Golden Legend* or some other source, his use of the story in his "Alexius" probably was suggested by Cooper's *Thesaurus*. In the first place, the title follows the dictionary spelling: A-l-e-x-i-u-s, not A-l-e-x-i-s as in other versions of the story. Then, too, in his free treatment of the legend, Pettie used only such details of the original as were available in Cooper's item, under *Alexius*. Also, the language of the *Thesaurus* suggests that of Pettie in certain passages of his story. Cooper writes, for example, "Alexius . . . hauing a wife of excellent beautie, for the loue of God left hir, and secretlye went sundrie pilgrimages in the habit of a poore man." Pettie says of Alexius, ". . . and seeing the sight of his sweet mistress to be a great hindrance to his heavenly cogitations, he altogether separated himself from her company, left friends and country, and spent the remainder of his life in pilgrimage and travel." (I, 165)

Finally, Pettie's allusions to the stories of Archimedes (138), to Zopyrus and Calisthenes (142), and to Semiramis (161) all seem to derive from entries under these names in the *Thesaurus*.

To sum up this part of the investigation, we may say that six of the stories in *A Petite Pallace* show definite use of the short biographical sketches and the legends recorded in Cooper's *Thesaurus*. Four of the six—"Germanicus and Agrippina," "Admetus and Alcest," "Minos and Pasiphae," and "Alexius"—appear to be expansions of dictionary items; and two others draw upon the same source for illustrative examples and classical allusions.

## 2. George Gascoigne

George Gascoigne, like his predecessors and contemporaries, did not hesitate to borrow or adapt matter from Cooper's *Thesaurus* when it suited his purpose to do so. Evidence of Gascoigne's indebtedness to Cooper may be found in *The Steel Glas* (1575), *A Delicate Diet for Daintiemouthde Droonkardes* (1576), and *The Complaynt of Phylomene* (1576). Consider, first, the parallels which follow as an indication of Gascoigne's debt in *The Steel Glas*:

| *The Steel Glas* | *Thesaurus* |
|---|---|
| (1) | |
| And *Paulus* he, (*Aemilius* surnamed) *Returnde to Rome, no richer than he went,* Although he had, so many lands subdued, *And brought such treasure, to the cōmō chests,* That *fourscore yeres,* the state was (after) free, From grevous *taske,* and imposition. (2.155-6)[14] | Paulus, A name of diuers Romaynes: one was moste excellent, named Paulus Aemilius, sonne of Lucius Paulus. He . . . *returned to Rome, not one grote the* rycher: . . . He *brought so much golde and siluer into the treasurie* of the Romaynes, that there needed no *taske* to be set on the people *.lxxx. yeares* after and aboue . . . . |
| (2) | |
| *Pericles* was, a famous man of warre, And *victor* eke, *in nine great foughten fields,* Wherof he was the general in charge. Yet at his death he rather did rejoyce Be still (quoth he) you grave *Athenians* (Who whispered, and tolde his valiant facts) You have forgot, my greatest glorie got. For yet (by me nor mine occasion) Was never sene, a mourning garment worne. (2.157) | Finally Pericles being sicke unto death, the noble men came to comfort him, speaking softly they communed of his prowes, where he had *victorie in nine great battayles.* He hearing what they spake, sayde vnto them, that he much maruyeled, that they so greatly extolled that thing, wherof the more part perteyned to fortune, and had happened to diuers other capitaynes as well as to him, and that they spake nothing of that which was most to be praysed. For neuer man, sayed he, . . . had cause to pute *mourning garment* vpon him. |
| (3) | |
| Bold *Manlius,* could close and wel convey Ful thirtie wounds, (and three) upon his head. . . . (2.157) | He [Manlius] had taken *.xxxiij. woundes in the fore part of his bodie.* |

Above are three of the illustrations which Gascoigne borrowed from the *Thesaurus* to adorn *The Steel Glas*. But this is not all. In his prose tract of the *Delicate Diet,* partly a translation from St. Augustine, Gascoigne departs from his original to supply certain illustrations. Where did he find them? Three successive examples come directly from Cooper's *Thesaurus.* The parallels from the *Delicate Diet* and the *Thesaurus* follow:

*Delicate Diet*

*Thesaurus*

(1)

*Alexander* the *Macedonian*, who by his valiaunce & prowesse, in lesse *then twelve yeeres*, conquered & subdued, *Illiria, now called Slavonia*, the Cittie of *Thebes*, with the Territories and Countreyes adjoyning: yea *al Greece, Asia, Persia*, and *India, with the East parts of the whole world*: being setled in peaceable possession of his dominions, gave himselfe over unto vanity & pleasures, and at the last to excessive droonkennesse: whereby *hee became so odious unto his people* generally, that they privily conspired his death, & executed the same. . . . (2.463)

Alexander, . . . the sonne of Phillip king of Macedonie, who . . . after the death of Phillip his father, being but .xx. yeares olde, he enterprised to conquere all the worlde. And first gat *Illyria, now called Slauonia:* And after subuerted the *citie of Thebes*, brought in subiection *al Greece*, entered into *Asia*, and vanquished the great and puissaunt Darius king of *Persia* . . . Finally he conquered *India, and all the east part of the worlde.* And all this did he in little more than *.xii. yeares.* But when he had pacified the worlde from all rebellions, he fell into such crueltie & pryde . . . that *he became odious to his owne people:* who desiring his destruction, at the last when he was in his most glori at the citie of Babilon . . . at supper with one of his phisitions, was poysoned by drinking out of a cup. . . .

(2)

*Lucullus a famous Romane, both for learning & skyl in Martial feats,* after a nomber of great victories, & exceding Fame got by temperaunce in justice, and pollitique goverment, dyd *geve him selfe over unto such* an *Epicures* lyfe, and soonke so deepe into the gulfe of this odious enormity, that in th'end he *lost his wyts* and memory, & with all his substaunce was lyke a chylde, *committed unto the charge & direction of others.* . . . (2.463)

*Lucullus, A famous and noble man of Rome, in rychese, learning, and martiall prowesse very excellent* . . . . After his returne out of Asia, *he gaue himselfe altogither to sumptuous and sensuall lyfe* . . . whereas dayly also he vsed such outragious fare, in feasting and banketting, that his deliciousnesse and sensualite is growne to a prouerbe. In the ende, he *beyng altered in his wittes,* was committed to the tuicion of his brother. . . .

(3)

*Apitius* not contented to distemper his owne body continually with wine & delicate fare, and after much & great consumption thereof, to find an hole in his bags, as bigge as *five hundreth fowre score & three thousand, fifty & fowre pounds sterlings, did yet infect the whole City of Rome,* with poison of y^t same abomination: which in times past had bene a perfect *Myrror of temperance* to other Nations: but in the ende he beastly & most ungodly, dyd *wilfully drink*

Apitius, A Romayne, which delighted in delicate meates, so much, that he professed cookerie, and *infected Rome* with gluttonie, which before was *the myrrour of temperaunce.* And when he had consumed in gourmandise, Millies sestertium, which amounteth . . . to two myllions, and .500000, crownes: which is after our rate *.583054. li.* When he grewe in debt, and . . . fearing in that substaunce to lyue in penurie he *wyllingly dranke poyson,* and dyed.

*poyson,* and destroyed himself, fearing lest
the remnant of his substaunce would not
minister sufficiently unto the plotforme or
foundation which he had layd in this ab-
hominable bybbing, banquetting, & quaff-
ing. . . . (2.463)

The parallels quoted above are sufficiently close to place beyond reasonable doubt Gascoigne's use, in *The Steel Glas* and the *Delicate Diet,* of
Cooper's *Thesaurus.* The familiarity with the *Thesaurus* which Gascoigne
shows in these two pieces establishes a fair presumption that he would resort to Cooper's text in the composition of other pieces. There is evidence
to indicate that he did so in writing *The Complaint of Philomene.*

The primary source of *The Complaint*—the tragic story of Philomela,
her sister Progne, and Tereus—is found in Ovid's *Metamorphoses* (6.412
ff.; see especially ll. 574-86). Gascoigne seems to have consulted the original Latin version as well as Arthur Golding's translation for the general
story. But the poet makes certain departures from the story as found in
the Latin and in Golding. Ovid relates, for example, that Philomela, after
her tragic experience, gave to *one* (person not specified) a web or cloth
woven with purple letters, as a means of revealing her wretched condition.
This web was to be carried to her sister Progne. Gascoigne has Philomela
send to her sister, by a "trustie servant," a "garment" made with "curious
needle work." In the conclusion of the story, Ovid (and Golding) have
Tereus transformed into a lapwing. The Ovid version does not specify into what kinds of birds the sisters are changed, and makes no mention of
Itys. Gascoigne tells us definitely, in this order, that Progne became a
swallow, Tereus a lapwing, Itys a "pheasaunt cocke," and Philomela, a
nightingale.

In an article[15] published a few years ago, one of the authors expressed
the opinion that Gascoigne had received suggestions for the changes he
made in the Ovid story, from the sketch of "Philomela" in Cooper's
*Thesaurus.* He stated also that the poet, in the composition of *The Complaint of Philomene,* had consulted Golding's translation of Ovid. C. T.
Prouty, in his *George Gascoigne: Elizabethan Courtier, Soldier, and Poet,*[16]
maintained in reply that Gascoigne had used neither Golding's Ovid nor
Cooper's *Thesaurus,* and that there was another explanation—to be given
below—of Gascoigne's departures from the original story. In a rejoinder[17]
to Prouty, evidence was presented of Gascoigne's knowledge of Golding—
a topic not necessary to pursue in the present discussion—and of the poet's

borrowing from Cooper's *Thesaurus.* Evidence of Gascoigne's indebtedness
to the *Thesaurus,* in two compositions, has been presented above. As
Prouty's book and the pertinent articles are easily available, it seems unnecessary to restate here the details of this minor controversy. We will
therefore state, in summary form, the relevant points of our conclusions,
omitting the discussion concerning Gascoigne's use of Golding.

Prouty would explain Gascoigne's departures from Ovid, in the Phil-
omela story, by assuming that the Elizabethan poet used a Latin text of the
*Metamorphoses,* published in Venice in 1565, with a commentary and
notes by Raphael Regius and synopses of the stories by Lactantius Placitus.
Drawing upon these authors and deriving additional matter from Henricus
Glareanus' notes on the Ovid text, Gascoigne would have found suggestions
for his variations from Ovid's narrative, Prouty maintains. He insists that
Lactantius Placitus' synopsis of the Philomela story, for example, is the
basis for the transformations at the end of Gascoigne's poem. Placitus'
Latin summary, the author quotes, omitting Cooper's account, in English,
of the same episode. He acknowledges, however, the similarity of the two
narratives, and suggests that Gascoigne and Cooper were both translating
from Lactantius Placitus. But we know that Cooper's source was the
"Philomela" entry in Charles Stephanus' *Dictionarium,* and, therefore,
Prouty's assumption of Placitus as a common source is not tenable.

To explain why Gascoigne employed "trustie servaunt" for Ovid's *uni,*
Prouty cites Raphael Regius' note—"uni: ex ancillis." Gascoigne's
"curious needlework" and "garment" trouble Mr. Prouty. Though he
labors hard, he finds for these terms no adequate explanation in Ovid's
Latin, in Regius' commentary, in Placitus' synopsis, or even in the additional notes of Henricus Glareanus. His investigation terminates in the
generalization that Ovid's meaning "is sufficiently loose to allow of the
idea of needlework." This is a complicated exposition, which fails to explain.

Our own position is that Gascoigne's use of the Philomela story as
summarized in Cooper's *Thesaurus*—a book which the poet borrowed from
in the composition of other pieces—would account adequately for the
variations from Ovid and would offer a simple and logical explanation of
them. Correspondences in content and phrasing between the relevant parts
of the poem and Cooper's summary of the story support this view. Compare the following:

*The Complaynt* (1576)

With *curious needle* worke,
*A garment* gan she make,
*Wherin she wrote what bale she bode,*
. . .
*This garment gan she give*
*To trustie Servants hande,*
*Who streight conveid it*
    *to the queen* [Progne].
When *Progne* red the writ,
. . .
She kept it close: *though malice made*
*Hir venging hart to swell.*

And *did deferre the deede,*
Til time and place might serve,
. . .
The thirde yeres rytes renewed,
Which *Bacchus* to belong,
And in that night the queene prepares
Revenge for al hir wrong.

*The Thesaurus* (1573)

. . . But she [Philomela] being very
*cunning in working and imbrodering, did*
in such sort *set out the whole matter* in
a *garment,* that any man might vnder-
stand it, and *sent the same by a seruaunt*
*to hir sister Progne,* Tereus hys wyfe.
    Who, *although she were greatly*
*mooued* with the matter, yet shee *did*
*deferre the reuengement,* vntill the solemne sacryfices of Bacchus.

(The two narratives here recount the rescue of Philomela by her sister,
the bizarre revenge which the sisters wreak on King Tereus by slaying the
son Itys and serving him as meat for the king, the king's discovery of the
deception and his attempt to slay the sisters. Then follow the transformations.)

*The Complaynt*

The *Thracian* prince stert up,
. . .
And armed (as he was)
He followed both the *Greekes,*
. . .
A sharpe revenge he sekes.
. . .
The *eldest dame and wife* [Progne]
A *Swallowe* was assigned,
. . .
The *king him selfe condemnde,*
*A Lapwing for to be,*
. . .
The *lad a Pheasaunt cocke*
*For his degree hath gaind,*
. . .
And *Nightingale* now namde
Which (*Philomela* hight)

*The Thesaurus*

With sight whereof Tereus being in a
great furie, ranne after his wife to haue
slaine hir: but *shee* with speede escaped
from him, and as Poetes feigne, *was*
*turned into a swallow,* and *he into a lap-*
*wing, Philomela into a nightingall,* and
*Itis into a pheasaunt.*

Comparison of the parallels above, especially the portions which we have
italicised, shows that Gascoigne's use of the "Philomela" story in the

*Thesaurus* would explain, in the proper context, the poet's "curious needle worke," the "garment," the "trustie servaunt(s)," and the transformation of the characters—features not accounted for by the text of Ovid. It would explain also the striking correspondences, in the same context, of the phrases "did deferre the revengement" and "did deferre the deede" (of vengeance)—phrases without basis in Ovid and not noted by Mr. Prouty. Add to these observations Gascoigne's use of the *Thesaurus* in other pieces of the same year and we can hardly escape the conclusion that the poet was drawing from the same source in the composition of *The Complaynt of Philomene.*

### 3. John Grange

In recent years Hyder E. Rollins and other scholars have pointed out numerous borrowings by John Grange in his *Golden Aphroditis.*[18] We now have to add to the list already noted a number of items which derive from Cooper's *Thesaurus.* Although Grange attempts to adapt borrowed matter to his context, he generally betrays himself by certain phrases from his source. This procedure is exemplified in the following verses from the *Golden Aphroditis*:

> . . . yet shal you neuer see,
> Nor know my senses, for to know the breath of any wight
> Saue thou alone, as *Biblia,* who when *Duellus* hight
> Him selfe to haue a *stinking breath* by open parlance mayde
> Of Roman dames vnto his face: *I haue not knowen* (she sayde,)
> But all mens breath haue bene alike, such was the vestal line
> Of that hir chosen path, as wel the stories doe define.[19]

This incident is, with variation, twice recorded in the *Thesaurus.* It appears in the item *Bilia* and in *Duillius,* and is referred to in *Biblia.* Though Grange was probably acquainted with both entries, he seems to have followed that under *Duillius,* which reads thus:

. . . When he was an olde man, in chidyng with his enimie it was cast in his teeth that hee had an yll sauouring breath. Wherewith he being somewhat abashed, went home to his wyfe and chidde with hir that shee neuer tolde him of it. Sir sayde shee, so woulde I haue done, had I not thought that all mennes breathes had sauoured in lyke maner. So farre were honest matrones in those dayes from clypping, kissing, and wanton daliaunce with straungers.

The same principle of adaptation is evident in Grange's use of the Admetus-Alcestis myth from Cooper: Grange's version follows:

. . . he fell from this treatise into the discourse of chaste Matrones, as in declaryng how that, when *Atropos, Lachesis* and *Clothoe,* beyng the *Ladies of the destenie had graunted* to *Admetus* kynge of Thessalia (*at the request of Apollo, being throwne into exile,* or rather banished from the stately throne of the potentiall Goddes *by force of Iupiters fearefull mace*) *that what tyme soeuer the turnyng spindle had thorowly twyned his fatall threede, if any one would take vpon him death* to awarde king *Admetus* his life, his proffer shoulde be accepted to reiourne his former wishe. *This day beyng common,* & none would yeelde his lyfe for *Admetus* his sake, then *Alceste* she *his* true and faythful *wyfe* did yeelde to death for to awarde hys life. (Sig. Fii)

Compare with the account just quoted Cooper's item on Admetus:

*Admetus,* Was king of a people called Pherei, vnto whom Apollo, *being exiled out of heauen by Iupiter,* came for reliefe, and kept his cattell, . . . which thing Admetus thankfully taking, entertayned him honorably. That being well considered of *Apollo, he obteyned of the destenies, called Parcae, that when the day of the death of Admetus should be wounde vpon their spyndels, if* he coulde *fynde anye other, that woulde wyllinglie die* for him, he himselfe should escape death at that time. *When the day was come,* that Admetus should finishe his lyfe, all men and women, yea father and mother, refused to die: onely *Alceste his wyfe,* preferred the lyfe of hir husband before hir owne . . . .

The italicized passages (italics ours) show, in our opinion, Grange's familiarity with the brief narrative of Admetus and Alceste in the *Thesaurus.*

Another of the "chaste Matrones" whom Grange briefly portrays is Artemisia. In this portrait, also, the author has recourse to the sketch of Artemisia in the *Thesaurus.* Without giving the accounts in full we shall quote a sentence or so from each as evidence of the close relationship:

GRANGE: . . . when *Mausolus* King of *Caria* had yeelded his lyfe to . . . death . . . yet did she [Artemisia] keepe his harte aboue the ground to keepe hyr company, vntill continuance of tyme had turned the same by course to moultrying duste. Then putting the same in a cup of wine, *she dranke it vp, saying;* whyle lyfe did last *his harte from hyrs asunder should not parte.* (Sig. Fii)

COOPER: . . . whan he [Mausolus] was dead, she [Artemisia] caused his heart to bee dryed in a vessell of golde into poulder, & by little and little *she dranke it vp,* saying: *Their twoo hearts should neuer depart a sunder.* . . .

Nearer to his source are Grange's remarks about Medusa. He writes:

. . . and ugly *Medusa, a Lady of whome* the *Poetes fayne, that by Minerua hir haires were turned into Adders, and they whiche behelde hir head were turned into stones.* . . . (Sig. Ni^v)

Compare the *Thesaurus* :

Medusa, a Ladie, of *whome fables doe report, that by Minerva hir heares were
turned into adders, and they which behelde hir, were turned into stones.* . . .

The discourse in the *Golden Aphroditis* about "Syrenes" (Sig. Ni$^v$)
follows in the main Cooper's account of "Sirenes," with possibly a few details from the *Dictionarium Poeticum* of Charles Stephanus.   Here follow
the brief narratives from Grange and Cooper, respectively :

GRANGE

. . . first the Syrenes appeared in number
three, *Parthenope, Lygea,* and *Lucosia,*
the daughter of *Achelous,* and *Calliope*
singing as sweetely . . . as doth an arbor
of Nightingales. . . . They shewed there
. . . their *habitation* to be *in a litle Isle
. . . it was betwixt Italie and Cicile,* where
thorow *their sweete musicke,* they allured . . . with their sugred bayte, *all
such as sayled by,* to come *vnto them,
whome* incontinently they slew.   The
Poetes fayne that none euer passed them
but Vlisses, who . . . escaped them, bindy-
ing himselfe to the maste of the shippe,
and stopping his Mariners eares with
waxe. . . . But they tooke such a dis-
pleasure at his escaping of them, and sor-
rowed so, that in shorte tyme after they
threwe themselves headlong *into the Sea,*
whome (*Neptune* foreseyng) *hath turned
into Marmaydes.* (Ni$^v$)

COOPER (*Thesaurus*)

Sirênes, *were three daughters* of Achelous
and Caliope, which dwelled *in an Ile
between Italy and Sicilie,* who *with their
sweete singing drewe such vnto them, as
passed that* sea, *and than slue them.* As
it happened Ulysses to sayle that way, he
stopped the eares of all his companie, to
the intent they should not heare the songes
of the Sirenes, and caused himselfe to be
bound to the maste of the shippe, and so
escaped.   Wherefore the sirenes sorowed
so much, that they were disapoynted, that
*they threwe themselues into the sea, whom
poetes feigned to be Mermaydens.*

The names of the three sirens and the detail of Ulysses stopping the ears
of his companions with wax may have come from Stephanus.   Such details
as the "isle betweene Italie and Sicilie," the "poetes feigned," the sirens
being turned into mermaids, etc., are common to Grange and Cooper, and
not in the Stephanus.

### 4. JOHN NORTHBROOKE

On account of its relation to the Elizabethan drama John Northbrooke's
*Treatise against Dicing, Dancing, Plays and Interludes* . . . (*ca.* 1577) is
probably better known than Grange's *Golden Aphroditis.*   Students familiar with the *Treatise* will remember that this work is somewhat of a
pastiche, drawing matter from many sources, some acknowledged and
some not mentioned.   Among the unacknowledged sources is Cooper's

*Thesaurus.* From this source, Northbrooke takes quite literally at least six passages.

One,[20] for example, consists of a half page, in which Age, personified, explains to youth the various kinds of plays. Age lists and explains the meaning of seven types of plays or games, as follows: *Ludi Circenses, Ludi Compitalitii, Ludi Florales, Ludi Gladiatorii, Ludi Gymnici, Ludi Lupercales,* and *Ludi Magalenses.* Under *Ludus* in the *Thesaurus* proper all these terms are defined in the order observed by Northbrooke. Comparison of the texts shows that Northbrooke followed, almost verbatim, the definitions in his source, supplying only the connections to convert the dictionary definitions into a paragraph.

The marginal note (p. 84) on *Histrix* is a good illustration of the way Northbrooke follows his source. He writes:

*Histrix* is a little beast with speckled prickles on his back, whiche he will cast off and hurt menne with them, which is, as Plinie sayth, a porkepine.

These are the exact words of Cooper in the *Thesaurus,* except that Plinie, as the authority, stands first, and the connective phrase "which is" does not appear in the dictionary.

From the same source comes Northbrooke's comment on Roscius (p. 84):

Roscius, a Romane and a player in comedies (whom for his excellencie in pronunciation and gesture, noble Cicero called his iewell): the Romaines also gaue him (as hystories reporte) a stipende of one thousand groates for euery daye (which is in our money xvi$^{li}$, xiij$^s$, iiij$^d$); Lucius Silla, being Dictatour, aue him a ring of gold, &C.

This language is that of the *Thesaurus,* excepting the parenthetical "as hystories reporte," which is obviously designed to mislead the reader.

# CHAPTER IV

# SPENSER AND THE DICTIONARIES

## I. SPENSER AND COOPER'S *Thesaurus*

THE SHEPHEARDES CALENDAR, PUBLISHED IN 1579, FOLLOWED BY three or four years the work of George Gascoigne and other writers discussed in Chapter III. This epoch-making volume was ushered into the world with an introductory letter and with annotations by E. K. Whether we think of E. K. as Spenser,[1] or, as some prefer, Edward Kirk, close friend and collaborator, we may agree that Spenser knew and approved the comments and explanations accompanying the various eclogues. He is, therefore, in a very real sense responsible for the annotations, including the exposition of classical myth and legend. Though in the discussion which follows we shall, for convenience, refer to E. K. as an independent being, we are justified in thinking of the annotations as essentially Spenser's.

In the gloss for "March" (1. 16) E. K. writes:

*Flora,* the Goddesse of flowres, but indede (as saith Tacitus) *a famous harlot, which, with the abuse of her body having gotten great riches, made the people of Rome her heyre*: who, in *remembraunce* of so great beneficence, *appointed a yearely feste* for the memoriall of her, calling her, not as she was, nor as some doe thinke, *Andronica,* but Flora: *making her the goddesse of all floures,* and doing yerely to her solemne sacifice.

On this item Mustard[2] comments, "Perhaps it derived from Lactantius *Inst.,* 1.20.6"; and about ten years later Renwick[3] writes, "The story is not in Tacitus but in Boccaccio, *de Genealogia Deorum,* IV, lxi, where it is copied from Lactantius' *de Falsa Religione,* 20. I can find no trace of Andronica." Lotspeich agrees that Boccaccio is the source of the gloss in question and suggests that "The conception of Flora found in E. K.'s gloss" reappears in the *Faerie Queene* (1.1.48).[4]

Whatever the ultimate basis of E. K.'s comment on Flora, his immediate source, hitherto unnoticed, is the following item in Cooper's *Thesaurus*:

*Flora, A notable harlotte, which with the abuse of hir bodie, hauing gotten* xceeding *great ryches,* at hir death *left the people of Rome hir heyre,* and *appoynted* a great summe of money to lye in a stocke, with the vsurie *whereof yearely to hir remembraunce* should be kept certaine playes called *Floralia.* This bicause in processe of tyme it seemed to the Senate a foule matter, they cloked it with this deuise, *feigning that Flora was a Goddesse that had the tuition of flowers,* and that she with such games must bee worshipped, for the better proofe of flowers, fruites and hearbes.[5]

A comparison of these lines with the gloss quoted above shows that E. K. depends absolutely on the dictionary entry under *Flora*, having in fact borrowed verbatim many of the phrases from the original. E. K.'s insertion of the parenthesis, "as saith Tacitus," and the name "Andronica," may be designed to mislead, since there is no such comment in Tacitus and no Andronica notorious as a harlot.

The gloss on *Latonaes seede*, "April" (1. 86), is another example of E. K.'s close adherence to the dictionary. His comment follows:

*Latonaes seed,* was Apollo and Diana. Whom when as *Niobe the wife of Amphion scorned,* in respect of the noble fruict of her wombe, namely *her seven sonnes, and so many daughters,* Latona, *being therewith displeased, commaunded her sonne Phoebus to slea al the sonnes, and Diana all the daughters: whereat* the unfortunate *Niobe being sore dismayed,* and *lamenting out of measure,* was *feigned of the poetes to be turned into a stone upon the sepulchre of her children.* . . .

According to Renwick (p. 193), "The story again comes from Ovid, *Met.* VI, 146-311"; Mustard cites the same source. True, Ovid has the original story, but the version which E. K. used, a comparison will show at a glance, is found in Cooper's *Thesaurus*, thus:

*Niobe* . . . Daughter of Tantalus king of Phrygia, *wife of Amphion,* a woman of much wisedome, who brought foorth *seuen sonnes, and as many daughters* of excellent beautie: whereof she vaunted and preferred hir self before Latona, *mother of Apollo and Diana.* Wherefore *Latona being angrie, commaunded Apollo to slea all the sonnes, and Diana all the daughters.* For which deede Niobe *(through discomfort and heauinesse)* lost hir speech and remayned without moouing. Wherefore the *Poetes feigned,* that she *was transformed into a stone vpon the sepulchre of hir children.*

Commenting on the "Geaunte," "May" (l. 142), E. K. writes:

*The Geaunte* is the greate Atlas, whom the poetes feign to be a huge geaunt, that beareth Heaven on his shoulders: being in deede a merveilous highe mountaine in *Mauritania, that now is Barbarie,* which, to mans seeming, *perceth the cloudes,* and seemeth to touch the heavens. Others thinke, and they not amisse, that this fable was meant of one Atlas, king of the same countrye, (of whome may bee, that hil had his denomination) brother to *Prometheus, who (as the Grekes say) did first fynd out the hidden courses of the starres, by an excellent imagination: wherefore the poetes feigned, that he susteyned the firmament on hys shoulders.*

On this passage Renwick's note reads (p. 196) "From Boccaccio, *de Montibus,* attached to *de Genealogia Deorum,* and that work IV, xxxi." Mustard (p. 198) quotes Servius on the *Aeneid,* i, 741, and remarks, "E. K. gives a rather confusing blend of two ancient stories, that Atlas was the brother of Prometheus (Hesiod, *Theog.* 507 ff.) and that he was an African king (Servius, *loc. cit.*)." Lotspeich (p. 41) writes, "E. K.'s euhemeristic interpretation of Atlas in the gloss to May 142 is found in Servius, *ad Aen.* 1.741, Bocc. 4.31, and N. C. [Natalis Comes] 4.7."

E. K. was quite capable of making a "confusing blend" and perhaps on occasion capable of "euhemeristic interpretation." But in his gloss on *Atlas* he did not need to do so. He found the blend and the interpretation ready made in the following entry in Cooper's *Thesaurus*:

*Atlas* . . . Of this name were three. One king of Italy, and father of Electra. An other of Arcadia, father of Maia. The thirde of *Mauritania,* called the greatest, *the brother of Prometheus, who as the Greekes suppose, did first finde out the course of the starres, by an excellent imagination. Wherefore the poetes feigned, that he sustayned the Firmament with his shoulders . . . . It is also the name of an hill in Barbaria,* high and small, *which pearceth the clowdes.*[6]

E. K. has two comments on Argus: one in the "July" (l. 154) gloss, and the other in the "October" (l. 32) gloss. These read,

"JULY": Argus was of the Poets devised to be full of eyes, and therefore *to hym was committed the keeping of the transformed cow, Io.* . . .

"OCTOBER": *Argus eyes.* Of Argus is before said, that Iuno to him committed hir husband Iupiter his paragon, Iô, bicause *he had an hundred eyes:* but afterwarde *Mercury, wyth hys musick lulling Argus aslepe, slew him and brought Iô away, whose eyes* it is sayd that Iuno, for his eternall memory, *placed in her byrd the peacocks tayle.* . . .

Renwick (p. 219) cites Ovid, *Met.* I, 623-722, as the general source.

The story is told by Ovid, but E. K.'s immediate source appears to be the following lines from Cooper's *Thesaurus*:

*Argus* . . . The Poetes feigne, that *he had an hundred eyes,* signifying thereby his wisedome and circumspection. Moreouer, that *Iuno appointed him to keepe Io, whome shee had transformed into a Cowe.* But *Mercurius* (being sent by Iupiter) *with his sweete harmony brought Argus on sleepe, slue him, tooke Io from him, and brought hir vnto Egypt.* Then Iuno tooke Argus eyes, and set them in the Pecocks tayle, wherefore the Pecocke is called *Auis Iunonia.*

Though E. K. may have read in Ovid's *Metamorphoses* the story of Argus, his notes show, as to details, arrangement, and language—such as "the Poetes devised," "the transformed Cow," "lulling Argus aslepe," "slew him"—that the glosser was familiar with Cooper's description of Argus.

E. K.'s gloss for "July" (l. 146) reads thus:

*Whom Ida, Paris, which being the sonne of Priamus king of Troy, for his mother Hecubas dreame, which, being with child of hym, dreamed shee broughte forth a firebrand,* that set all the towre of Ilium on fire, *was cast forth on the hyll Ida, where being fostered of shepheards,* he eke in time *became a shepheard,* and *lastly came to knowledge of his parentage.*

Renwick comments, "This and the following note (i.e. on *Helena*) almost reproduce the note of Badius on the place in Mantuan." The editor does not, however, quote the lines from Badius which would support his statement. Lotspeich (p. 97) remarks, "E. K.'s gloss on July 145-7, which tells the story of Hecuba's dream, is very close to Bocc., *loc. cit.,* (i.e., 6. 22)." Despite these ascriptions, it appears that E. K. has once again drawn from Cooper's *Thesaurus* for two successive annotations. With the passage quoted above, compare this entry from Cooper:

*Paris, King Priamus his sonne of Troy, whose mother being with childe dreamed,* that she *was deliuered of a fyre branne:* whiche thinge the soothsaiers interpreted, that the childe, she went with, should be the confusion of Troy. Wherefore, when he was borne, kinge Priamus commaunded him to be destroied, but Hecuba of motherly pitie, procured him to be *priuily brought vp of a sheepehearde in Mount Ida.* [Here follows the account of the judgment of Paris and the award of the golden apple to Venus.] After he had long time liued as a sheepeheard, *he was at the last knowen,* and *receiued into his fathers fauour.* . . .[7]

These passages are very much the same in substance and strikingly similar in certain phrases and spelling. Compare—

| E. K. | COOPER |
|---|---|
| Paris . . . sonne of Priamus king of Troy . . . | Paris, King Priamus his sonne of Troy. |
| . . . his mother . . . being with child of hym, dreamed . . . | . . . whose mother being with childe dreamed . . . |

Other likenesses the reader may see for himself.

The second of the two successive notes by E. K., "July" (ll. 147 ff.) reads thus:

*A lasse,* Helena, the *wyfe of Menelaus* king of Lacedemonia, was by Venus, for the golden aple to her geven, then promised to Paris, who thereupon with a sorte of lustye *Troyanes,* stole her out of Lacedemonia and kept her in Troye: *which was the cause of the tenne yeares warre in Troye,* and *the moste famous citye of all Asia most lamentably sacked and defaced.*

In this comment, the glosser retains the detail of the golden apple from the account of Paris, and adapts the following entry from Cooper:

*Helena* . . . (The daughter of Iupiter, and Leda wife to Tyndarus king of Lacedemonie) for hir wonderfull beautie, was twise rauished. First at the age of nine yeres by Theseus: afterward by Paris the *Troyan,* then being *wife vnto Menelaus, which was the onely occasion of the tenne yeres siege,* and *finall destruction of the most famous citie of Troye,* with the death and losse of most noble princes, and of people innumerable.

The italicised phrases and sentences (italics ours) in the quoted passages, the similarity of content and of spelling, as in "Troyanes" and "Troyans," place beyond a reasonable doubt the dependence of E. K. on the *Thesaurus.*

In the gloss of "October" (l. 28), E. K. writes,

*The shepheard that,* Orpheus: of whom is sayd, that by his *excellent skil in musick and poetry, he recovered his wife Eurydice from hell.*

According to Ovid and Virgil, Eurydice was only "half-regained." But Spenser generally refers to the recovery of Eurydice without condition, as in this passage in October, and the following in *The Ruines of Time,*

> And they [the muses] for pittie of the sad wayment
> Which Orpheus for Eurydice did make,
> Her back againe to life sent for his sake (ll.390-92).

Whether Spenser followed E. K. or the glosser's authority, we do not know. We feel fairly certain, however, that the source of E. K.'s gloss is a passage in Cooper's *Thesaurus:*

Orpheus . . . an auncient *Poet and Harper most excellent.* He (as the Poetes surmised) did with his *Musicke* delyte wilde beastes and infernall spirites, and

## DICTIONARIVM

# HISTORICVM

## GEOGRAPHICVM,

### POETICVM,

Gentium , hominum, deorum gentilium, regionum, locorum,
ciuitatum, equorum, fluuiorum, finuum, portuum, promon-
toriorum , ac montium , antiqua recentioráque ad Sacras &
prophanas hiftorias , poëtarúmque fabulas intelligendas,
neceffaria Nomina, quo decet ordine complectens.

*Ingenti Nominum acervo, hiftoriarum, ac rerum infignium copia, poftrema*
*hac Editione auctius & locupletius redditum, mendisq́*
*propemodum infinitis repurgatum.*

## LVGDVNI,

### SVMPTIBVS THOMÆ SOVBRON,

#### ET MOSIS A PRATIS.

ꝼ *M. D. XCV.* ƒ

Title page of Charles Stephanus' *Dictionarium Historicum, Geographicum,*
*Poeticum,* 1595, from a copy in the University of Texas Library.

mooued stones with his sweete harmonie: whereby *hee recouered his wife Eurydice out of hell. . . .*[8]

In the quoted passages, we note that E. K. follows Cooper in referring to Orpheus as excellent in musick and poetry, and, in almost identical language, repeats Cooper's unconventional and unconditional statement that the Thracian musician recovered his wife.

One of the longest and most interesting of E. K.'s comments is that on the Graces, "April" (1. 109). Here E. K. writes:

*The Graces be three sisters, the daughters of Jupiter, (whose names are Aglaia, Thalia, Euphrosyne; and Homer onely addeth a fourth, sc. Pasithea) otherwise called Charites, that is, thanks: whom the poets feyned to be the goddesses of al* bounti and comelines, which therefore (as sayth Theodontius) they make three, to wete, *that men first ought to be gracious and bountiful to other freely, then to receive benefits at other mens hands* curteously, and *thirdly, to requite them thankfully: which are three sundry actions in liberalitye.* And Boccace saith, that they be painted naked (as they were indeede on the tombe of C. Julius Caesar) *the one having her backe toward us, and her face fromwarde, as proceeding from us: the other two toward us, noting double thanke to be due to us for the benefit we have done.*

On this note Renwick comments,

The note on the graces may come from Servius, or Seneca *de Beneficiis;* the reference to Theodontius suggests that it comes direct from Boccaccio *de Genealogia Deorum,* V, xxxv (p. 193).

Mustard (*op. cit.,* p. 197) likewise suggests the *Genealogia* (V. 35) as a possible source, and quotes from this work. Lotspeich (pp. 64-65) refers to Spenser's sources as Hesiod's *Theogony* (907-11), Servius' *ad Aeneid* (1. 720), Seneca's *De Beneficiis* (1. 3). All of these studies seem to imply a composite conception of the Graces, made by Spenser on the basis of his knowledge of the authors cited—Hesiod, Seneca, Servius, Boccaccio, and possibly Natalis Comes. The truth is that E. K. and Spenser did not need to put themselves to so much trouble. They could have found at least eight composite descriptions of the Graces[9] easily accessible in contemporary reference works. One of these is especially apt in this discussion; it is indeed the main source of E. K.'s gloss on the Graces. We refer to the entry *Charites* in Cooper's *Thesaurus.* This item reads thus:

*Charites, The Graces,* which were supposed to *bee the daughters of Iupiter, three in number, whose names were Aglaia, Thalia, and Euphrosyne.* And where in speaking or wryting appeared to be a marueylous delectation or sweet-

nesse, it was sayde, that therein was a grace, in Greeke, *Charis.* Some men suppose that there were three Graces deuised to signifie *that men ought to be both
bountiful and gracious to other, and secondly to take benefites at other mens
handes, and thirdely, thankefully to requite benefites receyued: which are three
sundrie actes in the vse of liberalitie.* Other say they imagined three graces to
signifie liberal thankfulnesse, and that we shoulde plentifully requite benefite
with vantage more than we receyued. Wherefore they *paint the Graces in
this maner, that the ones backe should be towarde vs, and hir face fromwarde,
as proceeding from vs, the other twoo towarde vs: noting double thanke to bee
due for the benefite we haue done. They were also painted naked,* to doe men to
witte, that pleasures shoulde be done vnfaynedly without cloke or dissimulation. . . .[10]

A comparison of the phrasing and content of Cooper's exposition of the
Graces (Charites) with that of E. K. will, we think, convince the most
skeptical that, though the glosser may have read other authorities on the
subject, he draws most of his matter directly from Cooper's *Thesaurus.*
Possible indebtedness of E. K. and Spenser to Cooper in the *Shepheardes
Calender* and in other poems we shall consider below. We wish now to
show that in *The Faerie Queene* Spenser drew again from the same passage in the *Thesaurus* that had been used in glossing the Graces in the
April poem of the *Shepheardes Calender.*

In an earlier study[11] we have, in fact, pointed out at some length the
relationship between the "April" Eclogue (ll. 109 ff.) together with the
gloss, and the well-known stanzas on the Graces in *The Faerie Queene*
(6.10.9 ff.). The evidence of that relationship may be seen in the following
tabulation of similarities:

1. In each scene there is a company of ladies "raunged in a ring."
(*S. C.,* "April," ll. 100 ff.; *F. Q.,* 6.10.12).

2. In both, the Graces dance and sing.

3. In both, a maiden admired by the piper is the center of attraction.

4. In both, this maid is crowned: in "April" (l. 122), with an "olive
girland"; in *F. Q.* (6.10.14) with a "rosie girland."

5. In both, flowers are brought to the maid ("April," ll. 136 ff.; *F. Q.,*
6.10.14).

6. In both, she is referred to as worthy to be the fourth grace.

7. In the two scenes, also, are certain verbal parallels or near parallels.
Compare, for example,

A

And whither rennes this bevie of ladies bright,
Raunged in a rowe?   ("April," ll. 118-20)

An hundred naked maidens lilly white,
All raunged in a ring, and dauncing in delight.
                                        (*F. Q.*, 6.10.11)

B

Wants not a fourth Grace to make the daunce even?
Let that rowme to my Lady be yeven:
She shal be a Grace,
To fyll the fourth place,
And reigne with the rest in heaven.
                                        ("April," ll. 113 ff.)

But what so sure she was, she worthy was
To be the fourth with these three other placed . . . .
Another Grace she well deserves to be,
In whom so many graces gathered are
Excelling much the meane of her degree
Divine resemblaunce, beauty soveraine rare . . . .
                                        (*F. Q.*, 6.10.25-27)

All these similarities in details of scene and in language are but a prelude to a more striking relationship between E. K.'s gloss on the Graces in
the April poem and the very heart of Spenser's description of the Graces
at the center of the scene in *The Faerie Queene* (6.10.22-24).   In order
to make clear this relationship, we need to recall that E. K.'s gloss on
"April" (l. 109) is based primarily upon the entry of *Charites* in Cooper's
*Thesaurus,* as shown above.   A further tie-up of E. K.'s gloss on the
Graces with the dictionaries lies in the fact that Cooper's discourse on
*Charites,* which is the basis of E. K.'s, is itself a free translation of a part
of Charles Stephanus' *Dictionarium* on the same subject.   The Stephanus
entry follows.

Charites, seu Gratias, quidam ex Venere & Ioue genitas scripserunt, alij ex
Venere & Libero: Cicero ex Erebo & nocte ortas existimat. Lactantius in
primum Thebaidos, Iouis & Autonoes filias putat.  Hesiodus Iouis & Eurymones
[Eurynomes?] Oceani filias scribit.   Tres sunt, Aglaia (quae alio nomine
Pasithea dicitur) Thalia, Euphrosine.   Tot autem ideo esse prodiderunt, quia
& benefici esse in alios debemus, & aliorum beneficia suscipere: & iis qui in nos
fuerunt liberales, retribuere: quae tres actiones sunt separatae.  Alij ideo dicunt

tres Gratias esse, quia acceptum beneficium cum foenore reddi debet. Quapropter solebant veteres ita Gratias pingere, vt vna earum auersam faciem teneret, quasi à nobis profecta: duae vero nos aspicerent, vt duplex nobis beneficium rependi debere ostenderent. Nudae etiam pingebantur, quia beneficia fuco debent carere, & nullo velamine obtegi: iuuenes, ne beneficij memoria senescat: ridentes, quod hilariter dandum sit. Item connexae: quia insolubiles esse Gratias dicet: & beneficium, aliud semper beneficium parere, perpetuumque amicitiae foedus. Qui Veneris & Liberi filias arbitrantur (e quibus est Seruius) hac mouentur ratione, quod horum praecipue deorum muneribus, gratiae concilientur. Tradunt etiam eas in Acidalio fonte, qui est in Orchomeno Boeotiae vrbe, lauari, quoniam pura esse beneficia oportet, non sordida.

Cooper disregarded, apparently, the first two sentences of the Latin and the last two, in the Stephanus. He freely translated all sentences lying between.

It is now obvious that E. K.'s gloss on the Graces in "April" (ll. 109 ff.) derives directly from Cooper's *Thesaurus,* which in turn translates Charles Stephanus' *Charites.* Certainly Spenser knew E. K.'s gloss, and it is not an improbable assumption that he was familiar with the sources in Cooper and Stephanus back of this gloss on the Graces. We have noted a rather close relationship between the April poem, in which the Graces have a prominent role (and on which E. K. makes his gloss) and the scene in *The Faerie Queene* (6.10.9 ff.) in which the three sisters are even more prominent. An analysis of the three famous stanzas which most adequately describe and characterize the Graces will, we think, further establish Spenser's familiarity with Stephanus and Cooper on the Graces. These Stanzas follow:

### XXII

They are the daughters of sky-ruling Jove,
By him begot of faire *Eurynome,*
The Oceans daughter, in this pleasant grove,
As he, this way comming from feastfull glee
Of *Thetis* wedding with Æacidee,
In sommers shade him selfe here rested weary.
The first of them hight mylde *Euphrosyne,*
Next faire *Aglaia,* last *Thalia* merry:
Sweete goddesses all three, which me in mirth do cherry.

### XXIII

These three on men all gracious gifts bestow,
Which decke the body or adorne the mynde,
To make them lovely or well favoured show,

As comely carriage, entertainement kynde,
Sweete semblaunt, friendly offices that bynde,
And all the complements of curtesie:
They teach us, how to each degree and kynde
We should our selves demeane, to low, to hie,
To friends, to foes; which skill men call civility.

### XXIV

Therefore they alwaies smoothly seeme to smile,
That we likewise should mylde and gentle be,
And also naked are, that without guile
Or false dissemblaunce all them plaine may see,
Simple and true, from covert malice free:
And eeke them selves so in their daunce they bore,
That two of them still froward seem'd to bee,
But one still towards shew'd her selfe afore;
That good should from us goe, then come, in greater store.

Stanza XXII seems to owe nothing to E. K.'s gloss or to Cooper. The reference to Thetis' wedding with Aeacidee has no basis in any of the accounts of the Graces. This seems to be, in fact, Spenser's own expansion. The first two lines and a half, giving the paternity of the Graces, and the last three lines, revealing their names, could have come from Charles Stephanus' *Dictionarium*. Compare the Stephanus sketch above.

It is sometimes suggested that Stanzas XXIII and XXIV owe something to E. K.'s gloss on the Graces. In our opinion, the indebtedness is indirectly to the gloss, directly to the source which it suggested—Cooper's *Thesaurus*. References to the smiling or laughing of the Graces, for example, and to the league of love and friendship or friendly offices, not in the gloss, are common to Cooper and Spenser. So, too, the common use of the impersonal "men," and of "teach," and so on, suggests to us that Spenser had reread the Cooper and found additional suggestions in the lines not used by E. K. in the gloss. A few comparative passages will, however, better illustrate our point.

| COOPER | SPENSER |
|---|---|
| (1) | These three on men all gracious gifts bestow, |
| . . . Some men suppose that there were three Graces devised to signifie that men ought to bee both bountifull and gracious to other. | Which decke the body or adorne the mynde, |
| | To make them lovely or well favoured show. . . . (6.10.23) |

(2)

. . . finally their armes were painted as it were linked one within an other, to *teach* that *kindnesse should bee vndissoluble,* and one benefite so to prouoke an other, as it may make the league of loue and *friendship* sure and perpetuall.

As comely carriage, *entertainement kynde,*
Sweete semblaunt, *friendly offices that bynde,*
And all the complements of curtesie:
They *teach* us, how to each degree and kynde
We should our selves demeane, to low, to hie,
To *friends,* to foes; which skill men call civility.

(3)

. . . They were discriued laughing, because pleasures ought to bee done with a cheerefull and glad minde. . . .

Therefore they alwaies smoothly seeme to smile,
That we likewise should mylde and gentle be. . . .

(4)

They were *also* painted *naked,* to doe menne to witte, that pleasures shoulde be done vnfaynedly *withoute cloke* or *dissimulation.* . . .

And *also naked* are, that *without guile*
Or *false dissemblaunce* all them plaine may see,
Simple and true, from covert malice free.

(5)

Wherefore they paint the Graces in this maner, that the ones backe should be *towarde* vs, and hir face *fromwarde,* as proceeding from vs, the other twoo *towarde* vs: noting double thanke to bee due for the benefite we haue done.

And eeke them selves so in their daunce they bore,
That two of them still *froward* seem'd to bee,
But one still *towards* shew'd her selfe afore;
That good should from us goe, then come, in greater store.

It is noteworthy in No. 5, that Spenser has reversed the order so that two graces are moving away from us and one toward us. Commentators have noticed that this order departs from Servius, the source usually suggested. It also differs from the various other possible sources which we have discussed. The change was probably deliberate with Spenser, for the sake of changing what otherwise might be regarded as a mercenary motive. But the parallels in (3) and (4) together with the striking similarity of phrasing by Spenser and Cooper—all without basis in E. K.'s gloss on the Graces—show, I think, that Spenser's source of inspiration in these lines was the *Thesaurus.* And this book, with the suggestion from Stephanus that the Graces were the daughters of Jove and Eurynome, "The Oceans daughter" (Stz. XXII), contributed much, though not all, to the elaborate presentation of the fair daughters in Book VI of *The Faerie Queene.*

In Spenser's allusions to the Parcae, or fatal sisters, we see a similar manner of procedure. Spenser writes, in "November" (ll. 148-49),

> The Fatall Sisters eke repent
> Her vitall threde so soone was spent.

E. K.'s gloss on the allusion runs thus:

*The fatall sisters,* Clotho, Lachesis, and Atropos, daughters of Herebus and the Nighte, whom the poetes fayne to spinne the life of man, as it were a long threde, which they drawe out in length, till his fatal howre and timely death be come; but if by other casualtie his dayes be abridged, then one of them, that is, Atropos, is sayde to have cut the threde in twain.

For this gloss, E. K. appears to have drawn, in large part, from the following entry in Cooper's *Thesaurus*:

*Parcae,* Ladyes of destinie. The names of them bee *Clotho, Lachesis,* and *Atropos.* The first of them is deuised to beare the distaffe, the seconde to spinne out the threede of mannes lyfe so long as it doth continue, the thirde breaketh of the threede, and endeth the mans life. They are ymagined to bee the daughters of Erebus, and Nox.

Though E. K., apparently, attempted to conceal his indebtedness to Cooper, he has, in the naming of the sisters and ascription of paternity—in both of which there were other choices—followed the *Thesaurus.* Compare also,

| E. K. | COOPER |
|---|---|
| to spinne the life of man, as it were a long threde, which they drawe out in length. . . . | to spinne out the threde of mannes lyfe so long as it doth continue. . . . |

Spenser's most elaborate portrayal of the Fates occurs in *The Faerie Queene* (4.2.47-52). In Stanza XLVIII, we read,

> There she them found, all sitting round about
> The direfull distaffe standing in the mid,
> And with unwearied fingers drawing out
> The lines of life, from living knowledge hid.
> Sad Clotho held the rocke, the whiles the thrid
> By griesly Lachesis was spun with paine,
> That cruell Atropos eftsoones undid,
> With cursed knife cutting the twist in twaine.

Lotspeich suggests that in the association of the Fates with Daemogorgon and Chaos (Stz. XLVII) Spenser may have been indebted to Boccaccio or Natalis Comes, but that in 4.2.48 the poet "gives, with more elaboration than classical sources, the conventional picture of the three Fates spinning and cutting the threads of life." It may be noted that the elaboration in the phrasing *"drawing out The lines of life* from living knowledge hid" and "cruell Atropos" "with cursed knife cutting the twist in twaine," and the Fates entreating *"To draw them longer out"* (Stz. LI) depend upon E. K.'s gloss. Compare, for example, E. K.'s "Atropos . . . cut the threde in twain" and Spenser's "Atropos . . . cutting the twist in twaine." The mention of the "distaffe"—not in E. K.—the holding of the "rocke" (distaff) by Clotho, and the spinning of the thread by Lachesis, all indicate that Spenser remembered also E. K.'s original, Cooper's *Thesaurus* on the "Ladyes of destinie."

In E. K.'s gloss for "November" (l. 179) we read, *"Elysian fieldes* be *devised of poetes* to be a *place of pleasure* like Paradise, where the *happye soules* doe rest in peace and eternal happynesse." This gloss depends on Cooper's *Thesaurus,* in the following entries: *"Elysium, A place of pleasure,* where *poetes* did suppose the *soules of good men to dwell;"* and *"Elysij campi,* the same place that is called Elysium." On this gloss and its source in the *Thesaurus* Spenser draws again in *The Faerie Queene* (4.10.23):

> In such luxurious plentie of all *pleasure,*
> It seem'd a *second paradise* to ghesse,
> • So lavishly enricht with Natures threasure,
> That if the *happie soules,* which doe possesse
> Th' *Elysian fields* and *live in lasting blesse.*

In *The Faerie Queene* (4.11.16) Spenser writes of Albion,

> For Albion the sonne of Neptune was,
> Who, for the proofe of his great puissance,
> Out of his Albion did on dry-foot pas
> Into old Gall, that now is cleeped France,
> To fight with Hercules, that did advance
> To vanquish all the world with matchlesse might,
> And there his mortall part by great mischance
> Was slaine.

The poet is here writing of Albion as one of the founders of nations, "the most important one to Spenser" (Lotspeich, p. 35). Through Spenser may be, in general, following British chronicle history, as Lotspeich suggests, he seems likely to have remembered a remark about Albion in the

*Thesaurus.* After a long discussion, under *Albion,* concerning the founding and naming of Britain or Albion, Cooper concludes:

. . . Notwithstanding, Pomponius Mela maketh mention of a gyaunt called *Albion,* whome Hercules slue in Gallia, which was sonne of Neptunus, who mought with more reason be demed the first giuer of this name to this Ile, than that the other surmises should be likely.

There can be little doubt that Spenser would have read what was written about Albion and would have noted the emphasis upon Albion as the "first giver of this name." There are also in Cooper's item all of the details found in Spenser's allusion to Albion.

Another example of the indebtedness of *The Faerie Queene* to the *Thesaurus* is found in Spenser's reference to the temple of Diana at Ephesus and possibly in an allusion to the temple built by Herod, King of the Jews. The lines containing the allusions are these:

> Not that same famous temple of Diane,
> Whose hight all Ephesus did oversee,
> And which all Asia sought with vowes prophane,
> One of the worlds seven wonders sayd to bee,
> Might match with this by many a degree:
> Nor that which that wise king of Jurie framed,
> With endlesse cost, to be th' Almighties see.
> (*F. Q.,* 4.10.30)

Spenser's allusions derive from two entries—*Ephesus* and *Herodes*—in Cooper's *Thesaurus*:

Ephesus, . . . noble auncient citie in Asia the lesse . . . . In thys citie was the *famous temple of Diana, numbred among the seauen wonders of the worlde, edifyed by all* Asia in an hundred and twentie yeares.

Herodes, The sonne of Antipater, which in the tenth yeare of *Augustus,* was of the Romaynes declared king of the Jewes: and he reigned 37 years. To winne the fauour of the Jewes, he pulled downe the temple that after the captiuitie was buylded by Zorobabell, Jehosua, and Esdra, and *with exceeding great charges buylded* an other to the figure and paterne of that which Salomon erected.

As to Spenser's use of the Ephesus entry there can be little doubt. The reference to the temple "framed" by the "wise king of Jurie" may well be to Solomon's temple, as has been suggested (Cf. 1 Kings 5-6), but the Herodes entry containing the phrase "with exceeding great charges buylded" would be suggestive of Spenser's "framed with endlesse cost."

In *The Faerie Queene,* Spenser has two allusions to Hylas, the source of which has not been satisfactorily accounted for.  These are as follows:

> Or that same daintie lad, which was so deare
> To great Alcides that when as he dyde,
> He wailed womanlike with many a teare,
> And every wood and every valley wyde
> He fild with Hylas name; the nymphes eke Hylas cryde.
>
> (3.12.7)

> Such were great Hercules, and Hyllus deare;
> Trew Jonathan, and David trustie tryde.
>
> (4.10.27)

No one, so far as we can discover, has noticed Spenser's mistaken reference, in the second quotation, to "Hyllus," the son of Hercules, instead of "Hylas," his beloved companion.  This mistake, probably indicating not very great familiarity with the story, we shall try to explain below.  A striking feature of Spenser's version of the story, as adumbrated in the first excerpt above (3.12.7) is that the poet lets Hylas die.  This seems to be a departure from known classical accounts.  On this feature Jortin (*Var. Ed.* 3) comments, "It is unpoetical to make Hylas die.  The Nymphs gave him immortality."  We may add that Spenser's conception of Hylas and the manner of his death are far from the spirit of the treatment in Theocritus (*Idyll* 13) and the brief reference in Virgil (*Ecl.* 6.43.4), sometimes mentioned as contributory to Spenser's presentation.

A version of the story which would explain Spenser's apparent confusion of "Hylas" and "Hyllus" and account for the unromantic and unpoetic death of Hylas is that in Cooper's *Thesaurus*:

Hyla . . . or Hylas.  The companion of Hercules whom he lost in the borders of Ionia.  For when Hercules fled out of Caledonia, and came with his wife Deianira, and his sonne Hyllus to the Dropians, he desired of Theodamus some meat and drink to refreshe his sonne.  [The narrative then recounts the refusal of Theodamus, the slaying of the ox by Hercules, the resulting conflict, and Hercules' victory].  But in the ende he got the victorie, slue Theodamus, and tooke with him his companion Hylas, whom ever after he fauoured and loued as his owne.  In sayling to Colchos for the golden fleece, when Hercules had broken his Oare, he went to lande with his derlyng Hylas, in the woodes of *Mysia* to get him another Oare.  [Here Hylas is sent to the river Ascanius to fetch water] . . . And with his arms and body strayned so farre, that he fell into the riuer and there was drowned.  Whose losse Hercules tooke so greeuously that, not knowing the misaduenture, he lefte the Argonautes, and *went over all Mysia seeking and crying for Hylas.*

Cooper's version of the story is a free translation of the Hylas item in Charles Stephanus' *Dictionarium,* except in two sentences: Stephanus has in the first sentence of his entry "Hylas, filius Theodamantis, quem Hercules rapuit." Compare Cooper's first sentence above. Then Cooper omits from his translation the last sentence but one in Stephanus' Latin: "Quae res poetis occasionem praebuit famulandi Hylam a Nymphis fuisse raptum." And the last sentence in Stephanus, concluding "vt relictis Argonautis, Mysiam totam oberrans, Hylam quaereret," Cooper slightly expands to "he lefte the Argonauts, and went over all Mysia seeking and crying for Hylas."

We may now notice that Cooper's version with the first sentence (different from his source), introducing "Hylas" as the companion of Hercules, and the second sentence, referring to "Hyllus," the son of Hercules, could easily lead to the confusion of names observable in Spenser. The expanded last sentence of Cooper with the introduction of "crying" would suggest Spenser's use of the word in "eke Hylas cryde," and also the statement that Hercules "wailed womanlike with many a teare." And Spenser's "every wood and every valley wyde" may echo Cooper's "in the woodes of Mysia."

The allusions to Hylas in Theocritus and Virgil are, in spirit and content, altogether different from Cooper and Spenser. In Theocritus, Hylas is drawn into the fountain by the Nymphs and kept by them, but not drowned. In the classical authors there is no suggestion of Hercules' crying or wailing like a woman. Spenser's "the nymphes eke Hylas cryed" could be his own elaboration, or an echo of Stephanus, or Virgil, or Theocritus. Even so, he is, in the main, following Cooper.

Four times by way of illustration, Spenser alludes to the Castor and Pollux myth. Typical of the allusions are these:

> So raisde they eke faire Ledaes warlick twinnes,
> And interchanged life unto them lent,
> *That, when th' one dies, th' other then beginnes*
> To shew in heaven his brightnes orient.
>                                         (*R. T.* 386-89.)
> And eke the Bull hath with his bow-bent horne
> So hardly butted those *two Twinnes of Jove,*
> That they have crusht the Crab.
>                                         (5. Pr. 6)

In 7.7.34. the reference is to the "Twinnes of Leda," and in *Prothalamion*

(173-4.) to the "twins of Jove." For the allusion in *The Ruines of Time*, Lotspeich[12] cites for comparison the *Aeneid* (6.121-22) and Servius on the same. "The idea," he continues, "at 5. Pr. 6 that both are 'twinnes of Jove,' which contradicts the more common myth that Castor was son of Tyndarus, is supported by N. C[omes] 8.9." But contemporary diction-aries—C. Stephanus, Calepine, and Cooper—all make Castor and Pollux twins of Jove and of Leda. There is, then, no need to refer to Comes, especially since the language of Cooper seems definitely to suggest that of Spenser. Compare, for example, the *Thesaurus*:

*Castor*, and *Pollux*, *Two twinnes* begotten on Leda *by Jupiter* (as poetes feigne) in the forme of a swanne. [Here the compiler tells how the twins cleared the sea of pirates and were by sailors regarded as gods of the sea; how they took part in the Argonautic expedition to Colchos; and how, after their return, they stormed the city of Aphidna, and rescued their sister Helena, stolen away by Hercules. They were the war-like twins.] In the ende when Castor (who is sayde to be mortall, bicause he was not hatched of the same Egge that Pollux was) ended hys lyfe and dyed: Pollux being immortall, desired of his Father Iupiter, that hee might part his immortall state wyth his brother Castor. Which thing Iupiter graunted, and the two brothers lyued and dyed by course. Oc-casion of this fable was taken of the starres called *Gemini,* into the which it is feigned, those twoo brothers were turned. For the nature of them is, *that when the one ryseth, the other goeth downe.*

Here in Cooper is not only the story, but phrasing which closely parallels that of Spenser. Compare Spenser's "two Twinnes of Jove" and Cooper's *"Two Twinnes* begotten on Leda *by Jupiter,"* and Spenser's "That, when th' one dies, th' other then beginnes/To shew in heaven his brightnes orient," and Cooper's "that when the one ryseth, the other goeth downe."

## 2. SPENSER AND CHARLES STEPHANUS

Of the vogue and repute of the Stephanus dictionaries, we have treated above. Charles Stephanus' *Dictionarium Historicum, Geographicum, Poeticum* (1553, etc.) and Robert Stephanus' *Thesaurus Linguae Latinae* (1573) must have been of special value to Spenser and to other poets and scholars as well as to the readers of classical poetry and English poetry containing frequent allusions to classical mythology and history. Though there is no external evidence of Spenser's use of these dictionaries, there is a strong presumption that he would consult them repeatedly, and the internal evidence supports such a presumption. Even if the proof of Spenser's use of these reference books is not conclusive, we still have in them, as in Cooper's *Thesaurus,* most valuable illustrations of contemporary conceptions of classic myth and legend, and the matter for appropriate annotations. The value of the Stephanus lexicons in assessing the classical background of Spenser and his audience will emerge in the presentation of the illustrations which follow.

In "March" (ll. 95-97), Thomalin's account of Cupid's shaft wounding him "in the heele" elicits this gloss from E. K.:

> . . . I remember that in Homer it is sayd of Thetis, that shee tooke her young babe Achilles, being newely borne, and, holding him by the heele, dipped him in the river of Styx. The vertue whereof is, to defend and keepe the bodyes washed therein from any mortall wound. So Achilles being washed al over, save onely his hele, by which his mother held, was the rest invulnerable: therfore by Paris was feyned to bee shote with a poysoned arrowe in the heele, whiles he was busie about the marying of Polyxena in the temple of Apollo. . . .

Of this gloss, Renwick (p. 189) remarks,

> This is not in Homer, though it was perhaps natural for E. K. to refer all of the Achilles legend to him. He probably got it . . . from Boccaccio (xii, lii) who quotes Fulgentius, *Mythologia,* III, vii. . . .

Lotspeich, likewise, suggests Boccaccio as a probable source, though he thinks Renwick omits from the quotation "the part which would determine the allegory of 'lustfull love,' expounded by E. K.; '. . . et ideo per talum non mersum in Styge invictam in Achille libidinem voluerunt.' "

E. K. may well have had in mind the passage cited in Boccaccio. We think he had also refreshed his memory by reading the following entry in Stephanus' *Dictionarium*:

> *Achilles* . . . Pelei & Thetidis filius, quem adhuc infantem mater Stygiis vndis immersit: quamobrem [sic] inuulnerabilis toto corpore factus est, praeterquam in ea pedis parte, qua comprehensus ab ipsa fuerat, dum ablueretur . . . occisus est tandem à Paride, dum coniugium Polyxenes speraret . . . *De quo Plin.* 4.12.55 . . . & *Homerus in Iliade.* . . . Mythologi Achillem Imperatoris praestantissimi effigiem esse demonstrant. Fortes autem viri voluptatum illecebris potius quàm vi externa saepissimè obruuntur.

The mistaken reference to Homer, common to this entry and to E. K.'s gloss, seems to us significant, especially since the gloss contains the details and seems to echo the language of the dictionary item. The closing sentence in Stephanus' sketch may also have suggested the allegory of "lustfull love."

The gloss on "Maias bowre," "March" (l. 17), reads thus:

*Maias bower,* that is, the pleasaunt field, or rather the Maye bushes. Maia is a goddes, and the mother of Mercurie, in honour of whome the moneth of Maye is of her name so called, as sayth Macrobius.

Both Mustard[13] and Renwick[14] point to the *Saturnalia* (i, xii, 19) of Macrobius as the basis of this comment. Lotspeich[15] writes, on the other hand, that E. K.'s gloss on "March" (l. 17) is, in spite of his citing Macrobius, probably based on Boccaccio, 4.35, "Ei quidem, ut ait Macrobius, mense Maio eo quod ab ea denominatum putarent." It is not evident from this quotation that Boccaccio had all the details about Maia which are in E. K.'s gloss. The Macrobius, on the other hand, mentions that Maia was a goddess and was the mother of Mercury. This, as Mustard and Renwick suggest, could have been the source. So, also, could the following from Charles Stephanus' *Dictionarium*:

Maius, mensis, a maioribus dictus est, quia vt inquit Macrob.[ius] maioribus consecratus erat. . . . Sunt qui Maium a Maiestate dea denominatum velint . . . Alij a Maia Mercurij matre. . . .[16]

In this entry are all the details with the reference to Macrobius—"vt inquit Macrob."—and knowing E. K.'s habits in making other glosses, we suggest that the dictionary item is his most likely source.

In these lines in "October" (ll. 103-8) Spenser may have had direct suggestion from Charles Stephanus' *Dictionarium*:

> Who ever casts to compasse weightye prise,
> And thinks to throwe out thondring words of threate,
> Let powre in lavish cups and thriftie bitts of meate;
> For Bacchus fruite is frend to Phoebus wise,
> And when with wine the braine begins to sweate,
> The nombers flowe as fast as spring doth ryse.

On one phrase in the passage E. K. has this gloss: "*Lavish cups* resembleth that comen verse, 'Faecundi calices quem non fecere disertum?' "

Turning to *Bacchus* in the Charles Stephanus, we read the following: Hunc [i. e., Bacchus] Musarum Comitem censuerunt: quia vini calor excitet ingenium: nam & disertos & audaces, & fortes faciunt vini meracioris pocula, teste Horatio,

> "*Faecundi calices quem non* facere disertum?"

Idem & nudus & semper iuuenis habitus est, quod arcana effutiant facile vino madidi.

An analysis and comparison of the two passages shows, we think, that the Latin is the basis of the English. Compare, for example, "For Bacchus fruite is frend to Phoebus wise" and "quia vini calor excitet ingenium"; and "And thinks to throwe out thondring words of threate" and "nam & disertos & audaces, & fortes faciunt vini meracioris pocula"; "Let powre in lavish cups . . ." and "Faecundi calices . . ."; "And when with wine the braine begins to sweate,/The nombers flowe as fast as spring doth ryse" and "quod arcana effutiant facile vino madidi." And strangely enough E. K. quotes the line from Horace, "Faecundi calices, etc.," which is at the center of both passages.

One of the interesting E. K. glosses is that on "April" (1. 26), in which the annotator remarks that Hobbinoll should not be grieved that Rosalind should be commended in his verses for her rare virtue since she was no less deserving than Theocritus' Myrto or Petrarch's Laura,

. . . or Himera, the worthye poete Stesichorus hys idole: upon whom he is sayd so much to have doted, that, in regard of her excellencie, he scorned and wrote against the beauty of Helena. For which his praesumptuous and unheedie hardinesse, he is sayde by vengeaunce of the gods, thereat being offended, to have lost both his eyes.

It looks as if the mythical E. K. had deliberately distorted the story in this note to suit his purpose since Himera is a city in Sicily where Stesichorus lived and, of course, not the lady beloved of the poet. But Spenser employs the story also in *Colin Clouts Come Home Again,* avoiding the mistake of the "April" gloss. Here are the lines in the latter poem:

> And well I wote that oft I heard it spoken,
> How one that fairest Helene did revile,
> Through judgement of the gods, to been ywroken,
> Lost both his eyes, and so remaynd long while,
> Till he recanted had his wicked rimes,
> And made amends to her with treble praise.
>
> (ll. 919-24)

Though Spenser here corrects or avoids the error of the gloss, his phrase "Lost both his eyes" seems to show familiarity with it. It is reasonable to assume that the poet knew both the gloss and its source. What is the source?

In this connection Renwick's comment (Qtd. *Var. Ed.* 7.482) is apropos. Renwick suggests that the story is from Plato's *Phaedrus* (243). (Incidentally, there is only an allusion to the story, in *Phaedrus.*) He states also that Bembo quotes it in his *Asolani* (ed. 1540, p. 58), which Spenser probably knew, and following him, Castiglione in his *Cortegiano*: "Therefore to give M. Morello and Sir Fredericke warninge, that they lose not their sight, as Stesichorus did, a peine most meete for whoso dispraiseth beawtie . . . (Side-note:) A notable poet which lost his sight for writing against Helena, and recanting had his sight restored again."

"Himera," though wrongly applied by E. K., is absent from the sources cited by Renwick; so too are "by vengeaunce of the gods," in the gloss, and "Through judgement of the Gods" in *Colin Clout*. A version of the story which would account for all the details missing in suggested sources is this from Charles Stephanus:

Stesichorus poeta lyricus, ex Himera Siciliae vrbe, a qua & Himeraeus est cognominatus. Stesichorus autem dictus est ab eo, quod primus cum citharae cantu chorum coniunxerit: nam vero nomine Tisias dicebatur. Hic cum aliquando acerrimo carmine in Helenam, tanquam belli Troiani facem, esset inuectus, a Castore & Polluce luminibus dicitur orbatus, alioque rursus carmine cantata palinodia visum recepisse.

In the description of Donwallo (*F. Q.* 2.10.39) and Guitheline (2.10.42) Spenser draws upon the Aegerie-Numa legend. The stanzas run thus:

### XXXIX

Then made he [Donwallo] sacred lawes, which some men say
Were unto him reveald in vision,
By which he freed the traveilers high way,
The churches part, and ploughmans portion,
Restraining stealth and strong extortion;
The gratious Numa of Great Britany. . . .

### XLII

After him raigned Guitheline his hayre,
The justest man and trewest in his daies,
Who had to wife Dame Mertia the fayre,
A woman worthy of immortall praise,
Which for this realme found many goodly layes,
And wholesome statutes to her husband brought:
Her many deemd to have beene of the Fayes,
As was Aegerie, that Numa tought. . . .

Lotspeich points out that the material from classic myth in the quoted lines was not suggested by the English chronicles which Spenser was here following for his history, but probably by Ovid (*Fasti* 3.262 and 275-76).

The story of the Nymph who instructed the lawgiver and peacemaker is twice told with varying emphasis by Charles Stephanus—under *Aegeria* and *Numa Pompilius*.

Aegêria, nympha nemoris Aricini, colebatur prope Aricinum lacum, cum qua Numa Pompilius nocturnum colloquium se habere simulauit super cultu religionum, quo armorum & praedae studio flagrantem populum Romanum abstraheret, & leges à se conditas sanctiores redderet. Plutarch, in Numa. Alij dicunt fuisse vxorem Numae Pompilij secundi regis Romanorum, quae teste Ouid. lib. 15. Metamorphoseon, mortuo Numa ob dolorem flendo in fontem sui nominis versa est. Idem libro Fastorum tertio: *Aegeria est, quae praebet aquas, dea grata Camoenis, Illa Numae coniux, consiliúmque fuit.*
Numa Pompilius, . . . Romanorum rex, iustitia & pietate insignis: qui pacatis finitimorum odiis, quo truces efferatósque longa militia animos ad pacis artes traduceret, ad *Deorum cultum animum* adiecit. . . . Quae omnia quò maiore apud *imperitam plebem* in veneratione essent, simulauit sibi cum Ægeria Nympha nocturnos congressus esse, eiusque se monitu, quae acceptissima diis essent, sacra instituere. Postremò vbi maxima cum reuerentia & suorum, & finitimorum 40. annis regnasset, diem obiit. Liu. 1. ab vrbe condita. Plutarch.

The first half of the Aegeria entry would account for the comparison of Donwallo (Stz. XXXIX) with Numa, for the sacred laws, for "the churches part," for restraining stealth and extortion, etc. In the second part of the same entry is the suggestion that Aegerie was the wife of Numa, the clue for Stanza XLII with Dame Mertia, the adviser and lawgiver to her husband Guitheline. And in the Numa Pompilius entry the suggestion for Guitheline, "the justest man and trewest in his daies." (Compare "Numa Pompilius . . . Romanorum rex *iustitia & pietate insignis*," etc.) And the "goodly layes [laws] And wholesome statutes" could derive from either entry. The Stephanus then could easily be Spenser's immediate source, and surely the most compact exposition for his readers.

Since Spenser's most elaborate allusions to Aesculapius and Hippolytus are in the same stanzas (*F. Q.* 1.5.36-44) and since the poet is here concerned with the relationship of the two, they must be dealt with together, or in immediate succession.

The pertinent allusions to Aesculapius in the passage referred to are these:

(1)

In which [cave] sad Aesculapius far apart
Emprisond was in chaines remedilesse,
For that Hippolytus rent corse he did redresse.
(Stz. 36.7-9)

(2)

Tho, gathering up the relicks of his smart,
By Dianes meanes, who was Hippolyts frend,
Them brought to Aesculape, that by his art
Did heale them all againe, and joyned every part.

(Stz. 39.6-9)

(3)

Such wondrous science in mans witt to rain
When Jove avizd, that could the dead revive,
And fates expired could renew again,
Of endlesse life he might him not deprive,
But unto hell did thrust him downe alive,
With flashing thunderbolt ywounded sore.

(Stz. 40.1-6)

In stanza XLII, Aesculapius is referred to as the "far renowned sonne of great Apollo" of "might in medicine."

Commenting on these allusions, Jortin cites Virgil[17] (*Aen.* 7.765 ff.) as a possible source, though he observes that what Spenser says of Aesculapius' healing Hippolytus is the poet's own. Upton, noting that Spenser departs from strict adherence to old mythology, cites Euripides, Ovid (*Fasti* 6.475 and *Met.* 15.497) and also Virgil (*Aen.* 7.769). Lotspeich thinks that Spenser owes much, especially in Stanzas XXXIX and XL, to the *Aeneid,* but that he may have received also a hint from Natalis Comes, whom he quotes. There is thus some diversity of opinion as to the basis of Spenser's allusions.

In this connection editors and critics of Spenser have not considered the composite 400-word account of Aesculapius in Stephanus' dictionary. Supported by references to Virgil, Ovid, and Pliny, the compiler gives a coherent account of Aesculapius—his parentage, his Caesarean birth, his training by Chiron, his skill as a physician, his restoration of Hippolytus and consequent punishment by Jupiter, his being worshipped as a god in Epidauris, his family including Machaon and Podalyrius, distinguished physicians, and an allegorical interpretation of the myth. Familiarity with this entry would have enabled Spenser (or Milton) or any other author in the Renaissance to portray Aesculapius, without the information gathered piecemeal from two or three classical authors. As a basis for the quoted lines from Spenser, consider, for example, the following: after a statement at the outset of the Stephanus entry that Aesculapius was the son of Apollo and the Nymph Coronis, the compiler continues, a little further on,

Traditus est Chironi, sub quo medicinae studuit. Iamque huius artis peritus, Dianae precibus Hippolytum ab equis discerptum vitae restituit: qua re motus Iupiter fulmine eum occidit. Virgilius septimo Aeneid.

Compare with this the following from Stephanus, under *Apollo*. Apollo slew "deinde Cyclopes ob fabricatum fulmen, quo filius eius Aesculapius fuit ad inferos detrusus." And near the end of the Aesculapius entry, we read further,

Non defuerunt qui locum datum fuisse fabulae de Aesculapio tradiderint quod mortuos ab inferis reuocaret: quia nonnullos quorum conclamata esset spes vitae sanitati restituerit per vim medicamentorum. Vnde fabulati sunt antiqui Plutonem apud Iouem conquestum fuisse, quod suum imperium AEsculapius exinaniret. Idcirco fulmine percussum fuisse a Ioue inquiunt.

The story in the Spenser quotations (1 and 2, above) that Aesculapius restored Hippolytus to life could well have its basis in Stephanus, where it appears *s.v. Aesculapius, s.v. Apollo;* and, as we shall see, *s.v. Hippolytus.* Compare Spenser's (No. 1) "Hippolytus rent corse he did redresse" and Stephanus' "Hippolytus . . . discerptum vitae restituit." Jove's punishment of Aesculapius for restoring the dead to life and for the consequent threat to Pluto's kingdom may have its basis in the second quotation from the Stephanus ("Non defuerunt qui locum, etc.") as well as the first which, as in Spenser, asserts specifically that the penalty was for restoring Hippolytus. For Spenser as for his readers, no special knowledge of Virgil, Ovid, Euripides, and Comes was necessary beyond what they could find in Stephanus.

Just as in Stephanus' story of Aesculapius, Hippolytus has a definite and important place, so has he in Spenser's story (1.5.36-44). Hippolytus in Spenser is even more significant, taking, in fact, the leading role. These two stanzas relate the part of the Hippolytus narrative pertinent to our discussion:

> Hippolytus a jolly huntsman was,
> That wont in charett chace the foming bore;
> He all his peeres in beauty did surpas,
> But ladies love, as losse of time, forbore:
> His wanton stepdame loved him the more;
> But when she saw her offred sweets refusd,
> Her love she turnd to hate, and him before

His father fierce of treason false accusd,
And with her gealous termes his open eares abusd
(1.5.37)
Who, all in rage, his sea-god syre besought,
Some cursed vengeaunce on his sonne to cast:
From surging gulf two monsters streight were brought,
With dread whereof his chacing steedes aghast
Both charett swifte and huntsman overcast.
His goodly corps, on ragged cliffs yrent,
Was quite dismembred, and his members chast
Scattered on every mountaine as he went,
That of Hippolytus was lefte no moniment.
(1.5.38)

The narrative, continuing in the next stanza, tells how the "cruell step-dame," seeing her son's death, killed herself with a knife; and the father, gathering the members of Hippolytus, "by Diana's meanes" carried them to Aesculapius, who, as we have heard, restored Hippolytus to life and was for his work thrust down to hell, by Jupiter.

Jortin[18] comments that, according to Euripides, Ovid, Seneca, Hyginus, Servius, and Plutarch, Neptune sent against Hippolytus *one* monster, not *two*. He notes, however, that Virgil (*Aen.* 7.780) mentions monsters, without specifying the number. Lotspeich (p. 69) observes that Spenser's version of the myth "does not agree with any one classical version," and suggests that Spenser is following Boccaccio. Boccaccio, he asserts, "supplies all the material of Spenser's version, in Spenser's order, except two details: that Phaedra killed herself with a knife, and that Theseus, with Diana's help, gathered up Hippolytus' remains."

We have noticed above that Stephanus refers, under *Aesculapius,* to Hippolytus' restoration. The lexicographer relates the story in some detail, under *Hippolytus,* and repeats it with slight variation under *Phaedra,* and under *Virbius.* The fullest account (*s.v. Hippolytus*) in the Stephanus follows:

Hippolytus, Thesei & Hippolytae Amazonis filius, qui cum coelibem ducens vitam venatu sese exerceret, & constanti animo sperneret mulieres, a Phaedra nouerca absente patre amatus est: cuius turpi desiderio cum obtemperare noluisset, illa filium apud patrem detulit, tanquam de stupro eam appellasset. Quamobrem cum videret Hippolytus patrem nouercae dolo persuasum de nece sua cogitare, conscenso curru fugam arripuit. Sed dum phocae, quae tum forte in littus exierant, equorum & rotarum strepitu perterritae, magno impetu se in mare praecipitarent, exterriti equi frustra obluctante Hippolyto, currum per scopulos & saxa traxerunt, iuuenemque infoelicem loris implicitum varias in partes discerpserunt: in nemore autem Aricino Dianae sacro sepultus est. . . . Hunc postea AEsculapius, a Diana exoratus, reuocauit ab inferis, & pristinae incolumitati restituit.

The important additional details in the *Phaedra* entry are the response of Neptune to Theseus' entreaty to send punishment on Hippolytus, and the death of Phaedra by hanging herself.  In the Hippolytus entry quoted above, with some details from the closely related entries on Aesculapius and Phaedra, we have all the essentials of Spenser's narrative as to content and order of details, with phrasing near enough to have suggested that of Spenser.  Here too are the monsters (*phocae*) and the petition or prayers of Diana ("Dianes means") which elicited the services of Aesculapius.

In his treatment of Orion, Spenser refers to

> And huge Orion, that doth tempests still portend.
>
> (4.11.13.)

And in a later allusion he writes,

> Then came October full of merry glee:
> . . .
> Upon a dreadfull scorpion he did ride,
> The same which by Dianaes doom unjust
> Slew great Orion. . . . (7.7.39)

Sawtelle[19] observes that Spenser's account agrees with no one of those in Hyginus, Ovid, Homer, and Apollodorus, but on Orion's death, she cites Lucan (9.836) and Servius (*Aen.* 1.539) as possible sources.  Lotspeich suggests N. Comes, whom he quotes, and suggestions from Virgil (*Aen.* 1.535 and *Ciris.* 535), as a basis.  It is probable that Spenser knew more than one version of the story.  As to the allusions in the quotations above, he could have depended on the composite account in Stephanus.

According to Stephanus, Orion was born in the tenth month, which may be significant in Spenser's symbolizing October by Orion riding on a scorpion.  The dictionary further relates that Orion was a giant and a mighty hunter; and presents alternative accounts of the manner of his death, including that in which he was slain by the arrows of Diana, or by the sting of the scorpion sent by Diana.  The Stephanus entry includes also this statement: "Creditur autem hoc sidus ex ortu suo maximas concitare tempestates: Vnde nimbosum Orionem appellat. Virg.

1 *Aen.,"* which may be compared with Spenser's "huge Orion, that doth tempests still portend."

The parts of the Orion entry that would have been most suggestive to Spenser and his readers are here transcribed:

Orion . . . Iouis, Neptuni & Mercurij filius ex vrina procreatus. . . . Itaque decimo tandem mense puerum natum esse . . . Hic postea adultus, strenuus venator extitit, Dianaeque adhaesit. Verum cum corporis robori plus satis fidens, iactitaret nullam esse feram, quam conficere non posset. Terra hominis insolentiam non ferens, scorpionem peperit, cuius ictu Orion interiit. Diana autem comitis sui necem aegre ferens, in caelum eum transtulit . . . . Contra tamen Lucanus scorpionem hunc a Diana immissum tradit, aliorumque deorum miseratione in caelum fuisse translatum. Horatius autem Dianae eum vim inferre voluisse tradit, ideoque telis eius confossum occubuisse . . . . Creditur autem hoc sidus ex ortu suo maximas concitare tempestates: Vnde Nimbosum Orionem appellat. Virg. 1 *Aeneid* . . . . Sunt qui Graece ab aquarum inundatione sic dictum velint, quod habeat ortum hyeme, & mare ac terras tempestatibus turbet, ὁρίων enim, turbo & concito significat. . . . Plin. libro 7. capite 19. . . . N. Comes, *Mythol.* lib. 8. c. 13.

Spenser's rather frequent allusions to Proteus may indicate great familiarity with the myth. Quite possibly, he had read more than one account of this interesting sea-god, but not necessarily so. Proteus appears as a prophet, as a herder of Neptune's seals, and as a magician capable of transforming himself into various shapes. As a prophet, he appears in these lines:

> . . . she inquir'd
> One day of Proteus by his mighty spell
> (For Proteus was with prophecy inspir'd)
> Her deare sonnes destiny to her to tell. (3.4.25)

As shepherd of the seas, in these:

> Proteus is shepheard of the seas of yore,
> And hath the charge of Neptunes mighty heard,
> . . .
> His charett swifte in hast he thether steard,
> Which, with a teeme of scaly phocas bownd,
> Was drawn upon the waves . . .
> (3.8.30)

and,

> And Proteus eke with him does drive his heard
> of stinking seales and porcpisces together.
> (*CCHA.* 249-50)

As a transformer of himself, or quick-change artist, in these lines:

> As ever Proteus to himselfe could make:
> Sometime a fowle, sometime a fish in lake,
> Now like a foxe, now like a dragon fell.

(1.2.10)

And in the following:

> Then like a Faerie knight him selfe he drest;
> For every shape on him he could endew:
> Then like a king he was to her exprest.

(3.8.40)

> To dreadful shapes he did him selfe transforme,
> Now like a gyaunt, now like to a feend,
> Then like a centaure, then like to a storme,
> Raging within the waves . . . .

(3.8.41)

Homer, Virgil, Ovid, Boccaccio, Comes have been cited[20] as contributing to Spenser's conception and portrayal of Proteus. Not noticed hitherto is Stephanus' dictionary, which is comprehensive in the delineation of Proteus. Pertinent excerpts are these:

Proteus, deus marinus, Oceani & Tethyos filius, Neptuni phocas in mari pascens, idemque vaticiniorum peritissimus, & in quamlibet formam sese transmutans. Proteum aliquando in Carpatho insula regnasse . . . Alij ferunt hunc captum amore Pomonae, in omnigenam speciem se variasse. Hinc Latinis Vertumnus dicitur, a verso mutatoque cursu fluminis Tyberini. Propert. lib. 4. *Quid mirare meas tot in vno corpore formas? Accipe Vertumni signa paterna Dei.* . . . Vide prouerbium, Proteo mutabilior.

[The account then tells of a Proteus who was king of Egypt during the Trojan war, and protected Helena and her possessions, fallen into his hands after the war, until he could restore her to Menelaus. Then follows an exposition of Proteus' reputation for transforming himself.]

Quae vero de Protei mutabilitate poetae sunt commenti, ab AEgyptiorum regum consuetudine videntur emanasse. Illis enim, teste Diodoro, mos erat aut leonis, aut tauri, aut Draconis priorem partem in capite ferre, insignia principatus: quandoque vero arborem, aliquando ignem, quandoque redolentia supra caput vnguenta. Haec tum ad decorem spectabant, atque ornatum: tum stuporem ac superstitionem quandam aspicientibus iniiciebant. Vnde factus est locus fabulae, Proteum in ea omnia, quaecunque capite gestabat, solere transformari. . . . vt videre est apud Calcaguinum, & A. Bochium in Symbolicis quaestionibus. Vide etiam N. Comitem, mytholgiae. libro 8. cap. 8.

[See also Stephanus on *Vertumnus.*]

Proteus as a shepherd of the sea, caring for the phocae of Neptune, Proteus as a prophet ("vaticiniorum peritissimus"), Proteus, the self-transformer, emphasized and the custom explained, are all here in short space in the Stephanus. The single entry could be a basis for Spenser's presentation and an excellent exposition for his readers.[21] And the entry *Vertumnus*, suggested by the Proteus, could have suggested to Spenser Proteus' wooing of Florimell (3.8.39-41).

Spenser's reference to the "Lybicke Ocean" and Lybick sands in the following lines have elicited frequent comment:

> As when a beare and tygre, being met
> In cruell fight *on Lybicke ocean wide,*
> Espye a traveiler with feet surbet,
> Whom they in equall pray hope to divide. . . .
>
> (2.2.22)
>
> Full many yeares, and weetlesse wandered
> From shore to shore, emongst the Lybick sandes,
> Ere rest he fownd.
>
> (3.9.41)

Critics have noticed that Spenser, in his reference to "Lybicke ocean" and "Lybicke sandes" probably had in mind the Syrtes. As a basis for the allusions Jortin cited Lucan (9.903.); Upton, Plutarch's life of Crassus; and Kitchin, Virgil's *Georgics* (2.105).[22] A more convenient single version —a version which definitely suggests the phrasing "Lybicke ocean" and "Lybicke sandes" and gives the essential information underlying the allusions—for Spenser and his readers—is that in Stephanus. Here is the transcription:

Syrtes . . . duo sinus periculosissimi in *mari Libyco,* quia Africam propriam dictam alluit: quorum alter qui Carthagini propinquior est (minorem Syrtim vocant) CCC.M. pass. ambitum habet. Alter, qui in Cyrenaicā vergit, maior Syrtis dicitur: habetque circuitum DCXXXV.M. pass. Vtraque Syrtis nauigantibus est periculosissima, quòd mare ibi vadosum sit, *arenae vehens cumulos,* qui loci faciem vicissim immutant, dorsáque & breuia in alia atque alia loca transferunt. *Sunt & in terra Syrtes in eadem Africa,* vento arenas excitante, & proxima quaeque operiente. Vnde Solinus author est, iis in locis, *quamuis terra* iter facientes, cursum sideribus regere. Nam arenae cumuli, vento agitati, locorum faciem mutant: & quemadmodum in mari, nunc aggere sublimia faciunt, quae priùs desidebant, nunc vallibus profunda, quae priùs excelsa erant.

The "Lybicke ocean," which, in Spenser, refers to the land in the desert,

the "Lybick sandes," over which Aeneas wandered, and the adjective
"Lybick"—all have in Stephanus ample illustration.

Spenser's principal allusion to Titan is in these lines:

> For Titan (as ye all acknowlge must)
> Was Saturnes elder brother by birth-right;
> Both, sonnes of Uranus: but by unjust
> And guilefull meanes, through Corybantes slight,
> The younger thrust the elder from his right:
> Since which thou, Jove, injuriously hast held
> The heavens rule from Titans sonnes by might;
> And them to hellish dungeons downe hast feld . . . .
>
> (7.6.27)

The story of the usurpation of Titan's rights, as here adumbrated, by
Saturn and his son Jove is based on N. Comes, according to Lotspeich
(p. 111). It should be noticed, however, that the story is twice told (cf.
*Titan* and *Saturn*) in Stephanus' dictionary, and could have been well
known through this medium.

In Stephanus we read that Saturn was the son of Caelum (Uranus);
that he had an elder brother who should succeed his father ("Fratrem
habuit Titanem maiorem natu . . . vti par erat, succedere deberet."); that
Saturn was permitted to reign on the condition that he should slay any
male children born to him; that Ops with the help of the Corybantes
preserved Jove, Neptune, and Pluto ("Iunonem quidem Saturno ostendit,
Iouem vero clam nutriendum ablegauit, adhibitis interim Corybantibus,
qui cymbalorum tympanorumque pulsu obstrepebant, ne pueri vagitus
audiretur"); that Titan discovering the stratagem with his sons (called
Titans) defeated and imprisoned Saturn and his mother until Jove, grown
to manhood, overcame the Titans and liberated his brother, mother, etc.,
and resumed sway. The story, without reference to the Corybantes, appears
also under *Titan,* in Stephanus.

As for the Titans, Lotspeich rightly notes that Spenser does not dis-
tinguish sharply between them and the giants, especially in the battle against
the Olympians; that for Spenser, the Titans and Giants meant pride, rebellion against the established order, and revenge. To the battle of the
Titans and Giants on the Phlegrean plains, the poet refers three times
(V. G. 39-40; 2.10.3; 5.7.10). Comes and possibly Boccaccio, Lotspeich
suggests, would give hints for these details.

Full information also could have come from Stephanus. Under *Titanes*, for example, he writes, "Diodorus Sic. vocat illos gigantes tyrannos." In the item *Gigantes*, we read, "Alij namque illos Titani & Terrae filios fuisse scribunt." In the same entry Stephanus mentions the conflict of the giants with the gods on the Phlegrean fields (*"in campis Phlegraeis"*). And in the last named entry, he refers to their cruelty and pride (*"immanitas & superbia"*). In *Gigantes*, there is reference to their rebellion and attempt to displace Jupiter.[23]

One of the giants, or Titans, foremost in the rebellion, was Typhoeus. In 3.7.47 Spenser refers to him as among the Titans, who made

> Warre against heven, and heaped hils on hight,
> To scale the skyes, and put Jove from his right:
> Her syre [Argante's] *Typheous* was . . . .

Referring to the same Titan (7.6.15) Spenser writes,

> Doubting least Typhon were againe uprear'd . . . .

Spenser thus uses the names interchangeably. He would have had precedent in Stephanus, in these two successive entries:

Typhoeus . . . vnus e Gigantibus, Terrae & Titani filius, quem illa Ioui irata in perniciem coelestium fertur edidisse. Hic cum in ingentem corporis molem adoleuisset, eo vae cordiae prouectus est, vt Iouem de coeli possessione deiicere conaretur. Quapropter fulmine ab eodem ictus est, & sub Inarimen insulam detrusus, ut placet Homer in Catalogo.
Typhon, vnus ex Gigantibus, Titani & Terrae filius, qui alio nomine Tiphoeus dicitur.

### 3. Spenser and Robert Stephanus

The relationship of Spenser to Robert Stephanus' *Thesaurus* we have discussed in an earlier study.[24] We wish here to present two illustrations from *The Teares of the Muses* which seem to indicate the poet's familiarity with the *Thesaurus*. The first consists of two stanzas in the part of the poem devoted to Polyhymnia. Having observed that in ages past none but princes and high priests might profess the secret skill of poetry, the Muse continues (ll. 565-70):

> But now nor prince nor priest doth her maintayne,
> But suffer her prophaned for to bee
> Of the base vulgar, that *with hands uncleane*
> *Dares to pollute her hidden mysterie;*
> And treadeth under foote hir holie things,
> Which was the care of kesars and of kings.

Under *Musa,* Robert Stephanus relates that on a time Orpheus met, in the forest, Apollo accompanied on the right hand by the nine Muses and the three Graces, and on the left by a flock of chattering pies and furies. Orpheus cried out in amazement at the strange following.

Sed noli ô vates mirari Phoebus ait. Nempe quotidie multi mihi sacrificant, ut Musarum a me Gratiarumque munera impetrent. Ergo quicunque sacra puris manibus nobis faciunt, Musas a nobis Gratiasque gratis accipiunt. Quicunque vero *sacra manibus pollutis attrectare audent,* picas & furias inuiti reportant. Haec ille.[25]

The two stanzas in *The Teares,* only the second of which we have quoted, not only echo the thought of the R. Stephanus but, in the italicized words, reproduce the Latin phrasing. The account of Stephanus, striking in its imagery, must surely have been in the mind of Spenser when he wrote the lines quoted above.

A second passage in *The Teares* which may have been inspired by an entry in R. Stephanus, is this from Euterpe's monologue (ll. 253-58) :

> A stonie coldnesse hath benumbd the sence
> And livelie spirits of each living wight,
> And dimd with darknesse their intelligence,
> Darknesse more than Cymerians daylie night:
> And monstrous Error, flying in the ayre,
> Hath mard the face of all that semed fayre.

Under *Cimmerii,* R. Stephanus writes that these are people who inhabit lands filled with cold ("occupatas frigoribus")[26] such as was the region between Baiae and Cumae in which the valley was surrounded by high hills so that it was not touched by morning or evening sun. The Cimmerians in Italy lived in subterranean homes and were accustomed to come and go through underground passages. In these they lurked during the entire day only to come forth at night in quest of food and booty. He continues :

Penes hos *ingens* quondam *superstitio* increbruit, *loci natura erroribus suffragante.* Ibi sacra nemora venerata, fluminibus etiam & fontibus suus honor fuit. Specus praeterea famosi, & ad inferos crediti aditus, quos intrare fas non erat, nisi diis Manibus prius, quo auspicatior descensus foret, sacrificio placatis . . . .
Cimmeriae tenebrae, proverbium, pro Multa obscuritate, & animi caligine.

Notice the similarities of the English poem to the Latin lines. The central idea of Spenser's lines is expressed in the proverb quoted by Stephanus in which the Cimmerian shades symbolize intellectual darkness.

This idea Spenser might have had from Cooper,[27] or from Erasmus.[28] But neither of these sources would account for the imagery of the lines. The "stonie coldnesse" that benumbs the sense may reflect Stephanus' remark on the coldness ("occupatas frigoribus terras incolunt") of the country which the Cimmerians inhabit. "And monstrous Error flying in the ayre," etc., may well have been suggested by Stephanus' "Penes hos *ingens* quondam *superstitio* increbruit, *loci natura erroribus* suffragante . . . ." The whole Latin passage, at the end of which the proverb concerning Cimmerian shades is given prominence, seems indeed to have been familiar to Spenser.

## 4. SPENSER AND CALEPINE

The *Dictionarium* of Friar Ambrosius Calepine, first published at Bergamo, Italy, in 1502 as a Latin-Latin dictionary, continued to be issued with augmentations throughout the sixteenth and seventeenth centuries. Other languages were added to the Latin so that by the end of the sixteenth century the Calepine was a polyglot of some eight languages, Latin, however, retaining the dominant place. This was a general dictionary, with the proper names and their expositions distributed throughout the text. Though it could not give to proper names the space and elaboration that the Charles Stephanus dictionary, devoted wholly to proper names, could give, it retained these and was often consulted. There is some evidence of Spenser's acquaintance with it. Even if he did not actually consult the Calepine, it is sometimes the best illustration of allusions in his poems, as may be seen in the examples which follow.

Glossing *Calliope*, "April" (1. 100), E. K. writes,

*Calliope, one of the nine Muses;* to whome they assigne the *honor of all poetical invention* and the firste glorye of the heroicall verse. Other say that shee *is the goddesse of rhetorick*: and by *Virgile* it is manifeste, that they mystake the thyng. For there, in hys *Epigrams,* that arte semeth to be attributed to Polymnia, saying,

> *'Signat cuncta manu, loquiturque Polymnia gestu:'*

which seemeth specially to be meant of action and elocution, both special partes of rhethorick: besyde *that her name,* which (as some construe it) *importeth great remembraunce,* conteineth another part; but I holde rather with them, which call her *Polymnia,* or Polyhymnia *of her good singing.*

This note has elicited two comments which we here quote: (1) Mustard: "The verse quoted from Virgil's 'Epigrams' 'Signat cuncta manu, loquiturque Polymnia gestu,' comes from a short poem *De Musis,* or *De*

*Musarum Inventis,* which in the 16th century was ascribed to Ausonius. The poem is given in Scaliger's *Catalecta Virgilii,* etc., and in Riese's *Anthologia Latina,* No. 664";[29] (2) Renwick (p. 193): "Commenting on Mantuan, *Eclogue* IV, Badius Ascensius says: [Polymnia] a πολὺ i.multam, a μνεία i. memoriae, cuius filiae Musae sunt. Dicitur enim Polyhymnia multorum hymnorum, seu laudum."

Actually, E. K.'s procedure seems to be simpler than these comments suggest. He read what was written about Calliope and Polymnia in the brief entry in Calepine's *Dictionarium,* and with some hints from Cooper's *Thesaurus* made his comment, combining details from each, including the Latin quotation and the reference to Virgil's *Epigram.* The Calepine item, which is here quoted, would account for the essentials of E. K.'s gloss.

*Polymnia* . . . Vna musarum, *a memoriae magnitudine dicta.* Nam μνείαν *Graeci memoriam vocant* . . . Fuerunt qui corripi putarint, adducti *versu Virgilii ex Epigrammat.* 'Signat cuncta manu loquiturque Polyhymnia gestu' . . . . Sunt qui Polyhymnia scribant, vt a cantus multitudine dicatur . . . . Magis tamen placet superior scriptura.

E. K.'s mention of the name Polymnia which "importeth great remembrance" (cf. *"a memoriae magnitudine"*), the reference to the epigram, then supposed to be by Virgil, and the exact quotation of it, and finally the preference expressed for "Polyhymnia, of her good singing" (cf. *"Polyhymnia . . . vt a cantus multitudine dicatur"*)—all point to Calepine as the basis of E. K.'s note.

In another gloss for "October" (1. 111), E. K. writes,

*Wild yvie,* for it is dedicated to Bacchus, and therefore it is sayd, that the Maenades (that is, Bacchus franticke priestes) used in theyr sacrifice to carry thyrsos, which were pointed staves or javelins, wrapped about with yvie.

Commenting on this note, one editor[30] of the *Shepheardes Calender,* writes,

Badius on Mantuan iii: *"Dignus eras hederis:* quibus coronantur poetae, eo quod sunt in tutela Liberi patris, qui eis coronatus ex India rediit." Badius quotes Horace, Persius, Juvenal, and (most appropriate here) Virgil Ecl. viii, 12-13 & vii, 25:

                         hac sine tempore circum
          Inter victrices ederam tibi serpere lauros.
          Pastores, hedera crescentem ornate poetam.

A more probable source for E. K. than the Badius is found in Calepine's exposition of *Thyrus:*

*Thyrsus* . . . Alij accipiunt thyrsum pro hasta aculeata, hederis obtecta, quas in Orgijs Bacchis quatiebant. . . . Et Macrobius ait Liberum patrem tenere thyrsum, quod est latens telum, cuius mucro hedera lambente protegitur.

The description of Thyrsus and the reference to Bacchae, common elements in E. K. and Calepine, are not found in Badius.

The comment of E. K. on "November" (l. 53) is,

*Melpomene,* the sadde and waylefull Muse, used of poets in honor of tragedies: as saith Virgile,
"Melpomene tragice proclamat moesta boatu."

The Latin verse comes from the poem *De Musis,* attributed to Virgil, as Mustard (p. 202) notes. It should be added that E. K.'s readily accessible source was Calepine's dictionary. In this he would have found information about Melpomene, the reference to the Virgilian poem, and the quoted verse. See in Calepine,

*Melpomene* . . . Vna ex Musis, tragoediarum inuentrix à modulando nomen trahens. . . . *Virgil de Musarum inuentis,* Melpomene Tragice proclamat moesta boatu. *Vide Musa.*

Under Calepine's entry *Musa* we read,

. . . Quintam . . . Melpomenen à canendo . . . enim canto & modulor significat . . . hoc est à concentu faciendo: vnde & Tragoediis praesidere putabatur.

At the end of this entry, Calepine quotes the whole poem ascribed to Virgil. As E. K. has been shown to have used Calepine in other glosses, it is reasonable to assume that the same authority is the source of this gloss on Melpomene.

In *The Faerie Queene* (3.1.57) Spenser writes,

> By this th' eternall lampes, wherewith high Jove
> Doth light the lower world, were halfe yspent,
> And the *moist daughters of huge Atlas* strove
> Into the ocean deepe to *drive their weary drove.*

On this passage Upton cites Virgil (*Geo* 1.221) "Eoae Atlantides." Church[31] comments, "moist daughters of huge Atlas"—the Hyades. Lotspeich, citing N. Comes (4.7) as the authority for calling the Hyades the daughters of Atlas, suggests that the reference to their "weary drove" may derive from Ovid's *Fasti* (5.165), "Pars Hyadum toto de grege nulla latet."

Actually, the Hyades are called the daughters of Atlas in various Renaissance dictionaries—Calepine, Cooper, C. Stephanus, etc. There is little need to cite Comes. And Calepine's entry *Hyades,* which quotes the line cited from the *Fasti,* and gives ample basis for the epithet "moist" is, if not the source of Spenser, at least a most fitting illustration of his meaning. The Calepine reads:

*Hyades,* ὑάδες stellae septem, in cornibus & ore Tauri, quae quoties nascuntur, vel occidunt, pluuias creant, ἀπὸ τοῦ ὕω. Ouid. At simul inducent obscura crepuscula noctem, *Pars hyadum, toto de grege nulla latet* . . . . Alij tradunt Atlantem ex Aethra uxore Hyam filium suscepisse, quem a leone deuoratum, cum sorores miserabili lamentatione prosequerentur, & moerore vitam finirent. [Jupiter transformed the sisters to stars. Cf. also *Atlantides* in Calepine.]

The story of Sylvanus and Cyparissus is told (in outline at least) in *The Faerie Queene* (1.6.7 ff.), Stanza XVII containing what is pertinent as a basis of our discussion:

> By vew of her he [Sylvanus] ginneth to revive
> His ancient love, and dearest Cyparisse;
> And calles to mind his pourtraiture alive,
>
> . . .
>
> And how he slew with glauncing dart amisse
> A gentle hynd, the which the lovely boy
> Did love as life, above all worldly blisse;
> For griefe whereof the lad n'ould after joye. . . .

Sawtelle holds that the details of the story of Cyparissus correspond to those in Ovid (*Met.* 10.120) except that, in Spenser, it is Sylvanus who loves the youth, in Ovid, Apollo. Lotspeich thinks that Spenser may be following N. Comes or Boccaccio. An adequate exposition of the allusion with details of Sylvanus' relation to the Fauns and to Pan, part of the background of Spenser's portrayal, is this from Calepine:

*Sylvanvs,* syluarum Deus, quem Graeci πᾶνα uocant. Hic amauit puerum Cyparissum nomine, qui habebat mansuetissimam ceruam: Hanc cum Syluanus nescius occidisset, puer est extinctus dolore: quem amator deus in cupressum arborem eius nominis uertit, quam pro solatio portare dicit. Vergil 1. *Georgic.* Et tenerum ab radice ferens Syluane cupressum. haec Seruius. Est etiam adiect. Id quod ad syluam pertinet: ut, Syluanus deus Faunus, uel Pan, syluarum incola. Plin. lib. 12. cap. 1. Quin & Syluanos Faunosque & deorum genera syluis ac sua numina tanquam è coelo attributa credimus.

### 5. Spenser and Multiple Reference Books

Some of Spenser's classical allusions not already discussed in this study represent the poet's own synthesis of two or more sources; other allusions may be explained equally well by almost any one of a number of earlier accounts. It is necessary therefore to consider the poet's possible use of multiple sources.

We noted earlier that Spenser's most elaborate treatment of the Graces (*F. Q.* 6.10.6 ff.) seemed to draw most from Cooper's *Thesaurus*. But the poet's reference in that passage to Venus and the Graces playing and sporting in Mount Acidale (6.10.7,8) and the reference in 4.5.5—

> On Acidalian mount, where many an howre
> She with the pleasent Graces wont to play.

And to Maia, weary

> With bathing in the Acidalian brooke (*Epith.*, l. 310)

are not accounted for by Cooper. The key-word is "Acidalia." The mount in Acidalia appears to be Spenser's invention. There is a fount Acidale, and, for this, Lotspeich (p. 31) quotes Servius *ad Aen.* 1.720: "Acidalia Venus dicitur vel quia iniciit curas quas Graeci ἀχίδας dicunt, vel certe a fonte Acidalio . . . in quo se Gratiae lavant." Perhaps Spenser knew this note by Servius, but it was also easily accessible in the dictionaries. Charles Stephanus, for example, concludes his entry on *Charites* (the Graces) with these words: "Tradunt etiam eas in Acidalio fonte, qui est in Orchomeno Boeotiae vrbe, lauari, quoniam pura esse beneficia oportet, non sordida." And Stephanus' entry, it should be remembered, was the source of Cooper's *Charites*, which contributed so much to Spenser's long description (6.10.6 ff.). Under *Acidalia*, Stephanus is even more specific: he quotes the very language of Servius which Lotspeich cites. The entry in Stephanus runs thus:

*Acidalia*, Veneris epitheton, vel quia iniciit curas, quas Graeci ἀχίδας dicunt, vel certe a fonte Acidalio, qui est in Orchomeno Boeotiae ciuitate, in quo se Gratiae lauant quae Veneri sunt sacratae. Ipsius enim & Liberi filiae sunt, nec immerito. Gratiae enim per horum fere numinum munera conciliantur. Hactenus Servius Virg. 1. *Aeneid—at memor ille Matris Acidaliae, etc.* Vide Bocatium.

Two passages in *The Faerie Queene* (3.1.34-38 and 3.6.29 ff.) on Venus and Adonis and on the garden of Adonis have elicited considerable comment

and discussion.[32]   Our own contribution is primarily to point out some
contemporary sources of information on the Adonis myth which have been
generally neglected, and thus to fill in somewhat the background of Spenser
and his readers.  The concise comments of Lotspeich (pp. 32-33) on the
possible sources of the Adonis passages are most informative.  He rightly
observes that the story of Venus and Adonis told on the tapestry (3.1.34-
38) has much in common with Ovid's version (*Met.* 10, 519 ff.) and a
reminiscence (Stz. XXXVIII) of Bion's *Lament for Adonis* (7-9).  All
this matter, however, is found together in Natalis Comes (5.16), and
Comes has all the material of Spenser's passage in Spenser's order, except
the metamorphosis into a flower, which is found at *Met.*, 10.728.  Comes,
he thinks, is the main source for the passage.

To the stanzas on the Garden of Adonis (3.6.29 f.), Comes has made
a large contribution, Lotspeich *t*hinks.  Two distinctive features of this
passage—the Garden of Adonis as an earthly paradise, and Adonis conceived of as the "father of all forms . . . that living gives to all"—could
have derived from Comes' chapter on Adonis.  Comes, Lotspeich continues, says that Adonis is the author and nourisher of all seeds, and
"gives nutriment to all things."  Comes identifies Adonis with the sun,
and the boar as standing for winter.

Comes' chapter on Adonis may well have been known to Spenser and
would have offered many suggestions.  There are, however, other current
presentations of the subject not to be overlooked.  The story of Adonis,
with citation of various authorities, is summarized in Calepine's dictionary
(1542), in Robert Stephanus' *Thesaurus* (1573), and in Charles Stephanus'
poetic dictionary (1553, 1590, etc.).  Also, R. Stephanus has a special
entry on *Adonidis horti,* citing Erasmus *Adagia* (II, 26C-27B).  Of these
entries on *Adonis,* the most detailed, and, in this study, the most teasing, is
that of Charles Stephanus, which, gathered from various sources, includes
also a part of Comes' interpretation.

After a brief mention of Adonis' parents, C. Stephanus tells of Venus'
love for Adonis, of his hunting in the Idalian forest, of his slaughter by
the boar, of Venus' grief, and of Adonis' transformation into a flower.
Then follows brief comment on his name, the relation to the Adonius
river flowing from Mount Lebanon, the yearly commemoration of Adonis'
death, the lamentation for his death and rejoicing at his revival.  Then
follows the interpretation (citing Macrobius, Theocritus, Scaliger) of Adonis
as the sun, that which furnishes nutriment to all things, and is the author

of growth ("germinandi") ; and also the allegory of Adonis as the sun and the boar as winter, etc.

As to the tapestry story, familiarity with C. Stephanus' *Adonis* would have supplied Spenser with the detail of the metamorphosis into a flower— a detail missing in Comes. For the Garden-of-Adonis passage (3.6.29 ff.), Stephanus would have emphasized, through Macrobius and Theocritus, the identification of Adonis with the sun, and Adonis as the author of germination and the nourisher of all things. ("Macrobius vero accepit Adonidem pro sole . . . . Orpheus in hymnis, Adonin Solem esse sensit, cum illum rebus omnibus praebere nutrimentum, & esse germinandi autorem dixerit.") And the "Alij, inter quos Theocriti Scholiastes, Adonin semen tritici esse sentiunt" of the dictionary item is suggestive of Spenser's "there is the first seminary of all things that are borne to live and dye." C. Stephanus concludes with a reference to the gardens of Adonis, "Hinc horti Adonidis, pro instructissimis." And R. Stephanus enlarges on the topic of the gardens, referring to Erasmus' *Adagia.*

Whether Spenser used the dictionaries in his account of Adonis and the Garden of Adonis, we cannot determine. It seems very probable that such a description as that by Charles Stephanus would have attracted him, both for what it contains and for its references to other treatments of the subjects. The parallels of Stephanus with Spenser could be accounted for in part by Stephanus' overlapping Comes. At any rate, in these hand-books is the information at hand for poet and readers and of importance in a consideration of the materials from which authors could have drawn inspiration.

Spenser's treatment of the Agave-Pentheus story suggests a multiple or composite source. In *Virgils Gnat,* he translates,

> Came the bad daughter of old Cadmus brood,
> Cruell Agave, flying vengeance sore
> Of King Nictileus for the guiltie blood
> Which she with cursed hands had shed before;
> There she halfe frantick having slaine her sonne.
> Did shrowd her selfe like punishment to shonne.
>
> (171-76)

An allusion to the same story appears in *The Faerie Queene* (5.8.47).

> Or as that madding mother, mongst the rout
> Of Bacchus priests, her owne deare flesh did teare.

Would the rather free translation of Virgil's *Culex,* in the first quotation above, be sufficient basis for the second allusion? It is possible, though the "mongst the rout Of Bacchus priests" is hardly accounted for by the *Culex.* Was Spenser remembering other details about Agave from Ovid's *Fasti* (4.457), or *Met.* (3.701), or did he know this most interesting entry in the dictionary of C. Stephanus?

*Agaue,* Cadmi & Hermiones filia, Echioni Thebano nupsit, ex quo filium Pentheum suscepit, qui cum abstemius esset, ac propterea Bacchi sacra despicaretur, ab ipsa matre, reliquisque Maenadibus inter Bacchanalia, iam rex Thebanorum, membratim est discerptus. Virg. in Culice.

—*quo quondam victa furore,*
*Venit Nyctelium, fugiens Cadmeis Agaue*
*Infandas scelerata manus, et caede cruenta.*

Horatius, Serm. lib. 2 Satyra 3.

*Quid caput abscissum demens cum portat Agaue*
*Gnati infelicis, sibi tum furiosa videtur?*

We have transcribed this entry fully to show that familiarity with it would explain the reference to the mad mother "mongst the rout of Bacchus priests." As it quotes the very lines which Spenser had translated and cites other literary associations of the myth, it may well have attracted Spenser and it would be the annotation *par excellence* for Spenser's readers.

Writing of the portrait of Chastity (3.Pr.2.) Spenser has this allusion to "daedale,"

> But living art may not least part expresse,
> Nor life-resembling pencill it can paynt,
> All were it Zeuxis or Praxiteles:
> His *daedale* hand would faile, and greatly faynt,
> And her perfections with his error taynt.

Although the adjective "daedale" has received considerable attention from Spenser scholars,[33] no one has called attention to the exposition of the word in the Renaissance dictionaries. These give the contemporary conception of the word, which of course was in Spenser's mind and doubtless in that of his readers.

In Cooper's *Thesaurus,* we read, "*Daedala* was the generall denomination of Images wrought, of whome it seemeth to some, that *Daedalus* tooke his name." Under *Daedalus,* Calepine offers the following:

Dictus Daedalus (ut quidam existimant) ἀπὸ τοῦ δαιδάλλειν quod est variare. Alij hoc uerbum a *daedalo* deriuatum putant, ob multiplex variumque ingenium hominis, propter quod Graeci δαίδαλον varium dicunt. Et Lucretius terram ob rerum artificiorumque varietatem Daedalam nominat: Ennius simili modo Mineruam. Virg.

One of the most interesting and detailed allusions in *The Faerie Queene* is to the "faire Danae," in the following stanzas:

> Soone after that, into a golden showre
> Him selfe he chaung'd, faire Danae to vew,
> And through the roofe of her strong brasen towre
> Did raine into her lap an hony dew,
> The whiles her foolish garde, that litle knew
> Of such deceipt, kept th' yron dore fast bard,
> And watcht, that none should enter nor issew;
> Vaine was the watch, and bootlesse all the ward,
> Whenas the god to golden hew him selfe transfard.

(3.11.31.)

In the dictionaries of the period the Danae myth is presented with much detail. Charles Stephanus, for example, has the story three times, with slight variations: under the entries *Danae, Acrisius,* and *Perseus.* The first of these has most information on Danae, and cross-references to Acrisius and Perseus. It is the Danae entry that concerns us chiefly here, for this affords an adequate basis for all that is found in Spenser's stanza, quoted above. For example, referring to Danae as the daughter of Acrisius, king of the Argives, and the oracle that the king would be slain by his grandson, Stephanus states that the king inclosed his daughter in a strongly fortified tower, but "cuius [Danae] amore captus Jupiter, in imbrem aureum se conuertit, & per tegulas in puellae gremium sese demisit." A little further on, Stephanus, quoting Horace (*Carminum,* lib. 3.) uses these phrases: "*Inclusam Danaen turris ahenea,*" and refers to the guard at the door. Compare with this phrasing the first five lines of the quotation. The similarities are striking. Line six refers to "th' iron dore fast bard," with which compare Stephanus' "ferrea claustra," quoted in the same entry from an epigram of Paulus Silentarius. There is little doubt but that this composite entry could be the source of Spenser's allusions to the Danae story.

There is, however, another possibility. Stephanus' entry on *Danae* borrows freely from Comes' *Mythologiae,* the quotations from Horace and Silentarius apparently coming directly from that source. There, indeed, we find the phrases employed by Stephanus and paralleled by Spenser. Was Spenser then following Comes, or Stephanus, or was he familiar with both?

No conclusive answer can be given, though it seems probable that he knew both Comes and Stephanus.

Though Spenser was familiar with Britomartis[34] in Virgil's *Ciris,* the recurrent sketches of her in the contemporary dictionaries would have given vogue to the name and to characteristics associated with the person of Britomartis, and would thus have helped make the name the inevitable choice for a heroine of Britain.

In the Calepine of 1542, this brief entry appears:

Britomartes, nomen eius quam Diana fertur unice dilexisse, cuius patria fuit Gortina Cretae urbs.

Perhaps in competition with the Stephanus dictionaries, the later Calepines expand the entry, thus:

Britomartis, Puella fuit ex Gortyne Cretae ciuitate, Iouis & Charmes filia, Dianae in primis chara, alio nomine Dictynna appellata . . . hoc est, a retibus, quorum vsum in venatione traditur inuenisse. Hanc Minos Cretae rex fertur adamasse, cuius vim quum alioqui effugere non posset, ex altera sese rupe in mare praecipitauit. *Vide Virgillum in Ciri,* & Diodorum lib. 5.

Immediately following the Britomartis entry in the Calepine, and of no less interest is this:

Britona, *Puella* Cretensis fuit *insigni* forma, & Dianae in primis dilecta, quae quum Minois vim alioqui declinare non posset, in fluuium se praecipitauit: *leuius rata vitae, quam pudicitiae iacturam facere.* Haec à *Diodoro lib.* 5. & *Virg. in Ciri, Britomartis dicitur.*

In Robert Stephanus' *Thesaurus* (1573) the entry on Britomartis is almost the same as the longer entry from Calepine above, except that Stephanus adds, at the end, a reference to Scaliger and to Callimachus *Hymn. in Dianam,* v. 190., and these words: "Dicitur Diodoro lib. 6. *Britona.* Ipsam Dianam sic Cretensibus appellatam auctor est Solinus." A variation of these entries appears in Charles Stephanus' dictionary:

Britomartis, Nympha Cretensis *valde formosa,* Iouis & Charmes filia, Diodoro *Britona dicta,* retia ad vanādum inuenit, ex quo Dictynna est appellata, quòd causam praebuit, vt quidam Dictynnam & Dianam eandem esse putarint. Haec, vt quibusdam placet, á Minoe rege Cretensi adamata, cùm eiusdem concubitum fugere non posset, de rupe se in mare praecipitauit. Virgil. in Cyri. Bocatius.

From these dictionary sketches what suggestions could have come to Spenser and his readers? First there is the recurrence of the name, and it is worth noting that, though Spenser generally uses the English form *Britomart,* he employs *Britomartis* in the heading of the Book and once in the text (3.3.10). Also Calepine's remark that Britomartis thought more lightly of life than of sacrificing her chastity ("levius rata vitae, quam pudicitiae iacturam facere.") would have underscored Spenser's title: "The Legend of Britomartis *or of Chastity."* Though Britomartis must have had a masculine sort of beauty, the poet repeatedly refers to it. We read "faire Britomart" (3.1.52.), "fayre Britomartis" (3.3.19), "the fayre Britomart" (3.4.13), and

> Such was the beautie and the shining ray
> With which fayre Britomart gave light unto the day.
>
> (3.1.43)

With these complimentary epithets to Britomart may be compared the "insigni forma" of Calepine and the "valde formosa" of Charles Stephanus.

Spenser refers to his heroine as Britomart "from Britayne" (3.1.8), "the Britonesse" (3.1.58), and "this Briton maid" (3.2.4). It may be worth observing that in Calepine and in the Stephanus dictionaries "Britona" is used as an alternate name for "Britomartis."

Perhaps there would have been in the dictionary entries on Britomartis more suggestions for Spenser and his readers than would have been found in any one of the authorities cited by the lexicographers, more than in Virgil's *Ciris,* in Diodorus, in Callimachus. But Spenser's Britomart is a much more complicated character than the Britomartis of classical literature. Professor H. S. V. Jones writes, "Her lineage may be derived from the famous Amazons of the Trojan epic, Camilla and Penthesilea, through Boiardo's and Ariosto's Marfisa and Bradamante" (*Handbook,* 221). Others, A. S. Cook, for example, have noticed the general resemblance of Britomart, the warrior maid, to Camilla. Although Merritt Y. Hughes admits that Britomartis' love for Arthegall parallels the account of Sylla's love for Minos in Virgil's *Ciris,*[35] he maintains that "Camilla's story has nothing resembling the adventures of Britomart and they are alike in nothing except the quixotic chivalry common to all the daughters of Penethesilia."[36] In our opinion, Hughes minimizes the influence of Camilla's portrait in Spenser's conception of Britomart, but it is hardly pertinent to extend the discussion here.

We have seen above the indebtedness of E. K. and Spenser to Cooper's entry on the Graces. For certain of the longer allusions, the *Thesaurus* with some suggestions from C. Stephanus is an adequate basis. But Spenser throughout his work has about fifteen references to the Graces, not all of which Cooper would account for. Hesiod, Servius, Seneca, Boccaccio, and Comes have been cited by Spenser scholars as possible sources. But the content of these authors appears in a number of Renaissance treatises, not generally mentioned. The Graces are described and their significance explained, for example, not only in Charles Stephanus' dictionary and Cooper's *Thesaurus,* as seen above, but also in the *Thesaurus* of Robert Stephanus, the dictionaries of Calepine, Higgins' revision of Huloet (1572) ; in Perottus' *Cornucopiae* (1489, etc.), in Mirabellius' *Polyantheae* (1503), in Alciati's *Emblemata,* in Textor's *Officina* (1581), and in Cartari's *Imagines Deorum* (1581).

Spenser's familiarity with Cooper's *Thesaurus* and with the Stephanus dictionaries, we have shown above. From these, and from the other reference books listed, what information could the poet have acquired concerning the Graces? At least a partial answer may be made by a tabulation and brief discussion of topics.

1. Names of the Graces and significance of the names: In his gloss on "April," (1. 109) E. K. mentions in order Aglaia, Thalia, Euphrosyne ; "and Homer onely addeth a fourth, sc. Pasithea." E. K. follows the conventional order from Seneca through the various dictionaries. Both C. Stephanus and R. Stephanus mention Pasithea as another name for Aglaia ; and the later issues of the *Polyantheae* record that Homer called one of these graces Pasithea. E. K. apparently had no authority for calling her a fourth grace. He may have been trying to adapt his gloss to the text, in which a fourth grace is referred to. E. K. could, then, have got his information as to the names, including Pasithea, from the dictionaries and the *Polyantheae.* In *F. Q.* (6.10.22) the poet mentions the Graces in this order : Euphrosyne, Aglaia, and Thalia. For this order, the dictionaries offered no precedent.

Though Spenser does not formally comment on the meaning of the Graces' names, he shows by the phrase "daughters of delight" that he was familiar with the conventional epithets applied to them. Lotspeich (p. 64) suggests as a source N. Comes (4.15), who says that they stand for "hilaritas et laetitia" and are "laetitiae matres." Spenser doubtless knew Comes' *Mythologiae,* but he could also have known the characterization from various other sources. The *Polyantheae* writes "Gratiae a Graecis χάριτες dicuntur, eo quod *laetitiam* significent : nam & laetari videntur, qui dant & accipiunt beneficium." And the *Polyantheae* had borrowed this sentence from Perottus' *Cornucopiae*. Calepine (under *Gratia*) writes: ". . . quarum vnam Aglaiam nominarunt ab hilaritate, seu laetitia: propterea quod hilariter praestandum sit beneficium." C. Stephanus writes "Aglaia, Latine sonat Lux & laetitia, vna est Gratiarum. . . ," and "Euphrosyne, . . . vna Gratiarum soror Aglaiae & Thaliae, ab animi hilaritate . . . ita appellata." There was scarcely need for Spenser to go outside the dictionaries for the suggestion that the Graces were the "daughters of delight."

2. The paternity of the Graces: Spenser makes one definite statement as to the paternity of the three sisters. In *The Faerie Queene* (6.10.22), he writes,

> They are the daughters of sky-ruling Jove,
> By him begot of faire Eurynome,
> The Oceans daughter . . . .

The ultimate source of this passage is Hesiod's *Theogony,* and Lotspeich states definitely that "Spenser follows Theogony, 907-11, in making them the daughters of Jove and Eurynome." If the poet did follow the *Theogony,* he would not have got from the five-line account any suggestion of an alternative parentage or of the relationship of the Graces to Cupid—ideas with which Spenser was obviously familiar. On the other hand, he would have found in the dictionaries and polyantheaes from Perottus through the *Polyantheae,* the Calepine (under *Charites*), the Robert Stephanus, the Charles Stephanus, and the Huloet, the information, generally with a reference to Hesiod, that the Graces were the daughters of Jove and Eurynome, and the suggestion of another paternity. Under *Charites,* Robert Stephanus, for example, writes, "Hesiodus Iovis & Eurynomes Oceani filiae, filias scribit." And Charles Stephanus has the same statement; similar assertions are in the other volumes mentioned above.

But Spenser sometimes had in mind another of the traditional theories as to the paternity of the Graces. In *The Teares of the Muses* (l. 403) he refers to the graces as "ye three twins, to light by Venus brought," and in *The Faerie Queene* (2.8.6) he refers to the Graces as the sisters of Cupid. There is nothing in the Hesiod, where Spenser allegedly got part of his knowledge concerning the paternity of the Graces, to indicate that they are daughters of Venus. For this idea, Lotspeich cites Servius, Boccaccio, and N. Comes as mentioning the tradition that the Graces were daughters of Venus. It is noteworthy, however, that all the dictionaries which we mentioned above as making Jove and Eurynome the parents, record also the alternative paternity of Jove and Venus, or of Liber Pater and Venus. In the Charles Stephanus, for example, Spenser would have found the items together on paternity.  If he drew from Hesiod and Servius directly, he would have had to piece them together for himself.  In the dictionary, the account was already woven.

3. The Graces as Handmaids of Venus : This subject is closely related to, if indeed not inseparable from, the paternity of the Graces.  But for clarity a separate treatment may be desirable.  In *The Faerie Queene* (6.10.15) Spenser terms them the "Handmaids of Venus" and in *Epithalamion* (1. 103) the "three handmayds of the Cyprian Queene."  The same function seems to be implied in *The Faerie Queene* (2.8.6) and in *The Teares of the Muses* (1. 403).  In illustration of this idea, Lotspeich (p. 65) cites Servius, Boccaccio, and N. Comes without quoting them. Servius refers to the Graces, ". . . quas Veneri esse constat sacratas ; ipsius enim et Liberi filiae sunt : nec immerito ; gratiae enim per horum fere numinum munera conciliantur." This is scarcely different from the recurrent statements in the dictionaries (cf. Calepine, Robert Stephanus, Charles Stephanus), "Qui Veneris & Liberis filias arbitrantur (e quibus est Servius) hac mouentur ratione, quod horum praecipue deorum muneribus, gratiae concilientur." In the item on Aglaia, C. Stephanus writes of the Graces "Dicuntur esse in comitatu Veneris." Finally, Textor's *Officina* (1581) has this statement : "Finguntur Iovis & Eurynomes fuisse filiae & Veneris pedissequae." Spenser scarcely needed to go to Servius for his idea.

4. The Graces as companions of the Muses : Erato in *The Teares of the Muses* (1. 404) refers to the Graces as "The sweet companions of the Muses late." This association is represented also in *The Shepheardes Calender,* "April" (1. 100) and "June" (1. 25). Lotspeich cites *Theogony* (63-64). We have noted that Spenser was familiar with Robert Stephanus' item on the Muses, in which the author tells of the Muses and Graces together on the right hand of Apollo.  Erasmus' *Colloquy,* entitled "Epithalamium of Petrus Aegidius," depicts the Muses and Graces going together to celebrate the wedding.  Spenser seems to have known this piece and received from it some suggestions for his "Epithalamion." He could therefore have got from either Stephanus or Erasmus, or from both, the idea that the Graces were companions of the Muses.

5. Mount Acidale the haunt of Venus and the Graces : In two passages

in *The Faerie Queene* (4.5.5 and 6.10.6 ff.)   Spenser refers to Mount
Acidale as a place where Venus and the Graces were wont to sport.   We
find no Mount Acidale among the ancients or in the current dictionaries
of the Renaissance.   Lotspeich quotes Servius, *ad Aeneid,* l. 720, "Acidalia
Venus dicitur vel quia iniciit curas (cf. 6.10.8.6), quas Graeci ἀχίδας dicunt,
vel certe a fonte Acidalio . . . in quo se Gratiae lavant."   In his article on
*Gratiae,* Perottus has this: "Tradunt eas in Acidalio fonte, qui est
Orchomeni Boetiae vrbe, lauari, quoniam pura esse beneficia oportet, & ni-
hil sordidum, nullam spem retributionis habere.   Ab hoc fonte Venus
Acidalia dicitur: vel quia inijcit curas, quas Graeci ἀχυδίας vocant, vel
quae ἀχίδας spicula nominant, quibus vtitur Cupido."   The first sentence
"Tradunt eas," etc. recurs in the accounts of the Graces in *Polyantheae,*
Calepine, R. Stephanus, and C. Stephanus.   Under *Acidalia,* C. Steph-
anus and other lexicographers repeat the matter quoted from Servius.
Spenser would then have found in the detailed accounts of the Graces in
the dictionaries ample inspiration for his Mount Acidale.

In the dictionary articles, Spenser would also have found much more
information, as, for example, why there are three Graces, why they are
painted naked and with hands joined, why one has her face turned away
from us and two have theirs turned towards us, why they are depicted as
youthful and laughing.

All these show the possibility of multiple sources for Spenser and his
readers.   To these, however, must be added one other treatment of the
Graces current in Spenser's day—Vincentio Cartari's *Imagines Deorum.*
Cartari's six-page account (354-59) of the Graces, illustrated by wood-
cuts—one of Apollo leading the Graces and another of Mercury as
leader—was most likely to attract attention.   Having finished his discourse on Venus and Cupid, Cartari proceeded to treat of Venus' companions.   He pays tribute to the civilizing influence of the Graces, without
whose presence men would be inferior to other living creatures.   The
Graces, according to some authorities, are the daughters of Venus and
Bacchus.   Some hold that the Graces and the Hours are of the same
divinity.   The author here devotes a page to the discussion of the Hours
(Horae)—of which more below.   As there are four Hours, so there are
four Graces—and these are led by Apollo (woodcut).   Some maintain
there are only two Graces, but the more common opinion is that there are
three.   Then follows the conventional presentation of the three Graces,
excepting two or three slight departures.   (1) Benefits received, we should

## COLEBANTVR IMAGINES.        355

autem coronatæ,vna floribus,fru&ibufque terræ,altera fpicis,
& frumento,tertia vuis, & pampinis, atque pomis, vltima oliuis,cæterifque fimilibus; Apolloque manu dextera eas gefta-
re fingebatur;quod ex anni partes a Sole proueniant. Eædem *Gratiæ cur*
Veneri quoque comites funt allignatæ ; quod olim putarent, *Veneris co-*
ab eis proficifci, quod ad oris fpeciem, corporifque pulcritu- *mites.*
dinem fpectet; vt Diodorus refert. Earum quoque munus eft,
ne homines beneficiorum fint immemores, fed grato animo *Gratiæ*
gratiam rependant.Quare aliqui duas tantumGratias effe exi- *duæ.*

Yy    2

Apollo and the Graces, from a 1580 copy of the *Imagines Deorum,* in the
private collection of D. T. Starnes.

repay twofold: this is the reason why one grace is depicted facing away from us, two coming towards us (compare E. K.'s note on the Graces, quoted earlier in this chapter). To do a favor for remuneration is usury, not a benefit. (2) The usual order of listing the Graces' names is Aglaia, Thalia, Euphrosyne; Cartari has Euphrosine, Aglaia, Thalia, and mentions a fourth Grace which Homer called Pasithea. (3) Reference to *Eleois* Graces, one carrying in her hand a rose, a second a die, and a third a myrtle branch. (4) The identification of the Graces and the Hours, and the emphasis on the singing and dancing of the Hours, characteristics which, owing to the identification, could easily be applied to the Graces.

There is some evidence that, though E. K. in his annotations on the Graces "April" (1. 109) and Spenser in his presentation of these goddesses (*F. Q.* 6.10.9 ff.) were following in the main Cooper's *Thesaurus*, Spenser also had some suggestions from Cartari. (1) In *F. Q.* 6.10.24, for example, departing from Cooper, his immediate source, Spenser depicts two Graces going away from us and one coming toward us, indicating that "good should from us goe" in "greater store" than it should come to us. Though Cartari follows the conventional pattern in his picture of one Grace with her back turned and therefore going away, and two coming towards, he has the unconventional, though not illogical, interpretation for his picture that we should repay twofold any good or benefit received, and that doing a good with expectation of compensation is a form of usury. This is exactly the idea in Spenser's lines (6.10.24), and he rearranges the Graces to illustrate his meaning. As far as we can discover, Cartari is Spenser's only precedent for this interpretation. (2) In listing the names of the Graces (6.10.22) Spenser varies from the conventional order (Aglaia, Thalia, Euphrosyne) but follows exactly that of Cartari: Euphrosyne, Aglaia, and Thalia. In the same context (6.10.25), Spenser mentions a fourth Grace (and E. K. in his "April" gloss had referred to a fourth Grace whom Homer had called Pasithea). For the fourth Grace and the name Pasithea in a similar context, Spenser had a precedent in Cartari. (3) Spenser's frequent association of the Graces with song and dance and flowers ("April," ll. 109-14; "June," ll. 25-28; *F. Q.* 1.1.48; 6.10.14-15) has almost no suggestion in the conventional pictures of the three sisters. In Cartari these things are especially characteristic of the Graces in their depiction as Horae. And the Hours, or Horae, of Cartari suggest other anticipations of Spenser.

Spenser has two direct references to the Hours: (1) in *The Faerie Queene* (7.7.45); and (2) in *Epithalamion* (ll. 98-107). In the first the poet refers to their parentage—Jove and Night—to their "wondrous beauty," their virginity, and their function as "porters" of heaven's gate. In *Epithalamion* they appear as daughters of Day and Night; they allot the seasons of the year and "do make and still repayre" all that is fair in this world. They are here associated with the Graces and are termed daughters of delight.

As a basis for Spenser's treatment of the Hours, Lotspeich refers to Homer, Ovid, Boccaccio, and N. Comes. Less far afield would be contemporary dictionaries, especially Calepine and the Stephanus dictionaries. Typical of these is the entry in R. Stephanus, which seems to derive from Perottus. R. Stephanus explains that Hora signifies time—any part of eternity, embracing yearly, daily, or nocturnal space. After discussion of divisions of the day into 12 and then into 24 hours, Stephanus explains that Apollo was called Horus by the Egyptians, and from this name derive the 24 hours of the night and day, and also the four seasons. The Hours have charge of the horses of the sun; they preside over the gates of the sky and determine calm or cloudy weather; and, from them, derive the four seasons of the year, which the Greeks and the Romans call Horae. After more discussion of the way the Horae determine the seasons, the author concludes that they also are responsible for the fruits springing from earth and "Hora formosam quamlibet illa facit." Here are suggestions which Spenser could have used in his treatment of the Hours and in the pageant of the season.

Cartari has, however, more specific suggestions. He discusses the Horae under the heading of *Gratiae* (Graces) and with the Graces they are identified, and are therefore companions of Venus. The Horae are equated with the four seasons of the year; they are the porters of heaven's gates; they are companions of Janus in guarding the gates of the sky; they are also companions of Flora, the goddess of flowers; they are related to the Parcae, or Fates; they usher in the year and yearly make all things fair on earth; the seed of the earth is committed to them, which they return with interest. They are virgins, gifted with delightful song and dancing; and they are crowned with flowers and fruits and grains, and are led by Apollo (see woodcut in Cartari, p. 355).

Consider the following from Spenser,

> But first come ye, fayre Houres, which were begot,
> In Joves sweet paradice, of Day and Night,
> Which doe the seasons of the year allot,
> And al that ever in this world is fayre
> Do make and still repayre
>                                   (*Epith.* 98-103)

and compare Cartari,

Nec alius quidquam *Horae sunt,* quam *anni tempora*: hincque est, cur eas quattuor faciant, sicut & quattuor sunt anni partes, ita a Sole distinctae . . . *annum volutant, & tellus belle fert annua omnia.*

It is easy to infer from Cartari's Horae how fittingly Spenser introduced them into the midst of his pageant of the seasons (7.7.45). There the poet writes,

> Then came the Howres, faire daughters of high Jove
> And timely Night, the which were all endewed
> With wondrous beauty fit to kindle love;
> But they were virgins all . . .
> By mighty Jove; who did them porters make
> Of heavens gate. . . .

Compare Cartari,

Horas Homerus ait, caeli portis praeesse, curamque habere, vt modo serenum modo nubilum sit . . . Eusebius . . . scribit, Horae, quas quattuor anni tempora, ac caelum claudere, & aperire dicunt. . . . (pp. 353-54)

In other stanzas of the pageants of the seasons there may be echoes of Cartari. Spenser writes,

> So forth issew'd the seasons of the yeare:
> First, lusty Spring, all dight in leaves of flowres
> That freshly budded and new bloosmes did beare.
>                                   (7.7.28)

See also Stanzas XXXIII and XXXIV, on April and May, respectively, and their flowers, and compare Cartari,

(Horae) quattuor sunt anni partes, ita a Sole distincta, ac nominatae . . . interdum Soli tribuuntur, interdum & Cereri, atque ideo duos calathos ferunt, alterum *florum plenum, quibus ver innuitur.* (p. 354)

The Hours with their basket of flowers, to usher in the spring, could certainly have been suggestive to Spenser in his depiction of Spring and of the spring months, April and May, in each of which there is reference to the distribution. One other stanza (III) in the pageant may also have received hints from Cartari. Spenser in this stanza refers to "yellow clad" Autumn, "laden with fruits," and

> Upon his head a wreath, that was enrold
> With eares of corne of every sort, he bore.
>
> (7.7.30)

In the same chapter of Cartari, from which I have quoted above, the author speaks of the four Graces (identified with Horae), as

coronatae, vna floribus, fructibusque terrae, altera spicis [with grain or ears of corn as in the woodcut] & frumento, tertia uvis, & pampinis, atque pomis, vltima oliuis, caeteris que similibus . . . (pp. 354-55)

These words, illustrated by the cut of the Horae, with joined hands, and with garlands on their heads like those described, would not be difficult for Spenser or his readers to remember.

One of the best studies of early literature on the Muses, with special application to Spenser's poetry, is that by Lotspeich (pp. 83-85). Other studies and comments are found in Renwick's commentary in his edition of the *Complaints,* and in the articles by Mrs. Bennett and Professor Padelford, on Spenser's Muse in *The Faerie Queene.*[37] Most comprehensive is the compact sketch of Lotspeich. He first calls attention to the paternity (or paternities) of the Muses according to Spenser, as Apollo and Memory, ascribed to the influence of Comes; and Jove and Memory, in accord with the classical tradition as in Hesiod. Lotspeich then considers Spenser's conception of the function of the nine Muses, a conception based in part, Lotspeich thinks, on Virgil's Epigram or mnemonic verses (11 lines) and in part on hints from other sources, such as Boccaccio, Fulgentius, and Linocier. The exposition then extends to claims of Clio and Calliope as Muses of *The Faerie Queene;* the author on the basis of authorities mentioned above prefers Clio. He then notices briefly the idea of the Muses as sources of poetic inspiration, of their bringing poetic immortality, of their relation to learning and to music, and of their being crowned with the laurel.

Admitting the possibility of Spenser's familiarity with all that is said of the Muses by classical authors—Hesiod, Virgil, Plutarch, and by later writers—Boccaccio, Fulgentius, Lenocier, Comes—we think it is relevant to call attention to sixteenth-century disquisitions on the Muses, which, until recently, have not been noticed by Renaissance students.[38] The sixteenth-century books in which rather full information on the Muses was literally broadcast are Perottus' *Cornucopiae,* the dictionaries of Calepine, Charles Stephanus, and Robert Stephanus, and Cartari's *Imagines Deorum.* We may summarize as typical of the entries on Musa (*Musae*) that in Calepine.

According to Calepine's discourse, the poets feign that there are nine Muses, daughters of Jove and Memory, and they preside over music and poetry. They are essential to the learned man, who must be strong in intelligence and memory. They are variously referred to as Heliconides because of their residence in Mount Helicon, or Parnassides from Mount Parnassus, and so on through the appellations of Aonides, Cithaerides, Pierides, Thespiades, Hippocrenides, Castalides, etc. Here follow, in Calepine's account, the names of the nine and the significance of each: Calliope, from goodness of voice; Clio, from the glory and renown of the deeds which she sings; Erato, from singing of love; Thalia, from the voluptuous and lascivious character of her song; Melpomene, from the harmony of her song—she is thought also to preside over tragedy; Terpsichore, from delight in dancing; Euterpe, from the sweetness of her harmony, as if delighting well ("quasi bene delectantem")—by some she is called Tibicina, because she is believed to preside over the music of the flute; Polyhymnia (Polymnia), from her much singing and greatness or excellence of memory; Urania, as if celestial, from her song of heavenly affairs, or from the divine quality of her song. They are called Muses, some think, because among all disciplines (or learning) there is a similarity, or, as it were, a kind of chain of kinship, by which they are coupled and united; and so the Muses are painted as holding one another's hands, and as leading the dance. Some think the name signifies good and honest learning. At the end, the Epigram ascribed to Virgil, on the names of the Muses, is quoted in full.

The general entry *Musae* in C. Stephanus differs somewhat in detail from that of the Calepine, and the item in R. Stephanus contains much matter not in either of the other two. But the general discussions in the three dictionaries, together with the material under the individual names, constitute a fair-sized body of lore on the Muses which must have been known to the poets and to many of their readers in the sixteenth and seventeenth centuries.

In the light of new information from the aforementioned volumes and from one or two other sources, let us consider Spenser's ideas on the paternity, the functions, the general and individual characteristics of the Muses, and the possible relation of his presentation to the information available in the dictionaries and other neglected sources.

Apparently, Spenser makes no attempt to be consistent as to the paternity of the Muses. In some instances Apollo and Memory,[39] in others Jove and Memory[40] are represented as the Muses' parents. The first reference to Apollo as the father is by E. K. in his gloss on *The Shepheardes Calender,* "April," (p. 21). In subsequent passages, in which the poet represents Apollo as the father, he could have been following E. K. instead of, as Lotspeich suggests, Natalis Comes. Certainly, Spenser would not have needed to consult Hesiod or Cicero for the classical tradition of Jove and Memory as parents of the Muses. This information stands at the beginning of the entry *Musa (Musae),* as in the Calepine quoted above, and in three other current dictionaries with which Spenser was probably familiar.

As to the functions of the individual Muses the dictionaries are specific and detailed, but this topic is reserved for discussion later.

Among the haunts associated with the Muses Spenser employs Castalia, Helicon, Parnassus, Pieria, and Mount Cytheron. All these places are described, together with the derivative names applied to the sacred nine in the excerpt from Calepine, paraphrased above, and in other dictionaries. There is, in fact, a wide range of names for the various haunts, many of which Spenser never uses.

The relation of the Muses to music, to learning, to poetic inspiration, and poetic immortality is emphasized in the dictionary items. Notice the statements near the beginning and near the end of the matter paraphrased from Calepine. Similar assertions are to be found under *Musae* in Charles Stephanus' *Dictionarium.* More detailed treatment of these topics appears in the two-column entry in the *Thesaurus* (1573) of Robert Stephanus. Among other things, he writes:

1. Musae, pro Humanitate, doctrina quacunque, & literis accipiuntur . . . .

2. Musas Jovis & Mnemosynes, hoc est Memoriae filias poetae finxerunt, quod iis qui ad disciplinas & scientias pervenire cupiunt, duo haec in primis necessaria sunt, intellectus scilicet & memoriae facultas.

3. Eusebius . . . Musas tradit sic appellatas, quia μνέω apud Graecos honesta bonaque doctrina instituo significat . . . .

4. Musae in montibus dicuntur versari, ut ait Cornutus, quod secessu & solitariis maxime locis studiosi viri delectantur. Sunt & qui ideo in Heliconis & montium verticibus versari autument, quod ipsa sapientia atque intellectus, ex

quibus disciplinae ac scientiae nobis comparantur, quae per Musas intelliguntur, in hominis capite ut in puriori & eminentiori loco dicuntur esse.

5. Musae, a plerisque virgines esse dicuntur . . . quoniam disciplinae, uti virgines, abditae atque incomptae esse videntur, nativo scilicet decore contentae.

From the same source much more could be quoted to show the relationship of the Muses to learning and letters, but one more quotation must suffice. This is concerned with the use of the bay or laurel garland and the suggestion of poetic immortality.

6. . . . . Attribuitur & laurus Musis; vel quod ea arbor ad inspirationem & afflatum, & (ut Graeci dicunt) enthusiasmon conferat; quod Sophocles in Cassandra docet. Vel quod ejus arboris gustu poeticam se facultatem adipisci antiqui credidere, ut Lycophron innuit, qui poetam daphnophagon vocat, & de se canit Hesiodus; atque ideo etiam a Juvenale dictum, 7 Sat. 19.

. . . laurumque momordit.

Vel potius quod ea arbor semper sit virens; atque simili modo bonorum poetarum versus virescere perpetuo dicuntur per ora docta virorum. Quin & eadem causa in Musarum & Apollinis certaminibus poetas victores, quasi immortalitate quadam dignos, lauro coronari non solum apud antiquos, sed nunc quoque moris esse videmus.

To restate the substance of the discussion thus far, we may say that information on the paternity, the functions, and the haunts of the Muses was easily accessible to Spenser and other writers and students of the age in the standard reference dictionaries. In one of these—the *Thesaurus* of Robert Stephanus—are passages on the relationship of the Muses to learning, to poetic inspiration, and to the laurel crown or bay crown. Though Spenser's ideas on these topics are, as Lotspeich suggests, paralleled in the classics, they have also definite correspondences in the *Thesaurus* of Stephanus.

On the functions of the individual Muses Spenser has most to say in *The Teares of the Muses*. As a general pattern for this poem, Spenser seems to have had in mind Erasmus' colloquy of "The Conflict between Thalia and Barbarism." There are correspondences as to theme, characters, imagery, and general content.[41] Though the underlying thought in *The Teares* seems to owe much to Eramus' *Colloquy,* there is evidence, in the poem, of inspiration from other sources, particularly as regards the character and the functions of the various Muses. The functions are explained, for example, under the general entry in Calepine, as seen above, and in the Charles Stephanus. These compilers have the same order of listing, beginning with Calliope and ending with Urania, though they differ somewhat in the elaboration of individual duties. Calepine and Robert Stephanus place at the end of the general entry the mnemonic verses briefly describing the offices of the Muses. In the dictionaries, then, the poet could have found not only the exposition of the Muses' functions and the mnemonic verses in the main entry, *Musae,* but more detailed descriptions of the offices of each Muse under the individual entries, such as *Calliope, Clio,* and so on.

Lotspeich (p. 83) and Renwick (p. 206) observe that in *The Teares* the poet follows the order of the mnemonic verses *de Inventis Musarum,* ascribed to Virgil; and Lotspeich thinks that these lines offer sufficient explanation for certain of Spenser's delineations, to wit—Melpomene, Thalia, Euterpe, and Polyhymnia. Granted so, remember that Spenser could have read the pseudo-Virgilian poem in Calepine or in Robert Stephanus. It is to be observed, however, that Spenser generally says more concerning the function of each muse than he could have got from the single-line descriptions in the *de Inventis.* Even the words on Melpomene (*The Teares,* 151-56), which apparently do echo the Latin line, seem to show additional knowledge of this Muse's function, as if the poet had read the words of Calepine on Melpomene, concluding, ". . . unde & Tragoediis praesidere putabatur."

In the case of Thalia, the Latin line "Comica lasciva gaudet sermone Thalia" from the *de Inventis* affords little basis for characterization. Charles Stephanus' description under *Musae* offers much more: "Quartam a voluptate ac lasciuia cantus Thaliam: ϑάλλειν enim virere, germinare, florere est. Et vt ait Phurnutus, διὰ τὸ ϑάλλεῖν τὸν βίον αὐτων, i. quod reuiuiscere faciat ipsorum (poetarum) vitam. Vel, vt idem subiungit, quoniam & in conuiuiis ipsas virtutem habere, & honeste in eis conuersari suadet: vel, quoniam in longum tempus (vt alij scribunt) poetarum laus parta virescat. Nonnulli Thaliae comoedias attribuunt. . . ."

Euterpe, who, as Lotspeich states, becomes the Muse of the pastoral, could as well have become so on the basis of Calepine's characterization, or of Charles Stephanus' as on that of the *de Inventis.* Polyhymnia presides over rhetoric, and her complaint is, as Renwick and Lotspeich assert, chiefly a criticism of literary expression. Compare Robert Stephanus, who writes, among other things of Polyhymnia: ". . . Unde praesse rhetoribus dicitur, quibus opus est multa memoria. . . ." E. K.'s note (on "April," l. 100), to which Lotspeich refers in support of his statement, is a composite of Thomas

Cooper's item on Calliope—referred to as a goddess of rhetoric—and Calepine's entry under *Polymnia*.

Terpsichore's complaint simply develops the general theme that Ignorance and Barbarism have brought learning and letters to a low state. There is no reference to Terpsichore's function in the dance or chorus, nor can we find that she, more than ony other Muse, is presented as a patroness of letters, as Lotspeich suggests. She owes nothing to the mnemonic verses or to the dictionaries. The poet was developing his theme, which, as we have shown above, is based on Erasmus's "Conflict of Thalia and Barbarism."

For Erato and Urania, as for Terpsichore, Spenser took no suggestion from the pseudo-Virgilian poem on the functions of the Muses. He presents Erato as the Muse who presides over love poetry. For this information, he did not need to go to Linocier's *Mythologiae,* as Lotspeich suggests. Erato is presented as the Muse of love poetry under *Musae* in the Calepine paraphrased in the Charles Stephanus, in the individual entries under *Erato* in these lexicographers, and in the Robert Stephanus and the Thomas Cooper (*Thesaurus*). Some, or all, of these dictionary entries Spenser must have known.

Similarly, Urania is presented by the authorities mentioned, except Cooper, as the Muse concerned with heaven and divine song. See the characterization in the Calepine cited above. That in the C. Stephanus is almost identical. Under *Urania* in both of these appears this sentence: "Unde & Uraniam dictam putant quasi τά ἄνω ὁρῶσαν, hoc est, sublimis speculantem." Urania, in the Robert Stephanus is thus presented:

Una ex Musis, & apud nos Caelestis dicitur. Ovid. 5. Fast. 55. Excipit Uranie, fecere silentia cuncta, ὑρανὸς enim caelum dicitur, quod viros eruditos in caelum tollit. Uranos vero dicitur quasi *oranos* (ut ait Ambrosius libro Hexaemeron) ab ὁράω, quod sit visui pervium & minime densum, ut est aqua & terra. Catul, in *Epith.* Juliae, 59, 2.

If Spenser were familiar with the dictionary entries on Urania, and we must assume that he was, as they were standard reference works, he would not have needed to consult L. Gyraldus *de Musis Syntagma,* cited by Renwick (p. 215) or Plutarch's *Quaest. Conv.,* referred to by Lotspeich (p. 84).

As for Spenser's Muse in *The Faerie Queene,* an examination of Renaissance dictionaries together with other evidence will show that

Muse was Calliope. Concluding a former study on the subject—a conclusion we still maintain—we wrote these words: "In writing his longest poem Spenser was professedly following the tradition of heroic poetry as he understood it and as it had been expounded, with emphasis on its moral qualities, by all the major English critics of the sixteenth century, including Spenser's close friend, Sir Philip Sidney, whose comment on heroic poetry is a fitting characterization of *The Faerie Queene*. And the Muse for heroic poetry, according to standard Latin dictionaries of the sixteenth and seventeenth centuries, the pseudo-Virgilian verses on the Muses, and Drayton's *Muses Elizium,* was Calliope. That Spenser and his contemporaries believed that he had written a heroic poem, the commendatory verses and dedicatory sonnets show, we think, beyond a doubt. And all these harmonize perfectly with references to Calliope in *The Shepheardes Calender* and E. K.'s gloss for April (100) and with the majority of the formal invocations in *The Faerie Queene.*"[42]

Spenser's poetry is marked by scores of references to the Nymphs, in various situations and with various companions such as the Muses, Diana, fairies and elves, and bridal maids. The classes of Nymphs that Spenser refers to are Dryads or Hamadryads, Naiads and Nereids. Hesiod, Boccaccio, and Natalis Comes have been cited as most likely sources of information on the diverse kinds of Nymphs and their function. Spenser's sources were probably multiple, written and oral. Renaissance dictionaries, for example, contain explicit information on the Nymphs and probably helped to fix the conception. The dictionaries at any rate illustrate the character and function of the Nymphs as the poet conceived them. E. K., glossing "April" (l. 120), writes:

*Ladyes of the Lake* be Nymphes. For it was an olde opinion amongste the auncient heathen, that of every spring and fountaine was a goddesse the soveraigne . . . the Ladyes of the Lake, that is, the Nymphes. For the worde Nymphe in Greeke signifieth well water, or otherwise a spouse or bryde.

To gloss the glosser, we may quote from Friar Calepine's *Dictionarium* (1542):

Nympha, Νύμφη, Latine sponsa, Sed putauerunt antiqui Nymphas aquarum deas esse, quasi lympharum numina. Nymphae vero ab aquis deae sunt, quales sunt Dryades, Hamadryades, & Oreades. Quippe veteres Graeci Nympham dicebant, quam nos mutatione unius literal Lympham: hoc est, aquam. Aliquando Nymphae dicuntur Musae, quod aqua currendo musicos sonos efficiat.

Hinc saepenumero a poetis inuocantur.  Vergilius: Nymphae noster amor Li-
bethrides.[43]

E. K. seems to be fairly close to the entry in Calepine, though he employs
but little of his possible source in this gloss.  Deferring, for the present,
other ideas in the Calepine entry, let us notice more particularly the apparently superfluous detail (borrowed from Calepine) that the word
"Nymphe . . . signifieth a spouse or bride."

The association of Nymphs with brides and weddings appears in other
poems of Spenser.  In the *Epithalamion,* for example, he invokes the Muses
to "Helpe me mine owne loves prayses to resound," and

> Bring with you all the nymphes that you can heare,
> Both of the rivers and the forrests greene,
> And of the sea that neighbours to her neare.

(37-39)

The Nymphs are to bring with them a garland of lilies and roses and make
a great "store of bridale poses," and to strew flowers along the way and
"deck the bridale bowers."  In the *Prothalamion* the Nymphs are in a
similar rôle, but even more prominent.  The "flocke of nymphes" are
gathering flowers in wicker baskets,

> To decke their bridegromes posies
> Against the brydale day.

(34-35)

As the prospective brides, under the image of swans proceed on the Thames,
the Nymphs bring their baskets of flowers and "all the waves did strew."
Two of the Nymphs place garlands of flowers on the snowy foreheads of
the brides, while one sings a song of rejoicing for the prospective union.

If, as E. K. explains in the "April" gloss (l. 120), the word Nymph
means a spouse or bride, it would be quite natural for Spenser to associate
Nymphs with brides, as he did in the *Epithalamion,* the *Prothalamion,* and
elsewhere.  To Spenser and his readers this association of ideas must have
been almost commonplace.  E. K.'s gloss, for example, depends on Calepine, and Calepine seems to derive from Perottus's *Cornucopiae.*  R.
Stephanus elaborates Calepine, and asserts that brides are called Nymphs,
since formerly they went forth veiled but now allow themselves to be seen.
The *Bibliotheca Eliotae* (1559) defines Nymph thus: "Nympha doth signifie the bryde or spouse newe married, a nymphe or fayrie."  Thomas Thomas
gives the Greek word Νύμφη for Nympha and proceeds, "A nymph:

a bride or new married wife"; and Florio has "a new maried wife or bride."

On at least three occasions Spenser represents the Nymphs as Muses or in company of the Muses. In *Virgil's Gnat* we read,

> Wherefore ye sisters, which the glorie bee
> Of the Pierian streames, fayre Naiades. . . .
> (25-26)

And in *The Visions of Petrarch,*

> But manie Muses, and the nymphes withall,
> That sweetly in accord did tune their voyce. . . .
> (IV)

And in *Daphnaida,*

> Both Nimphs and Muses nigh she made astownd.
> (314)

The representation of the Nymphs as Muses, or in close association with the Muses, we have seen in the Calepine quoted above. The tradition is supported by Perottus, R. Stephanus, and Cooper in the *Thesaurus* and in the *Bibliotheca*. In the last named book are these words: "Nymphae, maydes of the sea, elfes, sometymes the muses."

"Spenser's nymphs," writes Lotspeich (p. 92), "have in many places become completely naturalized and are quite at home with English fairies." Illustrations of the Poet's presentation of the nymphs and fairies in association are many:

> . . . on whom did attend
> A fayre flocke of faeries, and a fresh bend
>    of lovely nymphs.
>                    ("May," 31-33)
> But frendly Faeries, met with many Graces,
> And lightfote Nymphes.
>                    ("June," 25-16)
> The joyous nymphes and lightfoote faeries.
>                    (*T. M.* 31)
> But nymphes and fairies by the bancks did sit.
>                    (*F. Q.* 6.10.7)
> Whether it were the traine of Beauties Queene,
> Or nymphes, or fairies, or enchaunted show.
>                    (6.10.17)

For the equation of Nymphs and fairies before Spenser, Lotspeich (p. 92, n 15) cites Gower and Chaucer; Latham[44] cites Douglas' translation of the *Aeneid* and Golding's translation of Ovid's *Metamorphoses*. Again we may say that the identification was common in Spenser's day. It is found in nearly all the contemporary dictionaries. We have noted above that the *Bibliotheca Eliotae* defines "Nympha" as "a bryde or spouse, a *nymphe or fayrie.*" The same lexicon refers to "Nereides" as "fairies of the sea." In Cooper's *Thesaurus* is a similar statement about Nereids; and these definitions of other kinds of Nymphes:

"Dryades were fayries of the woodes"
"Hamadryades, Nymphes or fayries of the woddes."
"Oreades, Nymphes of the Mountaynes."
(Cf. Thomas. "Oreades, Fayries of the mountaines.")
"Naides, Elfes or Fayries, haunting ryvers and fountaynes."

Florio (*A Worlde of Wordes: An Italian-English Dictionary*, 1598), has these:

"Náiade, elfes, nimphes or fairies, haunting rivers and fountaines."
"Driadi, certain wood-nymphs so called."
"Oreadi, mountain nymphes."
"*Nimpha* [1611 edit.], any kinde of Nimph, Elfe, or Fairie."

In "naturalizing" the Nymphs and making them "at home with the English fairies" Spenser was following the current practice.

The quotations from Cooper and Florio show the classes of Nymphs: Dryads, Hamadryads, Naiads, Nereids, and Oreads. These are the classes mentioned and described in other Renaissance dictionaries from Perottus through Calepine and Stephanus, and the other lexicons mentioned—and these also are the classes of Nymphs in Spenser's poetry.

Of these Nymphs, the Nereids receive the longest special reference in *The Faerie Queene* (4.11.48-53). The reasons for such emphasis are not far to seek. It would be natural for a poet of England or Ireland to give special attention to the mythical creatures of the sea and other waters. And this natural inclination would be re-enforced by authority. Perhaps all treatments of Nymphs available to Spenser and his public stressed particularly the association of these invisible beings with water; and as the Nereids more than any other class were of the sea, they would receive most attention.

To recall once more our entry on *Nympha* from Calepine, we notice the lexicographer states that the ancients regarded the Nymphs—all nymphs —as the goddesses of waters, for, he tells us presently, they are from [spring from] the water. C. Stephanus has a similar statement, characterizing the Nymphs, first of all as goddesses of the waters, though admitting the name was more widely extended to include goddesses of the trees, the woods, the mountains, etc. Earlier, Perottus had stressed the derivation of Nymphs from the waters, and had asserted that there are almost an infinite number of names for Nymphs of fountains, since every river and spring had its own Nymphs. (Col. 786.) Then Perottus gives considerable space to the Nereids as sea-nymphs, daughters of Nereus and Doris, and devotes a column and a half (folio) to listing the names, Latin and Greek, and indicating etymologies. Thus Perottus and his successor prepare us for the elaborate presentation of the Nereids by Spenser (4.11.48 ff.).

In his brief discussion of the stanzas just referred to, Lotspeich (pp. 89-90) holds that Spenser is following, in the main, Natalis Comes, with some suggestions from Hesiod on the epithets of Cymodoce, Glauconome, and Alimeda. The evidence does seem to show indebtedness to Comes and possibly to Hesiod. Even so, these originals do not explain all in the passage. For, we are told, Spenser has gone beyond his predecessors (Comes and Hesiod) in etymologizing, independent of sources. Among the independent etymologies listed by Lotspeich are these:

1. "swift Proto" (Πρώθεω)
2. "joyous Thalia" (Θάλεια)
3. "light foote Cymothoe" (Κυμοθοή)
4. "sweete Melite" (Μελιτόεις)
5. "speedy Hippothoe" (Θοή)
6. "Nemertea learned well to rule her lust" (Νημερτής)

It should be noted, however, that almost a hundred years earlier, Perottus (*Cornucopiae*, col. 785-87) had indulged in similar etymolygizing of forty odd names of Nereids and other Nymphs. And whether Spenser knew the *Cornucopiae* or not, there are some striking similarities in the etymologies. Compare, for example, with the tabulated list above, the following from Perottus:

1. Πρωτώ, proto a producendo.
2. Θάλια, hoc est *thalia,* quod virens seu *laeta* sit.
3. Κυμοθόη, Cymothoe a *velocitate* undarum.
4. Μελίτη, melite a *dulcore,* & suauitate μέλι *mel.*
5. Θοή, thoe à uelocitate currendi.
6. Νημερτής [*sic*], nemertes, quasi *incorruptibilis.*

Here from a single column (785) in the *Cornucopiae* is at least precedent for Spenser's individual etymologies. Nor is this all. In Stanzas XLVIII and XLIX Spenser refers to "Wondred Agave," "Light Doto," "Erato that doth in love delite," and "milkewhite Galathaea." Compare Perottus (785): "ἀγαυή, agaue a magnitudine splendoris"; "δωτὼ, doto a dando"; "ἐρατὼ, hoc est Eraten alteram nympham fuisse existimant, ab *amore*"; "Ταλήτεια, galatea a lactis colore."

In conclusion, we may state that though Spenser knew Comes and possibly Hesiod on the Nereids, he also shows in his treatment of the various classes of Nymphs familiarity with the great body of Nymph-lore duly recorded in contemporary dictionaries, a source of information important for Spenser's readers, past and present, and for the better understanding of the literary milieu of Spenser.

In two allusions, Spenser has confused Olympus with Olympia. The following passage illustrates the confusion:

> Or on the marble pillour, that is pight
> Upon the top of Mount Olympus hight,
> For the brave youthly champions to assay,
> With burning charet wheeles it nigh to smite.
>
> (3.7.41)

Compare also *The Ruines of Rome, 2.*

Jortin remarks that it is a strange mistake that Spenser should think the Olympic games were held on the top of Mount Olympus.[45] Church thinks there is a mistake in the text and suggests an emendation. Lotspeich suggests that Spenser made the inference from the account given by Comes. Though we cannot be sure of Spenser's source for 3.7.41, we know he had ample precedent in the period for placing the games on the top of Olympus. Polydore Vergil (*De Rerum Inventoribus*. 2.13) at the very beginning of the sixteenth century, writes of the various kinds of games among the Greeks, concluding one statement thus:

. . . quorum primi et longe celeberrimi olympici appellati sunt, ab omnibus fere poetis decantati, quoniam *in olympo monte* apud Pisam & Elidem oppida Arcadiae, Ioui dedicati Pelopis honore celebrantur . . . .

Here is a definite statement that the games were held on Mt. Olympus. The tradition persists in the *Bibliotheca Eliotae* of 1559, and the same entry, with slight changes in spelling, is found in Cooper's *Thesaurus*

(1565). This entry, here quoted in part, could have offered other suggestions to Spenser.

Olympicum certamen, was a game or pryce kept *on the hyll of Olympus,* by all the princes and cities of Greece, every fift yeare, in the honour of Hercules, who first began it. In the which were all these maysteries prooved: Running on foote to a gole. Also running foorth, and back again two furlongs. Also wrastling, fighting with fistes, running with horses, and leaping from one to the other, coursing with chariottes . . . . There was also contention and victorie of Poetes, Rhetoricans, Musitians, and subtile disputers. In the place did grow a wild Oliue tree: whereof Garlands were made, and giuen to the victours hereunto assembled.

Spenser's most detailed allusion to the sirens, or "mermayds" as he terms them, is in 2.12.30-34. The pertinent parts of the passage may be quoted.

> And now they nigh approched to the sted,
> Where as those mermayds dwelt . . .
> There those five sisters had continuall trade,
> And usd to bath themselves in that deceiptfull shade.
>
> (Stz. 30)

Defeated in their contest with the Muses, they were deprived of their beauty,

>                                       and th'one moyity
> Transformd to fish, for their bold surquedry;
> But th' upper halfe their hew retayned still,
> And their sweet skill in wonted melody;
> Which ever after they abusd to ill,
> T'allure weake traveillers, whom gotten
>          they did kill.
>
> (Stz. 31)

These stanzas have received from Spenser scholars considerable comment. (See *Var. Ed.* II, 364-65.) Lotspeich observes that Spenser makes no distinction between mermaids and sirens. Jortin calls attention to the poet's departure from classical tradition, in which sirens were part women and part birds. Upton thinks the sirens symbolize sensual pleasures. Lemmi interprets the mermaids as voluptuousness, after Comes; and Lotspeich, referring to Lemmi, and Comes, and adding Boccaccio, makes a similar interpretation. Few will disagree with the general interpretation of these critics, but we may query whether it was necessary for Spenser to hark back to Boccaccio or Comes for the particular conception of the sirens, or to Chaucer for the epithet of mermayds to apply to them.

On all these points, the current dictionaries may be consulted. Cooper, for example, concludes his brief account of the sirens with these words: "Whom poetes feigned to be Mermaydens." And the epithet was common in the period. So, too, in making his siren-mermaids part women and part fish, instead of part birds as in the classical tradition, Spenser had a basis in Calepine, Cooper, and the Stephanus dictionaries. Nor did he need to look elsewhere than in the dictionaries for the idea of the voluptuousness or lustfulness of the sirens. Note the following from Calepine (1542):

Siren . . . Sirena, monstrum maris, ab εἴρειν, quod connectere vel retinere significat. Vel ab σειρὰ catena, eo quod libidinis vinculum sirenes fuerint. Sunt qui & hoc nomen ab σύρω, traho deducant. . . . Fuerunt autem Sirenes Acheloi & Calliopes filiae, ore & pube tenus virgines reliqua parte corporis pisces, Siculum littus incolentes, quarum nomina fuerunt Parthenope, Lygia, & Leucosia.

The sirens or mermaids signifying a chain of lust ought to have been suggestive to Spenser. He would have found the figure of the chain repeated in Robert Stephanus' *Thesaurus* (1573), with added suggestions, such as:

. . . Secundum veritatem meretrices fuerunt, quae transeuntes, quoniam quos ducebant ad egestatem, his fictae sunt inferre naufragia: has Ulysses contemnendo deduxit ad mortem.

Charles Stephanus concludes his entry on the sirens by emphasizing the lesson of the story against the allurements of sensual pleasures (*"illecebras voluptatum"*) and the delights of the flesh (*"carnis delicias"*). But this entry has so much, besides, on the sirens, that we transcribe a large part of it.

Sirenes, monstra marina, poetarum fabulis celebrata, superiore sui parte virginis effigiem referentia, inferiore vero in piscis caudam desinentia. Hae tres fuisse finguntur, Acheloi fluuij, & Calliopes Nymphae filiae, Parthenope, Ligea, & Leucosia, quae cum littus Siculum incolerent, nautas praeternauigantes suauitate cantus in naufragiam pelliciebant. [Here follows the account of Ulysses' escape from the sirens and their casting themselves into the sea as a result. Homer. 12. Odyss. Then follows the alternate account (Ovid. 5. Met.) of the sirens as companions of Proserpine, of their search and failure to find Proserpine after her abduction, and of their being changed into sea monsters] . . . superiore corporis parte virgineam formam, inferiore pisces referentia: voce autem cithara & tibiis tam blande canentia, vt praeternauigantes sopirent, sopitos demergerent, demersos etiam deuorarent. Virg. 6. Aeneid. *Sirenum fabula docet voluptatum illecebras non posse nisi a sapiente superari, & carnis delicias in exitium detrudere miseros mortales demonstrat.*

The studies of Sawtelle and Lotspeich indicate that the range of Spenser's classical mythology was extensive and varied. Our discussion does not seek to minimize the importance of their work or that of other scholars who have studied Spenser's classical background. It seeks rather to show what helps Spenser and his contemporaries had in gaining and keeping fresh the knowledge of ancient myth and legend and to suggest that the poet was not writing in a vacuum. The reference books, besides original texts, which he had at hand were of course easily accessible to his readers. To avail himself of the reputable reference works was economy then as it would be now. Among the works which the evidence suggests that Spenser consulted are those with which he probably first became familiar as a student at the Merchant Tailors' School or at Cambridge. These are Cooper's *Thesaurus,* Robert Stephanus' *Thesaurus,* Charles Stephanus' *Dictionarium,* Calepine's *Dictionarium,* and Cartari's *Imagines Deorum*—to mention only those which hitherto have received scant attention. Study of these works as a part of the poet's heritage leads to a better understanding of Spenser's sources of information and his method of composition.

## CHAPTER V

# SHAKESPEARE AND THE DICTIONARIES

IN THE ANNUAL SHAKESPEARE LECTURE BEFORE THE BRITISH ACADEMY, 28 April 1943, F. S. Boas expressed his opinion that "the dramatist's classical lore was for the most part gained at second-hand"; that it was "curiously partial, both in its concentration and in its omissions"; that the "gods and heroes were known to him only under their Latin names"; that he "drew no line between the original old world legends and medieval accretions"; that "none the less, Shakespeare's classical knowledge, though second-hand, was not second-rate and should not be branded as superficial."[1]  Though he would not describe Shakespeare as a classical scholar, T. W. Baldwin, in his recent book *On the Literary Genetics of Shakspere's Poems & Sonnets* (Urbana, Illinois, 1950), assumes that the poet had sufficient knowledge of the Latin to read Ovid and Livy and other Latin authors in original contemporary texts, and that he actually did so, acquiring, besides the matter in the texts, many ideas from the notes and commentary by classical scholars in the Renaissance.  By implication, Baldwin's point of view is in sharp contrast with that of Boas.

Although Shakespeare was introduced to classical literature and mythology during the brief period at the Stratford grammar school, we may be certain that he did not have the facility in reading Latin possessed by Spenser, Marlowe, or Ben Jonson.  One may query indeed how far Shakespeare's knowledge of Latin enabled him to consult expeditiously the texts and their learned commentaries years after he left Stratford, and whether the information he might thus acquire could readily be gained from other sources.  Prominent among these was Cooper's Latin-English *Thesaurus,* which, Baldwin suggests, Shakespeare frequently consulted.[2]

In Part I of this chapter we shall present with appropriate comment an alphabetical list of persons, historical and mythical, in the manner of R. K.

Root's *Classical Mythology in Shakespeare*. Part II we shall devote to a more detailed discussion of certain sketches which Shakespeare may have read in Cooper's *Thesaurus*.

I

*Absyrtus*. In the *Second Part of Henry the Sixth* there is the following allusion to the story of Medea and Absyrtus:

> Meet I an *infant* of the house of York,
> Into as many gobbets will I cut it
> As *wild* Medea *young* Absyrtus did;
> In cruelty will I seek out my fame.
>
> (5. 2. 57-60)

Root[3] points out that the story is recounted in Ovid's *Tristia* (3.9). T. W. Baldwin[4] finds evidence of Shakespeare's acquaintance with this book. Citing the passage quoted above and the Latin lines from the *Tristia* as a possible source, Baldwin remarks that "this allusion may not be Shakspere's." Whether the lines are by Shakespeare or another, it is fairly certain that Ovid's *Tristia* is the ultimate source.

Cooper's summary of the story of Medea, in the *Thesaurus,* offers a suggestive parallel. Having told of Medea's assistance to Jason in securing the golden fleece, Cooper continues,

> After all which thinges atchieued, shee ranne away with Jason and tooke with hir *Absyrtus* hir *yong* brother. But Oetes . . . pursued them with such speede, that hee had well neere ouertaken them. Wherefore Medea seeing that nothing could stay hir fathers haste, fearing to bee taken, *kylled the yong babe* hir brother, and scattered his lymmes in the way as hir father shoulde passe. With sorrowe whereof and long seeking the *partes of hys yong sonnes bodye* the father was stayed, and Jason wyth Medea in the meane tyme escaped out of his realme.

The emphasis in *2 Henry VI* upon the infancy of Absyrtus is not found in Ovid.[5] In Cooper "yong" is thrice used, once in the phrase "yong babe" (suggestive of "infant" in the play). Other details, such as the suggestion for "gobbets" and even the epithet "wild" Medea (in the Cooper "wild fire," in part of the text not summarized)—all could have derived from the *Thesaurus*.

*Agamemnon*. Root[6] rightly observes that the character may have been drawn from Caxton, from Homer, or from mere tradition. He further observes that in *Henry the Fifth* (3.6.7) the Welshman, Fluellen, says that the Duke of Exeter is "as magnanimous as Agamemnon." Virgil and Ovid apply the epithet *magnanimus* to several of their heroes, but never to Agamemnon.[7] Keeping in mind Fluellen's epithet, we may notice also two passages in Shakespeare's *Troilus and Cressida:* Achilles speaks of procuring "safe-conduct for his person of the magnanimous and most illustrious six-or-seven-times-honoured *captain-general* of the Grecian army, Agamemnon" (3.3.277-280). And earlier Agamemnon himself had said to Aeneas,

> With surety stronger than Achilles' arm
> *'Fore all the Greekish heads,* which *with one voice*
> Call Agamemnon *head and general.*
>
> (1.3.220-222)

The epithet "magnanimous" applied to Agamemnon by Fluellen and by Achilles, the choice by all the Greeks of Agamemnon to be head and captain-general—all these could be explained by Shakespeare's knowledge of the sketch of the general in Cooper's *Thesaurus.*

*Agamemnon . . .* for his wisedome and *magnanimitie* was by *the consent of all the Greekes,* chosen to be their *generall Capitaine.*[8]

*Althaea.* In *The Second Part of King Henry the Fourth* the Page speaks thus of the red-faced Bardolph:

PAGE.  Away, you rascally Althaea's dream, away!
PRINCE.  Instruct us, boy; what dream, boy?
PAGE.  Marry, my lord, Althaea *dream'd she was delivered of a fire-brand;* and therefore I call him her dream.  (2.2.94-98)

On this, as Root notes,[9] Dr. Johnson comments: "Shakespeare is here mistaken in his mythology, and has confounded Althaea's firebrand with Hecuba's. The firebrand of Althaea was real; but Hecuba, when she was big with Paris, dreamed that she was delivered of a firebrand which consumed the kingdom." Dr. Johnson is right—the Page was mistaken. The Page seems, however, to have remembered the exact phrasing of Cooper's *Thesaurus* concerning Hecuba, under the item *Paris.*

*Paris,* King Priamus his sonne of Troy, whose mother being with child dreamed, that *she was deliuered of a fyre branne.* . . .

*Hercules.* Root (p. 71) observes that though Shakespeare's allusions to Hercules are quite numerous, his definite knowledge of the myth is exceedingly scanty. Of the labors, only four are alluded to in detail. In the passages which follow are the unusual references to the Hesperides.

Before thee stands this fair Hesperides,
With golden fruit, but dangerous to be touch'd,
For death-like dragons here affright thee hard.
*(Per.* 1.1.27-29)

For valour, is not Love a Hercules,
Still climbing trees in the Hesperides?
*(L.L.L.* 4.3.340-41)[10]

As Hercules
Did shake down mellow fruit.  You have made fair work.
*(Cor.* 4.6.99-100)

It is obvious from the quoted lines that Shakespeare regards the Hesperides as the name of the garden; and he represents Hercules as gathering the fruit himself, while, according to the traditional story, Hercules sent Atlas to do it for him.   These variations can be accounted for by positing Shakespeare's familiarity with the account of Hercules' labors in Cooper's *Thesaurus.* For example,

The twelfth and last labour was the taking of the *golden* Apples, out of the *gardeynes Hesperides,* and sleayng the terrible Dragon, which continually watching kept those Apples, which were *called golden* for the beautie of them.

Here the Hesperides are identified with the gardens, the apples are golden, and, by implication, Hercules gathers them for himself.

In preparing to celebrate the nuptials of Theseus and Hippolyta, the master of the revels refers to Hercules in the proposed song about the battle of the Centaurs.

"The battle with the Centaurs, to be sung
By an Athenian eunuch to the harp."
We'll none of that: that have I told my love
In glory of my kinsman Hercules.
*(M.N.D.* 5.1.44-47)

The occasion for the suggested story and the language used seem to indicate that the dramatist has confused the battle between the Centaurs and Lapithae at the marriage feast of Hippodamia with Hercules' battle with the Centaurs.   It is possible that Shakespeare was remembering again Cooper's account of Hercules' struggle:

The fourth labour was the battaile whiche hee had alone with the great number of men called Centauri, that were of great strength and swift as horses: all them he slue, when they assaulted him.[11]

In his semi-madness, Lear thinks, confusedly, of Goneril and Regan as she-Centaurs.

> I pardon that man's life. What was thy cause?
> Adultery?
> Thou shalt not die: die for adultery! No:
> . . .
> Let copulation thrive; for Gloucester's bastard son
> Was kinder to his father than my daughters
> Got 'tween the lawful sheets. . . .
> *Down from the waist they are Centaurs,*
> *Though women all above*:
> But to the girdle do the gods inherit,
> Beneath is all the fiends':
> There's hell, there's darkness, there is the sulphurous pit
> Burning, scalding, stench, consumption.
>
> (4.6.112-32)

The phrasing of Lear's reference to the Centaurs suggests that the dramatist remembered the account of these monstrous people as summarized in Cooper's *Thesaurus*:

*Centauri,* People of Thessalie by the mounte Pelion, which first deuised to breake horses and make them for warre and other vses: whereof it came to passe that they beyng seene on horsebacke by their borderers were thought to *haue the vpper parte of their bodies lyke men,* and *the neather lyke horses,* and therefore of their beginning Poetes fable in this wise. [Here follows the story of Ixion's adultery with Juno and his begetting the Centaurs of clouds.]

The part of Cooper's entry not here quoted shows that the genesis of the Centaurs was adulterous and that they were prone to be lustful, as indicated in the attempted rape of the bride at the marriage feast of Pirithous and Hippodamia; and, finally, that Ixion was their father. As Lear thought of his daughters as Centaurs, he did not forget that his role was that of Ixion, the father of the Centaurs. In the very next scene (4.7), for example, he indicates this relationship. Cordelia is attempting to nurse her father back to sanity, when, partially awaking from a long sleep, Lear imagines he is in hell and refers to himself as in the position of Ixion:

> You do me wrong to take me out o' the grave;
> Thou art a soul in bliss; but *I am bound*
> *Upon a wheel of fire,* that mine own tears
> Do scald like molten lead.
>
> (4.7.45-48)

Compare with this Cooper's story of Ixion:

*Ixion*, a king of Thessalie, who falsely brake promise with his wiues father, and threwe him into a pitte of fire. Hee also called by Iupiter vnto a feast, stirred Iuno to comit adulterie, which Iupiter perceyuing, made a cloude like vnto Iuno, and deliuered hir to him, on whome he begat the people called *Centauri*. But when hee had auaunted that he had companied with Iuno, he was *driuen downe into hell,* and there *bounde to a wheele alwayes turning* and full of Serpentes, as poetes feygne.[12]

The excerpts from the play and the *Thesaurus* show that Lear was father of the lustful daughters as Ixion was of the lecherous Centaurs; that Lear, like Ixion, was bound to a wheel (of fire), and that the story of Ixion and his adulterous offspring was in Shakespeare's mind through a good part of Act IV. Though the dramatist might have known the story from other sources, Cooper's *Thesaurus* offers most suggestive parallels.

*Cimmerian.* In *Titus Andronicus* (2.3.72) the dramatist refers to Aaron, the Moor, in these words:

> . . . your swarth Cimmerian
> Doth make your honour of his body's hue,
> Spotted, detested, and abominable.
> 
> (2.3.72-4)

Root notes that the land of the Cimmerians at the gate of Hades is described in the *Odyssey* (II, 14), but that the men are not depicted as of swart skin. He queries whether Shakespeare confuses them with the Ethiopians. Shakespeare probably does so. It must be remembered that Aaron, like Othello, is called a "Moor." For the "confusion" of "Moor" and "Aethiopian," Shakespeare had precedent in Cooper's *Thesaurus,* where "Aethiops" is defined as "a Mooren." In the proverb at the end of his entry "Aethiops," Cooper writes thus:

*Aethiopem lauas.* Thou washest a Mooren or Moore. . . . This prouerbe grewe out of one that bought a Mooren, and thinking that the blacknesse of his skinne happened by the negligence of his first mayster: he ceased not to washe the Mooren continually with such thinges as hee thought woulde make him whyte. By which labour and washing, he so vexed the poore slaue, that he brought him into a great sicknesse, his skinne remayning still as black as it was before.

The quoted proverb is a paraphrase from Erasmus, which could have been known to Shakespeare in the original. It should be observed, however, that in his interpretation of *Aethiopem lauas* Cooper introduces the word

*Mooren* as the equivalent of *Aethiops,* and this interpretation has no precedent in Erasmus. Shakespeare obviously has the same conception of the Moor as Cooper has, whether he learned it from the *Thesaurus* or elsewhere.

*Daedalus (Icarus, Minos, Minotaur).* Allusions to the story of Icarus and Daedalus, and other figures connected with that myth, are, as Root (p. 50) observes, limited to *The First Part of King Henry VI* and *The Third Part.* The story as told in *Met.* 8. 183-235, might account for all the allusions, except the following:

> Thou mayst not wander in that *labyrinth;*
> There *Minotaurs* and ugly treasons lurk.
> *(1 Henry VI.* 5.3.188-89)

As Root points out, neither the word *labyrinth* nor the name *Minotaur* appears in the story as told in the *Metamorphoses.* Shakespeare's familiarity with certain entries—*Minotaurus* and *Labyrinthus*—in Cooper could well be the basis of the quoted lines. Cooper writes:

*Minotaurus* . . . A monster in Creta, whome the poetes feigne to be borne of *Pasiphaë,* the wyfe of King Minos, being part like a man, part like a Bull, which being inclosed in the place called *Labyrinthus,* was *fedde with mannes flesh.* . . .

and

*Labyrinthus* . . . An other *Labyrinthus* was in Creta, made by Dedalus, by the commaundement of Minos, for a prison. . . . But by dyuers *doores, enterings,* and *issuings* out, it *deceyued them which came into it.*

Here are suggestions for Minotaurus in the Labyrinth, and "ugly treasons." Incidentally, the story of Minos' requiring seven Athenian youths yearly to be sacrificed to the Minotaur is told in Cooper in the Minos item, two entries above *Minotaur.* The sketch of Minos in the *Thesaurus* concludes with a *vide Aegeus.* In this last sketch is told how Theseus with the help of Ariadne overcomes the Minotaur and escapes from the Labyrinth. Also, under *Icarus* in the same text is a compact summary of the Daedalus-Icarus myth. Shakespeare's knowledge of these entries would account for all the allusions to the Icarus-Dedalus-Minos-Minotaur myth, without resort to the *Metamorphoses.*

*Phaethon.* Ovid tells the story of Phaethon in *Metamorphoses* (1.748; 2.238), and Shakespeare could have drawn his knowledge of the myth

**62**        A N D R E Æ   A L C I A T I

## In temerarios.

### EMBLEMA LVI.

Aspicis *aurigam currus Phaëthonta paterni*
  *Igniuomos aufum flectere Solis equos;*
*Maxima qui poſtquàm terris incendia ſparſit,*
  *Eſt temerè inſeſſo lapſus ab axe miſer.*
*Sic plerique rotis fortunæ ad ſidera Reges*
  *Euecti, ambitio quos iuuenilis agit;*
*Poſt magnam humani generis cladémq́, ſuámq́,*
  *Cunctorum pœnas denique dant ſcelerum.*

Furor

Phaeton, in Alciat's *Emblems*, 1608, from a copy in the University of
Texas Library.

from Ovid, though, as Root observes, there are no striking verbal similarities. The interesting feature of Shakespeare's use of the myth, however, is not his knowledge of the story—which he might have learned from
any of a number of sources—but, with a single exception, what the story
symbolizes in the contexts in which it recurs.

In *The Third Part of King Henry VI*, for example, Lord Clifford
says of the aspiring Richard Plantagenet, duke of York, as he is taken
prisoner,

> Now Phaëthon hath tumbled from his car,
> And made an evening at the noontide prick.
>
> (1.4.33-4)

Later, in this play, seeing King Henry at the point of defeat, Clifford employs the figure of Phaethon again.

> O Phoebus! hadst thou never given consent
> That Phaëthon should check thy fiery steeds,
> Thy burning car never had scorch'd the earth;
> And, Henry, hadst thou sway'd as kings should do,
> Or as thy father and his father did . . .
> And thou this day had kept thy chair in peace.
>
> (2.6.11-20)

Again, Richard the Second, about to submit to Bolingbroke, speaks.

> Down, down, I come; like glistering Phaëthon,
> Wanting the manage of unruly jades.
>
> (3.3.178-9)

And, finally, there is the speech of the Duke, rebuking Valentine in *The
Two Gentlemen*.

> Why, Phaëthon,—for thou art Merop's son,—
> Wilt thou aspire to guide the heavenly car
> And with thy daring folly burn the world?
> Wilt thou reach stars, because they shine on thee?
> Go, base intruder! overweening slave!
> Bestow thy fawning smiles on equal mates . . . .
>
> (3.1.153-58)

In three, probably four, of these quotations the story of Phaethon is used
to symbolize ambition for power to rule or, given the power, inability to
handle the "unruly jades." Of course the idea is implicit in Ovid's story.
In other books the symbolism is explicit. Alciati's emblem (No. LVI),

entitled "In Temerarios" has a woodcut of Phaethon falling headlong from his chariot with an inscription comparing his action and his ruin to that of an ambitious prince. And in an edition of Alciati with commentaries by Claudius Minois there is extensive elaboration of the figure, with examples of overweening rulers. The date of the commentaries (1608) is too late for the places under consideration. Perhaps Alciati's emblem and inscription would be sufficient suggestion for the dramatist. There is, however, another possible source for Shakespeare. In his *Dictionarium,* Charles Stephanus, gives a detailed summary of Phaethon's tragic experience, referring to Ovid and Lucian and Comes. Stephanus concludes,

. . . Fabula ad mores relata exprimit imaginem temerarij et ambitiosi principis, qui gloria & regnandi cupiditate incensus cogitat sublimia & concipit aethera mente.

Freely translated by Holyoke and Littleton in the seventeenth century, the passage was:

Howsoever it be, the fable doth present unto us the picture of an inconsiderate and ambitious Prince, who being touched with an eager desire of Majesty, before his time ascends the Throne, but shortly after, letting loose the reins by his undiscreet Government, he sets his subjects all in a combustion, and indangers his own downfall.

This paraphrase from Stephanus is the sort of interpretation of the Phaethon myth that Shakespeare, wherever he learned it, had in mind when referring to the story. The interpretation in the Stephanus dictionary, which derives from Comes' *Mythologiae* (6.1), is more explicit in its application than that cited by T. W. Baldwin (*Small Latine,* II, 195) from Erasmus' *De Copia* that the fable of Phaethon teaches that no one should undertake the performance of tasks above his powers.

*Prometheus.* In all his works Shakespeare has only four allusions to the Prometheus myth, two of these being in *Love's Labour's Lost.* The scarcity of allusions might show that the dramatist was not especially familiar with the details of the story. Only in *Titus Andronicus* (2.1.17) is Prometheus presented as the sufferer on Caucasus. As fashioner of the human race, Prometheus appears in *Othello* (5.2.12 ff.); twice in *Love's Labour's Lost* mention is made of "Promethean fire," which animates men and women.

108 ANDREÆ ALCIATI

Quæ ſupra nos, nihil ad nos.

EMBLEMA CII.

CAVCASIA æternùm pendens in rupe Prometheùs
Diripitur ſacri præpetis vngue iecur.
Et nollet feciſſe hominem: figulosq́; peroſus
Accenſam rapto damnat ab igne facem.
Roduntur variis prudentum pectora curis,
Qui cæli affectant ſcire, deûmq́; vices.

In

Prometheus on Caucasus, in Alciat's *Emblems,* 1608, from a copy in the University of Texas Library.

Root (101-102) notes that though Ovid (*Met.* 1.82) tells the story of Prometheus as the maker of man, the poet mentions only earth and water as the ingredients. But the myth of the making of man was early confused with the theft of fire, as Root shows in a quotation from the Scholia to Horace (Lib. 1, Ode 3), by reference to Fulgentius' *Mythologicon* (2.9), and to *The Faerie Queene* (2.10.70). We may add that the confusion was perpetuated in various other accounts, as in Erasmus' *De Conscribendis,*[13] in Alciati's *Emblema* CII (especially the commentary of Claudius Minois, 1608), in Calepine's *Dictionarium,* in Charles Stephanus' *Dictionarium,* and in Cooper's *Thesaurus.* With so many available sources of the myth (to say nothing of oral tradition) it must be admitted that the possibilities for the source of Shakespeare's allusion to this myth are almost legion.

In *Titus Andronicus,* Aaron refers to Tamora as his imperial mistress,

> . . . whom thou in triumph long
> Hast prisoner held, fetter'd in amorous chains
> And faster *bound to* Aaron's charming eyes
> Than is *Prometheus tied to Caucasus.*
>                                        (2.1.14-17)

Biron, in *Love's Labour's Lost,* says:

> From women's eyes this doctrine I derive:
> They sparkle still the right *Promethean fire;*
> They are the books, the arts, the academes,
> That show, contain, and nourish all the world.
>                             (4.3.350-53; cf. ll. 302-4)

And, last, are the well-known lines which Othello speaks as he prepares to murder Desdemona:

> Put out the light, and then put out thy light:
> If I quench thee, thou flaming minister,
> I can again thy former light restore,
> Should I repent me; but once put out thy light,
> Thou cunning'st *pattern* of *excelling nature,*
> I know not where is that *Promethean heat*
> *That can thy light relume.*
>                                        (5.2.7-13)

These are the principal allusions to the Prometheus legend in the plays. Two antecedents seem most pertinent in explaining Shakespeare's use of the myth. The first is that of Erasmus. Discoursing on classic myths which might serve as subjects for schoolboy exercises, he writes:

Of Prometheus' image of clay which he is feigned to have endowed with a little celestial fire; of the clay which the high God as a potter animated with his breath; of the particle of divinity, according to some, added to human bodies. For some have thought the soul to be nothing else than a spark from fire, or a little ray from that divine light.[14]

Of the Promethean fire as described by Erasmus Shakespeare might have learned in school. His allusions generally stress this aspect of the myth. But Erasmus does not narrate the story; of this the dramatist would learn elsewhere. The summary in Cooper's *Thesaurus* is suggestive.

*Prométheus.* The sonne of Iapetus, *firste inuented making of ymages*: wherfore the Paynyms supposed *that he made men,* and feigned that he went vp into heauen, and there did *steale fire to make his Image haue lyfe,* wherwith Iupiter being wrath, caused him *to be bounden on the hill called Caucasus,* and an Eagle standing by him eatyng his heart: by the which is signified, that he was studious, and a great Astronomer.

Aaron's figurative use of Prometheus bound to Caucasus, with phrasing similar to that in Cooper's account, may of course be inconsequential, but it is worth noting in the context of this discussion.

The "Promethean fire" which gives life and nourishment to all the world, as represented in *Love's Labour's Lost,* and which Othello knows he must vainly seek to "relume" Desdemona, once he has "put out thy light," is here of more consequence. Though Prometheus, according to the *Thesaurus,* stole fire from heaven "to make his Images have lyfe," Othello knows not where he may find "that Promethean heat" to make "the cunning'st pattern [image] of excelling nature" have life, "should I repent me."

Shakespeare's use of the Prometheus myth could be explained by his familiarity with Cooper's brief version of the story. But his emphasis upon the celestial fire suggests also Erasmus' discourse as a possible source of inspiration.

*Scylla and Charybdis.* In *The Merchant of Venice,* Launcelot speaking to Jessica, exclaims,

> . . . thus when I shun Scylla, your father, I
> fall into Charybdis, your mother.
>
> (3.5.18-20)

Root (p. 105) notes that both Vergil (*Aeneid,* 3.420 ff.) and Ovid (*Met.,* 13.730 ff.) describe Scylla and Charybdis, but thinks that Malone is right in referring the passage to the proverb "Incidis in Scyllam, cupiens vitare Charybdim," which Malone assigns to Philippe Gualtier, *Alexandreis*, 5. Erasmus, *Adagia*, (II, 183A) would be the natural source for Elizabethans.

It should be added that Cooper's *Thesaurus*, following Erasmus, gives a detailed account of Scylla, concluding

*Decidit in Scyllam cupiens vitare Charybdim*, prouerbially, to fall into one daunger, while he coueteth to eschewe an other.

*Sibyl.* Though Shakespeare probably knew Ovid's references (*Met.* 14, 126) to the Sibyls, there is some indication that he also drew from other sources. In the *First Part of Henry the Sixth*, he writes,

> The *spirit of deep prophecy* she hath,
> Exceeding the nine sibyls of old Rome.
> (1.2.55-56)

And in *The Merchant of Venice*, Portia says,

If I live to be as old as *Sibylla*, I will die as chaste as Diana, unless I be obtained by the manner of my father's will. (1.2.116-18)

In Cooper's *Thesaurus*, we read,

*Sibylla* . . . A generall name of all women which had the *spirite of prophecie*: of them (As Uarro and Lactantius doe write) were tenne: the first called Persica. . . .

The spelling of *Sibylla* in Portia's speech and the phrase *the spirit of deep prophecy*, both paralleled in Cooper, may show the poet's familiarity with this entry. And the discussion of Xantippe below may confirm this inference.

*Xanthippe.* Petruchio asserts that he will marry any woman for wealth, be she

> As old as Sibyl, and as *curst and shrewd*
> As Socrates' Xanthippe. . . . (*Shrew.* 1.2.71-72)

Compare in the *Thesaurus:*

*Xanthippe,* A passyng *shrewde, curst,* and a waywarde woman, wife to the pacient and wise philosoper Socrates. On a tyme she folowed hir husband from place to place scolding, in such sort, as he could not quietly abyde the house.

One can readily see the fitness of Cooper's description of Xanthippe for Petruchio's comparison.

## II

In Part I of this chapter we have presented evidence which indicates that Shakespeare was familiar with the proper-name section, or *Dictionarium Historicum et Poeticum* of Cooper's *Thesaurus*. We shall now discuss in some detail a few of the sketches which seem to have been even more significant for Shakespeare's poetry and drama.

The first sketch, or summarized story, is that of Lucretia. The poem *Lucrece* shows that its author was familiar with several versions of the story. He seems to have steeped himself in the Lucrece legend. Apparently, he had read the story in the Latin of Livy and in Ovid's *Fasti*, in the English of Chaucer and of Painter; and he may possibly have known Bandello's version of the story. It is not our purpose here to go into the whole complicated subject of the sources of the poem. Our aim is to show that, whatever other versions of the story Shakespeare may have heard or read, he had, in our opinion, read two short sketches which have been generally overlooked. We refer to the concise items on Lucius Tarquinius and Lucretia in Cooper's *Thesaurus*. These brief articles are as follows:

[Lucius] *Tarquinius,* For his proud and sterne behauiour surnamed *Superbus,* was the seuenth and last king of Rome. He married Tulla the daughter of Seruius Tullus, a woman of a naughty and cruell nature: by whose meanes he killed hir owne father, and by that horrible murder wickedly attayned that kingdom, which after cruelly he gouerned. . . . This king was afterward expelled out of Rome with all that were of hys stocke or line, because his sonne Sextus had wickedly rauished the noble and chaste matrone Lucrece. *Vide Lucretia.*[15]

*Lucretia,* A noble woman of Rome, wife to Tarquinius Collatinus, and a singuler paterne of chastitie, both to hir tyme, and to all ages following: whome Sextus Tarquinius, when by fayre meanes he coulde not obtaine, by force and violence did rauishe. For beeing intertayned for kyndreds sake in hir house, he brake into hir chamber, and with his sworde drawne, meanaced present death, vnlesse she would condiscende vnto his pleasure, adding moreouer, that he would kill one of hir seruaunts, and lay him in bed with hir, and so spread abroade that hee tooke them in aduoutrie and slue them. For feare of which shamefull reproch and infamie, rather than for dreade of death, as after appeared, shee suffered the violence of the wicked aduouterer. But the next day she sent for hir husbande, that was absent, and the residue of hir kinsfolke and friendes, and in the presence of them all, pitifully bursting out in weeping, declareth the cruell villainy of the tyranne: desiring them earnestly to seeke reuengement of the same, and therewithall pulleth out a knife, that for that purpose shee had hid vnder hir clothes, and strake hir selfe vnto the heart: affirming that the example of Lucrece shoulde neuer be a cloke for light women to excuse the vnfaythfull breache of wedlocke.  With indignation of this horrible acte, hir father and kinsfolke being mooued, raysed the people, and expelled both the prowde king Tarquine and his whole stocke out of the citie foreuer.[16]

Shakespeare's knowledge of these two items is, we think, exemplified in both the Argument to Lucrece and in the poem proper.  Consider, first, the Argument.  The phrasing of the first sentence of this piece as well as the content is strikingly similar to that of the first two sentences in the dictionary item on Lucius Tarquin.  Compare:

*Argument: Lucius Tarquinius, for his excessive pride surnamed Superbus,* after he had caused *his own father-in-law* Servius Tullius to be *cruelly* murdred, and, contrary to the Roman laws and customs, not requiring or staying for the people's suffrages, had *possessed himself of the kingdom,* went, accompanied with his sons and other noblemen of Rome, to besiege Ardea. . .

and

*Thesaurus:* [Lucius] *Tarquinius, For his proud and sterne behauiour surnamed Superbus,* was the seuenth and last king of Rome.  He married Tulla the daughter of Seruius Tullus, a woman of a naughty and cruell nature: by whose meanes he *killed hir owne father,* and by that horrible murder wickedly *attayned that kingdom,* which after *cruelly* he gouerned.[17]

The idea of Tarquin's pride and his murder of Servius Tullius, his father-in-law, Shakespeare could have got from reading several pages of Livy, but he would not have found there the two ideas in close proximity, or any suggestion for the particular phrasing of his first sentence.  In the *Thesaurus* he would have found in a few lines the ideas juxtaposed, and, what is more important, the initial phrase "[Lucius] Tarquinius, For his proud and sterne behauiour surnamed Superbus."  No other account of Lucius Tarquin has wording similar to this.  And to this phrasing, Shakespeare's seems to be too close to be regarded as coincidence.  The phrases "cruelly murdred," "possessed himself of the kingdom" may also be echoes of the *Thesaurus'* "horrible murder," "wickedly attained that kingdom," and "cruelly he governed."

In the dedicatory note to the Earl of Southampton, Shakespeare refers to *Lucrece* as a "pamphlet without beginning."  The Argument,[18] a composite, is apparently designed to supply for the reader the beginning and the outline of the story, with some information about Lucius Tarquinius.  The Tarquin sketch in the *Thesaurus* offered in compact form the precise information which the author wished in the first statement of The Argument. And the correspondence of phrasing and content points to Cooper's item on Tarquin as the source of the initial statement.

But even before the end of this statement Shakespeare is drawing from some other source for information concerning the siege of Ardea. And not until the end of the Tarquin sketch is there another suggestion for the poet. This sketch concludes

This king [Lucius Tarquinius] was afterward expelled out of Rome with all that were of his stock or line, because his sonne Sextus had wickedly ravished the noble and chaste matrone Lucrece. *Vide Lucretia.*

The general idea of the expulsion from Rome of Lucius Tarquin and his line is, of course, common to various versions of the legend, but the phrase "wickedly ravished" is at least suggestive of the "violently ravished" in The Argument. More significant are Cooper's phrases at the end of the sketch, "the noble and chaste matron Lucrece"[19] emphasizing the theme of chastity, and *Vide Lucretia,* neither of which is in the original of Stephanus. If Shakespeare were not already familiar with the Lucrece item in the *Thesaurus,* this reference would doubtless induce him to turn back the pages to this sketch. There is evidence that Shakespeare did so, or, at any rate, that he was familiar with the entry under *Lucretia.*

Though this familiarity is better exemplified in the poem, it seems, also, to be shown in The Argument. Shakespeare's emphasis, different from that of his sources, on the "incomparable chastity" of the heroine could have been suggested by "a singuler paterne of chastitie, both to hir tyme and to all ages following" of the Lucretia sketch;[20] his "violently ravished" by the *Thesaurus'* "by force and violence did rauish"; his *"withal* suddenly stabbed herself" by the *"therewithall* . . . strake hir selfe vnto the heart"; his "root out the *whole hated family* of the Tarquins," by the "expelled both the *prowde king Tarquine* and *his whole stocke* out of the citie forever"; his "wherewith the people were so moved," by "hir father and kinsfolke *being mooued, raysed the people."*

Once again, the content of these phrases could have come from some source other than the *Lucretia* of the *Thesaurus.* But in no other source is there so close a correspondence in actual phrasing to The Argument.

Of more importance, we think, are the correspondences in incident and language of the abridged Lucrece legend in the *Thesaurus* to passages in the poem proper. Analysis of the dictionary item, *Lucretia,* brief as it is, shows a close agreement as to essential incidents and phrasing with the story as told by Shakespeare in *Lucrece*. Cooper's concise summary could indeed have served as an outline, which the poet filled in with suggestions from various other sources and with his own invention.

Most versions of the Lucrece legend—Livy, Ovid, Painter, The Argument, for example—give details of a preliminary visit of Tarquin in company with Collatine and others to Lucretia, which marked the beginning of Tarquin's lustful desire. Neither Cooper nor Shakespeare, in the poem proper, gives the details of such a visit. In the first sentence of the dictionary account Cooper presents Lucrece as a model of chastity; so in the first stanza of his poem Shakespeare refers to "Lucrece the chaste";[21] and a few lines further on (l. 32), to the "singular" quality of her beauty and chastity, echoing perhaps the "singular paterne" of Cooper. Chastity indeed, as emphasized in the preliminary argument and as the leit-motif of the whole poem, may well have been inspired by the initial statement of the Lucretia sketch.

After the initial statement, Cooper's summary of essential incidents follows in rapid order : these are the entertainment of Tarquin because of kinship, the menace of death to Lucretia unless she yielded, the more terrible threat of reproach and infamy which would come from the discovery of her body and one of *her* murdered servants in bed with her, her yielding to forestall infamy, her sending for her husband and friends, the revelation, the request for revenge, the stabbing of herself so as not to be an example to excuse "light women" for unfaithfulness, and the expulsion of Tarquin and his stock from the city forever.

What could be a better introduction to the Lucrece story ? It is permissible to conjecture that this compact summary was indeed Shakespeare's introduction and that he may have first read it during his school days at Stratford. And whatever versions he later read, he held in memory the substance and phrasing of the dictionary version. We believe that the language of the poem supports this view.

Let us compare in order of appearance certain phrases from the *Thesaurus* account of Lucretia with those in the poem.

| *Thesaurus* | *Lucrece* |
|---|---|
| (1) | |
| Lucretia . . . a singuler paterne of chas-titie, both to hir tyme, and to all ages following. . . . | Of Collatine's fair love, Lucrece the chaste |
| | (l.7) |
| | What needeth then apology be made, |

To set forth that which is so singular?
(11.31-32)

(2)

The sundry dangers of his will's obtain-

when by fayre meanes he could not obtaine [his will of Lucrece]

ing,

Yet ever to *obtain* his will resolving
(11.128-29)

Pawning his honour to *obtain* his lust

(3)

(1.156)

. . . by *force* and violence did rauishe

If thou deny, then *force* must work my
way,                                   (1.513)

Yield to my love; if not, *enforced* hate,
. . . shall rudely tear thee

(4)

(11.668-69)

. . . and with his sworde drawne, menaced
*present death.*

. . . Assail'd by night with circumstances
strong

Of *present death,* and shame that might
ensue

By that her death, to do her husband
wrong.

(11.1262-64)

Two stanzas of the poem (11. 1625-38), in which Lucrece is recounting
the details of Tarquin's assault, seem to us especially to reflect, in content
and language, the poet's knowledge of the *Thesaurus* sketch.   These lines
tell of Tarquin's entrance into Lucrece's chamber with drawn sword, and
of his threats.   Only the second stanza with the precedent account from the
*Thesaurus* may here be quoted for comparison.

|              *Thesaurus*              |               *Lucrece*               |
|---------------------------------------|---------------------------------------|
| he [Sextus Tarquin] brake into hir chamber, and with his sworde drawne,[22] menaced present death, *vnlesse she would condiscende vnto his pleasure,* adding moreouer, that he would kill one of hir seruaunts, and lay him in bed with hir, and so *spreade abroade that hee tooke them in aduoutrie and slue them.* For feare of which shamefull reproch and *infamie* . . . shee suffered the violence. | " 'For some hard-favour'd groom of thine,' quoth he, 'Unless thou yoke thy liking to my will, I'll murder straight, and then I'll slaughter thee And swear I found you where you did fulfill The loathsome act of lust, and so did kill The lechers in their deed.   This act will be My fame and thy perpetual *infamy.'* " (11.1632-38)[23] |

It is of course possible that the stanza just quoted could have been based
upon a source or sources other than Cooper's summary of the story.   The
evidence suggests, however, that Shakespeare here remembered some of
the phrases and constructions found only in the *Thesaurus.*   Examine
closely the following phrases from matter already quoted:

*T.*: . . .*vnlesse* she would condiscende unto his pleasure. . . .[24]
*L.*: Unless thou yoke thy liking to my will,
*T.*: . . . and so spreade abroade that hee tooke them in aduoutrie and slue them.
*L.*: And swear I found you where you did fulfill
    The loathsome act of lust, and so did kill
    The lechers in their deed.
*T.*: For feare of which shamefull reproch and *infamie*. . . .
*L.*: . . . This act will be
    My fame and thy perpetual *infamy*.

We have here similar phrases in similar contexts, and for some of these phrases, such as "shamefull," "reproch," and "infamie" there is no basis in any other known source.[25]   The words listed, furthermore, are recurrent in the poem.   It is as if the poet knew Cooper's version so well and found certain words so apt that he inadvertently repeated them when association called them up.   The word "shameful," for example, appears four times[26] in *Lucrece,* in contexts very similar to that in which it is used in the *Thesaurus.*   And there is not a single example of its occurrence in any other poem or sonnet of Shakespeare.

"Reproch," so prominent in the Thesaurus account, appears six times in the *Lucrece,* once in the sonnets (121) and once in *A Lover's Complaint,* doubtfully ascribed to Shakespeare.   Compare the following:

*T.*: For feare of which *shamefull reproch* and infamie
*L.*: The orator, to deck his oratory,
    Will couple my *reproach* to Tarquin's shame (ll. 815-16)
    When life is *sham'd,* and death *reproach's* debtor (l. 1155)

The similarity of context and use of the terms "shameful," "shame," and "reproach" in the dictionary and in the poem seems not without significance in this study.[27]

The term "infamy" so conspicuous in the crisis of the story as summarized by Cooper and detailed by Shakespeare, is employed in similar contexts eight times in the *Lucrece,*[28] and not once in any other Shakespearean poem or sonnet.[29]

A comparison of *Lucrece* with its prefixed Argument shows that the poet did not consistently follow the summary.[30]   The Argument is a composite and the narrative of the poem is another composite, not always consistent with its Argument and not in fact consistent with itself.   The inconsistencies,[31] whether Shakespeare or another was responsible for them, betray the composite form of the poetic narrative.

One of the discrepancies is relevant to this discussion. In The Argument we are told specifically that Lucrece sent "messengers, one to Rome for her father, another to the camp for Collatine. They came, the one accompanied with Junius Brutus, the other with Publius Valerius." This is in exact accord with the account in, for example, Livy and Painter. Turning to the poem (ll. 1331 ff.) we hear that Lucrece sent only one messenger, and that to her husband at Ardea. He "brings home his lord and other company." The names of the accompanying friends are not mentioned until after the strange meeting of husband and wife, the revelation of Tarquin's attack, and the tragic death of Lucrece. We then discover that Lucretius, her father, is among those present though he has not hitherto greeted his daughter. Present also is Brutus, but Publius Valerius of The Argument is not mentioned in the poem. An example of the tradition nearest in time to Shakespeare is a part of the summarized story of Lucretia in the *Thesaurus*. This reads, "But the next day she sent for hir husbande that was absent, and the residue of hir kinsfolke and friendes. . . ." Compare the poem. On the day following, Lucrece orders,

> One of my husband's men
> Bid thou be ready, by and by, to bear
> A letter to my lord.
> (ll. 1291-93; see also l. 1331)

The summary in the *Thesaurus* continues, recounting concisely Tarquin's villainy and Lucrece's death by her own hand, ". . . affirming that the example of Lucrece shoulde neuer be a cloke for light women to *excuse the vnfaythfull breache of wedlocke.*" Compare with the words just quoted these in a similar context in the poem:

> "No, no," quoth she, "no dame hereafter living,
> By my *excuse* shall claim *excuse's* giving."
> (ll. 1714-15)

We know that Livy and Painter express almost the identical idea, and that with their stories Shakespeare was familiar.[32] But the *Thesaurus* and Shakespeare have in common, not only the idea, but the word *excuse* (twice used in the poem), for which there is no basis in other versions.

The same passage in the *Thesaurus,* furthermore, seems to be the source of another phrase in the poem. Lucrece, complaining to "uncheerful night," exclaims,

Make me not object to the tell-tale Day!
The light will show, character'd in my brow,
The story of sweet chastity's decay,
The *impious breach of holy wedlock vow*. . . .
(ll. 806-9)

The context here is such as to suggest the very language of the *Thesaurus*:
". . . to excuse the *vnfaythfull breache of wedlocke.*"

To argue that Shakespeare was thoroughly familiar with the sketches
of Tarquin and Lucretia in the contemporary *Thesaurus* compiled by
Bishop Cooper is not to imply that these were his only sources. He obviously had read other versions of the Lucrece legend, or possibly a composite form, from which he drew many details. Inconsistencies in his own
poetic narrative seem to be evidence of such procedure. But the evidence
shows that among his sources were the dictionary entries on Tarquinius
and Lucretia, the language of which he well remembered.[33]

Although Shakespeare found in Plutarch his principal source for
*Antony and Cleopatra*, it seems not improbable that he had also read and
remembered the sketch of Cleopatra in Cooper's *Thesaurus*. The entry
follows.

*Cleopâtra*, The name of diuers great Ladyes, speciallye Queenes of Aegypt.
Of whome one *excelling in pleasantnesse and sharpenesse of witte*, first allured
vnto hir Iulius Caesar, afterwarde Marcus Antonius, companion in the Empyre
with Augustus, whome shee brought into such *dotage*, that in following hir
appetite, he aspyred vnto the whole Empyre: wherefore he was afterwarde
destroyed by Augustus. This woman so exceeded in sumptuous gluttonie, that
she putting an excellent pearle into tarte vinegar (wherein being resolued)
receyued it into hir bodie, beeing esteemed at *Cênties*, HS, which is of ʋur
money 50000. li. This Lady after the death of Antonie, inclosed hir selfe in a
tombe, and *hauing twoo serpentes sucking at hir pappes so dyed.*

From this brief sketch Shakespeare may possibly have got two suggestions. The first is the application of the word *dotage,* one meʳning of
which, according to the *OED*, is foolish affection, or excessive fondness.
This is the sense of the word in the *Thesaurus* and in the play. All told,
Shakespeare employs the term with this meaning six times in the plays, two
of which are in *Antony and Cleopatra*. It is not, however, that this word
is common to Cooper's biographical sketch and the play that gives it
significance. Its importance lies in the fact that Cooper makes the term,
with all its implications, the key to Antony's character and the cause of

his ruin. In the play the dramatist does exactly the same. "Nay, but this *dotage* of our general's/ O'erflows the measure," exclaims Philo in the very first line of the play. And in the second scene (l. 121) Antony himself realizes his trouble: "These strong Egyptian fetters I must break,/ Or lose myself in *dotage*." And much of the meat of the play consists in the dramatist's study of Antony, whose dotage over Cleopatra brings him to ruin, in contrast with Octavius Caesar's restraint and freedom from passion, which give him mastery of the Roman world. It is the age-old theme of sensuality versus reason. And it is worthy of note that this particular theme is not explicit in Plutarch and that the word *dotage* does not appear in North's translation. It seems to us within the realm of probability that *dotage,* the key-word of the dictionary sketch with respect to Antony, was not only borrowed by Shakespeare but may also have been the cue for the poet's interpretation of Antony's character and for the emphasis, by way of contrast, on the restraint of Octavius Caesar.

The second suggestion which the dramatist may have got from the dictionary sketch appears in the manner of Cleopatra's death. In Plutarch's account and in that of Dion Cassius only one asp or serpent is used by Cleopatra to bring about her death, and this asp is applied to her arm. In the play the Egyptian queen employs two asps : one she applies to her arm ; another, and that which really proves fatal, she places on her breast. Almost at the moment of death, Cleopatra addressing Charmian, says,

> Peace, peace!
> Dost thou not see my baby at my breast,
> That sucks the nurse asleep?
>
> (5.2.311-13)

Perhaps it is not necessary to suppose that for this beautiful metaphor Shakespeare needed any suggestion other than that which might have come from North's Plutarch. Yet it is worthy of emphasis that the description in the *Thesaurus* closes with words that surely would be more powerful in suggesting the figure than those in any other known source. Here are the words, already quoted above: "This Lady after the death of Antonie, inclosed hir selfe in a tombe, and hauing twoo serpentes sucking at hir pappes so dyed."

Shakespeare's references to classic myth and legend are in the main of such a general nature that valid signs of indebtedness are relatively rare and it becomes difficult, if not impossible, to specify any one work as Shakespeare's source. He usually seems to have kept close to the knowledge probably acquired by any member of his audience who had attended grammar school,[34] and in general we believe that the dictionaries with one of the simpler texts of Ovid explain the vast majority of his allusions.[35] Be that as it may, the singularities in his references to classic myth and legend which have been pointed out in the preceding pages are adequate, we believe, to demonstrate his familiarity with entries in the lexicons. Such a conclusion need not minimize Shakespeare's learning. As the following pages will demonstrate, Ben Jonson, who was a much better classical scholar than Shakespeare, at times turned directly to the dictionaries. In all probability, Shakespeare used some of the lexicons when he was a schoolboy. Consciously or unconsciously he sometimes relied upon the "histories" which those works supplied in abundance.

# CHAPTER VI

# BEN JONSON AND THE DICTIONARIES

LTHOUGH JONSON MIGHT SPEAK CONTEMPTUOUSLY OF THE EPI-
grammatist Owen as "A pure Pedantique Schoolmaster sweeping
his living from the Posteriors of little children,"[1] he had the greatest admiration for his own teacher. The arrogant poet, otherwise proud of
his learning, could write that to Camden

> I owe
> All that I am in arts, all that I know,
> (How nothing's that?) . . . .
> *(Epigrams,* 14. 1-3)

To Camden—the "best parent" of the poet—Jonson dedicated *Cynthia's
Revels,* a drama by one who was "a pupil once, a friend forever." The
play, Johnson hoped, would provide a worthy scholar with youthful en-
joyment.

> GVLIELMVM CAMDENVM,
> Britanniæ Phœbum,
> Musarumque suarum Parentem Optimum,
> hic cum illis
> Beniamin Ionsonius,
> Alumnus olim, æternum Amicus
> iuuenari voluit.
> *Hor.*—Non ego te meis
> Chartis inornatum silebo.[2]

From Cooper to Camden to Johnson runs a sound pedagogical tradition and a love for scholarship and ancient literature. The dramatist attempted more than once to provide for his audience the solid "cates" of
"sound antiquitie," and he continually read and annotated his classical
texts.[3] His memory apparently was as good as his reading was wide.

Thus, at first glance, one might question the probability of information in the reference lexicons of the period being reflected in his writings. As part of his training, however, Jonson at one time probably had prepared "histories" of proper nouns. Indeed his memory of a particular phrase in the *Dictionarium Historicum* may be reflected in the burlesque lines celebrating the famous but unsavoury journey of Shelton and Heyden on Fleet Ditch from Bridewell Dock to Holborn (*Epigrams,* 133). The voyagers, writes Jonson, avoided one peril in the manner of Ulysses in the cave of Cyclops. Normally the situation is represented as in Chapman's translation:

> I then,
> Choosing myself the fairest of the den,
> His fleecy belly under-crept; embrac'd
> His back, and in his rich wooll wrapt me fast
> With both my hands. . . .[4]

But in Jonson's lines, Ulysses apparently is wrapped in a sheep's skin:

> as by Polypheme
> The slie Vlysses stole in a sheepes-skin,
> (ll. 112-13)

a phraseology almost identical with "pellibusque arietum inuolutis" in the account given by Charles Stephanus:

Inde rursus vela faciens, in Siciliam delatus est vbi Polyphemi antrum cum duodecim sociis intrauit: ex quibus cum Cyclops sex deuorasset, oculum ei eruit, praeusto stipite, *pellibusque arietum inuolutus,* cum superstitibus antrum euasit.

In *The Case is Altered* Jonson's *"Elizium,* Heere blessed Ghosts do walke" may reflect Robert Stephanus' "Elysium . . . vbi dicuntur esse animae bonorum" or Charles Stephanus' "Elysium . . . vbi piorum animae habitant." The phrase of Jonson's is of such a commonplace nature, however, that the expression in the lexicons of a similar idea in similar words probably means nothing. It is interesting to note, nevertheless, that Jacques, who so refers to Elysium, also connects it with Plutus. Jacques is, of course, the miserly figure based on Plautus' Euclio. To him Elysium would be the realm of the God of Gold. But the mature Jonson usually had some classical authority for any invention of his; and as entries in Charles Stephanus indicate, Elysium, or the Fortunate Isles, and Plutus might be connected specifically by place, if one subscribed to the Spanish theory about the position of the Islands.

> *Millaine* these od'rous and enfloured fields
> Are none of thine, no heres *Elizium,*
> Heere blessed Ghosts do walke, this is the Court
> And glorious palace where the God of gold
> Shines like the sonne . . . .
>
> (5.4.2-6)

*Elysium,* locus vbi piorum animae habitant . . . . Hunc locum . . . alij fortunatas insulas . . . esse dicunt . . . .
*Fortunatae insulae,* a fructuum vbertate, vel aeris bonitate dictae, contra Mauritaniae finem ad Occidentem sitae sunt. *Quam quidem ad partem et Hispaniae terminus concurrit.* Strabo lib. 3 . . . . Alias fortunatas insulas Diodorus, Mela, Solinus nominant circa Rhodum, et in Hispania.
*Plutus,* a Graecis fingitur diuitiarum deus . . . *Huius domicilium constituit Posidonius in subterraneis Hispaniae locis, eo quod regio ea metallorum foecunditate reliquis antecellat.*

A somewhat similar connection between two ideas appears in a reference to Rhadamanthus. In classical sources he is "sometimes a judge" and "at other times a torturer."[5] In *Poetaster,* the two ideas are combined and he appears as a severe judge who thoroughly punishes the vicious.[6] From his classical knowledge alone, Jonson might well have effected such a combination, but it is at least pertinent to note that the synthesis also appeared in Charles and Robert Stephanus. In Jonson's lines, Rhadamanthus is a just judge in Hell who "doth inflict strange vengeance"; in the lexicons, because of his severity on earth, in Hades Rhadamanthus pries diligently into the guilt of malefactors.

> Sir Rhadamanthvs, Rhadamanthvs, sir.
> There's one so cald, is a iust iudge, in hell,
> And doth inflict strange vengeance on all those,
> That (here on earth) torment poore patient spirits.
>
> (3.1. 146-49)

Rhadamanthus, Iouis ex Europa filius, rex Lyciae, qui quod seuerus fuerit iustitiae executor, fingitur a poetis apud inferos nocentum explorare culpas. (C. Stephanus)

Jonson's use of other proper names in *Poetaster* is also interesting. A generation of schoolboys who had consulted the *Thesaurus Linguae Latinae* might have had their attention called, for example, to the phrase "Phrygius Ganymedes" with the citation "Ovid .10. Met. 31 [(195)]."[7] That at least

one of them remembered the name from Ovid, or from the *Thesaurus,*
is attested by the lines Jonson gives to Tucca when that braggart speaks to
Pyrgus disguised as Ganymede,

> Well said, my fine *Phrygian* frie, informe, informe.
>
> (4.5. 109-10)

Or had Jonson, when studying Horace, for instance, been familiar with the
"history" of *Trebatius,* he would have known from Charles or Robert
Stephanus' description of the Roman as *iurisconsultus* that he was a
"great lawier"—as Tucca phrases it (3.4. 379)—even though Trebatius'
profession is not made clear in the particular dialogue (*Sat.* II, i) that Jonson was to dramatize.   And, of course, if Jonson and his contemporaries
had consulted the lexicons, they would have been directed to Cicero's
appropriate letters, also studied in the schools, for further information
about Trebatius (*Ep. Fam.,* II, 5-22).   Similarly, had Jonson utilized
either the *Dictionarium Historicum* or the *Thesaurus Linguae Latinae* for
the "history" of Laberius—who appears very briefly in Horace's satires
(I, 10, 6)—his attention would have been called to the passage in Aulus
Gellius which one modern editor of *Poetaster* has singled out as being
particularly pertinent in explaining the use of the name by a playwright
who would represent Marston in the guise of Rufus Laberius Crispinus.[8]
The same situation occurs with the *Fannius* of Demetrius Fannius.   Both
Charles and Robert Stephanus could have directed Jonson and his contemporaries to matter which modern editors believe to be reflected in the
play.[9]

Examples might be multiplied of instances in the plays and poems
wherein the dictionary entries could have supplied Jonson with particular
details of phraseology and association or could have directed him to classical passages that seem to be reflected in his lines.   As our second chapter
indicated, the lexicons contributed toward making commonplace certain
passages or ideas in ancient literature;[10] and such reference works always
illustrate contemporary conceptions of classic myth, legend, or history and
thus provide matter for appropriate annotation.   Furthermore, when a
considerable number of instances can be assembled of similarities between
the literature of the period and the lexicons—even if the information and
phrasing in any one passage may have such a variety of possible sources
that it amounts to no more than a commonplace—the probability increases
that the stimulus for some of the passages came from the one account com-

mon to all. However, to demonstrate indebtedness to the lexicons on the part of a writer who was continually reading the classics is extremely difficult. The thread at best is a fine one, as in the peculiar detail about Ulysses, but it seems to be there. Consequently, on two counts the masques of Jonson are more appropriate to our purpose than are the poems or the plays. In his courtly entertainments the poet at times brought to bear as much information as possible from the ancient and modern world. His reading of the classics, his reading of more recent Neo-Platonic literature, his reading of current literary, political, or alchemical writings, his reading of the best mythological compendiums was directed toward expressing doctrine that would be appropriate for the center of the kingdom. Particularly worthy of demonstration would be traces of the basic lexicons in such an ordered array of erudition. Secondly, Jonson himself sometimes aids those who would follow his acquisition of information. Fortunately for our purpose, Jonson was "y$^t$ kind of artificer, to whose worke is requir'd so much exactnesse, as indifferency is not tolerable";[11] thus the glosses he provided for his readers enable one to be much more confident about the material he utilized than one could be by relying only upon his poetic lines.

To discuss the basic conception of each masque and entertainment with which we shall be concerned is neither feasible nor necessary. Jonson believed that these "transitory" courtly devices in their "more remou'd *mysteries*" should develop sound doctrine that was suitable to participants, spectators, and occasion. They should be something more than an architect's spectacle that allowed the great persons of the realm to exhibit themselves and their riches in the intricate dances that formed the center of the masque, or the sumptuous tournament that formed the center of the barriers.[12]    To understand Jonson's purpose in some of the more complex pieces involves recognizing the existence of what modern critics might call various levels of meaning. In even the most intricate of the masques, however, the conceptions with which Jonson worked can be found in such current treatises as Cesare Ripa on iconology or Gyraldus, Comes, and Cartari on classical myth.[13] Usually Jonson's own glosses explain briefly the particular "invention" with which he is concerned. In his commentaries he may summarize matter in current compilations to justify or support his invention, and he may list confirmatory passages in ancient, medieval, or modern literature—passages which are often the ones also cited in the Renaissance compendiums. The marginal notes, in other words, frequently

indicate the material Jonson had in mind as he developed his basic conceptions, involving different levels of meaning, into "sound" and purposeful
texts.

To achieve his purpose Jonson found the three outstanding authorities
on classical mythology very useful, and we have already noted that some
reflection of the lexicons which were available in the common libraries seems
probable. For that matter, by the end of the sixteenth century no schoolboy could have used the *Dictionarium Historicum* very thoroughly without
running across some reference to Comes and Gyraldus at least. Editors
of Charles Stephanus occasionally referred their readers to Comes and
frequently summarized discussions in the *Mythologiae* for their own interpretations of a myth. Less frequently, Gyraldus will be mentioned; thus
the reader of the entry *Hercules* is referred to Macrobius and to Comes and
then to "Lylium Gyraldum, peculiari Syntagmate." At any rate, the
training we might have expected Jonson to receive—under Camden, for instance—is entirely congruent with the artistry of his courtly entertainments.
As the following pages will demonstrate, Jonson at times apparently
remembered material found in the basic lexicons with which we are particularly concerned; or he may have turned to those texts, as well as to kindred
compilations, in a manner inculcated by his early training, finding there
some of the information that fills out both gloss and text of the masques.
As such, although Jonson's artistry is based on wide reading and sound
erudition, it is also based to an appreciable degree upon what should have
been the education of his courtly audience.

The descriptions of the queens in the masque by that name afford
some revealing details. Nine of the twelve might be considered, but five
in particular show considerable indebtedness to the lexicons. On *"Penthesilea, the braue Amazon"* (l.399), Jonson writes (p. 306) :

She was Queene of the *Amazons,* and succeeded *Otrera,* or (as some will)
*Orythyia.* She liu'd, and was present at the Warre of *Troy,* on they$^r$ part,
agaynst the *Greekes,* where (as *Iustine* gives her testemony) *inter fortissimos
viros, magna eius virtutis documenta extitêre.* Shee is no where mentiond,
but w$^{th}$ the præface of Honor, and virtue; and is allwayes aduauncd in the
head, of the worthiest Women. *Diodorus Siculus* makes her the Daughter of
*Mars.* She was honord, in her death, to haue it the act of *Achilles.* Of w$^{ch}$,
*Propertius* sings this Triumph to her Beauty,
>    *Aurea cui postquam nudauit cassida frontem,*
>    *Vicit victorem candida forma virum.*

Of the sources cited by Jonson, Justin, II, 4, 31-2 gives the following facts:

Post Orithyam Penthesilea regno potita est, cuius Troiano bello inter fortissimos viros, cum auxilium adversus Graecos ferret, magna virtutis documenta extitere. Interfecta deinde Penthesilea exercituque eius absumpto paucae, quae in regno remanserant, aegre se adversum finitimos defendentes usque ad tempora Alexandri Magni duraverunt.[14]

Justin, however, does not mention "Otrera," nor the queen's death at the hands of Achilles. This last particular appears in Diodorus, who says that "she ended her life heroically at the hands of Achilles" (II, 37) and who also calls her the daughter of Ares.[15] The quotation from Propertius, said by Jonson to be from *"Lib. 3, eleg. 10,"* is from the *Elegies, 3,* xi, 15-6.

None of the sources so far considered, however, refers to Penthesilea's predecessor as *"Otrera,* or (as some will) *Orythyia."* The phase is a direct translation of *"Otterae,* sive (vt alij) *Orithyae"* in the *Dictionarium Historicum.* If Jonson, consequently, was sufficiently familiar with the entry for Penthesilea in Charles Stephanus' compilation to remember a detail of its phraseology from his school days, it is also probable that in the lexicon he first encountered the pertinent citation of Justin (given in the *Dictionarium Historicum* as "Iustino lib. 2"), the information that the queen was killed by Achilles, and the complete sentence which he has contracted for his first Latin quotation (*"inter fortissimos viros,* cum auxilium aduersus Graecos ferret, *magna virtutis documenta extitere"*). Moreover, any reader of the nearly identical article in Robert Stephanus' compilation would also find a citation from Virgil and then under "Moeotis Penthesilea" a reference to "Propert. lib. 3,"[16] the source from which Jonson got his last quotation. Thus the basic reference dictionaries could have provided Jonson with all the information needed for his description except for that in the brief reference to her parentage—information Jonson may have acquired from reading his 1604 edition of Diodorus.[17] We probably can never be sure that Jonson had utilized the "histories" of Penthesilea in the *Thesaurus Linguae Latinae* and the *Dictionarium Historicum* for one of his academic exercises; but we can be certain that prior to the publication of the *Masque of Queens* he had at least surveyed the following entry in Charles Stephanus:

*Penthesilea, Amazonum regina,* quae, *teste Iustino lib. 2. Otterae, siue (vt alij) Orithyae* successit in regno: eiusque Troiano bello *inter fortissimos viros,* cum auxilium aduersus Graecos ferret, *magna virtutis documenta extitere.* . . . Cum Troianis opem ferret, *ab Achille occisa est* . . . .

Obviously Jonson drew from the lexicons at least the "Otterae, siue (vt alij) Orithyae." Although he may likewise have consulted Justin, he did not need to.

The next description concerns "Swift-foote *Camilla, Queene* of *Volscia*" (l. 400). About her Jonson writes (pp. 306-7) :

Next, followes *Camilla,* Queene of the *Volscians,* celebrated by Virgil, about the end of the seuenth book; then whose *Verses* nothing can bee imagin'd more exquisite, or more honoring the person they describe. They are these, where he reckons vp those who came on Turnus part, agaynst *Æneas.*

> *Hos super aduenit Volscâ de gente Camilla,*
> . . . . [ll. 803-11.]

And, afterward, tells her attire, and Armes; w$^t$h the admiration, that the *Spectators* had of her. All w$^c$h if the *Poet* created out of himselfe, w$^t$hout *Nature,* he did but shew, how much so diuine a Soule could exceede her.

Virgil does not specifically refer to Camilla as "Queen of the *Volscians.*" Charles Stephanus, however, calls her "Volscorum regina," and Robert's first citation of authority is *"Eam Virgilius describit libro 7 his versibus, Hos super advenit Volsca de gente Camilla . . .* [ll.803-71]." Thus Jonson could have found all he needed for his note in the dictionaries. His gloss cites *"Aeneid, lib. 7.";* and the five lines quoted in the 1543 *Thesaurus* have been extended to the next full stop.

An indubitable example of Jonson's indebtedness to the reference lexicons occurs in his description of *"Candace,* pride of *Æthiopia"* (l. 405; pp. 309-10) :

The seuenth, that renowme of *Æthiopia, Candace;* from whose excellencye, the succeeding *Queenes,* of that *Nation,* were ambitious to be calld so. A woman of a most haughty spirit, agaynst enemies; and singular affection to her subiects. I find her, celebrated, by *Dion,* and *Plinie,* invading *Ægipt,* in the time of *Augustus;* who, though she were enforc'd to a peace, by his Lieutenant *Petronius,* doth not the lesse worthely hold her place, here; when euery where this *Elogie* remaynes of her Fame; that she was *Maximi animi Mulier, tantique in suos meriti, vt omnes deinceps Æthiopum reginæ eius nomine fuerint appellatæ.* She gouern'd in *Meroë.*

For the above facts Jonson cites Dio's *"Hist. Rom. lib. 54"* and Pliny's *"Nat. Hist. lib. 6, cap. 29."* Cassius Dio gives a somewhat detailed account of Petronius' victory over Candace but the passage show little, if any, verbal agreement with Jonson's description.[18] Pliny states only that many Ethiopian queens who governed in Meroe were named Candace: ". . . aedificia oppidi pauca. regnare [over Meroe] feminam Candace, quod nomen multis iam annis ad reginas transiit."[19]  The reference to Pliny, as we might expect, is given by both Charles and Robert Stephanus. But of much greater importance for understanding the description is the "history" of the Aethiopian queen in Charles Stephanus' compilation. Incorporated into the *Dictionarium Historicum,* the Latin "Elogie" may not have been "euery where," as Jonson phrases it; but it probably was in the common library of every Renaissance school:

Candace, *Æthiopum regina tempore Augusti maximi animi mulier, tantique in suos meriti, vt omnes deinceps Æthiopum reginæ, eius nomine fuerint appellatae. Plinius lib.* 6. c. 29.

It is this Latin passage which is also loosely translated in Jonson's first sentence. Cassius Dio and Pliny, at any rate, could not have provided anyone with the quotation given by Jonson; neither makes such a statement. Jonson, of course, was probably familiar with both authors; but one wonders if he would have referred to Pliny, or if he would have remembered both book and chapter number of a passage that here supplied him with little, if any, information, had not the *Natural History* been cited and the specific book and chapter numbers given by the reference lexicon that also gives Jonson's "Elogie" verbatim.

The description of Artemisia can be examined briefly (pp. 307-8):

The fourth was honord to life, in the time of Xerxes, and present at his great expedition into *Greece; Artemisia,* the *Queene* of *Caria:* whose vertue *Herodotus,* not w$^t$hout some wonder, records. That a Woman, A *Queene,* w$^t$hout a Husband, her Sonne a ward, and she administring the gouernment, occasion'd by no necessety, but a mere excellence of spirit, should embarque her selfe for such a Warre; and, there, so to behaue her, as *Xerxes,* beholding her fight, should say: *Viri quidem extiterunt mihi feminæ, feminæ autem viri.* She is no lesse renowm'd for her chastety and loue to her Husband, *Mausolus,* whose bones, (after he was dead) she preseru'd in ashes, and drunke in wine, making her selfe his tombe: and, yet, built to his memory a *Moniment,* deseruing a place among the seauen *Wonders of the World,* w$^{ch}$ could not be done by lesse then a Wonder of Women.

The authorities Jonson alleges for his description are Herodotus (*"in Polymn."* and "in *Vrania"*), *"Val. Max. lib.* 4. *cap.* 6," and *"A. Gell. lib.* 10. *cap.* 18." We need not stop to examine Jonson's indebtedness to Herodotus or to Valerius Maximus; and we need only note that the pertinent passages in the reference lexicons also refer to Gellius, the citation in the *Thesaurus Linguae Latinae* being exactly that of Jonson's. In the dictionaries likewise appear the details that Artemisia accompanied Xerxes as an ally (i.e., "by no necessety"), that she was "renowm'd for her chastity," that she drank her husband's ashes mixed with wine, and that the mausoleum was given "a place among the seauen *Wonders of the World.*"

But the preceding particulars are of much less interest and importance than is Jonson's basic conception of the life of this virtuous queen. As a recent annotator of the masque remarks, "Jonson has hopelessly confused two Artemisias." One, the heroine of Salamis, was queen of Halicarnassus and a "vassal of Xerxes." The other, the daughter of Hecatomnus, was the wife and successor of Mausolus of Caria.[20] That Jonson's account is confused is undoubtedly true; but the confusion also existed, long before he composed his masque, in the "history" of Artemisia as found both in the *Thesaurus Linguae Latinae* and in the *Dictionarium Historicum.*

*Artemisia, regina Halicarnasi, in auxilium Xerxis contra Graecos venit.* Inter primores duces bellum acerrime ciebat, quippe vt in viro muliebrem tunc rem, ita in muliere virilem audaciam cerneres. *Haec extincto viro Mausolo,* sepulchrum fecit, *inter septem orbis miracula connumeratum* a Graecis poetis: ad funus quoque ornandum primos Graeciae oratores accersiuit. Authores *Gellius lib. 10. cap. 18.* & Suidas, & Vitruuius lib. 2. (*Thesaurus.*)

*Artemisia, regina Halicarnassi, Mausoli Cariae regis vxor, in auxilium Xerxis contra Graecos venit:* inter primores duces bellum acerrime ciebat: *insigni pudicitia praedita, viri demortui cineres vino commistos ebibit:* ad funus quoque ornandum primos Graeciae oratores accersiuit: *huicque splendidum erexit sepulchrum,* vt magnifica omnia monumenta Mausolea deinceps ab illius nomine fuerint apellata. Gellius libro 20. Suidas. Vitruuius libro secundo. (*Dictionarium Historicum.*)

Thus for better or for worse, the two Artemisias were made one in the late sixteenth and early seventeenth centuries.

One more description of a virtuous queen, that of "fayre-hayr'd *Beronice, Ægipts* fame" (1.403), should be noted before we turn to other considerations (pp. 308-9).

The fifth was the fayre-hayrd Daughter of *Ptolomæus Philadelphus,* by the elder *Arsinoë;* Who (maried to her brother *Ptolomæus,* surnam'd *Euergetes*) was afterward *Queene* of *Ægipt.* I find her written both *Beronice,* and *Berenice.* This Lady, vpon an expedition of her new-wedded Lord, into *Assyria,* vowed to *Venus,* if he returnd safe, and conquerour, the offring of her hayre; W^ch vow of hers (exacted by the successe) she afterward þform'd: But her Father missing it, and taking it to heart [therewith displeas'd—Q, Ff.], *Conon,* a *Mathematician,* who was then in household w^th Ptolomæe, and knew well to flatter him, perswaded the King, that it was tane vp to Heauen, and made a

*Constellation;* shewing him those *seuen starres, ad caudam Leonis,* wᶜh are since call'd *Coma Beronices.* Wᶜh Story, then presently celebrated by *Callimachus,* in a most elegant *Poëme, Catullus* more elegantly converted; wherein they call her the *Magnanimous [euen] from a Virgin:* alluding (as *Hyginus* sayth) to a rescue she made of her Father, in his flight, and restoring the honor, and courage of his Army, euen to a victory. The words are,

> *Cognaram à paruâ virgine magnanimam.*

Jonson cites Hyginus *"Astronom. lib. 2, in Leo" and "Cat. de comâ Beronic."* as his authorities. In those works, it is true, there are three particulars which Jonson could not have found in the dictionary items: (1) Hyginus tells the story of Beronice's magnanimity,[21] and Catullus alludes to it (66, ll. 25-28); (2) Catullus gives Assyria as the locale of the expedition (l. 12); and (3) "fayre-hayred" is probably from Catullus (ll. 61-2): *"sed nos quoque fulgeremus devotae flavi verticis exuviae."*[22] There are, however, three particulars not in his alleged sources which Jonson probably found in the dictionary items: (1) the names *"Ptolemæus Philadelphus"* and *"Ptolomæus,* surnam'd *Euergetes";* (2) the translation of Callimachus' story by Catullus; and (3) the fact that Beronice was the daughter of the elder Arsinoë. The last detail Jonson could have found in Robert Stephanus under *"Arsinoë."* The other particulars are in the articles on *"Beronice"* (C. Stephanus) and *"Berenice"* (R. Stephanus). Charles Stephanus' article also gives the vast majority of the details in the story as it is reproduced by Jonson:

*Beronice, siue Berenice, Ptolemaei Philadelphi & Arsiones filia, quam cùm Ptolemaeus filius sororem suam in vxorem duxisset, nec multis diebus pòst cum exercitu* in Asiam *profectus esset, vouisse Berenicem tradunt, Si victor Ptolemaeus rediisset, se crinem detonsuram. atque eo voto damnatum crimen in Veneris Templum consecrasse: qui cúm* postridie *non apparuisset: aegrè id ferente rege, Conon Mathematicus gratiam regis captans dixit Ptolemaeo crinem inter sidera videri collocatum,* & quisdam vacuas figura *septem stellas ostendit cauda Leonis,* velut in triangulum collocatas: *de quo crine in stellas commutato Callimachus Graecus elegiam conscripsit, quam deinde Latinam fecit Catullus.*

Under *"Berenice vel Beronice,"* Robert Stephanus also cites Catullus' poem quoted by Jonson and writes

. . . Philadelphi filia, *quae deinde Ptolemaeo Evergeti fratri nupsit:* cuius crines in caelum relati putantur, persuasione Cononis mathematici. *De quibus elegiam composuit Callimachus, conversam deinde a Catul.*

Although Jonson might enlarge his notes, following the lead given him by Charles and particularly by Robert Stephanus, and although he might consult works not cited by the lexicons, the account of Beronice, considered with the other descriptions, clearly shows how Jonson utilized information in current reference dictionaries and indeed might err with them (the account of Artemisia) when he wished to substantiate his writing by "the particular *authorities*" found among ancient authors. His method and his materials were essentially those taught in the schools, and the two compilations which aided him here appear to be the cause of two errors that Jonson also unwittingly perpetrated when glossing his *Masque of Augurs*.

In writing about Linus (1. 286), he cites Pausanias as his authority: "Linus, Appollinus [*sic*] et Terpsichores filius. Paus." Although the *Description of Greece* contains separate genealogies for the two figures with such a name, neither agrees with Jonson's account of Linus' parents. One Linus, according to Pausanias, was the son of Apollo and Psammate (2.19.8) ; the other, the son of Apollo and Urania (9.29.5). The parentage given by Jonson could be found in both Comes and Gyraldus, but neither mythographer gave Jonson's erroneous citation of authority.[23]  A reader of the Linus entry in the *Dictionarium Historicum,* however, would find

Linus, Apollinis & Terpsichores filius, Musicae peritissimus, Thamyrae, Hercules & Orphei praeceptor.  Hunc ab Hercule occisum ferunt, impacta in caput cithara, quod ipsum rusticius canentem irrideret.  *Paus.* lib. 9.

The gloss to *The Masque of Augurs* obviously follows the preceding entry for both genealogy and citation, and thus errs with Charles Stephanus. The situation recurs in the note on Phoemonoë (1. 299).  A reader of the *Augurs* text would find that according to Hesiod's *Theogony,* she was the daughter of Phoebus and the first to sing heroic verse:

Phœmonoë, filia Phœbi, quæ prima carmen heroïcum cecinit.  Hesiod in Theog.

But in Hesiod there is no such information.  Wheeler has noted that Pausanias mentions Phoemonoë as the first prophetess of Apollo and the first to sing an hexameter verse ( 10.5.7), while Strabo writes that she was the first Pythian priestess (9.3.5).[24]  The lexicons by Charles and Robert Stephanus, however, give the words of the gloss verbatim, and, likewise incorrectly, cite Hesiod's *Theogony*:

Phoemonoë, filia Phoebi, et vates, quae prima carmen heroicum cecinit, vt est author Hesiodus in Theogonia.

A different sort of error appears in another gloss to *The Masque of Augurs* and has bothered modern editors. Concerning Branchus, the 1640 Folio reads:

Branchus, Apollinis & Janees filius, de quo vid. Strab. lib. 4. & Statium, Thebaid. lib. 3—*patrioque æqualis honori Branchus.*

*Janees* is usually corrected to *Jances;* but the reading, at best, "is doubtful."[25] It is understandable, nevertheless, when one turns to the basic Latin thesaurus of the period. Robert Stephanus' complete entry for Branchus in the edition of 1573 runs as follows:

Branchus, ut scribit Lactantius *Filius* fuit *Apollinis* ex filia *Iaucis* & Sucronis conjuge susceptus . . . post hoc ingens templum est ei aedificatum, quod Branchiadon nominarunt.
    Idem auctor alibi dicit Branchum, quendam Thessalum fuisse, ab Apolline maxime dilectum, cui post mortem in suo templo sacra fieri idem iussit. Hinc Apollo Branchiades dictus est, & Branchiadae communes Apollinis & Branchi sacerdotes.
    Branchi meminit *Stat. 3. Theb.* [479] *Strabo lib. 14.* . . .

Although the blame for the error "Strab. lib. 4" instead of "Strab. lib. 14" and for the error "Janees" instead of "Iaucis" may be put upon the printers, only by misreading such an item as the one in the *Thesaurus* is it likely that Jonson would write as he did. Thus in the note on Branchus, "Apollinis et Janees filius" apparently represents "Filius . . . Apollinis [ex filia] Iaucis [& Sucronis . . .".].

This last error might have resulted from Jonson's memory of material amassed under Camden's tutelage, or it might have resulted from his hasty perusal of the *Thesaurus* when he prepared his glosses. One suspects that the latter alternative is nearer the truth and that Jonson turned to one of the basic lexicons. In the first place, he enlarged his note on Branchus by citing Strabo with book number, as Robert Stephanus did, and by quoting from the first source cited in the *Thesaurus,* i.e., Statius, *Thebaid,* III (478-79). The glosses on Linus and Phoemonoë, moreover, point to such a conclusion; both repeat the authorities cited by the dictionaries, and the verbatim correspondence between the lexicons and the gloss on Phoemonoë is striking. The various figures named Linus, of course, might well have caused confusion; realizing that there were a number of singers with such a name, Jonson may have turned to the basic lexicons to find authority for using the one who, as the son of Apollo and a Muse, best suited his purpose.

As the appropriate passage from Comes indicates there were at least four possibilities:

Fabulantur Linum Amphimaro Neptuni filio & Vrania genitum fuisse: qui cum omnes mortales gloria musicae antecelleret, ab Apolline, cui se cantu conferebat, fuit extremo supplicio affectus, cui etiam parentant ante sacra Musarum. Fuit etiam Linus Apollinis & Terpsichores filius: vel, vt alij maluerunt, Vraniae & Mercurij, qui fuit ab Hercule cithara occisus, cuius discipuli fuisse memorantur Thamyras, Orpheus, Hercules. Hic natus est Thebis, vt in primo libro disciplinarum scripsit Hermodotus Platonicus . . . scriptum reliquit Dio in tertia compositione, Linum alium natum esse ex Apolline, & Psammate nympha, quam alij neptem, alij filiam fuisse Crotopi asserebant. . . . Fuit & alius Linus, qui lamentationes, ac fletus carmine prior edidit elegiaco, de quo mentionem fecit Phylarchus historicus.[26]

Even if we did not have Jonson's statement to the contrary, we would not expect a writer so outspoken about his learning to allow anyone else to gloss his erudite works. But the possibility should be met that the glosses discussed above were the result of peculiar circumstances. In writing the *Augurs* notes, Jonson may have been more hurried than usual. We do not know. If he was, he seems to have used the two lexicons that he utilized in writing his long literary descriptions of virtuous queens. The "histories" of these queens, however, are separated distinctly from the poetic text of the masque. This particular masque, moreover, was annotated at the request of Prince Henry; and Jonson wrote that it "prou'd a worke of some difficulty" to "retriue the particular *authorities*" for what he had written out of the "fúllnesse, and memory" of his former readings. In view of the preceding discussion, either his memory of pertinent entries in the lexicons was very good, or Jonson utilized the dictionaries after the Prince wished to read the text and "inquire into" the "beauties, and strengths" of such poetry. The question is not of great importance. Even if we assume that he consulted the lexicons after the masque had been presented, it is significant for our purpose that the dictionaries aided him in performing the Prince's "gracious command." The relationship between text and gloss in Jonson's courtly spectacles does, however, deserve some attention.

That Jonson was familiar with the lexicons lends probability to any assumption that he used them, or remembered information in their entries, when he developed the poetic text of his masques and turned to such kindred compilations as those by Gyraldus, Comes, and Cartari. As we have remarked earlier, the glosses in general explain the poet's "invention" and indicate the material he had in mind when he developed his conceptions into a purposeful and poetic text. The Neo-Platonic ideas reflected in *The Masque of Blacknesse* and *The Masque of Beautie,* as well as the tradition out of which arose the basic conception of *Hymenæi,* are understood as Jonson meant them to be only when gloss and text are considered together.[27] Some of the notes, consequently, which specify the source for concepts developed in the text, indicate that just as the compilations of the mythographers will leave traces of their phraseology and their authorities in both gloss and text, so may the basic lexicons, particularly the *Dictionarium Historicum* and the *Thesaurus Linguae Latinae.* The borrowing and inter-borrowing between editions of Renaissance reference works sometimes make it impossible to be confident as to the specific compendium from which Jonson derived his information. The lexicons, however—from which he drew for glosses and notes in *The Masque of Queens* and *The Masque of Augurs*—could have supplied him with material he has utilized. They are the same lexicons, of course, that contained entries reflected in *The Entertainment at Theobalds.*[28]

In the *Masque of Beautie,* the gloss to Proteus in the line "When Protevs, the gray *Prophet* of the sea, Met them . . ." (p. 183, l. 73) says, "Read his description, with *Virg. Georg. 4, Est in Carpathio Neptuni gurgite vates, Cæruleus Proteus."* Both Charles and Robert Stephanus have "Proteum aliquando in Carpatho insula regnasse . . . *Virg. 4. Georgic . . .Est in Carpathio Neptuni gurgite vates Caeruleus Proteus."* In the *Haddington Masque,* on the appearance of Pyracmon (p. 259, ll. 317-19), who later calls up Brontes and Steropes, Jonson writes, *"one of the* Cyclops; *of whom with the other two,* Brontes, *and* Steropes, *see* Vir. Æneid." His gloss is *"Ferrum exercebant vasto Cyclopes in antro, Brontesque Steropesque & nudus membra Pyracmon, &c."* Charles Stephanus gives the same information and quotes the same lines. Speaking of the Cyclops, he writes, "Ex his *tres potissimum a poëtis celebrantur. Brontes, Steropes, & Pyracmon,* quem Ouid. 4. Fastorum Acmonidem vocat. *Virg. 8. Aeneid. Ferrum exercebant vasto Cyclopes in antro,/ Brontesque, Steropesque, & nudus membra Pyracmon."* Robert Stephanus' article also includes the line quoted by Jonson and the citation of the *Æneid.* Just as he was undoubtedly familiar with the fourth book of the *Georgics,* Jonson of course knew at first hand the passage in the eighth book of the *Æneid* wherein Vulcan fashioned arms for the hero. But the

lexicons, as well as the more specialized treatises, by including the quotation from Virgil, could have recalled for Jonson a passage that aided him in
developing with "sound learning" a basic conception in one of his masques.[29]
Thus in celebrating the nuptials of John, Lord Ramsey, Viscount Haddington, and Lady Elizabeth Ratcliffe; Pyracmon, Brontes, and Steropes add
their art and "strike a time" with their sledge hammers to the dancing of
the masquers.  At any rate, the lexicons were probably instrumental in
making the passage from Virgil and the appropriateness of Jonson's invention relatively well-known to his audience.

A similar example occurs in *Hymenæi*.  Opinion disguised as Truth
naturally asserts that her parents are Truth's parents (1. 696): "Graue
*time,* and *industry* my parents are." A portion of Jonson's note upon his
poetic text runs as follows:

*Truth* is fained to be the daughter of *Saturne*: who, indeed, with the Ancients,
was no other then *Time,* and so his name alludes, Κρόνος. *Plut.* in *Quaest* . . . .
Charles Stephanus has

*Veritas Temporis filia* & Virtutis mater . . . *Plutarch in quaestionibus ait,*
*Veritatis parentem ac deum Romanos Saturnum habuisse,* & subdit causam:
An, inquit, quod vt plerique Philosophi putant, Κρό or Χρόνον, i. *Saturnum*
*tempus esse*: veritas vero tempore inuenitur, an illud potius quod Saturnus
iustissimus fuerit, & veritatem in primis etiam, quod verisimile est, coluerit.

The preceding information about Saturn is, of course, a thoroughgoing
commonplace and could be found, for example, in the compendiums by
Gyraldus and by Ripa—compilations that contain all of Jonson's materials
on Truth, as well as his reference to *Hippocrates uero in quadam ad Philo-*
*sopoemenen epistola* and the quotation describing Opinion, both of which
appear in the gloss (p. 234) that immediately follows the note on Truth
and Saturn.  Yet when Jonson encountered such material in the mythological and iconological treatises, certainly the information he repeated and
gave to his readers in the note quoted above may have been already familiar
to him and probably to at least some of his audience from entries in the
lexicons that had been utilized in the schools for at least one generation.[30]
Indeed elsewhere in *Hymenæi* two passages cited by Jonson occur in the
*Thesaurus,* while Comes would contain only one and Ripa might provide
the other.  Both passages concern Jonson's conception of Juno's appearance; and they are connected with material that seems to be taken verbatim
from Gyraldus.  Juno is described (ll. 215-16) as *"sitting in a Throne,*
*supported by two beautifull Peacockes; her attyre rich, and like a Queene.*

. . ." The second gloss on the passage runs as follows: "She was call'd *Regina Iuno* with the *Latines,* because she was *Soror & Coniux Iouis, Deorum & hominum Regis."* Wheeler, limited to classical sources, found Juno to be queen only "by implication" and by the Homeric epithet "queenly."[31] In his gloss, however, Jonson was quoting exactly the words of Lilius Gregorius Gyraldus: "Regina Iuno à Latinis cognominata, quòd soror et coniunx Iouis, deorum atque hominum regis." The dictionaries likewise state that Juno was the sister and wife of Jove and that she was a queen. Charles Stephanus' article on Juno begins "Saturni et Opis filia, soror et coniunx Iouis," while the *Thesaurus* of 1573 notes that she was "Iouis soror et conjunx" and adds later

Est Regina. Virg. I Æn. 50. Ast ego quae divum incedo regina. Et quia praeest nubentibus, Pronuba dicitur. Virg. 4 Æneidos . . . .

Of particular interest here, however, is the fact that the first sub-article after "Juno" in Robert Stephanus' compilation reads "Junonius, Adiectiuum . . . ut Auis Iunonia. Pauo. *Ovid* I. *de Arte,"* while under "Pavo" the last noticeable citation is "Ovid. 2. *Metam."* Consequently it is interesting to compare Jonson's gloss on the peacocks which supported Juno's throne when that goddess was "discovered" in the *"upper part of the Scene"*:

They were sacred to *Iuno,* in respect of their colours, and temper, so like the *Aire. Ouid. de Arte Amand. Laudatas ostendit auis Iunonia pennas.* And *Met. li. 2. Habili Saturnia curru Ingreditur liquidum pauonibus æthera pictis.*

Two noticeable citations in the *Thesaurus* are thus quoted by Jonson; one (the *De Arte Amandi*) is given by Ripa and the other (the *Metamorphoses*) is cited by Comes, while the *Mythologiae* might also supply Jonson's explanation of the reason for the peacock being sacred to Juno— "vtpote aereo temperamento."[32] Undoubtedly Jonson consulted both of the more specialized compendiums, but it is again interesting to note that his authorities for details about the birds were both prominently cited by the basic Latin thesaurus of the period and obviously were the ones commonplace to his age.

In the *Masque of Beautie,* again, one of Jonson's notes on Janus reads (p. 182, l. 48) "See the offices and power of *Ianus, Ovid. Fast.* I." Under "Janus" both Charles and Robert Stephanus cite *Fast.,* I, and quote lines therefrom. Similarly in the *Masque of Blackness,* for the account in the text of Phaeton, Jonson has (p. 174, l. 161) *"Notissima fabula,* Ovid. *Met. lib. 2."* Charles Stephanus just before the interpretation of the story of Phaeton gives the source of the preceding narration as *"Ouidius secundo Metamorphoseon,"* and Robert Stephanus' first citation reads *"De hoc vide finem primi, & initium secundi libri Met. Ovidii."* Finally, the first line of *Oberon* (p. 341, l. 7), spoken by the first Satyr, "Chromis, Mnasyl? None appeare?" has the following gloss: "They are the names of two yong *Satyres,* I find in *Vir. Eclog.* 6, that took *Silenus* sleeping. . . ." Here again, for a "history" of Silenus, Robert Stephanus, would have provided "Bacchi nutritius, vel paedagogus. De quo *Virg. ecloga* 6.3 [6 Ecl. 12]." Moreover, the *Thesaurus* is very probably the immediate source for a later gloss. Jonson writes on Lyaeus (p. 344, l. 78) : "A name of *Bacchus, Lyæus,* of freeing mens mindes from cares: παρὰ τὸ λύω, *soluo."* Robert Stephanus has *"Lyaeus dicitur Bacchus,* ut grammaticis placet παρὰ τὸ λύειν, id est *solvere,* quod *curas soluat, atque discutiat."*

The examples given above are sufficient to illustrate three points. The first has been made so frequently that there is perhaps no need to mention it again. The compilations noted above, with the exception of Ripa, were all subsidiary texts of long standing in the schools. In this instance, some of the most erudite poetry of the age arises in part from them. Certainly the modern scholar who would perceive the rapport between Renaissance author and audience must consider not simply the more specialized treatises but also the basic lexicons. The second point is in part related. Jonson's use of the dictionaries, or his memory of their contents, does not in any way preclude his use or recollection of material in the ancient classics or in the more specialized compendiums, and vice versa. Finally, as Opinion's line about her parents, or as the notes on the description of Juno, or as the glosses to *Oberon* indicate, there is usually a close enough connection between text and commentary to substantiate the assumption that by the time Jonson composed his poetic texts, he was thoroughly familiar with the works from which he drew the content and the authorities of his glosses.

The three points can be illustrated further. Just as Jonson erred twice with the dictionaries in writing glosses to the *Masque of Augurs,* so he incorrectly referred to material in Pomponius Mela when he wrote the Barriers of *Hymenæi*—the composition which includes the description of Juno and the reference to Opinion's parentage. And once again as in the *Augur* notes, or as in the descriptions of virtuous queens, Jonson errs with a lexicon—in this instance, with Charles Stephanus' *Dictionarium Historicum.*

The error, trivial in itself, but revealing for our purpose, occurs in Jonson's poetic text and neatly supports the three points made above. Such an indebtedness to the *Dictionarium Historicum,* moreover, occurs in one of Jonson's most intricate and carefully developed works. The pertinent lines, consequently, deserve to be discussed in some detail.

As part of Opinion's defense of virginity, Jonson writes (p. 235, ll. 766-73):

> And, where there is in *lifes* best-tempred fires
> An end, set in it selfe to all desires,
> A settled quiet, freedome neuer checkt;
> How farre are *married liues* from this effect?
> EVRIPVS, that beares shippes, in all their pride,
> 'Gainst roughest windes, with violence of his tide,
> And ebbes, and flowes, seuen times in euery day,
> Toyles not more turbulent, or fierce then they.

Jonson's gloss on Euripus describes the place as "A narrow sea, betweene *Aulis,* a port of *Bœotia,* and the Isle *Eubœa.* See *Pomp. Mela. li. 2.*"

The passage in Pomponius Mela (II, ix, 52-9) is as follows:

Euboea ad meridiem promuntorium Geraeston et Capharea, ad septentrionem Cenaeum extrudit et, nusquam lata duum milium spatium habet ubi artissima est, ceterum longa totique Boeotiae aposita angusto freto distat a litore. Euripon vocant, rapidum mare, et alterno cursu *septiens die ac septiens nocte fluctibus in vicem versis* adeo immodice fluens, ut ventos etiam ac plena ventis navigia frustretur.[33]

The wording obviously does not agree with that of Jonson's text or of his gloss. In addition, Pomponius Mela states that the sea ebbs and flows seven times a day *and* seven times a night. In the *Thesaurus* and in the *Dictionarium Historicum,* Pomponius Mela is cited as the authority for the lexicons' description of Euripus. Charles Stephanus' compilation, however, gives the exact wording of Jonson's gloss and also information which varies from that in Mela but which agrees with Jonson's statement that the sea "ebbs and flows seven times in every day." When Jonson writes that Eripus is "A narrow sea, betweene *Aulis,* a port of *Bœotia,* and the Isle *Eubœa,*" he repeats verbatim a passage wherein Euripus is described as "fretum angustum inter Aulidem Boetiae portum, & Euboeam insulam. . . ." The lexicon entry then continues with the detail in Jonson's text that the sea ebbs and flows seven times within the space of a day and a night:

. . . quod *vnius diei & noctis spatio septies recurrit eo impetu,* vt nauigia repugnantibus ventis secum rapiat.

The last bit of information just quoted, that the tide bears ships along with it against the wind, is also reflected in the poetic text.

The information in the *Dictionarium Historicum* is clearly Jonson's source, and such a borrowing in the text of his entertainment undoubtedly implies a great familiarity with the lexicon. At any rate, the verbatim correspondence of the gloss with the dictionary and the variation both in Jonson's text and in the lexicon from the original description in Pomponius Mela can be explained only by Jonson's reliance upon information in the *Dictionarium Historicum.* In the Masque of *Hymenæi,* as Mr. Gordon has pointed out, Jonson attempted to recreate an archaeologically exact representation of a Roman marriage; and the Barriers of that entertainment continue the topic and the symbolism of the masque proper, wherein the basic marriage image is extended to the union of the universe and its instance in the king's union.[34] Thus along with the wealth of classical allusion and Renaissance scholarship that is found in *Hymenæi,* appears related material clearly derived from one of the basic dictionaries that were designed almost a century earlier to aid all who would understand a Latin text. In this instance again, the reflection of a lexicon entry occurs in an ordered array of ingeniously careful erudition.

Elsewhere in the text of the masques there are indications, not as detailed perhaps, that Jonson was thoroughly familiar with the lexicons and that at least some of his audience probably encountered familiar material when they heard or read the lines of his courtly spectacles. Taken in conjunction with the preceding examples, as they must be, their cumulative effect is appreciable in demonstrating Jonson's knowledge of the dictionaries and also in indicating how consideration of entries in the reference lexicons can illumine the literature of the period and specify what knowledge was current during the era.

In *Mercury Vindicated from the Alchemists at Court,* Nature calls Prometheus "wise Prometheus" when invoking his aid for her twelve sons:

> How yong and fresh am I to night
> To see't kept day, by so much light,
> And twelue my sonnes stand in their Makers sight?
> Helpe, wise *Prometheus,* something must be done,
> To shew they are the creatures of the Sunne . . . .

(ll. 202-6)

Wheeler, who usually attempts to find a classical origin for such phrases as
"wise Prometheus," has not done so in this instance.[35]  The "wise," however, may very well be a reflection of the *vir prudentissimus* in the lexicon
entries, wherein Prometheus also appears as the thief of celestial fire and
the producer of men.  In the dictionaries likewise is an interpretation of
the myth that illumines these and other lines in the masque as well as the
basic conception of this courtly spectacle.

The speech of Nature quoted above is the first speech of the Masque
proper.  The conventional contrast between the main portion of a courtly
entertainment and the Antimasque had been underlined in this instance by
Mercury's words to Vulcan immediately preceding Nature's appearance:

Vanish, I say, that all who haue but their senses, may see and iudge the difference betweene thy ridiculous monsters, and his absolute features. (ll. 193-95)

The "ridiculous monsters" are the creations of Vulcan's "fire and Art,"
the imperfect figures of the alchemists' heat, who had performed the second
dance of the Antimasque; and "his absolute features" are those of "the
Maiesty of this light" (l. 191), that is, the Sun, who, with Nature, is the
creator of the twelve splendid figures referred to above:

> . . . each to other
> Is a brother
> And *Nature* here no stepdame, but a mother.
> (ll. 207-9)

As the entertainment continues, twelve masquers perform the usual dances
(the entrance dance, the main dance, a dance with the ladies, and a final
dance).  Prometheus and Nature are the commentators here, just as
Mercury, persecuted and pursued by Vulcan and his alchemists, had performed such a function in the Antimasque.  At the close of the entertainment as the dancers prepare to leave, Prometheus expresses a conventional
regret which allows the Chorus to assure him that each of Nature's sons
has left his heart with his lady (ll. 256-57).  Nature sings that they are
no sons of hers if they are not loth to part, though with a kiss that can be
refined (ll. 259-70).

The basic dramatic invention of the entire spectacle is obvious.  The
Antimasque figures created by fire and art are balanced against those
created by the sun and nature.  The absurd antics and doctrine of the
pseudo-Philosophers are balanced against the graceful motions and the Neo-
Platonic philosophy of the Main Masque.  The basic philosophical inven-

tion of the entire spectacle arises from the tradition which Jonson utilized in *Hymenæi, The Masque of Blacknesse,* and *The Masque of Beautie,* and is explicitly developed, as we shall see, in the lines of Prometheus, Nature, and their Chorus.

With such an outline in mind, one is aided further in understanding the development of the masque by knowing in what respect Jonson and his audience might consider Prometheus to be "wise," how Prometheus might well be represented as an opponent of seventeenth-century philosophasters, and how he might be represented as an ally of Nature and the Sun. To the Renaissance, Prometheus was not simply a figure who stole celestial fire to aid man and was in consequence bound to a mountain peak; his myth was thought to embody, among other things, the story of a truly wise philosopher who retired to the highest mountain in the Caucasus and there, eaten by care and solitude, discovered the motion of the planets. Quite fittingly, therefore, was Mercury, the god of wisdom and reason, represented as being the one who bound him to his task. Such an interpretation of the myth was widely disseminated, and it appeared in the *Dictionarium Historicum* in the following form:

Nam Prometheus vir prudentissimus fuit. Vnde etiam Prometheus dictus est, ἀπὸ τῆς προμηϑείας, id est, a prouidentia. Hic primus Astrologiam Assyriis indicauit: quam residens in monte altissimo Caucaso, nimia cura & solitudine deprehenderat. Hic autem mons positus est circa Assyrios, vicinis pene syderibus. Vnde etiam *maiora astra demonstrat, & diligenter eorum ortus occasusque significat.* Dicitur autem aquila cor eius exedere, quod à χος est solitudo, qua ille adfectus, *syderum omnes deprehenderat motus.* Et hoc quia per prudentiam fecit, duce Mercurio, qui prudentiae & rationis deus est, ad saxum dicitur esse religatus.

Comparable material in the *Thesaurus Linguae Latinae* is almost identical. Thus, for example, when Prometheus sings the conventional note of regret at the close of the masque and refers to his flight from the "ills" of womankind (ll. 252-55), Jonson just possibly may be glancing not simply at the creation of Pandora by Vulcan and others, but also at Prometheus' withdrawal from society, which was emphasized in the conventional interpretation of the myth.

Elsewhere in the masque, however, the astronomical-astrological aspects of the interpretation appear explicitly. Vulcan and those alchemists who would sublime and otherwise misuse mercury would persecute Mercury, the god of wisdom and reason. The results of their "art" are such abortions as a corrupt lawyer, "a master of the *Duel,*" and a pseudo-astrologer—a creature who is, in Jonson's words, "a fencer i'the *Mathematiques* . . . a supposed secretary to the starres." The culmination of Jonson's Antimasque, consequently, is quite fittingly represented by the dance of imperfect creatures, who are produced by those who trespass against the excellence of the Sun and Nature. Such creatures with *"helmes of lymbecks"* on their heads are appropriately dismissed by the god of wisdom and reason after he has been protected by the "Genius of the place," "the *Sol* and *Iupiter* of this spheare":

See, they begin to muster againe, and draw their forces out against me! The *Genius* of the place defend me! You that are both the *Sol* and *Iupiter* of this spheare, *Mercury* inuokes your majesty against the sooty Tribe here; for in your fauour onely, I growe recouer'd and warme. (ll. 104-9)

And here—as in the other similar masques—Jonson touches upon an immediate political application of his Neo-Platonic thought as it can be developed out of the conventional king-sun analogy. The absurdities which result from perverting wisdom and reason can vanish, and the god of wisdom and reason can present instead beautiful creatures when he is protected by the King at the center of his kingdom, for in such a mortal is embodied "the excellence of the Sunne and Nature":

Art thou not asham'd, *Vulcan,* to offer in defence of thy fire and Art, against the excellence of the Sunne and Nature, creatures more imperfect, then the very flies and insects, that are her trespasses and scapes? Vanish with thy insolence, thou and thy Impostors, and all mention of you melt, before the Maiesty of this light, whose *Mercury* henceforth I professe to be, and neuer againe the *Philosophers.* Vanish, I say, that all who haue but their senses, may see and iudge the difference betweene thy ridiculous monsters, and his absolute features.

*At which the whole Scene changed to a glorious bowre, wherein* Nature *was placed, with* Prometheus *at her feete; And the twelue Masquers, standing about them. After they had bene a while viewed,* Prometheus *descended, and* Nature *after him* . . . (ll. 186-200)

Thus the same god, who in the interpretation of the myth bound Prometheus to his task of understanding celestial bodies and their motion, appropriately brings to the audience "wise Prometheus," twelve of Nature's offspring who will move in graceful harmony, and Nature herself, who is

> The spring, whence order flowes, that all directs,
> And knits the causes with th'effects.

(ll. 243-44)

In other words, after the entrance dance, the singing commentary indicates
that the moving order of creation is transferred in representation to the
motions of the dance, for Nature is also "motions mother" (l. 242). Similarly, when the masquers were preparing to dance their first dance before
the court and before the ladies who were to become their partners—whereby
they might "make perfection vp," that is, become complete and show that
Nature is not their stepdame (ll. 206-12)—Jonson had utilized the conventional figure of stealing from ladies' eyes "the right Promethean fire,"[36]
but fittingly elaborated the idea with the circles, orbs, planets, and motions
associated in the interpretation of the myth with the "wise" figure from
whom Nature requested aid:

> But shew thy winding wayes and artes,
> Thy risings, and thy timely startes
> Of stealing fire, from Ladies eyes and hearts.
> Those softer circles are the yong mans heauen,
> And there more orbes and Planets are then seuen,
> To know whose motion
> Were a Notion
> As worthy of youthes study, as deuotion.
>                                        (ll. 213-20)

Jonson clearly knew and utilized the interpretation of the Promethean
myth quoted above from the dictionaries. To be sure, he could have found
it, as well as other interpretations, elsewhere—in the work by Natalis
Comes, for example, to which the reader of the account in Charles Stephanus' lexicon is referred. The number of those in Jonson's audience who
would appreciate the congruent details in his purposeful text, however,
would depend in large measure upon how many knew a particular interpretation of the Promethean myth. Whether many actually did or not, it
seems not unreasonable to suppose that Jonson knew which interpretation
he might assume to be disseminated most widely. Once again he might
well argue that his audience should be able to appreciate and understand
at least some of the poetic intricacies of his courtly entertainment if they
appeared with reason in the center of the kingdom to see *Mercury Vindicated from the Alchemists at Court*. At least one generation of those
trained to serve the body politic and attend its head might well have encountered the interpretation of the Promethean myth which Jonson utilized
in as basic a subsidiary school text as the *Dictionarium Historicum*.

In *Love Freed from Ignorance and Folly,* the major portion of the song after the last dance is as follows (p. 370, ll. 358-65) :

> What iust excuse had *aged Time,*
>   His *wearie limbes* now to haue eas'd,
> And sate him downe without his crime,
>   While euery thought was so much pleas'd!
> But *he so greedie to deuoure*
>   *His owne,* and all that hee brings forth,
> *Is eating euery piece of houre*
>   Some obiect of the rarest worth.

The identification of Time with Saturn was a conventional Roman concept and there are many references to the well-known myth of Saturn eating his own children. Robert Stephanus, however, has the following item as part of the article on Saturnus :

> Saturnum autem eum esse voluerunt, *qui cursum & conversionem spatiorum, ac temporum contineret,* qui deus Graece idipsum nomen habet: Κρόνος enim dicitur, qui est idem Χρόνος, id est *spatium temporis.* Saturnus autem est apellatus, quod *saturetur annis. Ex se enim natos comesse fingitur solitus, quia consumit aetas temporum spatia, annisque praeteritis insaturabiliter expletur.*

Jonson, to be sure, could have found such an interpretation of the myth elsewhere, for example in Cicero's *De Natura Deorum* (2.25.64), which is one of the sources cited by R. Stephanus for this item and the source alleged by Wheeler for Jonson's identification of Time and Saturn.[37]   A similar interpretation with the same citation of authority might also be found in Gyraldus and in Comes, but Jonson and his audience would have had in the basic Latin thesaurus of the period the ideas expressed in the major portion of the last song in *Love Freed*: i.e., "aged Time" with "wearie limbes," yet "greedie to deuoure his own" and continually eating.

   That Jonson may have been familiar with dictionary entries which dealt with Elysium and the Fortunate Isles was mentioned early in this chapter; and, as one might expect, matter appropriate for the annotation of a masque bearing such a title can be found in the lexicons. *The Fortunate Isles,* a revised version of the unperformed *Neptune's Triumphs,* was prepared when the engagement of Charles to Henrietta Maria was announced. After Johphiel has finally dismissed the principal character of the new antimasque, he indicates the nature of the coming main masque in a speech which begins with Jonson's utilizing a proverb cited by Cooper: "to sail to Anticyra."[38]

                                         Great King,
          Your pardon, if desire to please haue trespass'd.
          This foole should haue bin sent to *Anticyra,*
          (The Ile of *Ellebore,*) there to haue purg'd,
          Not hop'd a happie seat within your waters.
          Heare now the message of the Fates, and *Ioue,*
          On whom those Fates depend, to you, as *Neptune,*
          The great Commander of the Seas, and Iles.
          That point of Reuolution being come
          When all the Fortunate Islands should be ioyn'd,
          MACARIA, one, and thought a Principall,
          That hetherto hath floted, as vncertaine
          Where she should fix her blessings, is to night
          Instructed to adhere to your BRITANNIA:
          That where the happie spirits liue, hereafter
          Might be no question made, by the most curious,
          Since the *Macarij* come to doe you homage,
          And ioyne their cradle to your continent.
                                         (ll. 435-52)

The idea of a floating island is probably a survival from the earlier *Neptune's Triumph,* in which Delos was the name given the island that landed the masquers. But Jonson is too careful a writer not to have some authority for the moving of the Fortunate Islands—or, as he says, for the uncertainty "where the happie spirits liue"—and for a belief in the actual existence of such islands. In a number of contemporary reference works Jonson could have found the various locations of the Fortunate Isles discussed. Comes, for example, devotes a chapter in his *Mythologiae* to the Elysium Fields (III, xix), and a portion of Charles Stephanus' article on Elysium reads "Hunc locum alii inferorum foelicitatibus plenum, alii fortunatas insulas, alij circa lunarem circulum esse dicunt, vbi iam aër purior est." Robert Stephanus writes:

Fortunatae Insulae, [Μακάρων νῆσοι] a fructuum hubertate [*sic*] dictae sunt. de quibus Strabo lib. 1. sic inquit, Fortunatae insulae contra Mauritaniae finem ac Occidentem sunt. Quam quidem ad partem & Hispaniae terminus concurrit. Ex ipso autem nomine manifestum est, quoniam & has ipsas foelices existimabant, quia hujusmodi locis propinquae forent. Plin. lib. 4. cap. 22. Ex adverso Celtiberiae complures sunt insulae, Cassiterides dictae a Graecis, a fertilitate plumbi, & e regione Arrotrebarum promontorii, deorum sex, quas aliqui fortunatas appellavere. Vulgus autem nostrum hodie vocat *Insulas Cannarias,* a fertilitate cannarum, in quibus crescit saccarum. . . .[39]

That Jonson should name the islands "Macaria" and call the inhabitants "Macarij" seems, naturally enough, to be but an echo of Hesiod perhaps and a transliteration of the Greek μακάριος. This is what Wheeler's discussion amounts to; for without citing any source he says " 'Macaria' is the poetical name for several of the Grecian islands."[40] However, the association of the name "Macaria" with a definite island and with various sections of the world is found not only in Robert Stephanus' "Μακάρων νῆσοι" for "Fortunatae Insulae" but also, for example, in Charles Stephanus' item:

Macaria, Ptolem. Cypri insulae vrbs, quae Nigro Ialines appellatur. Est & fons in Marathone Atticae regionis, Pausan. Tractus Peloponnesi etiam, apud Strabonem. Et insula sinus Arabici. Ptolem.

In Robert Stephanus, moreover, under "Marcaria" one finds authority for the name's being applied to the isles of the blessed and for "Macaria" being a definite group of inhabited islands.

Μακάρων[νῆσοι,] i.e., Beatorum insulae, Asiatico littori oppositae & ad promontorium Tauri montis expositae, quas quidam dici sic putauere, siue quod fortunati admodum caeli solique sint, siue quod eas suo suorumque regno Macar occupauerat. Verba sunt Pomponii Melae lib. 2.[41]

Although the identification of England with the Fortunate Isles was a Renaissance commonplace, had Jonson, or anyone else, known the pertinent entries in the *Thesaurus,* the apt flattery of *Macaria* would have been obvious. Macaria is the isle of the blessed because it is ruled by *Macar,* the happy or blessed one(*"quod eas suo suorumque regno Macar occupaverat"*) and it is pertinent to note that the identification of Macaria with England is the basic idea not only of Johphiel's speech but also of the Main Masque.

A major portion of the last song in *Love Freed from Ignorance and Folly* has been mentioned above, and material elsewhere in this courtly entertainment is of even greater interest. In the directions at the beginning of the masque appear lines describing the entrance of the principal characters: ". . . *there was heard a strange Musique of wilde Instruments. To which a* Sphynx *came forth dauncing, leading* Love *bound."* Jonson's note on the Sphinx is as follows:

By this *Sphynx* was vnderstood *Ignorance,* who is alwaies the enemie of *Loue, & Beauty,* and lyes still in wait to entrap them. For which, *Antiquitie* hath giuen her the vpper parts, and face of a woman: the nether parts of a *Lion,* the wings of an Eagle to shewe her fierceness, & swiftnesse to euill, where shee hath power. (p. 359).

Classical sources suggested for the preceding description have been Apollodorus' *The Library* (3.5.8) and Seneca's *Oedipus* (99-102, 106).[42] Apollodorus' description of the Sphinx is that ". . . she had the face of a woman, the breast and feet and tail of a lion, and the wings of a bird."[43] Aside from 1. 106, in which the Sphinx is referred to as "monster," the pertinent passages in *Oedipus* are

> . . . saxaque impatiens morae
> revulsit unguis viscera expectans mea;
> nodosa sortis verba et implexos dolos
> ac triste carmen alitis solvi ferae.

All of the particulars in Apollodorus and Seneca, however, might well have been familiar to Jonson and his audience from the following items in the dictionaries of Charles and Robert Stephanus:

> *Sphinx, monstrum* ex Typhone & Echidna natum vt tradit Hyginus Fabularum poet. cap. 151. *caput & faciem habens puellae, alas vero auium, reliquo corpore canis referens effigiem.* Sedem habuisse dicitur in Sphincio monte iuxta Thebas, atque inde in viatores impetum facere solita . . . . (C. Stephanus)
>
> Poetae id *monstrum faciem habere virginis fingunt, pennas avium, pedes leonis.* . . . Lactant, in primum Theb. scribit, Sphinga *monstrum* fuisse, *alas & ungues habens in similitudinem Harpiarum* . . . . (R. Stephanus)

Not only are all of the details in both Apollodorus and Seneca found in the dictionary entries—which also include the story of Oedipus and the Sphinx—but also the word "monster," prominent in Jonson's masque (ll. 31, 99, 311), is decidedly prominent in the lexicons. Comes' description of the Sphinx, however, might have provided a reader with further information found in the gloss, for the *Mythologiae* specifies eagles' wings: ". . . cum alas haberet aquilae, citissimeque ad illos conuolaret. . . ." Yet one cannot ignore the information provided by the basic dictionaries of the period, for in Robert Stephanus' compilation appears the following statement that seems to be reflected in both text and gloss of the masque:

> Sphinx ab effectu nomen sortita: quod *homines suis quaestionibus ita stringeret,* ut se expedire non possent. Nam Graece σφιγγειν *constringere, vel vincere dicitur: vel quasi omnium mentes suis propositionibus ligare.*

The concept of the Sphinx as one who inextricably binds men's minds is clearly apparent (1) in Jonson's identification of her with Ignorance, an interpretation he may have found in Alciati's emblems, and one which the *Thesaurus* would confirm;[44] (2) in Love's appearing bound (*"omnium*

mentes . . . ligare"), one of the germinal ideas of the masque; and (3), to
a lesser extent, in such lines as

> 'Lesse they could the *knot vn-straine*
> Of a riddle, which shee put
> Darker, then where they are shut . . .
>
> (ll. 116-18)

or Love's further explanation that

> if I
> Did her riddle not *vntie,*
> I would freely giue my life
> To redeeme them, and the strife.
>
> (ll. 131-34)

Even from the text of *The Masque of Queenes,* with its careful and
learned background of witchcraft, there is evidence that Jonson knew his
pertinent "history" well, for he seems to have been thoroughly familiar
with the articles on Hecate in the lexicons which he utilized elsewhere.
The Dame, as she and the Hags begin their incantation, calls upon Hecate
(pp. 295-96, ll. 237-42):

> And thou, *three-formed Starre,* that on these nights
> Art only power-full, to Whose *triple Name*
> Thus *wee incline; Once, twise, and thrise-the-Same:*
> If, now, w^th *rites* profane and foule inough,
> Wee doe invoke thee; *Darken all this roofe,*
> *W^th present fogges* . . . .

Classical sources provide an explanation for details in the preceding lines
which is little better than Jonson's own gloss:

*Hecate,* who is calld, *Triuia,* and *Triformis* of whome *Virgil. Æneid, lib. iiij.*
*Tergeminamque Hecaten, tria virginis ora Dianæ.* She was beleeu'd to gouerne,
in witchcraft; and is rememberd in all they^r invocations . . . .

Wheeler has suggested that the following lines might be compared with
Jonson's phrases: "per triplicis vultus . . . Dianæ" (*Heroides,* 12.79), and
"ora vides Hecates in tres vertentia partes" (*Fasti,* I, 141-2).[45]

Both Charles and Robert Stephanus, however, cite Virgil's *Aeneid,* IV,
as a primary source for knowledge about Hecate. The first citation in the
*Thesaurus* is from line 511, and the first two words are quoted: "Tergeminamque Hecaten." "Triformis Hecate" is one of Robert Stephanus' sub-
headings, a phraseology that Jonson apparently had in mind when he wrote

"three-formed" in the text and "Triformis" in his gloss. Similarly, at the beginning of his article, Charles Stephanus writes about the line in Virgil that "Huic triplex nomen attribuitur," a passage that agrees with Jonson's "triple name." The comment in the *Dictionarium Historicum* continues as follows:

Huic triplex nomen attribuitur, vnde etiam a Virgilio *Tergemina* vocatur. Nam in coelo creditur esse Luna, in terris Diana, & apud inferos Proserpina.

Later in the entry, "Ovid, *Met.* lib. 9" is cited for information to the effect that Hecate had three heads; and after the reader is referred to Comes for an interpretation of the myth, Virgil's line is given in full, as it is in Jonson's note.

In the *Thesaurus*, moreover, a portion of the complete article on Hecate is of particular interest in editions of 1573 and thereafter.

Hecate . . . *cui* Jupiter elemente *subiecit, & caelo hereboque potentem fecit,* ut canit Maro. Unde & Hecate dicta est, ut discimus ex Hesiodo. Virg. 4, Æneid.

Ter centum tonat ore deos [*Aen.,* 4, 510]. Vt dicat *Hecaten a saga ter invocatam,* quam per centum deos obscure quidem, verum peritissime designavit, ad amplissimam deae potestatem, & nominis rationem simul alludens. Id ab ἔκατον trahitur: id est centum. Ternarius porro numerus in huiusmodi sacris adhibebatur ex ritu, vt ex Homero, Nasone, Tibullo, Papinio colligitur. et Porphyrius in Responsis abunde disserit.

The dictionary articles thus provide the following particulars: Hecate is called "three-fold," or "three-formed"; has a "triple Name"; has power in the lower world, the earth, and the heavens; controls the elements; and is invoked thrice *a saga.* The line from Virgil cited by the dictionaries appears in Jonson's footnote, and the above particulars are clearly reflected, as the italics show, in the Dame's speech when she invokes the goddess *"Once, twice,* and *thrise-the-Same."*

Finally, when the sixth charm of the Hags fails, Jonson, in the following speech of the Dame, once more refers to the triple invocation (p. 298, ll. 299-300):

> I call you once, and I call you twise,
> I beate you agayne, if you stay mee thrise.

He then has the Dame, when still unsuccessful, call for

> . . . a bough, that nere bare leafe,
> To strike the ayre; and Aconite
> To hurle vpon this glaring light.

(ll. 306-8).

Not only are Jonson's sources for his gloss on "Aconite" listed in Robert Stephanus but the dictionaries also definitely connect Hecate with such herbs—Charles with poisonous herbs in general and Robert with aconite specifically:

Hecate, herbarum veneficiorumque peritissima, quae in Taurica Cherroneso regnauit sub Dioynsio Milesio . . . . (C. Stephanus)

Sed ad venena mortifera conficienda summum studium operamque impendens, *prima aconitum invenit,* vim naturamque cujusque veneni in cibis quos aduenis dabat, experta. (R. Stephanus)[46]

That both Charles and Robert Stephanus give the Hecate connected with aconite a different parentage from that of the Hecate mentioned by Virgil is immaterial.[47] In both the dictionaries and the *Masque of Queens,* Hecate is associated with aconite, and only in such works as the compilations of Charles and Robert Stephanus could Jonson and his audience have encountered all of the preceding details in any one place. Comes and Gyraldus, to be sure, repeat much of the information. Neither, however, contains a statement that parallels the comment in the *Thesaurus* about "Hecaten a saga ter invocatam"; neither has the specific phrase "triplex nomen"; nor does Gyraldus connect Hecate with aconite specifically. From Comes, however, Jonson may have derived the idea of calling Hecate a star:

Eam Luciferam dictam fuisse constat, quia per sempiternos illos astrorum ignes descenderet.

Hecaten Iouis filiam & Asteriae finxerunt esse, quae credebatur vis esse per astra descendens, & occulte agens diuinitus in corpora haec inferiora. . . .[48]

But in addition to the details noted above as being in neither Comes nor Gyraldus, in the *Mythologiae* there is no passage corresponding with that in the *Thesaurus* which states that to Hecate "Iupiter elementa subjecit" —an idea important for the theatrical effect implied in the line "Darken all this roofe, W$^t$h present fogges." The poetic text of a learned courtly entertainment, in brief, indicates that for at least a portion of the "history" of Hecate, which might be derived from classical authorities, Jonson at one time was indebted nevertheless to the *Dictionarium Historicum* and the *Thesaurus Linguae Latinae.*

In *The Masque of Blacknesse* also, traces of the lexicons, more obvious than the one already noted,[49] seem undeniable—in spite of the fact that most of the mythology and iconology in this entertainment is drawn from

Comes, Ripa, Valerianus, or Gyraldus. Jonson derived from the *Mythologiae,* for example, the device whereby he initiates his plot, that is, the motivation of the journey of the Aethiopian nymphs to England. In brief, the plot develops as follows. A vision in the lake from which Niger springs had informed Niger's daughters that they would find the beauty they envied in a country whose name ended in *Tania.* Accompanied by their father and by twelve Oceanides, the nymphs are met by Oceanus, Niger's father, who in turn is accompanied by Tritons. They discover the vision in the lake to have been that of "Great Æthiopia," and the goddess informs them that here in "Britania" they have reached their destination. After songs and dances, the daughters of Niger are given directions for becoming white, and Niger alone is to return to his lake. The conception of the vision—of having Aethiopia's face and the "mysticke lines" reflected in a lake—was derived in all probability from Comes, as D. J. Gordon has pointed out.[50] Jonson also followed the *Mythologiae* in describing Oceanus and other characters. Ripa and Valerianus in turn provided him with material for his "Hieroglyphicks" and for his descriptions of the personages involved; and he repeated information in Gyraldus and in Cartari.[51]

For some of the details about Niger, however, particularly for the important one concerning his relationship to the lake in which the poet represents the vision as appearing, Jonson was probably indebted to the lexicon that specialized in all sorts of proper nouns. In the *Dictionarium Historicum,* Niger is linked with Nilus, Oceanus, and Aethiopia, both in entries under *Niger* and *Nigris* as well as in entries under *Aethiopia* and *Nilus.* Thus under *Nilus,* a reader might learn that

*Nascitur* in monte inferioris Mauritaniae, non longè ab Oceano, *stagnante ibi lacu, quem vocant Nilidem:* deinde condit se itinere aliquot dierum, rursumque erumpit alio lacu maiore in Mauritania Caesariensi, iterúmque arenis receptus, per deserta viginti dierum spatio *fertur ad proximos Æthiopas, & denuò prosilit fonte, que Nigris dicitur:* inde Africam ab Æthiopia disterminans, medios secans Æthiopas, sic plerásque insulas facit, quarum clarissima est Meroe . . . postquam se aquis omnibus auxit, Nilus appellatur. *Tandem septem ostiis in mare se exonerat. . . .*[52]

The passage ("Nascitur," etc.) is clearly reflected in lines that recount how the Aethiopian nymphs, the daughters of Niger, saw a vision one night

> . . . in the *Lake, where their first spring they gain'd.*
> As they sate, cooling their soft Limmes. . . .

(ll. 182-83)

Also pertinent are the following lines in Charles Stephanus' compilation:

*Nigir, fluuius Libyae* inferioris, eiusdem cum Nilo naturae, Ptolem. lib. 4. cap. 5.

*Nigris fons in Æthiopia,* quem nonnulli caput Nili esse autumauerunt, quòd sit cum Nilo naturae. . . . Plin. lib. 5. cap. 8 & Ptole. lib. 4. cap. 5.

*Nigris, fluuius est, à quo Nigrites, Steph. populi Libyae cognominati sunt.*

The information about the origin of Niger is combined with the passages just quoted when Jonson writes his introductory explanation of the masque and speaks of

. . . a river in *Æthiopia,* famous by the name of *Niger; of which the people were called Nigritæ,* now Negro's. . . . This riuer *taketh spring out of a certaine lake,* east-ward; and *after a long race, falleth into the westerne Ocean.*

Finally, in his text and glosses Jonson cites both the *"Lib. 4. cap. 5"* of Ptolemy as well as book five, chapter eight of Pliny's *Natural History* (1. 15, glosses a, c, and e)—authorities likewise cited in this respect by the *Dictionarium Historicum.*

For this masque, which marked the beginning of his collaboration with Inigo Jones, Jonson had received the Queen's command that the principal women participants be *"Black-mores* at first" (ll. 21-23). Although outweighed by a wealth of detail in an entertainment designed to inculcate Neo-Platonic doctrine, such particulars as those enumerated above are most revealing. They are so intricately linked to the basic plot of the entertainment that one is forced to conclude that when Jonson received the Queen's command and began to compose his masque, he utilized information in the *Dictionarium Historicum* as well as in the more specialized compilations. He may have turned to that dictionary directly, or details in Comes or Gyraldus might have called to mind particulars he had amassed when learning "histories" of proper nouns. In addition, the lexicons naturally contain some of the information pertinent to *The Masque of Blacknesse* which can also be found in the *Mythologiae* and the *De Deis Gentium.* In Charles Stephanus, as in Comes, one would find that Oceanus was the father of waters; as the *Dictionarium* words it "Oceanus, Coeli & Vestae filius, maris deus . . . fluuiorum fontiumque omnium pater." Thus Niger is "Fayre Niger, sonne to great Oceanvs" (1. 100). If Jonson had glanced at the entry under "Oceanides" in the *Thesaurus,* he would have found, as in Gyraldus, a reference to the fourth book of the *Georgics.* And it was *Georgics,* 4, that apparently supplied him with the additional names necessary to round out the Oceaniae to an even dozen—material not found in Hesiod's *Theogony*, the source which Jonson cites in his footnote.[53]

What Jonson's exact procedure was is pure conjecture. But when one runs one's eye down the entries among the *Aeth's* in the *Dictionarium Historicum*, one suspects that he is doing what Jonson did. For example, after a note that "Aethiope" was an island formerly called "Macaria," one reads as follows:

> *Aethiopia, Diana cognominata est, teste Steph.* Quidam sic appellatam putant, *a regiuncula quadam Lydiae:* ἀιϑιόποον nomine, *vbi coleretur:* nonulli, ab eo quod *cum apud Æthiopas versaretur,* inde ab Apolline abducta esset, alij παρὰ τὸ ἀιϑεῖν, ab ardore videlicet, *quod Luna sit,* vt ait Callimach. quidam, *quod ea Hecate* sit quae facibus vti putabatur.
>
> *Aethiopia,* Hebraeis Chus, quasi nigra vel nigredo, Graecis ardorem siue incendium significat. Regio est Aphricae, ab Æthiope Vulcani filio dicta. Alia pars Africae, torridae zonae subiecta, inter Arabiam & Ægyptum, *ab Indo flumine consurgens, inter Nilum & Oceanum,* & in meridie sub ipsa solis vicinitate, cuius gens primum Ætheria appellata est, deinde Atlantia, mox Aethiopia. . . .[54]

The entries then continue through "Aethiopia, Aegyptiorum armis attrita," "Aethiopia vnde dicta," "Aethiopiae duae," "Aethiopiae Magnes," "Aethiopici maris insulae plures," "Aethiopes quales," "Aethiopes Arotherrae," "Aethiopum gentis descriptio," "Aethiopum caput Meroe," until one reaches a passage that is once more clearly reflected in Jonson's words. Although the difference is slight, the wording of the following note from *The Masque of Blacknesse* is that of Charles Stephanus rather than that of the original source, Diodorus Siculus. Before citing Diodorus in his gloss, however, Jonson presumably checked the reference given by the dictionary. Consequently although he preserved Charles Stephanus' wording, he cited the ultimate source correctly, writing *"Diod. Sicul. lib. 3"* rather than Charles Stephanus' "Diod. Sicul. lib. 4" (p. 173, l. 138):

| | |
|---|---|
| . . . though they, [Aethiopian dames] were the first form'd dames of earth. . . . Read *Diod. Sicul. lib. 3.* It is a coniecture of the old *Ethnicks,* that they, which dwell vnder the *South,* were the first begotten of the earth. | *Aethiopes omnium hominum primi creati fuisse dicuntur,* cuius rei *coniecturam faciunt veteres ethnici* nonnulli . . . de quibus *Diod. Sicul. lib. 4* ita disserit. Et quidem simile veri est, *eos, qui sub meridiem habitant, primos e terra homines fuisse genitos.* |

The passage in Diodorus reads as follows:

Now the Ethiopians, as historians relate [ἰστοροῦσι], were the first of all men

and the proofs of this statement, they say, are manifest . . . .
. . . furthermore, that those who dwell beneath the noon-day sun were, in all
likelihood, the first to be generated by the earth [ὑπὸ τῆς ὄῆς ἐζωογονησϑαι]
is clear to all . . .[55]

When one considers all of the preceding details, there can be little doubt
that Jonson found the fullest proper-noun lexicon of the period useful in
composing a masque that would be based upon sound antiquity, inculcate
sound doctrine, and satisfy the Queen's command.

Before turning to another masque, moreover, we should note that
information quoted above and italicized under *Aethiopia* appears also in
*The Masque of Blacknesse* along with a reference to the same source cited
by the poet.    The Aethiopia-Diana-Luna identification and the worship
of that goddess by the Aethiopians is basic to Jonson's plot, and the pertinent gloss provided by the poet runs as follows:

> The *Aethiopians* worshiped the *Moone,* by that surname.    See *Stepha.* περὶ
> πόλεων. *in voce* ΑΙΘΙΟΠΙΟΝ and his reasons. (p. 176)

The same information about Aethiopia as that in the *Dictionarium Historicum* could be found in Robert Stephanus' *Thesaurus* and in Gyraldus' *De
Deis Gentium.*[56]   Jonson's indebtedness to material elsewhere in the *Aeth*
section of the compilation by Charles Stephanus, however, makes it pertinent at least to note one additional parallel.    When *The Masque of Beautie,*
the sequel to *The Masque of Blacknesse,* was finally performed, Jonson
utilized again the Aethiopia-Diana-Luna theme, but with the additional
identification of Aethiopia with Hecate.    The Aethiopian dames in *The
Masque of Beautie,* who come to meet their sisters, are released from their
wandering; Night's maleficent charms

> . . . being made vnto their *Goddesse* knowne,
> Bright *Æthiopia,* the siluer *Moone*
> As she was *Hecate,* she brake them soone . . . .
>                                    (ll.122-24)

The last two lines are very close to the phraseology noted above: "*Aethiopia*
. . . quod *Luna* sit . . . quod ea *Hecate* sit. . . ."

As we have remarked before, the lexicons with which we are concerned
existed in the schools as reference works common to all forms not simply
because they would aid those "stuck on the Latin word" but also because
they made a wealth of information more easily available than it would be if

it were left scattered throughout the glosses and texts of the ancient classics. Before discussing such a consideration in any detail, however, it might be well to consider how some of the more detailed entries, if surveyed, reread, or remembered by a mature and erudite poet, could (and perhaps did) start a train of associations that might result in a poetic text.

At the end of the second antimasque of Phantasms in *The Vision of Delight,* Phant'sie's speech introduces the contrasting main masque (p. 467, ll. 120 ff.) :

> But vanish away, I have change to present you,
> And such as (I hope) will more truly content you:
> Behold the gold-haird *Houre* descending here,
> That keepes the gate of Heaven, and turnes the yeare,
> Alreadie with her sight, how she doth cheare,
> And makes another face of things appeare.

*Here one of the* Houres *descending, the whole Scene changed to the Bower of* Zephyrus, *whilst* Peace *sung, as followeth.*

> Why looke you so, and all turne dumbe!
> to see the opener of the New-yeare come?
> My presence rather should invite,
> and ayd, and urge, and call to your delight.
> The many pleasures that I bring
> are all of youth, of heate, of life, and spring,
> And were prepard to warme your blood,
> not fixe it thus as if you Statues stood.

*The Quire.*
> ⌈ We see, we heare, we feele, we taste,
> | we smell the change in every flowre,
> ⌊ we onely wish that all could last,
>   and be as new still as the houre.

>             *The Song ended,* WONDER *spake.*
> WONDER must speake, or breake; what is this?  Growes
> The wealth of Nature here, or Art?  It showes
> As if *Favonius,* father of the Spring,
> Who, in the verdant Meads, doth reigne sole king,
> Had rowsd him here, and shooke his feathers, wet
> With purple-swelling Nectar? and had let
> The sweet and fruitfull dew fall on the ground
> To force out all the flowers that might be found?

Charles Stephanus' dictionary throws little light upon the above speeches; under *Horae,* he writes: "Iouis & Themidis filiae quarum nomina describit Hyginus, cap. 183 & decem numerat." Irene, or Pax, is, of course, listed by Hyginus as one of the Hours.[57]  The article under *Hora* in the 1573 *Thesaurus,* however, is very complete; and portions of it are relevant to our discussion:

Horas Homerus lib. 5. Iliad. ait *caeli portis praeesse, curamque habere ut modo serenum, modo nubilum sit, a quibus videri possunt quatuor anni tempora,* Horae appellata, non Graecis modo, sed & Latinis. Hor. de Ioue lib. I. Carm. 12.

Qui mare & terras variisque mundum.

Temperat horis. A quibus, ait Acron, velut *temperatur annus per ver, aestatem, autumnum, & hyemem.* Ouidius Homerum imitatus, *cum Iano foribus caeli adscripsit,* ita Iano loquente lib. I, Fastorum. Praesideo foribus caeli cum mitibus Horis. hinc ab ὡρέω, id est custodio, curo, dictas nonnulli putant, quod *sint ianuae caeli custodes.* Plato tamen in Cratylo: Horae, inquit, vocantur, quia ὁριζουι, id est *terminant hyemen atque aestatem, ventosque & fructus ex terra nascentes.* Pausanias in Eliacis: Homerus in Iliade scriptum reliquit, *Horus caelo etiam fuisse praefectas,* tanquam regiae aulae custodes.

Hora anni, pro Parte. Plin. lib. 9, cap. 35. Has *vbi genitalis anni stimulauerit hora,* pandentes sese quadam oscitatione *impleri roscido conceptu tradunt.*

There are, then, in the dictionaries three clear statements that the Hours keep "the gates of heaven"; once the phrase is *"ianuae caeli custodes."* Furthermore there are explicit statements that the Hours govern, separate, or are the seasons; hence the Hour "turnes the yeare" and "with her sight . . . makes another face of things appeare," while the chorus wishes "that all could last." The Hours are also associated with *"fructus ex terra nascente"* and, in the explanation of Pliny's synecdoche, with *"genitalis anni"*—an association also expressed under *Pax,* of whom Robert Stephanus says "Eodem quo Ceres habitu fingebatur, Spicam nimirum manu tenens." Hence the pleasures brought by Peace are "all of youth, of heate, of life, and spring,/ And were prepard to warme your blood." The rest of Wonder's speech, not quoted here, which begins by likening this vision of "the wealth of Nature" to spring, and therefore associating it with Favonius or Zephyrus, comes as a natural consequence and affords a contrast with the antimasque. Indeed, under *Favonius* in Robert Stephanus, Jonson could have found a reference to Claudian, a favorite author of his and the one used as the source for the long description of spring in the remaining part of Wonder's speech.

The Hours, who are twice mentioned in Robert Stephanus as overseeing the heavens, *"ut modo serenum, modo nubilum sit,"* and the dictionary's phrasing of the particulars from Pliny, *"impleri roscido conceptu tradunt,"* might also have raised associations in Jonson's mind with the passage in Claudian which he begins to follow when he speaks of the showers of Favonius, the "purple-swelling Nectar," which

> . . . had let
> The sweet and fruitful dew fall on the ground
> To force out all the flowers that might be found.
>
> (ll. 146-48)

Jonson's source runs as follows:

> . . . ille [Zephyrus] novo madidantes nectare pennas
> concutit et glaebas fecundo rore maritat,
> quaque volat vernus sequitur rubor; omnis in herbas
> turget humus medioque patent convexa sereno.[58]

The remainder of the main masque consists of (1) the rest of the vision of Spring described by Wonder, (2) the masquers' entrance dance with its prelude and choruses praising "a King Whose presence maketh this perpetuall *Spring,*" (3) the masquers' main dance praised by its chorus, (4) Aurora's appearance, who is urged "by the Day, Against my will, to bid you come away," and (5) the exit dance and chorus. This later portion of the spectacle, excluding the complimentary speeches, also indicates how a knowledge of "histories" in a reference lexicon might have aided a Renaissance poet in establishing common ground with his audience. In Robert Stephanus' article on "Hora" there is a passage that could easily have raised associations with Aurora, for the Hours are therein linked with the rising sun and consequently with Aurora, who appears to warn the masquers of the coming of day:

> Horae idcirco Solis equorum curam habere finguntur, quod ex cursu Solis oriantur, seu potius mensurentur & distinguantur. Ovid. lib. 2. Metam.
> Iungere equos Titan velocibus imperat Horis:
> Iussa deae celeres peragunt.

Moreover, in the song immediately preceding Aurora's speech (ll.224-27), there is perhaps a reflection of the dictionary items on Chloris (Flora), wife of Zephyrus (Favonius):

> In curious knots and mazes so,
> The Spring at first was taught to go;
> And *Zephire,* when he came to wooe
> His *Flora,* had their motions too . . . .

Here, as in his treatment of Chloris in *Chloridia,* Jonson avoids all mention of Zephyrus' rape of Chloris as recounted by the *Fasti* (5. 183-228). Al-

though Jonson referred to the poem by Ovid when writing *Chloridia,*
Wheeler has suggested that he purposely avoided mention of the assault
because the Queen was performing the role of Chloris.[59]   That may be
true; but here in the *Vision of Delight,* the wooing of Zephyrus is far
removed from Ovid's description:

> fortior ille fuit,
> et dederat fratri Boreus ius omne rapinae
>     ausus Erechthea praemia ferre domo.
> vim tamen emendat dando mihi nomina nuptae . . . .
>
> (ll. 202-5)

Consequently, Zephyr's gentle wooing of Flora, aside from being in accord
with the beauty and mildness of the main masque, may also be the result
of Jonson's reliance upon entries in the lexicons.   In both the *Thesaurus*
and the *Dictionarium Historicum,* although the *Fasti* is given as the source
of the information, there is no mention of any assault:

> Altera ab Ouidio dea florum ponitur: quae quum nympha esset non ignobilis,
> & Zephyro nuberet, quasi dotis loco id muneris a marito accepit, ut florum
> omnium potestatem haberet. [*Thesaurus,* s.v. *Chloris*]

Certainly Jonson was thoroughly familiar with Ovid and one might well
assume that he knew the account in the *Fasti;* yet here, as in his allotment
of time to the Parcae, his conception accords with information in the
lexicons.[60]

The poet's knowledge of Gyraldus, of Comes, and of Cartari also seems
to be reflected in *The Vision of Delight.*   The discussion of the Hours in
the *Imagines Deorum,* for example, probably explains Jonson's reference
to the Hours as "gold haird"—a description bothersome to anyone who attempts to find Jonson's details in classical literature alone.   In fact Cartari's
treatment is particularly apt; for the mythographer speaks of the Hours
descending to earth and of the pleasure they might give to anyone who saw
them turning the revolution of the year with their hands and heard them
singing very sweetly.

> A quoy venant, i'en feray seulement vn pourtrait selon que Philostrate en fait
> vn beau tableau, disant que les Heures descendues en terre font la reuolution de
> l'an, lequel est en forme d'vne certaine chose ronde, auec les mains: dont aduient
> que la terre produit puis apres, tous les ans, tout ce qui naist. Elles sont blondes,
> vestues d'habits tres-deliés, & cheminent sur les espics secs si legerement,
> qu'elles n'en rompent point, ny tordent seulement vne, elles sont d'vn regard

amiable & ioyeux: elles chantent tresdoucement, & en roulant ceste boule, ou
rondeur, il semble qu'elles donnent vn fort grand plaisir aux regardans. . . .[61]

Yet the information to be found in the basic Latin thesaurus of the period
is also pertinent.  Not only was it probably more widely diffused during
the period than the comparable account in the more specialized treatises,
but once known to Jonson, or once reread by him, it was of such a nature
that it might well have called to mind other material with which he was
familiar or confirmed a tentative plan and provided him with the means of
developing it—particularly with a reminder of material in Claudian, whose
lines Jonson paraphrased in Wonder's key speech.  In other words, Jonson's composition of this masque, which is without the learned annotations
that are otherwise so helpful to our purpose, may have been influenced by
his knowledge of dictionary entries; and his procedure in writing portions
of this poetic text may not have been greatly different from that which he
apparently followed in writing some of his longer glosses.

This last point deserves some attention, for the usefulness of the lexicons as a guide to a scholarly poet has not been discussed as yet in any
one place.  To be sure, it is implicit in a number of the particulars which
have been noted: in the instances which illustrate the relationship between
gloss and text of the masques, particularly when the glosses provide the
source for the conception Jonson develops in his poetic text.  It is also
implicit in such instances as the notes on Branchus, Penthesilea, Camilla,
and Berenice, wherein Jonson quotes material cited by the dictionary entries that he was following.  As part of our concern with the relationship
between the literature of the age and the basic lexicons, this particular point
can be examined and best illustrated perhaps by considering a single masque
*in toto*.  Of all his courtly entertainments, *The Masque of Augurs* seems
most appropriate for such a study.  All critics probably would agree that
the main masque of the spectacle is "a monument of Jonson's extraordinary
erudition"; yet here, as we shall see, the lexicons along with other scholarly
compendiums were probably most useful to Jonson, since they not only
provided him with specific information but also indicated where he might
find pertinent material in the classics.

In this Twelfth-Night masque for 1621-2, Jonson's learning is shown
in his handling of mythological particulars and in his including a wealth
of detail about ancient augurial practices.  Both bodies of material are so
carefully documented that the critic who attempted to reproduce Jonson's

details from the ancient classics alone would perforce conclude that the author had a well-nigh supernatural memory. What Jonson did, however, was to rely upon contemporary scholarly aids, the current short cuts to learning that were sometimes advertised as being "opera vtilissima a Historici, Poeti, Pittori, Scultori, & Professori di belle lettere."[62] The works that seem to have aided Jonson most in writing *The Masque of Augurs* are Comes' *Mythologiae,* Rosinus' *Antiquitates Romanæ,* Peucer's *Commentarius de Præcipuis Divinationum Generibus,*[63] and the two lexicons that have been previously noted in this chapter: Charles Stephanus' *Dictionarium Historicum, Geographicum, Poeticum* and Robert Stephanus' *Thesaurus Linguae Latinae.*

Three of the most obvious correspondences between *The Masque of Augurs* and sixteenth-century compendiums have already been noted:[64]

(1)

On Linus, Jonson writes "Linus Apollinis & Terpsichores filius, Paus." (Gloss f.)

(a) Pausanias has no such genealogy (I, xliii, 7; II, xix, 8; VIII, xviii, 1; IX, xxix, 6-9).
(b) C. Stephanus writes "Linus, Apollinis & Terpsichores filius. . . . Paus. 9."

(2)

On Branchus, Johnson writes "Branchus, Apollinis & Janees filius, de quo vid. Strab. lib. 4. & Statium, Thebaid. lib. 3—*patrioque æqualis honori Branchus.*" (Gloss h.)

(a) Although the quotation is from the *Thebaid* (III, 478-9), neither Statius, nor Strabo (XIV, i, 5), nor Lactantius on Statius[65] gives such a genealogy; *"Jances* corr. F: *Janees* F originally: the name, even in the corrected form, is doubtful."
(b) R. Stephanus writes *"Branchus,* ut scribit Lactantius, *filius fuit Apollinis* ex filia *Iaucis* & Sucronis conjuge, susceptus. . . . Branchi meminit *Stat.* 3 *Theb. Strabo* lib. 14."

(3)

On Phœmonoë, Jonson writes "Phœmonoë, filia Phœbi, quæ prima carmen heroïcum cecinit. Hesiod. in Theog." (Gloss k.)

(a) Hesiod gives no such information.
(b) C. Stephanus writes "Phoemonoe, filia Phoebi, & vates quae prima carmen heroicum cecinit, vt est author Hesiodus in Theogonia."

Two other glosses are likewise revealing. On Orpheus, Jonson writes (p. 639, gloss *g*) :

Orpheus, Apollinis et Calliopes, de quibus Virg. in Ecloga[4]scrip[si]t.

*Non me Carminibus vincet nec Thracius Orpheus, Nec Linus, huic mater quamvis, atque huic pater adsit, Orphei Calliopea, Lino formosus Apollo.*

The quotation, of course, "fixes only the parentage of Calliope," and Wheeler implies that Jonson, consequently, may have had Apollodorus in mind.[66] Jonson may have, but the article on Orpheus in the *Dictionarium Historicum* or in the *Thesaurus* supplies a much better explanation. There Jonson would have found not only the account of Orpheus' parentage but also the citation of the same three lines from Vergil:

> *Orpheus,* Musicus & poeta insignis, genera Thrax, *Calliopes & Apollinis filius . . . Virgil, Eclog.* 4.
> *Non me carminibus vincet, nec Thracius Orpheus*
> *Nec Linus, huic mater quamuis, atque huic pater adsit,*
> *Orphei Calliopea, Lino formosus Apollo.*

The other gloss, like the one on Branchus, is particularly apt for our immediate purpose, for Jonson seems to have enlarged his source by quoting from an authority cited by the *Thesaurus*. His familiarity with the dictionary entries, however, explains the resulting incongruity. In his note on Idmon, Jonson writes (p. 639, gloss *i*):

> Idmon, Apollinis et Asteries filius. De illo vid. Valer. Flac. lib. I. Argonautic—*Contra Phœb[e]ius Idmon Non pallore viris, non ullo horrore comarum Terrib[i]lis, plenus fatis, Phœboque quieto, Cui genitor tribuit [monitu] prænoscere Divum Omina, seu flammas, seu lubrica cominus exta, Seu plenum certis interroget aëra pennis.*

Here again Jonson's alleged source does not give the complete genealogy, but the items in the dictionaries do. Charles, like Robert, writes *"Idmon, vates inter Argonautas, Apollinis & Asteriae filius . . ."*; while Robert, under "Phoebeius Idmon," cites *"Valer. I. Argon. . . ."*[67] In this instance Jonson apparently used the dictionaries not only for an account of the parentage of Idmon but also for the citation of the authority which he subsequently quoted, but which gave only the name of Apollo. In writing the five notes just considered, Jonson apparently misread one dictionary item (Branchus), reproduced three almost verbatim (Linus, Orpheus, Phoemonoë), and twice erred with the lexicons (Linus, Phoemonoë). Three of his citations from the classics seem to have been lifted from the dictionaries (Linus, Orpheus, Phoemonoë), and two might very easily be the result of Jonson's turning to classical authorities in order to quote the lines cited by the lexicon (Branchus, Idmon).

Mythological particulars in the remainder of the masque can be found in the Stephanus' dictionaries again, or in Comes' *Mythologiae,* or in both Comes and Charles Stephanus. Probably the best example of Jonson's erudite handling of mythological details appears in the first speech of Apollo (ll. 275-83), with its five glosses explaining the conceptions expressed in the poetic lines:

> ([a]) Apollo descending sung.
> *It is no dreame, you all doe wake, and see;*
> *Behold, who comes!* ([b]) *far-shooting* Phœbus, *he*
> *That can both hurt, and* ([c]) *heale; and with his* ([d]) *voyce*
> *Reare Townes, and make societies rejoyce;*
> *That taught the Muses all their harmonie,*
> ([e]) *And men the tunefull Art of Augurie.*
> Apollo *stoopes: and, when a God descends,*
> *May Mortalls thinke he hath no vulgar ends.*

[glosses]
(a) Artes eximias quatuor Apollini acceptas tulit antiquitas.

(b) Sagittandi peritiam, unde apud Homerum, frequens illud Epitheton ἐκηβόλος, longe jaculans.

(c) Medicinam, unde Medici nomen adeptus.

(d) Musicam, unde μουσηγέτης appellatus.

(e) Et Divinationem (in quâ etiam Augurium) unde Augur Apollo dictus. Virg. Æneid. lib. 4. & Horat. Car. lib. 1. Ode. 2. *Nube ca<n> dentes humeros amictus Augur Apollo.* Et Car. sæcul. ult. ubi doctissimus Poeta has artes totidem versibus complectitur. *Augur & fulgente decorus arcu Phœbus, acceptusque novem Camœnis, Qui salutari levat arte fessos Corporis artus.*

Apollo's fourfold function, emphasized by gloss (a) and the last quotation in gloss(e), is pointed out in Comes' *Mythologiae,* a considerable portion of the discussion being reproduced verbatim by the article on Apollo in the *Dictionarium,* e.g.,

Et Plato in Cratylo, vbi nomenis rationem perquirit, *quæ ad quatuor facultates illius extenditur ad musicam, diuinationem, medicinam, peritiamque mittendarum sagittarum,* Apollinem, nunc quia non plures sint, nunc a soluendo, nunc a mittendo, nunc rerum simplicitate dictum contendit, quæ Soli conueniunt omnia ac nulli præterea.[68]

This information basic to the conventional interpretation of the Apollo myth, appears also in the *De Deis Gentium* and the *Imagines Deorum,* but in both compilations the wording is not as close to Jonson's as that in the passage just quoted.[69]

# NATALIS COMITIS

## MYTHOLOGIAE,

### SIVE EXPLICATIONVM FABVLARVM

*LIBRI DECEM.*

IN QVIBVS OMNIA PROPE
Naturalis & Moralis philofophię dogmata fub anti-
quorum fabulis contenta fuiffe
Demonftratur.

*CVM LOCVPLETISSIMIS INDICIBVS*
*eorum fcriptorum, qui in his libris citantur, rerumque*
*notabilium, & multorum nominum*
*ad fabulas pertinentium*
*explicationibus.*

OPVS NON TANTVM HVMANARVM,
*fed etiam facrarum literarum & Philofophia ftudiofis*
*perutile, ac prope neceffarium.*

CVM PRIVILEGIO.

# VENETIIS

## MDLXVIII.

Title page of Natalis Comes' *Mythologiae,* Venice, 1568, from a copy in the
private collection of D. T. Starnes.

*"Far-shooting* Phœbus" and Jonson's gloss (b) agree not only with *"peritiamque mittendarum sagittarum"* in the preceding quotation but also with the following passage from Charles Stephanus' article : ". . . ab Homero variis nominibus appellatur . . . ἐϰηβόλος. . . ." Both Comes and C. Stephanus also write "Hic longissimi e cœli in terras radios suos minime debilitatos iaculatur, vnde dictus est a poetis ἐϰάεργος, e longinquo operans. . . ." Apollo's curative powers, his being one that "can both hurt, and heale," are mentioned throughout Charles Stephanus' article and in Comes; while the following sentence from the *Mythologiae* specifically links together these two attributes of the god:

Tribuebatur Apollini ars medendi, et sagittarum scite emittendarum peritia, quod his verbis significauit Ouidius libro primo Metamorphos . . . .

That Apollo taught or presided over the Muses is frequently expressed in C. Stephanus, e. g., "Fertur accepisse citharam a Mercurio: & postea Musis præfuisse," and in Comes, e. g., "Fuerunt hac ipsa de causa Musae in eius tutela creditæ quarum et dux et pater Apollo fuit existimatus." The information in glosses (c) and (d), although hardly what one would call erudite, can be found in Robert Stephanus' *Thesaurus*.[70] As the linking together of Apollo's ability to hurt and heal may reflect material in Comes, so Jonson's lines that Apollo is the god that can:

> *Reare Townes, and make societies rejoyce;*
> *That taught the Muses all their harmonie,*

may reflect the arrangement of material in Charles Stephanus:

Ille muros & Troiæ, adiuuante Neptuno, Laomedonti rege ædificauit. . . . Author est carminis & Musices . . .

By these lines, of course, Jonson anticipates a later development in the masque, at which time he will refer in more detail to the founding of Troy. That Apollo also ruled over "the tunefull Art of Augurie" enlarges upon his presiding over divination in general, as the first sentence in gloss(e) points out: "Et Divinationem (in qua etiam Augurium) unde Augur Apollo dictus." In Comes' treatment of Apollo more than six columns are devoted to divination, and the discussion contains such specific details about the "tunefulness" of augury as the following particular:

Fama est Democritum non solum solita auguria intellexisse, sed etiam certo nomine aues quasdam nominare solitum, è quarum sanguine commisto anguis nasceretur, ex quo si quis edisset, auium omnium intelligeret idioma.

Under "Apollo" and "Augur" in the *Thesaurus,* moreover, "Augur" and "Apollo augur" are respectively the second and the first phrases appearing as subheads; and those subheads are followed by two of the three citations Jonson uses in gloss (e)—i.e., by "Virg. 4. AEn." and "Ho. 1. Carm. ode 2." Perhaps, in much the same manner as he seems to have composed other glosses, Jonson added the lines from the *Carmen Sæculare* along with their introductory sentence when he had been directed by Stephanus to Horace and turned to the edition in his library for the direct quotation.[71]

Finally, the last two lines of Apollo's first speech look forward to the foundation of a college of augurs and to his addressing the ruler who was watching the masque. Thus the god, whom, Comes reminds us, the Athenians considered to be "Deus patrius et ciuitatis defensor," has descended to bring an important message to the figurative center of the body politic, to the defender of the state of England. In other words, the conventional four-fold interpretation of the Apollo myth found, for example, in Comes and Charles Stephanus and embodied in the god's first speech provides a connection between Main Masque and prose foil that students of Jonson's courtly spectacles have heretofore felt to be lacking.[72] The appearance of Apollo, who *"taught the Muses all their harmonie,"* frightens away the absurd transgressors of his art—Notch, Slug, John Urson and his bears, the three "Gentlewomen" "that should have acted in that famous matter of *Englands joy* in sixe hundred and three," and particularly the conceited Van-goose and his "Antick-maske." This god, who in turn presents the Main Masque, can both hurt and heal. In Stephanus and Comes, for example, the abstract from Plato's *Cratylos* quoted above continues with the sentence: "Quid enim veritatem magis aperit quam Sol, et omnem *tenebrarum caliginem* ex humanis rebus *dispescit?*" In the interpretation of the Apollo myth, the beneficence of the rays of the sun is also a central idea. Apollo's killing of the Cyclops, for example, "nihil aliud significant nisi Solis beneficio *rabiem illam vaporem,* qui pestem excitauerant, fuisse *extinctam."* Thus the god, who also appears to interpret favorable auguries for the ruler of a state, disperses quite fittingly the "obscurity," "dullness," and injuriousness of the actors and dancers in the satiric Induction and Antimasque.

Elsewhere in the Main Masque other mythological details likewise indicate, I believe, that Jonson used these current compilations designed to aid the scholar, painter, or poet in finding and developing his inventions.

Utilizing Apollo's ability to rear towns, Jonson gives to the god the following lines addressed to James:

> Jove *hath commanded me*
> *To visit thee;*
> *And in thine honour with my* (¹) *Musique reare*
> (ᵐ) *a Colledge here,*
> *Of tunefull Augures* . . . .

(ll. 324-28)

Gloss(m) will be discussed later; gloss(1) reads

*Allusio ad illud Ovidij Epistol. Epist. Parid. Ilion aspicies, firmataque turribus altis Mœnia Apollineœ structa canore lyrae.*

Just as the glosses on Apollo's offspring sometime embody both the citation and the quotation of classical authorities as given by Charles Stephanus, so here Jonson may have lifted from the *Mythologiae* the material italicized in the following portion of Comes' discussion of Apollo:

At *Ouidius* non manibus Apollinis extructa fuisse mœnia Troiana scribit in *epistola Paridis,* sed per sonum lyræ, quam dum tractaret, saxa se sua sponte ait concinne accommodasse. Ita enim inquit:
> *Ilion aspicies, firmataque turribus altis*
> *Mœnia Apollineae structu canore lyræ.*

With the remaining mythological particulars, however, we have no detailed glosses to aid us in pinning down the possible source of the ideas expressed in Jonson's lines. Yet it seems very likely that the conception of the powers of Apollo as elucidated in the interpretation of the myth underlies the awakening and animation of his offspring in Jonson's masque. The beneficent force of Apollo, who is "generationis rerum et corruptionis vnicus autor" (Comes), may at times cause growth and animation; thus Jonson writes

> Branchvs.
> What sacred breath
> Doth re-inspire us?
> Idmon.
> Who is this we feele?
> Phoemonoe.
> What heat creepes through me, as when burning steele
> Is dipt in water?
> Apollo.
> . . . .

Let whole *Apollo* enter in you all,
And follow me.

(ll. 294-307)

With the exception of Phœmonoë, the names of the offspring that Jonson chose to have appear in his masque might be found in Comes' long list of Apollo's numerous progeny.

Finally, the omnipotence of Jove and his consequent control over the ratification of auguries—an idea Jonson expresses at the end of the masque (ll. 433-64)—although a mythological commonplace,[73] may have been suggested by at least one passage in Comes' discussion of Apollo that links the two gods together in a similar manner:

Fuerunt autem duo Dei tantum, quorum celebrabantur responsa, Iupiter & Apollo; quorum ita fecit mentionem Aeschylus in Eumenides:

κἄγωτε χρησμοὺς τοὺς
ἐμοὺς τε καὶ Διὸς
ταρβεῖν κελεύω
Oracula ipse Iouis, tum dein mea
Confidere imperio.

Veruntamen idem Aeschylus testatur in Sacerdotibus Apollinem a Ioue prius accipere responsa solitum, deinde eadem dare petentibus, vt est in his carminibus . . . .

For erudite mythological details in the *Masque of Augurs*, therefore, Jonson needed to know little more than the information available in current scholarly compilations. There he would have found either the learned particulars that he reproduced or a citation of the poems and lines which he quoted, except for one instance in which only the author was cited by the reference works.[74] That he was familiar with such aids to scholarship is indicated by the verbatim correspondences and frequent agreement between the reference works and the lines and glosses of Jonson's masque, as well as by the manner in which the Renaissance interpretations found in these current aids to learning explain Jonson's conception of the animation of Apollo's offspring and the connection between Main Masque and its prose foil.

With the material on augurial practices, the story is essentially the same, except that Rosinus' *Antiquitates Romanæ* and Peucer's *Commentarius de Præcipuis Divinationum Generibus* have to be considered. That Jonson should consult Rosinus and Peucer is not surprising. The *Antiquitates* had been on Jonson's desk when he wrote *Sejanus;* and Rosinus indicates his indebtedness to Peucer for his discussion of augury.[75] Charles Stephanus also used Peucer and cited his work as an excellent recent study in the group of authorities listed at the end of his article on "Augures."

Liu. lib. 1. Halicarnass. lib. 2. Plutarch. in Parall. & Problemat. Valer. Maxim. Cicero de Diuinatione. Varro, & alij. Augurum autem illorum deliria inter recentiores egregie confutauit G. Peucer. Commentario de variis diuinationum generibus.

The incorporation of much of Peucer's *Commentarius* into the *Antiquitates* makes it difficult and usually impossible to determine which work Jonson followed. Gloss (u), for example, elucidates the lines

> *It even puts* Apollo
> *To all his strengths of art, to follow*
> *The flights, and to divine*
> *What's meant by every Signe.*

(ll. 396-99)

The gloss clearly agrees with identical passages in the *Commentarius* and the *Antiquitates*:

| Jonson | Peucer and Rosinus |
|---|---|
| *Signa quæ sese offer[r]ent, era[n]t multifaria: nam si obijceretur avis aliqua, considerabatur quo volatu ferretur, an obliquo, vel prono, vel supino motu Corporis, quo flecteret, contorqueret, aut contraheret membra; qua in parte se occultaret; an ad dextram vel sinistram canerent Oscines, &c.* | *. . . si obijceretur avis aliqua, huc ne an illuc volaret, an prono, obliquo, supinove motu corporis ferretur, quo flecteret, contorqueret,* porrigeret, *contraheret membra:* an hac, vel in illa *se parte occultaret: a dextrane, vel sinistra parte canerent oscines.*[76] |

Jonson begins his poetic survey of augurial signs with

> *Which way, and whence the lightning flew,*

(l. 346)

and both Peucer and Rosinus begin their discussion of augurial signs with similar matter:

Ex cœlo tonitrua & fulmine, auguria dabant in hunc modum. Si aut lævum, aut impari numero intonuisset: aut si, ex Ortu emissa fulmina, cœli circumactu, in eandem partem redijssent . . . emicuissent prosperos eventus, & summam felicitatem, nunciare hæc a Dijs putabantur.[77]

At least twice, however, Jonson and Peucer agree where Rosinus has a different reading. As the following parallel passages show, there can be little doubt that the longest of Jonson's "erudite" discussions of augurial practices—gloss (o) on Apollo's statement that the augurs are *"closed in their Temple"* (l. 336)—is directly indebted to Peucer's *Commentarius;* for the two bracketed passages are omitted in Rosinus' *Antiquitates*:

| JONSON | PEUCER |
|---|---|
| *Auguria captaturi cœlum eligebant purum & serenum, aëreque nitido. Lituum (qui erat baculus incurvus, Augurale Signum) manu tenebat Augur. Eo cœli regiones designabat, & metas intra quas contineri debebant Auguria: & hæ vocabantur Templa: unde Contemplatio dicta est Consideratio, & meditatio rerum sacrarum, ut dextrum sinistrumque latus observaret. In impetrito sibi ipse regiones definiebat; inoblat[iv]o manum suam respexit lævam aut dextram. Regiones ab Oriente in occasum terminabat limite decumano, & cardine ex tran[s]verso signo metato, quo oculi ferrent quam longissime. Antica in Ortum vergebat. Postica regio a Tergo ad occasum. Dextra ad meridiem. Sinistra ad septentrionem. Observationes fiebant Augure sedente, capite velato, togâ duplici Augurali candidâ amicto, à mediâ nocte ad mediam diem, crescente, non deficiente die. Neque captabantur Aguria post mensem Julium, propterea quod Aves redderentur imbecilliores & morbidæ, Pullique eorum essent imperfecti.* | Talia *captaturi Augures* ex arce, *coelo non turbido, nec procelloso*, sed silenti, placido, *sereno*, & *puro aere, lituum* sine nodo, *hoc est, baculum a summo inflexum*, in parte, qua robustior est, *manu tenebant. Erat is insigne augurale, quo coeli regiones describebant, & designabant metas, intra quas, se obseruaturos signa constituerant, vt quod dextrum esset quodve sinistrum,* oculis animoque metiri possent. Manu enim haec spacia quae *templa vocabantur*, definire, & notare, saluis auspiciis non licebat.<br><br>Captato ergo prospectu in agros atque vrbem, & conuersa facie in Ortum, *regiones ab Oriente in Occasum terminabat, limite decumano, & cardine ex transuerso signo metato, quo oculi ferent quam longissime. Ex distinctis regionibus antica in Ortum vergebat, postica a tergo Occasum, dextra Meridiem, Boream sinistra respiciebat.*<br><br>His peractis, caesa victima, longum praefati carmen, preces effundebant. . . .<br><br>A precibus *considebant, velato capite, &, duplici amicti toga augurali*, quae læna dicta est, vel trabea, ex purpura & cocco, [vt Græcus Augur, *toga candida,*] defixisque in cœlum oculis, & attente soliciteque circumspectis ac perlustratis cardinibus omnibus, expectabant, nunquid alicunde ostenderet sese . . . .<br><br>[Ab auguribus in arce, vel ad veteres Curias, a Pontifice in post murio, & certis diebus, atque, *a media nocte, ad mediam diem* vsque, peragebantur.<br><br>Septima aut sexta diei hora non decebat; incipiente enim *die, aut crescente, non deficiente,* iusta auspicia fieri existimatum est: *Nec, post Sextilem mensem auspicari licuit, quod aues,* aut *imbecilles* tunc, aut *morbidae essent, & pulli imperfecti.* Homerus Orientem dextrum, Occidentem fecit sinistrum.][78] |

However, the *Antiquitates* of Rosinus, in turn, contains particulars found in Jonson but not found in the *Commentarius*. Peucer, for example, does not name Numa as one of the important augurs; Rosinus does,[79] and Jonson may have noted the name in the *Antiquitates* with the result that it appears in gloss (x) on *"princely* Augur" (l. 422). Again, it may be because of Rosinus' discussion that Jonson mentions *"parra"* in his list of birds, gloss (p), for the word does not occur in Peucer's description of augurial practices.[80] Finally, although the agreement in diction between Jonson and Rosinus may sometimes be coincidental and although Jonson's phraseology is derived from Peucer's as well, Jonson's wording sometimes seems to reflect a reading of Rosinus. Gloss (m), like gloss (q) and portions of gloss (n), is based on matter in Peucer and Rosinus with only an occasional verbatim correspondence.[81] Yet in one instance the wording of the first portion of an independent clause in Jonson's summary is closer to that in the discussion by Rosinus than it is to the comparable one by Peucer. In the remainder of the short clause, the situation is reversed and a summary without distinguishing verbatim correspondences follows:

Eorum officium fuit auspicia captare . . . . (Jonson)
   Officium *Augurum* fuit, ex avibus vaticinia observare . . . . (Rosinus, p. 201)
   Munus erat Augurum praecipuum, auspicia captare . . . . (Peucer, p. 377)

Fortunately a similar situation appears at the beginning of gloss (p), but on a larger scale:

Augurandi scientia ὀρνιϑομαντεία dicta. Divinatio per aves. (Jonson)
   Hic ὀρνιϑειαν . . . ὀρνιϑομαντεία Graeci nominarunt obseruatione rerum futura portendentium, interpretationesque, & diuinationes, ac responsiones aurispicium: Latini Aruspicinam, & Augurium. (Peucer, p. 375)
   (Rosinus has no comparable passage.)
Aves aut Oscines, aut Praepetes. Oscines, quæ ore, Praepetes, quæ volatu Augurium significant. Pulli tripudio. (Jonson)
   *Avium* aliæ erant *Oscines, aliæ Præpetes; Oscines,* aves dicebantur, *quæ ore* canentes faciebant . . . *Præpetes, quæ* secundo *volatu* ante eum, qui auspicabatur, volabant, & auspicium faciebant. (Rosinus, p. 206)
   Ex auibus oscines cantu augurium . . . praepetes seu τανυπτέρυγες volatu auspicium faciebant; *pulli tripudio* omina dabant. (Peucer, p. 381)[82]

Clearly Rosinus as well as Peucer contributed to the final result. The vast majority of Jonson's particulars on augurial practices, indeed, are not learned in the sense that they represent a compendium of details gleaned by Jonson from classical sources; they are erudite only in the sense that they were taken from two scholarly Renaissance compilations.[83]

For some of his particulars about augurial practices, however, Jonson seems to have consulted occasionally works other than the *Commentarius* and the *Antiquitates*. Brief reflections of Comes and of the Stephani appear again,[84] and it is interesting to note once more that, like Peucer's *Commentarius*, most of the other works probably consulted were cited as authorities by Charles and Robert Stephanus. Jonson, for example, links the college of Augurs with Salian rites:

> Jove *hath commanded me*
>    *To visit thee;*
> *And in thine honour with my Musique reare*
>    *a Colledge here,*
> *Of tunefull* Augures
>
>         .    .    .    .
>
> *Great* Mars *too, on these nights,*
>    *hath added* Salian *rites.*
>    *Yond, yond afarre,*
> *They closed in their Temple are.* . . . .
>
>                      (ll. 324-36)

Such a conception, although in keeping with James's peace policy, may perhaps be an echo of, or may perhaps have been confirmed by, Jonson's reading portions of Cicero's *De Divinatione* or Varro's *De Lingua Latina;* for both authors mention the college of augurs and the Salii within a single short passage.[85]   Varro and Cicero were cited by Charles Stephanus,[86] and Cicero's works are the most frequently cited authorities in the section of Robert Stephanus' *Thesaurus* which deals with "Augur" and related words.   The *De Divinatione,* moreover, was singled out as an authoritative study by Charles Stephanus.   Consequently, in view of Jonson's practice in handling some of his mythological citations, it is not surprising to find that in gloss *m,* Jonson's incomplete reference to "*Tull. lib.* I, Optimus Augur" is a reference to *De Divinatione,* I, 3.   Also in the same gloss, immediately preceding this reference to the *De Divinatione* with its brief quotation, Jonson cites another work singled out by Charles Stephanus, namely, Livy, I.[87]   Similarly, in his gloss on the Salii, gloss (n), Jonson's last citation and quotation of authority is the eighth book of Virgil's *Æneid:*

. . . *& Virg. Æneid lib.* 8.   Tum Salij ad Cantus incensa altaria circum Populeis adsunt evincti tempora ramis.

And Charles Stephanus' last citation of authority in his article on the

Salii is also the eighth book of the *Æneid*. Even more revealing is the passage that immediately precedes Jonson's citation of Vigil:

*Salius,* ὑμνωδὸς, *vet. gloss, & Pacuvi.* Pro Imperio sic Salisubsulus vestro excubet Mars . . . .

The authority cited by Charles Stephanus, also just before the citation of Virgil, runs as follows: "Vocantur etiam Salisubsuli a Catullo Epigram. 17. ad Coloniam." Robert Stephanus under *Salii* also cites Virgil and Catullus. Had Jonson turned to a current edition of Catullus, such as the one known to have been in his library,[88] he would have found in two of the commentaries upon the poem "Ad Coloniam" the possibly spurious line attributed to Pacuvius which he quotes, but with no mention of Catullus. From such commentaries likewise he could have derived the information (*Salius,* ὑμνωδὸς, *vet. gloss.*) which he gives in his note before citing Pacuvius and Virgil.[89]   Gloss (t) on "Auspice" agrees verbatim with a passage in Festus:

*Auspicium ab ave specienda.   Paul.   Nam quod nos cum præpositione dicimus ASPICIO, apud veteres sine præpositione SPICIO dicebatur.*[90]

Festus is the first authority cited in the *Thesaurus* under "Augur," and under "Auspicium," where the wording of Jonson's gloss can also be found, save that "Paul" and the phrase "sine præpositione" do not appear, while "inquit Festus" is added before "ab Ave."   Also in Robert Stephanus' *Thesaurus* the following note on the dove appears under the heading "Augurium":

Bene autem a columbis Æneae datur augurium, & Veneris filio et regi. Nam ad reges pertinet columbarum augurium: quia nunquam solae sunt, sicut nec reges quidem.   Haec Servius in illud libro 6.   Æneidos.

This note may have been the source for the lines

> The (ʳ) bird that brings
> Her Augurie alone to Kings,
> The Dove, hath flowne,

(ll. 372-74)

or rather it may have directed Jonson to Servius, where he found the passage he copied for gloss (r):

| JONSON | SERVIUS |
|---|---|
| *Columbæ auguria non nisi regibus dant; quia nunquam singulæ volant: sicut Rex nunquam solus incedit.* | . . . ut columbae non nisi regibus dant, quia nunquam singulae volant, sicut rex numquam solus incedit.[91] |

In view of Jonson's use of current reference works for mythological information and in view of his utilizing the volume singled out by the *Dictionarium* as an excellent recent authority on ancient augury, the correspondence between the authorities cited by Charles and Robert Stephanus and those cited by Jonson is, we believe, too consistent here, and in his mythological particulars, to be solely coincidental.

Once again Jonson apparently shows an indebtedness to entries in the lexicons which were utilized in the academic discipline of the age. The more specialized treatises that were frequently noted in the "concise bibliographies" of the dictionaries and the compilations by Charles and Robert Stephanus provided him with a storehouse of information. When Jonson wrote his first court masque, he probably turned to Charles Stephanus' *Dictionarium Historicum* soon after learning that "it was her Maiesties will" to have the principal actresses *"Black-mores* at first." The procedure he followed then, he apparently found useful when seventeen years later he approached the end of his masque-making career. As a learned poet he sensibly took advantage of the labors of preceding scholars. Thus in one sense the erudition displayed by *The Masque of Augurs,* for example, is less extraordinary than it might appear at first glance. Anyone with a reading knowledge of Latin and with five current reference works might have produced such learned particulars. Yet, paradoxically, Jonson's courtly spectacles are, in another sense, both "extraordinary" and "erudite." A few details from *The Masque of Augurs,* to preserve our example, cannot be explained by Jonson's use of the scholarly works mentioned above.[92] Even more important, no one other than Jonson so obviously and so carefully bothered to provide learned particulars for a "transitory" device.

Of all Jonson's dramas, only *Cynthia's Revels* shows striking similarities to his masques and entertainments. In the catastrophe of the play, the author has embodied two masques which are related closely to mythological material appearing earlier in the drama. Composed before Jonson devoted his energies to amusing and edifying the court of James I, *Cynthia's Revels* was produced by the children of Queen Elizabeth's Chapel, probably very late in 1600. Like his transitory devices, it, too, may have been designed for performance at Court. In the play, certainly, Jonson addressed the Queen and the center of the kingdom almost as clearly as he dedicated the drama to Camden.[93] It seems particularly suitable, therefore, to close the present discussion with the work whereby Jonson paid tribute to the pupil of Cooper and to the master who at one time supervised his academic training.

Even a brief summary of the course of the action makes clear the purpose and the structure of *Cynthia's Revels*.  In the first act the principal characters are introduced and the terminus of the action is stated (the "solemne revells" proclaimed by Cynthia which she "will descend to grace").  The theme of the play is broached by Echo's lamentation beside the Fountain of Self-love and is reinforced by the Senecan philosophy of Crites' soliloquy with which the act ends.

> O vanitie,
> How are thy painted beauties doted on,
> By light, and emptie ideots! how pursu'de
> With open and extended appetite!
> How they doe sweate, and run themselues from breath,
> Rais'd on their toes, to catch thy ayrie formes,
> Still turning giddie, till they reele like drunkards,
>
> .     .     .
>
> O how despisde and base a thing is a man,
> If he not striue t'erect his groueling thoughts
> Aboue the straine of flesh!  But how more cheape
> When, euen his best and vnderstanding part,
>
> .     .     .
>
> Floates like a dead drown'd bodie, on the streame
> Of vulgar humour, mixt with commonst dregs?
> I suffer for their guilt now, and my soule
> (Like one that lookes on ill-affected eyes)
> Is hurt with meere intention on their follies.
> Why will I view them then? my sense might aske me:
> Or ist a raritie, or some new obiect,
> That straines my strict obseruance to this point?
> O would it were, therein I could affoord
> My spirit should draw a little neere to theirs,
> To gaze on nouelties: so vice were one.
> Tut, she is stale, ranke, foule, and were it not
> That those (that woo her) greet her with lockt eyes,
>
> .     .     .
>
> Shee would betray, her loth'd and leprous face,
> And fright th'enamor'd dotards from themselues:
> But such is the peruersenesse of our nature,
> That if we once but fancie leuitie,
>           . . . yet will our muffled thought
> Choose rather not to see it, then auoide it:
> And if we can but banish our owne sense,

We act our mimicke trickes with that free licence,
That lust, that pleasure, that securitie,
As if we practiz'd in a paste-boord case,
And no one saw the motion, but the motion.
Well, checke thy passion, lest it grow too lowd:
"While fooles are pittied, they waxe fat, and proud.
                                              (1.5. 24-66)

The tenor of the speech clearly reminds one of passages in Seneca's *Naturalis Quaestiones* (I, prologus 5) and the *Epistles* (lix, 15).[94]

The entire second act is built around satirical sketches of the foolish courtiers, sketches which are divided by Mercury's eulogistic description of Crites (2. 3. 123-45). The act ends with the pages leaving to fetch the water of Self-love; but before they cross the stage, Cupid foretells the punishment of the vapid courtiers and points out that although Folly has thrust them into the center of the kingdom, they never appear in Cynthia's presence.

They are in her court (Mercvrie) but not as starres, these neuer come in the presence of Cynthia. The *Nymphs* that make her traine, are the diuine Arete, Timè, Phronesis, Thavma, and others of that high sort. These are priuately brought in by Moria in this licentious time, against her knowledge: and (like so many meteors) will vanish, when shee appeares. (2. 4. 105-11)

A certain balance between the good and the bad female courtiers, which is indicated in the preceding speech, runs as follows: Arete (Virtue), Timè (Honor), Phronesis (Good Sense), Thauma (Wonder) as against Philautia (Self Love), Argurion (Money), Phantaste (Fancy), Gelaia (Laughter). To the latter group should be added Moria (Folly), who has brought in such courtly female vices. Jonson also indicates a similar balance among the male courtiers: Crites (Judicious), Chrestus (Good), Euthus (Honest), Phronimus (Prudent) as against Amorphus (Deformed), Hedon (Pleasure), Anaides (Impudence), Asotus (Wasteful). As the names indicate, Jonson is concerned less with the virtues and vices of noble character than with those of the "body of *complement*" (5.9. 9), that is, those of good breeding or good manners in action and speech.[95] Of the good courtiers, three of the men are mentioned only (3.3. 18-9), and indeed only Crites and Arete have speaking parts. The emphasis, befitting a comical satire, is upon the presentation of folly and its final purge.

From the beginning of the third act until the catastrophe Jonson consequently continues to develop his satire upon absurd perversities of courtiers:

satire upon the pastimes of the vapid group, their parlor games and their contest in courtship (3.1 and 5; 4. 2 and 3) and satire upon their criticism and "groping" of one another (4.1 and throughout scenes 2. 3. 4). Although the major additions in the Folio version of the play occur in these sections, they in no way change the basic structure. Indeed they may represent material originally in Jonson's manuscript but left out for performance at Court on January 6, 1601. For the most part they sustain the satire on the court and italicize matter already noted by the dramatist, just as 5. 1 (Folio) repeats the praise of Crites and again serves notice of the punishment to be given courtly vice.[96] The stupidity of the gulls' actions in the fourth act is exceeded only by the complete fatuity of their subsequent bouts (5. 2, 3, and 4); for at the end of the fourth act, they have drunk water from the Fountain of Self-love.

Before drinking of the Fountain, the foolish courtiers have "groped" one another and have censured Crites (3. 2) and Arete; but once drunk with self-love, Amorphus refers to Cynthia herself as "humorous" (4. 5. 86), and the women's immediate reaction to the water is that they would not change places with that goddess (ll. 32-5). In contrast, for example, Philautia had earlier expressed a wish for "a little more command, and soueraignetie" (4. 1. 161 ff.). This self-satisfaction continues so that in 5.10 the courtiers compare themselves favorably with Cynthia:[97]

Amo. Cynthia (by my bright soule) is a right exquisite, and splendidious lady; yet Amorphus, I thinke, hath seene more fashions, I am sure more countries: but whether I haue, or not, what neede wee gaze on Cynthia, that haue our selfe to admire?

Pha. O, excellent Cynthia! yet if Phantaste sate where shee doo's, and had such a tire on her head (for attire can doe much) I say no more—but goddesses are goddesses, and Phantaste is as shee is! (ll. 42-50)

In other words, by the time of the masques (5. 7, 9, and 10) the gulls' perversity, instead of having been abated when Mercury and Crites made game of them (5. 1 and 4) has grown into a presumptuousness which belies their place, as indicated earlier by Cupid, and which allows them to masque themselves as virtues in the center of the kingdom and before Cynthia herself.

In contrast to such a presumptuous fatuity, in Crites, Jonson has been continuing his exposition of true virtue which he continually reminds the audience will be rewarded by the goddess (e.g., 3.4. 87-107; 4.5. 1-17; 5.4. 616-52; 5.5. particularly ll. 56-72). For Crites has many of the virtues of the Senecan man.  He throws off slanderous detraction with "a careless smile."

> What should I care what euery dor doth buzze
> In credulous eares?  it is a crowne to me,
> That the best iudgements can report me wrong'd;
> Them lyars; and their slanders impudent.
> Perhaps (vpon the rumour of their speeches)
> Some grieued friend will whisper to me, Crites,
> Men speake ill of thee; so they be ill men,
> If they spake worse, 'twere better: for of such
> To be disprais'd, is the most perfect praise.
> What can his censure hurt me, whom the world
> Hath censur'd vile before me?  If good Chrestvs,
> Evthvs, or Phronimvs, had spoke the words,
> They would haue moou'd me, and I should haue call'd
> My thoughts, and actions, to a strict accompt
> Vpon the hearing
>
> .        .        .
>
> And I doe count it a most rare reuenge,
> That I can thus (with such a sweet neglect)
> Plucke from them all the pleasure of their malice.
> For that's the marke of all their inginous drifts,
> To wound my patience, howsoe're they seeme
> To aime at other obiects: which if miss'd,
> Their enui's like an arrow, shot vpright,
> That, in the fall, indangers their owne heads.
>
> (3. 3. 8-44)

The preceding soliloquy, for example, echoes Seneca's *De Contumelia* and *De Remediis Fortuitorum Liber,* as well as such works as the *De Ira,* the *De Contumelia,* and Plutarch's *How to Profit by Our Enemies.* Similarly, Mercury's description of Crites in 2. 3. 127 ff. reflects matter in Seneca's *De Ira, De Vita Beata,* and possibly in Cicero's *De Officiis:*[98]

MER.  Crites.  A creature of a most perfect and diuine temper.  One, in whom the humours and elements are peaceably met, without emulation of precedencie . . . in all, so composde & order'd, as it is cleare, *Nature* went about some ful worke, she did more then make a man, when she made him. His discourse is like his behauiour, vncommon, but not vnpleasing; hee is prodigall of neyther.  Hee striues rather to bee that which men call iudicious, then to bee thought so: and is so truly learned, that he affects not to shew it. Hee will thinke, and speake his thought, both freely: but as distant from deprauing another mans merit, as proclaiming his owne.  For his valour, tis such, that he dares as little to offer an iniurie, as receiue one.  In summe, he hath

a most ingenuous and sweet spirit, a sharp and season'd wit, a straight iudg-
ment, and a strong mind. *Fortune* could neuer breake him, nor make him lesse.
He counts it his pleasure, to despise pleasures, and is more delighted with
good deeds, then goods. It is a competencie to him that hee can bee vertuous.
He doth neyther couet, nor feare; hee hath too much reason to doe eyther: and
that commends all things to him.

    CVP. Not better than Mercvry commends him.

    MER. O, Cvpid, tis beyond my *deitie* to giue him his due prayses: I could
leaue my place in heauen, to liue among mortals, so I were sure to be no other
then he. (2.3. 123-49)

Indeed, when Mercury says that he would be willing to become mortal
if he were sure to be another Crites, he expresses the idea that the Stoic
*sapiens* is above mankind in general and on a level with the gods—an idea
particularly pertinent to the play in that it balances the perverseness of
the foolish courtiers' final presumption. Likewise particularly apt, in view
of the reasons for Cynthia's appearance, is Crites' soliloquy about the
*sapiens* being slandered by the vicious, for the goddess has proclaimed the
revels "in regard of some black and enuious slanders hourely breath'd
against her, for her diuine iustice on Acteon." Moreover, as Crites is im-
pervious to slander, so Cynthia continues to be "gracious to the good" but

vnto the proud,
Or the prophane, perhaps indeede austere. . . .
(5.11. 12-13)

    In portraying Crites, however, Jonson has added attributes of the
Renaissance courtier-poet to features of the Stoical *sapiens*. Crites is one
whom "the Mvses, and Minerva loue" (5. 6. 90). Aided by Phoebus and
Mercury (the god of song who presides over the Muses and the god of
rhetorical fluency), he devises the masques that bring about the solution
of the play. In the first of the masques, Philautia, flattering self-love,
appears as Storge, an *"allowable selfe-loue"*; Gelaia, a fatuous laughter,
appears as Aglaia, *"delectable and pleasant Conuersation"*; Phantaste, an
egotistical fancy, as Euphantaste, *"a well conceited Wittinesse"*; and Moria,
a folly that guards the preceding vices, as Apheleia, *"Simplicitie; without
folds, without pleights, without colour, without counterfeit: and (to speak
plainly) Plainenesse it selfe."* Argurion, after fainting, had vanished from
the play (4.3. 442-50) because of the actions of Asotus. The whole group
appears as the four virgin daughters of Queen Perfection; to them nothing
is more odious than "false pretexts" (5.7. 23), and they are presented by

Cupid disguised as Anti-Cupid (the Love of Virtue). In the second masque, Amorphus, a stupid deformity, appears as Eucosmos, "*neate,* and *elegant*"; Hedon, a fatuous pleasure, appears as Eupathes, a "*fine humour*" that "without excesse, can make vse of superfluitie"; Anaides, impudence, as Eutolmos, "*good audacitie*"; and Asotus, wastefulness, as Eucolos, a "*good nature*" that "imparteth not without respect, but yet without difficultie." They are presented by Mercury as the sons of Eutaxia (Good Order).[99] After the two groups dance, Cynthia justifies her treatment of Actaeon, asserts that she does not intend to strike a note which jars with the revels but that she notices

> and can take reuenge
> Of these calumnious, and lewd blasphemies
> (5.11. 32-33)

that have been circulated about her action. She then requests that the courtiers unmask so that

> we not mis-take your seuerall worths,
> Nor you our fauour . . . .
> (ll.46-47)

The play, consequently, clearly develops toward a situation wherein Cynthia, appearing at her appointed revels, whose masques are devised by Crites, to justify her action upon Actaeon, is confronted, on the one hand, by presumptuous and fatuous courtiers who are punished and, on the other, by a poetical *sapiens* who has been slandered by the vicious courtiers but who is rewarded by Cynthia because of her love for virtue. Because their vices arise from qualities which through discipline may become virtues— just as the Aristotelian vice is an excess of that quality which in moderation becomes a virtue—the guilty are to be corrected, not destroyed, and an appropriate penance is devised by Crites.

In a manner to be typical of his later masques and entertainments, Jonson has manipulated all of the preceding material—allegorical and mythological figures, Renaissance concepts of courtly conduct, Stoic doctrine, his own and his fellow humanists' belief in the importance of poetry and the poet—so that the entire production not only sports with follies but also is applicable to the center of the kingdom. Thus Cynthia, addressing the judicious man, ends the play proper with a conventional maxim on the conduct of princes.[100]

And for this seruice of discouerie
Perform'd by thee, in honor of our name,
We vow to guerdon it with such due grace,
As shall become our bountie, and thy place.
"Princes, that would their people should doe well,
"Must at themselues begin, as at the head;
"For men, by their example, patterne out
"Their imitations, and reguard of lawes:
"A vertuous *Court* a world to vertue drawes.

(5. 11. 165-73)

In Jonson's masques and entertainments some relatively detailed aspects
of the tradition of Neo-platonic doctrine in which Ficino wrote appear frequently,[101] and indeed a case might be made out for the reflection in
*Cynthia's Revels* of Bruno's *De Gli Eroici Furori*. In the second part of
the Italian's work Diana appears as "the splendor of intelligible species,"
the goal of those who search for truth. If they do not see Amphitrite, "the
source of all number, of all species, of all reasons, which is the monad" in
absolute light, they do see the monad "in its seed" or in "its image." That
is, they do see Diana, the one who "is the same entity," "in which burns
the sun and the splendours of the higher nature, according to which, unity
is both the generated and the generating, the producer and the produced."
Thus a follower of Diana boasts that he is her prey and is happy as a captive and a subject. He envies no man for "there is none that can have
more," nor does he envy any god for he has "that species which is impossible to be obtained by an inferior nature. . . ."[102] And throughout Bruno's
explication of his poem, but particularly in the first portion of it, there is
emphasis upon the separation of those who seek after the truth from those
engaged in the vain pursuit of trifles. Bruno's work was dedicated to
Sidney and, of course, the conclusion to the dedication excludes from the
author's anti-Petrarchan tirade all women connected with Sir Philip.
They are of a celestial substance; they are divine nymphs reigned over by
a divine Diana. If one were searching for parallels to Cynthia's appearance
in Jonson's plays, one might also point to the way in which the moon according to Ficino might represent justice, and be "feminine inasmuch as
because of its inherent innocence it does no one any wrong, but masculine
inasmuch as it allows no harm to be brought to others, and with more
severe censure frowns upon unjust men."[103] Similarly just as the masques
and entertainments may reflect physical interpretations of a myth, one

might suggest that a portion of Cynthia's speech immediately following the
unmasking does likewise:

> In stead of med'cines, haue we maladies?
> And such impostumes, as Phantaste is,
> Grow in our palace, we must lance these sores,
> Or all will putrifie.
>
> (ll. 66-69)

Such a turn of thought, aside from reflecting the conventional idea of the
lancing, purging, or curative powers of satire, might reflect the medical
importance of the moon in effecting any beneficial influence on man—a
matter discussed in Ficino's writings and a medical commonplace of the
period, particularly when critical days, that is, days for lancing or blood-
letting, were considered.[104]

The preceding associations, although they do exist in the masques and
entertainments, may not be apposite to *Cynthia's Revels*. At least they are
not demonstrable, for the drama unlike the courtly spectacles contains no
gloss to elucidate the poet's concepts and cite his authorities. The prime
attribute of the ruler was conventionally justice and here, in contrast to
some of the masques and entertainments, the ruler-Cynthia-Elizabeth relationship is all that is essential for understanding Jonson's purpose in writing a drama in the year 1600—a drama, probably for Court performance,
to be produced by the boys of Elizabeth's Chapel. Jonson's utilization of
classic myth in *Cynthia's Revels* is, however, particularly apposite to our
purpose. Certain "morals" inculcated by some of the myths referred to
by the dramatist seem to be reflected in the play and do accord with its total
design. And in such a discussion of Jonson's technique, the basic lexicons
of the period must be given their appropriate place.

The material which is of particular interest concerns Echo, Narcissus,
Niobe, and Actaeon. Jonson's use of Cynthia, Cupid, and Mercury is easily
understood. They are major characters and their appearance necessarily
is well-integrated with the rest of the drama. The function of Cynthia as
virgin ruler is obvious; Jonson's conception, of course, was based on matter
conventional to the age and well-known to modern critics. Her actions
and her closing maxim, as noted above, reflect precepts conventional to
treatises *de regimine principum*.[105] Cupid and Mercury appear throughout
the play in rôles comparable to those of Brainworm or Macilente in Jonson's
earlier comedies, and for such a conception of the figures Jonson may well
have been indebted to Lucian. That Crites, embodying certain aspects of

the Stoic *sapiens,* should be beloved of Minerva, the goddess of wisdom, develops an obvious commonplace, as does the fact that Apollo and Mercury aid the judicious man when he becomes a courtier-poet. Jonson's use of Cupid in the first masque as "Anteros, or *Loues enemie"* repeats matter that can be found in the mythological treatises of the period and that is embodied, for example, in Alciati. As the one who introduces figures representing courtly female virtues, even though they are vices disguised, the Anteros of *Cynthia's Revels* reflects the *"amor virtutis"* that overcomes and binds Eros and destroys Love's weapons.[106] The relationship of Echo, Narcissus, Niobe, and Actaeon to the development of the play is not so obvious. Some of the expositions of their myths, however, illumine lines in the drama and indicate how Jonson probably conceived of these mythological figures as integrated with the rest of the composition. Indeed some of the moral interpretations of their myth are closely related to the ethical maxims Jonson attempts to inculcate by the entire drama.

In Cartari, Echo's wasting away for love of Narcissus is mentioned, as is her abode in desolate places, but she appears primarily as one loved by Pan. Though somewhat briefer, Gyraldi's account is similar. The Echo and Narcissus myths had been combined by Ovid (*Met.,* III, 339-510), and thus Comes in his interpretation neglects Echo for Narcissus. Elsewhere, however, interpretations of Echo can be found that are developed with a fair amount of detail. Boccaccio writes in a tradition embodied in the early fourteenth-century *Ovide Moralisé.* In this moralization of Ovid, attributed to Chretien Legouais de Saint-Maure, emphasis is placed upon Echo's being spurned by Narcissus; thus the nymph may be said to represent a virtue. To the author of *Ovide Moralisé,* she is "bone renomee" (III, 1465-1519). To Boccaccio she is true fame spurned by those who are entranced with their own glory reflected in the waters of worldly delight. Thus fame, being spurned, soon dies, and the reputation acquired otherwise fades as quickly as a flower.

Nam per echo: quae nil dicit nisi post dictum: ego intelligo famam: quae vnvmquemque mortalium diligit tanquam rem: per quam consistet. Hanc multi fugiunt et paruipendunt: et in aquis .i. in mundanis delitiis: non aliter quam aqua labilis seipsos .i. suam gloriam intuentur: et adeo a suis voluptatibus capiuntur: vt spreta fama post paulum tanquam non fuissent: moriuntur: et si forsan aliquid nominis superest in florem vertitur: qui mane purpureus et splendens est. sero autem languidus factus marcescit: et in nihilum soluitur. Sic et huiusmodi ad sepulchrum usque aliquid videntur habere fulgoris. sepulchro autem clauso euanescit: et in obliuionem perditur vna cum nomine.[107]

The version of Ovid's *Metamorphoses* written by Petrus Berchorius (Thomas Wallys) and printed in 1484, 1493, 1509, etc., has an interpretation greatly different from that found in Boccaccio. Instead of symbolizing a worthy object—true fame for which the worldly have little regard—Echo symbolizes a vice. She represents flatterers who repeat the words of those about them, or quarrelsome and troublesome women and servants who always wish to have the last word, or scoffers who augment or repeat derisively what is not favorable or pleasing to themselves.

Dic quod echo significat adulatores qui et montes i. prelatos; siluas, i. religiosos: flumina, i. seculares et delicatos frequentant, et circa ipsos resonant, et clamant: si enim contingat aliquid ab aliquo dici statim solent ad verba ipsius respondere: et verbum ejus tanquam benedictum replicare. . . . Vel dic quod tales echo sunt quedam litigiose et brigose mulieres, vel etiam quidam servitores queruli qui vltimum verbum semper volunt habere: et ad omnia que dicuntur a maritis atque Dominis respondere. Etsi ab eis reprehenduntur semper murmurant. . . . Vel dic contra derisores: qui verba aliorum deridendo referunt et resumunt ipsique si que sibi placentia vel placida non audiunt sepe multiplicant atque dicunt.[108]

The interpretation found in Berchorius is close to that in Charles Stephanus. After a brief résumé of the myth as found in Ovid, the *Dictionarium Historicum* reports that Echo signifies an empty boasting and thus she is fittingly represented as loving Narcissus. Echo is to Narcissus, as Boasting (Iactantia) is to Self-love (Philautia).

Echo allegorice significat iactantiam, haec spreta mutatur in sonum, hoc est, in rem inanem. Narcissus vero significat hominem sibi mire placentem, ac supra modum sui amantem: quod ex ipsius verbis intelligitur. Sic enim de seipso apud Ouid.

> *Iste ego sum sensi: nec me mea fallit imago*
> *Vror amore mei.*

Recte igitur Echo amat Narcissum, i. iactantiam φιλαυτίαν.

This last interpretation of the myth is the one chosen, for example, by Georgius Sabinus.[109]

Echo's symbolizing a reprehensible talkativeness is clearly reflected in *Cynthia's Revels*. Jonson modifies the moralization, however, in accordance with his plan for Diana's appearance, by having Echo censure the goddess severely. Thus he links his Echo materials with the myth of Actaeon, for Diana is to appear during the revels and defend herself against "some black and enuious slanders hourely breath'd against her, for her diuine iustice on

Actaeon" and "to intimate how farre shee treads such malicious imputations beneath her" (1.1.91-103). Criticism of Diana because of Actaeon's punishment is based upon the *Metamorphoses* (III, 253-55), wherein the goddess' treatment of the hunter is said to have caused "common opinion to fluctuate, some considering her more cruel than was just, others calling her act worthy of her austere virginity." Upon such a basis, Jonson represents Echo as considering Cynthia "more cruel than just." In spite of Mercury's attempt to silence her, she criticizes the goddess much more severely than do Philautia, Phantaste, and others later in the play. Diana, indeed, is proud, harsh, and vengeful.

> MER. Forgoe thy vse, and libertie of tongue,
> And thou maist dwell on earth, and sport thee there.
> Ecc. Here yong Acteon fell, pursu'de, and torne
> By Cynthia's wrath (more eager, then his hounds)
> And here, (ay me, the place is fatall) see
> The weeping Niobe, translated hither
> From *Phrygian* mountaines: and by Phœbe rear'd
> As the proud trophæe of her sharpe reuenge.
> MER.    Nay, but heare.
> Ecc. But here, O here, the *Fountayne* of *selfe-Louε*
> In which Latona, and her careless *Nymphs,*
> (Regardles of my sorrowes) bathe themselues
> In hourely pleasures. MER. Stint thy babling tongue;
> Fond Eccho, thou prophan'st the grace is done thee:
> So idle worldings (meerely made of voice)
> Censure the powers aboue them. Come, away,
> Ioue calls thee hence, and his will brookes no stay.
> Ecc. O, stay: I haue but one poore thought to clothe
> In ayrie garments, and then (faith) I goe.
> Henceforth, thou treacherous, and murthering spring,
> Be euer call'd the *Fountayne* of *selfe-Loue.* . . .
>
> (1. 2. 80-100)

The second and third of the interpretations in Berchorius certainly agree with the conception of the entire passage just quoted, which Jonson has cast into the repetitive form of the conventional Echo song. Echo's failure to be silenced by Mercury and her censure of Diana accord with the fact that the nymph may represent troublesome and quarrelsome women and inferiors as well as derisive speakers. Moreover, Charles Stephanus' interpretation of Echo as "iactantiam, *haec spreta mutatur in sonum, hoc est, in rem inanem"* may also be reflected in Mercury's "Stint thy babling tongue" and in his pointing out the worthlessness of such talk.

Jonson, indeed, seems to have been familiar with the various interpretations of the Echo myth and to have attempted to mold them into a coherent whole. Similarly, he has centralized the action in Gargaphie by bringing Niobe's statue thither; he has linked the Echo with the Actaeon myth by means of the nymph's talkative censoriousness; he has identified the water in which Narcissus saw himself with the water in which Diana was bathing when seen by Actaeon—the water that Echo christens the Fountain of Self-love (1. 2. 15, 27-29, 89-92). Furthermore, although the interpretation of Echo as a virtue (Boccaccio's true fame) is antithetical to that of Echo as a vice (Berchorius' talkative or derisive speakers), the interpretations can be synthesized if Echo describes herself as being excellent—that is, if both interpretations are put within the framework of a third moralization which emphasizes the conception that Echo-Iactantia dotes upon Narcissus-Philautia. Although such a consideration may seem forced, one must remember that the Renaissance writer and reader prized intricacy of invention, that Cordatus and Mitis explain in an equally ingenious manner some of the actions and speeches in *Every Man Out of His Humour,* and that Jonson's glosses on his masques and entertainments point out interpretations that are much more intricate. Consider, then, Echo's statement that

> Had Eccho but beene priuate with thy [Narcissus'] thoughts,
> Shee would haue dropt away her selfe in teares,
> Till shee had all turn'd water, that in her,
> (As in a truer glasse) thou mightst haue gaz'd,
> And seene thy beauties by more kind reflection:
> But selfe-loue neuer yet could looke on truth,
> But with bleard beames . . . .
>
> (1. 2. 31-37)

That Echo can speak of herself as "truth," whose tears would provide a "truer glasse" than the waters of the fountain in which Narcissus looked, may well be a reflection and a modification of the interpretation as found in Boccaccio, where the youth's spurning of Echo was said to represent the worldly and conceited man's turning from true fame to view himself in the waters of worldly delights. In the preceding lines, however, Echo is speaking—and speaking foolishly—as Mercury says. The situation which Jonson represents on the stage actually unites conflicting interpretations by modifying them in accordance with the moralization found in the *Dictionarium Historicum*. To sum up. Ovid says that Diana was censured by some for her punishment of Actaeon; the interpretations recorded by Berchorius provide the authority for Echo's being the derisive slanderer. The antithetical but more common interpretation found in Boccaccio also seems to be reflected in Echo's speeches. The moralization in the *Dictionarium Historicum,* however, makes the nymph symbolical of vain and empty boasting, which certainly accords, for example, with her considering herself "truth." She thus praises herself and derides others. Consequently when viewed against a background of current treatments of the myth, the speeches of Echo in *Cynthia's Revels* appear to be identical with Jonson's use of the other mythological elements so far considered. They are grounded upon Renaissance treatments of classic myth, and their author has handled his Echo story so that it broaches the theme of self-love in speeches which foreshadow the actions of those who later drink of the Fountain christened by the nymph. For our purposes, it is interesting to note that as part of the background surveyed above, one of the basic reference lexicons of the period provides the essential Iactantia-Philautia association. The account in the *Dictionarium Historicum* is the one with which Jonson's audience might be expected to be most familiar; it is one that Jonson seems to have known; and it is the one he seems to have emphasized.

In contrast with the treatment of Echo, the various interpretations of Narcissus do not differ greatly. The tragic result of his self-love was considered a warning to those who delight in the transitory glories of the world. Legouais, Berchorius, Comes, and emblem writers—all enlarge upon this interpretation. Alciati and Whitney, for example, place their emblems on Narcissus under "Philautia" and "Amor sui" respectively.[110] Comes notes that the myth is a warning to those who delight in corporeal forms, and that the dissolute and the proud are slowly but surely punished by God (IX, xvi). A similar but earlier exegesis in Legouais (III, 1504-1964) appears in Berchorius in a condensed but only slightly altered form. It is not good for one to know his own excellence in body, mind, or fortune; because of the intolerable pride likely to result, such a one will worship only transitory shades in the worldly fountain.[111] Boccaccio's interpretation of the Echo-Narcissus myth, it will be remembered, was very similar, as far as Narcissus alone was considered: the water in which he looked represented unsubstantial worldly delights in which those who gaze view only their own glory and soon pass away, leaving reputations as transitory as a flower. A brief exposition of this moralization also appears under "Narcissus" in the *Dictionarium Historicum,* with the additional information that the myth is a warning against an untimely assumption of wisdom. After the story in Ovid has been paraphrased, the entry runs as follows:

Sapienter ab Ouidio fingitur Nemesis, insolentiae & arrogantiae vindex, repetere poenas a Narcisso seipsum amante, vt suam ipsius vmbram admiretur. Diuinitus enim puniuntur sui amantes hac dementia, *vt etiam inscitiam suam esse sapientiam arbitrentur.* Mutatus in florem ostendit quam leuis et euanida sit inanis gloria mundi, et sero florescens *monet ne nimis mature et ante tempus sapere incipiamus,* neve nos aut nostra nimis amemus atque admiremur.

The preceding interpretation in the *Dictionarium Historicum* is again found, for example, in Sabinus' treatment of the myth, where it is given on the authority of the elder Winshemius.[112]

The interpretation of the Narcissus myth outlined above is clearly reflected in *Cynthia's Revels* when Echo laments Narcissus' fate:

> See, see, the mourning fount, whose springs weepe yet,
> Th' *vntimely fate* of that too beauteous boy,
> That *trophœe of selfe-loue,* and *spoile of nature,*
> Who (now transform'd into this drouping flowre)
> Hangs the repentant head, back from the streame,
> As if it wish'd, would I had neuer look'd
> In such a *flattering mirrour.*
>
>       . . . .
>
> Why did the gods giue thee a heau'nly forme,
> And *earthy thoughts, to make thee proud of it?*
> Why, doe I aske? Tis now the knowne disease
> That *beautie* hath, to beare too deepe a sense
> Of her owne *selfe-conceiued excellence.*
> O, *hadst thou knowne the worth of heau'ns rich gift,*
> *Thou wouldst haue turn'd it to a truer vse,*
> *And not (with staru'd, and couetous ignorance)*
> *Pin'd in continuall eying that bright gem,*
> The glance whereof to others had beene more,
> Then to thy *famisht mind the wide worlds store:*
> "So wretched is it to be *meerely rich.*
> Witness *thy youths deare sweets, here spent vntasted,*
> Like a faire taper, with his owne flame wasted
>                            (1.2. 23-53)

That Jonson meant Narcissus to symbolize self-love is obvious. The conventional interpretation that the waters in which Narcissus looked represent worldly delights is apparent in such phrases as "flattering mirrour" and "wide worlds store." In these waters the egotist sees his good fortune. The pride which results makes the self-lover, who was rich and fortunate by nature, worthy of punishment. Thus Jonson speaks of Narcissus as "the spoile of nature," or, as he expresses it in Echo's song, *"natures pride* is, now, a wither'd daffodill" (1. 2, 75). Indeed, Comes' warning against a delight in corporeal forms may be specifically reflected in the question, "Why did the gods giue thee a heau'nly forme, And earthy thoughts, to make thee proud of it?" Similarly when he composed the lines expressing the central thought of the passage quoted above, Jonson may have had in mind an interpretation of the Narcissus myth such as that in the *Dictionarium Historicum.* That Narcissus may represent a youthful bigotry which thinks its ignorance to be wisdom is apparently reflected in such lines and phrases as "Th'vntimely fate, of that too beauteous boy," "staru'd and couetous ignorance," "thy famisht mind," "So wretched is it to be meerely rich," "thy youths deare sweets, here spent vntasted," and the lines

> O, hadst thou knowne the worth of heau'ns rich gift,
> Thou wouldst haue turn'd it to a truer vse,
> And not (with staru'd, and couetous ignorance)
> Pin'd in continuall eying that bright gem. . . .

Once more, when Jonson's use of a myth is viewed in the light of its current treatments, the associations thereby provided relate it more closely to other features of the drama than does the unadorned theme of self-love. Echo's references to Narcissus accord with Jonson's treatment elsewhere of those fortunate but fatuous courtiers who are punished by a goddess and whose attributes with discipline might be virtues instead of vices. (*"Diuinitus enim puniuntur sui amantes hac dementia, vt etiam inscitiam suam esse sapientiam arbitrentur.* Mutatus in florem ostendit *quam leuis et euanida sit inanis gloria mundi,* et sero florescens *monet ne nimis mature et ante tempus sapere incipiamus,* neve nos aut nostra nimis amemus atque admiremur."—C. Stephanus.) Conventional exegeses of the Narcissus myth provide not only the obvious connection between Narcissus and egotism but also an interpretation of the waters into which the youth looked as well as an interpretation that apparently struck Jonson's humanistic mind—that is, that an untimely and immature assumption of wisdom results in a self-love that will be ultimately punished.  This last aspect of the conventional moralization was a feature of the entry in Charles Stephanus' *Dictionarium Historicum.*

Of Niobe very little need be said.  In *Cynthia's Revels* the derisive Echo includes her with Actaeon as an example of Diana's unjust austerity (1. 2. 84-7) ; and part of the courtiers' penance is to "March to your seuerall homes by Niobes stone, And offer vp two teares apiece thereon" (5. 11. 144-45).  Niobe's connection with any moralization against self-love is obvious.  That her *hubris* called for vengeance from the gods is clearly expressed by Ovid (*Met.,* VI, 165-315) ; consequently it was only natural that moralizers should fit Niobe into the schemata of virtues and vices and, among other interpretations, should see in her, as in Narcissus, a divine punishment of pride and temerity.[113]  This moralization amply explains and substantiates Jonson's linking Niobe's fate with the Fountain of Self-love.

But what connection has the Actaeon myth with the moralizations so far discussed?  Jonson himself points to the answer.  As we have seen, he utilized Echo's representing a derisive talkativeness to introduce the Actaeon myth; and that he saw a further relationship between the mythological materials so far discussed and the myth of Actaeon is indicated, for example, by Cynthia's speech in which she defends herself for her justice upon him.  Early in the speech Cynthia says:

> For so Actaeon, by presuming farre,
> Did (to our griefe) incurre a fatall doome;
> And so, swolne Niobe (comparing more
> Then he presum'd) was trophæed into stone
>                                   (5.11. 14-7).

Echo's derision of Cynthia, as we have seen, apparently manifests an ignorant presumption, that of querulous and derisive boasting.  Narcissus' fate resulted from a self-love which likewise produced an unwarranted assurance, an excessive concern with worldly inanities and an immature assumption of wisdom or judgment.  Niobe's fate referred to by Cynthia was also due to self-love and is again the result of an unlicensed effrontery.  As Cynthia's defense of herself indicates, Jonson must have had in mind a comparable presumption on the part of Actaeon.  And in the lines which follow the passage just quoted, Jonson obviously is referring to something more than Ovid's "mere mischance," whereby "with unsure footsteps" the hunter surprised Diana and her nymphs bathing :[114]

> But are we therefore judged too extreme?
> Seemes it no crime, *to enter sacred bowers,*
> *And hallowed places, with impure aspect,*
> *Most lewdly to pollute?* Seemes it no crime,
> To braue a *deitie?*
>
>                    (5.11. 18-22)

Most critics of the drama see in these lines only a reference to Essex's "tactless audacities" of September 1599, when he burst into the Queen's chamber.[115] At any time from the mid-sixteenth century, however, a person using the common libraries of a school for the history of proper nouns, or anyone turning to the basic Latin thesaurus of the period, would have encountered under "Actaeon," material that approximates Jonson's words at least as closely as do Essex's "tactless audacities." As part of his entry for Actaeon, Robert Stephanus had written

Actaeonum fabulantur a suis canibus discerptum, *quod Dianae concubitum,* quum venaretur in montibus *juxta templum* sitis, *appetierit.* Alii putant id ei accidisse, quod se illi Actaeon praetulerit in venandi arte.

The *Thesaurus* also gives the source for this statement as "Diod. lib. 5, cap. 14." The passage in Diodorus Siculus to which Robert Stephanus refers his readers is now numbered IV. 81. 3-5 and runs as follows:

After this, they say, Aristaeus went to Boeotia, where he married one of the daughters of Cadmus, Antonoê, to whom was born Actaeon, who, as the myths relate, was torn to pieces by his own dogs. The reason for this bad turn of fortune of his, as some explain it, was that, presuming upon his dedication to Artemis of the first-fruits of his hunting, he purposed to consummate the marriage with Artemis at the temple of the goddess, but according to others, it was because he represented himself as superior to Artemis in skill as a hunter. But it is not incredible that it was for both these reasons that the goddess became angry; for whether Actaeon made an improper use of the spoils of his hunting to satisfy his own desire upon her who has no part in marriage, or whether he was so bold as to assert that as a hunter he was to be preferred above her before whom even gods withdraw from rivalry in the chase, all would agree that the goddess was justified in having become indignant at him. And, speaking generally, we may well believe that, when he had been changed into the form of one of the animals which he was wont to hunt, he was slain by the dogs which were accustomed to prey upon the other wild beasts.

That the preceding version of the Actaeon myth underlies Jonson's lines seems very probable. Notice, for example, the similarity between Jonson's "with impure aspect most lewdly to pollute" and the lexicon's "quod Dianae concubitum . . . appetierit," between Jonson's "sacred bowers, And hallowed places" and the dictionary's *juxta templum,* drawn from the passage in Diodorus. Jonson may have encountered this version of the myth in reading Diodorus; some years after writing *Cynthia's Revels* he owned a copy of the 1604 edition of the *Bibliothecæ Historicæ,* which gave the Greek text, as edited by Stephanus, with a Latin translation. He may have noticed the preceding material if he turned to the *Thesaurus* to refresh his memory. Or he may have remembered such details from his school days. In Robert Stephanus, Jonson and his contemporaries would have encountered also a summary of the Ovidian fable, an interpretation of the myth, the pertinent passage in Diodorus cited and neatly summarized, and further references to the legend.

Jonson, of course, may have been struck with the application of the Actaeon myth to Essex's disgrace during the year from September, 1599, to late in 1600. Just as he found that the elder Seneca's words about Haterius paralleled his own opinion of Shakespeare, he may have perceived a striking parallel to contemporary events in the myths, which supposedly embodied the wisdom of the ancients. That Ovid's words about the grumbling of some against Diana could be applied to any popular clamor in favor of Essex would be, to Jonson, but one more string to the bow with which he continuously waged the battle of the scholar; but if so, it seems to have been a string used only briefly, if at all. The fundamental purpose of *Cynthia's Revels* is not to defend Elizabeth or criticize Essex but to lash folly and to promote sound ethical maxims—maxims similar to those inculcated by the Niobe myth, by interpretations of the Echo-Narcissus myth, and also, as we shall see, by current moralizations of the Actaeon story.

Three interpretations of the Actaeon myth seem to have been particularly popular during the late sixteenth and early seventeenth centuries. The one which was apparently the most popular, however, the so-called euhemeristic one, does not appear in *Cynthia's Revels.*[116] The other two were conveniently at hand in Charles Stephanus' *Dictionarium.* After a brief résumé of Ovid's treatment of the myth and an account of Fulgentius' interpretation, the dictionary article refers to the Actaeon in Apollonius, states that the Ovidian myth is better known, and gives the following interpretations:

[1] Haec fabula nos ad beneficia in bonos viros conferenda adhortatur, ac retrahit a bene merendo de ingratis, qui saepius pro acceptis beneficiis simultatis causas aucupantur, seque vel quauis leuissima de causa iratos fingunt, vt sic deletum appareat quicquid in eos collatum est. . . . [2] Monemur praeterea ne simus curiosi in rebus ad nos minime pertinentibus, quoniam multis perniciosum fuit res arcanas aliorum cognouisse, aut principum, ciuitatum, summorumque virorum, aut Dei praecipue quorum vel aliqua minima suspicio arcanorum conscium facile potest opprimere.

Both of the dictionary's interpretations were taken from Comes; the second practically verbatim, the first from the following discussion:

Per hanc igitur fabulam nos ad beneficia in viros bonos conferenda adhorta-bantur, ac retrahebant a benemerendo de ingratis & immemoribus acceptorum hominibus: quod etiam videtur significasse Theocritus in eo versu: τρέφε χύνας ὥϛε φάργωντι *nutri canes vt te edant.* Omnium sane beneficiorum optimum est illud, quod apud virum bonum & memorem & gratum collocatur: quod vero in maleficum & ingratum collatum est, omnino male collatum fuit: quippe cum improbi homines, ne parem gratiam referre cogantur, *Saepius pro acceptis beneficiis simultatis causas aucupentur, seque vel quauis leuissima de causa iratos fingant, vt sic deletum appareat quidquid in eos collatum sit.* Vt prudentiores igitur essemus in conferendis beneficiis, ne honori, facultatibus, vitaeque nostrae insidiatores nostris sumptibus aleremus, rationem conferen-dorum beneficiorum nos antiqui docuerunt: quippe cum beneficium viro bono-facere, sit prope accipere, atque haec nonnulla pars est iustitiae, vt traditum est in officiis.[117]

Strictly speaking, the two interpretations are antithetical. In the first, Actaeon represents the victim of ingratitude; in the second, he stands for the overly curious who concern themselves with things which pertain to illustrious men, princes, or gods. Mythographers, however, as our discussion of the Fates indicates,[118] did not attempt necessarily to unify all aspects of a myth; they were interested primarily in the morals to be derived from various aspects of the narrative or of the figures involved. If they were acute enough, they might perceive in one myth a number of maxims that were conventional and appropriate to their world and suited to various readers. The precepts *qua* precepts, of course, would not be incompatible. Thus the first moral noted above, which exhorts one to bestow benefits upon the good and withdraw them from the ungrateful, since the latter search for occasions to be angry and malicious and thereby destroy what has been given them, can exist concomitant with the maxim that one should refrain, particularly in matters political or divine, from an unwarranted concern with the affairs of great men or gods.

A number of the speeches in *Cynthia's Revels,* which are clearly developed in accordance with the design of the entire play, seem to indicate that Jonson knew the second interpretation of the Actaeon myth given above. Consider the speeches of Mercury and Cynthia, parts of which have been quoted elsewhere. Both speeches point out the presumptuousness of those who would pry into or judge of higher truths:

> Stint thy babling tongue;
> Fond Eccho, thou prophan'st the grace is done thee:
> So idle wordlings (meerely made of voice)
> Censure the powers above them.
>
> (1.2. 92-5)
>
> Let mortals learne
> To make religion of offending heauen;
> And not at all to censure powers diuine.
> To men, this argument should stand for firme,
> "A Goddesse did it, therefore it was good. . . .
>
> (5.11. 22-26)

The first of these quotations, it will be remembered, was the final portion of the passage in which Jonson utilized Echo's derision to link the Narcissus-Echo myth with the Actaeon myth. The second appeared immediately after Cynthia's reference to Actaeon's effrontery. As far as we know, only in such interpretations as those recorded by Comes and Charles Stephanus could Jonson have found the association of myth and maxim which he has here preserved—that is, the specific association of Actaeon with the admonition that men should not be too curious or presumptuous about the arcana of civil, political, or divine activity. Such effrontery, the moralizers point out, will probably be punished. And indeed before *Cynthia's Revels* ends the bad courtiers satirized throughout the play are punished at the command of Cynthia. They have compared themselves favorably to the goddess; and in addition they would attach themselves to the court in Cynthia's presence, that is, to the very center of the body politic. While they appear as virtues, the goddess says that she construes their actions as an "acceptable zeale"; for they are not those who censure her as too severe. To the good she is gracious; but to the proud or profane, perhaps indeed severe. Thus Actaeon and Niobe were punished. She for "com-

paring more Then he presum'd." She insists she is not cruel, but she
notices and can avenge calumnious and lewd blasphemies. Although she
now appears so that mortals may see her without injury, they should not
"challenge to themselues" immunity from the gods (5.11. 1-43). Thank-
ing the dancers again and asking them to unmask so that she may not mistake their "seuerall worths," she cries out angrily when she sees them,

> Is there so little awe of our disdaine,
> That any (vnder trust of their disguise)
> Should mixe themselues with others of the court?
> And (without forehead) boldly presse so far
> As farther none?

> (5.11.51-5)

Like the Actaeon of the interpreters, the bad courtiers would press into
affairs of state, of princes, and of gods. Their self-love has led them to a
presumption of the same kind as that of Niobe and Actaeon; but since it
is less in degree, it is punished much less severely.

Throughout the play, moreover, Jonson has been emphasizing the necessity to bestow benefits upon the worthy. During the catastrophe, Crites,
the Stoic *bonus vir,* is rewarded when the vicious courtiers are punished.
Consider, then, the interpretation in Comes and Charles Stephanus which
uses the myth of Actaeon to inculcate the maxim that benefits should be
bestowed upon good men and not upon the unworthy who wrong the bounty
done them. Although Jonson wisely attempts no strict application of this
moralization,[119] it apparently remained in his mind. Notice particularly
Diana's first speech:

> When hath Diana, like an enuious wretch,
> That glitters onely to his soothed selfe,
> Denying to the world, the precious vse
> Of hoorded wealth, with-held her friendly aide?
> Monthly, we spend our still-repaired shine,
> And not forbid our virgin-waxen torch
> To burne, and blaze, while nutriment doth last:
> That once consum'd, out of Ioves treasurie
> A new we take, and sticke it in our spheare,
> To giue the mutinous kind of wanting men,
> Their look't-for light. Yet, what is their desert?
> "Bountie is wrong'd, interpreted as due;
> "Mortalls can challenge not a ray, by right,
> "Yet doe expect the whole of Cynthias light.
> But if that *Deities* with-drew their gifts,
> For humane follies, what could men deserue

But death, and darknesse? It behooues the high,
For their owne sakes, to doe things worthily.
ARE. Most true, most sacred *Goddesse;* for the heauens
Receiue no good of all the good they doe
                                        (5.6. 19-38).

As Jonson develops this speech of Diana's from a typically anti-acquisitive sentiment, he merges the maxim that the ungrateful wrong the bounty done them with a reference to the moon's service to "Diana's foresters" and with Senecan precepts. Arete's speech, for example, is clearly taken from the *De Beneficiis* (4. 9. 1). But the precepts of Seneca are free from any association with Cynthia and Actaeon. Only in the moralizations of the myth does one find those figures associated with a maxim about wronged bounty in a manner very similar to the way in which Jonson's goddess speaks when she comes to defend her action against Actaeon. As for the rewarding of good men (*"Haec fabula nos ad beneficia in bonos viros conferenda adhortatur"*), the entire comical satire leads up to just such a conclusion. Thus Cynthia says when speaking of Crites,

Our selfe haue euer vowed to esteeme,
(As vertue, for it selfe, so) fortune base;
Who's first in worth, the same be first in place.
                                        (5.6. 105-7)

With his predilection for Stoicism and for the particular theme of the bestowal of benefits, it would be surprising if Jonson had not remembered a kindred mythological interpretation which appeared in the standard reference works of Comes and Charles Stephanus. Certainly, there can be no doubt that the moralization of the Actaeon myth accords perfectly with the Senecan cast of the entire drama, particularly with the sentiments taken from the *De Beneficiis.*

When viewed in the light of conventional interpretations of classic myth, the mythological elements in *Cynthia's Revels* are far from being an "embryonic or fragmentary" action extraneous to the plot,[120] nor can the play be denounced as Swinburne castigates it: "the most noticeable part in this studiously wayward and laboriously erratic design is that the principle of composition is as conspicuous by its absence as the breath of inspiration."[121] The principle of composition is all-embracing. Even the minor mythological elements in the play accord with Jonson's design. By ridiculing the fatuous vices, the dramatist is attempting to inculcate the love and practice of a virtue which leads to the serenity of the *sapiens* and to purposeful poesy, and which is "by gods protected" "not of bountie only, but of right" (5.5. 71). For the gods, like the best of rulers, will not waste their bounty by conferring it upon the unworthy. A cultivation of the effeminate and superficial forms of conduct brought in by folly, when heightened by self-love leads to the *hubris* of Niobe and, if related to the center of the body politic, to the presumption of Actaeon. For that matter, the cultivation of superficial forms of conduct, a vice the courtiers were guilty of before they drank of the Fountain of self-love, is similar to Narcissus' concern with worldly inanities and to his assumption of wisdom; for both produce a perversion of one's natural gifts.

A popular audience would probably miss many, if not all, of the intricacies pointed out above; but no great harm would have resulted, for the emphasis throughout the play is upon the ridiculousness of the fatuous courtiers. Jonson probably was writing primarily for courtly spectators, however, for an audience similar to that which later viewed his masques and entertainments. At any rate the mythological elements in the play which have been discussed are a congruent adornment closely linked to the masques of the fifth act and to the moral and the maxims of the entire play. When the drama is considered in the light of the preceding discussion, one can understand more clearly than before why Jonson might dedicate *Cynthia's Revels* to his master Camden and why in referring to this work he insisted that "By God 'tis good, and if you lik't, you may" ("Epilogue," 20). Indeed the interpretations which seem to underlie Jonson's use of his mythological material were not in themselves esoteric. They could have been found in current reference works in the academic tradition of the period.

Most interesting for our purpose are the following facts. The *Thesaurus Linguae Latinae* indicates what version of the Actaeon myth Jonson seems to have had in mind. The *Dictionarium Historicum* preserves the two interpretations of that myth which are apparently reflected in the play. In Charles Stephanus' lexicon also appears a specific detail in the moralization of Narcissus' fate that likewise elucidates lines in *Cynthia's Revels*. The same basic reference work gives a moralization which Mercury's censure of Echo seems to reflect and which also provides the means of unifying conflicting interpretations of that myth. These particulars—in this instance details that are important for an understanding of Jonson's principle of composition—should be considered in conjunction with matter found elsewhere in the plays and poems, with Jonson's allotment of time to the Fatal Sisters in the *Entertainment at Theobalds,* and with the relationship between lexicons and masques. When this is done, traces of the basic reference lexicons in Jonson's ordered array of erudition are both meaningful and considerable, even though much of his information on proper nouns, particularly in the plays and poems, had become too much of an academic commonplace to be earmarked as derivative from any one work. Fortunately for us who attempt to follow his trail, however, Jonson's zealous scholarship produced certain annotations and certain peculiarities of information that point directly to the lexicons. Nor should his erudition be disparaged because he used sound dictionaries any more than it should be disparaged because he utilized Rosinus or Peucer or Gyraldus or Comes. At an early age, Jonson probably acquired a substantial core of the mythological, geographical, and legendary particulars in the compilations by Charles and Robert Stephanus. Some such information was expected of all students, even if they read no more than the prescribed grammar school texts; and Jonson seems to have been particularly aware of the information in those Latin lexicons when he wrote the play dedicated to his schoolmaster and when he composed sound entertainment for the court of James. Indeed, we might have expected an erudite poet to remember pertinent "histories" from his school-days; but in addition—perhaps as a check upon possible errors, perhaps as a means of refreshing his memory—Jonson seems to have turned to Charles and Robert Stephanus for an authority, a phrase, or a line apposite to his purpose, or for further information with which to round out his or Inigo Jones' inventions. The method again is one inculcated by the schools.

Socrates can be ironic when speaking to Hermogenes of his inability to recall information in Hesiod, but the Greeks and Romans themselves had difficulty in remembering details of their mythology. Few people, if any, could carry in their memory the mass of information with specific book numbers that Jonson utilizes. Fewer could keep that information so fresh that it might be transferred to paper without any aid from scholarly compilations. Very infrequently did Jonson err, and when he did he was liable to err with the scholarly lexicons that provided basic information for the age. That such a poet would show his knowledge of entries in lexicons when he was being most erudite gives added weight to the pertinence of other instances wherein there is a close correspondence between the dictionaries and the verses of less learned, less obviously erudite writers who did not attempt to gloss their lines.

# CHAPTER VII

# THOMAS HEYWOOD AND THE DICTIONARIES

I N THE FOREGOING CHAPTERS WE HAVE OBSERVED THAT VARIOUS authors have employed contemporary dictionaries, without naming them, for the annotation of proper names, for convenient references to primary sources, and, on occasion, for the essentials of the myth or legend which was made an organic part of the composition. The work of Ben Jonson, for example, illustrates the diverse ways in which the proper-name dictionaries were used. In the present chapter we shall see Thomas Heywood, a contemporary of Jonson, making similar use of the current reference lexicons as a means of expediting his writing.

For annotations, the most obvious and extensive dependence of Heywood upon the dictionaries may be seen in the following parallels between the dictionaries and *Earth and Age*.[1]

H.

The Sibils were in number ten. *Persica, Libyca, Delphica, Erithraea, Samia, Hellespontiaca, Tiburtina, Albinaea, Cumaea, Cumana:* of these you may read *Varro, Gellius,* etc. (6. 148-49).

*Ascraean,* so titled from *Ascra,* a Towne in *Boetia,* neare unto the mount *Helicon,* where the famous poet *Hesiod* was borne, from which place hee had the sirname *Ascraeus.* (6. 149)

It [Canna's field] hath reference to the great battaile fought by Hannibal against the Romanes neare unto the village *Cannas,* where he slew 80. thousand in that one conflict: from thence the people of *Italy* are call'd *Cannenses.* (6. 149)

S.

*Sibyllae,* fatidicae mulieres omnes dictae ... Decem fuisse, scribit Varro, Persicam, Libycam, Delphicam, Cumaeam, Erythraeam, Samiam, Hellespontiacam, Tyburtinam, Albuneam, & Cumanam. . . .[2]

*Ascra,* vicus Boetiae . . . in dextra parte Heliconis, Hesiodi patria . . . Stephanus Boeotiae vrbem ait esse, inde Ascraeus Hesiodus dictus.

*Cannae,* vicus Apuliae, non procul ab Aufidio fluuio, circa quem Annibal Paulum Aemilium & Terentium Varronem consules ingenti clade superauit, caesis quadraginta Romanorum millibus, tantoque equitum numero. . . .

*Cannenses,* Italiae populi, Corinensibus & Collatinis vicini, Romana clade insignes.

You may read the like of *Niobe* the daughter of *Tantalus,* and wife to *Pelops:* who had sixe Sonnes, and six Daughters, all which *Latona* the mother to *Apollo* and *Diana* . . . caused to be slaine, for the pride of *Niobe,* who presumed to compare with her : for griefe whereof shee lost her speech, and remained stupid and without motion, which gave the Poets occasion to feigne that she was changed into a marble statue. (6. 149)

*Niobe,* filia Tantali, soror Pelopis, vxor autem Amphionis, regis Thebanorum, quae cum viro suo sex filios, totidemque filias peperisset, animo elata, Latonae sese praeferre non dubitauit. Quamobrem indignata dea, Apollinis & Dianae sagittis liberos eius ad vnum omnes interficiendos curauit. Niobemque ipsam . . . in saxum transformauit . . . . Per saxum in quod Niobe mutata est, intelligitur immodicus dolor, qui tandem in stuporem & indolentiam conuertitur, fecitque vt Niobe deriguerit, & veluti lapis immota steterit : vel lapidea statua.

*Astianax* was the Sonne of *Hector* and *Andromache,* who after the taking of *Troy,* was by the Grecians precipitated from an high tower and so slaine. (6. 150)

*Astyanax* . . . vnicus fuit filius Hectoris ex Andromache, natus post inchoatum bellum inter Troianos & Graecos, quem Ulysses naues e Sigeo soluens, e turri dedit in praeceps.

*Daedalus* was the sonne of *Micion* borne in Athens, the most excellent Artificer of these times. He made the Labyrinth into which *Minos* put him, and his sonne *Icarus,* at length having got feathers and wax, he made therof artificiall wings for himselfe and his sonne, and so flew from Crete into Sardinia, and thence to Cuma, where he built a temple to Apollo, but *Icarus* in the way soared so high, that the beames of the Sunne, melted the wax, and his wings failing him, by that disaster he fell into the Sea, from it hath still retained the name of *Mare Icarium,* the Icarian Sea, according to that of Ovid.
    *Icarus Icarijs nomina fecit aquis.* (6. 150-51)

*Daedalus,* faber Atheniensis, Micionis filius, artificum omnium suae aetatis ingeniosissimus. . . . In Creta item Labyrinthum construxit . . . in qua & ipse vna cum Icaro filio a Minoe fuit inclusus. . . . Pennas & ceram poposcit : quibus impetratis, sibi & Icaro filio alas confecit, atque ita ex Creta in Sardiniam euolauit. Deinde & Cumas delatus est, vbi Apollini templum erexit : Icarus vero cum patris consilium spernit, iustoque altius euolat, cera radiis Solis liquefacta in mare decidit, quod deinde a nomine eius Icarium est appellatum. Ouid. lib. 8. Metamorph.
    [Under the entry *Icarus,* Stephanus concludes : Ouid. *Icarus Icariis nomina fecit aquis.*]

*Colossae vel Colossis,* was a towne of Phrygia, neare unto Laodicea, which was demolished by an earth-quake in the time of Nero. (6. 151)

*Colosse,* siue *Colossi* . . . oppidum Phrygiae prope Laodiceam, quod teste Orosio, temporibus Neronis cum Laodicea & Hierapoli vrbibus Asiae, terrae motu cecidit.

Memphis was built by King *Ogdous,* and tooke the name of his daughter . . . it is

*Memphis,* vrbs AEgypti regia ab Ogdoo rege condita, & a nomine filiae eius ita

a great and spacious City in Egypt, famous for the Pyramides and stately sepulchers of Kings there set up: it is at this day called Alcayrum, or Grand-Cayre. (6. 151)

appellata. Haec inter omnes AEgypti vrbes . . . pyramidibus, regum sepulchris imprimis insignis . . . Vulgus hodie *Alcayrum* vocat. . . . Gall. *le Grand Caire.*

*Mausolus,* was King of Caria, to whose memory his wife *Artimesia* reared a most sumptuous Tombe which was reckoned one of the seven wonders of the world . . . . (6. 151)

*Mausolus,* Cariae rex . . . Artemisiae maritus . . . . Ad haec sepulchrum eidem sumptuosissimum extruxit, quod a nomine eius Mausoleum est appellatum, ob operis magnificentiam inter septem orbis miracula numeratum. . . .

[Herostratus] It hath reference to the stately Temple of *Diana* in the City of Ephesus: which was afterward maliciously burnt down by *Herostratus.* (6. 151)

*Herostratus,* Ephesius, homo ignauus & scelestus, qui celeberrimum illud Dianae Ephesiae templum suis manibus incendit, vt ea re nominis immortalitatem sibi compararet.

*Tarpeian* alludeth to *Tarpeia,* a Vestall virgin in Rome, who covenanting with the Sabines their enemies, to betray the Capitoll, for the bracelets they wore on their left armes, when they entred the City, and she stood ready to receive that which she had contracted for, instead of their bracelets, they cast their Targets upon her, by which she was smothered and pressed to death. . . . The Tarpeian Mount was so called because she was there buried, and *Iupiter* was sirnamed *Tarpeius,* because there worshipped. (6. 151-52)

*Tarpeia,* virgo Vestalis . . . quae arcem Capitolinam, patris sui Tarpeij custodiae commissam Sabinis prodidit: a quibus cum proditionis mercedem peteret (pacta enim erat, quicquid in sinistris brachiis gestarent, armillas intelligens, quas illi aureas gemmatasque laeuo in brachio ferebant) scutis illorum obruta Tarpeio monti nomen fecit, qui prius Saturninus dicebatur. Virgil. a quo etiam monte Iupiter Tarpeius dictus est: quod ibi coleretur.

*Atrides,* were the two brothers, *Agamemnon* and *Menelaus,* so called from their father *Atreus.* (6. 152)

*Atridae,* Atrei filij, Agamemnon and Menelaus. Virg. 1. Aeneid.

*Dido* was otherwise called *Elisa,* the daughter of *Belus* King of Tyre, and espoused to *Sychaeus,* one of *Hercules* Priests, whom her brother *Pigmalion* slue for his wealth, she after built the famous Citty Carthage, and in the end . . . kild herselfe for the love of *Aeneas.* (6. 152-53)

*Dido,* siue Eliza, filia Beli Tyriorum regis, quae primis nuptiis Sichaeo Herculis sacerdoti iuncta fuit: quem cum Pygmalion, Elizae frater, thesauris eius inhians, ante aram obtruncasset . . . . [Dido] vrbem condidit, quam Carthaginem appellauit . . . cum praeter spem desereretur, mortem sibi consciuisse . . . .

*Hippolitus,* the sonne of *Theseus* and *Hyppolita* the Amazon, who when his father was abroad, his stepmother *Phaedra* sollicited him to incestuous love,

*Hippolytus,* Thesei & Hippolytae Amazonis filius . . . a Phaedra nouerca absente patre amatus est: cuius turpi desiderio cum obtemperare noluisset, illa filium

which he refusing, she accused him to his father that he would have forced her, but when hee perceived him to give credit to her false information, he tooke his Chariot and horses to flie his fury, but by the way his steeds being frighted with Sea-calves, ran with him to the mountaines, and dashed the Coach in pieces, and him also . . . . (6. 153)

apud patrem detulit, tanquam de struprc eam appellasset. Quamobrem cum videret Hippolytus patrem novercae dolo persuasum de nece sua cogitare, conscenso curru fugam arripuit. Sed dum phocae, quae tum forte in littus exierant, equorum & rotarum strepitu perterritae, magno impetu se in mare praecipitarent, exterriti equi frustra obluctante Hippolyto, currum scopulos & saxa traxerunt, iuuenemque . . . varias in partes discerpserunt . . . .

In his annotations of *Aegeus,* Heywood seems to depend wholly on Cooper's *Thesaurus,* as the parallels below will suggest. His comment on Marcus Crassus derives from both Cooper and Stephanus. Compare the following:

|                          H.                          |                          C.                          |
| --- | --- |
| *Aegeus* was the sonne of *Neptune,* and King of *Athens,* in whose raigne King *Minos* of *Creete* to revenge the death of his Sonne Androgeus, made most cruell warre on the Athenians, forcing them yearely to send seven Noblemens Sonnes into *Crete,* to bee devoured by the monster *Minotaurus.* . . . at length knowing his sons shippe, and seeing the same sable flagge in the top, with which they first launched from that shoare, supposed hee had beene dead, and therefore surcharged with griefe, cast himself headlong from the rocke into the Sea, which was after cald by his name *Aegeum mare.* (6. 150) | *Aegeus,* Neptunes sonne, was king of Athens . . . In this mannes reigne king Minos of Crete, in reuengement of his sonne Androgeus his death, had made most cruell warre on the Atheniens, and had set upon them this penaltie, that yerely they should sende into Crete, seuen noble mens children to be deuoured of the monster Minotaurus. . . . But at the length seing the ship flitting homewarde as it went forth with a black sayle, thinking his sonne and the residue to haue beene slaine, for sorrow did cast himselfe into the sea, that afterward of his name was called *Aegeum.* |

| H. | C. | S. |
| --- | --- | --- |
| *Crassus* surnamed *Marcus,* the richest man amongst the Romans, who held no man Worthy to be cald rich, who could not within his yearely revenue maintaine an Army : hee was extremely covetous, and managed warre against the Parthians, by whom, both hee and thir- | Crassus, Called Marcus. was the richest priuate person of the Romaynes . . . . He would say, he ought not to be called a rich man, except hee could with his yearely rent maintaine a legion . . . . He was exceeding couetous and vnstable. . . . Finally, being steered with couetousnesse and | Crassus, praenomine Marcus, P. Crassi filius, Romanorum omnium ditissimus, negauit quempiam habendum, qui annuo reditu exercitum alere non posset. . . . Et quoniam auri cupiditate expeditionem eam suscepisse credebatur, Barbari mortuo liquefactum aurum in os infuderunt, iubentes. |

ty thousand Romanes were slaine, and because the barbarous enemy conjectured that hee made an assault upon them for their gold: therefore they melted a great quantity, and powred it into his dead body, to sate him with that, with which in his life time, hee could never be satisfied. (6. 153)

enuie . . . he procured warre agaynst the Parthians, by whome both he and his sonne with 30,000 Romaynes were slain.

vt saltem mortuus se auro satiaret, cuius famem viuus nunquam sedare potuisset.

Though Heywood's annotations on *Earth and Age* are more extensive than on other pieces, the author did supply notes on the classical names in various other of his writings. In these too he constantly had recourse to the dictionaries, as the following transcriptions show:

### H.

*Pindus,* was a mountain in Thessaly, sacred to Apollo and the Muses, &c. (Fr. Annotations upon "Iupiter and Io," 6. 279)

*Erix,* Promontory: *Erix* was the sonne of *Venus,* slaine by *Hercules,* and buried in a mountaine of Cicilia, so called after him, in which place *Venus* had a Temple erected unto her, and from that she had the denomination of *Eriana* [*sic*] (Apollo & Daphne," 6. 296)

*Python,* was a mighty huge Serpent, which *Iuno* sent unto *Latona* when she was with child by *Iupiter,* to devoure her, but she went to her sister *Astrea,* who protected her, and she was after delivered of two twins, *Apollo* and *Diana.* ("Apollo & Daphne," 6. 296)

*Salmoneus,* was said to be the sonne of *Eolus,* not he whom the Poets feigne to be the god of the winds, but one of the name, who raigned in the Citty of Elis in Greece. He willing to appeare unto his subjects to be a God, and no man, and so to assume unto himselfe divine adoration, made a bridge of brasse over a great part of the Citty, over which he

### S.

*Pindus,* Lapitharum sedes, mons Thessaliae, Apollini Musisque sacer, Acarnaniam, ab AEtolia diuidit, vt inquit Solinus.

*Eryx,* Butae & Veneris filius . . . ab Hercule ex Hispania redeunte superatus occubuit: atque in monte, in quo Veneri matri templum condiderat, sepultus est: vnde mons ipse Eryx, & Venus Erycina appellatur.

*Python,* serpentis mirae magnitudinis proprium nomen . . . . Hic a Iunone Latonae ex Ioue grauidae dicitur fuisse immissus, nullamque ei pariendi quietem concessisse, donec illa ad Asterien sororem suam peruenisset . . . a qua suscepta, Dianam & Apollinem peperit.

*Salmoneus,* AEoli filius, non regis ventorum, inquit Seruis, sed cuiusdam apud Elidem, vbi regnauit, qui cum regia maiestate contentus non esset, conatus est se Deum suis ostendere, & fabricato aeneo ponte sublimi, adeo vt Elidis partem desuper tegeret, super eo agitabat currus ad imitanda tonitrua: & in quem iaculatus esset facem, eum iubebat occidi.

used to hurry his Chariot, whose wheeles were shod with rough iron, thinking thereby to imitate *Joves* thunder, for which insolence, *Iupiter* being justly incenst against him, stroke him with a true thunderbolt, and sent him quicke to hell. A type of pride justly punished. ("The Man-hater," 6. 195)

Ob quam superbiam Iupiter iratus, eum vero fulmine ad inferos deturbauit. Virgil. AEneid. libro 6.
*Superborum principum typus.*

The parallels quoted above, from Heywood and Stephanus, respectively, offer concrete evidence of Heywood's dependence upon the *Dictionarium*. Further proof of such dependence may be found by comparison of the annotations of the following words from Heywood's works with exposition of the corresponding terms in Stephanus.

Cassiopeia, Andromeda (4. 291); Proteus (5. 264-66); Janus (5. 363-64); Orpheus (5. 366); Jason, Medea (5. 368-69); Iocasta (6. 150); Autonoe, Antigone (6. 151); Getae, Helena, Alcinous (6. 152); Driades (6. 153); Marius, Mezentius, Calpe (6. 154); Deucalion, Epimenides (6. 195); Phineus, Harpiae, Tantalus, Danaus (6. 196); Cyclopes, Dis, Nireus, Cecrops, Erichthonius (6. 197); Alcmena, Maia (6. 218); Iapygium, or Iapyges (6. 231); Menippus (6. 242); Naiades, Pierides, Syrinx, Styx (6. 279); Tithonus (6. 296).

Further analysis of his writings shows that Heywood employed the dictionaries not only in making annotations but also in developing and illustrating ideas in his text proper. Some of the more obvious examples are found in the dialogue of "Earth and Age" (6. 133-148). Earth speaks:

Ev'n such [i. e., sorrow] was thine, (k) Aegeus, to behold
Thy sonnes *blacke sailes returning*: which so cold
Strook to thy heart, thou *thinking Theseus slaine,*
Leapt *from a rocke,* and *gav'st the sea thy name.*
(6. 134)

In the annotation (k; 6. 150) Heywood summarizes the story of Aegeus as found in Cooper's *Thesaurus*. The lines of the text just quoted are even nearer, in phrasing, to Cooper's account than to Heywood's paraphrase in the annotation. Compare with the four quoted lines above the following from the *Thesaurus*:

Wherefore the olde Prince passingly desyrous of his sonnes safe returne . . . was daylie *on the top of an high rock,* to see whether he could espie *the ship returning* with the token of his sonnes victorie. But at the length *seing the ship flitting homeward* as it went forth *with a black sayle, thinking his sonne* and the residue *to have beene slaine,* for sorrow did cast himselfe *into the sea,* that afterward of his name was called Aegeum.[3]

Though Heywood does not gloss *Sardanapal,* the lines in his text indicate that he is again following Cooper's *Thesaurus.* Heywood has Sardanapal speak thus:

> Lest soft effeminacie, lust, and abuse
> Of Natures gifts might pleade the least excuse;
> I am that Sensuallist *Sardanapal,*
> Who to myself thinking to ingrosse all
> Voluptuousnesse, *deckt in their womanish sutes,*
> *I spent my time 'mongst common Prostitutes. . . .*
> And being man, the shape of woman bore.
>
> (6. 147)

Compare Cooper's *Thesaurus:*

Sardanapalus, An Emperour of Assyria, so exceedingly given to effeminate wantonnesse and follie, as he maye seeme to haue chaunged his sexe or kinde, and *by nature being framed a man, in conditions to be a verie woman.* For hee *was wonte continually* in some inner part of his palaice, *to sitte in the companie of light women, arrayed in womens apparayle,* spinning and carding as they did, and in lightnesse of countenance and wanton gestures farre passing the most shamelesse strumpets.[4]

In the annotations, Heywood writes of Helena,

Helena was in her Nonage first rap't by Theseus before her marriage to *Menelaus* King of Sparta, and after by Paris ravisht, and carried to Troy. (6. 152)

This gloss is based upon Stephanus' account of Helena. In the text proper ("Earth and Age," 6. 143) Heywood seems to have drawn other details from Stephanus. The lines in Heywood's text, not his annotations, are,

> Behold . . . that Grecian *Hellen,* shee
> Rap't *Menelaus,* in his prime from thee:
> Me (a) Theseus ravisht first, and *left me so,*
> *That saving kisses I did nothing know.*
> False *Paris* last (by Fate or Fury led)
> *Hosting with me, made stealth into my bed . . .*
> This putrified Coarse by him so bought,
> *Was after by a thousand ships resought.*
>
> (6. 143)

The source for this passage as well as for the annotation is the following from *Helena,* in Stephanus:

. . . Helena, cum caeteris suae aetatis foeminis formae elegantia praestaret,

A    C

*Qui ficcis oculis moſtra natātia,Qui vidit ma-*
*re turgidŭ,& infames ſcopulos Acroceraunia.*
Hodie Cimariotti, & monte de Chimera, vulgò appellant.
Acrôcon.Vide ATHO, & ACROTHON.
Acrocomæ, ſunt populi Thraciæ à capillorum
longitudine dicti, quòd Antas in fronte mu-
lierum more demiſlas geſtarent Author Homerus in catalogo nauium.
Acrocorinthus,mons Peloponneſi excelſus, inter duo maria, Ægeum ſcilicet & Ioniŭ,ſta-
diorum trium & dimidiati : ſub cuius radice
in plano inſtar menſæ, loco iacet oppidum
Corinthus. Vertex ipſe Acrocorinthi,Veneri
facram habet ædiculam:infra verticem,Pyre-
nem fontem, haud affluentes, ſed perſpicuas
aquas habentem. Plin. 4.12.Steph. Plutarch.
in Arato dicit eum è media Græcia enaſci.
Acroliſſus, arx eſt in colle ſupra Liſſum Illirici
vrbem,Strabo lib.7.
Acrolóchias, promontorium Aegypti ad Pha-
rum.Strabo lib.17.
Acron,Ceninenſium rex,quem ob raptus virgi-
num Sabinarum Romulus ſingulari certamine vicit, telóq; traiecit, & eius ſpolia opima
Ioui Pheretrio dicauit : eíque nomen dedit.
Plutar.in vita Romuli.Etenim(inquit) Ferire
apud Latinos, erat Vulnerare ſagittis, Pro-
pert.lib.4.
*Tempore quo portas Ceninum Acrona petētem.*
Acron,medicus Agrigentinus Athenis vnā cum
Empedocle philoſophatus eſt:antiquior Hip-
pocrate : ſcripſit lingua Dorica De medicina
librum vnum. Suidas.
Acron, nobilis Grāmaticus, Horatium poëtam
enarrauit.
Acron, ciuitas in tribu Dan, quæ & Accaron.
Ioſue 13.19.
Acroneus, nomen principis Phæacum. Odyſſ.
lib.1.
Acrónius, in Alpibus lacus eſt, qui deſcendens
à fronte Rhenum facit:noſtri lacum Côſtan-
tienſem vocant. Pomp.lib.3. Brigantinus La-
cus Plinio, Brigantia Ammiano, Podamicus
recentioribus nonnullis.Lacus Heluetiorum
Maximus, quem Bodenſee Germani appellāt.
Acrópathos,Mediæ maioris ſinus,&Suſianę rex.
Acrópolis, arx Athenienſium. Athenæ enim in
tres partes diuiduntur, ἀκρόπολιν, ἄςυ, & Py-
ræum portum.
Acrorei,vrbs Triphyliæ.Steph.
Acrotádus,inſula in ſinu Perſico.Plin.6.23.33.
Acrotatus filius Cleomenis:poſt defunctum pa-
rentēm Lacedæmoniis imperauit. Plutarc. in
Agide,& Pauſ.lib.1.
Acrothon, oppidum. Plin. lib.4. capit.10.ſuper
montem Athon collocatum.Steph. Acrothy-
nos vocat.Thuc.lib.4.
Acrouentum Mamboleium, in Italia locus Ior-
nádi,vbi Mincius amnis cômeantiŭ frequen-

A    C     II

tatione tranſitur,hodie Gouerno. G.Merula.
Acta, apud Thucyd. 4. lib. locus eſt vicinus
Atho monti ad Aegeum pelagus.
Actacottes, populi feroces, qui inſulam Britanniam, vulgò Angliam, totam diripuerunt.
Am.Marcel. lib.27.
Actæa, Athenienſium regio, dicta ab Actæo,
quòd primus in ea regnauit:deinde,verò Attica denominata ab Atride filia Cranai.Pauſ.
lib.1.
Actææ,nympha,ab Actæ.i.littore maris dicta.
Actæon,filius Ariſtæi, ex Autonoë aut Antonoë
coniuge vnde *Autonoius heros* ab Ouidio Dictus eſt,venationi addictus,cùm in valle Gar-
ganoë ad fontem limpidum receſſiſſet,à Diana nuda conſpecta conuitiis laceſſitus eſt, atque in ceruum mutatus, quem ſui ipſius canes diſcerpſerunt De quo figmento ſic ſcribit
Fulgentius, Anaximenes (inquit) qui de pi-
cturis antiquis diſſeruit, ait lib.2. Actæonem
venationem dilexiſſe, cui cùm ad maturam
perueniſſet ætatem,conſideratis venationum
periculis,id eſt,quaſi nudā artis ſuę rationem
videns,timidus factus eſt. Et paulo pòſt : Sed
cùm venandi periculum fugeret, affectū tamen canum non depoſuit : quos inaniter pa-
ſcendo,penè omnem ſubſtantiā perdidit : ob
hanc rem à ſuis canibus deuoratus eſt. Hæc
ille de Ouid.ſententia li.Metamorph.3.Quā-
quam de Actæone aliter in commentariis
Apollonij lib.4.ipſum nó Ariſtix, ſed Meliſſi
filiŭ : nec à canibus ſuis pro ceruo,ſed à Bacchi orgia celebrantibus laniatum fuiſſe tra-
ditur.Sed receptior eſt Ouidij ſententia.
*Inſcius Actæon videt ſine veſte Dianam,*
*Prada ſuis canibus non minus ille fuit.*
Hæc fabula nos ad beneficia in bonos viros
côferenda adhortatur,ac retrahit à bene merendo de ingratis,qui ſæpius pro acceptis beneficiis ſimultatis cauſas aucupantur,ſeq; vel
quauis leuiſſima de cauſa iratos fingunt,vt ſic
deletī appareat quicquid in eos collatum eſt.
Et canibus certè eiuſmodi adulatores aptiſſi-
mè comparantur. Monemur præterea ne ſi-
mus curioſī in rebus ad nos minimè pertinentibus, quoniam multis pernicioſum fuit
res arcanas aliorū cognouiſſe,aut principum,
ciuitatum, ſummorūmve virorum, aut Dei
præcipuè quorum vel aliqua minima ſuſpicio
arcanorum côſcium facilè poteſt opprimere.
Actæonis oſſa Orchomenios olim horrendo
phantaſmate liberarunt, quod ſaxū magnum
geſtans, totam regionem vaſtabat:vnde ac-
colæ Delphos profecti,acceperunt ab oraculo,vt omnia Actæonis oſſa abſportarent,eáq;
ſepelirēt:quo facto,illico liberati ſunt. Pauſa-
nias. Plutarchus in Sertorio, duos ait Actæo-
nes fuiſſe,alterum à canibus,alterum ab ama-
toribus diſcerptum.
Acte, Neconis liberta quam parum adfuit quin

B 3

*a Theseo rapta est* adhuc virguncula, non multo tamen post . . . *citra iniuriam restituta est,* & Menelao vxor tradita . . . . Post haec fama pulchritudinis eius illectus Paris . . . in Graeciam se contulit: vbi a *Menelaeo hospitio susceptus, clam se in amorem Helenae insinuauit; tandemque* absente hospito *Helenam rapuit, et in patriam abduxit.* . . . *Nec multo post mille contractis nauibus in Asiam nauigarunt,* multisque expugnatis oppidis, tandem Ilium obsederunt. . . .

In Heywood's dialogue "Misanthropos, or the Man Hater" the author's annotation of *Salmoneus* (6. 195) follows closely the Latin of Stephanus, on the same word. Likewise, in the text (6. 157) Heywood appears to have in mind the same entry in Stephanus. Heywood has Timon address Jupiter in these words:

> From hence it comes, that (a) *Salmoneus* dare
> *With thee in thy loud thunders to compare:*
> Nor strange; he a man that bold and daring is,
> And thou a god so sufferant and remisse.
>
> (6. 157)

Compare Stephanus,

Salmoneus . . . qui cum regia maiestate contentus non esset, conatus est se Deum suis ostendere, & fabricato aeneo ponte sublimi, adeo vt Elidis partem desuper tegeret, super eo agitabat *currus ad imitanda tonitrua*: & in quem iaculatus esset facem, eum iubebat occidi . . . .

As Calepine, and Cooper translating him, has Salmoneus imitate Jupiter's lightnings, and as Heywood, like Stephanus, has Salmoneus imitate Jupiter's thunder, it seems probable that Heywood was following Stephanus.

In the same dialogue ("The Man Hater," 6. 168) Heywood bases his annotation of *Danaus* (6. 196-97) on Stephanus, but in the text proper, he seems to have consulted Cooper, under *Danaus* and *Belides*. In the dialogue Plutus addresses Timon:

> But thinke you that at length he will forbeare
> To poure me into leaking vessels, where
> Though *with great labour you maintaine it still,*
> The liquor *runs out faster than you fill* . . .
> I shall be as in (i) Danaus daughters *tunnes,*
> *No sooner ought pour'd in, but out it runnes;*
> So *many holes being in the bottom drild,*
> *That it drains faster than it can be fild.*
>
> (6. 168)

Cooper concludes the exposition under *Danaus* with "vide Belides." **Under**

"Belides," having told of the murders by the fifty daughters, he continues,

In punishment of this cruell murder, the Poetes feigne that the daughters of Danaus were put to *this continuall labour,* to fill with water a *great tunne full of holes, so that it ranne out faster than they coulde pour it in.* Whereof ryseth this prouerbe, *Danaidum dolium,* spoken of an vnsatiable man whose greedie desire is never satisfied.

In his dialogue "Nereus, Thersites, Menippus" Heywood has Nereus speak thus to Menippus:

> Am not I descended
> From *Charopes* and *Aglaia,* fam'd so far
> *'Bove all that came vnto the Trojan war*
> *For my rare beauty?* . . .
> Ask *Homer,* of what fame Nereus was then,
> And he will answer, *The most faire of men;*
> Ascribing Beauties praise fully to me.
>
> (6. 241)

Sufficient basis for the reference to Nereus is found in the following entry in C. Stephanus:

*Niraeus,* rex Naxi, *Charopi & Aglaiae filius* quem *omnium formosissimum ad Troiam venisse Hom. tradidit.*

Cooper refers to the surpassing beauty of Nireus but has no mention of Aglaia or Homer. Robert Stephanus (*Thesaurus*) has the necessary details for Heywood's allusion, but he refers to all the Greeks that sailed (*navagerunt*) to Troy. The entry in C. Stephanus' *Dictionarium* is nearest in phrasing to Heywood's lines.

In the compilation of *Gunaikeion, or Nine Books of Various History Concerninge Women* (London, printed by Adam Islip, 1624) there is evidence that Heywood drew from a wide range of sources. Among these are C. Stephanus' *Dictionarium* and Cooper's *Thesaurus.* Heywood writes, for example, of Cybele:

Cybele's priests were called Curetes, and Coribantes; as also *Idaee Dactili,* who *like mad-men wagging their heads* and playing on Cimbals *ran about the streets, provoking others to do the like*: They came from Ida in Phrygia into Creete, in which Island they called a hill by the name of Ida.

For these lines, Heywood seems to have consulted both Stephanus and Cooper. Under *Corybantes,* Cooper translates Stephanus, in part. Cooper's account runs thus:

Corybantes, The priestes of the Idole Cybele, which *as madde men, wagging their heades* and daunsing, playing on Cymballes, *ranne aboute the streetes, prouoking other to doe the lyke.* They first inhabited the mounte Ida in Phrygia, and afterwarde passing into Crete, tooke for their abyding an hill, which of their olde habitation they called also Ida.

Here Heywood is copying the language of Cooper, and though Cooper was translating Stephanus, he omitted such details as the following:

Sunt qui Curetas, & Corybantes . . . & Idaeos Dactylos eosdem esse putent.

Heywood apparently consulted Stephanus and added this detail to Cooper's account, which he was following.

In his *Gunaikeion* (p. 169) Heywood has a short essay on Canace and Macareus, in which he refers to Valeria Tusculana as if this were his source. The story of Canace and her brother is told concisely in both Cooper and Stephanus though it is not certain that Heywood used either for information on the two principal characters. In the reference to Aeolus, incidental in the story, Heywood expands by borrowing from Stephanus. The story begins thus:

Macareus and Canace were brother and sister, the sonne and daughter to AEolus king of the winds (for so the Poets feigned him, because the clouds and mists rising from the seaven AEolian Islands, of which he was king, alwaies pretended great gusts and tempests) hee is reported to be the sonne of *Iupiter* and *Alceste,* daughter to Hyppotes the Tyrian, of whom he had the denomination *Hippotides* . . . .

This part of Heywood's discourse may be compared with Stephanus' entry on *Aeolus*:

*Aeolus,* Iouis filius & Sergestae (alias Acestae,) Hippotae Troiani filiae, a quo dicitur Hippotades. . . . Hic regnauit in insulis Aeoliis quas nonnulli Vulcanias. . . . Fingitur ventorum rex, eo quod ex nebulis & fumo Vulcaniae insulae futurum ventorum flatum praedicebat . . . .

Heywood's version of the Candaules story (*ibid.,* 251) illustrates another way in which he used the dictionaries. In the margin the author has the references "Herodotus in Clio" and, underneath, "Plato 2 de Repub." Examination of his text shows that Heywood has a fairly close translation of Herodotus' story of Candaules and Gyges. He has, however, none of the details ascribed to Plato, and, in fact, no further reference to Plato in the story. Why then the citation of Plato in the margin of Heywood's version? Stephanus does not have this reference to Plato, under

*Candaules* or *Gyges*. Under *Gyges,* however, Thomas Cooper cites Herodotus, then relates his story in condensed form. Immediately after the summary of the Herodotus version, Cooper cites Plato *libro. 2. de iusto,* and gives the account of Gyges' magic ring. These details are absent from Heywood's version of the story. The suggested explanation is that Heywood first read Cooper's account of the Candaules-Gyges story, took the references cited by Cooper, then turned to Herodotus, or possibly a translation, such as that ascribed to Barnabe Rich (Books I-II), for the original story. Having transcribed this, Heywood did not follow up the reference to Plato, though he left the citation in the margin.

In the same work (*Gunaikeion,* 325) there appear in the margin of the text "Heliades" and "Phaetontides." In the accompanying text we read,

> . . . the sisters of *Phaeton,* called by some *Heliades,* by others *Phaetontides;* who with such funerall lamentation bewayled the death of their brother, that the gods in commiseration of their sorrow, turned them into trees. Lib. 1. Met. & Virg. in Culice . . . their names were Phaethusa, Lampitiae, Phoebe, &c.

This passage apparently derives from Stephanus' *Heliades.*

> *Heliades,* filiae Solis & Clymenes, sorores Phaethontis, quarum nomina sunt Phaethusa, Lampetusa, & Lampetia. Hae cum iuxta Padum mortem Phaethontis fulmine deiecti insolabiliter deflerent, in alnos siue (vt alij volunt) in populos versae sunt, electrum lachrymantes. Vocantur autem Heliades a patre Sole . . . Ouid. lib. 2. Metamorph. Eaedem & Phaethontiades appellantur a fratre Phaetonte. Virg. Ecloga. 6.

Under the general heading "Of Cleobule Lindia, & other Poetesses" (*Gunaikeion,* 394), Heywood has in the margin "Cleobulina" and opposite, in the text, these words:

> Shee was the daughter of *Cleobulus Lindius,* one of the seven wise men of Greece; shee was called also *Eumite,* and Cleobulina; in her writing, shee imitated her father. Shee was eminent for AEnigmaes, and Riddles; of which, this one was redeemed from oblivion, and remembered of her,

> > Est vnus genitor, cui vni sunt pignora bis sex,
> > His quoque triginta natae, sed dispare forma.
> > Hae niuiae aspectu, nigris sunt vultibus illae,
> > Sunt immortales omnes, moriuntur & omnes.

> > One father hath twelue children, great and small,
> > They beget thirtie daughters, vnlike all,
> > Halfe of them white, halfe blacke, immortall made,
> > And yet we see how euerie houre they fade.

For the discourse on Cleobulina, Heywood seems to have depended on the following two entries in C. Stephanus:

*Cleobulus,* Euagorae filius, Lindius, vnus e septem Graeciae sapientibus. . . .
*Cleobulina,* Cleobuli filia, hexametris aenigmata quaedam prescripsit: quorum vnum ad huc extare fertur.

> Est unus genitor, cuius sunt pignora bis sex,
> His quoque Triginta natae, sed dispare forma.
> Aspectu hinc niue nigris sunt vultibus inde
> Sunt immortales omnes, moriuntur & omnes.

In conclusion we may say the evidence shows that Thomas Heywood regularly consulted two dictionaries: the Latin-English *Thesaurus* of Bishop Thomas Cooper, and the poetic, geographic, historic Latin dictionary of Charles Stephanus. These lexicons he uses in three ways: (1) as sources of annotations of his own classical allusions; (2) as ready references to original classical sources, which the author may consult for himself; e. g., the Candaules story in Herodotus; (3) as direct sources for allusions in the text of his writings. Heywood's use of the dictionaries as reference works and as sources of classical learning has a definite parallel in the method of Ben Jonson.

# CHAPTER VIII

# MILTON AND THE DICTIONARIES

I N AN EARLIER CHAPTER WE GAVE AN ACCOUNT OF REFERENCE WORKS in the Renaissance, especially the dictionaries, and we have observed in the course of this study that English authors not infrequently made use of myths and legends and biographical and geographical matter found in the dictionaries of Calepine, Elyot, Cooper, Robert Stephanus, and Charles Stephanus. As a classical scholar Milton may well have been familiar with all these, but there is evidence that, with respect to proper names, the poet most frequently consulted the *Thesaurus* of Robert Stephanus and the *Dictionarium Historicum, Geographicum, Poeticum* of Charles Stephanus —the former probably because of its comprehensive character and its exact citation of classical sources; and the latter because of its convenient size (8vo) and because it is devoted exclusively to proper names.

Though compact, the *Dictionarium* is broad in its range. It embraces, as the title suggests, information on mythology, history, and geography, and it is supported by the best authorities, ancient and modern. Furthermore, the periodic revisions introduce new matter from current authorities. In the first edition (1553), for example, there is no mention of Comes' *Mythologiae*. Later editions of Stephanus quote Comes at length in various places, and often cite him as an authority on mythology and its interpretation. Similarly in geography: Strabo, Ptolemy, Pomponius Mela, Pliny, are among the classic standbys. But also Mercator, Ortelius, and others are drawn upon when they become known. In Charles Stephanus' *Dictionarium* we have, in short, a scholarly work given over entirely to mythology, history, and geography as these are associated with proper names; wide in range, citing and often quoting original sources, such as Virgil, Horace, Lucan, Ovid; making free use of secondary sources and interpretations from Cicero, Gyraldus, Hyginus, Boccaccio, Comes, and Cartari;

and from time to time brought up-to-date by the addition of fresh information. Milton nowhere mentions the *Dictionarium* of Charles Stephanus.
It is worthy of note, however, that Edward Phillips, the poet's nephew,
whom Milton tutored as a youth, drew freely from Charles Stephanus in
the compilation of *The New World of Words, a General* [English] *Dictionary* (1658). His first acquaintance with Stephanus' dictionary may
have come through his uncle. The annotations which are presented below
seem to indicate that the poet kept the *Dictionarium* at hand.

The poet's knowledge of the lexicographical works of Henry Stephanus
and Robert Stephanus is easily demonstrable. Among Milton's marginalia
on Aratus' *Phoenomena* is a definite reference to Henry Stephanus' *Thesaurus Graecae Linguae* (1572-3) :[1] and from the anonymous life, attributed by
Miss Darbishire to John Phillips, we learn that after his blindness and
during the composition of *Paradise Lost,* Milton "began that laborious work
of amassing out of all the classic authors, both in Prose and Verse, a *Latin
Thesaurus* to the emendation of that done by Stephanus. . . ."[2] Edward
Phillips is more explicit; after Milton moved into "a pretty Garden-house
in *Petty-France* in *Westminster* (1652) and disposed of Alexander More,
he had leisure again for his own Studies and private Designs; which were
his foresaid *History of England,* and a New *Thesaurus Linguae Latinae,*
according to the manner of Stephanus; a work he had been long since
collecting from his own Reading. . . ."[3]

There can be little doubt about Milton's familiarity with the tools of his
trade, including books of rhetoric and dictionaries. His interest in education, his high and serious conception of the poetic art, his zeal for the
mastery of language—English as well as Latin, Greek, and Italian—all
would lead him to a study of the best authorities on the meanings and uses
of words; consequently, the texts that dealt with these subjects. And of the
lexicons available in Milton's day, those compiled and published in the
sixteenth century by the Stephani, the French classical scholars and
printers, had most to offer.

The explanation of his use of source materials is not simple. We have
to remember that, before the period of his blindness, Milton was a voracious
reader of classical literature and history and that he had a prodigious
memory. The result was that a given passage employing a classical myth
might well be the synthesis of several originals or the poet's own adaptation of a myth to his purpose. But even Milton's memory was not infalli-
ble, and we may well believe that he not infrequently refreshed it in the

most expeditious manner—that is, by consulting a standard dictionary. There he would find, especially in the Stephanus dictionaries, compact summaries, often of more than one version of a myth or legend, together with precise references to original sources, not only to classical poetry and prose, but also to ancient and modern authorities on history and geography, and even to Biblical persons and places.

The primary purpose of this part of our study is, then, to present annotations of important passages in Milton's poetry and to emphasize the value of the dictionaries and other current reference works in an explanatory and illustrative capacity. Through these, we may better understand what Milton's readers, as indeed the readers of Spenser and Jonson, might be expected to know, or readily to discover for themselves. In other words, we shall come to understand better the Renaissance poet's point of view in his free use of classical allusions; and, it is hoped, we shall find for ourselves new light on certain passages which, hitherto, have puzzled readers and commentators alike.

In presenting the matter we employ a modified alphabetical order, choosing as the key word the important personal or place name in the myth or legend under consideration. Deviation from a strict alphabetical arrangement occurs in the treatment of a name like Aesculapius, for example. Under this heading it seems desirable, for the sake of unity, to deal with the legends of persons, such as Coronis, Machaon, and Chiron, closely associated with Aesculapius. To the allied characters thus treated there will be cross-references in the appropriate places.

The annotations set forth below are meant to be representative, not exhaustive. And the annotations are concerned with two groups of proper names found in Milton's poetry: (1) those applicable to persons, real or mythical, and (2) place names, including those pertaining to countries, towns, mountains, rivers, etc.

## I. PROPER NAMES OF PERSONS, INCLUDING THE LEGENDARY AND MYTHICAL

ADES (ORCUS)

> . . . with him Enthron'd
> Sat Sable-vested Night, eldest of things,
> The Consort of his Reign; and by them stood
> *Orcus* and *Ades*.
>
> (*PL.* 2. 961-64)

An apt annotation for the word *Orcus* as well as for the atmosphere of the passage may be found in these two entries in Charles Stephanus:[4]

1. Ades, a Graecis inferorum deus, quem nos Ditem & Plutonem appellamus: ita dictus ab α priuatiua, & εἰδειν videre: quod in densissimis inferorum tenebris, nocteque profunda perpetuo agens nihil cernere videatur. Non enim absque lucido aere (qui apud inferos nullus est) visio potest fieri.

2. Orcus, a veteribus inferorum deus est existimatus, quem & Plutonem & Ditem patrem vocabant. Aliquando tamen figurate pro ipso inferorum loco ponitur.

For *Orchus,* compare also Calepine (1542) ". . . Proprie autem Orcus, obscuritas inferorum," and Elyot-Cooper (1559), "A ryuer of hell . . . It is sometyme taken for hell, or the darknesse of hell."

ADONIS

> Thammuz came next behind,
> Whose annual wound in *Lebanon* allur'd
> The *Syrian* Damsels to lament his fate
> In amorous ditties all a Summer's day,
> While smooth *Adonis* from his native Rock
> Ran purple to the Sea, suppos'd with blood
> Of *Thammuz* yearly wounded: the Love-tale
> Infected Sion's daughters with like heat,
> Whose wanton passions in the sacred Porch
> *Ezekiel* saw, when, by the Vision led
> His eye survey'd the dark Idolatries
> Of alienated *Judah.*
>
> (*PL.* I. 446-57)

Editors and critics have referred to diverse early writings—Ezekiel, Strabo, Lucian, Ovid, Theocritus, the Orphic hymn to Adonis—which give information on Adonis, without however, urging any one of these as a direct source. By implication the poet made his own synthesis on the basis of various originals. A simpler explanation might be found by positing Milton's knowledge of the accounts of Adonis in Renaissance dictionaries. The myth of Adonis is related in the various issues of Calepine (1510, 1542, 1609), in Robert Stephanus' *Thesaurus* (1572), and in Charles Stephanus' *Dictionarium* (1553, etc.). It is the Adonis story in the last named volume which offers most in common with Milton and is therefore the best annotation. The entry in the Charles Stephanus begins, "Adonis, idis, filius Cynarae Cypriorum regis et Myrrhae eius filiae, quem Venus in deliciis habuit"; it recounts Venus' love for Adonis and his death, and then continues as follows:

Ideo autem Venerem amasse dicunt, quod hoc genus pigmenti sit valde feruidum. Lucianus *Adonium fluuium ex Libano monte profluentem, singulis annis sanguinolentum fieri commemorat per eos dies, quibus Adonis fuit interfectus.* Hieronymus in *Ezechielem.* Quem nos Adonidem interpretati sumus, et Hebraeus et *Syrus sermo Thamuz vocat.* Vnde quia iuxta gentilem fabulam in *mense Iulio, Amasius Veneris* et pulcherrimus iuuenis occisus, et deinceps reuixisse narratur, eundem *Iulium mensem* eodem appellant nomine, et anniuersariam ei celebrant solennitatem, in *qua plangitur quasi mortuus,* et postea reuiuiscens *canitur* atque laudatur. Vnde apud *Ezechielem prophetam* legitur, *Ecce ibi mulieres sedebant plangentes Adonidem.* Vbi intelligi vult fuisse *idolatriam celebratam in honorem Adonidis,* quanquam nonnulli fortasse rectius exponant de *planctu qui fiebat* propter mortem Osiridis ab AEgyptiis, *quorum ritus imitabantur Iudaei.* . . .

*Adonis* Phoeniciae *fluuius* est Ptol. et Luciano qui scribit eum *oriri ex Libano* et circa Byblim *in mare effundi, quotannisque cruore infici, ipsumque* mare magna parte *purpureum efficere.*

As the italicized passages indicate, all of Milton's details are present in this dictionary entry, with the exception of those which a person familiar with Ezekiel 8 would naturally know.[5] Milton's "amorous ditties" and "love-tale" seem to be a reflection of the well-known story of the love of Venus for Adonis (e.g., *"Amasius Veneris"*) and the singing in celebration of the rites. His "a summer's day" probably reflects the *mense Iulio* of the dictionary entry. The annual nature of the celebration and its reasons are mentioned twice by Milton and by the dictionary. The name Thammuz appears in both accounts, while the *Syrian* damsels' lamenting Adonis' fate under such a name is explained by the dictionaries. The locale in both accounts is specified as Lebanon; both refer to Ezekiel; and the "idolatries of alienated Judah" is perhaps a reflection of the dictionary's *idolatriam* and *ritus imitabantur Iudaei.* Adonis running purple to the sea could be a paraphrase of the last sentence quoted from Charles Stephanus.

The matter from Stephanus has more correspondences to Milton's lines than any other cited by students of Milton. It should be noted, however, that in his composite entry under *Adonis,* Charles Stephanus drew some of his matter from Natalis Comes' *Mythologiae* (5. 16), especially the allegorical interpretation of the myth, omitted from the quotation and not essential to the exposition of Milton's lines. Absent from the Comes are the references to Jerome and Ezekiel and Thammuz and the river Adonis flowing purple to the sea. In brief, the passage quoted above from the Stephanus *Dictionarium* owes relatively little to Comes. Yet this passage would amply explain Milton's detailed allusion to Thammuz (Adonis); the account in Comes' *Mythologiae* would not do so.

AEOLUS (HIPPOTADES)

> And sage Hippotades their answer brings,
> That not a blast was from his dungeon stray'd,
> The Air was calm, and on the level brine,
> Sleek Panope with all her sisters play'd.
>
> (*Lycidas.* 96-99)

Professor Osgood notes that Aeolus is called Hippotades by Homer (*Od.* 10. 2, 36), that Virgil and Ovid refer to Aeolus' confining the winds; and that "the epithet 'sage' seems to go back to a passage in Diodorus, who speaks of Aeolus as reverent and just," and also as one who taught the use of sails and forecasting of winds.[6] Of Hippotades, Merritt Y. Hughes writes, "Aeolus, the son of Hippotas and god of the winds, is called *sage,* perhaps because Diodorus Siculus says that he invented sails and taught the art of predicting storms."[7]

In the *Dictionarium* of Charles Stephanus, under the entry *Aeolus,* the compiler employs the term "Hippotades," explains his mastery over the winds, his skill in astronomy, the value of his prognostications to mariners, and characterizes him as *vir sapiens.* Incidentally, this account quotes Ovid and Homer and refers to Virgil and Diodorus. The pertinent lines from the 300-word item by Stephanus follow:

> *Aeolus,* Iouis filius et Sergestae . . . Hippotae Troiani filiae, a quo dicitur *Hippotades,* Ouidius,
> *Aelon Hippotaden cohibentem carcere ventos.* . . .
> Quod attinet ad mores, *AEolus est vir sapiens,* qui irae, moderatur pro opportunitate temporum, et praesentium negotiorum, quando nunc simulare iram nunc dissimulare vtilissimum est: is autem putatur ventos refraenare et emittere cum libuerit. N. Comes, *Myth.* li. 8. c. 10.

These words from the dictionary might serve as an apt annotation of Milton's reference to "sage Hippotades." But Stephanus is indebted to Comes, as his citation suggests, for at least a part of his matter on Aeolus. The last four lines of the Latin quoted are almost verbatim from the *Mythologiae.* Either Comes or Stephanus or both could have been known to Milton.

AESCULAPIUS (CORONIS, MACHAON, CHIRON)

In his Latin poems, especially Elegy 2 and 4 on the Death of the Vice-

Chancellor, a Physician, Milton exhibits familiarity with the Aesculapius legend and with the persons, Coronis, Machaon, Chiron, related to the renowned legendary physician. As the English poet echoes Ovid in these early poems, some students urge that Ovid is the principal, if not the sole, source of inspiration. But as the Roman poet does not account for some of the allusions, critics have cited Homer, Quintus Smyrnaeus, and others to explain the details missing in Ovid. We are left to infer that Milton, when he composed Elegy 2 on the Vice-Chancellor, at the age of seventeen, was synthesizing matter from a wide range of ancient authors. With Milton this procedure may have been possible.

It is well to remember, however, that there were at least two available accounts of the Aesculapius legend with all the essential details—accounts not mentioned by editors and commentators—easily available to the young poet. Comes' *Mythologiae* devotes a chapter (4. 11) to Aesculapius and another (4. 12) to Chiron, drawing from various earlier sources. More compact and perhaps more practicable to use are the narratives *s.v. Aesculapius* and *Chiron* in the *Dictionarium* of Charles Stephanus. The dictionary, borrowing freely from Comes, puts the essentials of the legendary biographies in more concise form. To posit Milton's familiarity with Comes or with Stephanus, or both, would be a simpler explanation of his use of the Aesculapius legend. Of the two books, the *Dictionarium* seems a more likely source of information than the *Mythologiae* though the latter is not to be ruled out.

Under the entry *Aesculapius* Stephanus informs us that the physician was the son of Apollo and the Nymph Coronis, that the infant was cut from his mother's womb, that when he grew up, he studied under Chiron and became skilled in the art of medicine, that, with the prayers of Diana, he restored to life Hippolytus torn to pieces by his runaway horses, and, for his trouble, was slain with a thunderbolt by Jupiter. Aesculapius was worshipped first at Epidaurus (whence called Epidaurius). He delivered Rome from the plague, and a temple was built in his honor and he was worshipped in the likeness of a serpent.

He had two sons—Machaon and Podalyrius—who became renowned in the art of medicine. These accompanied Agamemnon to the Trojan war and were of no little service to the Greek soldiers. (Then follows an allegorical interpretation of the myth after Comes.)

As Aesculapius, through the potency of his medicine, restored to health men who had abandoned hope of life, some say that he was calling the dead back from the lower world (*"mortuos ab inferis revocaret"*). Therefore, the ancients feigned that Pluto complained to Jove that Aesculapius was emptying his kingdom; whereupon Jove slew the physician with a thunderbolt.

This is the substance of the principal entry. Characters mentioned within the entry *Aesculapius*—Chiron, Hippolytus, Machaon—are each sketched in more detail under their individual entries. We learn, for example, that Machaon became a distinguished doctor, went with the Greek leaders to Troy, and was slain by Eurypylus. We learn also, *s.v. Chiron*, that this Centaur knew the power of herbs and was a skilled physician; that he taught Aesculapius medicine and Hercules astronomy; he was tutor of Achilles and taught him, among other things, to play the cithern and sing, and thus made him an expert *citharoedus*. Keeping in mind the information available in the composite accounts of the dictionary, let us examine a few of Milton's allusions to the myth.

| MILTON | C. STEPHANUS |
|---|---|
| Dignus quem Stygiis medica revocaret ab undis <br> Arte, Coronides, saepe rogante dea. (*Eleg.* 2. 9-10) (Worthy that Coronides, at the frequent prayer of a goddess, should with his healing art recall you from the waves of the Styx. [MacKellar's translation]) | Aesculapius, Appollinis ex Coronide nympha filius. . . . Iamque huius artis [medicinae] peritus, Dianae precibus, Hippolytum ab equis discerptum vitae restituit. <br><br> Hippolytus, Thesei & Hippolytae Amazonis filius. . . . Hunc postea Aesculapius, a Diana exoratus, reuocauit ab inferis, & pristinae incolumitati restituit. |

The quotation from Elegy 2 above alludes to Aesculapius' restoring Hippolytus to life. The story is told by Virgil (*Aen.* 7. 937 ff., Cranch's translation), by Ovid (*Met.* 15. 533 ff.), Spenser (*F.Q.* 1. 5. 38 ff.), and by Comes (*Mythologiae.* 4. 11). According to Virgil, Hippolytus was restored by "Paeon's herbs and Dian's love"; there is no mention of her prayers. In Ovid there is no reference to Diana in this particular episode; Hippolytus is revived by the potent remedies of Apollo's son. In Spenser Apollo gathers up the "relicks" by "Dianes meanes" and brings them to Aesculapius. Comes does not refer to Diana in recounting this episode. It is interesting to see that in two entries—*Aesculapius* and *Hippolytus*—Stephanus refers definitely to the entreaties or prayers of Diana and that the language of Milton's Elegy 2 is quite close to that of Stephanus.

It is in his poem on the Death of the Vice-Chancellor, A Physician, that Milton has the most extensive allusions to the Aesculapian myth. (*Procanc.* 21-28, 37-40.) For convenience in discussing the different episodes alluded to, we divide into three parts the twelve lines and consider each group separately below.

MILTON

Numenque trinum fallere si queant
Artes medentum, ignotaque gramina,
Non gnarus herbarum Machaon
Eurypyli cecidisset hasta. (*Procanc.* 21-24)
(If mysterious herbs and the arts of the physicians could thwart the triple goddess, Machaon with his skill in simples had not fallen by the spear of Eurypylus. [MacKellar])

C. STEPHANUS

*Machaon,* filius AEsculapii & Arsinoes . . . *medicus insignis,* qui vna cum reliquis Graeciae principibus ad Troiam profectus, tandem ab *Eurypylo occisus* . . . cuius tumulus templo colebatur magnifico, quod variorum morborum hinc peterentur remedia. . . .

Machaon and his death at the hands of Eurypylus are not mentioned in the story of Aesculapius as told by Ovid (*Met.* 2. 629 ff.). Comes (4. 11) refers to Machaon's skill as a physican and to his presence with other Greeks before Troy, but not to his death by Eurypylus. Homer (*Iliad,* 11. 506 ff.) relates that the physician was struck in the shoulder by an arrow from the bow of Prince Alexander. Both MacKellar[8] and Hughes[9] cite Homer and both recall that Quintus Smyrnaeus (*The Fall of Troy.* 6. 391 ff.) recounts Machaon's death by Eurypylus. Thus Milton at the age of seventeen would have drawn together in the brief allusion suggestions from Homer, Virgil, Quintus Smyraneus, and others. The parallels quoted above suggest the more direct procedure of his reading one or two entries in Stephanus (or possibly Comes) for the pertinent details.

Let us note succeeding lines from Milton's poem on the death of the Vice-Chancellor. Compare,

MILTON

Laesisset et nec te, Philyreie,
Sagitta echidnae perlita sanguine. (25-26)
(And the arrow smeared with the serpent's blood had done you no injury. [MacKellar])

STEPHANUS

Chiron, Centaurus, Saturni & phillyrae . . . filius . . . . Postremo cum grauiter vulneratus esset, Herculis sagitta Lernaeo veneno perlita casu decidentem in eius pedem, optauit mori . . . .

For an account of Chiron and the manner of his death Hughes refers to Ovid (*Met.* 2. 596-654).[10] This passage contains Ocyrhoe's prophecy concerning the manner of Chiron's death, but there is nothing in the phrasing to suggest Milton's words. Ocyrhoe refers to the time when Chiron "shall be in agony with all thy limbs burning with the fatal Hydra's blood" ("tum cum cruciabere dirae sanguine serpentis per saucia membra recepto," 2. 651-2). Comes (4. 12) more nearly anticipates Milton in the following words: "Cum postea Herculis sagittas veneno Lerneae hydrae perlitas Chiron sequentibus temporibus tractasset, in alterum pedem eius vnam illarum cecidisse affirmant. . . ." Charles Stephanus, apparently, paraphases Comes' account. In doing so, he makes changes which bring his language strikingly near to that of Milton. It will be noted that Comes employs the plural forms "sagittas" and "perlitas." C. Stephanus uses the singular for these two words—and Milton, likewise, reverts to the singular forms.

From the same poem on the Vice-Chancellor, we quote the following lines for comparison with Stephanus:

| MILTON | C. STEPHANUS |
|---|---|
| Nec tela te fulmenque avitum, | Aesculapius, Apollinis ex Coronide |
| Caese puer genitricis alvo. . . . (27-28) | nympha filius . . . sed is [Apollo] postea |
| | facti [the killing of Coronis] poenitens, |
| At fila rupit Persephone tua | *secto eius vtero conceptum ex se eduxit* |
| Irata cum te viderit artibus | *infantem, eumque AEsculapium appel-* |
| Succoque pollenti tot atris | *lauit.* . . . Non defuerunt qui locum datum |
| Faucibus eripuisse mortis. . . . (37-40) | fuisse fabulae de AEsculapio tradiderint |
| (Nor had the arms and bolts of your | *quod mortuos ab inferis reuocaret:* quia |
| grandsire harmed you, O son, who were | nonnullos quorum conclamata esset spes |
| cut from your mother's womb . . . . | vitae sanitati *restituerit per vim medica-* |
| But Persephone broke the thread of life, | *mentorum.* Vnde fabulati sunt antiqui |
| angered when she saw how many souls | Plutonem apud Iouem conquestum fuisse |
| you snatched from the black jaws of | quod, suum imperium AEsculapius exin- |
| Death by your arts and your potent | anerit. Idcirco *fulmine percussum* fuisse |
| juices. [MacKellar]) | a Ioue inquiunt. . . . |

The quotation above from Milton refers to two critical episodes in Aesculapius' life: his being cut from his mother's womb, and his being struck down by Jove's thunderbolt because he was saving so many people from death. Ovid (*Met.* 2. 629) relates that Apollo snatched (*"eripuit"*) the unborn child from his mother's womb (*"natum flammis uteroque parentis eripuit"*). Comes (4. 11) writes, "Mercurius e ventre mortuae Aesculapium *extraxit,* vel Phoebus ipse," citing Ovid (lib. 2 *Met.*). Neither "eripuit" nor "extraxit" has the meaning of *cut.* In both Milton and C. Stephanus the word used in the same context means *cut:* Milton has *"Caese* puer genitricis alvo" and Stephanus *"secto* eius *utero* conceptum ex se eduxit infantem. . . ." Was Milton remembering the dictionary account of Aesculapius?

Referring to the death of Aesculapius (*Met.* 2. 643-646), Ocyrhoe prophesies that mortal bodies shall often owe their lives to Aesculapius, but as a result of the scorn of the gods, he "shall be stayed by his grandsire's lightning" (*"flamma prohibere avita"*). The reason for Jove's wrath, namely, that Aesculapius was restoring too many bodies to life, is not mentioned. Milton refers definitely to the legendary physician's snatching so many souls from the black jaws of death and, as a result, Jupiter's striking him with lightning (*"fulmine"*). C. Stephanus states that because Aesculapius was recalling the dead from the lower world (*"mortuos ab inferis reuocaret"*) and, by the power of his medicines, restoring them to health and thereby emptying Pluto's realm, Jove struck him down with lightning (*"fulmine"*). Milton is nearer to this version of the story than to any other which we know.

AETHON

> Flammeus at signum ter viderat arietis Aethon
> Induxitque auro lanea terga novo.
>
> (*Elegia Quarta.* 33-34)

The usual citation for information and names of the horses of the sun, including Milton's "Flammeus . . . Aethon," is Ovid (*Met.* 2. 153-5). For a rather full contemporary annotation which quotes Ovid, compare the entry in C. Stephanus' *Dictionarium*:

*Aethon,* Solis equus, quorum quatuor sunt, quatuor diurniae circuitionis qualitates demonstrantes. Pyrois, id est, rubeus, eo quod primo mane surgentibus a terra vaporibus sol rubeat. Eous, id est, splendidus, eo quod exhalatus sol iam dissolutis vaporibus splendens sit. Aethon, id est, ardens: nam sole iam medium coeli tenente, lux eius corusca est, & cunctis feruidior videtur. Phlegon autem quartus, ex croceo colore in nigrum tendit, & in tempore terram amans, ostendens aduesperascente die solem terram petere, id est occasum. Oui. lib. 2 Metam. *Interea volucres Pyrois, Eous, & Aethon solis equi, quartusque Phlegon, hinnitibus auras flammiferis implent.*

Calepine (1542) lists the names of the horses of Phoebus, indicating that these signify four periods of the day: "nam φλέγω inflammo significat, πυρόεις ardens. Ἐωός splendens, ἀιϑών ardens, & splendidus."

AMMON

Milton's treatment of Ammon is another example which suggests that he consulted a dictionary entry and then turned to another work. On *Ammon,* Charles Stephanus writes:

*Ammon,* alij *Hammon,* dicitur *Iupiter* in specie arietis, sicut colebatur in *Lybia:* quod sitienti *Libero* patri in Arabiae desertis, Iouemque imploranti apparuerit in forma arietis, qui terram concutiens pedibus, fontem ostenderit. . . . Vide Curtium lib. 4. *Diodor.* li. 17. . . . Alij autem rectius interpretantur [the name], qui *Ammonem seu Chammonem à Chamo,* Noachi patriarchae filio, verae religionis deprauatore et superstitionis in Africa inuentore deductum tradunt. . . .

Ammon, Tritonis filius, rex Lybyae, pater Dionysij, qui & *Bacchus* dicitur.

Robert Stephanus gives about the same information with a slight variation in wording (e.g., "Liber quum Indos peteret, et per Libyam exercitum duceret: fatigatus siti, Iovis patri sui imploravit auxilium"), but adds, "De Ammone longe plura vide apud *Diod. Sicul.* lib. 4. cap. ult." It seems to us very probable that Milton was familiar with the dictionary entries and that he read the long account to which Robert Stephanus, and presumably Charles, refer. One of the four places with which Milton compares Paradise is

> . . . that Nyseian isle
> Girt with the river Triton, where *old Cham,*
> *Whom Gentiles Ammon call and Libyan Jove,*
> Hid Amalthea and her Florid Son,
> Young *Bacchus* from his stepdame *Rhea's* eye.
> (*PL.* 4. 275-79)

As Whiting points out, a number of the details in this description of the "Nyseian isle" seem to be derived from Diodorus:[11] yet in Diodorus, Milton would have found no mention of "old Cham," while the various forms of "Ammon" occupy a considerable space in the dictionary entries. Considering the passages discussed earlier, which clearly seem to be indebted to contemporary works of reference, can we not assume that Milton read one of the dictionary entries quoted above and then turned for further information to a source which the dictionaries cited? May he not have followed such a procedure early in his poetic career and perhaps have associated the description of the beautiful Nysaean isle in Diodorus with the description of Adonis' garden, which he could have read in Robert Stephanus or elsewhere—the fruit of the association being the following lines from *Christ's Nativity?*

> The Libyc *Hammon* shrinks his horn,
> In vain the *Tyrian* maids their wounded *Thammuz* mourn.
>
> (ll. 203-4)

Such a question verges into the realm of pure conjecture; but that Milton returns to the figures of Ammon and of Thammuz in *Paradise Lost* and that he preserves Diodorus' unconventional account of Bacchus' genealogy and of the jealous Rhea make the question at least pertinent.

ANTAEUS

> But Satan smitten with amazement fell
> As when Earth's Son *Antaeus* (to compare
> Small things with greatest) in Irassa strove
> With *Jove's Alcides,* and oft foil'd still rose,
> Receiving from his mother Earth new strength,
> Fresh from his fall, and fiercer grapple join'd,
> Throttl'd at length in the Air, expir'd and fell.
>
> (*PR.* 4. 562-68)

Pindar and Lucan have been cited as the classic sources of this description.[12] Very suggestive of Milton's language is the narrative in Comes' *Mythologiae* (7.1.), which is paraphrased in Charles Stephanus' dictionary. Here are the pertinent lines from Comes:

Hic [Antaeus] cum Herculem ad luctam prouocasset, ab eo pene extinctus ter prosternitur, at erat ea virtute, vt quoties Terram matrem attingeret: toties fortior resurgeret, quod sentiens Hercules hunc comprehensum sublimen a terra tamdiu sustinuit, quamdiu spiraret, donec vi Herculea brachiisque denique strictus, expirauerit. . . .

More compact is the passage from Stephanus:

. . . Is quoties membra labore defessa essent, tactu Terrae recreabatur, quem Hercules palaestra pectori astrictum expirare coegit. . . .

Comes' lines offer more of the essential details for Milton.

The Calepine dictionaries, with matter similar to that in C. Stephanus, place Antaeus in Libya near the town of Lixus.

ARCHILOCHUS

> Graiusque vates parcius
> Turpem Lycambis execratus est dolum,
> Sponsamque Neobulen suam.
>
> (*In Obitum Praesul. Eliensis,* 20-22).

There needed no licensing of Books among them [the Spartans], for they dislik'd all, but their own Laconick Apophthegms, and took a slight occasion to chase Archilochus out of their City, perhaps for composing in a higher straine then their owne souldierly ballats and rondels could reach to. ("Areopagitica," *Works,* IV [N. Y., 1951], 300.)

Apparently the story of Archilochus and the power of his iambics was well known in the Renaissance. Masson[13] and Hughes[14] and other editors tell briefly the story of this Greek poet, without citing a reference to any original source. MacKellar (p. 288) cites Ovid (*Ibis,* 45), Horace (*Epod.* 6. 11-3), and Plutarch (*Cato the Younger, 7*). According to C. Stephanus, brief mention of Archilochus appears in Horace, Cicero, and Quintilian. In Stephanus, the story is summarized in at least three places —under *Archilochus, Lycambes,* and *Neobule.* The fuller account in the entry *Archilochus* is perhaps the best annotation for Milton's allusions.

Stephanus' version of the story runs thus:

*Archilochus Graecus, poëta* Parius, *persecutus est Lycambem socerum suum,* quod ei *filiam pactam* nomine *Neobolon* alteri collocauerat: eumque ad laqueum, ob Iamborum petulantiam in eum scriptorum, compulit. Horat.:
*Archilochum proprio rabies armauit Iambo.* Ouidius. *Tincta Lycambeo sanguine tela madent.* Quintilianus, Archilochus primus inter eos qui Iambos scripsere: summa in eo vis, elegantes sane, vibrantesque sententiae plurimum sanguinis atque neruorum: adeo vt videatur quibusdam, quod quidem veneni est, materiae, esse, non ingenij vitium. Emicuit regnante Romulo, vt ait Cicero in *Tuscul. Huius libros ob inuerecundiam & obscoenitatem Lacaedaemonij ex vrbe tolli iusserunt, authoremque eorum in exilium miserunt . . . .*

(Cf. *ibid.,* under *Lycambe,* where S. cites Horace, *Epodes,* Ode. 6 & Ouidius, in *Ibis.;* and *Neobule.*)
Perottus, *Cornucopiae* (C. 421. 3-15) appears to be the source of Stephanus.

ARIMASPIAN

> As when a Gryfon through the Wilderness
> With winged course o'er Hill or moory Dale,
> Pursues the Arimaspian, who by stealth
> Had from his wakeful custody purloin'd
> The guarded Gold.
>
> (*PL.* 2. 943-47)

On this passage Osgood cites Herodotus (3. 116 & 4. 13) and quotes the Latin of Pliny (*N. H.* 7. 2).[15] Whiting quotes Holland's translation of Pliny.[16] Milton was doubtless familiar with both authors on the subject of the Arimaspians and the griffins. Had he needed to refresh his memory on the subject, he could have consulted Robert Stephanus' *Thesaurus* on *Arimaspii*, where are cited both Pliny and Herodotus, or C. Stephanus' *Dictionarium*, in which Lucan and Herodotus are cited, and Pliny, apparently, summarized.

Here are parts of two entries from the *Dictionarium*.

Arimaspus, fluuius est Scythiae in Asia ad Septentrionem, aureis arenis abundans. Lucanus lib. 3.

*Arimaspi,* eiusdem fluminis accolae, vel populi Scythiae Europae, habentes vnum oculum in fronte, qui perpetuo bella gerunt cum gryphibus, aurum & smaragdos colligentibus. Lucan. lib. 3

> . . . auroque ligatas
> substringens Arimaspe comas.

ASTARTE

> With these in troop
> Came *Astoreth,* whom the *Phoenicians* call'd
> *Astarte,* Queen of Heaven, with crescent Horns;
> To whose bright Image nightly by the Moon
> *Sidonian* Virgins paid their Vows and Songs;
> In *Sion* also not unsung, where stood
> Her Temple on th' offensive Mountain, built
> By that uxorious King, whose heart though large,
> Beguiled by fair Idolatresses, fell
> To Idols foul.
>                           (*PL.* 1. 437-46)

Milton was familiar with the Scriptural references to Astarte (Jer. vii. 18; 1 Kings xi. 4, 5; 2 Kings xxiii, 13), and probably, as Whiting suggests (207) with Raleigh's discussion of the worshipers of Baal and Ashtaroth. These lines from C. Stephanus serve also to illustrate the meaning

*Astarte,* Syriorum numen non aliud quam Veneris fortasse aut Iunonis: sacrae literae Astartem Sydoniorum deam vocant: cui Salomo rex vni concubinarum suarum obsequi volens, altaria condidit.

See Calepine (1542, 1609), *s.v. Astarte,* for almost identical entries.

BELLEROPHON

> With like safety guided down,
> Return me to my Native Element:
> Lest, from this flying Steed unrein'd, (as once
> Bellerophon, though from a lower Clime)
> Dismounted, on th' *Aleian* Field I fall
> Erroneous there to wander and forlorn.
>                           (*PL.* 7. 15-20)

Osgood points out that Milton is not exactly accurate in his statement, although he might quite logically "infer" that Bellerophon fell into the Aleian plain from Homer's conclusion to the story: "But when even he became hated of all the gods, he went wandering along through the Aleian plain, consuming his heart, shunning the path of men."[17] Certainly Milton could have made such an inference from Homer's naming the field "of wandering" or "of error." It is interesting to note, however, that the inference had already been made. That Bellerophon fell into the Aleian field is expressly stated both in the 1609 edition of Calepine's *Dictionarium* and in even earlier editions of Charles Stephanus' dictionary. In his article on Bellerophon, Stephanus has the following statement:

Bellerophontes autem foelici rerum successu elatus, cum in coelum euolare cum Pegaso conaretur, immisso a Ioue oestro equo excussus est, *deciditque in eum campum, qui postea Aleius appellatus est.*

Compare Comes (*Mythologiae.* 9. 964. Hanoviae, 1605), cited also by Hughes: . . . "Cum in Aleiam Ciliciae planitiem is cecidisset, caecusque factus fuisset, tamdiu errauit per illam planitiem, quamdiu vixit."

BoÖTES

> Non me Boötis terruere lucidi
> Sarraca tarda frigore . . . .
> (*In Obit. Praesul. Eliensis,* 51-52)

MacKellar (*op. cit.,* 292) observes that Milton's lines are reminiscent of Juvenal 5.23:

> Frigida circumagunt pigri serraca Boötae

Hughes (*Par. Reg., Minor Poems,* 47) quotes the same passage from Juvenal.

Charles Stephanus, *Dictionarium, s.v. Boötes,* has the most nearly adequate annotation. After explaining the derivation of the name and identifying Boötes with Arctophylax, Stephanus quotes from Cicero (*de Natura deorum*) and Ovid, and then the passage from Juvenal, "*Frigida circumagunt pigri Sarraca Boötae,*" using the spelling *Sarraca,* as in Milton. Stephanus continues

Habet quatuor stellas in dextra manu quae non occidunt. Gel. [Aulus Gellius] lib. 2. c. 21 Aratus.

*Tardus in occasum, sequitur sua plaustra Bootes.*

He then quotes Manilius

*A tergo venit Arctophylax, idemque Boötes.*

Milton's knowledge of the entry *Boötes* in Stephanus, or in the 1609 Calepine which has the same matter, might account for the spelling *Sarraca* and his use of *tarda* in this context.

BRIAREOS

> Lay floating many a rood, in bulk as huge
> As whom the Fables name of monstrous size,
> *Titanian* or Earth-born, that warr'd on *Jove,*
> *Briareos* or *Typhon,* whom the Den
> By ancient *Tarsus* held. . . .
>
> $\qquad\qquad\qquad\qquad$ (*PL.* I. 196-200)

Conventional notes on these lines may or may not attempt to explain an apparent confusion. Masson points out that the Titans, who were the progeny of Heaven and Earth, were distinct from the Giants, who sprang from the Earth itself or who were the sons of Tartarus and the Earth.[18] Moody in his Cambridge edition says, "Briareos was one of the Titans, Typhon one of the giants. . . . It was the giants only who 'warred on Jove.' "[19] Osgood calls attention to the fact that in Homer, Briareos aids Zeus; but that in Virgil, he is Zeus' enemy.[20] Fletcher writes that Briareos, a son of Uranus, is "meant to represent the Titans and later the Giants."[21] The dictionaries, however, offer a solution to Milton's apparently confused references. At the beginning of Charles Stephanus' article on the giants, for example, they are called "Telluris filij," Tellus being "terrae dea, rerum omnium mater et alumna"; and later in the article when their genealogy is specifically discussed, the following passage occurs:

> De Gigantum autem origine variae sunt priscorum opiniones. Alij namque *illos Titani et Terrae filios* fuisse scribunt, alij *ex sanguine Titanorum* a Ioue interfectorum *e terra esse natos* aiunt.

Furthermore, at least four contemporary reference works call Briareos a giant. Robert Stephanus simply states "Briareus . . . Gigas, Caeli et Terrae filius fuit, alio nomine AEgaeon dictus, quem perpulchre his versibus depinxit Virg. 10. AEn. 565. . . ." Cooper repeats the information without the reference to or the quotation from Virgil. A reader of either an early seventeenth-century edition of Calepine or the *Dictionarium* of Charles Stephanus, however, would have found not only that Briareos was sometimes numbered among the giants who plotted against Jove but also that he was connected with monsters and underground dens:

Alij Briareum inter eos numerant gigantes, *qui aduersus Iouem conspirarunt*: vnde a Vergil. lib. 6, *cum aliis monstris in vestibulo inferorum collocatur.* . . .

The association of the giant Briareos with *monstris* and *vestibulo inferorum* certainly agrees with his being linked with "Typhon, whom the den By ancient Tarsus held"; and it is tempting to conjecture that Milton's knowledge of Briareos' connection with *vestibulo inferorum* might have called up in his memory Aeschylus' line describing Typhon as living in a "Cilician den." At any rate, in the passage quoted above from *Paradise Lost* Milton obviously refers only to giants, "Titanian or Earth-born"; and the aforementioned dictionary entries explain his lines without qualification. From Virgil, Milton might have derived the idea of treating Briareos as a giant; but neither Virgil nor any other source that we know of gives all the information found in the dictionaries—information, moreover, which varies from that in conventional classical accounts. Consequently it is hard to believe that Milton is not definitely indebted here to such a contemporary reference work as that by Charles Stephanus.

CADMUS (HERMIONE)

> . . . Pleasing was his shape,
> And lovely; never since of *Serpent* kind
> Lovelier—not those that in *Illyria* chang'd
> *Hermione and Cadmus*
>
> (*PL.* 9. 503-6)

The story of the transformation of Cadmus and Harmonia is told in Ovid's *Metamorphoses* (4. 562 ff.), as Osgood, Masson, and Hughes point out, each noting, however, that Ovid uses the word *Harmonia,* not *Hermione.* Osgood cites also Nonnus (*Dion.* 44. 107-118) as a possible suggestion for the elaboration as to the beauty of the serpents.[22] It is probable that Milton had read the account in Ovid, and he may have known Nonnus. But none of these would account for the poet's deviation from classical sources in the use of the word *Hermione;* nor is this term employed by Comes, Calepine, or Robert Stephanus, all of whom recount the story of Cadmus.

Once again the best illustration of Milton's allusion, and a possible source of suggestion is found in the *Dictionarium* of Charles Stephanus. The pertinent lines of this account read:

Cadmus . . . Postremo ab Amphione & Zetho regno pulsus, ad *Illyrios* transiuit, ibique deorum commiseratione vna *cum vxore Hermione,* quam Ouidius Harmoniam vocat, Martis & Veneris filia, *in serpentem est commutatus* . . . .

CALISTO, CYNOSURA

> In Wood or Grove by mossy Fountain side,
> In Valley or Green Meadow, to way-lay
> Some beauty rare, *Calisto* . . . .
>
> *(PR. 2.* 184-86)
>
> And thou shalt be our star of *Arcady,*
> Or *Tyrian* Cynosure.
>
> *(Comus,* 341-42)
>
> Where perhaps some beauty lies,
> The Cynosure of neighboring eyes.
>
> *(L'Allegro,* 79-80)

Apollodorus, Hyginus, and Ovid have been cited as telling the story of Calisto; and Hyginus as relating that of Tyrian Cynosure.[23]

Appropriate annotations, possible sources, are entries in Stephanus:

Calisto . . . vna ex Nymphis celeberrima. Lycaonis *Arcadiae regis filia,* quae a Ioue compressa grauidaque effecta, cum simul cum Diana lauaretur tumore vteri prodita, & ab ea repulsa Arcadem filium in syluis peperit: a quo postea Arcadia dicta est. Haec postea a Iunone in vrsam commutata, & Iouis miseratione in coelo collocata, maiorem efficit Vrsam: quae & Helice a Graecis dicitur. Propertius. lib. 2.

> *Calisto Arcadias errauerat vrsa per agros:*
> *Haec nocturna suo sidere vela regit.*

Cynosura . . . sidus Septentrionale, ex septem constans stellis, quod & Vrsam minorem appellamus. Hanc poëtae fabulantur Nympham fuisse Idaeam vnam ex Iouis nutricibus, postea ab Ioue rerum potito in hoc sidus translatam, vt ex Aglaosthenis sententia refert Hyginus in Astr. poët. Alio nomine etiam Phoenice appellatur teste eodem Hygino, eo quod a Phoenicibus inter nauigandum potissimum soleat obseruari, quemadmodum & Helice, hoc est, Vrsa maior, a Graecis nautis. Ouid. de tristibus,

> *Esse duas Arctos, quarum Cynosura petatur*
> *Sidoniis, Helicen Graia carina notet.*

Calepine (1609) has a similar account of Cynosura.

CASSIOPEA

> Or that *Star'd Ethiop* Queen *that strove*
> To *set her beauty's praise* above
> The *Sea Nymphs, and their powers offended.*
>
> *(Il Penseroso.* 19-21)

Moody, Osgood, and Hughes all note that Cassiopeia, according to classical tradition, boasted "not her own but her daughter Andromeda's beauty was greater than that of the Nereids." Comes (8. 6.) relates the story, states that Cassiopea preferred herself before the Nereids, and mentions that Cassiopea was "inter sidera relata." Comes' account could be the basis of Milton's allusion. Somewhat nearer to him in phrasing is the composite narrative in Charles Stephanus' *Dictionarium*:

> *Cassiope* . . . Cephei *regis AEthiopum vxor*, & Andromedes mater, *quae, quod gloriaretur, Nereidibus sese corporis pulchritudine praestare, illarum indignationem incurrit.* Nymphae enim iactantia eius irritatae incredibilis magnitudinis cetum immiserunt, filiamque eius vnicam, nomine Andromedam saxo alligarunt . . . *Cassiope* vero tandem generi meritis in *coelum translata traditur* . . . . In capite eius stella ostenditur vna, in vtroque humero singulae, in mamilla dextra clara vna, in lumbis vna, in sinistro femore duae, in genu vna, in pede ipsius dextro vna: in quadrato, quo signum eius circunscribitur, vna: in utrisque angulis singulae, caeteris clarius lucentes. Hyginus *de Signis caelest.*

In the first ten lines of his account Stephanus runs parallel to Comes, may indeed be paraphrasing the *Mythologiae* or using a common source. One difference in phrasing is noteworthy: the *"foeminae* irritatae" in Comes becomes "Nymphae . . . irritatae" in Stephanus. The corresponding phrase in Milton is "Sea Nymphs . . . offended." Comes writes that Cassiopeia "ausa est se Nereidibus etiam praeferre," and Stephanus that Cassiopeia boasted that "Nereidibus *sese corporis pulchritudine praestare."* This latter seems nearer to Milton's "To set her beauty's praise above the Sea Nymphs." Finally, though Comes mentions Cassiopeia's translation to the stars, Stephanus, following Hyginus, emphasizes this aspect of the translated Cassiopeia, and thus affords the stronger suggestion for the epithet "Starr'd."

Calepine (1609), *s.v. Cassiopeia,* has most of the details contained in Stephanus' account.

Hyginus *Poeticon Astronomicon* (in *Mythographi Latini,* Amsterdam, 1681) has a woodcut of Cassiopeia (p. 427) seated in the *siliquastro,* with stars placed on her body as described in the lines quoted above from Stephanus.

CHALYBEAN

Samson's strength made "arms ridiculous" and

> *Chalybean temper'd steel,* and frock of mail.
>
> (*SA.* 133)

Osgood cites Apollonius (2. 375) : "The Chalybeans are workmen and busy themselves with the working of iron." A scholium on the passage, the account continues, says that they were a Scythian people. Hughes remarks that "The Chalybes lived in Pontus . . . and were famous for their skill in forging iron."[24]

Two entries in the *Dictionarium* would have been most suggestive to the author of *Samson Agonistes* :

1. Chalybes, Plinio, populi Ponto vicini, ad Thermodoontem fluuium. . . . Divites hi sunt, victumque ex argenti venis, & ferri metallis, quaerunt. . . . Flaccus, lib. Argonaut. 4

> Non ita sit metuenda tibi, saevissima quanquam
> Gens Chalybum, duris patiens cui cultus in arvis,
> Et tonat adstricta semper domus ignea massa

. . . Hi optimo ferri genere olim celebrabantur, quod nudi effodiebant. Virg. primo. Georg.

> India mittit ebur, mollis sua thura Sabaei :
> At Chalybes nudi ferrum, etc.

2. Chalybs, fluuius in Hispania, *in quo ferrum optime temperatur* : iuxta quem & Chalybas populos collocat Iustinus . . . .

Compare also Calepine, *Dictionarium* (1609).

CLEOMBROTUS

> . . . and hee who to enjoy
> *Plato's Elysium,* leap'd into the Sea,
> *Cleombrotus.*

(PL. 3. 471-73)

In a note on these lines, Hughes cites Plato's *Phaedo* (68, B) as the book that Cleombrotus had read. Most apt contemporary annotations for Milton's allusions are those in current dictionaries. The following is from C. Stephanus :

Cleombrotus, adolescens Ambraciota, qui cum ei nihil accidisset adversi, è muro *se in mare abiecit,* lecto Platonis libro de animarum immortalitate. Cic. in Tuscul.

Cooper (*Thesaurus*) has a free translation of this entry. R. Stephanus' entry (*Thesaurus*) is identical with that of his brother. Calepine (1609) has Cleombrotus jump from the wall to his death, but makes no mention of the sea.

COTYTTO (BAPTAE)

> Hail, *Goddess of Nocturnal sport,*
> Dark-veil'd Cotytto, whom the *secret flame*

*Of mid-night Torches burn;* mysterious Dame
*That ne'er art call'd but when the Dragon womb*
*Of Stygian darkness spets her thickest gloom,*
And makes one blot of all the air,
                                        . . . befriend
Us thy vow'd Priests, till utmost end
Of all thy dues be done . . .
[Ere . . . The nice Morn . . .] to the tell-tale Sun descry
Our *conceal'd Solemnity.*
Come, *knit hands, and beat the ground,*
In a light fantastic round.

                              (*Comus.* 128-44)

In commenting on this passage Osgood refers to Strabo, Suidas, Hesychius, Juvenal, and the scholium on Juvenal. He writes that "It is evident that Milton had this passage [Juvenal, II, 91-2] and its scholium in mind." Here again he points out, however, that Cotytto's being worshipped at night is only implied in classical sources, "most directly in 'secreta taeda' [Juvenal], though the few cases in which the goddess is mentioned would seem by their association to point to nocturnal rites." Certainly, Milton might have made this implication, but the dictionaries expressly state that Cotytto was worshipped in nocturnal rites—a fact which Milton empha- sizes—and the dictionaries also refer specifically to Juvenal, quoting a portion of the pertinent lines. Robert Stephanus, Charles Stephanus, and early seventeenth-century editions of Calepine write under "Cotytto" ("Cotyto") :

> Cotytto . . . dea impudentiae, cui Athenis *a Baptis* (*eo nomine vocabantur eius sacerdotes*) *nocturna sacra fiebant,* quae ab illa vocabantur Cotyttia. Hanc Probus saltatricem fuisse existimat: vnde etiam *sacerdotes eius lasciuis salta- tionibus mores eius referebant.* Iuuenal Satyr. 2. [92]
> Cecropiam soliti Baptae lassare Cotytto.

The same information is given under "Baptae," "sacerdotes Cotyttus . . . *cui nocturna sacra peragebant, saltationibus, & omni voluptatum generi indulgentes,"* and again the line from Juvenal is quoted. Is it not logical to assume that Milton read the entries just quoted and then perhaps turned to the passage specifically cited by the dictionaries? There he could have found the one detail lacking in the dictionary articles—the "secret flame" from Juvenal's "secreta taeda" ("talia secreta coluerunt orgia taeda Cecropiam soliti Baptae lassare Cotyton"). Neither the dictionaries nor Juvenal alone nor Juvenal and the scholium have all the details in Milton

Only the dictionary entries and Juvenal's verses, which the dictionaries cite and partially quote, explain Milton's lines without qualification.

Apparently, the source of the matter on Cotytto and Baptae in the Stephanus dictionaries is found in the *Cornucopiae* (1518 edition) of Perottus. As in this account the author gives the full quotation from Juvenal, including the "secreta taeda," Milton would have needed no other source. Pertinent excerpts from the *Cornucopiae* follow:

A cocyto palude & Pluto ipse cocytus dicitur. & Proserpina cereris filia, quā in insula Sicilia raptā uxorē duxit. Iuue. Talia secreta coluerunt orgia teda Cecropiā iussi baptae lassare cocytū, a qua cocytia sacra dicta sunt. (C. 572. 22-26)

. . . Celebrabantur autem Proserpinae sacra Athenis nocturno tempore a solis mulieribus, crinibus passis, & ad tedarum lumina, nec fas erat alicui viro introire. (*Ibid.* 59-62)

DEUCALION

> . . . nor important less
> Seem'd their Petition, than when the'ancient Pair
> In Fables old, less ancient yet than these,
> *Deucalion* and chaste *Pyrrha to restore*
> The *Race of Mankind drown'd,* before the Shrine
> Of *Themis* stood devout.
>                     (*PL.* II. 9-14)

Milton could have read the story of Deucalion and Pyrrha in various books, one of the more obvious being Ovid's *Metamorphoses* (1. 260-412), as Osgood and others have pointed out. With the Ovid, the poet was doubtless familiar. Comes (*Mythologiae.* 8. 17) devotes five columns to the Deucalion myth, the episode of Deucalion's consulting the oracle being about the middle of the narrative. The *Mythologiae* also was a book known by Milton. More compact accounts are found in the dictionaries of C. Stephanus and of Calepine (1609). The following is from Stephanus:

Deucalion, filius Promethei, cui adulto Epimetheus patruus Pyrrham filiam coniugio iunxit. Porro cum hic apud Thessalos regnaret, ingens diluuium uniuersum terrarum orbem inundauit, genusque humanum ad internecionem deleuit, Deucalione tantum & Pyrrha seruatis: qui in Parnassum montem nauicula delati, ubi primum aquae desedissent, *Themidis oraculum consulerunt, quanam ratione genus humanum posset reparari* . . . .

In the more elaborate account by Comes, apparently the source of Stephanus, are these pertinent phrases:

... quare Deucalion eo cum scapha traiecit, quo egressus eum Pyrrha Themidis oraculum adiuit sciscitaturus quo pacto, si ita Diis placeret, posset humanum genus reparari.

## ECHO

In the story of Milton's *Comus* the Lady, lost from her brothers, sings a song addressed to Echo, which, she hopes, they may hear and thereby be led to her. Here are the pertinent lines from the song:

> Sweet *Echo*, sweetest *Nymph,* that liv'st unseen
>     Within thy airy shell . . .
> Canst thou not tell me of a gentle Pair
>     That likest thy Narcissus are?
>       O if thou have
> Hid them in some flow'ry Cave,
>     Tell me but where,
> Sweet Queen of Parley, *Daughter of the Sphere!*
>     So mayst thou be translated to the skies,
> And give resounding grace to all Heaven's Harmonies.
>
>                             (230-43)

The conventional myth of Echo and Narcissus never refers to Echo as daughter of the sphere or associates her with heavenly harmony. This characterization in *Comus* is indeed rare; and no commentator, so far as we can discover, has ever given a satisfactory explanation of it. Turning to Charles Stephanus' *Dictionarium,* we find *one* entry (under *Echo*) summarizing the traditional story; a *second* entry is, however, very suggestive for this study. It runs thus:

*Echo, Nympha, nullo oculo visa,* et a Pane, pastorum deo, mirum in modum adamata: quae quidem physice *coeli harmoniam significare* dicitur, Solis amicam, tamquam domini, et moderatoris *omnium corporum coelestium, ex quibus ipsa componitur atque temperatur* . . . .

The italicised passages in the quoted selections (italics ours) show not only similarity of phrasing but almost exact correspondence in meaning. In Stephanus and Milton, Echo is the Nymph that lives unseen, she is the daughter of the sphere, she gives "resounding grace" to "all Heaven's Harmonies." It seems beyond a reasonable doubt that the immediate inspiration for the unusual conception of Echo in Milton's song is the entry quoted from Stephanus.

EMPEDOCLES

> . . . hee who to be deem'd
> A God, leap'd fondly into *AEtna* flames,
> *Empedocles.*
>
> (*PL.* 3. 469-70)

The traditional story of Empedocles appears in the various dictionaries of the period—in Calepine, in R. Stephanus, in C. Stephanus, and in Cooper. This from C. Stephanus is an apt annotation:

Empedocles . . . Ferunt hunc, cum lacum AEtnae montis investigare contenderet, decidisse in foueam igneam, & incendio consumptum. Vel vt alij, noctu a sociis clam discendentem, *in ardentem caminum montis AEtnae se demississe, vt deus immortalis haberetur* . . . .

The immediate source of Milton's lines may be, as Gilbert suggests, from Horace:

> Deus immortalis haberi
> Dum cupit Empedocles, ardentem frigidus AEtnam
> Insiluit.
>
> (*Ars Poetica.* 464-66)

EREBUS (NOX, CHAOS)

> (1)         and on thir hinges grate
> Harsh Thunder, that the lowest bottom shook
> of *Erebus.* (*PL.* 2. 881-83)
>
> (2)         . . . where eldest Night
> And *Chaos,* Ancestors of Nature, hold
> Eternal *Anarchy.* (*PL.* 2.894-96)
>
> (3) The luminous inferior Orbs, enclos'd
> From *Chaos* and th' inroad of Darkness old,
> *Satan* alighted walks. (*PL.* 3. 420-22)
>
> (4)         Darkness now rose,
> As day-light sunk, and brought in louring night,
> Her shadowy off-spring. (*PR.* 4. 397-99)

The entry from the dictionary of C. Stephanus serves to illuminate the quoted lines:

Erebus, inferorum deus, & pater Noctis ex Chao & Caligine progenitus, vt refert Hyginus, Fab. poet. cap. 1. Cicer, tamen de. Nat. deor. Noctem Erebi vxorem facit, id quicquid est, Poëtae frequenter Erebum pro ipsa inferorum sede collocant. Virgil. 4. AEneidos.

*Pallentes umbras Erebi, noctemque profundam.* Ouid. lib. 5. *Meta.* Proserpinam Erebi reginam appellat.

The statement in Stephanus that the poets frequently use Erebus for the seat or bottom of hell explains its meaning in the first (1) quotation. Night and Chaos as ancestors of Nature (2) might also be inferred from the relationship established in the dictionary. Perhaps, too, what appears to be the identification of Chaos and Darkness (3) is clarified by the dictionary statement that Erebus is the father of Night *"ex Chao & Caligine."*

With respect to the fourth (4) quotation, from *PR.* 4. 397, Hughes' comment, that "Through Boccaccio's *Genealogy of the Gods* (I, V) and similar mythological works Milton inherited his interest in Hesiod's personification of Night as the wife and sister of Erebus or Darkness (*Theogony,* 748-57),"[25] does not apply. Osgood remarks more aptly: "In *PL.* 3. 421 Darkness seems to be identical with night as the latter is represented elsewhere. In two places, however (*PR.* 4. 397; *L'Al.* 6), there is a suggestion of Erebus, though Night was not his offspring but his sister and wife."[26] But Stephanus, citing Hyginus as his authority, states explicitly that Erebus was the father of night. It is this tradition that Milton seems to be following in *PR.* 4. 397. In *In Quintum Novembris* (69), however, the poet seems to make Night the wife of Erebus. For this, too, there is authority in Stephanus, who cites Cicero.

It is not necessary to urge the dictionaries as a source for all Milton's references to Erebus and Night and Darkness, but the Stephanus as typical, illustrates the poet's use of the myth.

EUPHROSYNE

> But come, thou Goddess fair and free,
> In Heaven yclep'd *Euphrosyne,*
> And by men, heart-easing Mirth,
> Whom lovely *Venus* at a birth
> With two sister Graces more
> To ivy-crowned *Bacchus* bore. . . .
> (*L'Allegro.* 11-16)

Osgood quotes Servius (on *Aen.* 1. 724) as Milton's authority for making Venus and Bacchus parents of the Graces. It is not necessary, however, to assume that the poet had directly in mind the commentary by Servius. In at least ten different manuals or reference books in the period Milton could have read accounts of the Graces, and in more than one of these, he could have found authority for the Venus-Bacchus paternity. A typical entry is this from the C. Stephanus *Dictionarium:*

(1) Charites, seu Gratiae, quidam ex Venere & Iove genitas scripservnt, alij
ex *Venere & Libero*. . . . Tres sunt Aglaia . . . Thalia . . . & Euphrosyne. . . .
(2) Euphrosyne . . . vna Gratiarum, soror Aglaiae & Thaliae, ab animi
hilaritate . . . ita appellata. . . .

EURYBATES

> Talis et Eurybates ante ora furentis Achillei
> Rettulit Atridae iussa severa ducis.
>
> *(Elegia Secunda,* 15-16)

The reference to Eurybates is, as Hughes points out, based ultimately
on Homer (*Iliad.* 1. 320-33).[27]  Milton would have had at hand also
Stephanus' dictionary with the following lines:

Eurybates, praeco Ithacensis, ex Vlyssis comitatu, ab Agamemnone missus, vt
ab Achille auferret Briseidem.  Ouidius Epistol. 6. Homer. Iliad.

R. Stephanus and Calepine have the same information on Eurybates.

FAMA (MAEOTIS, MAREOTIS)

> Esse ferunt spatium, qua distat ab Aside terra
> Fertilis Europe, et spectat Mareotidas undas;
> Hic turris posita est Titanidos ardua Famae.
>
> *(In Quintum Novembris,* 170-73)

The tower of fame, as described by Milton, extends from lines 170 to
193 in the poem *In Quintum Novembris*.  Scholars have pointed out,
notably MacKellar (280 ff.) and, in somewhat more detail, Harding[28]
that Milton's description is a synthesis of matter from Virgil and Ovid,
and possibly others.  It is of course natural that Milton should think of
the pertinent passages on *Fama* in the *Aeneid* and in the *Metamorphoses*.
It is, however, worth noting that long before Milton, Perottus, in his
*Cornucopiae* (1489, 1518, col. 909. 30 seq.), had brought together, *s.v.*
*Fama,* the lines from Virgil (*Aeneid* 4. 173-187) and from the *Metamorphoses* (12. 39-63), preceded by an account of the birth and character of
Fama and referring to her as the sister of the giants Coeus and Enceladus
and the avenger of Terra, her mother.  Perottus' *Fama* contains all the
lines from Virgil and Ovid which scholars have cited as underlying Milton's
own description of the goddess and her action, and in the introductory
statements based on neither of the Latin authors, Perottus gives an account of the birth of Fama, brought forth as the avenger of her mother,
which motivates the action of Fama.  Translated, the prefatory lines run
thus:

It is reported that Fama was a goddess, the daughter of earth, and that when Jove, ambitious of sovereign power, made war on the Titanian giants, sons of earth, and these, far and wide were being slaughtered by Jove and the other gods, Earth was much grieved since she had no weapons against such powerful enemies. But plotting how to avenge in any way possible the injury inflicted upon herself she gave birth to Fama, forced from her womb, Fama who should broadcast the crimes of the gods through the whole world.

Such a goddess was well suited to Milton's purpose, and one line in *In Quintum Novembris* suggests that the poet had a hint from Perottus' initial remarks.

Ipsa quidem summa sedet ultrix matris in arce (180)

Fama as the avenger of her mother—*ultrix matris*—not accounted for by the lines in Virgil and Ovid, could have been suggested by Perottus.

The phrase in Milton's description of Fama which, from the eighteenth century to the present day, has provoked most discussion is the *Mareotidas undas*, appearing in the lines quoted at the beginning of this comment. Warton, Keightley, and after them Masson hold that "Milton cannot have meant Lake Mareotis, which is in Egypt, but the great Lake Maeotis, now the sea of Azof, north of the Black Sea." Gilbert ("The Tower of Fame in Milton," *MLN.* 28 (1913). 30) thinks that Milton uses *Mareotidas,* figuratively, to mean Egyptian and that *Mareotidas undas* might signify literally Egypt. MacKellar and other scholars seem to be in agreement with Gilbert. No one has, so far as I know, pointed out an exact parallel to Milton's *Mareotidas undas* or, to what Keightley and others have said Milton should have written: *Maeotidas undas.*

Renaissance dictionaries seem to throw light on the subject. In the *Thesaurus* of Robert Stephanus we read:

Maeoticus, a, um. Adj. 3 Georg. 349.
    At non qua Scythiae gentes *Maeotica unda.*

(For otherwise is it where dwell the tribes of Scythia by the waters of Maeotis. [Tr. Fairclough, Loeb Classical.])

More informative is the following entry in the *Dictionarium* of Charles Stephanus:

Maeotis, palus Scythica, in regione Septentrionali iuxta Phasidis ostium, Cimmerio Bosphoro a Ponto Euxino discreta, hyeme congelascens, Tanaim, aliosque innumeros fere recipiens fluuios: ita dicta ab accolis, qui Maeotae appellantur. Lucan. lib. 3.
    *Quaque fretum torrens Maeotidas egerit vndas.*

Compare the phrase *Maeotides . . . vndas* and Milton's *Mareotidas undas.*
For the context of the line, we turn to Lucan's Civil War (3. 271-78) :

> Colchorum qua rura secat ditissima Phasis,
> Qua Croeso fatalis Halys, qua vertice lapsus
> Riphaeo Tanais *diversi nomina mundi*
> *Inposuit ripis Asiaeque et terminus idem*
> *Europae, mediae dirimens confinia terrae,*
> Nunc hunc, nunc illum, qua flectitur, ampliat orbem;
> Quaque, fretum torrens, *Maeotidas egerit undas*
> Pontus.   [Italics ours]

([Men came] from the regions where the Phasis cleaves the rich land of the
Colchians, where flows the Halys that brought doom to Croesus, and where
the Tanais, falling down from the Riphaean heights, gives *the names of two
worlds* to *its two banks, bounding Asia and Europe as well—it keeps the
central part of earth from union,* and, according to its windings, enlarges now
one continent and now the other—and where the Euxine drains the rushing
waters of the Maeotian Mere through the strait. [Tr. J. D. Duff, Loeb Classical.])

Granted Milton's general indebtedness to Ovid and Virgil for his description of Fame and the Tower of Fame, the lines from Lucan, with the
*Maeotidas undas* phrase, are nearer in language and meaning to the beginning of Milton's description, "Esse ferunt," etc. than any others thus
far cited.   Compare Milton's

> Esse ferunt spatium, qua distat ab Aside terra
> Fertilis Europe, et spectat Mareotidas undas (170-71)

and Lucan's

> . . . qua vertice lapsus
> Riphaeo Tanais diversi *nomina mundi*
> *Inposuit ripis Asiaeque et terminus idem*
> *Europae, mediae dirimens confinia terrae. . . .*
> Quaque, fretum torrens, *Maeotidas egerit vndas*
> Pontus.   (3. 272-78)

and Ovid's

> Orbe locus medio est inter terrasque fretumque
> Caelestesque plagas, triplicis confinia mundi.
>
> (*Met.* 12. 39-40)

The evidence thus far suggests that whether Milton originally wrote
*Mareotidas* or *Maeotidas,* he was thinking of the position of *palus Maeotis,*
and the thought might have come directly from Lucan, or, indirectly,
through the dictionaries.   It is generally conceded that Milton gives a

central location to the tower. Though he does not specify an exact location, it is between Europe and Asia and—if we accept Maeotidas as his adjective—in the vicinity of Lake Maeotis, possibly at the mouth of the Tanais river, which flows into Maeotis on the north, or at the Cimmerian Bosporus on the south. And what could be more nearly central than Maeotis and its immediate surroundings to the then known world—*tres partes orbis?*

In the first chapter of his *De Situ Orbis,* Pomponius Mela writes of the World and its Parts (*De Mundo et Partibus ejus*). After a few preliminary remarks the author begins with *Fretum* (now the Straits of Gibraltar) which opens the lands (*"terras"*) and enters, carries us through the *Mare nostrum* (the Mediterranean), and then, in the order listed, to the Hellespont, the Propontis, the Thracian Bosporus, the Euxine, the Cimmerian Bosporus, which joins the Lake (*"palus"*). The Lake itself is Maeotis— termed by the Scythians "maris finis," "mater maris." From this central location, the author indicates the three parts of the world, each of which is described in subsequent chapters. The lines which immediately follow the mention of Maeotis are these:

Hoc mari [that is, the Mediterranean and the adjoining waters mentioned above] et duobus inclytis amnibus, Tanai atque Nilo, in tres partes universa dividitur. Tanais, a septentrione ad meridiem vergens, in mediam fere Maeotida defluit; et ex adverso Nilus in Pelagus. Quod terrarum jacet a Freto ad ea flumina, ab altero latere Africam vocamus; ab altero, Europen: ad Nilum, Africam; ad Tanain, Europen. Ultra quicquid est, Asia est.
(By this sea and by two renowned rivers, the Tanais and the Nile, the world is divided into three parts. The Tanais, running from north to south, flows almost into the middle of Maeotis; and on the opposite side, the Nile into the Sea (Mediterranean). The land which lies between the straits [Gibraltar] and these rivers, on one side we call Africa; on the other Europe—that which extends to the Nile, Africa; that which extends to the Tanais, Europe. Whatever land is beyond is Asia.)

Opposite the page on which Pomponius describes the World is a map with the title *Orbis Totius Forma,* showing the *tres partes Orbis*—Europe, Africa, and Asia—the Mare Nostrum, and the *palus Maeotis* between Europe and Asia, with the Tanais coming into it on the north, and directly south, the Nile going into the Mare Nostrum. About the central location of *palus Maeotis* as conceived of by Pomponius—and still acceptable in the seventeenth century—there can be no doubt. Pomponius in fact makes

Maeotis the center from which he describes the threefold world and each continent thereof.

In his *Etymologiae,* Isidore of Seville is even more explicit as to the division of the world and the central location of Lake Maeotis. Under "De Orbe" Isidore writes,

The world is triply divided: one part is Asia, another Europe, and a third, Africa, which also is called Libya. These three parts of the world the ancients did not equally divide; for Asia extends from the south through the east and to the north; Europe from the north to the west; and Africa from the west to the south. Evidently Europe and Africa occupy half of the world, and Asia alone the other half. The reason why the former are made into two parts is that from the ocean the Mediterranean Sea comes between them and separates them. Therefore, if you divide the world into two parts, of east and west, Asia will be in one, Europe and Africa in the other.

In a copy of Isidore (Paris, Iehan Petit, 1520) this discussion of the world is illustrated by a drawing of circle within circle. About the outer circle we read: OCEANUM MARE. The circle within has the east-west division of the world (*orbis*), indicating the positions of Europe, Africa, and Asia according to the exposition recorded above. At the exact center of the inner circle is printed *MAEOTIS PALUS.*

Ovid in his "orbe locus medio" and, after Ovid, Lucan in a more specific way, were doubtless thinking of the east-west division of the ancient world—a division which placed *Maeotis palus* at the center. Now Milton could have departed deliberately from this traditional conception, but those who hold that he did so and that he wrote, intentionally, *Mareotidas undas* have not given a convincing explanation. Milton's phrasing in the two lines (170-71) appears, in fact, to echo that of Lucan as transcribed above, one phrase, if we substitute *Maeotidas* for *Mareotidas,* corresponding exactly to that of Lucan. The evidence seems to indicate that Warton, Keightley, and Masson were right in suggesting that *Mareotidas* in Milton's text was a mistake or a misprint for *Maeotidas.* This is the simpler explanation. Revised and translated, the reading should be:

There is a place, men say, which faces (or lies on) the waters of Maeotis, equidistant from Asia and the fertile land of Europe. Here is located the lofty tower of Fame, the Titanian goddess.

The dictionaries, once more, specify the knowledge current during the era, cite a pertinent line in a classical author, and refer the reader to a fuller discussion which elucidates the poetic lines of a major Renaissance author.

GENIUS

Milton's use of this term is limited to the idea of a Genius or divinity of place, generally the Genius of the wood, as in *Christ's Nativity* (186), *Il Penseroso* (154), *Arcades* (26 ff.), and *Lycidas*. The wider application of Genius as the lord of generation, or as the good or evil spirit influencing the life of the individual, though used extensively by Spenser, has little place in Milton's poetry. His most extensive and characteristic employment of the term is in the "Genius of the Wood," in *Arcades,* as in these lines:

> For know by lot from *Jove* I am the pow'r
> Of this fair Wood, and live in Oak'n bow'r,
> To *nurse* the Saplings tall, and curl the grove
> With Ringlets quaint, and wanton windings wove.
> And all my Plants I save from nightly ill,
> Of noisome winds, and blasting vapours chill.
> > (*Arcades.* 44-49)

So well known, in Milton's day, was the lore on Genius that it is hardly necessary to posit the author's knowledge of Servius' comment on Virgil's *Georgics* as a possible source of inspiration. Even the excellent studies of Professor E. C. Knowlton[29] in tracing the allegorical figure of Genius in the Middle Ages and the Renaissance are by no means exhaustive. Not mentioned by Knowlton, or any other scholar so far as we know, are the treatments of Genius by Polydore Virgil (*De Inventoribus Rerum,* lib. 1. C. 1), Erasmus (*Adagia.* 2. 55 F), Cesare Ripa (*Iconologia,* "Genio"), Perottus (*Cornucopiae*), and the dictionaries of Calepine, and the Stephanus brothers, Valeriano (*Hieroglyphica,* 2. 496.), and Cartari (*Imagines Deorum*).

Annotations for the lines in *Arcades* might come from almost any one of the sources cited. In widest circulation perhaps was the poetic dictionary of C. Stephanus, from which we quote:

Genius, dicebatur a priscis deus naturae, & qui omnium rerum gignendarum vim haberet, vnde cuiusque rei dicebatur suus Genius: hominique duos Genios assignabant, bonum & malum. Accipitur pro ipsa natura. Quidam ipsam animam vel deum, vel spiritum esse volunt, qui mortales ad voluptatem incitet: vnde Geniales ab antiquis appellabantur, qui ad curandam cuticulam erant promptiores. Inde prouerbium, Indulgere genio. Fuerunt etiam qui aquam, terram, ignem, aerem, item duodecim signa, & solem & lunam, deos genios facerent: & a gerendo, quod multa gerere possent, primum Getulos, deinde Genios appellatos esse putarent.

GRATIAE, HORAE (GRACES, HOURS). See EUPHROSYNE.

With the exception of the mention of Euphrosyne (*q.v.*) and the Graces in *L'Allegro* (12, 15, etc.), all Milton's allusions are to the Graces and the Hours in association. It seems logical therefore to consider the passages involving the two allied groups, especially since the Graces are discussed above, with Euphrosyne:

> Along the crisped shades and bow'rs
> Revels the spruce and jocund Spring,
> The Graces and the rosy-bosom'd Hours,
> Thither all their bounties bring.
>
> (*Comus.* 984-87)
> . . . airs, vernal airs,
> Breathing the smell of field and grove, attune
> The trembling leaves, while Universal *Pan*
> Knit with the *Graces* and the *Hours* in dance
> Led on th' Eternal Spring.
>
> (*PL.* 4. 264-68)
> . . . till Morn,
> Wak't by the circling Hours, with rosy hand
> Unbarr'd the gates of Light.
>
> (*PL.* 6. 2-4)

The Graces (*Charites; Gratiae*) are discussed in the various dictionaries, from Perottus through Calepine and Stephanus, and Cooper, as are the *Horae* (Hours) generally. With the exception of Perottus (1518), none of these definitely associate the Hours and the Graces. Characteristic of the descriptions of Horae is the entry in Robert Stephanus' *Thesaurus*. Stephanus asserts that *Hora* signifies time, any part of eternity embracing yearly, daily, or nocturnal space. He explains the divisions of the day into 12 and then 24 hours. Among the Aegyptians, Apollo is called Horus, and from him, the Horae, into which the night and day are divided, receive their name. The four seasons of the year likewise are called Horae. The Horae have charge of the horses of the sun; they preside over the gates of the sky and determine the weather as well as the seasons. According to Plato, the Horae determine winter and summer and the winds, and the fruits springing from earth, and "Hora formosam quamlibet illa facit." Similar information is found in Calepine.

All this information, and more, appears in Cartari's *Imagines Deorum*
(1581). Here the Graces and the Horae are described under the same
heading. They are closely associated; by some indeed regarded as identical. The Horae care for the horses of the sun; they are the companions
of Janus in guarding the sky; they determine the seasons and the hours
of the day; they bring with them wickers, one filled with flowers, ushering
in the spring; the other with figs, signifying summer. They are the companions of Flora. Beautiful in body and sweet in voice, they come dancing
and singing and roll in the year, and make fair all things on earth. (pp.
353-54)

HERMIONE.  See CADMUS.

HIPPOLYTUS.  See AESCULAPIUS.

[ISOCRATES]

> . . . as that dishonest victory
> At *Chaeronéa,* fatal to liberty,
> Kill'd with report that Old man eloquent.
> *(To the Lady Margaret Ley.* 6-8)

A likely source of information on that "Old man eloquent" is found in C.
Stephanus.

*Isocrates,* orator Atheniensis, vnus e decem, dulcis & numerosus in dicendo
fuit. . . . Decessit annos fere centum natus, post Atheniensium cladem ad
Cheroneam acceptam, non sustinens nuntium tantae cladis. Ex. Philostrato.

The *Thesaurus* of R. Stephanus gives a more detailed account of Isocrates,
concluding, however, in the language of the entry quoted above.

IAPETUS, JAPHET, JAVAN

> (1)  Parere fati discite legibus
>       Manusque Parcae iam date supplices,
>          Qui pendulum telluris orbem
>             Iapeti colitis nepotes.
>                                        *(Procanc.* 1-4)
> (2)            . . . O! too like
>       In sad event, when, to the unwiser Son
>       Of *Japhet* brought by *Hermes,* she ensnar'd
>       Mankind with her fair looks, to be aveng'd
>       On him who had stole *Jove's* authentic fire.
>                                        *(PL.* 4. 715-19)
> (3)  Th' *Ionian* Gods, of *Javan's* Issue held

> Gods, yet confest later than Heav'n and Earth
> Thir boasted Parents . . . .
>
> (*PL.* 1. 508-10)

As Verity,[30] Osgood,[31] MacKellar,[32] and Hughes[33] point out and as is obvious from the first two quoted passages above, Milton identifies Iapetus with Japhet of Genesis x, 2, the son of Noah. Hughes maintains that this identification is traditional, but cites no earlier example than that of Milton. A suggested explanation of such an identification we shall see below.

Osgood cites Jerome (*Hebr. Quaest. in Gen.* 10.2) to the effect that "from Javan, the son of Japhet are sprung the 'Iones, qui et Graeci.' " Two entries in Stephanus' dictionary will show that Milton did not need to look back even to Jerome to find Japhet and Javan identified as ancestors of the Ionians or Hellenes.

Iaphet, i. dilatatus, aut pulcher, siue persaudens, filius Noe, Gen. 5. Hic Aphricam tenuit secundum Berosum, a quo Gentiles. Hic pater fuit Hellech. a quo Graeci originem, & nomen duxerunt: hi enim primum Hellenes dicti sunt.

Iauan, filius Iaphet, Genes. 10. a quo Iones, siue Graeci, Ezech. 27. Lat. decipiens, vel contristans, aut coenosus, vel columbus.

These entries, especially *Iauan,* might account for Milton's reference, in No. 3 above, to the relation of the "Ionian Gods" and "Javan's Issue." The poet's reference, in the same passage, to "Heav'n and Earth Thir boasted Parents" confirms his identification of Japhet with Iapetus. The entry of *Iapetus,* in Stephanus, begins "Iapetus, *Coeli siue Titani* & *Terrae filius* (vt inquit Hesiodus). . . ." Immediately following the *Iapetus* item is the entry *Iaphet,* as quoted above. One may well wonder whether Milton having read or heard read these two entries together, had thus suggested to him the interesting identification of Iapetus and Iaphet. As far as we have been able to discover there is no earlier example of such identification. But the dictionaries of Adam Littleton (1678) and Thomas Holyoke (1677) do make the names apply to the same person.

JOSHUA

> But *Joshua* whom the Gentiles *Jesus call,*
> *His Name and Office bearing,* who shall quell
> The adversary Serpent. . . .
>
> (*PL.* 12. 310-12)

On this passage Verity (II, 650) comments "His name and office bearing" is that, as Joshua led the Jews through the wilderness and brought them

to the Land of Promise, so Christ brings men, after their journey through
the world into the presence of God, as being their Mediator (XI, 32-34)
and Advocate (Smith's Bible Dictionary)."

More relevant is Masson's comment 1. 310: "Jesus is used as the
Greek equivalent to Joshua in the Septuagint, and also in Acts vii. 15, and
Heb. iv. 8."

For the language of his allusion to Joshua, Milton may have had in
mind Stephanus' comment on *Iosue*:

*Iosue, & Iesus, idem est nomen*: cognominatus est autem a patre, Iesus Naue, vel
Iosue Bennum, i. filius Naue, vel Nun, quod idem est: dictus est autem sic, ad
differentiam Iesu filij Sirach pronepotis Iesu magni sacerdotis, qui Ecclesiasti-
cum scripsit, Comest. in praefa. libri. *Iosue, Typum Iesu Christi non solum in
gestis, verum etiam in nomine gerens,* transiit Iordanem. . . . [1595 ed.]

The language of Milton in the lines quoted seems almost a translation
of Stephanus' Latin. Compare "Joshua whom the Gentiles Jesus call, His
Name and Office bearing" and "Iosue, & Iesus, idem est nomen . . . Josue,
Typum Iesu Christi non solum in gestis, verum etiam in nomine gerens."
Lycaonius. (Boötes)

> Iamque Lycaonius plaustrum caeleste Boötes
> Non longa sequitur fessus ut ante via . . . .
> *(Elegia* V. 35-6)

*Lycaonius* in this context has caused the commentators a good deal of
labor without very satisfactory results. MacKellar writes that "Keightley
says this is not a proper epithet for Boötes, which had nothing to do with
Lycaon, whose daughter was turned into the *plaustrum caeleste.*" But
Lycaonius, MacKellar adds, has the transferred meaning of northern (see
Ovid, *Tr.* 3. 2. 2).[34] Mary Campbell Brill reproduces MacKellar's note
and writes out the cited quotation from Ovid's *Tristia*: "*Quaeque Lycaonia
terra sub axe iacet.*"[35] Davis P. Harding, obviously not satisfied with the
earlier annotations, writes, "A good example of a phrase which has never
been fully explained is *Lycaonius . . . Boötes* in *Elegy* (5. 35)."[36] Harding then quotes the two lines from the *Elegy*, as above, reproduces annotations from Regius and Micyllus, and returns to MacKellar as the first
scholar to suggest a parallel between Milton's expression and the phrase
in Ovid's *Tristia*—"*Lycaonis terra sub axe iacet.*" Harding then comments (p. 47) that *Lycaonius* in its context is used to emphasize the position of the axis in the northern part of the sky. He notes further that

Forcellini and other lexicographers have inferred that *Lycaonius* had the transferred meaning of "northern"; and that though "the word is not defined in the Renaissance dictionaries . . . a note in the Chipping edition of the *Opera* strongly suggests that this transferred meaning was known to the Renaissance. . . . In any case, Milton would have had sufficient authority for *Lycaonius* . . . *Boötes*. It was a perfectly logical variation."

Despite the two-page comment, Harding has added little, if anything, to MacKellar's annotation. And one wonders what Renaissance dictionaries Harding consulted. The *Thesaurus* of Robert Stephanus, a work with which Milton was demonstrably familiar, has this entry:

*Lycaonius* . . . Adj. . . . ut,
    Axis Lycaonius, Septentrionales, Ovid. 3. Trist. 2. 2
    Astra Lycaonia. Claud. Cons. Mall. Theod. 299
    Calisto Lycaonia. Catull. de coma Berenices. 64. 66
    Mensae Lycaoniae foeda convivia. Ovid. 1 Met. 165

In Calepine (1609 edit.) we read: "*Lycaonius*, Adiectuum . . . vt Axis Lycaonius, Septentrionales. Ovid. 3 Tr. Eleg. 2. *Quaeque Lycaonis terra sub axe iacet.*" And, in the same text, *s.v. Boötes,* we read that Boötes was the son of Jove from Calisto and the grandson of Lycaon, and "Septentriones autem sequitur Arctophylax, vulgo qui dicitur esse Boötes."

Charles Stephanus' *Dictionarium . . . Poeticum* (1638 edit.) reads "*Lycaonius* . . . Vt Axis Lycaonius, hoc est, Vrsa maior, in quam Calysto Lycaonis filia creditur transformata. Ouidius 1. Trist. *Quaeque Lycaonis terra sub axe iacet.* Idem 1 Metamorph. *Foeda Lycaoniae referens conuiuia mensae.*" In the same lexicon *s.v. Arctophylax,* we find "Simili etiam ratione Boötes appellatur, quod in modum bubulci plaustrum sequatur: rustici enim Septentrionem plaustra vocant."

The upshot of the discussion is that the meaning of *Lycaonius* as it appears in Milton's context with Boötes was so well known in the sixteenth and seventeenth century, as revealed in the Calepine and Stephanus dictionaries, that a single citation, say to Robert Stephanus' *Thesaurus, s.v. Lycaonius,* should have been adequate annotation. (For Milton's use of Boötes in *On the Death of the Bishop of Ely,* see *s.v.* Boötes)

HORAE. See GRACES.

MUSAE (THE MUSES)

    Spenser, Jonson, Milton, and other poets of the Renaissance could have found in concise form all that had ever been said about the Muses, in contemporary handbooks. Calepine, Charles Stephanus, Thomas Cooper, Robert Stephanus, Comes, and Cartari all treat of the subject. In Calepine (1609), for example, we are told under *Musae,* of their parentage, their habitations, the various general names applied to them as a group, the number of Muses, the particular name and function of each, and, at the conclusion, the epigram of Ausonius (ascribed to Virgil) on the role of each. Similar is the matter in Charles Stephanus; and that in Robert Stephanus' *Thesaurus,* extends the discussion much further. With any, or all, of these works Milton may have been familiar. In the case of Robert Stephanus' book, we know that Milton was using it as a basis for a Latin dictionary which he himself had under way, but left unfinished. With this *Thesaurus,* the poet must have been well acquainted.

In *Elegy VI,* to Charles Diodati, Milton writing of the qualifications of him who would write heroic poetry, urging an abstemious and innocent life, continues:

> Additur huic scelerisque vacans et casta iuventus,
> Et rigidi mores, *et sine labe manus.*
> Qualis veste nitens sacra, et lustralibus undis,
> Surgis ad infensos augur iture Deos.
>
> (63-66)

A most apposite annotation on these lines is found in Robert Stephanus' item on the Muses. The story runs that Orpheus once met in the forest Apollo with the Muses and the Graces on his right and chattering pies and furies on the left. Orpheus expresses amazement at the sight, and the account continues,

Sed noli O vates mirari Phoebus ait. Nempne quotidie multi mihi sacrificant ut Musarum a me Gratiarumque munera impetrant. Ergo quicunque sacra puris manibus nobis faciunt, Musas a nobis Gratiasque gratis accipiunt. Quicunque vero *sacra manibus pollutis attrectare audent, picas & furias inviti reportant.*

Milton's "Heavenly Muse" in *Paradise Lost* is Urania, not, the poet informs us "of the Muses nine." Yet descriptions of Urania, in the dictionaries, as one of the nine Muses would be a basis for Milton's elaboration. His longest description of her appears in Book VII:

> Descend from Heav'n, *Urania,* by that name
> If rightly thou art call'd, whose Voice divine
> Following, above the *Olympian* Hill I soar,
> Above the flight of Pegasean wing.

> The meaning, not the Name I call: for thou
> Nor of the Muses nine, nor on the top
> Of old *Olympus* dwell'st, but Heav'nly born
> . . . .　　　　　　　　　Up led by thee
> Into the Heav'n of Heav'ns I have presum'd,
> An Earthly Guest, and drawn Empyreal Air,
> Thy temp'ring. . . .
>
> （1-7; 12-15.）

Of Urania, Calepine writes,

> . . . Nonam Oὐρανίαν Vraniam, quasi coelestem, vel a coelestium rerum cantu, vel a cantus diuinitate. Oὐρανὸν enim Graeci vocant coelum.

Similar is the language of C. Stephanus under *Musae;* and under Urania, he writes, among other things, "unde & Uranium dictam putant quasi τὰ ἄνω ὁρῶσαν hoc est, sublimia speculantem." Urania, in the Robert Stephanus is thus described:

> Una ex Musis, & apud nos Coelestis dicitur.　Ovid. 5. *Fast.* 55.　Excipit Uranie, fecere silentia cuncta οὐρανος enim coelum dicitur, quod viros eruditos in coleum tollit.　Uranos vero dicitur quasi *oranos* (vt ait Ambrosius libro Hexaemeron) ab ὁράω quod sit visui pervium & minime densum, ut est aqua & terra.　Catul. in Epith. Juliae. 59. 2.

In the dictionaries as in *Paradise Lost,* Urania is the heavenly Muse who lifts learned men to the sky.

Nimrod (Nemrod, Nembroth), Babel, Senaar, etc.

A long passage in *Paradise Lost* (12. 24-63), alluding to Nimrod and the building of the tower of Babel, is a good example of the way Milton frequently synthesizes information derived from various sources, including probably contemporary dictionaries. Though the passage of about forty lines is too long to quote here, some parts will be given in the remarks which follow.

The basic source of Milton's lines on Nimrod is found in Genesis (10. 8-10; 11. 2-9), the language of which the poet clearly echoes. Compare, for example,

> . . . they cast to *build*
> *A City and Tow'r, whose top may reach to Heav'n;*
> And *get themselves a name, lest* far disperst
> In foreign Lands thir memory be lost,
> 　　　　　　　　　(*PL.* 12. 43-46)

and

And they said, Go to, let us *build a city and a tower, whose top may reach unto heaven;* and let us *make us a name, lest* we be scattered abroad upon the face of the whole earth. (*Gen.* 11. 4.)

There are, also, other parallels; but the Biblical source by no means accounts for all of the matter in Milton's lines. The poet has echoes of Sylvester's Du Bartas, as Taylor points out;[37] and Milton may have read Raleigh's *History of the World,* on Nimrod, as Whiting suggests.[38] But even these sources lack some important details seen in Milton's lines, such as associating Nimrod with the building of Babel, the idea that brick in the Tower of Babel was "cemented together with mortar, made of bitumen," Nimrod's deriving his name from rebellion, etc. Hughes cites Josephus *Antiquities* (I, iv, 2, 3, etc.) as a possible source.[39] The gist of Josephus, and much besides, the poet could have read in Charles Stephanus' dictionary, under *Nembroth.* Here Stephanus cites Josephus, Berosus, and Comestor on the subject of Nimrod and places associated with his name.

To begin the discussion of the possible relation of Milton to Stephanus on the subject of Nembroth, let us look first at an earlier reference, in *Paradise Lost,* to Babel and Sennaar. Milton writes,

> The builders next to *Babel* on the Plain
> Of *Sennaar,* and still with vain design
> New *Babels,* had they wherewithal would build.
> (*PL.* 3. 466-68)

In the scriptures, it will be remembered, the plain is referred to as "Shinar," not "Sennaar." Compare, however, this from Stephanus:

Sennaar, campus Babylonis, in quo regnauit Nemrod. Gen. 10. quae Babylonia siue Chaldea interdum dicitur.

Here is authority for the use of Sennaar as the Babylonian plain. Keeping in mind this association, let us recall certain lines of Milton in *PL.* 12:

> Hee [Nimrod] *with a crew, whom like Ambition joins*
> *With him* or under him to tyrannize,
> Marching from *Eden* towards the West, shall find
> The Plain, wherein a black bituminous gurge
> Boils out from under ground, the mouth of Hell . . . .
> (ll. 38-42)

These lines are suggested, in part, by *Genesis,* 11. 2. But Genesis employs the word "Shinar," and it is not evident that Nimrod was the leader

Title page of Calepine's *Dictionarium*, printed at Paris, 1516, from a copy
in the University of Texas Library.

or who the sojourners are, other than descendants of Noah. Milton may have remembered what he had read in Stephanus, *s.v. Nembroth* or *Babylonicus populus*:

. . . *Nembrotus* [Nimrod] (inquit Berosus li. 3) assumpto filio Ioue Belo, *cum coloniis*, furatus est rituales Iouis Sagi, & *cum populo venit in campum Sennaar*, vbi designauit vrbem, & fundauit maximam turrim . . . .

This quotation from Stephanus definitely places Nimrod as the leader of those who come into the plain, as Milton does; calls the plain *Sennaar*, as the poet does in an earlier passage; and in the "cum coloniis" may suggest the "crew, whom like Ambition joins with him [Nimrod]."

The line, referring to Nimrod,

And from Rebellion shall derive his name,
(*PL.* 12. 36)

may be compared with Stephanus'

Nemrod, filius Chus. Gen. 10. Lat. *rebellis*, vel dormitio descensionis, aut dormiens dominans,

and Milton's

. . . thus was the building left
Ridiculous, and the work Confusion nam'd,
(*PL.* 12. 62)

with Stephanus'

Babel, civitas, Gen. 11, Lat. *Confusio*, seu Commistio . . . .

Referring to Babel, under the entry *Babylon*, Stephanus writes,

. . . *Murum* habuit *coctili* latere, atque *interfuso bitumine* compactum . . .

which may recall Milton's

. . . a black bituminous gurge . . .
Of *Brick*, and of *that stuff they cast to build*
A City and Tow'r . . . .
(*PL.* 12. 41-44)

A reading in Stephanus of the entries *Nembroth, Babel*, and *Babylon* strongly suggests these as a source of information, supplementing the poet's knowledge of the Scriptures, Du Bartas, etc. The fact that, later in *Paradise Regained* (3. 254 ff.), he reverted to the Stephanus' accounts of Babylon and related words, may be some confirmation of his early use of them. For further comparison by the reader, we quote here C. Stephanus' discourse on Nembroth (Nimrod) :

Nembroth, filius Cham, filij Noae post diluuium cum homines a Dei timore, aquarum vim interminantis, avocare conaretur, spem suam in virtute propria ponendam ratus, turrim altissimam aedificandam suadebat, quam aquae superare non possent. His itaque opere iam incoepto ita insanientibus, Deus discordiam immisit linguarum: vt per multas obsonasque voces intellectu inter se carerent. Haec igitur tot linguarum, quibus etiam nunc homines vtuntur, diversitatis est origo, Ioseph lib. i. antiq. Nembrotus (inquit Berosus li. 3) assumpto filio Iove Belo, cum coloniis, furatus est rituales Iouis Sagi, & cum populo venit in campum Sennaar, vbi designauit urbem, & fundauit maximam turrim, anno salutis ab aquis diluuij centesimo primo: regnauitque annis quinquaginta sex: ac deduxit turrim ad altitudinem & magnitudinem montium, in signum atque monumentum, quod primus in orbe terrarum est populus Babylonicus, & regnum regnorum dici debet. Haec Berosus. Itemque Comest. in cap. 10. Gen. de ipso sic ait: Nembroth, gigas 10 cubitorum, qui coepit primus potens esse in terra, & robustus venator coram Deo, id est, oppressor, & extinctor hominum, dominandi & regnandi cupiditate: & cogebat homines ignem adorare. Unde prouer. Fortis & malus ut Nembroth.

NISROCH (NESROCH)

> He sat; and in th' assembly next upstood
> *Nisroch,* of Principalities the prime;
> As one he stood *escap't* from cruel fight
> Sore toil'd.
> > (*PL.* 6. 446-49)

Masson (III, 365) believes that *"Nisroch"* (perhaps "Great Eagle") is from 2 Kings xix. 37. Hughes, following Verity, explains Nisroch as an Assyrian deity and remarks, "Milton may have derived the word from the Hebrew 'Nesher,' 'eagle,' or have made the mistake of identifying Nisroch with the vulture-god of the Assyrian bas-reliefs."

Stephanus' dictionary offers the following suggestive lines for Milton:

*Nesroch,* Hebr. *Nisroch,* i. *fuga* vel tentatio tenera aut delicata vel vexillum delicatum: aut Syriace, tabula tua, idolum quod adorabat Sennacherib. 4 Reg. II, 19. Isai. 37-8

The ultimate source of this entry is perhaps Robert Stephanus' *Hebraea, Chaldaea, Graeca et Latina nomina virorum* . . . (Paris, 1537), p. 205 The language in this text and the *Dictionarium* of C. Stephanus is identical.

OPHION

> And Fabl'd how the Serpent, whom they call'd
> *Ophion* with *Eurynome,* the wide—
> Encroaching *Eve* perhaps, had first the rule
> Of high *Olympus;* thence by Saturn driv'n
> And Ops. . . .
>
> (*PL.* 10. 580-84)

None of the editors or commentators satisfactorily account for Ophion as a serpent. Masson (3. 381) has the interesting suggestion that the word "Ophion" implies "serpent," and that Milton treats the myth of Ophion and Eurynome as a tradition of the story of the Serpent and Eve, kept up among the Heathens by the Devils themselves. Osgood (34) points to Apollonius of Rhodes (*Arg.* 1. 503) as the source of the Ophion-Eurynome story and observes that the poet suggests an etymological connection between "Ophion" and ὄφις, serpent. Similar observations are made by Verity and Hughes. Comes' version of the story (*Mythologiae.* 2. 122) makes no association of Ophion and the serpent. Two entries in both Charles Stephanus' dictionary and Robert Stephanus' *Thesaurus* suggest a plausible explanation of the poet's allusion:

(1) Ophion, socius Cadmi ex illis qui e dentibus serpentinis nati fuerunt: ideoque & nomen habet a serpente, qui Graece ὄφις dicitur.
(2) Ophion, vir qui cum Eurinome vxore, quam genuit Oceanus, ante Saturnum rerum potitus est, quem Saturnus fugauit. Claud. 3. de raptu Proserp.

Suppose Milton did know the story as told by Apollonius of Rhodes and sought to refresh his memory by consulting the Stephanus dictionaries; he would have been impressed by the two successive entries, in the first of which is the authority for Ophion as a serpent. It would have been quite in keeping with the poet's practice deliberately to fuse the two Ophions, having in mind, as Masson suggests, the story of the Serpent and Eve as a striking parallel.

In the Calepine (1609) the two items quoted above are placed under a single entry—*Ophion.*

PANDORA

Referring to the nuptial day of Eve, Milton writes that the genial angel:

> Brought her in naked beauty more *adorn'd,*
> More lovely than *Pandora,* whom the Gods
> *Endow'd* with all thir gifts, and O too like
> In sad event, when to the unwiser Son

> Of *Japhet* brought by *Hermes,* she ensnar'd
> Mankind with her fair looks, to be aveng'd
> On him who had stole *Jove's* authentic fire.
>
> (*PL.* 4. 713-19)

In the *Doctrine and Discipline of Divorce* (3), Eve is referred to as "a consummate and most *adorned* Pandora."

Hesiod (*W & D.* 50 ff; *Theog.* 511) tells the story of Pandora, as Osgood and others have noted. Hesiod could have been Milton's source. There are, however, other versions which may have contributed to Milton's knowledge of the legend. Comes (*Mythologiae.* 4. 316) recounts it. Some of Comes lines run ". . . id cum resciuisset Iupiter, Vulcano imperauit, ut foeminam e luto componeret, quae cum astutissima esset, & *omnibus artibus a Diis donata,* vocata fuit Pandora." Stephanus' version, in which he refers to Hesiod as his source, is in phrasing nearer to Milton than is Hesiod or Comes. Stephanus writes

Pandora . . . Hesiodo fingitur *prima mulier,* a Vulcano *Iovis* iussu fabricata, *quam singuli dij donis suis ornaverunt* . . . inde dicta fuit Pandora, quasi *omnium donum,* vel quasi *ab omnibus donata,* vel omnium rerum genere *dotata.* Hanc postea cum pyxide clausa missam fuisse tradunt ad Epimetheum (cum humano generi male cupiebat Iupiter, ob Promethei audaciam, qui ignem e coelo furatus, ferulae inclusum detulerat in terras) qui illa recepta, & pyxide aperta, cui omne malorum genus inerat, terram morbis calamitatibusque repleuit.
. . .

Whatever accounts of Pandora Milton had read, it looks as though that of Charles Stephanus was most vivid in his mind when he was writing the lines quoted above (4. 713-715, especially). He employs the active voice as contrasted, for example, with the passive of Comes. The *prima mulier* in the first line of Stephanus would have suggested the comparison with Eve; "ornauerunt" supplies the "adorn'd" (1. 713); "donata" or "dotata" suggests "Endow'd" (715); the "singulis . . . donis suis" and "omnium donum" emphasize "with all their gifts."; and "quam singuli dij donis suis ornauerunt" (cf. "donata" and "dotata") is parallel in structure and meaning to "whom the Gods Endow'd with all their gifts."

PARTHENOPE

> Credula quid liquidam Sirena, Neapoli, iactas,
> Claraque Parthenopes fana Achelöiados,
> Littoreamque tua defunctam Naiada ripa
> Corpora Chalcidico sacra dedisse rogo?
>
> (3 Ad Leonoram. 1-4)

The best explanations of the allusion to Parthenope are found in the Stephanus dictionaries.   Charles Stephanus writes,

*Parthenope,* vna Sirenum . . . Harum aliae alia in loca.   Parthenope autem eo delata est, vbi postea condita fuit Neapolis, praeclara vrbs Campaniae, quae ab eius nomine etiam Parthenope est appellata . . . Neapolis haec vrbs appellatur, & ciues ipsi Neapolitani: quos scribit Lycrophon quotannis *ad tumulum Parthenopes faces ferre consueuisse.*   Verisimilior est itaque aliorum opinio, qui hanc vrbem a Cumanis conditam tradunt: qui quum in eo loco Parthenopes corpus in vetere monumento conditum reperissent, nomen eius vrbi indidere.

R. Stephanus has substantially the same account, but he adds "Ab hoc igitur Sirene Neapolis est appellata, a virgine Parthenope."   The *Cornucopiae* of Perottus appears to be the source for the Parthenope item in the Stephanus dictionaries.

PARTHIANS

> (1) Me nequit adductum curvare peritius arcum,
>     Qui post terga solet vincere, Parthus eques.
>                          (*Elegia Septima.* 36-37)
> (2) They issue forth, Steel Bows and Shafts their arms,
>     Of equal dread in flight, or in pursuit:
>     All Horsemen, in which fight they most excel.
>                          (*PR.* 3. 305-07)
> (3) He saw them in their forms of battle rang'd
>     How quick they wheel'd, and flying behind them shot.
>     Sharp sleet of arrowy showers against the face
>     Of their pursuers, and overcome by flight.
>                          (*PR.* 3. 322-25)

An annotation from Stephanus is

Parthia . . . *Hi arcu plurimum valuerunt,* quo *vel fugientes hosti plurimum detrimenti afferebant.*

PHOENIX

In describing Raphael's flight to Paradise, Milton uses the story of the Phoenix in these lines:

>                          . . . till within soar
> Of Tow'ring Eagles, to all the Fowls he seems
> A *Phoenix,* gaz'd by all, as that sole Bird
> When to enshrine his reliques in the Sun's
> Bright Temple, to *Egyptian Thebes* he flies.
>                          (*PL.* 5. 270-74)

Having reached the cliff of Paradise, Raphael assumes his own shape,

A Seraph wing'd; six wings he wore, to shade
His lineaments Divine; the pair that clad
Each shoulder broad, came mantling o'er his breast
With regal Ornament; the middle pair
Girt like a Starry Zone his waist, and round
Skirted his loins and thighs with downy Gold
And colours dipt in Heav'n; the third his feet
Shadow'd from either heel with feather'd mail
Sky-tinctur'd grain.

(*PL.* 5. 277-85)

Since the classical writers agree that the phoenix visited Heliopolis, scholars have wondered what Milton's authority was for saying that the phoenix flew to Thebes. One suggestion has been made for what seems to be Milton's mistake that in the Bible Heliopolis is called *On* and Thebes *No,* and, with more relevance, that Diodorus reports the Egyptians called Thebes Heliopolis. Another comment states flatly, "Milton changed 'the city of the sun,' i.e., Heliopolis, to the neighboring Egyptian city of Thebes." It is not likely, however, that Milton or his readers would have thought of Thebes (274) as a mistake. They would have known from various current dictionaries that, in ancient times the names were frequently interchangeable—Thebes was called Heliopolis, and Heliopolis, Thebes. So in Calepine, in Charles Stephanus, and Robert Stephanus. Compare, for example, Calepine:

Thebe . . . nomina quarundam urbium, quarum una fuit in Aegypto, a Busyride Aegypti rege condita, quae Graece, Ἡλιούπολις id est, solis ciuitas . . .

and

Heliopolis, Ἡλιούπολις . . . ciuitas Aegypti, inter Alexandriam & Coptum, a Graecis Thebae dicta: quasi ciuitas Solis.

But the dictionaries could have done more for Milton and his readers than explain Thebes and Heliopolis: they presented various versions of the phoenix legend. Here are two, from Friar Calepine and Robert Stephanus, respectively, which could have offered definite suggestions to the poet. The first is from Calepine (1542):

Phoenix. . . . Similiter Phoenix auis a purpureo pennarum colore dicta, toto orbe celeberrima, in Arabia nascens, aquilae magnitudine, quae annis sexcentis & sexaginta uiuere dicitur, generis tam masculini quam foeminini. Hieronymus in expositione Symboli: Quid mirum uidetur, si virgo conceperit, cum Orientis auem, quem Phoenicem uocant, in tantum sine coniuge nasci, vel renasci constet, ut semper una sit, & semper sibi ipsa nascendo, uel renascendo succedat? Idem ad Praesidium: Phoenix auis est in India, & per quingentos annos de Libano implet se aromatibus, & sic nidificat, & indicat sacerdoti Heliopolitano, mense famenoth, aut famurth. Implet aram sacerdotis sarmentis, & ibi confert Phoenix aromata, et electrum arae imponit. Et primo Solis ortu Phoenix quidem mouet pennas, Solis vero calore accenditur electrum, & sic exurūtur aromata, & ipsa Phoenix incenditur. Crastino die de cinere gignitur vermis, secundo pennas affert, tertio ad antiquam redit naturam, & sic ad sua loca reuertitur. De hac aue uide Pli. lib. 10. cap. 2. . . .

And the second from Robert Stephanus:

Phoenix . . . Avis. Plin. lib. 10. ca. 2. . AEthiopes & Indi, discolores maxime & inenarrabiles ferunt aves, & ante omnes nobilem Arabia phoenicem: haud scio an fabulose, unum in toto orbe, nec visum magnopere. Aquilae narratur magnitudine, auri fulgore circa colla, caetera purpureus, caeruleam roseis caudam pennis distinguentibus, cristis fauces, caputque plumeo apice honestante. Primus atque diligentissimus togatorum de eo prodidit Manilius Senator ille maximus, nobilis doctrinis doctore nullo: neminem extitisse qui viderit vescentem: sacrum in Arabia Soli esse, vivere annis DIX senescentem casia thurisque surculis construere nidum, replere odoribus, & superemori. Ex ossibus deinde e medullis ejus nasci primo ceu vermiculum, inde fieri pullum, principioque justa funeri priori reddere, & totum deferre nidum prope Panchaiam in Solis vrbem, & in ara ibi deponere. Ouid. 15. Met. 393. . . . Et viuax phoenix vnica semper auis. Ouid. 2. Amor. 6. 54.

The suggestion of "Tow'ring Eagles" (1. 271), in close proximity to "Phoenix," could have come from the "aquilae magnitudine" of either version; so could the ideas of the sole Bird and enshrining his reliques in the bright temple of the sun. In the second part of the quotation (ll. 277 ff.), the conception of Raphael as a Seraph with six wings is doubtless indebted to *Isaiah* (6.1), but the elaboration and coloring in the description has no basis in *Isaiah*. Definite suggestions may have come, however, from Robert Stephanus' version of the Phoenix story or from Stephanus' source in Pliny. (*N. H.* 10. C 2).

Referring to the indescribable (*"inenarrabiles"*) colors of the birds of Africa and India, and before all those of the renowned Phoenix in Arabia, Stephanus continues that this bird, the size of an eagle, is of gleaming gold (*"auri fulgore"*) about the neck, of purple on the rest of the body, the tail of cerulean or sky-color adorned with rosy feathers, the throat with tufts embellished, and the head with a downy crown (*"plumeo apice"*). Compare with this description of the phoenix, Milton's descriptive phrases applied to the wings of Raphael the Seraph—Raphael, who had a moment before been compared to a phoenix. The wings from the shoulders of the Seraph mantled "o'er his breast." With regal (purple, *"purpureus"*) ornament; the middle pair girt his waist "like a Starry Zone" (*"ceruleam"*) and skirt his loins and thighs with downy (*"plumeo"*) gold "And colours dipt in Heav'n" (*"ceruleam"*) ; and the third shadows his feet "with feather'd mail Sky-tinctur'd grain" (*"caeruleam roseis caudam pennis distinguentibus"*). The likenesses as to color and application are so striking as to suggest that Milton had in mind Robert Stephanus' description of the phoenix (or that by Calepine after 1609), or Pliny, the source of Stephanus and Calepine.

Milton has pressed into service another allusion to the phoenix, in which he may be following a different version of the legand. Of Samson, he writes,

> . . . but as an Eagle
> His cloudless thunder bolted on thir heads.
> So virtue giv'n for lost,
> Deprest, and overthrown, as seem'd,
> Like that self-begotten bird
> In the *Arabian* woods embost,
> That no second knows nor third,
> And lay erewhile a Holocaust,
> From out her ashy womb now teem'd,
> Revives, reflourishes, then vigorous most
> When most unactive deem'd
> And though her body die, her fame survives,
> A secular bird ages of lives.
>
> (*Samson Agonistes,* 1695-1707)

It is interesting to see that Milton again employs the figure of the eagle in juxtaposition to that of the phoenix, as in Calepine and Stephanus. With the "self-begotten bird" "that no second knows nor third," we may compare Calepine's "ut semper una sit, & semper sibi ipsa nascendo." And with the poet's reference to the phoenix, "from out her ashy womb" reviving, reflourishing, and becoming most vigorous, we may compare Calepine's "Crastino die de cinere gignitur vermis, secundo pennas affert, tertio *ad antiquam redit naturam,* & sic ad sua loca reuertitur."

This last sentence from Calepine is in keeping with Milton's conception of the phoenix in the Samson allusion: "the new phoenix is not represented as a young bird, but as the old one rejuvenated by the fire." Calepine's bird, like Milton's, *"ad antiquam redit naturam."* The alternate version of the legend, too, must have been well known in the sixteenth and seventeenth century. In the *Bibliotheca Eliotae* (1559), for example, we read:

Phoenix . . . a birde, which liueth aboue .600. yeres: and finally cariyng sweete spices up to a highe mountayne, by the heate of the sonne, and labour or hir wynges, kindleth fire, wherwith *she beynge all bourned, of hir asshes riseth a nother lyke byrde.*

Of particular interest is the entry in the *New World of Words, or a Generall Dictionary* (1658) of Edward Phillips, Milton's nephew and sometime protégé:

Phoenix (Greek), an Arabian Bird of which it is reported that there is one of them in the World at a time, and that having lived 500 years, it builds a nest of combustible spices, which taking fire from the Sun, she fans it with her wings, and burns herself therein, *out of whose ashes there springs up a new Phoenix.*

Milton's use of the Phoenix legend in *Epitaphium Damonis* (186-189) might also reflect his knowledge of entries cited above.

PHLEGETON. See RIVERS OF HELL.

PLEIADES

> First in his East the glorious Lamp was seen,
> Regent of Day, and all th' Horizon round
> Invested with bright Rays, jocund to run
> His Longitude through Heav'n's high road: the gray
> Dawn, and the *Pleiades* before him danc'd
> Shedding sweet influence.
> 
> (*PL. 7.* 370-75)
> 
> Some say the Sun
> Was bid turn Reins from th' Equinoctial Road
> Like distant breadth to *Taurus* with the Sev'n
> *Atlantic* Sisters, and the *Spartan* Twins
> Up to the *Tropic* Crab.
> 
> (*PL.* 10. 671-74)

On the subject of the Pleiades, Osgood cites Hesiod (*W. & D.* 383), Aratus (*Phoen.* 254-67), Athenaeus (2. 489, 490) and Hyginus (*Astr.* 2. 21). Less widely dispersed, and apt as exposition of Milton's allusions are the accounts in the dictionaries. Charles Stephanus has the following:

Pleiades, septem stellae inter os Tauri, & caudam Arietis sitae. Higyn. in Astron. poëtico, quae ortu suo primae nauigationis tempus ostendunt, vnde Graece Pleiades dicuntur . . . Latine Vergiliae dicuntur, a verni temporis significatione, quo oriuntur. Nam circa aequinoctium vernum, earum ortus matutinus est. Has poëtae Atlantis filias faciunt ex Pleione Nympha: vnde & Pleiadum nomen tractum esse quidam existimant. Sunt qui putent Pleiades dictas, quasi πλείονας, hoc est plures, quod nunquam singulae appareant, sed omnes simul, praeter Meropen, quae vix conspici potest. Phericides has tradit septem sorores fuisse, Lycurgi filias, ex Naso insula, Liberi patris nutrices, ab Ioue inter sydera relatus. . . . Alij ferunt eas in caelum assumptas, & in stellas esse mutatas ob pietatem, quod Atlantis calamitatem perpetuo fletu prosecutae sint: vel quod, cum perpetuam virginitatem seruare decreuissent, & ob id Dianae studia sequerentur: Orionem vero, qui illarum amore captus eas persequebatur, effugere non possent, implorato Iouis auxilio, in stellas mutatae sunt . . . Comes, *Mythologiae*. lib. 4. c. 7.

The association of the Pleiades with the vernal equinox, with morning and sunrise, with Taurus, and the Pleiades as the "Sev'n Atlantic Sisters," all are illustrated here.

For a similar exposition of *Pleiades,* see Calepine (1609).

PROSERPINA (ENNA)

> . . . Not that fair *field*
> *Of Enna, where Proserpin gath'ring flowers,*
> Herself a fairer Flow'r, by gloomy *Dis*
> Was gather'd, which *cost Ceres all that pain*
> To seek her through the world.
>
> (*PL.* 4. 268-72)

Hughes suggests that "Milton thought of Ovid's account of the perpetual spring in the Sicilian fields of Enna where Dis (Pluto) kidnapped Proserpina (*Met.* 5. 385-391)."[40] But in Ovid Proserpina is gathering lilies in a beautiful "grove"; no field is mentioned. Comes (3. 247-8) tells the story, but Milton's phrasing is not near to that of the *Mythologiae*. Ortelius' map, in which "Enna" is marked with the legend "Campus Ennensis" may have been known to Milton, as Whiting (108) suggests. But more suggestive of the content and phrasing in Milton's allusion are the very first lines in Stephanus' account of Proserpina.

*Proserpina,* Iovis & Cereris filia, quae *cum in campis Ennaeis flora legeret,* a Plutone rapta est. *Quam cum Ceres diu frustra toto terrarum orbe investigasset . . . .*

Compare Calepine (1609) for a similar account of Proserpina.

PYGMIES

> . . . For never since created man,
> Met such imbodied force, as nam'd with these

Could merit more than that *small infantry*
*Warr'd on by Cranes* . . . .
(*PL.* I. 573-76)
Now less than smallest Dwarfs, in narrow room
Throng numberless, like that *Pigmean Race*
*Beyond the Indian Mount* . . . .
(*PL.* I. 779-81)

Whiting (81) cites Pliny, which Milton may have read. He would have found in compact form the substance of Pliny (from two different books), in Charles Stephanus' account of the Pygmaei. And this concise item suggests the language of Milton.

Pygmaei, populi in extremis Indiae montibus habitantes. Plin. li. 7. c. 3. salubri coelo, semperque vernante fruentes, ternos dodrantes non excedentes: vnde & Pygmaei dicti sunt, quasi πηχυσίοι, hoc est cubitales. . . . Fama est, insidentes arietum caprarumque dorsis, *armatos sagittis,* veris tempore *vniuerso agmine* ad mare descendere, & oua pullosque *gruum* consumere, ternis eam expeditionem mensibus confici: aliter futuris gregibus non resisti. . . . Plin. praeterea libr. 4 c. 2. in Thracia Pygmaeos fuisse scribit, vrbemque Geraneam tenuisse, donec a gruibus fugati, nouas sibi sedes quaerere sunt coacti.

R. Stephanus, *s.v. Pygmaei* has a very similar account, adding, at the end, these lines from Juvenal .3. Sat. 167:

Ad subitas Thracum volucres, nubemque sonoram
Pygmaeus parvis currit bellator in armis,
Mox impar hosti, raptusque per aera curvis
Unguibus a saeva fertur grue, si videas hoc
Gentibus in nostris, risa quatiere: sed illic
Quanquam eadem assidue spectentur praelia, ridet
Nemo, ubi tota cohors pede non est altior uno.

PYTHON

Having recounted that the fallen angels, including Satan himself, are changed into hissing serpents, Milton continues:

. . . but still greatest hee [Satan] the midst
Now Dragon grown, larger than whom the Sun
Ingender'd in the *Pythian* Vale on slime,
Huge *Python,* and his Power no less he seem'd
Above the rest still to retain . . . .
(*PL.* 10. 528-32)

Osgood (71) notes that the story of Python was first told in *Hom.* (*Hy. to Pyth. Ap.* 122 ff.) and that it appears also in Ovid (*Met.* 1. 434-440), a part of which Osgood translates. Hughes comments: "Milton alludes to Ovid's story of the earth's unwilling engendering of the serpent Python, of mountainous size, from the mud left after Deucalion's flood. (*Met.* 1. 438-440.)"[41]

Three entries in Charles Stephanus' poetic dictionary offer the most appropriate annotations and are most suggestive as a source for Milton. In order of entry these are as follows.

(1) Phythia . . . ludi Apollinares, in Apollonis honorem instituti *in Pythio Macedoniae loco,* ob caedem Pythonis serpentis nocentissimi: aut, vt Strabo li. 9. scripsit, *hominis sceleratissimi, cognomento Draconis.*

(2) Python, serpentis mirae magnitudinis proprium nomen, ex putredine terrae post diluuium nati. [Here follows a detailed story, concluding] . . . Cuius rei memoria ne ullo temporum lapsu obliteraretur, sacra certamina instituit, quae a nomine serpentis Pythia apellauit. Ouid. 1 Met.

(3) Python draco post diluuium e terra natus, significat immensam exhalationis vim, quae extitit post inundationem, donec a Sole consumeretur. Iouian. Pontan. in Vrania. Dicitur autem Pytho a putredine seu putrefactione. Et quia Sol consumit omnem putredinem terrae eiusque circulo emicant radii in modum sagittarium, ideo Apollo fingitur sagittis Pythonem interficere.

The conception by the poet of Satan, first, as a serpent and then as a dragon is similar to Python as a serpent (Entry 2); and Python as a dragon (Entry 3), in the Charles Stephanus. To have fused the matter of the two entries to suit his own purpose would have been a characteristic procedure of the poet. And the blending would have been suggested by Strabo's reference (No. 1 above) to Draco as the cognomen of a most wicked man.

SATURN (RHEA, VESTA)

> *Titan* Heav'n's first born
> With his enormous brood, and birthright seiz'd
> By younger *Saturn,* he from mightier *Jove,*
> His own and *Rhea's* son, like measure found;
> So *Jove* usurping reign'd . . .
> > or who with Saturn old
> Fled over *Adria* to th' *Hesperian* fields. . . .
> > > (*PL.* 1. 510-14; 519-20)
> Thee [Melancholy] bright-hair'd Vesta long of yore,
> > To solitary Saturn bore;
> His daughter she (in Saturn's reign,
> Such mixture was not held a stain).
> > > (*Il Penseroso.* 23-26)

The story of Saturn in his relation to Titan, his elder brother, and to his wife and children, especially Jupiter, is concisely outlined by Milton, in the first quotation above. For the ancient accounts of the myth that Milton might have known, see Osgood (74-5). In Milton's own day the story was current in the dictionaries. Typical is the following from C. Stephanus:

Saturnus, Coeli & Vestae filius, qui Opem sororem suam matrimonio sibi coniunxit. . . . Fratrem habuit Titanem maiorem natu. [Stephanus' narrative here relates how, though Titan was heir to the throne, he agreed to cede the rule to Saturn, on condition that Saturn produce no male offspring to succeed him; how through the strategy of Ops, the male children, including Jove, Neptune, and Pluto were preserved; and how when Titan discovered the fraud, he with his sons, made war against Saturn, defeated him and put him and Ops in prison until Jupiter, at length grown up, defeated the Titans and freed his parents. Then the Latin narrative continues:] Post haec Saturnus cum ex oraculo didicisset, fore vt a filiis regno pelleretur, cum ob hoc Ioui insidias strueret, ab eo regno pulsus, in Italiam profugit, vbi aliquandiu apud Ianum regem laetitauit: vnde ea pars Italiae Latium dictum est. Hoc regnante aetatem auream fuisse fabulantur. . . .

The story with the Latin form of the proper names, as in Milton, is all here, including the reference to Saturn's reign as the golden age in Italy (the "Hesperian fields"). In fact, the Stephanus version would account for most that is in the two quotations from Milton, except perhaps what seems confusion with respect to Vesta and Rhea.

Although Milton himself may not have been confused in the way he employs Rhea and Vesta in the two passages, it would not be strange if he were. The ancients themselves seem to have been somewhat confused. Under the entry *Rhea* (C. Stephanus), for example, we read that Rhea, daughter of Heaven and Earth, is also called Cybele, Ops, Vesta, magna mater, Dindymene, and Berycynthia. Under *Ops,* we note that Ops is the daughter of Coeli and Vesta—that is, Vesta is the mother of Ops, as under *Saturn.* The entry *Cybele* tells us that Cybele, the daughter of Heaven and Earth, and wife (*"uxor"*) of Saturn, is also called Ops, Rhea, Vesta, etc. Under *Vesta,* we read first that Vesta is the daughter of Saturn from Ops. And here seems confusion doubly and trebly confused. In the same entry, further on, appears the information (and here we translate) that the ancients affirmed that there were two Vestas: the one the mother of Saturn, the other his daughter. These the poets, however, confuse, using the one for the other. It is to be understood, however, that when they take Vesta for the earth, they mean the mother of Saturn; but when they call her a virgin, they mean his daughter.

This explanation is the answer to the implied stricture of Osgood that "Vesta never bore any other relation to Saturn than that of daughter (Hes. *Theog.* 454)," and it shows how Milton could make Rhea (Vesta) the mother of Saturn in the first selection above and the daughter in the second.

Compare also Comes, *Mythologiae* (p. 907 ff., 1605 edit.), "De Vesta," a probable source of C. Stephanus.

Summanus

> Talibus infestat populos Summanus et urbes,
> Cinctus coeruleae fumanti turbine flammae.
>
> (*Q. Nov.* 23-24)

The appropriate annotation could be found in the Charles Stephanus: Summanus, Pluto, deus inferorum, ita dictus, quasi summus deorum Manium, vt in Nup. Philologiae docet Martianus. Huic Romani nocturna fulmina assignabant, quemadmodum diurna Ioui. Plin. li. 2. C. 51. Ouid. 6. Fast.

Calepine (1609) employs the same language in describing Summanus.

Titan

> *Titan,* Heaven's first-born,
> With his enormous brood, and birthright seiz'd
> By younger *Saturn*: he from mightier *Jove,*
> His own and *Rhea's* son, like measure found. . . .
>
> (*PL.* 1. 510-13)

The conventional note on these lines is, for example, that "Milton's scholarship seems at fault here in supposing that there was an individual giant named Titan, who, instead of Uranus, was father of the twelve Titans." In Cooper, Calepine, Charles Stephanus, and Robert Stephanus, Titan appears as "the brother of Saturnus," "Saturnus frater, Coeli et Vestae filius"; while in seventeenth-century editions of Calepine and in Charles Stephanus' *Dictionarium* the following information is found:

*Titan* . . . *Caeli et Vestae filius, frater Saturni natu maior,* ad quem quamius paternae hereditatis ius pertineret, quoniam tamen matrem et sororem in Saturnum propensiores esse sentiebat, suo illi iure ea cessit lege, ne quam sobolem masculam educaret, sed caeli imperium ad liberos suos rediret. Verum cum postea Opis dolo factum intelligeret, vt primum Iupiter, deinde et Neptunus et Pluto clam essent educati, *eaque via liberos suos auita successione deictos*

*videret, vna cum filiis suis (qui et ipsi Titanes dicebantur) bellum aduersus
fratrem suscepit. . . .*

Titan is then represented as being temporarily successful in capturing and
imprisoning Saturn, but Jupiter defeats the Titans and releases Saturn, who
"post haec . . . cum ex oraculo didicisset, fore vt a filiis regno pelleretur,
cum ob hoc Ioui insidias strueret, ab eo regno pulsus, in Italiam profugit.
. . ."

Stephanus' account of Titan seems, however, to be based upon that in
Comes' *Mythologiae* (6. 20). Either affords an adequate explanation of
Milton's lines, though neither has been noticed hitherto in exposition of
Titan as an individual in the roll of pagan gods.

TITYOS

Referring to Satan in hell with uplifted head and blazing eyes, Milton
continues the description in these words:

> his other parts besides
> Prone on the flood, extended long and large
> Lay floating many a rood, in bulk as huge
> As whom the fables name of monstrous size
> Titanian or Earth born, that warr'd on *Jove,*
> *Briareos* or *Typhon.* . . .
> *(PL.* I. 194-99)
> So stretcht out huge in length the Arch-Fiend lay
> Chain'd on the burning Lake.
> *(PL.* I. 209-10)

It has been argued, not without reason, that in the description of Satan,
Milton was thinking of Typhon. Commenting on the passage, D. P. Harding writes: "There is, first of all, the concrete fact that Milton compares
the size of Satan with that of Typhon."[42] Harding notes also that Typhon
was a type of ambition, a leader of the giants who warred against Jupiter
in heaven and were defeated and driven down to hell (85-86). The
analogue is, in general, sufficiently striking, though it is not so certain that
in describing the size of Satan, Milton had in mind Typhon, and Typhon
alone. In some particulars he may have been thinking of Tityos.

So far as we can discover, the story of Tityos in this connection has not
hitherto been cited. The story is first told by Homer (*Od.* 11. 570) in the
account of Odysseus' visit to the lower world where, "I saw Tityos, son
of renowned earth, lying on a levelled ground, and he covered nine roods
as he lay." Parallel is Aeneas' remark on a visit to the underworld (*Aen.*

6.595) : "Likewise one might see Tityos, nursling of Earth, the universal mother. Over nine full acres his body is stretched, and a monstrous vulture with crooked beak gnaws at his deathless liver and vitals fruitful for anguish." A similar reference appears in Ovid (*Met.* 4. 455-58). In the sixteenth century Natalis Comes (*Myth.* 6. 19) relates Tityos' story in more detail, adding that the giant was driven down to hell, and there prostrate and tied so that he cannot move, his body covers nine acres of ground. Any of these versions of the story Milton may have known and, by association, called to mind in the story of Satan.

The Tityos story appeared with slight variations in most Renaissance dictionaries—in Calepine, in Cooper, in R. Stephanus, and in C. Stephanus. Cooper writes,

*Tityus,* The sonne of Earth, whom poetes feigned to be slain by Apollo, because he would have rauished Latona his sister : and therefore lieth in hell, hauyng an eagle alway eatyng his lyuer. And it is also sayde that his bodie was in length nine furlongs . . . .

Most suggestive of all for Milton's purpose is the story as recounted in the *Dictionarium* of Charles Stephanus. It may be translated thus :

Tityus was the son of Jove by Elara, the daughter of Orchmenus. When Jupiter had embraced Elara and made her pregnant, he concealed her in the earth, fearing the wrath of Juno. When the time for delivery came, Elara gave birth to a boy of such enormous size that, the ground having opened when he was born, he was believed to be the son of Earth. When he was grown and, by the prompting of Juno, attempted to ravish Latona, he was struck by the lightning of Jove, or (as some suppose) pierced by the darts of Apollo and driven down to hell. There, stretched out on the ground, he is said to cover nine acres of earth, and his liver ever growing again with the moon, is eaten by a vulture or, as Hyginus thinks, by a serpent. Ovid. 4 *Metam.* This fable may be fitly applied to the hatred which can never be destroyed and it depicts excellently the eternal punishment of those that cherish hatred.

The story as thus recounted together with its moral application seems especially pertinent to Milton's Satan, of the first two hundred lines or so, both as to motivation and size. Satan is inspired by hate that cannot be destroyed. The poet refers to Satan's "obdurate pride and steadfast hate" (1. 58), to his "unconquerable will, And study of revenge, immortal hate." (1. 107). As Tityos, having offended Jupiter, was struck with his lightning and driven down to hell, so Satan and his companions, for their rebellion against the Almighty, were pursued with "thunder Winged with red lightning" (1. 174-76) and thrust into hell. As Tityos, stretched out on the ground (*"humi exporrectus"*) in hell covers nine acres, so Satan "extended long and large," lies floating "many a rood" (1. 195-96). As the fable of Tityus applies to those suffering everlasting punishment for hatred that cannot be removed, so Satan, cherishing "immortal hate" and with "A mind not to be chang'd by Place or Time" (1. 254) is doomed to endure his suffering "without hope of end."

TRISMEGISTUS

> Where I may oft outwatch the *Bear*,
> With *thrice great Hermes*, or unsphere
> The spirit of *Plato* to unfold
> What Worlds, or what vast Regions hold
> The immortal mind that hath forsook
> Her mansion in this fleshly nook:
> And of those *Daemons* that are found
> In fire, air, flood, or under ground,
> Whose power hath a true consent
> With Planet, or with Element.
>
> (*Il. Pens.* 87-95)

> Non ille trino gloriosus nomine
> *Ter magnus Hermes* (ut sit *arcani sciens*)
> Talem reliquit Isidis cultoris.
>
> (*Idea.* 32-34)

Comments on the lines from *Il Penseroso* are generally concerned with Plato and the demons. Milton could have found in the dictionaries, Calepine, C. Stephanus, R. Stephanus specific information on Hermes Trismegistus. Compare Robert Stephanus:

Trismegistus . . . qui etiam 'Ερμῆς Τρισμέγιστος. Mercurius, *quasi ter maximus dictus,* vel valde maximus, qui fuit nepos majoris Mercurii quem fabulantur fuisse filium Nili. Hunc tamen secundum adferunt occidisse Argum, AEgyptiisque praefuisse, & leges literasque tradidisse: sed literarum characteres, animalium arborumque figuras habuisse. Hic condidit vrbem, quam a se Hermopolin nominauit. Dictus est autem Trismegistus, quod & philosophus maximus, & sacerdos, & maximus denique rex fuerit. Consueuerunt enim AEgyptii ex omni philosophorum numero sacerdotes, ac rursus ex sacerdotibus regem eligere. Hic autem ut philosophos sapientia, ita religione sacerdotes excelluit, ac mox in imperio ministrando superiores omnes reges superauit. Hic primus a physicis ad diuinorum speculationem se erexit. Primus de majestate Dei, *de Daemonum ordine animarumque mutationibus* sapientissime disputauit. Scripsit multa volumina quibus *arcana mysteria & oracula* panduntur. Non enim vt philosophus solum, sed vt propheta futura praedicit. Haec ex Didoro Siculo.

Cf. Calepine (1542, 1609) and Charles Stephanus for similar matter on Trismegistus.

The quoted passage from R. Stephanus could have offered suggestions to Milton. It serves at any rate to show the readily available information concerning Trismegistus and to illustrate the meaning of the poet's allusion.

VULCAN (MULCIBER)

> Men call'd him *Mulciber;* and how he fell
> From Heav'n they fabl'd, *thrown by angry Jove*
> Sheer o'er the Crystal Battlements: from Morn
> To Noon he fell, from Noon to dewy Eve,
> A Summer's day, and with the setting Sun
> Dropt from the Zenith, like a falling Star,
> On Lemnos, th' AEgean Isle.
>
> (*PL.* 1. 740-46)

More than one commentator has pointed to Homer's *Iliad* (1. 588 ff.) as the possible source of this episode. Though Homer does not employ the term "Mulciber," it does appear often in Ovid (*Meta.* 2. 5. 9. 263; 14. 533). Perhaps no further comment is needed. There are, however, two other analogues which have not been recorded in this connection. The first is in Comes (*Mythologiae.* 2. 6), where are found these suggestive words: "Fuerunt, qui dixerint, Vulcanum Iouis fuisse filium, qui cum deformis natus est, fertur a Ioue in Insulam maris, Aegae Lemnum praecipitatus Hom. Iliad. lib. 1." Comes does not use the name "Mulciber."

Another account not to be overlooked is that in Charles Stephanus' dictionary:

Mulciber . . . idem qui Vulcanus, deus ignes praeses, a mulcendo dictus, quod ignis omnia mulceat, id est, molliat, vincat, ac domet. . . . Fuit enim Mulciber Iouis ex Iunone filius, quem cum parentes infelicissima forma esse vidissent, ex coelo in Lemnum insulam praecipitarunt: ex qua ruina intorto pede fertur claudicationem contraxisse. Homerus fingit eum a Ioue ideo praecipitatum, quod Iunonem matrem ex eius irati manibus eripere conaretur.

In this quotation the name *Mulciber* is emphasized by its position as the heading and by elaboration of the meaning of the word, and Mulciber is identified with Vulcan. At the same time the story as recounted by Homer is compactly related.

> . . .
> *Xerxes*, the *liberty of Greece to yoke,*
> From Susa, his Memnonian Palace high,
> Came to the Sea, and, *over Hellespont*
> *Bridging his* way, *Europe with Asia joined.*
> (*PL.* 10. 307-10)

Herodotus (7. 33) is cited as Milton's source: "After this he prepared to march to Abydos; and meanwhile his men were bridging the Hellespont from Asia to Europe" (Loeb translation). Neither in the translation nor in the original is expressed the idea of *joining* one continent with the other. Though Milton probably knew the Herodotus, the specific idea could have come from Stephanus:

*Xerxes,* Persarum rex fuit filius Darij . . . *Graeciae bellum intulit* . . . tantum autem habuit nauium apparatum, vt totum *Hellespontum operiret,* & *Asiam Europae ponte coniungeret.* . . .

Compare also Calepine, *s.v. Xerxes.*

## II. NAMES OF PLACES

In an illuminating article on "Pierre Davity: His Geography and Its Use by Milton"[1] Allan Gilbert shows how the poet emphasizes the necessity of the study of geography in a well-rounded scheme of education. A French edition of Pierre Davity, the poet employed to teach his scholars a knowledge of French and geography at the same time. Apparently, Milton selected the Davity's *Les Etats,* not because it was adapted to his personal use but because it was suitable to his pupils. Milton's own knowledge of geography depended upon many of the writers, especially the Greek and Latin, whom Davity knew. The point of interest for this study is the insistence on a knowledge of geography, supplemented by travel and observation, as an educational requirement. In passing, we may note that at least one of his pupils, Edward Phillips, showed later his own interest in geography by the inclusion of proper names in his *New World of English Words: a General Dictionary* (1658).

In his preoccupation with geography, ancient and modern, Milton was of course not unique. His was a full manifestation of the Renaissance spirit, of the enhanced interest in the physical world which was stimulated by the revival of learning in the fifteenth and sixteenth centuries, and by travel and exploration for a hundred years before he was born. We might say, indeed, that the general interest in geography had constantly exhibited itself since antiquity. It was, however, in the Renaissance that this interest became especially pronounced, and Milton shares it to the full.

Easily accessible to him, of course, were the works of the ancient geographers and historians—Strabo, Ptolemy, Pomponius Mela, Pliny, Solinus, Herodotus, Diodorus Siculus, to mention a few: and such later cartographers as Mercator, Munster, Ortelius, and Purchas. And most of these Milton doubtless read at one time or another, probably before the period of his blindness (1652). Many of these were, however, large volumes, often thick folios, inadequately indexed, or indexed not at all, so that ready reference to them, even if they were easily available, was difficult. What books, if any, would serve to supplement the knowledge or refresh the memory, or give specific reference to the originals for Milton and other authors of the sixteenth and seventeenth centuries?

A partial answer to this question is found in Chapters I and II, above. There is the account of general dictionaries with proper-name sections or with distribution of such names throughout, as well as dictionaries devoted exclusively to proper names. Among these are Perottus' *Cornucopiae*, Torrentinus' *Vocabularius Poeticus*, Calepinus' *Dictionarium*, Robert Stephanus' *Thesaurus*, the Elyot-Cooper dictionaries and their successors in the seventeenth century, and, most popular of all, Charles Stephanus' *Dictionarium Historicum, Geographicum, Poeticum*.

As the 1638-edition of Stephanus has approximately the form and content in vogue during the period of Milton's composition, we may consider further the geographical aspects of this volume. On the title-page, following the general title and the author's name, there appears in somewhat smaller print a statement that the book contains all the proper names of regions, places, states, oceans, rivers, bays, ports, promontories, and mountains, both ancient and modern necessary to the understanding of sacred and profane histories. Then follows a word concerning this last edition (1638), indicating the increase of information concerning hills, forests, deserts, islands, peoples, gathered from printed books, and geographical records (*"chartis geographicis"*).

In the printer's address to the reader, we are told, among other things, that there have been added in this edition an almost infinite number of geographical names, ancient and modern, drawn from the *Geographical Thesaurus* of A[braham] Ortelius, and others. Also Hebrew names of men and places, with their Latin interpretation, have been supplied from the Old Testament.  The Latin runs thus:

nominibus vrbium, insularum, populorum veterum, quorum frequens apud Geographos occurrit mentio, nouas nomenclaturas ex A. Ortelij doctissimi Geographi Thesauro aliisque collectas coniunxit, infinitis pene tum recentioribus tum vetustis Geographiae vocibus nunc primum huic Indici insertis, Vrbium hodie florentium & praecipuarum partium accuratas descriptiones haud pratermisit.  Nominibus Hebraeis, ex veteri Testamento potissimum diligenter excerptis, Latinam adtexuit interpretationem. . . .

Examination of the text-proper of C. Stephanus' *Dictionarium* shows that the claims of the printer as regards the geographical features are well substantiated.  The original compilers and the subsequent revisers ranged widely for their information, among ancient Latin and Greek authorities, and periodically inserted new matter resulting from recent travel and exploration, and new studies of the ancient and modern world.  Among the authorities cited are Strabo, Ptolemy, Pomponius Mela, Pliny, Dionysius Perigetes, Herodotus, Homer, Pausanius, Diodorus, Volaterranus, Mercator, Munster, and scores of others.  Probably of most frequent reference are, in the order listed, Strabo, Pliny, Mela, and Ptolemy; and of the later geographers, Ortelius, Munster, Mercator.  As a rule, these authorities are followed closely and specific citation is made to the work, section, and chapter.  Thus those who wished could verify the data and could, if desired, read further on the subject.

Though the *Dictionarium* was originally intended to be helpful to young men in the reading of classical literature and history, it obviously proved to be useful to adult readers, to scholars and writers generally; and it could be most serviceable to readers as well as to editors and commentators of the present day.  The alphabetical arrangement, the concise information, the citation of original sources—all are features which greatly expedite the search for information.  Suppose, for example, one wished to learn about "Achelous."  If he consulted Strabo, as one of the earlier authorities on geography, he would find that there are three rivers of the name "Achelous," and the data on them are dispersed at widely separated intervals (through two volumes in Bohn's translation).  If he turned to the Stephanus, he would discover the essential matter about the three rivers in less than one column.  "Acheron" provides a similar illustration.  If one knows something about "Acheron" but wishes to reassure himself, he should go to Strabo.  He would find one Acheron described in I, 382

(Bohn), another in I, 497, and a third in II, 17. (Though sixteenth- and seventeenth-century editions of Strabo may have been in a single large tome, our illustration is still apt.) The dictionary has the descriptions, with reference to Strabo and other authorities in one column of an octavo edition.

In the entry *Memphis,* in Stephanus, we find an illustration of another kind. Though not built on the site of ancient Memphis, as Gilbert points out, Cairo is near and is the successor of the ancient city. Milton identifies it with Memphis in his reference to Alcairo (*PL.* 1. 718), and in his use of the adjective "Memphiticus" to indicate Cairo (*Lit. Oliv.* (57). 6. 306). Milton's identification is explained by the Stephanus. Under "Memphis," Stephanus wrtes, "Vulgus hodie Alcyrum vocat. Hinc sit Gentile, Memphites . . . Item Memphiticus . . . Gall. *le grand Caire."* Whether Milton had his information directly from Stephanus or not, Stephanus affords the apt illustration of the poet's meaning.

Stephanus also affords much information on Hebrew and Biblical names of men and places. Suppose, for example, Milton, or a contemporary reader of Milton, or for that matter, a present-day reader or editor wished to learn something more about "Azotus" (*PL.* 1. 464) or "Ashdod," as it appears in the Old Testament. In *Paradise Lost* Milton refers to the "Temple high" of Dagon "Rear'd in Azotus," and in *Samson* (976 f.) Dalilah asserts that though her name may be defamed in Dan and Judah and among the bordering tribes, it will be renowned in her own country, in Asdod and elsewhere. As the form "Asdod" does not appear in the Bible, and "Azotus" only in the New Testament, there might be a query as to Milton's use of the terms. Consulting Stephanus, one finds "Azotus, Hebr. Asdod . . . a renowned city of Palestine, situated between Ascalon and Joppa in the tribe of Dan. It was ceded by lot (*"sorte"*) to the tribe of Judah. This was one of the five cities of the Allophyli, or Philistines, and was renowned for the temple of the idol Dagon. . . ." These statements and others, here omitted, are supported by ten Scriptural references, and on to Volaterranus. For the poet, had he wished to renew his knowledge about Azotus-Ashdod, Stephanus was the most direct authority; and if Stephanus were not adequate, it would offer all the necessary references to the Scriptures.

In the light of these examples, it is evident that Charles Stephanus might have been an invaluable reference work and guide for authors, and especially for Milton with the handicap of blindness and of consequent dependence upon readers. It would have been a matter of common sense and economy for an author to have recourse to such an authority. Whether or not the poet did so proceed, the *Dictionarium* affords so much for apt illustration and annotations of the geography in his poetry that present-day students may not disregard it. For these reasons, we here present more examples of the value of contemporary dictionaries, especially the Stephanus, in the study of Milton's poetry.

AETNA

Describing Satan rising from the lake of fire, Milton writes,

> . . . on each hand the flames
> Driv'n backward slope their pointing spires, and roll'd
> In billows, leave i' th' midst a horrid Vale.
> . . . till on dry Land
> He lights, if it *were Land that ever burn'd*
> *With solid,* as the Lake with liquid *fire;*
> And such appear'd in hue, as when the *force*
> *Of subterranean wind* transports a Hill
> Torn from *Pelorus,* or the shatter'd side
> Of thund'ring AEtna, *whose combustible*
> *And fuell'd entrails thence conceiving Fire,*
> *Sublim'd with Mineral fury,* aid the Winds,
> And leave a singed bottom all involv'd
> With stench and smoke. . . .
>                         (*PL.* 1. 222-37)

Hughes' suggestion that the allusion to Aetna and Pelorus may be reminiscent of Virgil (*Aen.* 3. 570-77)[2] seems to be well founded. The "thund'-ring Aetna" and "fuell'd entrails" may indeed echo the *"horrificis iuxta tonat Aetna ruinis"* and *"avulsaque viscera montis"* of the *Aeneid.*

Current Latin dictionaries offered pertinent information on Aetna. Compare the following from Charles Stephanus' *Dictionarium*:

Aetna, mons Siciliae, prius Inesia appellatus, vt tradit Volaterranus, *perpetuo igni terribilis,* & *quandoque globos igneos longius emittens,* circa radices amoenissimus est multis fontibus & fruticibus. Sub hoc monte Iupiter Gigantes deiecit fulmine, vt fabulantur poëtae. Quare autem *Aetna flammas euomat,* Trogus lib. 4. explicat. Sicilia terra est cavernosa & fistulosa, quo fit vt ventorum flatibus pateat, *vnde ignis concipitur*: *intrinsecus sulphur habet & bitumen*: *vbi ventus per spiramenta cauernarum incubuit,* diu luctatus *concipit ignem*: sic AEtnae durat incendium: Motus ergo ventorum causa incendij est.
. . .

This description could have suggested to the poet a number of phrases. Compare a "Land that ever burn'd With solid . . . fire" and "Aetna . . . perpetuo igni terribilis"; "the force Of subterranean winds" and "ventus per spiramenta cauernarum incubuit"; "thence conceiving Fire" and "vnde ignis concipitur"; "And fuell'd entrails . . . Sublimed with Mineral fury" and "intrinsecus sulphur habet & bitumen."

The Calepine dictionaries contain the matter in Stephanus, quoted above, from "Quare autem Aetna" to the end.

ALPHEUS

> Of famous *Arcady* ye are, and sprung
> Of that renowned *flood*, so often sung
> *Divine Alpheus*, who by secret sluice,
> Stole under Seas to meet his *Arethuse*.
>                    (*Arcades.* 28-31)
> *O Fountain Arethuse*, and thou honour'd flood. . . .
>                    (*Lyc.* 85)
> Return *Alpheus*, the dread voice is past,
> That shrunk thy streams; Return *Sicilian Muse*. . . .
>                    (*Lyc.* 132-33)

Homer, Virgil, Seneca, Statius, and Ovid, among classical authors, have been suggested as offering a basis for Milton's allusions to Alpheus and Arethusa.[3] Of these authors, Ovid (*Met.* 5. 572-641) tells the story of Alpheus' love for Arethusa. The poet's recollections of his reading in Ovid and Virgil might adequately account for the brief allusions in the lines quoted above. Apt annotations may, however, be made on the basis of accounts in the current dictionaries of Calepine, Robert Stephanus, and Charles Stephanus. In the proper-name lexicon of the last named compiler, we read

*Alpheus, fluuius Elidis Arcadiae* ciuitatis, iuxta Pisas defluens longo cursu in Achaiam, & ibi a terra absorptus, atque *subter mare* defluens, ex Graecia in *fontem Arethusam* apud Syracusas in *Sicilia* se attollit, inde in *mare Siculum* cadit. Virg. 3. Aeneid.
>     Alpheum fama est huc Elidis amnem
>     Occultas egisse vias subter mare, qui nunc
>     Ore Arethusa tuo Siculis confunditur vndis.
. . . Hunc fluuium non nulli Ethnici pro Deo coluerunt, cui & statuam & communem aram cum Diana erexerunt . . . .

This entry, here quoted in abbreviated form, owes much to Comes' *Mythologiae* (8. 21). In diffuse form (four and a half columns of Latin)

in the Comes, Milton would have found all the available information on Alpheus and Arethusa. The first ten lines of the Stephanus entry, which owe less to Comes than do the remaining lines, have all information essential to Milton's allusions, and, in close proximity, the proper names employed by him—Arcady, Sicily, the "divine" Alpheus, the quotation from the *Aeneid* concerning the relationship of Alpheus and Arethuse.

ANGLESEY (MONA)

> For neither were ye [Nymphs] playing on the steep,
> Where your old *Bards,* the famous *Druids,* lie,
> Nor on the shaggy top of *Mona* high. . . .
> (*Lyc.* 52-54)

In his account of Anglesey, Allan H. Gilbert observes that this island is also known as Mona. He queries, "Yet what does Milton mean by calling Mona 'high'? The island nowhere rises to any great elevation. 'High' might be properly applied to the Isle of Man, also sometimes called Mona." Professor Gilbert suggests that Milton is possibly giving a composite picture made up of accounts of both Anglesey and Man, neither of which he had ever seen.[4]

In the dictionaries of the sixteenth and seventeenth centuries Mona and Man were generally identical. As early as 1542, Calepine writes that *Monaeda* is an island near the western region of Ireland called *Monarina,* or in the common speech *Man.* Thomas Cooper, *Thesaurus,* 1565) speaks of "Mona, called of the Greeks Monna," as "an Ile nighe to Britaine . . . I suppose it to be the Ile nowe called Man, and not Anglesey, for as much as that is ioined to Britaine." Thomas Thomas (1631) : "Mona, The Ile of man between England and Ireland. Mona Taciti, Anglesey. Mona Caesaris siue Mannia & Menovia, The Isle of Man." The Rider-Holyoke dictionary of 1649, copies the first statement of Thomas verbatim, and continues, "Others make it the Ile of Anglesey in the north Wales, as may appear by Tacitus." What Milton's nephew, Edward Phillips, puts into his English dictionary (1658) may be of special interest. He has "*Anglesey,* an Island lying over against Caernarvon in Wales, it was anciently the seat of Druides, and was called by the Brittains, Ynis Dowil, and the land of *Mon,* in Latin *Mona.* . . ." Charles Stephanus' description (1638) is fuller than those cited. It begins "Mona, insula inter Angliam & Hiberniam sita, vt Ptolemaeus, Caesar. & Plinius eam describunt. . . . Haec olim Druidum sedes fuit, Tacito auctore. Hodie incolis Britannis,

qui auitam linguam retinent, *Mon* vocatur : Angli vero Saxonica lingua im-
buti, *Anglesey* vocant teste H. Luydo & Laelando . . . Haec insula . . . eam
quam Anglo Saxones hodie Man nominant."

Whiting, citing Ortelius, Camden, Lhuyd, and Leland, reaches similar
conclusions as to Mona, Man, and Anglesey, and supplies additional information to account for "the shaggy top of Mona high."[5] Independently,
Whiting utilizes the same sources as those cited in the Charles Stephanus.

ARAXES

> here thou behold'st
> *Assyria* and her Empire's ancient bounds,
> *Araxes* and the *Caspian* lake, thence on
> As far as *Indus* East, *Euphrates* West. . . .
> (*PR.* 3. 269-72)

Under *Caspium mare,* C. Stephanus has these words : "denominatum
Lacus totius orbis maximus est."

Gilbert comments that "Virgil refers to the force of the river [Araxes]
in the words, 'Araxes that spurns a bridge' (*Aeneid* 8. 728), which occur
in an historical and geographical passage like that of Milton."[6]  On Araxes,
with an allusion to the *Aeneid,* compare R. Stephanus' *Thesaurus* :

> Araxes . . . Armeniae fluuius, ex eo monte ex quo Euphrates nascitur,
> contrario tamen ei cursu, versus Orientem tendens, vsque ad Atropatiam :
> deinde in Boream conuersus, Azaram praeterlabans, in mare desinit Hyrcanum
> ut author est Strabo.  Herodoto tamen secus visum est.  Porro Araxem ἀπὸ
> τῶ ἀράσσειν vocari, quod opera Jasonis & labore Penei Thessalici, montium
> continuationem disrupit, Stephanus & item Strabo authores sunt. . . . Pontem
> indignatus Araxes. Virg. 8.  AEn. 728. non ab re dictum est : nam (ut refert
> Isidorus) cum Alexander eum transgredi vellet ponte fabricato, tanta vi inunda-
> vit, ut pontem dirueret.  Servius notat id Xerxem conatum fuisse facere.

ARCADIA

> Nymphs and Shepherds dance no more
> By sandy *Ladon's* Lillied banks.
> On old *Lycaeus* or *Cyllene* hoar,
> Trip no more in twilight ranks,
> Through *Erymanth* your loss deplore,
> A better soil shall give ye thanks.
> From the stony *Maenalus,*
> Bring your Flocks and live with us . . .
> Though *Syrinx* your Pan's mistress were,
> Yet *Syrinx* well might wait on her.

> Such a rural Queen
> All *Arcadia* hath not seen.
>
> (*Arcades.* 96-109)

On the mountains and rivers of Arcadia, its pastoral life and the association with Pan, C. Stephanus offers informative comment *s.v. Arcadia*.

*Arcadia*, Peloponnesi regio intima, a mari vndique remota: ab Arcade filio Iouis & Calistonis Lycaonis Arcadiae regis filiae sic appellata. . . . Oppida eius praecipua sunt Mantinea, Tegea & Stymphalus, Montes praecipui, Pholoë, *Cyllene, Lynceus, Maenalus* & Nonacris. Fluuij, *Ladon* & *Erymanthus*. Fuit autem tota haec regio pastioni potius pecoris, quam aut negotiationi aut agriculturae dedita: ideoque *Pana,* pastorum Deum, velut peculiare numen sibi vendicarunt. Virg. Ecloga. 4. 58-9.

> Pan Deus Arcadiae mecum si iudice certet,
> Pan etiam Arcadiae dicat se iudice victum.   [1595 ed.]

ARNON

> Him [Moloch] the *Ammonite*
> Worshipt in *Rabba* and her wat'ry Plain,
> In *Argob* and in *Basan,* to the stream
> Of utmost *Arnon*.
>
> (*PL.* 1. 396-99)

According to recent geography, the Arnon is so far away from the country of the Ammonites that it is impossible to see why Milton made it one of their limits, though the maps of the time make the passage clear.[7] Clear, too, is the entry in C. Stephanus, which definitely states that the Arnon is the boundary between the Ammonites and the Moabites, and may suggest the "utmost Arnon." The entry from Stephanus follows.

*Arnon*, i. exultans, siue arca eorum, aut Lux filij, vel Lux, aut maledictio permanens vel aeterna, fluuius Moabitarum, Iosepho lib. 4, Antiquit. Iudaic. ca. 4. de montibus Arabiae fluit, ac per totam solitudinem labens in Asphaltitem lacum erumpit, seiungens Moabitidem & Ammonitida. Hieronymo vero est rupes excelsa in limite Amorrhaeorum & Moabitarum. Num. 21. Deut. 2. Iosue. 12 & 13 Iudicum 11. Iere. 46.

On Arnon and other places mentioned in the passage quoted above, Whiting (202 ff.) cites Raleigh, Fuller, and Purchas.

AROER

> Next Chemos, th' obscene dread of *Moab's* Sons,
> From *Aroar* to *Nebo,* and the wild
> Of Southmost *Abarim*.
>
> (*PL.* 1. 406-8)

As Gilbert notes, there are two Aroers: one a city of Palestine, now ruined, on the north bank of the river Arnon; the other, less famous, apparently situated not far from Rabba. In Milton's time the two were considered as one, which was placed near Rabba, but still on the Arnon, which was mistakenly supposed to rise near Rabba. Though Milton's reference properly indicates the more famous Aroer, supposed to lie far northeast of its true site, the poet thought that in the successive mention of Aroer, Nebo, and Abarim he was passing from north to south, whereas Aroer is south of Nebo. Perhaps the entry in Stephanus gives the notion of Aroer in Milton's day:

*Aroer,* i. Myrica, siue suscitatio vigiliae, aut denudatio pellis, aut denudatio aemuli, vrbs Moabitarum, sita est super ripam torrentis Arnon extructa a filiis Gad. Deut. 2, Ios. 12 & 13. Ier. 46. contra Rabbath. Ios. 13. cessit tribui Gad. Iud. 11. sit eius mentio, i. Reg. 30. 2 Reg. 24. Num. 21. 32. 33. 4. Reg. 10.

ASPHALTUS (SODOM)

(1)

. . . many a row
Of Starry Lamps and blazing cressets fed
*With Naphtha* and *Asphaltus yielded light*
*As from a sky.*

(*PL.* 1. 728-30)

Compare Charles Stephanus:

*Asphaltus* . . . lacus Iudaeae in Pentapoli . . . Huius lacus aqua *Asphaltum* appellatum, Graecis *Naphtha, quae eminus igni admota flammam concipit,* ea capitis Medeae involucrum ad Iasonem missum intinctum fuerat.

Note the spelling of the word *Asphaltus* as employed by Milton, its proximity to Naphtha and the convenience of the latter, which could be lighted from a distance.

(2)

. . . greedily they plucked
That Fruitage fair to sight, like that which grew
Near that bituminous Lake where Sodom flam'd;
. . . they fondly thinking to allay
Thir appetite with gust, instead of Fruit
Chew'd better Ashes. . . .

(*PL.* 10. 560-66)

(3)

Thus these pious flourishes and colors examin'd thoroughly, are like the Apples of *Asphaltis,* appearing goodly to the eye, but look well upon them, or at least but touch them, and they turne into Cinders. ("Eikonoklastes," *Works* [Columbia edit.], V. 263)

Josephus (*Wars*. 4. 8) is sometimes cited as Milton's source.[8] What Josephus and others wrote about the Dead Sea and the fruit growing near is concisely recorded in the dictionaries and constitutes a fitting annotation. In Stephanus, for example, we read,

*Asphaltus,* vel Asphaltites, lacus Iudeae in Pentapoli: in quo nihil grave submergi potest. In eo fuerunt Sodoma & Gomorrha, & tres aliae vrbes, quae propter nefandam populi luxuriam & libidinem caelitus exustae sunt. Mortuum mare ab historicis dicitur, nihilque praeter bitumen gignit: animal nullum habet, nec in eo aliquid viuum mergi potest Solin. & Iustin. libro 36. Huius lacus aqua Asphaltum appellatum, Graecis Naptha, quae eminus igni admota flammam concipit, ea capitis Medeae inuolucrum ad Iasonem missum intinctum fuerat.

Similar information, and more besides, appears under the entry *Sodoma,* which concludes:

Multis in locis iste lacus nigras glebas bituminis vomit: & ideo lacus Asphaltidis dicitur. Poma item in arboribus nata si incidas, fauillas intus inueniens. Comest. in cap. 18. Gen.

ATHENS (ACADEMIA)

    . . . *on* the *Aegean shore* a City stands
    Built nobly, pure the air, and light the soil,
    *Athens,* the eye of *Greece, Mother of Arts*
    *And Eloquence,* native to famous wits
    Or hospitable, in her sweet recess,
    City or Suburban, *studious walks and shades;*
    See there the Olive Grove of *Academe,*
    *Plato's retirement.* . . .
        . . . within the walls then view
    The schools of *ancient Sages;* his who bred
    Great *Alexander* to subdue the world,
    *Lyceum there,* and painted *Stoa* next.
                  (*PR.* 4. 238-53)

We may assume that Milton, familiar with classical antiquity, could have drawn freely from his store of knowledge concerning Athens. Yet the details in the allusions above as well as the phrasing suggest that dictionary accounts, such as those in Calepine (1609) and Charles Stephanus, on *Athens* and *Academia* may well have stimulated his memory.

Compare the following items from Charles Stephanus:

*Athene, civitas Graeciae* inter Macedoniam & Achaiam, in ea littorali regione quae olim Actae deinde Attica vocata. . . . *Fuit haec civitas omnium bonarum artium inventrix, Philosophorum & Oratorum mater, & Poëtarum alumna.* Virg. in Aetna [sic] *Nunc hic Cecropiae variis spectantur Athenae / Carminibus, gaudentque sui victrice Minerva.* . . .

*Lyceum,* gymnasij celeberrimi nomen iuxta Athenas, in *quo Aristoteles frequentissimo* auditorio philosophiam profitebatur, *quemadmodum Plato in Academia.* . . . Qui erant cum Aristotele, Peripatetici dicti sunt, quia disputabant inambulantes in Lyceo . . . .

*Academia locus nemorosus,* ab Athenis mille passus distans: ab Academico Heroe, vt Eupolidi placet . . . hoc est, *in ambulacris vmbrosis* Academi Dei. Horat. *Atque inter syluas Academi quaerere verum* . . . *Ibi natus est Plato*: vbi cum philosopharetur, studendi vsu & discipulorum frequentia morumque celebritate insignis fuit. Vide Laert. in vita Platonis. Erat Academia gymnasium inferius, *cum superiori gymnasio nomen esset Lycaeum.* Nam *inferior ambulatio* & superior dicebantur. Lyceum vero nomen *fuit Scholae Aristotelicae.* Alii . . . Academiam à Cadmo Phenice, literarum & liberalium studiorum in Graecia instauratore dictam probant . . . .

A comparison of some of the phrases in Milton's reference to Athens with those in the dictionary items is suggestive. Compare, for example "on the Aegean shore a City stands . . . Athens" and "Athene, civitas Graeciae inter Macedoniam & Achaiam, in ea litorali regione"; "Athens, the eye of Greece, Mother of Arts And Eloquence, native to famous wits . . ." and "Fuit haec civitas omnium bonarum artium inventrix, Philosophorum & Oratorum mater, & Poetarum alumna"; "in her sweet recess, City or Suburban, studious walks and shades; See there the Olive Grove of Academe, Plato's retirement . . ." and "Academia locus nemorosus, ab Athenis mille passus distans . . . in ambulacris umbrosis . . . *Atque inter sylvas Academi quaerere verum* . . . Ibi natus est Plato"; "within the walls then view The schools of ancient Sages; his who bred Great Alexander to subdue the world, Lyceum there . . ." and "Erat Academia gymnasium inferius, cum superiori gymnasio nomen esset Lycaeum . . . Lyceum vero nomen fuit scholae Aristotelicae."

ATHOS

    Hic turris posita est Titanidos ardua Famae,
       . . . rutilis vicinior astris
    Quam . . . Athos. . . .
               (*Quint. Nov.* 172-74)

According to Strabo, Athos is a mountain so high that those on its summit see the sun rise three hours earlier than those at its foot (7. Frag. 33).[9]

Here is the apposite description of Athos, by Stephanus, in which he represents its great height in another manner:

Athos, vel Athon, mons quem Xerxes abscidisse fertur, & velis fecisse peruium: vnde a Iuuenale velificatus dicitur. Hunc leporibus abundare testatur Ouidius. *Quot lepores in Atho, quot apes pascuntur in Hybla.* Situs est inter Macedoniam & Thraciam, altitudinis mirandae, vt vsque ad insulam Lemnon vmbram porrigere dicatur. Nonnunquam mons Thraciae dicitur, vt Homero in Hymno Apollinis. Nonnunquam etiam Macedoniae & AEmoniae. Plin. & Pompon. Fuit & nomen Gigantis, a quo mons nomen habet. Virgilius AEneidos 12. *Quantus Athos, aut quantus Eryx.* . . .

ATLANTICAE. See ELYSIAN FIELDS.

AVERNUS

> Magna sepulchrorum regina, satelles Averni,
> Saeva nimis Musis, Palladi saeva nimis,
> Quin illos rapias qui pondus inutile terrae?
> (*Elegia Secunda.* 17-19)

Avernus infrequently appears in Milton's poetry. The contemporary description of it is in Stephanus.

Auernus, lacus Campaniae prope Baias, quem Plutoni dicatum, & inferorum limen esse rudis vetustas credidit. Dictus quasi ἄορνος, hoc est, auibus carens, siue quod aues superuolantes graui eius odore enecarentur siue quod sulphureae exhalationes aerem vsque adeo extenuarent, vt aues sustinere non posset. Virg. lib. 6. AEneid.

> *Quem super haud vllae poterant impune volantes*
> *Tendere iter pennis,* &c.
> Vnde locum Graij dixerunt nomine Aornum.

. . . Capitur plerunque pro ipso inferorum loco, vel propter foetorem, vel propter Necromantiam, quae ibi exercebatur. . . . (Avernus is associated with Aornus and Styx, and also is said to be near to Lucrine Bay.)

AZOTUS (ASDOD)

See the discussion above in the introduction to this division of the study and compare with Milton's use of "Azotus" (*PL.* 1. 464) and "Asdod" (*Samson.* 981), the following from the *Dictionarium* of Stephanus.

Azotus, Hebr. Asdod. i. depredatio, siue ignis dilecti aut ignis patrui, insignis Palaestinae vrbs inter Ascalonem & Ioppem in tribu Dan, in qua gigantes habitarunt, capta a Iosue duce, Ios. 11. Sorte cessit tribui Iudae. Iosue 15. Haec vna e quinque ciuitatibus Allophylorum, templo Dagon idoli nobilitata, 1 Reg. 6. Quam vt ait Steph. condidit quidam e mari rubro profugus, ex nomine uxoris suae Azes. Volater. lib. 11. Cuius in Scripturis multa est mentio.

Ier. 25. Amos 1 & 2. Sophona 2. Zach. 9. Isa. 20. 2. Par. 26. In hac Philippus praedicauit Christum. Act. 8. Est & Azotus vrbs Achaiae, Pompon. Strabo. Steph.

BOSPORUS (SYMPLEGADES)

> And more endanger'd than when *Argo* pass'd
> Through *Bosporus* betwixt the justling Rocks.
>
> (*PL. 2.* 1017-18)

Readers familiar with the *Argonautica* of Apollonius Rhodius would need no gloss or annotation for this allusion. Gilbert quotes at length from the *Argonautica* (2. 549-602) to show the nature of the "justling rocks."[10] Keightley writes, "There is a slight slip of memory here, for it was after emerging from the Bosporus into the Euxine that the Argo had to pass through the Symplegades, which he properly translates 'the justling rocks.' "[11]

Two entries in C. Stephanus serve as annotations:

(1) Bosphorus, vel Bosporus, a bouis meabili transitu dictus, propter angustias freti, quasi bouis transitus. Plin. Soli. Duo sunt autem Bosphori, alter iuxta Byzantinum, qui Thracius dicitur estque ostium Ponti, per quod in propontidem influit, dictum a traiectu Iouis in vaccam deformati. Valer. Flac. lib. 4. Argon.

> *Iamque dies auraeque vocant, rursusque capessūt Aequora, qua rigidos eructat Bosphorus amnes.*

Alter est Bosphorus in introitu Maeotidis paludis, per quem in Pontum defluit. . . .

(2) Symplegades, quae & Cyaneae, insulae duae, siue potius scopuli, trans Bosphorum Thracium in ipso Ponti Euxini ostio mille quingentis passibus ab Europa distantes: tam modico autem inter se discretae interuallo, vt ex adverso quidem intrantibus geminae cernantur, paulum vero deflexa acie, coeuntium speciem praebeant. Quae res occasionem praebuit poëtarum fabulis, qui eas olim inter se concurrisse tradunt. Unde & nomen acceperunt ἀπὸ τῶ συμπλήγαδαι, hoc est, a concurrendo, siue conflictando. v. Cyaneae.

CARMEL

> Mount *Hermon*, yonder Sea, each place behold
> In prospect, as I point them; on the shore
> Mount *Carmel*.
>
> (*PL.* 12. 141-44)

"On the shore Mount Carmel" is often regarded as an echo of "Carmel by the sea," in Jeremiah (46. 18). The suggestion, with much additional information about "Carmelus maris" and another Carmel in Judea, together with the Biblical references, appears in the following entries in C. Stephanus:

(1) Carmelus, mons Tyriorum, Ptolemaidi ad mare imminet. Inde cognomen Carmelus maris accepit, versus ortum extensus tantum, vt campum magnum, quem Esdrelon vocant ab vno latere claudat. Ideoque a Iosepho tribui Issachar ascriptus, finisque Zabulonitarum ad mare Galilaeae, sicut Asseritarum ad mare magnum traditur. Ferax est admodum vini. Ios. 19. In hoc Elias videns frequenter versabatur, 3 Reg. 18. In hoc etiam Nabal habitauit, 1. Reg. 25. Isaiae 33, Ierem. 36. Amos 1. & 9. . . . Ioseph. libro 3. capite 2. de bello Iudaico. (2) Carmelus, alius in Iudaea, qua itur Aegyptum ad meridionalem plagam, de quo Isaiae 29. Ios. 15. in quo ciuitas eiusdem nominis extructa videtur. Quibus duobus locis posterioribus legitur Charmel.

CAUCASUS (HYRCANIAN)

Referring to the places from which the Parthian horsemen come, Milton writes,

> . . . from *Candaor* East,
> And *Margiana* to the *Hyrcanian* cliffs
> Of *Caucasus.*

>                                        (*PR.* 3. 316-18)

Commenting on "Caucasus" as here employed, Gilbert (79) suggests that Milton's reference to the "Hyrcanian cliffs of Caucasus" is dependent on the lines of Virgil quoted in the *Logic.* He translates, "Neither was a goddess your mother, nor Dardanus the founder of your race, traitor! but Caucasus bristling with rugged rocks begot you, and Hyrcanian tigresses gave you suck." (*Aen.* 4. 365-7.) It is interesting to find that in his entry *Caucasus,* Stephanus refers to the steep cliffs and quotes the identical passage of Virgil, and under *Hyrcania* he gives much information, including a reference to the tigers and panthers. The two entries are, then, the pat contemporary illustrations.

(1) *Caucasus,* mons editissimus in Septentrionali Asiae tractu, Indiam dirimens a Scythia, cacumina habens praerupta, perpetuisque niuibus tecta. Verg. 4. Aeneid.
> sed duris genuit te cautibus horrens
> Caucasus.

[Here follows a column of information on the Caucasian mountains, with references to the Prometheus myth, the *"Caucasiae portae vel pylae,"* the height, boundaries, etc.] Cf. Hyrcania.

(2) *Hyrcania,* regio Asiatica, variis nominibus hodie denominata, magna ex parte plana, & praeclarissimis vrbibus adornata, quarum celeberrimae sunt Talebrota, Samaria, Carta & Tape: adeo autem fertilis & opulenta, vt vitis vini metretam ferat, & ficus sexagenta modios ficuum, frumentum ex semine nascatur, quod cadit ex culmo, in arboribus mellificetur, profluat mel ex oleis: Dicta Hyrcania, ab Hyrcana sylva, quae Scythiae subiacet. Habet ab Oriente mare Caspium, a Meridie Armeniam, a Septētrione Albaniam, ab Occasu Iberiam. In ea regione pantherae, pardi, & tygres abundant, cum syluis aspera sit. Hinc Myrcanus, adiectiuum. Hyrcanum mare, & Caspium, idem.

There is also a separate entry on *Hyrcanum mare.*

CHALCIS (CHALCIDICA)
> Haec, et plura simul; tum quae mihi
>      pocula Mansus,
> Mansus, Chalcidicae non ultima gloria ripae.
>               (*Epitaph. Damon.* 181-82)
> Corpora Chalcidico sacra dedisse rogo?
>                  (3 *Ad Leonoram.* 4)

The Stephanus dictionaries have explicit information on "Chalcis" and "Chalcidica," with references to the use of the terms by Virgil.[12] This from R. Stephanus is probably the best annotation.

Chalcis, Vulgo *Negroponte,* Euboeae urbs praecipua, ab Aulide Boeotiae portu, exiguo Euripo diuisa, vetus Atheniensium colonia: ita dicta, si Stephano credimus, a Chalcide filia Asopi: aut certe, quod aerariae fabricae ibi primum fuerint repertae. . . .
Chalcidicus . . . Adj. Qui est ex Chalcide vrbe, vel Chalcidica regione. ut Arx Chalcidica. Verg. 6. Aen. 17.
Chalcidica levis tandem superastitit arce. Idem 10. Ecl. 50. Ibo, & Chalcidico quae sunt mihi condita versu Carmina, &c.

CHERSONESUS (OPHIR)
> To *Agra* and *Lahor* of great *Mogul*
> Down to the golden *Chersonese.*
>                 (*PL.* 11. 391-92)
> And *Sofala* thought *Ophir,* to the Realm
> Of *Congo.*
>                 (*PL.* 11. 400)
> From *India* and the golden *Chersonese.*
>                 (*PR.* 4. 74)

Milton would have been familiar with the "golden Chersonese" and Ophir from many sources, including the Scriptures and Ortelius and Purchas.[13]

Concise and adequate information is found also in the dictionaries under
*Chersonesus* and *Ophir*. These entries in C. Stephanus afford ample
illustration.

Cherronesus, seu Chersonesus . . . terra est, insula modum mare cincta,
vno tantum, eoque angusto spatio continenti adiuncta; Latini Peninsulam
vocant. Quinque autem insigniores commemorantur Cherronesi. [Here is
given some information about the first four] . . . Quinta, quam Auream
cognominant, in India sita supra Gangem, Ortum versus, iuxta sinum, quem
magnum appellat Ptolemaeus. (Cf. *Ophir.*)

Ophir, I. ciuis, vel incineratio, aut fructificatio, filius iectan. Gen. 10. Inde
Ophira regio. 3. Reg. 9. quae, vt refert Ioseph. lib. 8 etiam aurea terra nun-
cupatur, vnde aurum Ophirizum, quod Obrizum vocant. Quidam Auream
Chersonesum esse existimant, i. omnem eam oram, quae Pegusiis, Malaca &
Sumatra continetur. Cephala est aliis. Goropius, Arias Montanus & alii
Peruanam regionem nuper inuentam esse autumant. Regio illa aurifera Ophir
etiam scribitur in sacris literis celebris, vnde Salomoni aliisque Hebraeorum
regibus ternis annis (vt 2. Paral. cap. 9. habetur) magna vis auri aduehebatur.
Sed vbi terrarum sita sit haec regio, & an alio etiam nomine cognita esset, hactenus ignoratum fuit. Iosephus eam in India ponit, & Terram Auream suo
tempore vocatam addit. Eupolemus auctor apud Eusebium libr. 9. c. 4. prae-
parationis Euangelica, Vrphen appellat, & dicit insulam maris Rubri esse, &
naues cogi solere Melanis Arabiae vrbe. Hesion Gaber vocat hanc sacra scriptura, etsi Epiph. Ailon dici in sacris literis prodat. Hinc Marius Niger eam
Auream Chersonesum Ptolemaei interpretatus est, non parum enim ad terram
auream alludit, & Rubri maris huc vsque pertingere, ex classicis auctoribus
potest doceri, sed hanc Chersonesum auri diuitem olim fuisse nemo veterum
auctor est. Cephalam AEthiopicam regionem pro Ophir malunt quidam accipere, vt colligunt ex eius annalib. Tomas enim Lopesius in sua Indica nauigatione tradit Cephalenses habere libros patria lingua scriptos in quibus legitur
Salomonem regem hinc tertio quoque anno aurum tulisse. Abundatque haec
regio etiamnum hodie aurifodinis, adeo vt nihil praeter aurum, vt Lusitanorum
peregrinationes testantur, exteris mercatoribus communicet. Postello *Peru*
videtur, cui suffragatur. Goropius in sua Hispania: idem affirmat Arias.
Montan. Edidit tamen Gaspar Varrer. Lusitanus nuper opusculum, de Ophyra
regione, in quo constanter asseuerare, multisque argumentis persuadere cona-
tur, Sacrae scripturae Ophyram esse Auream Chersonesum, aut potius omnem
eam oram quae Pegusiis, Malaca & Sumatra continetur. Pro Ophir Ophat
legit Ioannes Tzetza, & insulam siue paeninsulam auream in India esse dicit.

This Ophir item is from the 1638 C. Stephanus, and is expanded to about
three times the length of that in the 1596 edition.

CHOASPES

> There *Susa* by *Choaspes,* amber stream,
> The drink of none but kings.
>
> *(PR.* 3. 288-89)

Hughes writes, "Herodotus (I, 188) says that on all his marches the Great King took with him water of the Choaspes boiled . . . of which alone and no other river the king drinks."[14]　More suggestive for Milton is the following entry in the Stephanus:

Choaspis, Medorum fluuius, ad fines Persidis in Tigrum defluens: *cuius aquae tam sunt suaues, vt finitimi reges non alia aqua ad potum vtantur.*　Tibullus. lib. 4.

Nec qua vel Nilus vel regia lympha Choaspis, profluit.

Milton's use of the plural form "kings" and the phrasing of the line are near to Stephanus.　Compare "The drink of none but kings" and "reges non alia aqua ad potum vtantur."　In the phrasing of Stephanus, which seems to anticipate Milton, we have also a statement of the reason why royalty chose the water of the Choaspes.

Compare Gilbert (84) for detailed discussion.

CIMMERIAN

> Cereaque in manibus gestant funalia caeci,
> Cimmeriis nati in tenebris vitamque trahentes.
>
> *(In Quintum Novembris,* 59-60)
>
> Est locus aeterna septus caligine noctis,
> Vasta ruinosa quondam fundamina tecti,
> Nunc torvi spelunca Phoni, Prodotaeque bilinguis. . . .
>
> *(Ibid.,* 139-41)
>
> . . . exanguisque locum circumvolat Horror,
>
> .　.　.
>
> Ipsi etiam pavidi latitant penetralibus antri
> Et Phonos et Prodotes, nulloque sequente per antrum,
> Antrum horrens, scopulosum, atrum feralibus umbris,
> Diffugiunt sontes . . . .
>
> *(Ibid.,* 148, 151-54)
>
> Hence loathed Melancholy
>   Of *Cerberus* and blackest midnight born,
> In *Stygian* Cave forlorn
>   'Mongst horrid shapes, and shrieks, and sights unholy,
> Find out some uncouth cell,
>   Where brooding darkness spreads his jealous wings,
> And the night-Raven sings;
>   There under *Ebon* shades, and low-brow'd Rocks,

As ragged as thy Locks,
In dark *Cimmerian* desert ever dwell.

(*L'Allegro*. 1-10)

Long before Milton's day the association of Cimmeria with darkness, physical and mental, had become proverbial, and there is little need, so far as the general idea is concerned to cite specific passages as a basis for the poet's allusions. Though the common idea pervades the quoted lines, the associated ideas of melancholy, of horror, of crime, as well as the imagery require further comment.

Lines from Homer (*Od*. 2. 13) and Ovid (*Met*. 2. 592) have been aptly cited as possibly offering suggestions to Milton as to imagery and details. Items from contemporary reference works which would be equally felicitious as illustrative annotations have been neglected. Characteristic of the current items is this from C. Stephanus:

Cimmerij, populi in Italia ad Baianum & Auernum sinum, qui in subterraneis domiciliis habitantes, & per cuniculos commeare soliti, toto in illis die delitescebant, noctu tantum ad latrocinia egressi, cum victum ex metallorum alioqui effossione, diuinationum mercede, & prouentibus a Rege designatis quaererent, vt ex Ephoro scribit Strabo. Penes hos ingens quondam superstitio increbuit, loci natura erroribus suffragante, ibi sacra nemora venerata, fluminibus etiam & fontibus suus horror fuit. Specus praeterea famosi, & ad inferos crediti aditus, quo intrare fas non erat, nisi diis manibus prius, quo auspicator descensus foret, sacrificio placatus. Vnde Homero suae fabulae Oeconomia, quam Odyss. libro 2. comminiscitur, desumpta est, & Virg. libro 6. . . . Hinc *Cimmeriae tenebrae* pro *densissima caligine*.

This entry could have been suggestive for the lines in *In Quintum Novembris*. Here are people living in eternal darkness in their subterranean homes, inclined to crime. Here are superstition and horror associated with the place, a cave believed leading to the lower world, the citation of Homer and Virgil. In a subsequent entry, Stephanus describes the Cimmerian Bosphorus, according to Herodotus, refers to the proverb ("Hinc Cimmeriae tenebrae prouerbio celebrantur, pro densissima caligine"), and quotes Ovid's:

Est prope Cimmerios longo spelunca recessu
Mons cauus, ignaui domus, & penetralia Somni.

Cooper partially paraphrases the entries in Stephanus, thus:

(1) *Cimmerij,* people inhabytyng the furthest parte of Europe, not farre from the fennes called *Paludus Maeotidis,* about the sea *Bosphorus Cimmerius,* north east from Grecia. Plinie and other affyrme, that by the farre dystance

of the sonne from it that country is alwaie veraie darke, wherof hapned this prouerbe, *Cimmerijs tenebris atrior,* blacker than the darkenesse of Cimmeria, applied to much darknesse, dulnesss of witte, or lacke of wisdome.

(2) *Cimmerij,* were also people of Italy, in the country betwene Baiae, & Cumae, whiche was so enuyroned with hylles, that the sonne came not to it, neyther in the mornynge nor at nyght. There was supposed to be a descente into hell. And the people dwelled only in caues.

### CITHAERON

Referring to the shrieks of Bacchus and the Bacchae as they chant their orgies, Milton continues,

> Dum tremit attonitus vitreis Asopus in undis,
> Et procul ipse cava responsat rupe Cithaeron.
> *(Quint. Nov.* 66-67)

On Cithaeron the Stephanus dictionaries give explicit information, with references to Ovid, Virgil, and Servius. This is from the *Thesaurus* of Robert Stephanus:

Cithaeron. . . . Mons Libero sacer. De quo Servius Aen. 10. 192. Parnassus, mons est Thessaliae juxta Boeotiam, qui in duo finditur juga, Cithaeronem Liberi, & Heliconem Apollinis & Musarum. Hunc Lactan. lib. 1. cap. 22. Divinarum institutionum, quia super ipso frequenter Orpheus citharae cantu personaret, Cithaeronem appellatum scribit. Ovid. 2. Met. 223. . . . Ibi enim sancte colebatur Bacchus. Servius alibi censet esse partem montis Parnassi refertam animalibus, ex illo Virg. 3. Georg. 43. . . .
Nocturnus, Nocte celebratus. Virg. 4, Aen. 303. . . .

Cf. also, *Bacchae,* from C. Stephanus:

Bacchae mulieres, tertio quoque anno ad Cithaeron montem cateruatim cum Thyrsis conuenientes, vt ibi Bacchi Orgia magno cum vlulatu celebrarent. Ouidius libro nono Meta.

### CNIDOS

> . . . Venus
> Huic Cnidon, et riguas Simoentis flumine valles,
> Huic Paphon, et roseam posthabitura Cypron.
> *(Elegia Prima.* 82-84)

Apt annotation, with a suggestive quotation from Horace is this from C. Stephanus:

Cnidus, siue Cnidos, vrbs in signis in extremo cornu peninsulae Cariae adhaerens, Praxitelis Venere imprimis nobilis. Hor. 1. car. Ode 30.
*O Venus regina Cnidi Paphique,*
hodie *Cabocrio,* quibusdam. Moletius *Chio* appellat.

CRETA

> . . . these first in *Crete*
> And *Ida* known. . . .
> (*PL.* 1. 514-15)
> Their wines of *Setia, Cales,* and *Falerne,*
> *Chios* and *Crete.* . . .
> (*PR.* 4. 117-18)

There is no extensive reference to Crete, by Milton, though he does refer to its wines. In the Stephanus entry below is a reference to the excellent wine—and much besides.

Creta, tae, & Crete, tes, vulgo *Candie:* insula in medio Ponto, centum vrbium fama clara: vnde a Graecis ἐχατόμπωλις appellatur, quae (vt scribit Strabo) ad Septentrionem AEgeo alluitur, simul & Cretico Pelago, ad Austrum Aphro, aliis Libyco: ad occidentem Aegliam & Cytheram spectat, ad Orientem Carpathum. Habet in longitudine 279 millia passuum, in latitudine quinquaginta millia. Circuitus eius 1589. millia passuum complectitur. Insignes in ea vrbes sunt, Gortyn, Cydonia, Gnossus Minois regia, & Strabonis Cosmographi patria. Nullum in Creta animal noxium viuit, optimique vini fertilissima est, de qua Virgilius 3. AEneid.

> *Creta Iouis magni medio iacet insula Ponto,*
> *Mons Idaeus vbi & gentis cunabula nostrae:*
> *Centum urbes habitant magnas, vberrima regna.*

Here follow various accounts about the derivation of the name Crete.

CTESIPHON

Among the places built by "Parthian hands," Milton writes of

> The great *Seleucia, Nisibis,* and there
> *Artaxata, Teredon, Ctesiphon.*
> (*PR.* 3. 291-92)
> . . . for now the *Parthian* King
> In *Ctesiphon* hath gather'd all his Host
> Against the *Scythian.* . . .
> (*PR.* 3. 299-301)

The source of Stephanus' description is Strabo and Pliny, and this condensation current in the dictionaries, illustrates Milton's allusions.

Ctesiphon, locus Parthorum, Strabo li. 15. Prope Seleuciam vicus maximus est, nomine Ctesiphon, in quo Parthorum reges hyemabant. Hic vicus vrbis potentia & magnitudine est adeo, vt Parthorum multitudinem & apparatum omnem recipiat, ac venalia necessariaque artificia illi suppeditet. Ibi Parthorum reges in hyeme propter aeris temperiem degere solebant, aestatem vero in

Hyrcania & Ecbatanis agebant. Quin. & Ctesiphontem Babylonici regni caput fuisse, Plin. lib. 6. scribit ca. 26. Gentile Ctesiphontius.

CUSCO

> And *Cusco* in *Peru,* the richer seat
> Of *Atabalipa.* . . .
>
> (*PL.* ii. 408-9)

Milton may have read of Cusco in Purchas' *Pilgrimes.* The short entry from Stephanus shows something of the range of the *Dictionarium,* and may have been of service to Milton's readers.

Cusco, metropolis & praecipua ciuitas in ea noui orbis parte, quae meridiem magis respicit, quam Hispani terram firmam appellant, & quae Brasiliam Peruuiamque comprehendit. Haec ciuitas, cum pulcherrimis Galliae & Hispaniae vrbibus, amplitudine, inuicta arcis munitione, & hominum, potissimum nobilium frequentia, aedificiorum serie & dispositione, situsque amoenitate contendit. Delectantur incolae rebus depictis: panno, plumbi, stannique fondinis abundant. Argenti apud eos vis magna, auri non item. Vide noui orbis descriptores.

CYDON (CYDONIUS)

> Qui post terga solet vincere, Parthus eques.
> Cydoniusque mihi cedit venator. . . .
>
> (*Elegia Septima.* 36-37)

Milton's use of Parthian and Cydonian in close conjunction and in the same context as Virgil may point to the *Aeneid* as a source. But Stephanus, who quotes the *Aeneid,* illustrates the allusion:

Cydon, Plinio, vrbs insignis Cretae insulae, cuius incolae Cydones dicuntur, & poma Cydonia. Virg. Aeneid. 12.
> *Parthus, siue Cydon telum immedicabile torsit.*
Cydonia, insula ante Lesbon. Plinius libr. 2. c. 103. Cretae insulae vrbs. Ptol.

Compare Calepine (1609) :

*Cydon* . . . Insigne Cretan oppidum, a quo Cydonius . . . Ouid. 2. Meta. Cydonio fundebat spicula cornu. Vergil 4. Eclog. 10. Ite liber, Partho torquere Cydonio cornu Spicula. . . .

CYLLENE

> On old *Lycaeus* or *Cyllene* hoar,
> Trip no more in twilight ranks.
>
> (*Arcades,* 98-99)

Gilbert (95), commenting on Cyllene, writes, "With Milton's adjective 'hoar,' or snow-covered, cf. Virgil's 'gelidus vertex.'" (*Aeneid* 8. 139)

As Stephanus quotes the lines of Virgil referred to by Gilbert and gives information about Cyllene and Cyllenius, his lexicon affords the apposite illustration.

Cyllene, mons Arcadiae, in quo Maia a Ioue compressa, Mercurium peperit. Virg. lib. 8. Aeneid.

> *Vobis Mercurius pater est, quem candida Maia*
> *Cyllenes gelido conceptum vertice fudit.*

Cyllenius, peculiare Mercurij cognomen, inde impositum, quod omnem rem sermone, sine manibus conficiat. . . . [Other reasons are given for the name Cyllenius, but the article returns to Virgil's reason, that Mercury was born in a mountain Cyllene in Arcadia.]

## Delphos (Delphi)

> The Oracles are dumb,
> No voice or hideous hum
> Runs through the arched roof in words deceiving.
> Apollo from his shrine
> Can no more divine,
> With hollow shriek the steep of *Delphos* leaving.
> (*Nativity.* 173-78)
> . . . henceforth Oracles are ceast,
> And thou no more with Pomp and Sacrifice
> Shalt be inquir'd at *Delphos* or elsewhere,
> At least in vain, for they shall find thee mute.
> (*PR.* 1. 456-59)

Apollo at Delphi, the steep cliffs, and the muting of the oracles on the birth of Christ—all in the entry *Delphi* of Stephanus—make this the ample gloss and illustration of the allusions to "Delphos."[15]

Delphi, ciuitas in Boeotia iuxta Parnassum, dicta a Delpho Neptuni filio, magis rupibus & loci natura, quam humana arte munita, vbi clarissimum templum habuit Apollo, reddebatque oracula, vnde & Delphicus vocatus est. Nomen autem accepit a Delpho Deucalionis filio, ex Melantho eiusdem filia suscepto. In hac ciuitate, nato Christo, obmutuit oraculum.

## Dodona

Surveying the cult of the Olympian gods, Milton has the following allusions:

> . . . or on the *Delphian* Cliff.
> Or in *Dodona,* and through all the bounds
> Of Doric Land.
> (*PL.* 1. 517-19)

The speaking tree, the sacred oak of Jupiter, appears in the *Odyssey* (19. 296), as Gilbert notes.[16] The story is aptly summarized by C. Stephanus, and is richly suggestive for the background of the allusions to Dodona.

Dodona ciuitas Chaoniae regionis Epiri, iuxta quam propinquum erat nemus Iouis sacrum querneum totum, vbi Iouis Dodonaei templum fuisse dicitur, & in eo oraculum omnium quae apud Graecos fuerunt, vetutissimum.   In quo duas columbas consulentibus responsa dedisse quidam fabulantur, quarum altera Delphos, altera vero in Ammonis Iouis templum volauit.   Alij arbores ipsas vocales fuisse volunt, & consulentibus oracula edere solitas.   Hinc Dodonaeus Iupiter, qui in Dodonaea nemore colebatur.   Item Dodonaeum aes, tintinnabuli quoddam genus, die noctuque continuo crepitans: vnde & ad homines iusto loquaciores prouerbiali metaphora transferre solet Ausonius. Vide Epirus.

                    *Nec Dodonaei cessat tinnitus aheni.*
. . . Steph. vel potius a Dodanim, filio Iauan, quorum posteri suis superstitionibus veri Dei cultum a Noa sincere traditum foedarunt.

ELYSIUM (BLESSED ISLES, FORTUNATE ISLES, HESPERIAN GARDENS)

> *Spirit.* To the Ocean now I fly,
> And those happy climes that lie
> Where day never shuts his eye,
> Up in the broad fields of the sky:
> There I suck the liquid air
> All amidst the Gardens fair
> Of *Hesperus,* and his daughters three
> That sing about the golden tree:
> Along the crisped shades and bow'rs
> Revels the spruce and jocund Spring,
> The Graces and the rosy-bosom'd Hours,
> Thither all their bounties bring,
> That there eternal Summer dwells,
> And West winds with musky wing
> About the cedarn alleys fling
> *Nard,* and *Cassia's* balmy smells.
> *Iris* there with humid bow,
> Waters the odorous banks that blow
> Flowers of more mingled hue
> Than her purfl'd scarf can shew,
> And drenches with *Elysian* dew . . .
> Beds of *Hyacinth* and Roses
> Where young *Adonis* oft reposes,
> Waxing well of his deep wound

> In slumber soft, and on the ground
> Sadly sits th' *Assyrian* Queen.
>
> (*Comus.* 976-1002)

The lines quoted are from the epilogue spoken by the Attendant Spirit. If we add to these a passage which Milton crossed out in the Trinity College Manuscript, between lines four and five of the received text,[17] we have more information about the poet's conception of the Hesperian gardens and, incidentally, a sort of framework for the whole poem. The deleted passage follows:

> Amidst the Hesperian gardens, on whose banks
> Bedewed with nectar, and celestial songs
> Eternal roses grow, and hyacinth
> And fruits of golden rind, on whose fair tree
> The scaly harnest dragon ever keeps
> His unenchanted eye, and round the verge
> And sacred limits of the blissful isle
> The jealous ocean that old river winds
> His far extended arms till with steep fall
> Half his waste flood the wide Atlantic fills
> And half the slow unfathomed Stygian pool . . .
> Yet thence I come and oft from thence behold.

For information about the Hesperides, especially in the second quotation, Milton could have got suggestions from the entry *Hesperides* in Charles Stephanus. In translation a pertinent part of the entry is thus:

The Hesperides are the daughters of Hesperus, the brother of Atlas, and are called Aegle, Arethusa, and Hesperethusa. The poets feign that these daughters had very precious gardens in which was an orchard bearing golden fruit, and guarded by an ever wakeful dragon. Him Hercules is said to have slain and to have taken the golden apples to his step-father Euristheus. Pliny and Solinus report that there was an inlet of the sea, with a winding course in the form of a dragon, which encompassed the gardens of the Hesperides.

The garden, the golden fruit, the watchful dragon are common elements in the myth—details which the poet could have known from almost any version of the story. Less common and more important for Milton are the details ascribed to Pliny and Solinus concerning the inlet which, winding its course in the form of a dragon, surrounds the gardens. Here may be the suggestion for Milton's "and round the verge/And sacred limits of the blissful isle/The jealous ocean that old river winds/His far extended arms." But in placing the fair gardens on a "blissful isle" and supplying them with perennial roses and hyacinths Milton is thinking in terms of the traditional Elysium.

In the epilogue by the Attendant Spirit (quoted first above) the tendency to make the Hesperian gardens central in his description of an ideal clime, or earthly paradise, is fully developed. These lines (976 ff.) constitute a synthesis of ideas and details associated with the Fortunate Isles, the Blessed Isles, and the Elysian fields. Here is eternal summer, the "West winds with musky wing," flowers of many colors, drenched with *"Elysian* dew." What is most striking in the passages from *Comus* is Milton's identification of the Hesperian gardens with Elysium and the Islands of the Blest. For this identification, there seems to be no precedent in the ancient poets. But the identification is definitely made in the *Dictionarium* of Charles Stephanus, *s.v. Atlanticae Insulae*—an entry which could have given many additional suggestions to Milton. This entry, translated, reads as follows:

The *Atlanticae* are two islands which they call the Blessed and the Fortunate. These, separated from each other by a small space of sea, are a thousand miles distant from Africa. There the showers are rare and gentle and the winds most pleasant and dew-bearing. The fertile soil, cultivated without human effort, produces delicious fruit for the care-free people. The air is pure and temperate and undergoes little change in the course of the year; for the north winds, Boreas and Aquilo, which blow from the land, move over vast open spaces and are exhausted before they reach these islands. Winds from the southwest and the west, Argestae and Zephyri, which blow from the sea, bring cool and refreshing showers. There, as Homer and other poets say, are the Elysian fields and the homes of the Blest. Pliny seems to call these islands the Hesperides. . . .

Here is the indication that the Hesperides are islands, which, on the authority of Pliny, are identified with the Elysian fields, the Islands of the Blest, and the Fortunate Isles, as in Milton. It should be noted also that, *s.v. Elysii Campi,* the *Dictionarium* has the cross-reference: "Vide Atlanticae Insulae." But this entry in the Stephanus owes much—excepting the identification of the Hesperian gardens with the Elysian fields—to Comes' *Mythologiae.* (See "De campis Elysiis," 3. 19.) In Comes' text Milton could have found many of the details which appear in his descriptions of his earthly paradise.

At the outset Comes summarizes speculations as to the location of the Elysian fields, indicating that these have been identified with the

Fortunate Isles, and the Islands of the Blest. The latter, located in the Atlantic Ocean, he writes about as follows:

These two are said to be small islands, separated from each other by a small tract of sea. There the winds, most sweet and fragrant, blow gently, as if crossing over an incredible variety and sweetness of flowers. For, as is the perfume from many roses, violets, hyacinths, narcissi, myrtles, laurel, cypress, such is the sweetness of the breathing breezes. Here in the wood, the whispers of the gently moving leaves are most pleasing. The soil is so fertile that it may be easily cultivated, and indeed produces much of its own accord, without any human effort. It can, without difficulty, support a great many people, for it yields crops three times yearly.

Here it is always spring. No wind is wont to blow except the West, and the place is adorned with all kinds of flowers and tame plants. The vineyards bear fruit every month. Pure and temperate is the air and undergoes almost no change in the course of years. The North wind, and other sharp winds, are exhausted over the open spaces and cease before they reach these islands. But those winds which do come, the West and the Southwest, sometimes stir up the gentlest showers. This place does not, however, often need rain, since with the moisture and goodness of the air, it can sustain almost all animals and plants. Here are said to be wonderful songs of various birds as they fly hither and thither in the branches of the trees. Here are heard also the sweetest songs of human beings. Girls with boys lead the choir, and with these the most skillful singers with their musical instruments take part— singers such as are said to have been Arion of Methymna, Eunomus of Locris, Stesichorus of Himera, and Anacreon of Teius.

A little further on in the same chapter Comes quotes Tibullus, associating Venus with the Elysian fields.

But me, because I am always affable to tender love, Venus herself leads into the Elysian fields. Here are dancing and singing, and the ranging birds echoing the sweet song in their throat. The untilled land brings the odors of casia and the benign earth blooms with fragrant roses. A train of youth plays in the company of maids, and assiduously Love embroils the battle.

To take stock of the investigation thus far, we may say that Milton seems to have read Stephanus on the Hesperides and to have reflected his knowledge of the entry in the deleted lines of the Trinity College Manuscript. In the same entry he would have found a reference to Comes' *Mythologiae* for further information on the subject. If, as seems likely, he also consulted the dictionary on *Elysii campi,* he would have observed a cross-reference to *Atlanticae Insulae.* In this entry is the definite identification of the Hesperian gardens with the Elysian fields and the Islands of the Blest, together with details concerning the temperate climate, the pure air, and the dew-bearing and sweet-scented breezes.

But, in these entries, Stephanus is, in part, paraphrasing Comes' chapter on the Elysian fields. In the *Mythologiae* Milton would have found many details lacking in the dictionary. The idea of Elysium, for example, is closely associated, in the mind of Milton, with that of flowers, as Osgood notes (31-32). For this association, Milton had precedent in Homer, Pindar, and Plutarch, all of whom, however, refer to flowers in general terms. It will be noted in the translation above that Comes emphasizes the abundance of flowers in the Islands of the Blest, referring specifically to roses and hyacinths—flowers which appear in Milton's descriptions—and to violets, and myrtle and laurel, etc. Here it is always spring, according to Comes, the gentle breezes are redolent with perfume; there are youth, song and dance and Venus and love-making. In brief, two entries—*Hesperides* and *Atlanticae Insulae*—in C. Stephanus' *Dictionarium,* and part of the chapter on the *Elysian fields* in Comes' *Mythologiae* offer the essential elements found in Milton's picture of an earthly paradise, as first presented in *Comus*.

Some parallels between *Comus* and the *Dictionarium* and *Comus* and the *Mythologiae* have been suggested above. Other correspondences, in confirmation of these relationships, are here presented. Compare the following:

| *Comus* | *Dictionarium* |
|---|---|
| But beauty, like the fair Hesperian Tree Laden with blooming gold, had need the guard Of dragon-watch with unenchanted eye, To save her blossoms and defend her fruit. . . . | Hesperides, appellatae sunt Hesperi fratris Atlantis filiae, Aegle, Arethusa & Hesperethusa, quas poetae fabulantur habuisse hortos, nemore aurifero pretiosos, a dracone pervigili servatos. |

(ll. 393-396)

More striking, perhaps, are the correspondences between the epilogue in *Comus*—the composite sketch of the Hesperian gardens, or Islands of the Blest—and certain passages in the *Mythologiae*. Notice the following:

| *Comus* | *Mythologiae* (3. 19) |
|---|---|
| There [in the "happy climes"] I suck the liquid air | Nam locus imbribus plerumque non indiget, *cum ipso aeris humore ac bonitate omnia & animalia & plantas fere sustentare possit.* (pp. 275-76.) |

(l. 980)

| Comus | Mythologiae (7. 7) |
|---|---|
| Of Hesperus, and his daughters three That sing about the golden tree. (ll. 982-83) | Anguis terrigena, hic vbi caelo attollitur Atlas. Illum curabant nymphae praedulce canentes Hesperides truncum amplexus. (Qtd. from Apollonius. lib. 4. p. 735.) |

| Comus | Mythologiae (3. 19) |
|---|---|
| That there eternal summer dwells, And West winds with musky wing About the cedarn alleys fling Nard and Cassia's balmy smells. (ll. 986-89) | Hic semper est ver, neque vllus ventus praeter Zephyrum aspirare solet, locusque ipse omnibus florum generibus & mansuetis plantis vestitur. (p. 275.) . . . Fert casiam non culta seges, totosque per agros Floret odoratis terra benigna rosis. (p. 277.) |

| Flowers of more mingled hue Than her [Iris's] purfl'd scarf can shew, And drenches with Elysian dew . . . Beds of Hyacinths and Roses. (ll. 994-98) | . . . atque ventos ibi plurimum suaues & oderiferos leniter spirare, tanquam per incredibilem florum varietatem & amoenitatem transeuntes. Nan qualis odor est multis rosis, violis, hyacinthis, narcissis, liliis, myrtetis, lauris, cyparissis, talis aspirantium ventorum est suauitas. . . . (p. 275.) |
|---|---|

| Comus | Mythologiae (3. 19) |
|---|---|
| Where young Adonis oft reposes . . . and on the ground Sadly sits th'Assyrian Queen. (ll. 999-1002) | Sed me, quod facilis tenero sum semper amori, Ipsa Venus campos ducet in Elysios. Hic choreae, cantusque vigent. . . . (p. 277.) |

Correspondences of *Comus* and the *Mythologiae* as to the "liquid air," singing about the golden tree, the eternal spring or summer, the fragrant west wind, the flowers of mingled hue, especially hyacinths and roses, and the presence of Venus and love—are in number, details, and order of appearance too significant to be ignored. They strongly suggest Milton's recollection of Comes' chapter on the Elysian fields.

This suggestion is further confirmed by a number of passages in *Paradise Lost,* passages which seem to echo Milton's conception of a terrestrial paradise as pictured at the end of *Comus* and also to reflect

ideas and details from the *Dictionarium* and the *Mythologiae,* which lie
back of that conception. Consider first the excerpts which follow:

> . . . far off *Atlantic Seas* . . .
> Or other Worlds they seem'd, or happy Isles,
> Like those *Hesperian* Gardens fam'd of old,
> Fortunate Fields, and Groves and flow'ry Vales,
> Thrice happy Isles. . . .
>
> *(PL.* 3. 559, 567-70)

And these lines in the description of Paradise,

> And higher than that Wall a circling row
> Of goodliest Trees loaden with fairest Fruit,
> *Blossoms* and *Fruits* at once *of golden hue*
> Appear'd. . . .
>
> *(PL.* 4. 146-49)

And then more about paradise, a little further on,

> A happy rural seat of various view:
> Groves whose rich Trees wept odorous Gums and Balm,
> Others whose fruit burnisht with Golden Rind
> Hung amiable, *Hesperian* Fables true.
>
> *(PL.* 4. 247-50)

These three passages all refer to paradise, and each associates with that
happy place the Hesperian gardens and the golden fruit, just as the poet
had done in *Comus.* And the suggestion for the association in *Comus*
may well have derived from the *Atlanticae Insulae* in Stephanus. If so,
this is an interesting clue to the way a hint from the dictionary may become an organic part of many lines of poetry.

Two other examples may be of interest here. Compare:

> But I can now no more; the parting Sun
> Beyond the Earth's *green Cape* and *verdant Isles*
> *Hesperian* sets, my Signal to depart.
>
> *(PL.* 8. 630-32)

And Stephanus:

Hesperium ceras . . . Africae extremum promontorium, vbi scilicet veluti in
fronte circumaguntur naues in occasum ac mare Atlanticum. Sonat haec vox
occidentale cornu. Hodie vocant Caput viride. vulgo, *Le cap verd.* Merca-
tori est *Cabo blanco.*

And, finally, the following, in which there is a partial description of
paradise as first seen by Satan; and Stephanus' lines on Elysium:

. . . so lovely seem'd
That Lantskip: *And of pure now purer air*
Meets his approach, and to the heart inspires
Vernal delight and joy. . . .

(*PL.* 4. 152-55)

Elysium, locus vbi piorum animae habitant ἀπὸ τῆς λύσεος, a solutione. Nam animae post solutionem vinculi corporei deueniunt ad Elysios campos. Hunc locum alij inferorum foelicitatibus plenum, alij fortunatas insulas, alij circa lunarem circulum esse dicunt, *vbi iam aer purior est.*

The passages transcribed below suggest the threefold relationship existing in *Comus, Paradise Lost,* and Comes' *Mythologiae:*

(1)

| *Paradise Lost* | *Mythologiae* (3. 19) |
|---|---|
| . . . now *gentle gales* Fanning their *odoriferous* wings dispense Native perfumes, and *whisper* whence they stole Those balmy spoils. <br><br> (4. 156-159) | atque *ventos* ibi plurimum *suaues* & *oderiferos leniter* spirare, tanquam per incredibilem florum varietatem & amoenitatem transeuntes. Nam qualis odor est multis rosis, violis, hyacinthis, narcissis, myrtetis, lauris, cyparissis, talis aspirantium ventorum est suauitas. Hic in syluis motorum sensim foliorum iucundissimi sunt *sussuri.* (p. 275.) |

(2)

| | |
|---|---|
| Their glittering tents he [Raphael] pass'd and now is come Into the blissful field, through Groves of Myrrh, And flow'ring Odours, Cassia, Nard, and Balm; A Wilderness of sweets; for Nature here Wanton'd as in her prime. . . . <br><br> (5. 291-5) | . . . Hic semper est ver, neque vllus ventus praeter Zephyrum aspirare solet, locusque ipse omnibus florum generibus & mansuetis plantis vestitur. At vineae fructum ferunt singulis mensibus. <br><br> (p. 275.) |

Compare with these *Comus,* ll. 986-95.

The phrasing in the examples under (1) above is so similar as to suggest more than coincidence. Compare: "now gentle gales Fanning their oderiferous wings" and "atque ventos ibi plurimum suaues & oderiferos leniter spirare"; "Native perfumes" and "incredibilem florum varietatem & amoenitatem"; "whisper" and "sussuri," in their contexts.

In summary we may say that in the concluding lines of *Comus* (976-1002) Milton first developed in detail his picture of an earthly paradise. A central feature of his picture is the Hesperian gardens, which are identified with the Elysian fields and the Isles of the Blessed. It is a synthesis of much that had been written, from Homer to the authors of the sixteenth century, on these happy climes. Such a synthesis had been partially effected by Natalis Comes in his *Mythologiae* and by Charles Stephanus in his *Dictionarium, Historicum, Geographicum, Poeticum.* From these compilers, the evidence seems to show, Milton drew suggestions and some concrete details in completing his picture.

Once complete, the description in *Comus* colors all subsequent passages in Milton's poetry which are concerned with the idea of an earthly paradise. Such passages appear, naturally, in *Paradise Lost* (3. 567 ff.; 4. 145 ff. and 245 ff.; 5. 292 ff.). In these recur the central idea, the imagery, often details and phrasing of the lines in *Comus.* Apparently, the conception of the happy climes, inspired by Comes and Stephanus, and felicitously sung by the Attendant Spirit, remained in the poet's mind and, by association, was more than once recalled and put into service in *Paradise Lost.*

Eshtaol (Esthaol)
> We come thy friends and neighbors not unknown
> From *Eshtaol* and *Zora's* fruitful Vale. . . .
> > (*Samson.* 180-81)

One could run down the word Eshtaol in Milton's scriptural sources (*Judges* and *Joshua*). Stephanus offers this interesting item, together with the Biblical references.

Esthaol, vrbs tribus Iudea, siue Dan, inter Azotum & Ascalonem in Palaestina, Ios. 15 & 19. Vbi filij Israel posuerant castra contra Philisthiim. Iud. 13. iuxta quam sepultus erat Samson. Iud. 16. Hieronym. villula Asco dicta. Lat. postulans, aut mulier fortis vel stulta, siue ignis laboris.

Gades
> From *Gallia*, Gades, and the *British* West.
> > (*PR.* 4. 77)

In *Samson*, Milton refers to the approach of *Dalila*, like a stately ship
> Of *Tarsus*, bound for th' Isles
> Of *Javan* or *Gadire*
> With all her bravery on. . . .
> > (ll. 715-17)

Charles Stephanus offers much information on the Gades Islands; Gades, now Calix [Calais]; Gadire; etc.; and has the interesting reference to the lascivious character of Gaditanian girls. (C. Stephanus has six entries concerned with Gades, Gadire, etc. The first, a half column in length, runs in part as follows:)

Gades . . . duae insulae. Plin. li. 4. c. 22. vltra finem Baeticae prouinciae, & in extremo nostri orbis, versus Occidentem, extra freti angustias, quibus Africa ab Europa dirimitur. [Each island is here described, and the conclusion runs:] Inde Gaditanus, vt mare Gaditanum, & Gaditanae puellae, quae agilitatis lasciuiaeque nomine olim in pretio fuerunt.
(2) Gades, nunc Calix, Hispaniae Baeticae, seu Gadirae insulae oppidum, quod Cicero in oratione pro L. Corn. Balbo, quia Herculeo freto vicinum, itinerum ac laborum Herculis terminum vocat, & a L. Marineo Siculo Baeticae prouinciae initium statuitur. Vide Strab. lib. 3.
(3) Gadira urbs, quae prius Cotinusa dicta fuit. Steph.
(4) Gadira, locus iuxta Hispaniam extremam, ad quem profectus Hercules, & pertransire non valens columnas ab incolis sumptas infixit.

GEHENNA (HINNOM, TOPHET)

> . . . the wisest heart
> Of *Solomon* he led by fraud to build
> His Temple right against the Temple of God
> On that opprobrius Hill, and made his Grove
> The pleasant Valley of *Hinnom, Tophet* thence
> And black *Gehenna* call'd, the Type of Hell.
>                               (*PL.* 1. 400-5)

Milton was familiar with passages in the Scriptures (I Kings xi, 7; II Kings xxiii, 13; Jer. xix, 5), as Hughes notes,[18] and the Scriptural allusions are a part of the background for Milton's reference. The poet may well have known other accounts of Moloch, Hinnom, and places associated with them. Verity (II, 383) quotes Sandys' *Relation of a Journey* (1615): "We descended into the valley of Gehinnon, which divided the Mount Sion from the Mountaine of Offense. . . . This valley is but streight (*i.e.,* narrow); heretofore most delightful, planted with groves and watered with fountains." Whiting (*N. & Q.* 192.225) notes the correspondences between Milton's lines and those of Henry Greenwood's description of hell, in his tract "Tormenting Tophet."

Under the entry *Geena,* or *Gehenna,* Renaissance dictionaries—Cooper, Calepine, Charles Stephanus—give concise accounts of the place. Typical is the following from Stephanus:

*Gehenna,* i. vallis deceptionis, vel tristiae, siue divitiarum: aut *Syriace infernus,* nomen loci apud Evangelistas. Hoc nomen proprium, inquit Hieronymus, a Servatore nostro ponitur hac occasione. Erat idolum Baal iuxta Hierusalem, ad radicem montis Mora, unde Siloa fluit. Haec vallis & parua campi planities irrigua & nemorosa, plenaque deliciis, & lucus in ea idolo consecratus. In tantam autem populus Israel venerat dementiam, ut deserto templo ibi hostias immolaret filiosque suos incenderent, demonibus vel initiarent. Appellabatur autem locus ipse Gehennon, id est, vallis Hennon. Hoc regum volumina, & Paralipomenon, & Hieremiae plenissime scribunt. Et comminatur Deus se locum illum impleturum cadaveribus mortuorum, ut nequaquam Tophet & Bahal, sed vocetur Polyandrium. Futura ergo supplicia & poenae perpetuae, quibus impij cruciandi sunt, huius loci vocabulo denotantur. Duplicem autem esse Gehennam, nimij ignis & frigoris, in Iob legitur.

For his *Thesaurus,* Thomas Cooper paraphrased, with some omissions, the entry from Stephanus in these words:

*Gehenna,* A name in the Scripture giuen to hell, uppon this occasion. At the roote of the mountayne Mora by Hierusalem, is a valley and small plaine fielde, and in it a groue dedicated to the ydoll Bahal. In this groue or wood, the people of Israel fallen to Idolatrie, became so foolish that they burned their children, or dedicated and consecrated them to the deuyll. The place itself was called Gehennon, that is the valley of Hennon, and for the wickedness therein used, God threatned that he would fyll the place with dead mens carkasses, so that it shoulde no more be called Tophet and Baal, but Polyandrium. Wherefore the euerlasting punishments appointed for euyll men, are noted by the name of that place.

The dictionary accounts show what information on Gehenna Milton might reasonably expect his readers to have, or to find easily in the available reference works.

HAMBURGA, HAMA

Ditis ad Hamburgae moenia flecte gradum,
Dicitur occiso quae ducere nomen ab Hama,
Cimbrica quem fertur clava dedisse neci.
(*Elegia IV.* 14-16)
(Turn your course to the walls of rich
Hamburg, which, as the legend runs, derives
its name from Hama, slain, it is said, with
a Cimbrian club. [MacKellar])

At the age of eighteen Milton addressed to Thomas Young, his tutor, the lines quoted above with the allusion to the legend about the founding of Hamburg. Warton annotated the passage thus:

Krantzius, a Gothic geographer, says that the city of Hamburg in Saxony took its name from Hama, a puissant Saxon champion, who was killed on the spot where the city stands, by Starchater, a Danish giant. (*Saxonia* I.C. xi). The *Cimbrica clava* is the club of the Dane.

Editors and commentators to the present day have quoted Warton,[19] apparently without questioning his authority or consulting the source of his information. And yet all that is contained in Warton's note and all that Milton would have needed to know about the legend may be found in two entries in Charles Stephanus' *Dictionarium*. The first is *s.v. Hama*.

*Hama,* pugil nobilis apud Saxones qui tamen satis infeliciter pugnauit cum Starcathero altero pugile iam sene. De quibus Saxo libro. 6.

A few entries further on, in the same column of the *Dictionarium*, we find:

*Hamburga,* maxima inferioris Saxoniae vrbs, nomen habet ab Hammone, qui eam instaurauit, vnde Latine Hammonis burgum, F. Irenico dicitur. At Alb. Crantzius ab Hama insigni pugile nomen accepisse existimat, qui a Starcatero Dano gigante hoc loci ante vrbis aedificationem occisus perhibetur. Aquis est instructissima & ad mercaturam situ admodum opportuno, & Anglorum frequentatione hodie celeberrima. Moenibus, fossis, vallo, diuitiis & incolis nihil Hamburga cultius, nihil munitius videri potest.

It seems obvious that, in these two entries, Milton could have found a basis for his allusion; Warton, an explanation of the allusion; and subsequent scholars, if they had consulted Stephanus, the probable source of Warton.

HEBRUS

> His gory visage down the stream was sent,
> Down the swift *Hebrus* to the *Lesbian* shore.
> (*Lycidas*. 62-63)

Though Ovid (*Met.* 11. 1 ff.) has been suggested as a possible source of these lines, it is interesting to see how well Stephanus, with the quotation from Virgil, illustrates the allusion.

Hebrus fluuius Thraciae, aureas voluens arenas, in Rhodope monte nascens, supra Philippopolin, & e regione Samothraciae insulae in mare AEgeum sese exonerans. Fabulantur poëtae Orphei caput in hunc fluuium proiectum fuisse, cum a Ciconum mulieribus fuisset discerptus: vnde & Oeagrius dicitur ab Oeagro Orphei patre. Virg. lib. 4. Georg.

> Tum quoque marmorea caput a cervice revulsum
> Gurgite quum medio portans Oeagrius Hebrus
> Volueret, &c.

## HERMON (SENIR, SANIR)

> From *Hermon* East to the great Western Sea,
> Mount *Hermon,* yonder Sea, each place behold
> . . . but his Sons
> Shall dwell to *Senir,* that long ridge of Hills.
> (*PL.* 12. 141-42; 145-46)

The identification of Hermon and Sanir, the suggestion of two mountains of the name, and other details in Stephanus throw light on the poet's meaning.

Hermon mons, quem Sidonij *Sarion,* Amorrhaei *Sanir* vocant. Deut. 3. Iosue 33. Psalm 88. 1. Par. 5. Alias dicitur & Sion. Deut. 4. A nonnullis traditu duos esse hoc nomine montes, vnum non procul a Gelboa iuxta Iordanem: alterum vero multo altiorem, altero supra Trachonitidem regionen. Quod equidem haud obscure etiam Dauid Psalmo 42. innuere videtur, dum inquit, De terra Iordanis & Hermoninim a monte modico. Idem significat quod Herem.

## HESEBON (HORONIAM)

> . . . in *Hesebon*
> And *Horoniam, Seon's* Realm, beyond
> The flowr'y Dale of Sibma . . . .
> (*PL.* 1. 408-10)

Identification of Hesebon and Horoniam, or Oroniam, with the Scriptural references Stephanus makes, is as follows:

Hesebon, i. numerus, siue cogitatio, aut festinans intelligere vel aedificare, ciuitas in Galaad Moabitarūm, in qua habitauit Sehon rex Amorrhaeorum, Isa. 13. Num. 21. quam aedificauerunt filij Ruben. Num. 31. 1 Par. 6.

Oroniam, duo vici, qua via est ad Assyrios, siue duae vrbes Moabitarum: vna superior, altera inferior, Isa. 15. Lat. irae, vel furores, aut Syriace, libertates.

## HYPERBOREUS

Milton twice uses the term—*Quint. Nov.,* 95; *Mansus, 26*—to refer to the northern sky. Though the poet does not employ "Hyperborei," Stephanus' item on this word illustrates the full force of the meaning and has an interesting, if mythical, account of the Hyperboreans. See the beginning of the dictionary entry below.

Hyperborei, populi Septentrionales, ita dicti, quod supra Boreae statum siti esse crederentur: Festus docet Hyperboreos esse supra Aquilonis flatum habitantes: ita dictos, quoniam humanae vitae modum excedant, viuendo ultra centessimum annum. . . .
[More follows about their happy situation and felicitous life.]

IDA, MOUNT

> . . . or the fairest Goddess feign'd
> Of three that in Mount *Ida* naked strove. . . .
>                                   (*PL.* 5. 381-82)

Milton here alludes, obviously, to the story of the judgment of Paris in the Mt. Ida about Troy. Elsewhere (*PL.* 1. 515; *Il Pens.* 29) his brief allusions are to Mt. Ida of Crete. Although Stephanus gives only brief mention of Cretan Ida, he is more circumstantial concerning Trojan Ida—both in the same entry, thus:

Ida . . . mons altissimus, qui ad Troadem spectat. Latus eius Septentrionale, ex angustiis Abydi vsque ad Esapum & Cyzicenum agrum ad Propontidem pertinet: Occidentale ad Hellespontum respicit. Australe promontorium facit, quod Lectum appellatur. Orientalia Idae ad Mysos declinant, abundatque mons aquis, & multa flumina ex eo descendunt, parva quidem, cum mox a mari absorbeantur: celeberrima vero propter ea quae gesta sunt apud Ilium. In hoc quoque monte Paris sententiam tulit pro Venere, de pomo aureo aduersus Palladem & Iunonem. Homerus libro octavo Iliados, ferarum parentem esse dixit, in cuius summitate locus fuit, Gargarus appellatus: est etiam, Ptolameo teste, Cretae Insulae mons. Idaeus mons Plin. dicitur, hodie Petro Belonio *Psiloriti* vocatur.

IMAUS

> Here walk'd the Fiend at large in spacious field.
> As when a Vulture, on *Imaus* bred,
> Whose snowy ridge the roving *Tartar* bounds,
> Dislodging from a Region scarce of prey,
> To gorge the flesh of Lambs or yeanling Kids
> On Hills where Flocks are fed, flies toward the Springs
> Of *Ganges* or *Hydaspes, Indian* streams,
> But in his way lights on the barren Plains
> Of *Sericana,* where *Chineses* drive
> With Sails and Wind their cany Waggons light;
> So, on this windy Sea of Land, the Fiend
> Walk'd up and down alone, bent on his prey. . . .
>                                   (*PL.* 3. 430-41)

Although most of the pertinent details in the Satan-Vulture simile were probably suggested by Ortelius' maps, dictionary entries under Tartaria, Scythia, and Imaus constitute illuminating annotations; and that of Imaus may possibly have contributed details to the picture. It runs thus:

Imaus, *mons Indiae, qui extenditur vsque ad fontes Gangis,* vltra quem sunt Scytharum gentes. Est et pars Caucasi & Tauri, vt Plin. et Ptol. tradunt. De eo enim Orosius *Emaon* Arriano dicitur. *Semanthini* montes Ptolemaeo sunt, Mercator *Inifia* interpretatur: cuius Paulus Venetus meminit, argentique fodinas in eo esse scribit Castald. *Altai* putat, vbi omnes Tartariae imperatores sepeliuntur. Ramusius hunc *Altai,* eundem esse putat cum *Belgian* monte, in quo Haythonus Tartaros ait habitasse. Hic Imaus mons videtur Postello *Sephar,* cuius in sacris literis memoria est. *Imaus* Ptolemaei ab hoc Imao longe alius est, nempe qui ex radicibus Tauri montis exoriens, & *vsque ad mare Glaciale progrediens, Scythiam* (quae ab eo intra et extra Imaum cognominatur) *bifariam diuidit.*

Important in this entry is the explanation of the division of Imaus into two parts and the connection of the Tartars and Imaus. More striking is the parallel between Milton's

> . . . flies *toward the Springs*
> *Of Ganges* or Hydaspes, Indian streams . . .

and the dictionaries' "mons Indiae qui extenditur *vsque ad fontes Gangis."*

Under *Tartaria* and *Scythia* the nomadic life of the Tartar is emphasized. A third entry under Scythia explains further about outer-Imaus and inner-Imaus, thus:

Scythia, apud Ptolemaeum duplex est, quae Imao monte distinguitur. Inde intra & extra Imaum cognominatur. Regnum *Cathay* has Scythias hodie obtinere scribit Villanouanus, in suo Ptolemaeo. Quae intra Imaum est, videtur mihi magnam partem Tartariae occupare, inquit Ortelius. Quae extra Imaum sita antiqua dici tradit M. Niger. Scythiam intra Imaum Ar. Montanus *Dicla* Hebraeis esse putat, in suo appa. Biblico: Iornandes scribit Gothos Scythiam regionem (Europaeam innuens) *Ouim* eorum lingua appellare pro Ouim legit ex hoc authore *Ocimnin* Conradus a Lictenauu.

ISMENUS (ISMENIUS)

> And as that *Theban* Monster . . .
> Cast herself headlong from the *Ismenian* steep.
> (*PR.* 4. 572-75)

The story of the Sphinx could have been known to Milton from many sources. There is a detailed summary of the legend in Stephanus, begin-

ning "Sphinx, monstrum ex Typhone & Echidna natum," and a little
further on "Sedem habuisse dicitur in Sphincio monte iuxta Thebas."
But in this entry there is no mention of the "Ismenian steep." Under
*Ismenus* there is mention of the Ismenian (Theban) hill. Compare the
following.

Ismenus, Fluuius Boeotiae, non procul Aulide in Euripum Euboicum illa-
bens, Dictus autem putatur Ismenus, ab Ismeno Pelasgi filio. Ouid. 2. Metam.
Inde Ismenius, a, um, i. Thebanus. Ismenides, mulieres Thebanae, & Apollo
*Ismenius.* Stepha.

Ismenius, Apollo dictus est ab Ismenio colle Thebano vbi templum habet.

JORDAN

> . . . here the *double-founted stream*
> *Jordan*, true limit Eastward. . . .
> (*PL.* 12. 144-45)

Verity (II, 646) writes, "It is quite likely therefore that Sandys [*Relation of a Journey*, 1615] was responsible for *double-founted* here." Gilbert (163) thinks that Milton's reference to Jordan as the "double-
founted stream" probably depends ultimately on Jerome, who writes:
"Dan is one of the fountains of Jordan. For the other is called Jor . . .
that is brook. Hence, when the two springs, which are not distant from
one another, unite in one stream, it is called Jordan."

The accounts in Calepine and C. Stephanus, with the phrase "duobus
fontibus," is most suggestive of Milton's "double-founted stream."

*Iordanes*, Heb. Iarden, fluuius Iudaee, aquas habens suauissimas, Peraeam
a reliqua Iudaea disterminans, Plinio lib. 5. cap. 14. Oritur ad radices Libani
*duobus fontibus:* alteri nomen est Ior. alteri Dan, qui simul iuncti Iordanem
efficiunt, Gen. 13. Lat. fluuius indicij, aut demonstratio vel proiectio siue
defensio iudicij.

LUCRINUS (LUCRINE BAY)

> . . . all Fish from Sea or Shore,
> . . . for which was drain'd
> Pontus and Lucrine Bay. . . .
> (*PR.* 2. 344-47)

Even Horace and Martial had referred to the shell fish of Lucrine Bay
(Gilbert, 177). The brief account in Stephanus and in Calepine emphasizes the same feature, after supplying other interesting details concerning
the Bay.

Lucrinus, lacus campaniae in sinu Baiano, contra Puteolos, tam propinquus Auerno lacui, vt mari tempestatibus concitato quandoque soleant coniungi. Dictus a lucro, propter multitudinem piscium qui ibi capiebantur.

MEANDER

Milton writes that the Nymph Echo lives

> By slow Meander's margent green. . . .
>                              (*Comus.* 232)

This seems to be Milton's only reference to Meander. If there were any question as to the character of the river and the reason for its "margent green," Stephanus has an illuminating answer.

Maeander, fluuius Asiae clarissimus, qui ortus e lacu in monte Aulocrene, plurimisque affusus oppidis, & repletus fluminibus crebris, ita sinuosus redditur flexibus, vt saepe ad fontem credatur reverti. Apamenam primum peruagatur regionen, mox Eumeneticam, ac deinde Bargylieticos campos, & Cariam alluit: omnesque eos agros fertilissimo rigans limo, ad decimum a Mileto stadium illabitur in mare. Plin. libro. 5. ca. 29. Vnde obliquitates omnes. Maeandros veteres appellarunt, vt cum res agitur non simpliciter, sed variis & obliquis consiliis, sumpta metaphora a fluuio Maeandro, qui sinuosus ac flexuosus labitur, vnde & nomen habere videtur quasi oberret, quaerens hominum consortia, more Maeandri illud fieri dicitur, quod tortuose flexuoseque sit. Hunc poetae fingunt Oceani & Terrae filium fuisse, & Cyaneen Nympham genuisse, quam postea Miletus Solis filius compressit, & ex ea Caunum & Byblidem suscepit.

MEMPHIS (ALCAIRO)

> Not *Babylon,*
> Nor great *Alcairo* such magnificence
> Equall'd in all thir glories. . . .
>                              (*PL.* 1. 717-19)

Perhaps no better annotation could be found than that of Stephanus in the entry *Memphis.* (Cf. also *Cairo.*)

Memphis, vrbs AEgypti regia ab Ogdoo rege condita, & a nomine filiae eius ita appellata. Haec inter omnes AEgypti urbes secundum ab Alexandria locum obtinuit, pyramidibus, regum sepulchris imprimis insignis. Eius ambitus traditur fuisse centum & quinquaginta stadiorum. Sita est in loco totius AEgypti opportunissimo, vbi Nilus in duas scissus partes: literae Δ speciem praebet: quo sit, ut portuosissima sit, omnibusque pene nauigiis aditum praebeat. Vulgus hodie *Alcayrum* vocat. Hinc sit Gentile, Memphites, phitae. Item Memphitis, tidis. Item Memphiticus, ca, cum. Gall. *le grand Caire.* Memphin Arcadiae vrbem in qua Astragalam nascitur memorat Dioscorides lib. 4. sed haec Arcadia cuius mentionem faciunt Eustathius, liber Notitiarum & Steph.

MEROE (SYENE)

> Syene, and where the shadow both way falls,
> Meroe, Nilotic Isle. . . .
>
> (PR. 4. 70-71)

Whiting (88) and Gilbert (189-90) quote Pliny as a possible source of this passage. Under the entries *Meroe* and *Syene* Stephanus offers much information concerning the two places, including the reference to the shadow (*umbra*) which "both way falls," and the reference to Pliny. Here, for the reader or modern editor is the comment *par excellence* for Milton's lines.

Meroe . . . insula Nili omnium, quae eo fluuio ambiuntur, longe maxima: quippe cuius longitudo ad tria millia stadiorum latitudo ad mille extendatur. Vrbem habet eiusdem nominis insulae totius caput, a Cambyse conditam, & de nomine sororis ibi defunctae, Meroe appellatam. De hac ita scribit Herodotus: Meroe fuit olim regni caput: clypei figuram ea insula imitatur, ad tria millia stadiorum cum Nilo protensa. Accolunt pastores eam qui passim venantur, & agricolae qui & aurifodinas habent. Effodiuntur in ea aurum, argentum, aes, ferrum, ebenum: praeterea fert & lapidum multiplex genus: distatque a Syene quinque millibus stadiorum, vltra quam est ad torridam Zonam. Alia est Meroe Antiochiae iuxta Daphnem orientem versus. . . .
Syene, vrbs in confinibus AEthiopiae atque AEgypti, non procul a Nilo supra Alexandriam, versus Meridiem quinque millibus stadiorum sub tropico Cancri directe locata: vnde Sole existente in Cancro, medio solstitij die supra verticem ciuitatis, nullam prorsus ibi corpora vmbram faciunt, vt est author Plin. libro 2. cap. 73.

MESOPOTAMIA

> A spacious plain outstrecht in circuit wide
> Lay pleasant; from his side two rivers flow'd,
> . . . and left between
> Fair Champain with less rivers intervein'd. . . .
>
> (PR. 3. 254-57)

The rivers alluded to are the Tigris and the Euphrates, and the "spacious plain" and "Fair Champain" indicate Mesopotamia, lying between. In Stephanus' *Mesopotamia* is a clear description of the boundaries, and reference to the Tigris and Euphrates and other names familiar to readers of Milton's poetry.

Mesopotamia, regio Asiae latissima, Tigrim habens ab Oriente, Euphratem ab Occidente, a Meridie Babyloniam, a Septentrione Caucasum. Mesopotamia dicta ab eo, quod media sit inter duos fluuios, Tigrim & Euphratem. Haec regio etiam dicta est Seleucia, vt refert Plin. lib 6. Gentile, Mesopotamites. Ab Hebraeis dicitur *Aram Naharaim,* i. Syria fluuiorum s. duorum: nam dictio ipsa dualis est numeri. Item dicitur *Padan Aram,* i. redemptio aedis. . . . Nunc dicitur *Helapia,* teste Olivar. in Melam. Mesopotamiam fertilem efficit Euphrates, in quam quotannis quasi nouos agros inuehit. Cicer. 2. de Nat. deorum, Steph. *Adiabene* est: recentiores *Azamia* habent *Diarbech* Bellenio dicitur.

MEXICO

. . . in Spirit perhaps he also saw
Rich *Mexico* the seat of *Motezume.* . . .
(*PL.* ii. 406-7)

On this passage Gilbert quotes Francis Lopez de Gomara.[20] Stephanus' reference to Mexico [City] as the most opulent city of Mexico and other interesting details chosen from recent writers about the New World would illustrate Milton's allusions. This entry is a good example also of the way the dictionary seeks to keep its geography up to date. See the entry on "Cusco" with the references to Brazil and Peru.

Mexico, siue Temixtita, in Hispania noua Mexicanae prouinciae opulenta & celeberrima ciuitas, vliginoso & salso in lacu mirabiliter constituta, ampla & visu iucundissima, vici omnes suos habent exitus, vt ab uno ad alium aquam permeare possit. Maior (quam vocant) platea, porticibus vndique cincta est, vbi quotidie vltra 60. hominum millia, vendentium, ementiumque cernuntur. Idola ex farina & humano sanguine conficiunt, quibus multa hominum corda ex viuentium corporibus extracta quotidie offerunt. Dominus Ciuitatis Muterzuma appellatur. Huic maior pars noui orbis paret. Plura lege apud noui orbis neotericos descriptores. Theatr. vrb.

MINCIUS

. . . and thou honour'd flood,
Smooth-sliding *Mincius,* crown'd with vocal reeds. . . .
(*Lycidas.* 85-86)

Apropos of Mincius in this line, Gilbert aptly quotes and translates Virgil (*Ecl.* 7. 12-13). It is interesting to see that Stephanus, after brief remarks concerning the course of this river, quotes the Latin of Virgil which Gilbert cited.

Mincius, Venetorum fluuius, qui ex Benaco lacu profluens, alium prope Mantuam lacum efficit & inde rursus, multis torrentibus auctus, influit in

Padum. Virgil. 4 Georg. *Hic viridis tenera praetexit arundine ripas Mincius,* &c.

OETA (TRACHINUM)

> . . . non ferus Hercules
> Nessi venenatus cruore
> Aemathia iacuisset Oeta.
> *(Procancel.* 10-12)
> . . . nutat Trachinia rupes,
> Nec sentit solitas, immania pondera, silvas. . . .
> *(Mansus.* 66-67)

For concise information on Oeta and Trachin, available to Milton and his readers, compare these entries from Stephanus.

Oeta, mons in finibus Thessaliae, Doridi a tergo incumbens, morte & sepulchro Herculis nobilitatus; vnde factum est nomen Tragoediae Senecae, quae Hercules Oetaeus inscribitur. Ibidem elleborum optimum nascebatur. Plinius lib. 15. cap. 5. a Parnasso vsque Pindum pars in Thermopylas vergens, proprie Oeta vocatur. Hinc Oetaeus, taea, taeum . . . Stephanus qui Oetam montem iuxta Trachinum esse scribit: & ciuitatem Meliensium eiusdem nominis. . . .

Trachin, inis, vel Trachis, Straboni oppidum in finibus Phthiotidis, ad Oetam montem & Thermopylarum angustias, a loci asperitate nomens habens . . . .

OLYMPUS

> Milton refers to Ophion with Eurynome who
> . . . had first the rule
> Of high Olympus. . . .
> *(PL.* 10. 583-84)
> Donec nitentes ad fores
> Ventum est Olympi, et regiam Crystallinam, et
> Stratum smaragdis Atrium.
> *(In Obitum Praesul. Eliensis.* 62-64)

These are two of Milton's five references to Olympus as heaven. For this practice he had precedent and the sanction of authority. Compare C. Stephanus:

Olympus, mons editissimus, in ea parte Thessaliae, quae in Macedoniam vergit, cuius vertex vsque adeo attollitur, vt nubes penetrare, caelumque ipsum attingere credatur. Quo factum est, vt Olympum poëtae pro ipso accipiant coelo. Dictus Olympus, quasi ὅλος λαμπρὸς, eo quod claros habet solares radios, nullisque amnino nubibus offuscetur. [The article then mentions and

describes four mountains called Olympus, the first and highest being that between Thessaly and Macedonia.]

OPHIUSA

> . . . (not so thick [with serpents] swarmed once
> the Soil
> Bedropt with blood of Gorgon, or *the Isle
> Ophiusa*). . . .
>
> (*PL.* 10. 526-28)

Masson writes (III, 381) "*Ophiusa* or *Colubraria* (both names meaning
'Snake Island') is now Fomentaru, south of Iviza." The entry in Stephanus gives specific information on the topic:

*Ophiusa, insula* in mari Balearico, Ptolmeo, ex duabus Pytiusis minor, nam
maior Ebusus dicitur, *propter serpentum copiam inculta:* unde & Colubraria
a Latinis appellatur. Rhodus quoque insula, *aliquando propter serpentum
copiam Ophiusa dicta fuit.* . . .

ORCADES (ORCHADES)

> . . . et extremis me discant Orcades undis.
>
> (*Damon.* 178.)

According to Gilbert (220), Milton thought of the Orcades as a northern
limit. The quotation seems to support such a conclusion. Yet Milton
also knew Thule, characterized by Virgil and others as "ultima Thule,"
the farthest north. According to Stephanus, the Orcades was near Thule
and might also be regarded as "extremae." The dictionary entries of
*Orcades* and *Thule* show what the allusions may have meant to Milton's
readers.

Orchades . . . insulae Oceani Septentrionalis vltra Britanniam & Hyberniam,
numero triginta, secundum Pomponium, parum inter se distantes, non longe ab
insula Thule. Hodie parent regi Scotorum. Incolae lingua Gottica utuntur.
*Orcknai,* vulgo & *Orcano* dicuntur.

Thule, es, hodie *Island* [Iceland?], insula in ditione Scotorum, in Septentrionem vergens, vltra Orcadas, latitudinem habens graduum LXIII. . . . Haec
extrema fuit earum, quae in Septentrionale Oceano Romanis fuerunt cognitae:
vnde etiam a Virg. vltima Thule appellatur. . . .

OREB (SINAI)

> . . . that on the secret top
> Of *Oreb,* or of *Sinai,* didst inspire
> That Shepherd, who first taught the chosen Seed. . . .
>
> (*PL.* 1. 6-8)

God from the Mount of Sinai . . .
descending, will himself

. . .

Ordain them Laws. . . .

(*PL.* 12. 227-30)

The phrase "Of Oreb, or of Sinai" seems to have been troublesome to a few editors. Typical of the comment is this by Verity: "Milton may be referring to two occasions on which Moses received a divine communication—(1) when the Lord appeared to him in a burning bush, Exod. iii; (2) when he was given the Law, Exod. xix-xxxi. Myself, I believe that only the latter is intended, and that Milton contrasting Exodus xix. 20 with Deut. iv. 10, does not decide whether the mountain where Moses received the Law should be called 'Oreb' or 'Sinai.'"[21] Hughes distinguishes "Mt. Horeb and its spur, Sinai." Gilbert (270) cites Adrichomius, who thinks the two mountains are distinct, rejecting Jerome's opinion that one mountain is known by two names (Oreb and Sinai). Milton, Gilbert thinks, identifies the two in *PL.* 11. 73-76 and in 12. 227-30, "though *PL.* 1. 7 gives the opposite impression."

The lexicographers make clear that Milton and his readers thought of Oreb and Sinai as one and the same; and, if so, in *PL.* 1. 7 the poet was thinking of one place but offering the alternative names. Cooper's *Thesaurus* has this entry:

*Sina or Sinai,* A mountaine in the desert of Arabia, called also Oreb. It is of Solinus called Casius: Iustinus calleth it Synaeus. On that hil God appeared to Moises, and deliuered to him the tables of the law.

The two entries which follow are from Charles Stephanus:

*Oreb,* mons Arabiae, qui & Sinai dicitur. Iuxta hunc montem Moyses tactu virgae e saxo summam aquarum copiam erumpere fecit in omnium Hebraeorum salutem. D. Hierony.

*Horeb,* nomen montis in regione Madianitarum. Exod. 3. Psa. 105. Sinai alias dicitur, in quo data fuit lex Mosi. Est & nomen petrae, Exod. 17. Lat. desertum, vel solitudo, siue destructio, aut siccitas, vel gladius.

In the same lexicon Sinai and Oreb are again made identical, *s.v. Arabia felix.*

ORMUS

High on a Throne of Royal State, which far
Outshone the wealth of *Ormus* and of Ind. . . .

(*PL.* 2. 1-2)

Readers familiar with Purchas' *Pilgrimes* (cf. Gilbert, 220) would have appreciated at once the allusion to the wealth of Ormus. Current in the Stephanus also was the description of Ormus which would illustrate fully the allusion.

Ormus, Persiae inclyta ciuitas, situ elegantiore, ac unionum copia, nulli urbium secunda, sita est in insula, & omnibus maritimis ciuitatibus praeferenda, abest a continenti, spatio duodecim mille passuum, aquarum potu suauium, annonaeque mira caritas: inuehuntur ferme omnia quae victum incolis suppeditant. Illinc itinere trium dierum leguntur conchae, quae pariunt margaritas venustiores, grandioresque caeteris baccis. Expugnata est haec vrbs anno 1560. a Lusitaniae regis praefecto marino, qui eam Lusitanico rege ingens pendere tributum annuatim coegit.

PALESTINA (PALESTINE)

> . . . dreaded through the Coast
> Of *Palestine,* in *Gath* and *Ascalon,*
> And *Accaron* and *Gaza's* frontier bounds.
> (*PL.* 1. 464-66)

Milton followed Scriptual usage in applying the name Palestine to the land usually called Philistia. Afterwards the whole Land of Promise took the name of Palestine (Gilbert, 224-5). Besides widely dispersed passages in the Scriptures, the best contemporary brief exposition of Palestine is probably that in two successive items in Stephanus.

(1) Palaestina prouinciae Syriae, Arabiae contermina, Ebraeis Philistim, vrbe metropoli. In ea, inquit Plin. lib. 5. ca. 3 & 20. (nam & Herodo. Syriam alteram Palaestinam vocat.) quinque ciuitates continebantur, Gaza, Ascalon, Geth, Acaron & Azotum. Palaestina etiam (inquit Steph. in Iope) Phoenicia dicebatur. Est altera Palaestina prope Phaeaciam: de qua Lucanus lib. 5.

(2) Palaestina, olim Chanaam dicta, Iudaeam, Samariam & Galilaeam complectitur: tametsi Iudaeae nomine tota Palaestina saepius accipiatur. Ea ab Ortu habet Libanum montem, ab Occasu mare Phaenicium, a Septentrione Phaenicenia, a Meridie Arabiam Petraeam. Olim terra Promissionis, nunc Sancta appellatur. Eam post sacra Biblia descripserunt. Iosephus Vadianus, Zieglerus, & alij D. Hieron. in locis Hebraecis ait esse notandum, apud Historicos, quod *Iudaea* ad Palaestinam, *Galilaea* vero & *Samaria,* ad Phoenicen pertineant, hodie ab Europaeis omnibus variis vocabulis pro linguarum differentia vocitatur.

PANEAS (DAN)

> From *Paneas* the fount of *Jordan's* flood
> To Beërsaba. . . .
>
> (*PL.* 3. 535-36)

The identification of the town of Paneas with Caesarea Philippi and with Dan would be known to Milton's readers who consulted their Stephanus; and Milton's reference to the fountain of Paneas "rather than to the city incorrectly" would not have been perplexing in the light of Stephanus.

Paneas, fons sub Libano monte, in quo si qua natantia proiiciantur, in lacu, cui Phiala nomen est, cuncta reperiuntur. Vide Iordanem & Panium. Est etiam hoc nomine Colchorum fluuius, Bocatio, cui oppidum imminet sui nominis, habens post se Homochorum multimodas gentes.

Panias, fons, e quo Iordanis amnis profluit, inque Asphaltitem lacum prolabitur. Plin. lib. 5. ca. 15. . . .

Panium, specus Palaestina, e quo Iordanes fluit. Inde Paneius, Vide Paneada.

Paniada, quae & Caesarea Philippi vrbs Iudeae, a Philippi filio Herodis condita.

Cf. Robert Stephanus (*Thesaurus*) : "Panias. Fons e quo Iordanis amnis profluit."

PARADISUS (PARADISE)

See in this study "Elysian Fields," for a consideration of certain features in Milton's conception of Paradise. The description proper of Paradise is most detailed and elaborate in Book IV of *PL*. The conception of the garden as on a high hill or mountain with a river running through it is best expressed in ll. 223 ff. This feature of the celestial garden finds expression also in Stephanus.

Paradisus . . . Est & locus in Oriente longo tractu maris distans a continente, de quo Augustinus ad Orosium scribit sic, Paradisus in Oriente situs est, interiecto Oceano, & a nostro orbe longe remotus, *in altissimo loco* constitutus, pertingens vsque ad Lunarem circulum: vnde illuc aqua diluuij minime peruenisse dicitur. Hanc opinionem D. Augustinus ex Platonis Phaedone sumpsit quam & Beda secutus est. Hic locus a primi hominis reatu interclusus est, nec vlli animantium datur in eum aditus. Amnis item Paridisi meminit Capella libro 6. . . . Paradisus terrestris, natale solum Adami. quod Hebraei *Ganeden* vocant.

PARNASSUS

> Primus ego Aonios illo praeeunte recessus
> Lustrabam, et bifidi sacra vireta iugi,

Pieriosque hausi latices, Clioque favente
Castalio sparsi laeta ter ora mero.
(*Elegia Quarta.* 29-32)

The quoted lines with reference to various names associated with Parnassus is characteristic of Milton's allusions to Parnassus. In four out of six allusions (*El. Quart.* 29-31 ; *El. Quint.* 9; *Ad. Patrem.* 3.16; *Mansus.* 92; *Ad Rous.* 66) the poet has reference to the twin peaks.

For Milton's readers Parnassus and all the associated names in his poetry would be explained by Stephanus.

Parnassus, mons Phocidis, Apollini & Musis sacer, duos vertices habens, quorum unum Tithorea vocari, alterum Hyampeum, author est Herodotus in Vrania. Cithaeron autem & Helicon, quos Seruius male putauit esse parnassi iuga, montes ab hoc diuersi & disiuncti sunt: ille circiter quindecim passuum millia: Cithaeron vero triginta, ab eo distans. Ovid. 1. Meta. In hoc monte rupes vel maiestate numinis, vel situ ipso horrorem visentibus facit, vndique fere praeceps, in formam theatri: hic est Apollinis Delphici templum: hic fons Castalius, Musis sacer. Hic habitauere Pieres, natio Thracia, vnde Pierius mons, & Pierides Musae. Sub Parnasso habitauerunt Hyantes populi. Vnde aquae Parnassi fontis Hyantides dicuntur. Hic fontes Atticam versus, Hippocrene & Aganippe. Hinc Parnassius. . . .

PELLA (PELLEAN)

Remember that *Pellean* Conqueror,
A youth, how all the Beauties of the East
He slightly view'd. . . .
(*PR.* 2. 196-98)

The most appropriate annotation for the lines might come from Stephanus.

Pella, vrbs Macedoniae, in littore AEgaei maris illustrata, maxime natalibus Philippi Macedonum regis & Alexandri. Vnde vterque Pellaeus a poëtis cognominatur. *Bunomos* antea dicta, vt Steph. tradit. Huius Liuius meminit lib. 44. *Ieniza* Sophiano, *Zuchria* Nigro hodie dici videtur.

PHLEGRA

. . . though all the Giant brood
Of *Phlegra* with th' Heroic Race were join'd
That fought at *Thebes* and *Ilium.* . . .
(*PL.* 1. 576-78)

Three entries—Pallene, Phlegra, and Phlegraei—afford information about Phlegra and the fight of the giants with the gods. The Phlegraei entry is fullest.

Phlegraei, campi duo fuere, alter in Graecia, a Phlegra Thessaliae valle, vbi Gigantes cum caelestibus pugnauere. Vel ἀπὸ τῇ φλέγειν, quod est vrere atque inflammare. Alter in Campania prope Cumas, in quo Gigantes Herculem superasse dicuntur. Plin. lib. 3. c. 5. & Strabo lib. 5. Theagenes vero & Eudoxus, qui ad historicam fidem pugnam hanc conantur reducere: Pallenem, inquiunt, quae veteri nomine Phlegra vocabatur, homines tenuerunt, quibus immanitas, & suberbia morum, Gigantum cognomen peperit. In hos ineunte praelium Hercule, fulmina de coelo missa sunt, donec ii fugere coacti sunt, ipsique ingenti victoria superati. Ex hac re rumor in vulgus ortus, vt Gigantes mouerint bellum diis. Id autem ideo fictum est, quoniam ea regio tota sulphure plurimo scatet. Hinc sit, ut ventorum impulsu excitetur passim ignis, qui cum exitum e cauernis natura expetat, dum lucatur assidue, terram tandem quatit & commouet, exuritque frequenter: vnde & nomen fortitur: φλέγειν, enim Graece exurere, ardereque significat.

PIERUS (PIERIDES)

Pieriosque hausi latices. . . .

(*Eleg. Quarta.* 31)

Nunc mea Pierios cupiam per pectora fontes
Irriguas torquere vias. . . .

(*Ad Patrem.* 1-2)

Haec quoque, Manse, tuae meditantur carmina laudi
Pierides. . . .

(*Mansus.* 1-2)

Two short entries in Stephanus constitute an explanation of the meaning of the term *Pierides* to Milton's readers.

Pierus, mons Thessaliae post Pheras in Macedoniam vsque protensus, Plin. lib. 4. c. 8. In hoc monte quidam Musas natas volunt, atque inde Pieridas appellatas, quanquam alij a Pieriae regione, & alij rursum a Pieri filiabus, quas cantu vicerunt, dictas malunt.

Pierides, Musae dicuntur propter amoenitatem ac solitudinem Pierij montis, quod eae secretis locis, propter studia liberalia delectantur, vt inquit Sextus Pompeius. . . .

RABBA (RABBATH)

Him the *Ammonite*
Worshipt in *Rabba* and her wat'ry Plain. . . .

(*PL.* 1. 396-97)

In writing "Rabba," not "Rabbah," Milton uses the Vulgate form, as he does in many other Biblical words. It is interesting to see that the Vulgate almost always is employed also by Stephanus.

Rabba, licet diuerse a Rabbath scribatur, videtur tamen eadem esse ciuitas. Ier. 49. Lat. multa, siue magna, aut iurgium, siue impugnatio. Rabbath, idem metropolis filiorum Ammon, a rege AEgypti Ptolemaeo cognomento Philadelpho, qui Arabiam tenuit cum Iudaea, Philadelphia nominata.

RED SEA (MARE RUBRUM)

Milton's half dozen references to the Red Sea apparently have their basis in Scripture, though in *Damon* (185) *Mare Rubrum* is probably used to mean Arabian and Persian Gulfs together. This, and much more, Milton's readers would understand by consulting Stephanus.

Mare rubrum, Pomponio dicitur, siue quia eius coloris est, siue quia ibi Erythras regnauit, ἐρυθραν θάλασσαν appellant, procellosum, asperum, profundum, & magnorum animalium, magis quam caetera capax. Vide Pomponij Enarratorem Vadianum. Mare rubrum in duos diuiditur sinus, *Persicum & Arabicum,* in quos varii fluunt amnes. Dionysio *AEthiopicum,* Plinio & Melae *Indicum,* & Herodoto *Persicum* appellatur inter Africam & Taprobanam insulam Asiae meridionalem partem alluit. Strabo illud sub *Atlantici* nomine comprehendit: huius pars quae Persiam & Arabiam foelicem lambit, *Azanium* apud Plin. lib. 6. ca. 14. nuncupatur. Dominicus Niger scribit etiam sic nominari. *Mar d'India,* a Lusitanis dicitur, vt quidam volunt: maris rubri vocabulum tam late apud bonos auctores extendi fugit Guilandinum in suo de Papyro libello, vbi Eustathium reprehendit, quod scribat Indiam ad Rubrum Oceanum pertingere. Item Martinum del Rio, apud quem male audit Seneca, quod dicat *Tepidum rubenti Tigrin immisces freto,* sed hic error illis communis est cum his qui Mare Rubrum tantum pro Arabico sinu intelligunt, idque male. Indum enim, Tigrim & Euphratem flumina in hunc sinum minime exonerari cunctis pene notissimum est, eaque tamen in mare Rubrum se exonerare apud classicos auctores luce clarius ostenditur.

RIVERS OF HELL (ACHERON, COCYTUS, LETHE, PHLEGETON, STYX)

> Abhorred *Styx* the flood of deadly hate,
> Sad *Acheron* of Sorrow, black and deep;
> *Cocytus,* nam'd of lamentation loud
> Heard on the rueful stream; fierce *Phlegeton*
> Whose waves of torrent fire inflame with rage.
> Far off from these a slow and silent stream,
> *Lethe* the River of Oblivion rolls
> Her wat'ry Labyrinth, whereof who drinks,
> Forthwith his former state and being forgets,
> Forgets both joy and grief, pleasure and pain.
>
> (*PL.* 2. 577-86)

Information on the infernal rivers was widespread during the Renaissance. The text of Milton here quoted could be amply illustrated by reference to Perottus' *Cornucopiae;* and the Perottus is drawn upon by the dictionaries of Calepine, Charles Stephanus and Robert Stephanus. Besides, the mythographers, Gyraldus, Comes, and Cartari (cited by C. Stephanus) discourse on the various rivers of Hades.

Among these authorities, Perottus offers perhaps the best illustration of the passage from Milton. In the *Cornucopiae* the rivers are described in immediate succession in a single passage (cols. 572-5, 1518 ed.), and a portion of the discussion gives the Greek root and meaning of each river; examples of the appearance of the names in classical literature, as in Virgil, Seneca, etc.; and words derived from the originals, as "Lethean," "Lethal," or "Stygian." Such a presentation would make a strong appeal to Milton. Here follow the pertinent quotations from the *Cornucopiae:*

*Acheron*
Praeterea acheronta alium inferorum amnem commemorant dictum ab a priuatiua particula & χαίρων, quod significat gaudens, quasi sine gaudio. Seneca. At hinc tumultu rapitur ingenti ferox, Et saxa fluctu uoluit acheron inuius Remigrari. (c. 574. 37-40.)

*Cocytus*
Sunt etiam qui Cocytum ἀπὸ τοῦ κωκύω deductum putant, quod apud graecos gemos significat propter gemitum animarum. Virg. Continuo auditae uoces, uagitus et ingens, Infantumque animae fluentos in limine primo. Nec procul hinc partem fusi monstrantur in omnem Lugentes campi, sic illos nomine dicunt. (c. 572. 20 seq.)

*Lethe*
. . . lethen quoque flumen apud inferos esse prodiderunt, cuius latices siquis gustauerit omnium praeteritarum rerum obliuiscitur. idcirco ἀπὸ πῆς λήϑης, hoc est obliuione nomen habet. Datus autem huic fabulae locus est, quia morientes rerum omnium obliuio subrepit. . . . Quam iuxta Lethes tacitus praelabitur amnis Infernis, ut fama trahens obliuia uenis. (c. 573. 30 sq.)

*Phlegethon*
Item aliud inferorum flumen, quod Phlegethon dicitur, flammis aestuantibus rapidum, unde ἀπὸ τῶ φλέγω, quod est ardeo deriuatur. Vir. quae rapidus flammis ambit torrentibus amnis Tartareus phlegethon torquetque sonantia saxa. (c. 574. 54.)

*Styx*
Postremo aliam quoque apud inferos paludem esse, quae Styx dicitur, poëtarum carminibus celebris, hoc nomen aliij ἀπὸ τῶ ςτυγῶ deductum existimant, quod est timeo. odi, quod terrori omnibus sit, alij ἀπὸ τῶ ςτυγνῶ, quod moestum, tristemque significat. De his aquis multa poëtae finxerunt. Quippe cocytum stygis filium esse dixere, ex eo Phlegethonta genitum, huius filium esse lethen, Stygem vero Acherontis, & terrae filiam secundam aliquos. (c. 574. 58.)

An examination of these lines from Perottus shows the etymology of the names of the rivers, similar to what seems to have been in Milton's mind. In describing Phlegeton, Perottus gives not only the derivation but the quotation from Virgil ("quae rapidus flammis," etc.) which, scholars have pointed out, is back of Milton's "waves of torrent fire inflame"; and on Lethe, Perottus has "Lethes *tacitus* praelabitur amnis Infernis . . ." with which may be compared "a slow and silent stream, Lethe . . . rolls."

Perottus, if not a primary source, is an excellent illustration of what was in Milton's mind. But the poet here, as elsewhere, seems to have synthesized matter from various authors. Compare, for example, the following, on Lethe:

> Her wat'ry Labyrinth, *whereof who drinks,*
> Forthwith his former state and being forgets,
> *Forgets both joy and grief, pleasure and pain.*
>                              (*PL.* 2. 584-86)

And Comes,

. . . *Bibebatur* autem duplici de causa aqua *Lethaei fluminis, tum* ut *obliuiscerentur* animae *illarum deliciarum, quibus fruebantur* in campis Elysijs, *tum* etiam ut *fierent immemores earum molestiarum,* quas antea in vita pertulissent. (3. 20.)

In phrasing and content these passages offer striking similarities. Did Milton know the Comes? The answer becomes perhaps more difficult when we add another parallel from C. Stephanus:

*Lethe* . . . fluuius inferorum apud poëtas, cuius aquam *si quis gustasset, omnium statim praeteritorum obliuisci* eum voluerunt. Id circo ἀπὸ τῆς λήϑης, hoc est, ab obliuione nomen creditur accepisse, quoniam morientes *praeterita omnia tum dicta tum factu* obliuione tradunt.

Compare "si quis gustasset omnium *statim* praeteritorum obliuisci" and "whereof who drinks, *Forthwith* his former state and being forgets." It would be difficult to say what exactly is the relationship of Milton's lines to the parallels quoted. At any rate Perottus, Comes, and Stephanus are once more of importance in annotating and illustrating the poetry of Milton.

SABA (SABAEAN)

> . . . off at Sea North-East winds blow
> *Sabean* Odours from the spicy shore
> Of Araby the blest. . . .
>                              (*PL.* 4. 161-63)

Though Milton, as Hughes suggests, may have been thinking of what he had read in Diodorus (3. 45),[22] his readers would have found in Stephanus suggestive description and satisfactory explanation of "Sabean Odours."

> Saba, Arabum metropolis in monte sita, hoc vocabulo appellata, quod est reuereri, seu venerari: quia thus mittit, quo in sacrificiis utimur, ut notat Seruius: & ideo thuriferam vocat Ptolem. Vel ἀπὸ τῶ ϛάβειν, quod est sacrificare. vide Sabaea & Sabaei. *Mariaba* videtur eam Strabo appellare. *Saua* in Arriani periplo.
> Sabaea, regio Arabiae foelicis, in qua sola thus nascitur.
> Sabaei, populi foelicis Arabiae, ditissimi thuri, & syluarum fertilitate odorifera: corpora mortuorum non pluris faciunt quam stercora. Quinetiam reges ipsos inter sterquilina reiiciunt. Horum metropolis est Saba, quam Strabo li. 16. Mariabam vocat. vide Strabonem li. 6.

SARRA (MELIBAEA)

> . . . over his lucid Arms
> A military *Vest of purple* flow'd
> Livelier than *Melibaean,* or the grain
> Of *Sarra,* worn by Kings and Heroes old
> In time of Truce. . . .
>                    (*PL.* II. 240-44)

Two entries in Charles Stephanus constitute concise and apt annotations of these lines:

> (1) Sarra, urbs in Phoenicia, deinde Tyrus dicta, a pisce quodam qui illic abundat, quem Sara appellant, ex cuius sanguine *sericum in purpuram tingebatur.* Inde *Sarranae vestes,* Tyriae dictae sunt, quae & ostrinae & purpureae.
> (2) Meliboea, littoralis urbs Magnesiae, vel secundum aliquos, Thessaliae. Herod. lib. 6. patria Philoctetae Paeantis filii: a quo Meliboeus . . . : nobilis *ob purpuram* quae illic inficiebatur . . . .

SILOA (SION)

> . . . Or if *Sion* Hill
> Delight thee more, and *Siloa's Brook that flowed
> Fast by* the Oracle of God. . . .
>                    (*PL.* I. 10-12)
> . . . chief
> Thee *Sion* and the flowr'y *Brooks* beneath
> That wash thy *hallow'd* feet, and warbling flow. . . .
>                    (*PL.* 3. 29-31)

Verity (II, 369) comments: "*Siloa's brook;* more familiar to us in the description 'pool,' through John ix, 7, 11; but Isaiah's words of which

M. may be thinking—'the waters of the pool overflowed into the garden below and so formed a streamlet which would find its way into the Kidron.'" "Shiloah" and "Siloam" are the Biblical words. Nearer to Milton's language and a better explanation of his allusion are the following entries in Stephanus:

Siloe . . . *fons, piscina,* aut amnis est *ad radices Montis Sion, perennibus aquis ebulliens,* cuius sit mention Isai. 8. 6 . . . .
Sion, i. a cervus, aut tumulus, vel specula mons Ierosolymne qui alias *mons Domini,* item & *mons sanctus* dicitur, in cuius vertice erat arx constructa, quae a Davida, civitas Davidis est vocata. 3 Reg. 4.

SUSA

> Cedite Achaemeniae turrita fronte puellae,
> Et quot Susa colunt, Memnoniamque Ninon.
> > (*Elegia* I. 65-66)
> *Xerxes,* the Liberty of *Greece* to yoke,
> From *Susa his Memnoniam palace high*
> Come to the Sea.
> > (*PL.* 10. 307-8)

Stephanus' record of Susa runs thus:

Susa . . . urbs nobilissima inter Persidem, & Babyloniam sita, Persarum olim regia, a Dario, Hystaspis (si Plinio credimus) aut (ut Straboni placet) a Tithono Memnonis patre condita, trans Choaspem fluvium: a cuius urbis nomine circumiecta regio dicta est Susiana. In hac urbe fuit nobilis illa Cyri regia, e candido varioque marmore, columnis aureis, magnaque gemmarum copia exornata, coeli in lacunaribus habens simulachrum, stellis micantibus insignitum. . . .

The entry *Xerxes,* in Stephanus, begins:

Xerxes, Persarum rex fuit filius Darij, & Cyri ex Atosa filia nepos . . . .

TAENARUS

In the Latin poems—*Eleg.* 5.66; 4 *Prod. Bomb.* 2; and *Procancel.* 5— Taenarus refers to the lower world, or adjectivally, pertaining to the lower regions.

The following entry from Stephanus illustrates the meaning of the word.

Taenarus . . . siue Taenara . . . promontorium Laconicae regionis, circa medium meridionalis lateris Peloponnessi, quam longissime in mare procurrens, oppidum habens eiusdem nominis. Suidas ait Taenarum promontorium esse Laconiae, in quo fauces erant ad inferos deducentes, vbi & Neptuni praesidiis templum: illic supplicantes in sacello Neptuni Helotes, nihil veriti Lacedaemonij interfecerunt. Circa Taenarum antrum ostendebatur, per quod Herculem ab inferis rediisse poëtae fabulati sunt, Cerberumque vinctum ad superos traxisse, vulgoque creditum est, eas inferorum esse fauces. Ibidem marmor Laconicum effodiebatur, coloris viridis, quod & a loco Taenarium cognominatur.

## TAGUS

> Ditior Hesperio flavet arena Tago.
> (*Eleg. Tertia.* 46)

Compare Stephanus on Tagus rolling golden sands.

Tagus, Lusitania fluuius, aureas voluens arenas, vt Plinius ait. Circa hunc fluuius (si eidem credimus) equae in Fauonium obuersae concipiunt, equosque ita gignunt pernicissimos, sed tertium aetatis annum non excedentes. Oritur in Celtiberis, diuidit Lusitaniam & vltra Vlysiponam in Oceanum prorumpit, & accolis *Tayo* vocatur.

## TAPROBANE

> From *India* and the Golden *Chersonese,*
> And utmost Indian isle *Taprobane.* . . .
> (*PR.* 4. 74-75)

Among the ancients, Pliny (cf. Gilbert 284) gives the most complete account.

The sketch in Stephanus with references to Pliny and Ptolemy is the concise illustration for Milton's contemporaries.

Taprobane, vulgo *Sumatra,* insula omnium quae Veteribus cognitae fuerunt, maxima, a Colaico Indiae promontorio in austrum quatridui nauigatione recedens, in qua Septentriones negant conspici posse. Lucet ibi Canopus, sidus clarum & amplissimum. Homines corporum magnitudine alios antecellunt, caeruleis oculis, atroci visu, terrifico sono vocis. Viuunt vltra annos centum. Nascuntur in ea berylli & hyacinthi, vt Ptol. lib. 6. refert. Plin, 6 cap. 21. item aurum & argentum & marmor testudini simile praeterea gemmae & margaritae praecipuae bonitatis. Apud eos annona nunquam augetur: neque sunt fora, neque lites, Herculem colunt. Populus regem elegit, senecta, clementiaque venerandum & liberos non habentem. Etsi postea gignat, abdicant, ne fiat haereditarum regnum. . . . [Nine lines are omitted which are concerned with former names of Taprobane and of the inhabitants, etc.]

Compare also

India, regio Orientalis . . . Insulas tanto numero habet India, vt merito Orbis insularum appellari queat. Celebriores sunt, Iapan, Moluccae, Sumatra (olim Taprobana) Iaua maior & minor. . . .

# APPENDIX I

# THE FATES

T HE READER SHOULD REALIZE WHAT THE AUTHORS ARE ONLY TOO aware of; namely, that the material dealt with might well be described *in toto* as academic or literary commonplaces. Conversely the reader should also realize that the commonness of the material does not per se lessen its importance. If anything, as we have attempted to indicate above, it increases the pertinence of that material for anyone interested in understanding a tradition out of which grew some undeniably excellent literature. These pages, consequently, are meant to illustrate the preceding statement in some detail and at the same time to indicate that the authors are only too cognizant of a two-fold difficulty inherent in their work. In the first place, reflections of wording or of the arrangement of materials can be shown only by parallel passages; and the dangers of such a method are well known. The second difficulty, indeed, is closely related; for the parallel becomes particularly deadly when it is concerned with matter that was the common property of the age, with coin that passed current during a particular period. Of all the proper nouns occurring in Renaissance literature, certainly those of classic myth appear most frequently; and it is with just such material, for example, that the chapters in the text of this study are concerned.

The frequent use of classic myth and legend is quite in accordance with the academic tradition of the era, but the dictionaries were naturally not the only compilations devoted to elucidating the classics. Good texts in both Greek and Latin suitable for various levels of accomplishment were made available and were in general overloaded with critical and explanatory materials. The classics were translated, and there were prepared a considerable number of scholarly treatises devoted entirely or in part to such subjects as classic myth. A copy of Comes was in the library of James I and in that of Richard Stonely as well as in the library of the Merchant Taylors' school by 1599.[1] The *Mythologiae* is also listed by Hoole in his discussion of the work of his fourth form, that is, when his students begin to study Ovid. He groups it, as we have seen, with the seventeenth-century mythological treatises by Bacon and by Alexander Ross; with Sandys' translation of Ovid; and with Antoine du Verdier's *Imagines Deorum,* which was the basic Latin translation of the *Le Imagini dei Dei degli Antichi* by the Italian Vincenzio Cartari; and, of course, with Charles Stephanus' *Dictionarium Historicum, Geographicum, Poeticum.* Such a group of texts in one place was meant to invite the students "like so many bees to busie themselves sucking up matter and words to quicken their invention and expression."[2]

Specialized compendiums like the *Mythologiae,* consequently, were undoubtedly known to literary men by the end of the sixteenth century. Between the covers of such works the information on proper nouns that appeared in a dictionary might also be found, and, as we have noted elsewhere, sometimes the discussion is more detailed than was suitable for a dictionary entry. Two of the compilations John Marston names, and the nature of a third he indicates when satirizing a pseudo-satirist.

> My wit is stricken blind, hath lost his sight;
> My shins are broke with groping for some sense,
> To know to what his words have reference.
> Certes, *sunt* but *non videntur* that I know;
> Reach me some poets' index that will show.
> *Imagines Deorum,* Book of Epithets,
> *Natalis Comes,* thou I know recites,
> And makest anatomy of poesy;
> Help me to unmask the satire's secrecy. . . .[3]

"*Imagines Deorum*" refers, in all probability, to a Latin translation of Vincenzio Cartari's *Le Imagini dei Dei degli Antichi,* and quite possibly to the translation by Antoine du Verdier recommended by Hoole.[4] "Natalis Comes" means the *Mythologiae.* "Book of Epithets" indicates such a compilation as that by J. Ravisius Textor entitled *Epithetorum Opera Absolutissimi,* wherein descriptive entries on mythological figures were followed by apposite quotations from the writings of ancient, medieval, and modern authors.[5] The passage from Marston, consequently, is frequently adduced as proof of the popularity of such reference works, and the subtitle of one of the editions of Cartari also indicates how such works might be used.  Since their scholarly completeness was generally recognized, such a compilation might well be advertised as "opera vtilissima a Historici, Poeti, Pittori, Scultori, & Professori de belle lettere."[6]  When Thomas Lodge, for example, translated Simon Goulart de Senlis' commentary on the immensely popular work by Du Bartas, he ran across a statement that once again indicates the popularity of the works compiled by Comes and Cartari.  And in the same passage, Goulart de Senlis refers his reader to the third major mythological treatise of the period, the *De Deis Gentium* by Lilius Gregorius Gyraldus:

> Qui voudra cognoistre cela par le menu, & à quoi toutes les parties de la fable de Bacchus . . . lise le troisiesme chapitre du cinquiesme liure de la Mythologie de Noel des Comtes, le huictiesme liure de l'Histoire des dieux Payens, de Lilius Giraldus, & Cartari en ses images des Dieux: car ceux-là ont presques recueilli tout ce que les anciens en ont dit.[7]

From the middle of the sixteenth century, the compilations of Cartari and Comes had undergone numerous editions in various cities and countries, as had the *De Deis Gentium*.  By the end of the century, knowledge of classic myth had been disseminated also by such varied and widely current texts as Boccaccio's *Genealogiae Deorum,* Perottus' *Cornucopiae,* and Textor's *Officina*.  Similar and related material could be found in the extremely popular emblem books, particularly in such an edition of Alciati's *Emblems* as that made by Claudius Minois, or in kindred compilations like the *Iconologia* of Cesare Ripa or the *Hieroglyphica* of Giovanni Pierio Valerianus.  In Johannes Rosinus' *Antiquitates: Romanarum Antiquitatum Libri Decem,* for example, or in Onuphrius Panvinius' *Reipublicae Romanae Commentarii,* or in Caspar Peucer's *Commentarius de Praecipuis Divinationum Generibus,* the religions and rites of ancient times were described, sometimes with learned detail, as were other matters of classical antiquity dealing with historical figures.[8]  In brief, more and more of the matter to which we are limited approached the commonplace as the age advanced.

Consequently it may not seem supererogatory if we consider a particular commonplace of mythology in order to supplement our discussion of dictionary entries that seem to be reflected in the works of individual authors.  Such a discussion will illustrate the relationship between the proper noun entries in standard reference dictionaries of the period and the similar material in more specialized treatises.  The myth of the Fates has been chosen, not simply because mention of the Fatal Sisters is one of the most frequent references to classical mythology, but also because the pertinent material in Renaissance compendiums is brief enough to be surveyed in a relatively short space. Thus the pages that immediately follow outline representative material on the Parcae found in the dictionaries with which we are concerned, and in such current compilations as those more specialized treatises mentioned above. Passages in vernacular literature that parallel the material outlined and that appear, for the most part, in the writings of Spenser, Shakespeare, Jonson, and Milton are then discussed. The material in the reference works to be surveyed will indicate the wealth of information on such a subject that was available to the Elizabethan or the Jacobean—the learned digests, the numerous quotations included in discussions of the Fates, and the pertinent illustrations found in current works of reference.

If a schoolboy were not already aware of current conceptions of the Parcae, he might well have had his attention directed to the myth of the Fatal Sisters when he read the fable of Ocyroë in the second book of the *Metamorphoses*. Therein Chiron's daughter, after prophesying the fate of Æsculapius, is transformed into a mare because she had spurned her father's art in order to sing the secrets of the Fates or Destiny. Although Elyot questioned the wisdom of spending much of the student's time on Ovid when the hours might be occupied with "eloquence, ciuile policie, and exhortation to vertue," he believed that the *Metamorphoses* and *Fasti* should be "declared abundantly" by the master and found even in Ovid's "mooste wanton bokes" "righte commendable and noble sentences."[9] In England, Ovid was nearly always the first classical poet to be encountered in the grammar school and, as a rule, after his *Tristia* had been studied, a student read in the *Metamorphoses* for the next half-year or year.[10] What and how much information about the Fatal Sisters the average schoolboy was expected to amass, we do not know; certainly the relative pedantry of his master would have much to do with the nature of his knowledge. Yet even if emphasis were placed upon what Pico della Mirandola calls "light trifles"—that is, upon such mythological details as questions "concerning the mother of Andromache or the sons of Niobe"[11]—both master and pupil, as the following pages will demonstrate, could have found sufficient material for discourse or theme without much trouble. Even moot points of mythological genealogy could have been used in a discourse that would have pleased Elyot; for to the

Renaissance, as to the Middle Ages, there was "no one tale among all the Poets", that did not embody "some thing that parteineth, either to the amendment of manners, to the knowledge of the trueth, to the setting forth of Natures work, or else the vnderstanding of some notable thing done."[12]   In some form or another the schoolboy undoubtedly encountered the doctrine that "whatsoever either Virgil did write of his gnatt or Ovid of his fley was all couertly to declare abuse."   In writing this last statement, Lodge's tongue may have been somewhere in the direction of his cheek; he was twitting Gosson on being a *"homo literatus."*[13]   Yet the general attitude, even of the learned, toward the significance of the myths was that of Bacon's when he compiled his *De Sapientia Veterum:*

. . . I do certainly for my own part (I freely and candidly confess) incline to this opinion,—that beneath no small number of the fables of the ancient poets there lay from the very beginning a mystery and an allegory.  It may be that my reverence for the primitive time carries me too far, but the truth is that in some of these fables, as well in the very frame and texture of the story as in the propriety of the names by which the persons that figure in it are distinguished, I find a conformity and connexion with the thing signified, so close and so evident, that one cannot help believing such a significance to have been designed and mediated from the first, and purposely shadowed out.
Upon the whole I conclude with this: the wisdom of the primitive ages was either great or lucky; great if they knew what they were doing and invented the figure to shadow the meaning; lucky, if without meaning or intending it, they fell upon matter which gives occasion to such worthy contemplations.[14]

As we shall see, even a schoolmaster's pedantic emphasis upon the ancestry of the Parcae might be utilized for a discussion concerned with "the setting forth of Natures work"; or a consideration of the Fates might well have involved the question of the malevolence or beneficence of "fate" or the problem of the freedom of man's will.   If master and pupils paused on the fable of Ocyroë, for example, the pupils might be encouraged, as with all such fables, to "strive (who can best) to turn the Fable into English prose, and to adorn and amplifie it with fit Epithetes, choice Phrases, acute Sentences, wittie Apophthegmes, livelie similitudes, pat examples, and Proverbial Speeches, *all agreeing to the matter of moralitie therein couched. . . ."*[15]   Some, indeed, might have enlarged the fable along the lines suggested by Georgius Sabinus in his interpretive treatment of the *Metamorphoses.*   After a student had considered the text that related Ocyroë's tranformation, the Koeningsberg professor apparently would have the student's attention called first to Plato's representation of the Fates as the daughters of Necessity, then to the way in which the Fates, "fate," or "necessity," signifies a divine Providence, which by the movements of the heavens or the elements, or by the managing of men, effects its just beneficence without destroying the freedom of the will. Such an interpretation, it will be seen, was conventional among mythographers.   Only briefly does Sabinus discuss the name "Ocyroë."[16]

Any interpretation of a myth, of course, would arise from the traditional conception of the figures involved; and from such conceptions a scholarly teacher like Sabinus would draw or develop his explication or gloss.   Thus we should expect such an edition of Ovid's works as that published in 1601 at Frankfort to embrace material that was current at the turn of the century and would be appropriate for mature students of Ovid's poetry—as well as for the pupil who may have encountered the edition sometime before 1662 in the library of the Merchant Taylors' school.[17]   Obviously an attempt at a definitive edition, it includes the commentaries, notes, and readings of a variety of scholars and editors: Raphael Regio, Jacob Molsheym of Strassburg, Ercole Ciofano, Gregor Bersmann, Aldus, Antonio Constantino, Paolo Marso, Gaudenzio Merula, Gregorio Merlini, Philip Melancthon, Desiderius Erasmus; and it indicates that in general the Renaissance was familiar with three distinct conceptions of the Parcae.   They might appear as the three sisters who draw out and cut the thread of life; or they might appear as the secretaries of the Gods; or as the singing daughters of Necessity.[18]

That the first of these conceptions passed as current coin during the period hardly need be commented upon, when one recalls the lines that Pyramis and Thisbe spoke "obscenely and courageously" before the court in Athens, or the braggadocio rhetoric of Pistol:

> Ha! art thou bedlam? dost thou thirst, base Troyan,
> To have me fold up Parca's fatal web?
>
> (*Henry V*, 5.1. 20-21)

All the current works of reference with which we are concerned contain at least a short digest of the classical conception of the Fates as the three sisters who draw out and break the thread of life.   Charles Stephanus' immensely popular dictionary, for example, contains an account that is relatively brief.   The longer entries in the *Dictionarium Historicum, Geographicum, Poeticum* usually cite more authorities than two, and as a rule give specific lines from classical authors to support such a sentence as that ending the first quotation below: "Hinc sorores lanificae a poetis appellantur." The account, however, might well represent the kernel of other fuller digests that deal with the Fates as *lanificae*.

In the *Dictionarium Historicum* the entry begins by noting that the Parcae are the fatal goddesses who order or control the threads of human life. It then gives two derivations of the word *Parcae*. One, attested by Varro, relates the word to *partus,* a "bringing forth" or "parturition." The reason for this is that the Fates are thought to bestow both fortune and misfortune upon men at birth. The other derivation relates *Parcae* to the verb meaning "to spare"; for the Fates spare no one. The initial sentence is then enlarged upon: the Fates, called *lanificae* by poets, are the daughters of Erebus and Night; they are represented as three in number and are named Clotho, Lachesis, and Atropos. The first or eldest holds the distaff; the second spins the thread and determines the end of human life; the third cuts the thread, or breaks off life at the appointed time.

Parcae, deae fatales, humanae vitae stamina dispensantes. Dictae autem putantur Parcae a partu, teste Varonne, eo quod nascentibus hominibus bona malaque conferre censeantur. Alij a parcendo κατ' ἀντίφρασιν dictas putant, propterea quod nemini parcant. Hae autem tres esse finguntur, Clotho, Lachesis, et Atropos, Erebi et Noctis filiae: quarum primam colum volunt gestare, secundum nendo humanae vitae terminum praefinire, tertiam filum incidere, hoc est, vitam tempore statuto abrumpere. Hinc sorores lanificae a poetis appellantur.

Charles Stephanus then cites his second authority, Apuleius, for an explanation of the triple number of the Fates. Such a statement in effect constitutes a germinal "interpretation" of the myth of the Parcae, for the spinning of the Fates corresponds to the triple division of time. The past is represented by thread on the spindle; the present, by thread being spun; the future, by that which is still on the distaff.

Apuleius ternarium Parcarum numerum a triplici tempore ductum existimat. Nam quod in fuso perfectum est, praeteriti temporis habet speciem: et quod torquetur in digitis, momenti praesentis indicat spatia: et quod nondum ex colo tractum est, futuri et consequentis seculi posteriora videtur ostendere.

The derivation of the name for each of the Fates is then given. *Lachesis* is derived from the Greek word meaning "to allot" or "to choose" (*"sortior"*); *Atropos,* from the Greek meaning "not to be averted"; *Clotho,* from the Greek also, meaning "to spin" or "to turn around."

Lachesim dictam esse putant, ab eo quod λαγχάνω Graece, sortior designat. Atropon, quia verti, hoc est mutari aut flecti non possit, ab α priuatiua particula, et verbo τρέπω, quod est verto. Clotho quoniam contorta, et conuoluta omnia teneat: a verbo Graeco κλόθω, quod significat neo vel circumuoluo.

The entry in Charles Stephanus' *Dictionarium Historicum* ends with the notation that ancient Latins gave to the Parcae the names Nona, Decima, and Morta: "Latini veteres earum tria nomina fecerunt, Nona, Decima et Mortam."

The corresponding entry in Cooper's *Thesaurus,* to be quoted later, is briefer than the account found in the dictionary of Charles Stephanus, although it may well have been derived from the digest quoted above. The pertinent material in Calepine's dictionary, on the other hand, is very similar to the account found in Charles Stephanus' compilation but is somewhat longer than the entry in the *Dictionarium Historicum.* Although the length of the entry in Calepine's lexicon, and the details found therein, vary with different editions, the material in the *Dictionarium* is, in turn, not as detailed as that found in Robert Stephanus' *Thesaurus.* Nor do later editions of Calepine necessarily provide a fuller account than do earlier redactions—in contrast with what is usually true for editions of Charles Stephanus' proper-noun dictionary. The account of the Fates in the 1548 edition of Calepine printed by the house of Aldus, for example, agrees almost verbatim with the major portion of the entry in the 1543 *Thesaurus.* It gives slightly more information on the derivation of the names of the Parcae, but it does not contain the last thirteen quotations given by the *Thesaurus,* nor does it include the brief statement which indicates the duties of the three sisters. In contrast, the account in the 1581 Calepine that also was printed by the house of Aldus is even less detailed than the account in the 1548 edition.[19] Consequently, a comparison of the entries by Charles and Robert Stephanus will serve our turn.

Robert quotes lines from classical authors that Charles, in this instance, has neglected to include. A passage from Martial, for example, is quoted in the *Thesaurus* to substantiate the cognomen *lanificae:*

Quapropter lanificas sorores appellat Martialis lib. 6. 58.
>Si mihi lanificae ducunt non pulla sorores
>Stamina, nec surdos vox habet ista deos.

Elsewhere the entry under *Parcae* in the *Thesaurus* also gives in more detail the information found in the *Dictionarium Historicum*.

The entry in Robert Stephanus' compilation of 1543, accordingly, begins by noting that the derivation of *Parcae* from *parco* is "by the contrary"; "Parcae, a parco, per contrarium, quod nemini parcant." For this information, which a student might be expected to know as part of his exercise on "the Derivations and Differences of some words," the edition of 1543 gives no authority. In later editions, however, Julius Caesar Scaliger, "Poet. 3. 90," is cited; for Scaliger had objected to such an etymology in view of the fact that only one of the sisters did not spare mankind, that is, did cut off life; while two, Clotho and Lachesis, preserved it. Robert Stephanus in the edition of 1543 also gives the alternate derivation noted in the *Dictionarium Historicum,* but the citation of Varro ("Varro, apud Gell [ius]. 3. 16," in later editions) is supported by a reference to Hesiod ("Th[eogony]. 218 & 904," in later editions). This last reference substantiates the derivation and its reason; for as Charles Stephanus pointed out in almost identical words, the Fates were thought to confer the good as well as the bad upon men at birth. In the *Thesaurus,* however, the statement is followed by an appropriate quotation from Juvenal.

Varro a partu, vnius literae mutatione, deduci putat: quoniam (vt scribit Hesiodus) hae nascentibus hominibus bonum malumque conferre censeantur. Iuuen. Saty. 9. 14,

> Haec exempla para foelicibus: at mea Clotho
> Et Lachesis gaudent, si pascitur inguine venter.

Between the accounts of the two conventional derivations of *Parcae,* that is, just before the passage quoted above, Robert Stephanus inserts a sentence briefly indicating that the Fates are three in number and that they are thought to be so represented because of the three divisions of time on which all things turn, or in which all things are rolled along or considered: "Ideo tres esse Parcas arbitrantur quoniam tria sunt tempora, in quibus omnia voluuntur."

A reader of the edition of 1543 would then encounter matter also found in the *Dictionarium Historicum,* that the Fates, whose names are given, are the daughters of Erebus and Night; but in Robert Stephanus, as in Calepine, the citation of Cicero as an authority is added, the specific location of the pertinent passage is given ("3. de Nat. deor. 59"), and

the fact is noted that the Parcae signify Fate. The *Thesaurus* then refers
to a statement which the Stoic Cleanthes ascribed to Seneca: the Fates
lead (*"ducunt"*) the willing, or the well-inclined; but drag or draw along
(*"trahunt"*) the unwilling, or the ill-inclined:

Tres autem fuisse Parcas, Clotho scilicet et Lachesin et Atropon finxerunt
antiqui, quas Cicero 3. de Nat. deor. 59, Erebi et Noctis filias fuisse scribit,
et easdem fata esse existimat. Vnde est illud Cleantis, Ducunt volentem fata,
nolentem trahunt.

The differentiation between *duco* and *traho,* wherein the idea expressed
by *duco* might involve the drawing of another only as a result of his free
will, was thoroughly conventional to the sixteenth century, as the following sentences from the definitions of the two words in the *Thesaurus*
testify:

Duco . . . Manifestae significationis. Differt a traho: quod ducimus eum qui
sponte sequitur: Trahimus autem nolentem.
Traho . . . Per vim ducere. Trahimur enim inuiti: Ducimur volentes.

In Boccaccio's account of the Fates a similar distinction had been made
when Cleanthes' words were referred to. Boccaccio emphasized, however,
the inexorable rule of necessity and referred in some detail to the Senecan
*Œdipus*.[20] By itself, the quotation of Cleanthes' brief maxim in the *Thesaurus,* might well start a train of associations in the mind of a Renaissance reader. Stoic doctrine, of course, was singularly pervasive; and
the educated were raised on the difference between "inclining" and "com-
pelling," particularly as the configuration of celestial bodies at birth was
concerned. Moreover the difference between those of good intent (*"volentem,"* in its context) and those of "perverse wit" (*"nolentem"*) might
well have associations with doctrines concerning the omnipotence and fore-
knowledge of a just and beneficent Deity.

With the sentence that the Parcae are feigned to preside over and
spin out the lives of men ("Fingunt vitae hominum praeesse, et nendo eam
ducere"), the entry in the *Thesaurus* passes on to a statement that briefly
indicates the duties of each of the three sisters: "Clotho, colum baiulat:
Lachesis, net: Atropos, filum frangit." It is this sentence that is supported
by the passage from Martial quoted above.

Apuleius ("de Mundo ad fin" in later editions) is then cited for the
relationship between the myth of the Parcae and time; and the account
that follows enlarges upon the sentence inserted between the brief dis-

cussions of the derivation of the word *Parcae*, i.e., "Ideo tres esse Parcas arbitrantur quoniam tria sunt tempora, in quibus omnia voluuntur." Again the material in the *Thesaurus* is slightly more detailed than that in the *Dictionarium Historicum*, and, like the moral implicit in the quotation of Cleanthes, it also constitutes a germinal interpretation of the myth which has affinities with more detailed treatments of the Fatal Sisters in other works of reference:

Apuleius, Tres Parcae tria fata sunt numero, cum ratione temporis facientia, si potestatem earum ad eiusdam similitudinem temporis referas. Nam quod in fuso perfectum est, praeteriti temporis habet speciem. Et quod torquetur in digitis, momenti praesentis indicat spatia. Et quod nondum ex colo tractum est, subactumque curae digitorum, futuri et consequentis seculi posteriora videtur ostendere.

Such a synopsis of Apuleius, however, taken with the sentence which briefly enumerates the respective duties of the three sisters, results in a curious distortion of the thought in the *Liber de Mundo* (XXXVIII). After writing the words quoted by the *Thesaurus*, Apuleius continues the discussion by allotting to Atropos the past, to Lachesis the future, and to Clotho the present.[21] In the *Thesaurus*, the inclusion of the sentence "Clotho, colum baiulat: Lachesis, net . . ." would demand that Clotho be allotted the future and Lachesis the present. Such a minor distortion of the thought of Apuleius—of some importance, however, for a portion of the discussion to follow— is possible but less obvious in Charles Stephanus and in Calepinus. In the *Dictionarium Historicum*, after the names Clotho, Lachesis, and Atropos were given, the entry read that the first, or eldest, (*"prima"*) held the distaff. In Calepine there was no *prima*, and no sentence concerning the respective duties of the Parcae; but Clotho was named before Lachesis. Thus unless a reader consulted Apuleius, he would probably allot future and present time in accordance with the order in which the entry listed the Fates, for past time would obviously belong to Atropos.

The discussion of the derivation of the three names of the Parcae is slightly briefer in the 1543 edition of Robert Stephanus than is the corresponding passage in the *Dictionarium Historicum*. In the *Thesaurus*, however, Clotho is said to be so called because she keeps or holds everything twisted together and arranged together in order (*"contorta et coordinata"*), while the elucidation of the name as it is derived from the Greek word meaning 'to spin' or 'to turn' is omitted.

The major portion of the entry in the *Thesaurus* then closes with another quotation from Martial on the implacability of the Three Sisters:

Lachesin dictam esse putant, quia λαγχάνω Graece, sortior designat. Atropon, quia reuerti non possint. Clothon, quoniam contorta et coordinata omnia teneat. Haec enim, nomina ipsa lingua Graeca ostendunt. Mart. lib. 1. 162,

> Lanificas nulli tres exorare puellas
> Contigit: obseruant quem statuere diem.

The final bit of information about Nona, Decima, and Morta that appeared in Charles Stephanus' entry can be found under "Nona" but is missing in the 1543 article on "Parcae," although it appears there also in later editions of the *Thesaurus*.

After this last quotation from Martial, appear other appropriate passages from Latin authors—a feature of all entries in the *Thesaurus*. In addition to the quotations and citations mentioned above, the article on the Parcae in the edition of 1543 quotes lines from Virgil ("4. eclog. 10"), three lines from Ovid ("5. Trist. eleg. 4.3"; "5. Metam. 107"; and "epist. 11. 21"), and a line from Juvenal ("Saty. 12.7"). It gives descriptive phrases of two or three words from a poem by Statius ("5. Sylu. 2. 17"), three poems by Horace ("2. Carm. ode 16.8"; "Carm. seculari, 5"; and "2. Carm. ode 6.2"), and poems by Valerius Flaccus ("5. Argon. 107") and Virgil ("12. AEneid. 30"). Later editions of the *Thesaurus* increase the number of lines or phrases so quoted; and in general the lines cited express protests against a cruel or lamentable fate, against the anger of the wicked Fates, the sad nature of their gifts, against their ferociousness, or their hostile unjustness. Thus side by side with statements that the Fates confer fortune and misfortune upon men, whereby they may be conceived of philosophically, and side by side with such an interpretation of the myth as that ascribed to Apuleius, wherein they are linked with the eternal course of time, appear lines and phrases wherein the Parcae are represented as merely capricious or vengeful. Such conflicting points of view, apparent even in the 1543 edition of the *Thesaurus,* are natural and understandable when one considers the varying nature of the classical materials upon which any such entry must be based; it is nevertheless an interesting aspect of the treatment of the myth in Robert Stephanus, and it is one that appears in other current treatments of the Parcae.

In later editions of the *Thesaurus,* moreover, the phrases of two or three words (followed by the author's name and an indication of where the phrase or line may be found) tend to be introduced by a key word. Thus the words "Saevae," "Veraces," "Hilares," or "Iniquae," for example, are followed by the appropriate phrase and its citation—in these instances, from the works of Valerius Flaccus, Horace, Juvenal, and Horace again. Of the other reference works enumerated above, this use of key words is especially characteristic of the method employed by Textor in his popular epithet book, which also includes epitomes on the figures of classical mythology.

A description of the brief digest on the Fatal Sisters given by Textor need not detain us. The key words and the nature of the authorities cited, however, deserve some attention, for although some of the passages cited by Robert Stephanus also appear in the *Epithetorum Opera Absolutissimi,* the number of the descriptive key words and the range of the authorities are greater than in the *Thesaurus Linguae Latinae.* Under such descriptive words as "Concordes," "Iniquae," "Veteres," "Nentes," "Durae," "Celeres," "Crudeles," and "Tenaces," Textor quotes twenty-nine classical, medieval, and contemporary authors. The passages cited range from the "licentious Naso" to Strozius Pater, the ecclesiastical historian; from the impassioned Propertius to Crinitus, the late fifteenth-century compiler. In the order of their occurrence they are "Virgil"; "Horace, 2. Carm."; "Horace, Carm. Saec."; "Ovid. 15"; "Ovid, Trist. 5"; "Stat[ius], 6, Theb." (two passages); "Propert. 4"; "Stat [ius], 5, Theb."; "Stat[ius], 11"; "Stat[ius], 2, Syl." (two passages); "Hier. Ang[erianus]"; "Mart[ial] 4"; "Mart[ial] 5"; "Seneca"; "Pont [anus]"; "Polit[ianus]"; "Marull[us]"; "Faust[us Andrelinus]"; "Stroz [ius] Pat[er]" (two passages); "Sabell[icus]"; "Crinit[us]"; "Remaclus"; "Calentius"; "Hier. Argent. Bon."; "Tibull[us], 13"; "Vinc. Astell. Nouar."; and "Theod[oritus] Cyr."[22]

Similarly, material found in the dictionaries on the Fates as *lanificae* is also found in the compilations by Gyraldus, Comes, and Cartari. Therein the particulars outlined above are sometimes developed by consonant ideas and discussed in greater detail than they were in the dictionary entries. Gyraldus, Comes, and Cartari limit themselves to ancient mythology, whereas the lexicons also provide information on historical and legendary figures and on a great variety of geographical names. Thus in five of the one hundred and fifteen lines on folio pages that Gyraldus devotes to the Parcae, he can write about the word *lanificae* more specifically than did Charles Stephanus, Cooper, Calepine, or

Robert Stephanus.   Actually he simply enlarges upon the implications of the passage in Martial that Robert quoted:

Lanificae Parcae à nostris cognominatæ sunt, quod pensa et stamina uitæ humanæ trahant candida, uel argentea, id est felicia, uel ferrea et pulla: uel nigra, id est infelicia.   *Martialis:*
> Si mihi lanificæ ducunt non pulla sorores
> Stamina.

The number of authorities listed in these compilations, however, seems at first glance not to accord with the relatively detailed treatment the mythological figures receive.   Gyraldus alone surpasses Textor, citing or quoting in his digest on the Parcae some thirty-nine passages from twenty-three authors.   Nevertheless, in contrast with the *Epithetorum Opera* and the dictionaries, the compilations by Gyraldus, Cartari, and Comes frequently quote Greek; and thus the reader of their compilations, if he wished to ornament his discourse with Greek as well as Latin, would find at hand apt quotations concerning the Fates as *lanificae* from such classics as the Orphic Hymns, Homer, Plato, Aeschylus, and Euripides, as well as from the Greek mythographer Phurnutus.   In Comes all the Greek lines were conveniently translated into Latin immediately after they had been quoted.[23]

Moreover, in editions of Cartari after 1569 at least, and in early seventeenth-century editions of Comes, one also finds illustrations of the various mythological figures, the *imagines deorum* that could be derived from references and descriptions in ancient literature.   The illustration of the Fates as *lanificae* (Plate I) is based, for example, upon the full description of the Parcae found in the compilation by Cartari, which is here quoted from the French translation and augmentation of the *Imagines Deorum* made by Antoine du Verdier (Lyon, 1581).   Similar material is found in Comes; and in both instances, the basic conception of the discussion is that briefly expressed by Charles and Robert Stephanus, Calepine, and Cooper.[24]   In Cartari, however, the passage illustrated by the plate begins by noting that inasmuch as the Parcae spin the thread of human life, they are fittingly associated with Pluto.   The nature of the thread determines the nature of a man's life, and because of their control over man's destiny, the Fates were represented as three: one concerned with birth, the other with life, and the third with death.   Cartari then proceeds to develop this remark in some detail.   The three Fates are said to reside together; to differ in age as in function (the youngest

PLATE I

holding the distaff) ; to be winged, according to Homer ; and to have white fillets around their heads.   On the authority of Catullus, quoted in full in the Italian and Latin versions, their trembling limbs are said to be covered by white robes with a purple border :

Et n'est de merueille que les Parques seruent à Pluton.   Car on estimoit qu'elles filoient la vie de l'homme, laquelle dure peu ou prou, selon que le corps fragile est idoine à viure plus ou moins : et ceci en l'homme est la matiere representee par Pluton.   Des changements donques que reçoit en soy la matiere, vient la mort, et la vie, laquelle selon la mesure dicelle les Parques font longue ou courte.   Pour ceste cause les anciens faignoient qu'elles estoient trois, et que l'vne auoit le soin de faire naistre, l'autre de faire viure, et la troisieme de faire mourir.   A cause dequoy toutes trois demeurent ensemble à filer la vie des hommes, l'vne, qui estoit la plus ieune, tenoit la quenoille, et tiroit le fil, l'autre plus aagee, le tournoit à l'entour du fuseau, et la troisieme desia vieille, le coupoit.   Pour ce Virgile en Dante parle ainsi de Dante, s'esmerueillant de le voir si auant en purgatoire. . . .

. . . et autres leur ont bandé la teste auec vne bande blanche, comme fait Catulle, lequel les descripuant vieilles de visage, dit qu'elles sont vestues d'vne robe blanche qui leur couure les membres tremblans, et est ceinte et enuironnee de pourpre, et ont à la teste vne bande blanche.   Et combien qu'elles soyent vieilles, sont neantmoins tousiours prestes à filler de leur main en diuerses manieres, et par leur trame et ouurage la vie de l'homme vient, et s'en va pour la derniere fois.   Homere chantant les louanges de Mercure, dit que les Parques sont trois seurs vierges, qui ont des ailes, et de farine fort blanche respandue par dessus leurs testes.

The mythographers, as they abstract material from previous authors, are not always consistent about which of the Parcae held the distaff.   The Latin and French versions, as well as early Italian editions of Cartari, do not involve any specific division of labor by name.   In later Italian editions, however, one will find that Clotho, Lachesis, and Atropos are named in that order : thus Clotho, the youngest, holds the distaff and controls the future, while Lachesis turns the thread on the spindle.[25]   Boccaccio, following Apuleius, at one point reverses such an allotment and gives to Clotho the present (which corresponds to the thread and the spindle) and to Lachesis the future (or distaff) ; so at one point does Gyraldus.   But when both mythographers recount Fulgentius' interpretation of the myth, they repeat material that would again give to Clotho both the future and the distaff, and to Lachesis the present.   Elsewhere Gyraldus also repeats what we shall hereafter refer to as the Latin tag,[26] in a form slightly different from that in the *Thesaurus,* whereby Clotho is again said to hold the distaff and Lachesis to spin.

Although the Fates as *lanificae* were associated with Pluto by Cartari, no mythographer of the period, as far as we know, ever suggested that the infernal god was their parent. Both Comes and Cartari note that the Parcae are sometimes called the daughters of Jove and Themis (Justice), and Comes and Gyraldus also note that they may appear as the daughters of the Sea. Such genealogies, however, were apparently less well known to the English authors with whom we are concerned than were two others: that the Fates were, as the lexicons pointed out, the daughters of Erebus and Night (sometimes simply of Night), and that they were the daughters of Demogorgon and associated with Chaos (or simply the offspring of Chaos).

The first genealogy, aside from being in the lexicons, is also found in the compilations by Boccaccio, Gyraldus, Comes, and Cartari, wherein it is used as the basis for an interpretation of the myth. In other words, just as Gyraldus and Cartari in the passages quoted above enlarged upon the nature of the thread spun by the Fates and applied it to the nature of a man's life, so here an account more detailed than that in the dictionaries results from the mythographers' elaborating upon the implications of a parentage connected with Erebus and, or Night. As in the entries for "Erebus" in the dictionaries, so in the *Imagines Deorum,* for example, appears the statement that Erebus indicates obscurity, the deepest and darkest place of the earth. Thus such a genealogy, by the nature of both parents, shows how secret, or difficult to discover, are the causes of things.

Autres ont dit que les Parques sont filles de Herebe (qui fut le lieu le plus profond et plus obscur de la terre) et de la Nuict, pour monstrer par l'obscurité du pere et de la mere, combien sont occultes les causes des choses.

The same idea is expressed by Comes when, for example, he mentions that the Parcae live in an obscure cave, gives the reasons for their having such an habitation, and emphasizes the immutable though obscure vengeance of God which the wicked cannot escape.

Hae dictae sunt in spelunca quadam obscura habitare solitae, quoniam occulta sunt Dei iudicia, neque statim ad sceleratos homines conuolant supplicia: verum vbi opportunum tempus vindictae Dei accesserit, nulla neque arx munitissima, neque legio peditum, aut cataphractorum equitum praesidia possunt ab homine nefario Dei vindictam depellere vel retardare.

In the *Genealogiae Deorum* one might also find a kindred idea expressed when Boccaccio writes that the Parcea were sometimes said to be the daughters of Demogorgon and thus, quite appropriately, coeval with the beginning of things. For Demogorgon might represent the primal deity, the "grandfather" of the gods, who abides in the deepest part of the Earth, surrounded by cloud and vapor and with whom, consequently, caves are associated "apud rusticos."[27]  Textor also had noted briefly that the Parcae might be represented as the daughters of Demogorgon; and Comes writes that the Fates are sometimes said to be the offspring of Chaos.  The passage in the *Mythologiae* which discusses the Fatal Sister's connection with the beginning of things[28] also includes the congruent detail that the Parcae as *lanificae* abide in the cave of Chaos: "seque in illam speluncam recepisse, vnde quocunque liberet facile conuolarent." The way in which the Demogorgon-Chaos genealogy emphasizes the beginning of things but is also akin to the idea of obscurity, expressed by the Erebus-Night parentage, is best illustrated perhaps by Cartari, when he develops the idea that poets make the Fates three in number because everything must have "un principe" at the beginning and continue thereby until its destined end.  Thus the Parcae born of Chaos represent the way in which the cause inherent in the first great separation of things is effected; that is, the Three Sisters may be said to represent beginning, middle, and destined end of the determining principle:

. . . aucens ont dit, que les Poëtes . . . en feirent trois, parce que chascune chose commence par vn principe, et cheminant par son moien, qui luy est approprié, elle paruient au but et fin à laquelle elle est destinee, et ces Parques nasquirent du Chaos: car en la premiere separation, qui fut faite à toute chose, fut asignee sa propre cause.

The passage is then followed by the genealogy also given in the lexicons, that is, by the reference to the Erebus-Night parentage, wherein Cartari says that such a genealogy shows how secret or difficult to discover are the causes of things.

As the myth of the Parcae might be related to the beginning, middle, and destined end of all things, the name and function of the first of the Fates may receive particular attention.  Thus in Boccaccio's *Genealogiae Deorum* and Gyraldus' *De Deis Gentium,* the reader is provided with a summary of Fulgentius' discussion of the name *Clotho.*  Gyraldus' account is condensed and more applicable to the life of man only, but in Boccaccio one reads that *Clotho* means "a summoning" or "a calling forth," and thus the Fates are concerned not simply with the life of man but also— as the preceding passage from Cartari indicates—with the "seed of each thing" as it emerges into the light:

Et ait idem Fulgentius Cloto [*sic*] interpretari evocationem, eo quod suum sit iactoque cuiscumque rei semine, illud adeo incrementum trahere, ut aptum sit in lucem emergere.

Lachesis, interpreted as *pertractio,* then draws out into life that which Clotho has put together: ". . . eo quod qcqd a Clotho compositum est: et in lucem euocatum: a Lachesi suscipiatur et pertrahatur in uitam."[29]

There is no need to enlarge upon the way in which the statements enumerated above might be made to accord with doctrine that stretches back at least to Lucretius and expounds concepts about "nature's germens" or the "seeds of time." On the other hand, although the representation of the Fates as offspring of Demogorgon and Chaos and such details as *Clotho* meaning *evocatio* are not found in the lexicons, it is equally revealing to note how the kernel of the interpretations just surveyed might well be represented by the way in which Charles Stephanus, Calepine, and Robert Stephanus abstract material from Apuleius and represent the Fates as standing for time in its triple division. In the *Thesaurus* of 1543, moreover, one of the Fates was called Clotho "quoniam contorta et coordinata omnia teneat."

Perhaps as a result of the way in which the Fates might be related to the beginning of things, they were sometimes associated with certain major deities. Indeed, a student, school-master, editor, or writer who knew both Comes and Gyraldus would be able to cite authorities for saying that Lucina or Venus or Vesta or Minerva or Martia was sometimes thought to be the name of one of the Parcae.[30]  As the daughters of Jove and Themis, moreover, the Fates might be linked with the Hours and the Graces and, in Valerianus' *Hieroglyphica,* with Janus *quadrifrons* as well.[31] The relationship of the myth of the Parcae with that of Lucina will appear later in this discussion, but other similar ramifications of the myth will have to be dismissed for the present.  For that matter, of the goddesses mentioned above, only the association of Venus with the Parcae is enlarged upon by the major mythographers.

The Fates' association with Love or Cupid, however, must be mentioned briefly, inasmuch as Love, or Phanes, was frequently represented, in accordance with Neo-Platonic tenets, as being the first major deity to arise from Chaos. This appearance of Love, according to Cartari, for example, was occasioned by the pleasure Nature felt for all things, represented by Pan, which she had created. With such a possible association between the Fates and Love, consequently, runs a very definite one between the Fates and Pan. Comes mentions this definite relationship only briefly, in a manner that links the Fates once more with the beginning of things. He writes that the Parcae, whose Chaos parentage he interprets in a manner very similar to that of Cartari, are sometimes thought to have been born with Pan from the same unformed chaotic matter: "Alii putarent has [Parcas] ex illa confusa et informi materia cum Pane pastorum Deo natas fuisse, quae Chaos ab antiquis fuit appellata." For Pan, according to Comes, is all-embracing nature, the nature of things, the gigantic universal mass that makes up natural bodies ("universam naturam," "rerum natura," "universa corporum naturalium moles").[32] Thus he should be represented as appearing at the first great separation concomitant with the determining cause effective in beginning, middle, and end.

As was true for the digest in the dictionaries based on Apuleius' interpretation, so in discussions of the origin of the Parcae, the compilers do not emphasize "cruel Atropos." Seldom, if ever, can all the details of a myth be worked out within the pattern of a single interpretation or a single group of references; for the handling of any myth in a work of art is dependent upon the particular purpose of a writer, and the résumés with which we are concerned are in turn dependent upon passages in various works by many authors. The ramifications of the myth of the Fates as they are concerned with beginnings grew out of the basic concept of the spinning *lanificae*. With a shift in emphasis toward the function of Atropos, or Morta, the same concept, particularly as it may concern the thread of man's life and destined end, gives the Parcae an entirely different group of associates. In the *Imagines Deorum,* the discussion of the Fates was part of the general discussion of Pluto. A similar classification occurs in Comes as well as in Gyraldus' *De Deis Gentium,* wherein the sixth syntagma is concerned with figures of the mythological underworld:

> Pluto & Persephone, dei silentum,
> Et Parcæ, & Furiæ, deique Manes,

Omnis denique cœtus inferorum,
Hoc Syntagmate sunt breui notati.

The concept that the Fates control the thread of man's life, its white-
ness or blackness, its fortunate or unfortunate nature, and its destined
end, makes their association with the Furies not surprising. Indeed a
1542 and a 1548 edition of Calepine's dictionary, indicate that the two
groups were perhaps being confused, for the entry on *Furiae* concludes
with these words: "Ne furias easdem esse cum Parcis existimes, quae
Parcae sint, suo loco cognosces." The close association between the
two groups is illustrated further by a passage in Comes that immediately
follows his genealogical discussion of the Fates. After noting that the
Parcae are called triform, Comes refers to Aeschylus' *Prometheus*, a
tragedy wherein the Fates are associated with the Furies (1.516). He
then continues his discussion by drawing from Pausanias a statement
that they were worshipped as gods with the same ceremony used for evok-
ing the Eumenides—a remark that might lead to an identification of the
two groups:

Has parcas triformes nominauit Aeschylus in Prometheo: quae pro Diis
summa religione colebantur apud Sicyonios, & eodem prope ritu, quo vocatae
Eumenides, vt testatur Pausanias in Corinthiacis.

The discussion in Cartari, moreover, includes a description of Morta,
or Atropos, pursuing Eteocles as he ran to kill Polynices, a description
which might well remind the reader of the pursuing and avenging Eumenides. The appearance of Morta is said to be more cruel than that
of any fierce beast, and Cartari considers the grouping of the figures to
mean that Polynices so died because of destiny but that Eteocles died
as he deserved because of his guilt.

Ceste cy [Morta] est descripte par Pausanias, quand il recite les choses grauees
et entaillees en l'arche de Cipsele. En ceste sorte la estoit (dit-il) Polynice
tombé à genoux, sur lequel couroit son frere Etheocle, pour le tuer, et derriere
estoit vne femme, ayant les dens et les ongles fort longues, qui sembloit à la
voir beaucoup plus cruelle que toute autre fiere beste, et estoit ceste la (ainsi
que les lettres qui y estoient grauees designoient) MORTE, l'vne des Parques, et vouloit signifier, que Polynice mouroit par tel destin, mais Etheocle
mouroit par sa coulpe, et l'ayant merité.

A similar account of the appearance of Morta, also taken from Pausanias'
description, occurs likewise in Comes immediately after the passage

wherein he refers to the *Prometheus,* although there are not as many details therein as in Cartari's account. Indeed, if the reader of the preceding account were familiar with other passages in Cartari's compilation, he might have encountered elsewhere another detail that referred to the same tragedy and that thereby might associate Fate with Fury more closely in his mind; for like Morta, one of the Furies, Tisiphone, was specifically connected in the *Imagines Deorum* with the story of Polynices and Eteocles.

The warning given in Calepine's dictionary might well have been needed, particularly after the publication of Comes and Cartari (i.e., after 1551, 1556), not simply because of such passages as those pointed out above, but also because of further associations of the Fatal Sisters with the realm of darkness and death. In Cartari, for example, after the correspondence in number between the Fates and the Furies had been pointed out, the passage in Claudian was cited wherein one of the Parcae, in addressing the king of the underworld, referred to the Fates as being under Pluto's rule:

Ces Parques furent en nombre tel que les Furies, et seruoient aussi à Pluton, comme vne d'elles le dit en Claudian, quand elle prie ce Roy d'enfer de ne faire point de guerre à Iupiter.

The association of the Fates with tribulation and death was emphasized, moreover, by their Latin names; and when mythographers discuss *Nona, Decima* and *Morta,* the information briefly noted in Charles Stephanus' *Dictionarium Historicum* is developed in some detail, particularly as Gyraldus, Comes, and Cartari follow the etymology attested by Varro which derives *Parcae* from *partu.* In this respect, the fullest discussion and the citation of the greatest number of authorities is found in Gyraldus:

Sed quoniam Parcas diximus ex eruditorum sententia appellatas, quòd minimè parcant: Varro tamen apud Gellium libro tertio, nomina Parcis antiquos ait fecisse à pariendo, & à nono atque decimo mense. nam Parca, inquit, immutata litera una, à partu nominata. item Nona & Decima, à partus tempestiui tempore. Cesellius autem Vindex in lectionibus suis antiquis: Tria, inquit, nomina Parcarum sunt, Nona, Decima, Morta. Et uersum hunc Liuij antiquissimi poëtæ ponit ex Odyssea,
Quando dies adueniet quem profata Morta est.
Sed homo minimè malus Cesellius, Mortam quasi nomen accepit, cùm accipere quasi μοῖζαρ deberet. atque hæc quidam ille.

Cartari in a corresponding passage emphasizes the connection of Nona and Decima with childbirth, and Comes goes even further. Following Pausanias, he notes that Lucina, the goddess of parturition, was thought by some of the ancients to be one of the Parcae:

. . . Lucinam ἑυηινοις, quasi Lanificam dixerim, vnam esse putauit e Parcis, quae dicta est Pepromene; quae Saturno multo fuit antiquior: quod etiam sensit Lycius Delius antiquissimus poeta, qui hymnos cum in alios Deos, tum in Lucinam composuit.

Indeed, Fulgentius' general interpretation of the myth of the Fates as it is repeated in the *Imagines Deorum* also links the Parcae with the ruler of the underworld. Fulgentius, as Cartari phrases it, meets the question of the relationship between Fate and God by making the Fates subservient to Pluto, since their force is over only terrestial things and Pluto represents the world:

Fulgence dit que les Parques sont promptes au seruice de Pluton, parce que leur force est seulement sur les choses terrestres, et nous auons desia dit que par Pluton est signifiee la terre.

A similar abstract of the material in Fulgentius might be found also in Boccaccio. In neither instance, of course, does the thought expressed agree with all statements made by ancient poets. Not infrequently even the supreme gods were said to be controlled by Fate or Destiny. At one point Comes, for example, writes "Arbitratus est Herodotus fatum non hominibus solum, sed etiam Dijs ipsis dominari"; but elsewhere in his compilation the force of Fate is sometimes said to be inferior to Jove or to be a symbol of his power.[33]

The report of Fulgentius' interpretation, however, does suggest once more that discussions involving the myth of the Parcae might well be concerned with considerations that Elyot would consider "right commendable and noble," in this instance, with *dicta* about the omnipotence of God and the freedom of man's will. The obvious identification of the Parcae with Fate—an identification for which Robert Stephanus cited Cicero[34]—provided such excellent material for moralizing that all of the mythographers with whom we are concerned devote considerable attention to explaining the force that might be symbolized by the Fatal Sisters. To such a discussion Georgius Sabinus, it will be remembered, devoted the longest portion of his interpretation of the fable of Ocyroë, and his analysis of the problem was thoroughly conventional when he wrote that the Parcae might signify divine providence, effective through celestial or elemental compulsion or through the managing of men.[35] Cartari, for example, expresses the basic assumption of the mythographers. He writes that by the fable of the Parcae, ancient poets meant to express the same idea philosophers did when they gave to the providence of God the power to dispose and order everything at one time. From such a power arose the force of Destiny, or as the Latins called it "Fatum":

Mais parce que plusieurs Philosophes anciens ont voulu que la prouidence de Dieu, ait disposé et ordonné vne fois toutes les choses, de maniere qu'elles ne se peuuent changer, parce que les causes d'icelles sont ainsi ordonnees ensemble, que d'elles mesmes elles les produisent, d'où vient la force de Destin, que les Latins appellent *Fatum:* aucuns ont dit, que les Poëtes ont entendu la mesme chose sous la fiction des Parques, et qu'ils en feirent trois, parce que chascune chose commence par vn principe, et cheminant par son moien, qui luy est approprié, elle paruient au but et fin à laquelle elle est destinee. . . .

The passage then continues as it was quoted above in the discussion of the Fates' Chaos parentage.

That the power of the Fates was derived from God, however, was not always apparent. Comes, for example, writes that the ancients, to whom the wisdom of Christianity had not been revealed, believed that each terrestial thing not only had a Genius to govern it but also was under the inexorable sway of "Fatum, vel Parcam":

Existimarvnt antiqui, quibus Christianae sapientiae semina nondum innotuerunt, omnia quae nascerentur siue animalia, siue essent plantae, siue aedificia, ac ciuitates, non solum proprium habere Genium, a quo perpetuo gubernarentur: sed etiam sub Parcarum atque fati potestate esse sita, ita vt quoties nasceretur aliquid, illi post certum dierum numerum ex ordine fatorum vel ferro, vel igne, vel aegritudine, vel sideratione, vel alio mortis genere esset pereundum: quam necessitatem nulla ratione, nullaque hominis prudentia deuitari posse putarunt: atque eandem vim in omnia sese extendere. Hanc vim Latine scriptores Fatum, vel Parcam: at Graeci μοῖραν, vel αἶσαν dixerunt: de cuius fati necessitate ita scripsit AEschylus in Prometheo. . . .

Furthermore, a "physical" interpretation of the myth results when moralizers consider such statements as the following ones by Juvenal: "For it makes all the difference by what stars you are welcomed when you utter your first cry, and are still red from your mother's womb," "What made their fortunes but the stars and the wondrous potency of secret Fate? The Fates will give kingdoms to a slave, and triumphs to a captive."[36] The myth of the Parcae, in other words, may be interpreted also as representing astral influence and the influence of other supraterrestial elements. Gyraldus, for example, includes such an interpretation in his summary when he writes that Clotho may be considered to be the seven planets; Lachesis, "res sublimares" (apparently all celestial things not included under Clotho and Atropos); and Atropos, the sphere of the fixed stars:

Sunt ueró qui Parcas ita interpretentur. per Clothon septem planetas, per Lachesin res sublimares: per Atropon autem Aplanen, id est interrantem sphæram.

Of all the reference works mentioned earlier, Valerianus' *Hieroglyphica* develops such an interpretation in the greatest detail. Although the discussion in the *Hieroglyphica* develops from Plato's *Republic,* wherein the Fates are represented as the singing daughters of Necessity, the interpretation accords with that for the myth as a whole, and the following passage occurs under the section "De Colu et Fuso":

Lachesin quippe firmamentum esse (vt superiorem fabulam apertius interpretemur) in cuius stellis vires sortesque inferiorum omnium contineantur. Clotho vero Planetarum coetum, in euoluendis rerum sortibus firmamento subministrarem. Atropon denique Saturnam, qui stabilitate sua eductas in effectum sortes immutabiliter confirmet: quae quoniam late apud eos disputantur, a me nunc praetereuntur.[37]

As one might surmise, the discussion concerning the immutability of Fate that is referred to in the preceding passage ("vt superiorem fabulam apertius interpretemur")[38] is too long for quotation here.  It pointed out that a star might signify Fate; began with a reference to Egyptian priests; and, among other things, referred to Plotinus, Augustine, Ambrose, as well as to recent writers—particularly Giovanni Pico, who objected severely to the conclusions of "mathematicians," that is, of astrologers.

Suffice it to say that after discussing the way in which the power of the Fates might represent the force of celestial configurations, the Christian mythographers usually conclude as does Comes.  He repeats the lines from Juvenal quoted above and argues that whatever happens is justly determined and governed by the highest God.  Nor is the force of the stars or of supraterrestial elements so powerfully in control of human affairs that it can master man's will or reason:

Nullam tamen vim astrorum esse putamus tantam, quae vim inferre vel nolentibus nobis possit, vel rationis consiliique potentiam opprimere: si quidem corpus animi habenis, at non contra corporis animus paret et obtemperat. Neque me tamen praeterit, quidquid ex anteactis rebus accidat, illud fatum a vulgo sapientum [*sic*] vocari solitum, quod alii Fortunam vocarunt, cum minime viderent omnia diuino quodam ordine gubernari ac nihil frustra accidere, neque e nullis antecedentibus principiis.[39]

Comes then continues by explaining why there are different origins assigned to Fate, that is, why there are a number of genealogies given to the Parcae. The various parents, in brief, represent various attitudes among men, ranging from that which wisely recognizes the justness of Destiny (the Parcae as the daughters of Jove and Themis) to that which foolishly emphasizes the cruelty of the Fates (the Parcae as the daughters of the Sea):

At nunc, quid ad morum probitatem sub his occultari senseruit antiqui, ex his discutiamus. Cum Parcas Iouis et Themidis, quae iustitia est, filias esse dicerent: illud significare voluerunt, quidquid vnicuique eueniret, illud et iure et pro meritis, rerumque gestarum dignitate contingere, et altissimi Dei consilio. Qui vero minus erant perspicaces, et in his magis caecutiebant, illi non pro meritis singulorum, sed ex inordinato fortunae cursu mala et bona hominibus euenire putarent: quare ex illa prima confusa materia Parcas euocatus dixerunt. Qui ex inscitia hominum mala contingere putarunt, ij Noctis filias Parcas appellarunt. Illi vero etiam qui obtusiore adhuc fuerunt ingenio, neque diuina prouidentia res humanas gubernari, neque quidquam diuino consilio regi putarunt, sed solam suppliciorum acerbitatem considerantes, minime perpendentes scelerum grauitatem, quia omnes maris filij crudeles et inordinati fuerunt, Parcas maris esse filias sunt arbitrati.

In other words, just as the dictionaries provided a kernel for interpretations of the myth previously mentioned, so here the lexicons by Calepine and Robert Stephanus summed up the moral of the myth by repeating Cleanthes' maxim: "Ducunt volentem fata, nolentem trahunt."

Finally, as we might expect, Renaissance mythographers point out that the Fates can also be connected with the figure of the goddess Fortuna and that Phurnutus—or rather Cornutus—joined the Parcae with Adrastia and Nemesis. For the present, however, we shall dismiss these ramifications of the interpretation of the myth with Gyraldus' words:— "Tu inde petas."

Adrastiam et Nemesin cum his [Fates] coniugit Phurnutus. Sed ipse in eo, in quo de Fortuna egi, eas copiose sum executus. Tu inde petas.

Before we turn from interpretations of the myth of the Parcae as *lanificae,* however, one section of Gyraldus' discussion deserves to be quoted in full, for it is a good example of the scholarly treatment a reader would find on turning to such a work as the *De Deis Gentium*. From even such a brief discussion, the Renaissance writer, editor, or scholar might ornament his discourse and refer to numerous authorities: Cicero, Phurnutus, Aristotle, Apuleius, Proclus, Hesiod, Boethius, Hesychius:

εἱμαρμενη etiam Parca, et Fatum dicitur. sed cuius uerbis potius eam describemus, quàm M. Tullij; qui Velleium inducit ita loquentem: Hic, inquit, nobis existit primùm illa fatalis necessitas, quam εἱμαρμενην dicitis, ut quicquid accidat, id ex æterna ueritate, causarumque continuatione fluxisse dicatis. Sed de Imarmene etiam plura Phurnutus de Deorum natura, item Aristoteles, et Apuleius de mundo. Proclus in Commentarijs Hesiodi in ἔργοις, Stoicos ait appellare Imarmenen διὸς νοῦν, super ea Hesiodi verba . . . id est, nusquam est Iouis mentem aufugere. Chrysippus: *Imarmene, inquit, sempiterna quaedam et indeclinabilis rerum series, et catena, sese uoluens et implicans per æternos consequentiæ ordines, è quibus connexa est.* His conformia scribunt et Phurnutus, et Boëtius in Topicis, εἱμαρμενη uero dicta . . . quoniam trahat et cedat consequenter. Hesychius ait, Imarmenen à Cretensibus uocari ἀμεργὸν. Plurimi etiam ἀνάγκην, id est necessitatem, cum Imarmene describunt, inter quos Phurnutus, qui ait: Anance est, quam cogere aut uincere non possumus, si quidem ei omnia ut ad causam referuntur.

Also interesting to note in this connection is the fact that once more the kernel of a discussion in the basic mythological treatises might be found in the lexicons. The *Dictionarium Historicum* alone fails to include material drawn from Cicero's *De Divinatione*. In other mythological entries, the editors of Charles Stephanus frequently abstract pertinent interpretative material, generally from Comes; but perhaps in this instance they felt that the obvious connection between *Parcae, Fata* and the common noun *fatum* made further elucidation unnecessary. Be that as it may, among the lexicons the fullest account comparable to the passage quoted above from the *De Deis Gentium* occurs, as might be expected, in Robert Stephanus' *Thesaurus*. There the long entry under *fatum* in the 1543 edition lists at least seventy-nine citations and quotations from classical authorities before *fatalis* and other derivative words are considered. An equal number of citations can be found in Cooper. Although the passage based on the *De Divinatione* is greatly condensed in the Latin-English *Thesaurus*, in three of the basic lexicons might be found material that referred to Cicero's discussion of *heimarmenē*, or εἱμαρμένη, and that repeated his definition of Fate as being the series of causes linking cause with cause and flowing eternally from eternity by which "ea quae praeterierunt, facta sint; et quae instant, fiant; et quae sequuntur futura sint."[40]    The concept expressed agrees, of course, with such statements under *Parcae* as the following from Robert Stephanus' lexicon: "Ideo tres esse Parcas arbitrantur, quoniam tria sunt tempora, in quibus omnia voluuntur."

Although the lexicons provide no such array of authorities upon the word εἱμαρμένη as did the *De Deis Gentium,* they certainly were instrumental in making Cicero's thought an academic commonplace.    Whether or not a student were familiar at first hand with material in the *De Divinatione* (I, lv-lvi), the thought expressed there and repeated sometimes verbatim in reference lexicons of the age might easily be related to the myth of the Parcae and could appear in a discussion expounding doctrine that the most moralistic of educators would find commendable.    More specifically, however, some such information as that italicized above in the passage from Gyraldus—but with implications less universal—was perhaps in Donne's mind when he wrote:

> She who was such a chaine as Fate employes
> To bring mankinde all Fortunes it enjoyes;
> So fast, so even wrought, as one would thinke,
> No Accident could threaten any link.
> (*Second Anniversary,* 143-46)

Bacon, too, was probably familiar with similar information when he moulded much of the material we have been discussing into a brief résumé:

To the Nature of things [*i.e.,* Pan], the Fates or destinies of things are truly represented as sisters.  For natural causes are the chain which draws after it the births and durations and deaths of all things; their fallings and risings, their labours and felicities: —in short all the fates that can befall them.[41]

A discussion of such parallels, however, must await a brief survey of the way in which the Parcae might appear as scribes or as the singing daughters of Necessity.

As commentaries on the *Tristia* and *Metamorphoses* indicate, the Renaissance also conceived of the Fates as those who wrote down the immutable decrees of the Gods and as those who turned the gigantic spindle of Necessity.    Both of these conceptions can be treated briefly, for the Renaissance compiler, when making his résumé of this material, found only a few authorities to abridge.    Perottus, for example, cites Martianus Capella as the authority for the first of these conceptions: "Martianus non ignobilis author has deorum scribas esse inquit, et sententias Iovis studio veritatis excipere." Gyraldus gives essentially the same information about the Parcae as scribes or keepers of the celestial archives. He also adds the detail that one speaks, the second writes, while the third spins out the threads, i.e., elaborates, perhaps:

> Parcas tres existimabant ueteres: unam loqui, alteram scribere, tertiam fila deducere. propterea Parcas, scribas ac librarias superum uocat Martianus: Clotho, inquit, Lachesis, Atroposque, quoniam sententias Iouis orthographæ studio ueritatis excipiunt, utpote librariæ superum, archiuique custodes.

Comes includes in his discussion an explanatory comment about the Fates as scribes and cites Homer for repeating the commonplace that they bestow man's fortune upon him at his birth: "Creditae sunt Parcae esse Deorum scribae atque quidquid euenturum esset nascentibus iam tum hominibus impartiri, vt testatur Homerus in lib. η Odysseae. . . ." The passage in the *Odyssey*, however, supports only the latter half of the statement: when Odysseus is in his land, he will receive whatever fate the Parcae wove into his thread at birth (VII, 197).[42] The *Imagines Deorum* enlarges upon the Fates as "librariæ superum, archiuique custodes." Cartari writes that Jupiter's control over them, or over Destiny, may be the reason that some writers consider them the chancellors of the gods. Their duty would be to understand the will of Jupiter and the decisions of the celestial senate and to write down the decrees in anticipation of the day when they would be put into execution:

> . . . car luy [Iupiter] seul tient les Parques en sa puissance, et luy seul fait ce que le Destin, ou (pour mieux dire) l'ordonnance de Dieu ordonne: d'où il aduient parauenture, que quelques vns l'ont appellé chancellier des Dieux, comme que ce soit son office d'entendre la volonté de Iupiter, et les ordonnances de tout le Senat celeste, et les mettre par escript, à fin qu'elles se puissent estendre en apres au temps de les mettre en execution.

Cartari's illustration, consequently, includes paper, pen, and ink bottle on a stone slab at the feet of the Three Sisters (Plate I). The statement at the beginning of the quotation to the effect that Jupiter controls the Fates is, of course, entirely in keeping with a Christian interpretation of the myth; for Jove as the ruler of the gods may represent the true God's attribute of omnipotence. Indeed, the basic conception of the Parcae as *fatum*, applies not simply to the Fates as *lanificae* but to these two other representations as well.

The *Thesaurus Linguae Latinae* and the other dictionaries, however, neglect both the conceptions with which we are here concerned. Inasmuch as the compilations of Robert and Charles Stephanus show an indebtedness to Perottus, the exclusion of the Fates as scribes may have been a conscious one, dictated by the need for compression perhaps, or perhaps by the fact that this representation of the Parcae was not found in the best classical authors; for according to later reference works the conception of the Fates as scribes rested primarily upon Martianus Capella. The exclusion from the lexicons of the third conception of the Fates, i.e., the Parcae as the daughters of Necessity, is clearly understandable in a work like the *Thesaurus* which is concerned only with the Latin tongue. Indeed, most of Charles Stephanus' citations are likewise from Latin authors. And this third conception rests upon a portion of Er's vision in Plato's *Republic,* although Comes, after speaking of the Parcae as daughters of Necessity, also cites the Orphic hymns for their living in a cavern on high whence their influence is felt on human affairs.

Alii Necessitatis, siue (vt aiunt Graeci) ἀνάγκης filias esse Parcas crediderunt. Has in spelunca quadam sublimi habitasse scripsit Orpheus, atque inde ad humana opera, vbi libuerit, euolare solitas. . . .

As Gyraldus points out, the conventional *locus classicus* for this third basic conception of the Fates was the tenth book of the *Republic,* wherein is described the revolving spindle moved by the Fates who sing of past, present, and future.[43] That the Parcae control the revolution of things is, of course, not incompatible with statements already encountered in the lexicons.

A résumé of the pertinent matter in Plato that is most nearly complete is found in Cartari's compilation.

Platon les fait estre filles de la Deesse Necessité, entre les genoux de laquelle il met ce grand fuseau de diamant, qui tient d'vn pole iusques à l'autre, et les Parques qui demeurent assises pres de la mere, egalement distantes l'vne de l'autre sus vn siege haut et esleué, qui chantent auec les Sirenes, qui sont par dessus les Spheres du ciel, asçauoir Lachesis du passé, Clothon du present, et Atropos de l'aduenir, et toutes semblablement mettent la main au fuseau, auec la Deesse Necessité, leur mere: en ceste sorte, Clothon y met la main droite, Atropos la gauche, et Lachesis auec les deux mains, le touche deçà et delà, et sont toutes trois vestues de drap blanc, et ont la teste enuironnee d'vne couronne. Poursuit en apres Platon, disant que comme les sorts ou aduentures de la vie de l'homme viennent de Lachesis, et quelques autres choses qui con-

PLATE II

tiennent sens et intelligences fort haultes, et tresgrands mysteres, comme ie declareray, quand i'escriray de l'ame. . . .

The preceding abstract, however, omits Plato's detailed description of the spindle, whose large hollow whorl has seven others fitted within it. The peculiar motion and appearance of the eight correspond to Plato's conception of the movement and appearance of the spheres of the seven planets and the fixed stars. Consequently, a later passage that depends upon this description is also omitted by Cartari; namely, Plato's statement that Clotho assists the revolution of the outer circle, Atropos those of the inner ones, and Clotho "either in turn." As part of this last detail, the "deçà et delà" of the preceding passage is a poor substitute. Omitted likewise from Cartari's description is Plato's assertion that the Sirens on the upper surface of the spheres revolve with the whorls, each "uttering a single tone or note" and all eight producing the harmony of the spheres. Otherwise the account given by Cartari is accurate, save for a few details. In the *Imagines Deorum,* the Parcae have crowns instead of Plato's chaplets, and the spindle of diamond or adamant is slightly more complicated in the *Republic* than in the preceding description. In Plato, the spindle has a staff and a hook of adamant, and a whorl, partly of adamant and partly of other material. The appropriate illustration in Cartari is accordingly based clearly upon the compiler's words rather than upon Plato's (Plate II). Cartari also adds to Plato's description the obvious detail that the throne upon which the Fates sit is on high ("haut et esleué"). His allotment of the past to Lachesis, the present to Clotho, and the future to Atropos agrees with the *Republic.*

The details just considered are not of particular importance here, save as they fill in a background against which some of the literature of the period can be projected. The particular function of each Fate in the *Republic* after the souls have made their choice from the sample of lives need not detain us. Nor need we stop for a final, different representation of the Fates described by Cartari. Concerning its illustration (Plate III) the French version of the *Imagines Deorum* gives an abbreviated account that is sufficient:

Il ne souuient d'auoir veu autresfois, au liure des antiquailles recuillies par Pierre Appian, les Parques peintes en ceste sorte, comme il dit qu'elles estoient en vne lame de plomb, qui fut iadis trouuee au païs de Stirie, (maintenant dicte Sclauonie, vers Hongrie) en l'an 1500.

PLATE III

That all of the material just surveyed was known to the average school-boy is very doubtful. Most of the students were probably of a "rurall humor," being satisfied, as Abraham Fraunce phrases it, with "a pleasant and plausible narration." Others who could "reach somewhat further then the external discourse and history" might have become interested in the "morall sence" of the myth, which would be "euery way profitable for the institution of a practicall and commonwealth man." Yet all of the preceding material by the latter part of the sixteenth century was easily available to mature writers, and at least a few schoolboys might have sucked matter and words "like so many bees" from the compilations mentioned above. In contrast to those of a "rurall humor," or to those who might become "practicall and commonwealth" men, at least a few students, even in the myth of the Parcae, might have found "hidden mysteries of naturall, astrologicall, or diuine and metaphysicall philosophie, to entertaine their heauenly speculation."[44] Regardless of Fraunce's classification of contemporary readers of poetry, however, what was encountered in Cooper, Calepine, Charles and Robert Stephanus was sound germinal knowledge of a myth; and to those lexicons the average school-boy probably turned when in his study of Ovid he was expected to "relate such Histories as the proper names will hint at." If anything, the abstracts on the Fates are less complete than are the majority of mytho-logical entries in the dictionaries, and yet as the preceding discussion clearly shows the information found in the reference lexicons provided a thoroughly adequate basis for details and ramifications of the myth found in the more specialized treatises of the period. Although the lexi-cons, for instance, do not mention the Parcae as secretaries of the gods or as the daughters of Necessity, those two conceptions of the Fatal Sis-ters are entirely congruent with the seminal interpretations in the diction-aries and with the material devoted to the better known conception of the Fates as *lanificae*.

On the basis of such considerations, Jonson appears to be much less esoteric than sometimes has been thought when he quotes from Comes or refers to Gyraldus or parallels matter in the *Imagines Deorum,* or when in his references to the Fates he refers to Martial, for example. He was, of course, thoroughly familiar with the Latin poet; and his annotated copy of Scriverius' edition (1619) shows that he was a "keen lover" of that writer.[45] Jonson likewise may have known that Gyraldus enlarged upon implications in Martial's lines when writing about the Fates as *lani-ficae,* or that Cartari referred to the thread of life being long or short as it was made of strong or weak material. But even when reference lexicons did not quote lines from Martial, they at least repeated the idea expressed by

> Si mihi lanificae ducunt non pulla sorores
> Stamina, nec surdos vox habet ista deos.

And this commonplace aspect of the myth Jonson frequently utilized when he referred to a blessed life of even thread or of the whitest wool; or when, as in the following verses, he combined both ideas with that of the Parcae conferring benefits at birth upon mankind:

> . . . the destin'd heire
> In his soft Cradle, to his Fathers Chaire,
> Whose even Thred the Fates spinne round, and full,
> Out of their Choysest, and their whitest wooll.
>                      (*The Vnder-wood,* LI, "Lord Bacons
>                      Birth-day," 13-16)

In other words, in spite of Jonson's admiration for Martial, during the English Renaissance an appreciation of the mythological reference expressed in such lines actually demanded of writer and reader no recollection of any one classical writer per se. Current mythological compilations, even current reference lexicons, would have sufficed. Similarly, all listeners with a grammar-school education probably appreciated the humor in Lancelot Gobbo's "Fates and Destinies and such odd sayings, the Sisters Three and such branches of learning," or the drunken rhetoric of Pistol, wherein "grievous, ghastly, gaping wounds untwine" the Parcae, or the comical incongruity in referring to Bottom-Pyramus' life as a "thread of silk."[46]

Even a passage that at first glance might seem to involve the reflection of a number of classical texts can sometimes be shown to be adequately represented in dictionary entries. Consider the learned Jonson's invocation of the Fates:

> Daughters of night, and secrecie, attend;
> You, that draw out the chayne of *Destinie,*
> Vpon whose threds, both liues and times depend,
> And all the periods of mortalitie.
>                      (*Entertainment at Theobalds,* 48-51)

The parentage of the Fates agrees with that given by the dictionaries: ". . . Cicero .3.de Nat. deor. 59, Erebi et Noctis filias fuisse scribit, et easdem fata esse existimat." For "Erebus" Jonson has written "secrecie"—an interpretation of the name that, like the preceding genealogy, could be found in classical authors and in the works of Renaissance mythographers but that could also be found under "Erebus" in the lexicons. Moreover, Cicero's discussion of Fate appears when the lexicographers discuss *Fatum* as the word or command of God and go on to give the meaning of the Greek εἱμαρμένη. It is the eternal series linking cause with cause whereby effect is produced and the future and past connected. Robert Stephanus, for example, reproduces Cicero verbatim:

Vnde fatum, iussum, & dictum dei. Cic. 1. de Diuinat. 203, Fieri igitur omnia a fato, ratio cogit fateri. Fatum autem id appello quod Graeci εἱμαρμένην, id est ordinem, seriemque causarum, quum causae causa nexa, rem ex se gignat. ea est ex omni aeternitate fluens veritas sempiterna. quod quum ita sit, nihil est factum quod non futurum fuerit: eodemque modo nihil est futurum, cuius non causas idipsum efficientes natura contineat. ex quo intelligitur vt fatum sit, non id quod superstitiose, sed id quod Physice dicitur causa aeterna rerum, cur et ea quae praeterierunt facta sint: et quae instant, fiant: et quae sequuntur, futura sint.

That the Fates draw out the chain of destiny and thereby control the threads upon which the lives of men depend repeats matter that refers, in Cooper's words, to the way in which the Fates "spinne out the threede of mannes lyfe so long as it doth continue." That the Parcae control not simply the lives of men but "times" and indeed all "periods of mortalitie" agrees, of course, not only with the preceding passage from the *Thesaurus* but also with the way in which the lexicons turn to Apuleius' interpretation of the myth after discussing the *lanificae*. All of the preceding details, of course, can be found in classical literature; but they were also in the compendiums by Gyraldus, Comes, and Cartari; and the particulars in Jonson's invocation would be familiar also to anyone who had perused the "history" of the Parcae in the reference dictionaries available in grammar school libraries.

At times, indeed, the entries in the lexicons seem to explain, and do elucidate, features of an author's reference to the Fates. Consider the speeches Jonson wrote for the Fates in his *An Entertainment of the King and Queen at Theobalds*. The Parcae are speaking to the Genius of Theobalds. In the audience are King James, Queen Anne, the Prince of Lorraine, and Prince Henry. Under the latter, England, of course, looked forward to a continuous reign by the House of Stuart. In such a context Jonson gives Clotho's speech the form of a prophecy:

> When, vnderneath thy roofe, is seene
> The greatest King, and fairest Queene,
> With Princes an vnmatched payre,
> One, hope of all the earth, their heyre;
> The other styled of *Lorraine,*
> Their bloud; and sprung from CHARLEMAINE:
> When all these Glories iointly shine,
> And fill thee with a heat diuine,
> And these reflected, doe beget
> A splendent Sunne, shall neuer set,
> But here shine fixed, to affright
> All after-hopes of following night,
> Then, GENIVS, is thy period come,
> To change thy Lord: Thus, Fates doe doome.
>                                       (59-72)

Referring only to James and Anne, however, that is to the present rulers of England, Lachesis applies Clotho's speech to the immediate occasion:

> The person, for whose royall sake,
> Thou must a change so happie make,
> Is he, that gouernes with his smile,
> This lesser world, this greatest Isle.
> His Ladies seruant thou must be;
> Whose second would great NATVRE see,
> Or FORTUNE, after all their paine,
> They might despaire to make againe.
>                                       (95-103)

Finally, Atropos, in paying a courtly compliment to James' queen, refers to the past and to the queen whom the founder of Theobalds had served most loyally:

> She is the grace of all, that are:
> And as ELISA, now a starre,
> Vnto her crowne, and lasting praise,
> Thy humbler walls (at first) did raise,
> By vertue of her best Aspect;
> So shall BEL-ANNA them protect:
> And this is all, the *Fates* can say;
> Which first beleeue, and then obay.
>                                       (105-12)

From the preceding discussion, it will be remembered that among the mythographers there was no general agreement about the allotment of future and present to Clotho and Lachesis. Nor was there any agreement among classical authors, between Apuleius and Plato, for example. Information to the effect that Clotho controlled the future (and held the distaff) and that Lachesis controlled the present could be found in late Italian editions of the *Imagines Deorum,* in the *Genealogiae Deorum,* and in the *De Deis Gentium;* but Boccaccio and Gyraldus also gave the alternate allotment of time. In the dictionaries, however, particularly in Robert Stephanus' *Thesaurus,* the division found in Jonson's entertainment appeared most forcefully. Whether or not the particular entry in Robert Stephanus' lexicon was in Jonson's mind when he wrote the preceding lines, whether or not he reflected knowledge acquired during his school-days from the dictionaries with which we are concerned, the fact remains that the idea Jonson chose to utilize here was, consciously or unconsciously, the one that in all probability would be most familiar to his audience. With Jonson, indeed, one expects a conscious and purposeful use of such details.

A comparable situation results when one examines two instances of the treatment of the Parcae in the *Faerie Queene.* Spenser's fullest description of the Fatal Sisters appears in the fourth book and concerns the fate of Agape's sons:

> Therefore desirous th'end of all their dayes
> To know, and them t'enlarge with long extent,
> By wondrous skill and many hidden wayes
> To the three Fatall Sisters house she went.
> Farre under ground from tract of living went,
> Downe in the bottom of the deepe Abysse,
> Where Demogorgon, in dull darknesse pent,
> Farre from the view of gods and heavens blis,
> The hideous Chaos keepes, their dreadfull dwelling is.
>
> There she them found, all sitting round about
> The direfull distaffe standing in the mid,
> And with unwearied fingers drawing out
> The lines of life, from living knowledge hid.
> Sad *Clotho* held the rocke, the whiles the thrid
> By griesly *Lachesis* was spun with paine,
> That cruell *Atropos* eftsoones undid,

With cursed knife cutting the twist in twaine:
Most wretched men, whose dayes depend on thrids so vaine.
(4. 2. 47-48)

In the succeeding stanzas, Spenser speaks of the short and thin threads of Agape's children and of the immutable decrees of the Fates.

As others have pointed out, Spenser's references to the abode of the Fatal Sisters seem to reflect material in Boccaccio and Comes. Comes speaks of the Fates' being received into the cave of Chaos; both Boccaccio and Comes associate Demogorgon with caves; and other similar details can be found in the *De Genealogiae Deorum* and *Mythologiae*.[47] In view of the preceding survey, however, to the mythographers mentioned, one might add Textor, Cartari, and Gyraldus as writers whose works also contain particulars that might be considered pertinent to an elucidation of the preceding stanzas. Although Spenser does not specifically call the Parcae daughters, or offspring, of Demogorgon or Chaos, Textor as well as Boccaccio names Demogorgon as their parent and Cartari as well as Comes names Chaos. Gyraldus and Comes, for example, as well as Boccaccio, give information that would make the Fates coeval with the beginning of things (in Gyraldus also Clotho's name is interpreted as *evocatio*). From a consideration of Stanza XLVII, consequently, there can be little doubt that Spenser knew material not found in the dictionaries but found in current mythological compendiums, as well as in classical literature—although it would be difficult to specify any one or any two works as his immediate source. Even more commonplace than the details mentioned above are Spenser's references to the thread of life and to the immutable decrees of the Fates and his association of the Parcae with darkness. This last feature of the myth, emphasized by Spenser, was connected with the Fates' Erebus-Night parentage, a genealogy found in all the works surveyed above.

In Stanza XLVIII, however, the only image of the Parcae which Spenser enlarges upon is obviously the common one found in the Latin tag that is repeated in slightly different form by Gyraldus and Robert Stephanus ("Clotho colum retinet, Lachesis net, et Atropos occat"; "Clotho, colum baiulat; Lachesis, net; Atropos, filum frangit"). Such a conception of the Fates had been developed earlier in E. K.'s gloss ("November," 148), which in comparison with Spenser's stanza lacks only the detail of Atropos' knife:

Atropos . . . With cursed knife cutting the twist in twaine.. . .
(Spenser)
Atropos, is said to have cut the threde in twain.. . .
(E. K.)

Except for the Latin tag, moreover, the conception as developed by E. K. in its length, the extent of its information, and its phrasing, finds its closest counterpart in Cooper's Latin-English *Thesaurus*. E. K. writes

The fatall sisters, Clotho, Lachesis, and Atropos, daughters of Herebus and the Night, whom the poetes fayne to spinne the life of man, as it were of a long threde, which they drawe out in length, till his fatal houre and timely death be come; but if by other casualtie his dayes be abridged, then one of them, that is Atropos, is sayde to have cut the threde in twain. Hereof commeth a common verse.
"Clotho colum bajulat, Lachesis trahit, Atropos occat."

Cooper's entry is as follows:

*Parcae,* Ladyes of destinie. The names of them bee *Clotho, Lachesis,* and *Atropos.* The first of them is deuised to beare the distaffe, the seconde to spinne out the threede of mannes lyfe so long as it doth continue, the thirde breaketh of the threede, and endeth the mans life. They are ymagined to bee the daughters of *Erebus,* and *Nox.*

Once more a mature writer of the Renaissance has apparently chosen to utilize information about the Parcae which in all probability was best known to his age—and one suspects best known to the author. E. K. at any rate was glossing the *Shepheardes Calender* in the manner approved by the schools and thus relating "such Histories as the proper names shall hint at." When placed against the mythological information available to the period, his note on the Fates is closest to an entry in the reference lexicon that was frequently worn out by hard use.

Spenser's description of the Parcae and his reference to the immutable decrees of Fate, should be considered also in the light of a passage in the third book where Britomart and Glaucé go to Merlin for advice. There the reader learns that the warrior-maid had loved "by fatall lore." She looked into the enchanted glass by

. . . the streight course of heauenly destiny
Led with eternall prouidence

to bring "his will to pass." Spenser, consequently, represents Glaucé as asking not simply how Britomart will find and recognize the man who

will sire her illustrious progeny but also why there is any need of action
since all has been ordained,

> . . . sith fates can make
> Way for themselves, their purpose to partake.

The result is that Merlin's words provide a moral inculcating, as previous
commentators have noted, the Renaissance Platonism and vigorous Virgilian ethics which went into Spenser's ideal of chastity.

> Indeede the Fates are firme,
> And may not shrinck, though all the world do shake:
> Yet ought mens good endeuours them confirme,
> And guyde the heauenly causes to their constant terme.
>
> (3. 3. 25)

As a portion of the preceding survey indicates, however, Merlin's words
also reflect the conventional moral of the myth of the Parcae, particularly
as it might inculcate the doctrine that men of good will are led by the
Fates—or, as Spenser expresses it even more positively, that such men
attempt to further the decrees of eternal providence. The closest parallel
to Merlin's advice, consequently, are the words of Cleanthes, found in
Boccaccio, Calepine, and Robert Stephanus. Boccaccio, however, had
developed his reference to Cleanthes into a discussion wherein the emphasis was different from that in Spenser's lines. He stressed man's
impotence in the hands of Fate and, among other things, referred to the
Senecan *Œdipus*.[48]   In Seneca's epistle wherein Cleanthes' words appear,
the thought was developed in a manner similar to Comes' exposition of
the myth: the great soul surrenders itself to fate while the puny and de-
generate one struggles and sees only evil in the universe. The maxim inculcated by the discourse was essentially negative: what can't be cured
must be endured.[49]   The words of Cleanthes by themselves, consequently,
as they are expressed in reference lexicons ("Ducunt volentem fata, nolentem trahunt") appear to be closest to Spenser's even more positive emphasis. The confronting counsel of Merlin is, of course, thoroughly in
accord with Spenser's doctrine throughout the *Faerie Queene*. But there
can be little doubt that in Merlin's reference to the Fates, Spenser struck
a note which would be meaningful, and would have at least a degree of
familiarity, for his average reader. The reference lexicons, indeed, may
have influenced the poet to develop in such a manner the conventional
moral of the myth of the Parcae.

Certain other conventional aspects of the myth are likewise revealing. Consistently in Renaissance literature, for example, protests against the Fates appear side by side with reflections of the moral or philosophical interpretation of the myth. Such key words in Textor and Robert Stephanus as "Crudeles," "Durae," "Feroces," "Immites," "Impiae," "Iniquae," "Malignae," "Nocentes," "Rapaces," "Saevae," and "Tristes" correspond to such phrases and lines as Spenser's *"cruell* fates," (*F. Q.* 1. 7 22), "Fates *perverse* with *Guileful* love," (*F. Q.* 4. 7. 15), "Th' *importune* Fates, which *vengeance* on me seeke," (*Daph.*, 386-87), the

> Fatall Sisters, whose *sad* hands
> Doo weave the *direfull* threds of destinie,
> And in their *wrath* breake off the vitall bands.
> (*Daph.* 16-18)

And elsewhere in Spenser and in Renaissance literature there are many passages in which the Parcae "seem to be regarded as merely capricious or vengeful." Yet in other verses in the same work, they may often appear "in a philosophical sense":[50]—as in "The Fates divine decree," (*F. Q.* 4. 3. 21), "The eternall doome of Fates decree," (*F. Q. 7. 6.* 33), or in

> . . . for what the Fates do once decree
> Not all the gods can chaunge, nor Jove him selfe can free....
> (*F. Q.* 4. *2.* 51-2)

For Fates as *fatum* was simply a common interpretation of the myth of the Parcae, who bestow all things on men and who are described differently by men wise and foolish, fortunate and unfortunate. A realization that fate made fortune what it was, as well as the specific association of the Parcae with the goddess Fortuna, also illuminates the neat appropriateness of "the whore Fortune, and her bawds the Fates." To Renaissance author and reader—in view of statements in mythological compendiums—it might well be sound antiquity and not "Elizabethan license" when Cethegus so referred to the fickle goddess.[51] With a knowledge that *Parcae* equalled Fate, which was the command of the gods or a manifestation of God Himself, one can perceive that Tamburlaine's "I hold the Fates fast bound in iron chaines" might well have had blasphemous implications for at least some members of an Elizabethan audience.[52] Conversely, a Renaissance poet might base his lines upon *fatum* or Destiny, upon "the true meaning of the myth," but write in the plural of the Fates or even of the Destinies. Thus in his "Progresse of the Soule," John Donne shifts between "Fate" and "Fates," and Jonson writes of "Destinees"

(l. 186) in his poem "To Elizabeth, Countess of Rutland." The relationship between the Three Sisters and fate may also involve a reference to the power of the Parcae. Even the gods may be ignorant of all their ordinances, or their power may depend upon Jove. Such logically conflicting statements were reconciled by the moral found in the myth; and a recognition of the fact that its Christian interpretation was probably very well known, aids one sometimes in understanding an author's purpose.

In the *Masque of Augurs,* for example, Apollo is represented as singing the following verses, wherein he states that the Fates ordain events which they keep hidden from the gods:

> *Doe not expect to heare of all*
> *Your good at once, lest it forestall*
> *A sweetnesse would be new:*
> *Some things the* Fates *would have conceal'd*
> *From us the Gods, lest, being reveal'd,*
> *Our powers shall envy you.*
>
> (412-17)

The lines, of course, are addressed to the principal person in the audience, James I. They follow predictions of success for whatever course of action might be undertaken by James. Linus, Orpheus, Branchus, and Idmon say that he shall control "the course of things" which are now "with tumult carried" and that he shall live free from hatred, conspiracy, and the fear of having to break his peace policy ("the feare/To blast the Olive thou dost weare"). The year 1622 was the third after the Bohemian revolt; the first after Spain's truce with Holland had ended; and James' peace policy, as it applied to Spain, was becoming increasingly unpopular. The lines which had been addressed to the king immediately preceding Apollo's speech recognize the possibility of war; but express the thought that if it occurs it will be a just war—that is, a war, which in accordance with precepts *de regimine principum,* would be for the purpose of peace and good rule over those who had been subjects of a tyrant instead of a king:

> *Thy neighbors at thy fortune long have gaz'd,*
> *But at thy wisdom, all doe stand amaz'd,*
> *And wish to be*
> *O'ercome, or governed by thee!*
> *Safetie it selfe so sides thee, where thou go'st,*
> *And* Fate *still offers what thou covet'st most!*
>
> (404-9)

Jonson's audience, however, included foreign ambassadors as well as the principal rulers of England. As James' opponents knew only too well, no law could be passed in Parliament without the English king's assent, even though the course of events, which was controlled thereby through the king's nod, might make any particular act necessary; and the question of abandoning a peace policy, as far as a declaration of war itself was concerned, theoretically rested solely in the hands of James. Consequently, Jonson well might liken attributes belonging to James as the center of the court and the ruler of the English commonweal to attributes given by ancient poets to Jove. When read in such a light, the final mythological conception of the masque (in which Fate is said to become effective with the approval or nod, the "beck," of Jove) becomes congruent with preceding passages in the masque and like them can be made applicable to the audience and the occasion. Although the future and the total course of events may be unknown to gods and men and is controlled by the Fates as *fatum* or destiny, which derives its power from God's word, Jove and James must with a nod approve any immediate or present action for a decree to become effective—particularly, as far as James is concerned, if it be a declaration of war.

> Jove *is that one, whom first, midst, last, you call,*
> *The power that governes, and conserveth all;*
> *Earth, Sea, and Ayre, are subject to our checke,*
> And Fate, *with Heaven, moving at our beck.*
> *Till* Jove *it ratifie,*
> *It is no* Augurie,
> *Though utter'd by the mouth of* Destinie.
>
> (444-50)

Touching upon a delicate subject with which James and other members of the audience were concerned at the time, Jonson handles the matter with consumate skill and caution. By utilizing conventional poetic materials, he manages to rule out neither war nor peace; and he also pleases James, who insisted upon his supremacy.

Although such mythological references tell us nothing about an author's indebtedness to any other author or to any one compilation, the material found in current reference works does at times provide a backgroud against which the literature of the period appears to be more concretely or more skillfully conceived than it might seem to be at first glance. Such a background likewise aids one in appreciating a contemporary audience's understanding of Renaissance literature. To enlarge upon other references to the Parcae, however, would have little bearing upon the purpose of a study concerned primarily with the basic reference lexicons of the period. A few final examples will perhaps suffice. The relationship between the Parcae and the Furies as surveyed above illuminates some of Milton's lines in *Lycidas.* There Atropos or Morta appears as the Fury with "abhorred shears" (73-76) and reminds one of matter that can be found in Cartari—material, for example, which is based on Pausanias' description of Morta pursuing Eteocles.[53]   Such a description in the *Imagines Deorum* probably had a much wider circulation, among Milton's readers at least, than did the text of Pausanias or the *Prometheus* of Aeschylus, a work to which some of Milton's contemporary readers might also have been referred by Comes.[54]   Similarly a connection between Lucina and the Fates might well have been known to those who had used the *Mythologiae,* and such a relationship is also encountered in Milton's "Epitaph on the Marchioness of Winchester" (23-30).   Jonson's note on Love, or Phanes, being awakened by Clotho and emerging from Chaos, appears to have been taken from the *De Deis Gentium*[55] and the same information can be found in Spenser's "An Hymne in Honour of Love." Jonson's merging of two conceptions of the Parcae likewise illustrates how the material surveyed above is paralleled in the literature of the period.   In the *Entertainment at Theobalds*—portions of which have been discussed above—and also in *Lovers Made Men,* the poet gives the Fates not simply the distaff, spindle, and shears of the spinners but also the book of the scribes.[56]   Such a combination, of course, might have been suggested by the stone slab and the writing utensils in Cartari's image of the Parcae as *lanificae.*   But only Milton's merging of two of the three conceptions of the Fates can be discussed in any detail.

When one remembers Milton's own feeling for the "sweet compulsion" that "doth in music lie," his references to the music of the spheres, and his second Prolusion, one might well expect him to represent poetically the conception of the Fates as the singing daughters of Necessity.   When he does so in the *Arcades,* there can be little doubt that he was familiar with Er's vision in Plato's *Republic.*[57]   His description of the spindle alone substantiates such a conclusion in comparison with the abridged version of Plato found in the *Imagines Deorum;* and his statement that the "fate of gods and men" is wound on the spindle reflects Er's account of the Fates' action after the souls have made their choice from the lots of life offered to them. Details not in the *Republic* appear when Milton adds the fate of gods to the fate of men, quite in accordance with the Christian interpretation of the myth; when his enfolded spheres are nine in number instead of eight; and when his daughters of Necessity turn the spindle around instead of only assisting in the revolution of the spheres. Consideration of such minor variations between the *Arcades* and the *Republic* need not detain us, however. Of particular interest is the way in which Milton has strengthened the association which might be found in Plato between the Fates as daughters of Necessity and the Fates as *lanificae*. In Er's vision the spinning of the Parcae appears in such details as the "lots and patterns" of men's lives and the actions of Atropos "to make the web . . . irreversible."[58] But to his daughters of Necessity, Milton has given "the vital shears" that belonged to the *lanificae* and that were the cause of much elegiac poetry. Thus Milton's Fates do not take part in the celestial harmony; they are "lulled" by the singing of the Sirens, just as "unsteady Nature" is kept to her law by "sweet compulsion" and the "low world" is drawn after the heavenly tune "in measur'd motion."

> But else, in deep of night, when drowsiness
> Hath locked up mortal sense, then listen I
> To the celestial *Sirens'* harmony,
> That sit upon the nine enfolded Spheres,
> And sing to those that hold the vital shears,
> And turn the Adamantine spindle round
> On which the fate of gods and men is wound.
> Such sweet compulsion doth in music lie,
> To lull the daughters of *Necessity,*
> And keep unsteady Nature to her law,
> And the low world in measur'd motion draw
> After the heavenly tune, which none can hear
> Of human mold with gross unpurged ear.
>                   (*Arcades.* 61-73)

In other words, in handling a conception of the Parcae which was less of a commonplace than that of the Fates as *lanificae,* Milton's major variation emphasizes one of the most familiar aspects of the myth. His Fatal Sisters, even though they are the figures in Er's vision, still carry with them the connotations of "Durae," "Immites," "Malignae," "Nocentes," "Saevae"—a feature of the myth which would strike anyone who had studied or used such key words as those supplied by Textor or Robert Stephanus.

The conclusion of this appendix has been expressed at the end of the second chapter. It might be well, nevertheless, to point out once more that the preceding discussion illustrates how the lexicons with which we are concerned supplied their readers with sound kernels of information that might be developed elsewhere in greater detail. During the Renaissance knowledge was associative and homogenous in a sense not known to the specialized and diversified twentieth century. It began with the basically simple out of which might develop the most complex ramifications. Much less well-known than the importance of the academic curriculum, or than the influence exerted by any one of the specialized treatises, have been the nature and the contents of the material supplied by the major dictionaries of the era. Yet those works clearly specify what was well known to the period and, as a result, indicate even more clearly than do the specialized treatises, how frequently and meaningfully mature writers utilized the commonplace as a basis for their own poetic conceptions.

APPENDIX II

# GEORGE SANDYS' *OVID* (1632)

GEORGE SANDYS (1578-1644) FIRST PUBLISHED HIS OVID'S *Metamorphoses Englished, Mythologiz'd,* etc., in 1626. That edition included an alphabetical list of proper nouns which were meant to aid anyone who might "bee confounded with the many names that are giuen to one person." The information after each name was so scanty, however, that many readers probably welcomed the edition of 1632. Therein the author explains that "in this second Edition of my translation, I have attempted . . . to collect out of Sundrie Authors the Philosophicall sense of the fables of Ovid. . . . I have also added Marginall notes for illustration and ease of the meere English Reader, since diuers places in our Author are otherwise impossible to be understood but by those who are well versed in the ancient Poets and Historians." Elsewhere in the preliminary matter and in a note immediately preceding his comment on the First Book of the *Metamorphoses,* Sandys lists some of the authors which, he says, afforded aid in the expository comment on each book.

Among the listed authors both "profane" and "Christian" are Raphael Regius, Iacobus Micyllus, Muretus, Stephanus, Hyginus, Plutarch, Diodorus, St. Augustine, Macrobius, Palaephates, Fulgentius, Vives, Comes, and Francis Bacon. It is probable that the author consulted many, if not all, of the authorities listed, as well as some not mentioned. His use of the Regius-Micyllus commentary, which appeared in standard editions of Ovid's text, has been commented upon by previous students of the period. Of the other works mentioned, those by Comes and Bacon were recognized as authoritative reference books, and grouped by Hoole with Sandys' own work as texts to be "reserved for your Scholars use in the Schoole-librarie."[1] Perhaps it was taken for granted that in making annotations and comments an author also would have at hand, as a matter of convenience, an equally authoritative dictionary, and there is evidence in the marginal notes and in the comment at the end of each book of his translation of the *Metamorphoses* that Sandys made frequent use of Charles Stephanus' *Dictionarium Historicum, Geographicum, Poeticum.* The parallels which follow suggest the relationship of Sandys' marginal notes to the Stephanus and to the most frequently used commentary of the period, which might also supply readers with information paralleling that in Charles Stephanus.

In a number of instances it is difficult or impossible to tell from which work of reference Sandys drew his material: [Abbreviations: *Sa.,* Sandys; *St.,* Stephanus; *R.-M.,* Regius-Micyllus.].[2]

### CITHAERON

*Sa.*    [Cithaeron]   In that there the orges of *Bacchus* were celebrated.  (p. 50e.)

*St.*    Cithaeron. . . . Hic mons Libero patri sacer erat: vnde etiam ibi eius Orgia celebrabant.

*R.-M.* . . . *Cythaeron*) mons est Boetiae Baccho dicatus, ad cuius orgia celebranda.

### HELIADES

*Sa.*    [Heliades]   The daughters of the Sunne (for so the name signifies) and sisters unto *Phaeton.* (p. 52f)

*St.*    Heliades, filiae Solis & Clymenes, sorores Phaethontis. . . . Vocantur autem Heliades a patre Sole, qui Graecis ἥλιος dicitur.

*R.-M.* [Heliades]  Solis filiae Heliades dicuntur ἥλιος hoc est, a Sole, quae etiam a fratre Phaethontides fuerunt appellatae.

### NAXOS

*Sa.*    [Naxos]  An Iland of the *AEgean* Sea; among all the *Cyclades* the most fertile in Vines: & therefore sacred to *Bacchus.* (p. 95b)

*St.*    Naxos, insula in mari AEgeo, vna ex Cycladibus caeteras superans.... Hanc Dionysiam a vinearum fertilitate dici scribit Plin. lib. 4 cap. 12.

*R.-M.* Naxos insula est AEgei Cycladum clarissima, quae & Dionysias dicta fuit, vt inquit, qui Dionysius cognominatur, vel quod vini fertilitate alias Cyclades vincat.

### AEOLUS

*Sa.*    [Hippotades]  *AEolus* the sonne of *Acesta,* daughter to *Hippotes:* King of the winds. (p. 148a)

*St.*    AEolus, Iouis filius & . . . Acestae Hippotae Troiani filiae, a quo dicitur Hippotades. . . . Fingitur ventorum rex.

*R.-M.* . . . *Hippotades*) AEolus Hippotae nepos.   Nam AEolus Iouis fuit filius ex Acesta Hippotae Troiana filiae.  Is idcirco rex ventorum esse perhibetur, quod. . . . (p. 84, D)

CALAURIA

Sa. [Calauria] An Iland betweene *Creet* and *Peloponesus,* where *Latona* was worshipped. (p. 239p)

St. Calauria, insula est iuxta Cretam a Calauro Neptuni filio denominata. Est etiam vrbs Locrorum, in qua Latona maxime colebatur. . . .

R.-M. Calauria, insula est iuxta Cretam a Calauro Neptuni filio declinata. Est etiam vrbs Locrorum, in qua Latona maxime colebatur. . . . (p. 136, C)

CICONES

Sa. [Cicones] People of *Thrace,* by the River *Hebrus.* (p. 337a)

St. Cicones populi Thraciae, iuxta Hebrum. . . .

R.-M. Cicones populi sunt Thraciae iuxta Hebrum fluuium habitantes. . . .

There are, however, a number of instances wherein the wording of the *Dictionarium* is closer to Sandys' gloss than is the comparable material in the commentary.

ZEPHYRUS

Sa. [Zephyrus] The West wind importing a nourisher of life; for all the vegitables by the temperature thereof more luxuriously prosper. (p. 2e)

St. Zephyrus, ventus flans ab Ocassu . . . dictus Zephyrus, quasi . . . hoc est, vitam ferens: eo enim plantae omnes germinant & pullulant.

R.-M. Zephyrus ventus est occidentalis . . . hoc est a ferenda satis omnibus vita. (p. 6, D)
. . . nullae tunc inquit erant variationes temporum, sed Zephyri assidue flantes, sine vllo semine nascentes [*sic*] fouebant flores, ut ver semper esse videretur. (p. 8, D)

BALEARES

Sa. [Baleares] The inhabitants of the *Balaries* (two Ilands now called *Maiorca* and *Minorca*) renowned for their slings. (P. 61 h.)

St. Baleares, vulgo *Maiorque* & *Minorque,* duae insulae ante Hispaniam . . . . Dictae Baleares . . . a iaculando, propterae quod fundae & iaculationis Baleares peritissimi habiti sunt.

R.-M. *Balearica funda*) qua Balearium insularum incolae maxime vtuntur. Baleares autem insulae sunt duae Hispaniae adiacentes, quarum incolae optimi sunt funditores. (p. 47, I)

AONIA

Sa. [Aonia] The mountainous part of *Boeotia;* and taken for the whole country. (p. 88d)

St. Aonia, pars montana Boeotiae, cuius meminit Steph. vnde totam Boeotiam prius Aoniam dictam scribit . . . .

R.-M. *Ille per Aonias*) Boetias. Aonia enim pars est Boetie montana ab Aone

rege cognominata. Haec autem inseruntur, vt commodius fabulae con-
iungantur. (p. 59, F)

CHIMAERA

*Sa.* [Chimaera] A Monster, with the head of a Lyon, the body of a Gote,
and the taile of a Serpent. (p. 208f)

*St.* Chimaera . . . monstrum esse, quod flammas euomat, caput & pectus
leonis habens, ventrem autem caprae, & caudam draconis.

*R.-M.* [Chimaera] Fingitur autem a poetis fera esse pedes habens serpentinos,
caprae ventrum, caput leonis flammas vomens. . . . (p. 114, I)

Among passages that show a wording closer to that in a dictionary
entry than to the comparable material in Regius-Micyllus, the gloss on
*Palici* is particularly revealing. In Sandys' description, the height of the
spouting water is given as three cubits:

[Palici] Hot lakes by *Palica* a citty of *Sicilia,* which spouted up their waters
three cubits high. (p. 181a)

The information in Regius-Micyllus runs as follows: "Iuxta Palicos autem
fons est Palicene, qui aquam in altum sex cubitis eiaculari dicitur . . ."
(p. 98, A). Not only is the height different but the wording varies con-
siderably from that in Sandys. Closer to the Ovid gloss is the wording
of the *Dictionarium.* Not until the edition of 1620, however, have we
been able to find "tres . . . cubitus" instead of "sex . . . cubitus":

Palici, qui & *Delli* & *Crateres* nominantur, lacus siue fontes in Sicilia sunt,
qui continua eructatione, ad tres circiter cubitus in altum. . . .

Apparently Sandys, knowing that new information was continually being
embodied in the *Dictionarium,* was referring to a fairly recent edition of
the work that in all probability he first encountered as a schoolboy.

Revealing also is Sandys' gloss on "Hypaepa." The name, as the
Regius-Micyllus commentary points out, was given to a little town situated
near a mountain in Lydia and was named "quasi ὕπαιπα, hoc est, sub cacumine & vertice sita." The next gloss concerns "Timoli": "Timolus, qui
et Tmolus dicitur, mons est Lydiae vitibus consitus." Sandys, however,
writes as if the word "Hypaepa" were derived from "Tmolus."

[Hypaepa] A little towne at the foote of the mountaine *Tmolus,* from whence
it taketh that name. (p. 201c)

Had Sandys not been sure of the derivation of the word to be glossed
or of the relationship between *Hypaepa* and *Tmolus,* his curiously distorted etymology might well have resulted from a hurried glance at the
entry in the *Dictionarium:*

*Hypaepa . . . Lydiae oppidum,* Veneri sacrum, quod occurrit *a Tmolo monte* ad Caystri campestria iter facienti: *nomen ei est . . .* ab eo quod sub Aepo monte situm sit.

Occasionally one also encounters instances wherein Sandys utilizes information not found in the Regius-Micyllus but in the *Dictionarium.* The three following examples are typical:

### OLYMPUS

*Sa.* [Olympus] A Mountaine betweene *Macedon* & *Thessaly,* whose top is neuer reached by the Clouds, therefore so called by the inhabitants, and vsed for heauen by the Poets. (p. 5d)

*St.* Olympus, mons editissimus, in ea parti Thesaliae, quae in Macedoniam vergit, cuius vertex vsque adeo attollitur, vt nubes penetrare, caelumque ipsum attingere credatur. . . . Olympum Poëtae pro ipso accipiant coelo. . . .

### AVERNUS

*Sa.* [Avernus] Infernall: of *Avernus* a lake in *Campania,* ouer which no bird could fly for the poysonous exhalations, and thereof so called a supposed entrance into Hell. (p. 183f)

*St.* Auernus, lacus Campaniae prope Baias . . . Plutoni dicatum, & inferorum limen esse rudis vetustas credidit. Dictus . . . quod aues superuolantes graui eius odore enecarentur: siue quod sulphurae exhalationes aërem vsque adeo extenuarent, vt aues sustinere non posset.

The word "Infernall," in the last example may well have been taken from the basic Ovid commentary of the period: *"Auernales* infernales" (p. 101, F). Yet Sandys' next note on "Avernus" (p. 338g) has no counterpart in the commentary, and the passage in Sandys at times shows verbatim correspondence with the passage from the dictionary quoted above:

[Avernus] A lake of *Campania* consecrated to *Pluto,* and belieued to be an entrance unto Hell, because the birds fell in that attempted to fly ouer it (and thereupon called *Auernus*) proceeding either from the impoysoning damps, or aire extenuated by sulphurus exhalations.

There can be no doubt, however, about Sandys' use of the basic Ovid commentary. Consider, for example, the eight following passages in which, although the differences are slight, Sandys seems to be drawing from Regius-Micyllus rather than from the similarly worded *Dictionarium:*

### INACHIDES

*Sa.* [Inachides] *Perseus* the *Argiue:* the *Argiues* so called of *Inachus* their first King; and of the River which carried his name. (p. 149f)

*R.-M. Inachides*)  Perseus Argiuus. Inachidae namque Argiui dicuntur ab Inacho, qui primus apud Argos regnauit, ac fluuium Achiae Inachum de suo nomine appellauit. (p. 85, G)

*St.*  Inachus, primus Argiuorum rex, qui Inacho fluuio nomen dedit: a quo Argiui ipsi, Inachidae appellati sunt.

PLUTO

*Sa.*  [Dis]  *Pluto:* both signifying riches; treasure being digd out of the bowels of the earth, his supposed empire. (ᵽ. 123f)

*R.-M.* Plutonis . . . sic Latini a diuitiis ditem nominant.  Est n[omen] terrae deus Pluto, diuitiae autem ex terra effodiuntur. (pp. 78-9)

*St.*  Pluto . . . Dictus Pluton . . . a diuitiis, eo quod opes omnes ab inferis, hoc est, ex intimis terrae visceribus eruantur. . . .

ATTICA

*Sa.*  *Attica* once called *Mopsopia;* of *Mopsopus* their King. (p. 186c)

*R.-M.* Attica enim etiam Mopsopia a Mopsopo rege fuit appellata. . . . (p. 104, E)

*St.*  Mopsopia, Attica regio, a Mopso rege sic dicta.

CYTORUS

*Sa.*  *Cytorus* is a mountaine of *Papalagonia,* abounding with Box. (p. 204, k)

*R.-M.* Cytorus mons est Paphlogoniae buxis abundans. . . . (p. 110, A)

*St.*  Cytorum, vrbs Paphlagoniae . . . Cytorus, mons Galatiae, in quo buxus plurima nascebatur. . . .

CINYPS

*Sa.*  [Cynips or Cyniphis]  Of *Cyniphus* a River of *Libya* which runnes into the Sea betweene the two Sy[r]tes. (p. 237c)

*R.-M.* Cinyps fluuius Libyae qui inter duas Syrtes in mare Libycum exit. . . . (p. 132, D)

*St.*  Cynips, siue Cniphis, siue Cyhiphos, fluuius Africae, inter duas Syrtes . . . in mare Libycum se exonerant.

TAENARUS

*Sa.*  [Taenarus]  A Promontory of *Laconia,* wherein a Caue, as they held, descended to Hell. (p. 337e)

*R.-M.* *Taenaria porta*)  Taenarus Laconiae promontorium est, in quo specus esse dicitur, per quem ad inferos descenditur. (p. 189)

*St.*  Taenarus . . . promontorium Laconicae regionis. . . . Suidas ait Taenarum promontorium esse Laconiae, in quo fauces erant ad inferos deducentes. . . .

The two remaining examples involve passages in the commentary which are somewhat too long for quotation here; their relationship to the Ovid glosses, nevertheless, can be briefly demonstrated.  About "Tempe," Sandys writes:

Not the *Thessalian,* but the *Boeotian Tempe;* called also the *Teumesian* . . . here called *Cygnean,* of that boyes conversion into a Swan (p. 239m)

The pertinent passage in the *Dictionarium* runs as follows:

Tempe, Thessaliae loca. . . . Sunt & Tempe in Boeotia, quae Teumessia dicuntur a Teumesso monte Boeotiae, ab Ouid. Cygneia dicta.

In contrast, the gloss in Regius-Micyllus contains all of the information in both Sandys and Stephanus and such occasional verbal similarities as "Cygneia autem Ouidius vocasse videtur ab euentu, quod circa haec puer de quo hic dicitur, in cygnum conuersus fuerit." A similar situation occurs with the note on "Caphareus":

[Caphareus] Promontory of *Euboea,* where *Nauplius* in the revenge of the death of his son *Palamedes* hung out a light in a tempestuous night, when the Graecians imagining that it directed to the harbor, fell upon the rocks. (p. 465r)

In the *Dictionarium* one finds only

Caphareum, Euboeae promontorium.
Caphareus, mons altissimus Euboeae Hellespontum versus. . . . Hic Nauplius, Euboeae rex, mortem filij Palamedis Ulyssis dolo interfecti vltus est. Nam cum Graeci Troia diruta redirent, Nauplius facem in montis vertice, vt locus fidem portus haberet, quo cum venissent, multi naufragium fecerunt.

In the Regius-Micyllus, one finds the information in the *Dictionarium* as well as such revealing details as those concerning the "tempestuous night" and the ships striking the rocks:

Nauplius enim cum caedem Palamedis filij insidiis ac fraude Vlyssis interfecti, vlcisci vellet, ea nocte, qua Graeci a Troia redeuntes, circa Caphareum, tempestate periclitabantur, conscenso scopulo, et face accensa, ad cuius lucem Graeci, tanquam in portum nauigarent, naues illorum in saxa et radices montis impingere, atque ita perire fecit.

As the immediately preceding examples indicate, when balanced against the nine which are close to the *Dictionarium,* Sandys' glosses sometimes reflect information and wording in both the Regius-Micyllus and the Stephanus. Similarly, evidence of the use of both works is apparent within a single annotation. In even his brief note on *Lyrcaeus,* "A Mountaine of *Arcadia,* where Inachus hath his head" (p. 146), the author is following Regius-Micyllus when he writes "Mountaine," but his phrase "where Inachus hath his head" is closer to the phrasing in the *Dictionarium* than to that in the commentary.

Lyrceus, siue Lyrceum, fons Arcadiae sub Cynuria monte, ex quo Inachus fluuius oritur. (Steph.)

The Regius-Micyllus passage discusses whether the reading should be *Lycaea, Lyncea,* or *Lyrcaea.* It gives, as part of the discussion of the first reading, the following information "Temetsi hactenus Lycaeo Arcadiae monte Pano dicato," while in a portion of the discussion of the third reading one finds ". . . dubitet, vtrum Lynceium, a Lynceo rege, an potius Lyrceium a monte, vnde Inachus fertur, legendum sit."

About "Dictynna," Sandys writes:

[Dictynna] *Diana* so called of the toiles wherewith they take wild beastes, by her first invented. (p. 55a)

The opening phrase reflects the wording of the commentary's discussion of Dictynna, "Diana dicitur . . . a retibus," but the information that toils or nets were first invented by Dictynna appears in the *Dictionarium:*

Dictynna, Nympha Cretensis, quae casses venatorios prima creditur inuenisse. . . . Ferunt autem hanc in Creta Dianae consuetudine familiarissime vsam fuisse, quae & ipsa ob id a poetis nonnunquam Dictynna appellatur.

About "Styx" Sandys writes

Poysonous: such as the water of that infernall River; or of *Styx* the Arcadian fountaine, which nothing could containe but the hoofe of an Asse. (p. 83a)

The information is a combination of the short gloss in Regius-Micyllus and the longer entry in Stephanus:

*Ore stygio)* venenato. qualis est styx inferorum palus. (*R.-M.,* p. 53 E)
Styx, fons ad Nonacrin Arcadiae, e saxis profluens, exitiosus omnibus animalibus . . . solaque mulae vngula possit contineri. . . . (Steph.)

The lists of parallels are not intended to be exhaustive but exemplary; they show *in toto* the way in which we think Sandys employed the Stephanus in making marginal annotations for the translation of Ovid's *Metamorphoses.*

Immediately before his "Comment" on the First Book of Ovid's *Metamorphoses,* Sandys acknowledges indebtedness to a number of authors, ancient and modern. Though he does not include among the listed sources the poetic and historic dictionary of Charles Stephanus, there is evidence that in writing the Comments on the various books, just as in composing the marginal notes, Sandys frequently consulted this dictionary. Below are some excerpts from the Comments paralleled with entries from

Stephanus' dictionary, and from other reference works that happen to be pertinent—from Comes, the Regius-Micyllus, and the Lactantius commentary on Ovid.[3]

### 1. LUCIFER

*Sa.* Lucifer . . . is here said to fore-runne *Aurora,* or the morning; and last of all to resigne his place, in that the last starre which shineth. This is the beautifull Planet of Venus; which, when it riseth before the Sunne, is the Morning starre, and setting after it, the Evening. (p. 68)

*St.* Lucifer, vna errantium stellarum, quem & Venerem appellamus, quae mane Solem praecedens, vnaque cum Aurora sese ostendens (vnde & Aurorae filius fingitur) Lucifer dicitur: vesperi autem Solem subsequens, Hesperus nominatur.

*R.-M.* Lucifer enim, qui Graeci φώσφορος dicitur, vltimus est qui desinat fulgere Sole oriente, priusque incipit lucere, illo occidente, tunc quod Hesperus vocatur. Veneri autem haec stella dicata esse perhibetur. ["Aurora" is mentioned in the notes immediately preceding and following.] (p. 33, C)

### 2. ERICHTHONIUS

*Sa.* *Erichthonius* is here fained to have had no mother: for *Vulcan,* as they fable, intending to ravish Minerva, defiled the ground, from whence he had his beginning: expressed in his name which signifies Earth and Contention. . . . They giue Erichthonius the hinder parts of a Dragon. . . . He was the fourth King of the Athenians. . . . Pausanias writes that Erichthonius was the first that invented Chariots to conceal his deformity: and Virgil;

> First *Erichthonius* with foure horses drew
> Swift Chariots; on hot wheeles the victor flew.

[The Latin of this couplet is quoted in the margin and assigned to Virgil, Georg. 1.3] (pp. 71-72)

*St.* Erichthonius. . . . 4. Atheniensium rex, ex semine Vulcani in terram proiecto editus. Vnde & nomen habet . . . id est, certamine atque humo. . . . Tum in illa colluctatione Vulcanum in terram profudisse aiunt semen, atque inde editum esse puerum draconum pedibus, nomine Erichthonum: qui cum adoleuisset, vt pedum deformitatem tegeret, primus currus vsum adinuenit, Seruius in illud Virg. lib. 3. Georg.

> *Primus Erichthonius currus, & quatuor ausus,*
> *Iungere equos, rapidisque rotis insistere victor.*

[Note: Comes (IX, xi), however seems to be the main, if not the sole, source for this note, supplying, *i. a.,* the interpretation which Sandys has here used: *e. g.,* "huic patrem fuisse neminem mortalium, sed quoniam ex terra et contentione sit genitus, Vulcani ita fuisse nominatum." (Ed. 1616, p. 515.) See

also under II, vi (p. 78) for a discussion of the meaning of the Vulcan myth:
*e. g.,* ". . . quod nomen et contentionis et terrae nomen intra se continet. . . ."]

### 3. BATTUS

*Sa.*  *Battus* for a double reward betraying *Mercury* to himselfe was transformed into a Touch-stone . . . the meed of his avarice and periury.
By *Battus* our *Ovid* intends a foolish poet of that name, redounding
with vaine and tedious repetitions, whereof he here giueth an example:
the like of him being called Battologia. (p. 76)

*St.*  Battus, pastoris cuiusdam Pylij nomen, quem Mercurius in Indicem
commutauit . . . ob quam perfidiam Mercurius eum in lapidem, qui
Index dicitur, commutauit. Ouid. 2. Met. . . . Haec fabula docet
fraude sermonis ac periurio abstinendum.

Battus, ineptus poeta, qui in carmine conficiendo eadem saepius
repetabat, & ineptam iterum occinebat cantilenam, inde Battologia, verborum redundantia, eiusdemque rei vitiosa repetitio.

[Note: Fabulantur Batto pastori cuidam Mercuriam vaccam largitum esse,
vt taceret, qui solus furtum illud cognouerat. Deinde cum hominis, fideni
vellet experiri mutatis vestibus, *duplici praemio* pro indicando furto proposito
inconstantiam ac perfidiam Batti cognouit, eumque in saxum indicem conuertit. . . . (Comes, V, v, p. 237.)][4]

### 4. CYCLOPES

*Sa.*  [Cyclopes] Ioues fearfull artillery he faines to be forged by the *Cyclopes:* whereof Virgill more fully.
    The *Cyclop's* in vast caues their anvills beat:
    *Steropes, Brontes,* nak'd *Pyragmon,* sweat.
[These and seven additional lines Sandys translates from the Aeneid,
lib. 8. In the margin he quotes the nine lines of Latin from the
*Aeneid,* beginning "Ferrum exercebant vasto Cyclopes in antro."]
(p. 102)

*St.*  Cyclopes . . . fuerunt ministri autem Vulcani, Ioui sua fulmina fabri-
cantes. Cyclopes dicti ab eo, quod vnicum habuerit oculum, eumque
orbicularem media in fronte situm. Ex his tres potissimum a poëtis
celebrantur. Brontes, Steropes, & Pyracmon . . . Virg. 8. Aeneid.
    *Ferrum exercebant vastro Cyclopes in antro,*
    *Brontesque, Steropesque, & nudus membra Pyracmon.*
[Note: The additional details in Sandys can be found throughout a discussion,
too long for quotation here, in Comes, IX, viii. There one encounters, *i. a.,*
the interpretations of names used by Sandys as well as the entire passage
of nine lines from the *Aeneid.*]

### 5. LYCURGUS

*Sa.*  [Lycurgus] The Thebans sing of the miserable fate of *Lycurgus;* the
sonne of *Dryas,* and king of Thrace: who perceiving that the Thracians

addicted themselves wholly to drunkennesse, commaunded the vines throughout all his kingdome to be cut downe: whereupon it was fained that he pursued Bacchus with such deadly hatred; killing his Frowes who lay hid in Nysa, and forcing the affrighted God to fly unto Nazos. For which fact deprived of his sences, instead of a vine, he cut his thigh asunder: but according to Homer struck blind by Iupiter. [There then follow 10 lines in English, translating a Latin version of Homer which is given in eleven lines in the margin.] (p. 154)

*St.* Lycurgus, Thraciae rex, filius Dryantis, qui quod Thracos immoderate vino deditos conspiceret, vites omnes toto regno excidi iussit. Plutarchus . . . Hinc datus est poetis locus fabulae, Lycurgum infestissimo Bacchum odio prosecutum esse, adeo ut nutrices illius in Nysa latentes persequeretur, & Baccho ipsi tantum terroris incusserit, ut praecipiti fuga traiecto mari, in Naxum se receperit: ideoque iusta numinum ira Lycurgum in furorem conuersum, cum vites quoque, ne Baccho in posterum libaretur, excidere vellet, tibias sibi succidisse. . . .

[Note: Comes (V, xiii) supplies a long and detailed entry on Lycurgus, of which the following passage seems to have been used by Sandys: "Fuerunt qui dixerint Lycurgus praeterea cum sacra Liberi patris spreuisset, caecum factum fuisse e Ioue . . . atque de Lycurgi, supplicio ita scripsit Homerus lib. 3 Iliad. . . ." The pertinent lines are then given in the Greek, with a Latin translation, which does not agree, however with that in Sandys. Information similar to that in Comes also appears in Regius-Micyllus: "Videtur Ovid. ad Homeri locum respexisse, qui est Ilia. 6. Ibi enim Lycurgus dicitur Bacchi . . . nutrices bipenni, siue securi persecutus esse, eoque postea a Ioue oculis priuatus. Versus Homerii sunt. . . ." The same lines as in Comes are then quoted. (p. 69, H)]

### 6. AESACUS

*Sa.* One *Aesacus* the sonne of *Priamus* by the Nymph *Alixothoe*. Who hating the glorious miseries of the Court; enioyes his freedome in the open fields and Forrests of *Ida*. . . . But Loue, who is winged with excesse and ease, finds Aesacus out amidst his homely fare, and laborious exercises. When pursuing the Nymph *Eperia:* by the biting of a serpent her flight and life were at once suppressed. He, distracted with sorrow, threw himselfe from a rock, into the sea; and by the pitty of Tethis was turned into a Cormorant. . . . (p. 397)

*St.* Aesacus, Priami filius ex Alyxothoe Dimantis filia, plus syluis, quam ciuitatibus delectatus: hic cum Hesperiem seu Eperiem liberali forma puellam videret, adeo eius amore captus est, vt in syluis illam sequeretur, quae fugiens morsu serpentis est occisa: ipse autem amoris impatiens, acrique dolore concussus, se de scopulo in mare praecipitem dedit, cuius Thetis miserata eum in mergum transformauit. Ouid. lib. 11. Meta.

[Note: AEsacus natus Priami et Alyxothoes Cebrenidis filiae, sub monte Ida furtim editus cum vrbanum apparatum cultumque syluis et labori postposuisset, incidit in conspectum Eperies nymphae, cuius captus pulchritudine dum fugientem persequitur causa interemptus eius extitit. Confusa enim timore per ignorantiam serpentem calce pressit, cuius morsu concidit: eius desiderio AEsacus ne diutius dolorem sentiret e monte in subiectum pelagus se praecipitauit, qui priusquam mergeretur, in auem cessit. Haec aequora amat, nomenque Mergi tenet, qui amne mergitur illo. (Lactantius, p. 219, L)]

## 7. HERSILIA

*Sa.*    *Hersilia* the wife of *Romulus* (one of these maids which were ravished from the *Sabines*) was also for her coniugall love assumed by Iuno, the president of nuptials, into heaven to her husband; her name changed into *Ora;* the same with the *Latines,* that *Hebe* is with the *Grecians,* the Goddesse of Youth; called also *Horta,* in that, according to Plutarch, she exhorteth young men to virtue and noble indeavours. This Goddesse was placed in one shrine with Quirinus; signifying that an Empire is not to be purchased nor conserued by sloth; but by vertue and fortitude, the flowre of youth best suting with warfare. Thus changed they the names of those whom they deified, that they neuer might be thought to haue been mortall. (p. 487)

*St.*    Hersilia, vxor Romuli, Liuio lib. 1. quam rapuerat Sabinis inter alias virgines, cum iidem ex inuidia filias suas Romanis collocare recusarent. Haec postea in Oram deam mutata est, Ouidius Metam. 1. 14. huius mutationis meminit. Porro mortuis honore Deorum consecratis nomina immutabantur, ne crederentur mortales fuisse. Sic Romulus mutato nomine dictus est Quirinus: & Hersilia eius vxor dicta est Ora, quae apud Romanos erat, qualis Hebe apud Graecos, Dea iuuentae, & Horta etiam dicebatur, vt Plutarchus refert in libro Problematum, eo quod iuuenes ad virtutem & res gerendas hortatur. Hanc Romani suo Quirino, perinde vt vxorem consecrarunt: significantes imperium non desidia & otio, sed virtute & fortitudine parari atque conseruari: virtutem vero bellicam niti flore iuuentutis.

[Note: Information on "Hersilia" is not in Comes, and only brief mention of her appears in Cartari; while the Lactantius commentary, with much else lacking that is found in Sandys, adds only the Juno detail: "Hersilia coniunx Romuli, cum fleret amissum coniugem, post datam ei a Iunone immortalitatem, Ora Quirini nuncupata est: quorum templa a populo Romano in colle Quirinali constituta sunt." (p. 273)]

Sandys' discussion of "Phineus" is particularly interesting:

## 8. PHINEUS

The *Argonautes* now sailing to Colchos, touch by the way at Paphlagonia, where *Phineus* the sonne of Agenor then reigned: deprived of his sight and spending his old age in penury. For he, having pulled out the eyes of Crambus and Orythus, his sons by Cleopatra daughter to Boreas and Orythia, at the instigation of their stepmother Idaea, the daughter of Dardanus, was struck blind himself by the divine vengeance for his unnaturall cruelty: the Harpies being sent to devoure his food and contaminate his table.

> More horrid monsters, direr plagues then those,
> Or wrath of Gods, from Styx yet never rose:
> Like foule with virgin faces, purging still
> Their filthy panches: arm'd with talons, ill,
> And ever pale with famine.

[This is Sandys' translation of lines from the Aeneid lib. 3, which are quoted by Sandys in the margin of his text.]

But now the Argonautes, being nobly entertained by Phineus . . . sent Calais and Zetes, the winged issue of Boreas (now reconciled for the iniury don to their innocent nephews) to chace them away. Who pursueing them as far as the Strophades, were commanded by Iris to offer no farther violence to the Dogges of Iupiter. The Harpyes are so named of Rapine: said to be virgins in that barren; because goods so gotten descend but seldome to posterity: to fly, in that swift in extorting: to be covered with plumes, for cloking their prey: and to have the talons of vultures, of griping and fast-holding their ill-got riches. These qualities are also charactered in their names, Aello, Ocipetes, and Celeno: signifying a taking away that which is an others, celerity in the act, and subtilty in concealing. . . . (p. 251)

For at least five particulars, Sandys apparently is indebted to the *Mythologiae*. Under "De Harpyis" (VII, vi), Sandys might have found the Latin lines, cited in the margin, which he translates in his text. There too are details about the Harpies which appear in the "Comment": "Has igitur Iouis canes fuisse memorant poetae, ac rapaces daemones . . . (p. 382)." Comes notes that the birds were chased away by "Boreae filios," but he does not give their names; one finds there, however, details of the reconciliation "for the iniury don to their innocent nephews." Material in Sandys concerning Iris is also in the *Mythologiae:* "Reuersi sunt autem Boreadae, et ab insequendis Harpyis destiterunt Iride illos reuocante. . . ." Comes, finally, is the source for the rest of Sandys' information about the myth—not quoted here—as well as for its interpretation. Yet Sandys, perhaps, found the detailed discussion in Comes somewhat too complicated; for the wording in the *Mythologiae* is not as close to that of Sandys[5] as is the pertinent account in the *Dictionarium:*

Phineus, Agenoris filius. . . . Hic igitur rex . . . Paphlagoniae, vxorem duxit Cleopatrem . . . ex qua genuit Orythum & Crambum . . . cui etiam Apollonij Commentarius subscribit, qui li. 1. dicit, Phineum Cleopatrem Boreae & Orythiae filiam vxorem duxisse, secundam vero Idaeam Dardani filiam nouercam superinduxisse: cuius suasu filios suos ex Cleopatra susceptos excaecauit. Quapropter & ipse excaecatus est a diis, & Harpyiae contra eum missae, quae cibos & mensam turpissime foedarent. Postea vero, deuenientibus ad ea loca Argonautis, a Calai & Zethe fratribus alatis rursus ad Strophades insulas fugatae sunt. . . .

Once more, the preceding parallels are exemplary; but they indicate, we believe, how Sandys utilized the *Dictionarium Historicum* in writing the Comments to his translation. One can find instances (nos. 1, 6) wherein the information and phraseology of Stephanus is closer to Sandys than very similar material in other related works; instances (nos. 7 and 3, Battus the poet) wherein Stephanus provides matter used by Sandys which does not appear in kindred reference books; instances, on the other hand, (no. 2) wherein the English Ovid is closer to such a compendium as Comes than it is to the *Dictionarium;* and, most interesting of all, instances (nos. 3, 4, 5, 6, 8) wherein both the *Dictionarium* and at least one other work of reference contributed to Sandys' discussion and interpretation of classic myth.

When one considers the closeness of the parallels between Sandys and Stephanus and the distribution throughout Sandys' marginal annotations and his Comments of matter so near to the entries in the basic proper-name dictionary of the period, one is certainly justified in concluding that a convenient reference book which Sandys kept at hand was Charles Stephanus' *Dictionarium Historicum, Geographicum, Poeticum.*

# APPENDIX III

# THE *MYSTAGOGUS POETICUS* AND THE

# *DICTIONARIUM HISTORICUM*

JUST AS SANDYS UTILIZED AUTHORITATIVE REFERENCE WORKS FOR HIS scholarly notations, and just as Bacon was indebted to the Comes when writing the *De Sapientia Veterum*,[1] so the Scottish schoolmaster Alexander Ross used works discussed in the preceding chapters when he compiled his own reference work, the *Mystagogus Poeticus* (London, 1647). His dependence upon Charles Stephanus is particularly interesting, for at the outset of his roughly alphabetical discussion, he draws sparingly from the *Dictionarium Historicum, Geographicum, Poeticum*. Beginning with the letter H, however, he apparently found the process of eclectic revision too wearisome. At any rate, he then began to use Charles Stephanus consistently, and sometimes slavishly, for the introductory descriptions of his mythological figures, each of which is followed by an "Interpreter." In the interpretation of his myths, he utilized Comes and Cartari frequently; but at times he apparently branched out on his own, and at times one again finds clear traces of the *Dictionarium*.

In Ross's "Interpreter" to "Alpheus," for example, at two points there is a slight reflection of material in the dictionary. [Abbreviations: R. = Ross, *Mystagogus Poeticus; S.* = Stephanus, *Dictionarium Historicum*]

### ALPHEUS

R.  1. *Alpheus* was worshipped as a God, and his image was placed upon the same altar with *Diana*. . . . 2. *Alpheus* is a River of *Elis* in *Arcadia:* through secret passages running under the Earth and Sea, it empties it self in the spring *Arethusa* in *Sicily,* which though Strabo denieth it, cannot be otherwise. . . . (pp. 18-19)

S.  Alpheus, fluuius Elidis Arcadiae ciuitatis . . . defluens longo cursu in Achaiam, & ibi a terra absorptus, atque subter mare defluens ex Graecia in fontem Arethusam . . . in Sicilia se attollit. . . . Strabo libr. 6.

ait Alpheum sumere originem in Peloponeso & per mare sub terra in Arethusam fontem terminari. . . . Hunc fluuium non nulli Ethnici pro Deo coluerunt, cui statuam, & communem aram cum Diana erexerunt.

In a number of mythological discussions, the pertinent dictionary item is reflected not simply in the interpretations but also in portions of the introductory descriptions:

### CEPHALUS

*R.*　　He was the son of Eon, and husband to Procris, the daughter of Hyphilus King of Athens. Aurora was so in love with Cephalus, that she carried him away; but admiring his constancy, sent him back to his wife in a disguised habit, in which he found out her dishonesty, but afterward being reconciled to her, gave himself to hunting in the woods, where he shot his wife unawares, supposing she had been some wild beast.

4. In *Procris,* who was sollicited by *Cephalus* in a disguised habit to prostitute her body for a great sum of money, we see. . . . 7. But withal we have a fearful example of matrimonial jealousy . . . for Procris. (pp. 59-60)

*S.*　　Cephalus, Eonis filius, qui Procrin Erechthei vel Hyphili, Atheniensium regis filiam vxorem duxit. Huius amore capta Aurora . . . vi eum dicitur rapuisse. Verum cum ne sic quidem constantiam eius posset labefactare, ad vxorem eum remisit, in negotiatoris similitudinem transformatum: cuius erga se fidem cum explorare vellet, ingentibus muneribus pudicitiam eius solicitauit, cumque illa pretij magnitudine iam succumberet, Cephalus recepta pristina forma perfidiam ei exprobauit. . . . Tandem tamen viro reconciliata, iaculum ei ineuitabile . . . dedit. . . . Cephalus, syluis sese assidue oblectabat . . . venatione sese exercebat.

### CHIMERA

*R.*　　This was the monster, having the head of a Lion, breathing out fire, the Belly of a Goat, and the tail of a Dragon, which did much hurt, but was killed at last by Bellerophon.

2. Some think that this was a Hill, on the top whereof were Lions and *Vulcans* of fire, about the middle was pasture and goats, at the foot Serpents. . . . (p. 72)

*S.*　　Hinc factus est locus fabulae, Chimaeram monstrum esse, quod flammas euomat, caput & pectus leonis habens, ventrem autem caprae, & caudam draconis. . . . Et quoniam Bellerophon Glauci filius montem hunc habitabilem reddidit, Chimaeram fingitur occidisse.

Chimaera, mons Lyciae igniuomus, in cuius cacumine leones habitant: in medio autem, vbi pascuis abundat, caprae: in radicibus autem serpentes.

FERONIA

R.    This was the Goddess of the Woods, who had a Grove under the Hill
Soracte in Italy, which casually once being on fire, and the neighbouring
inhabitants endeavouring to rescue her image, and to carry it away
thence; the Grove (as they say) grew suddenly green again.

    5. *Strabo* and others record, that the Priests of this goddess *Feronia,*
used every year in her solemnities, to walk without any hurt bare-foot
upon hot burning coals. . . . (pp. 121, 123)

S.    Feronia, nemorum dea a ferendis arboribus dicta. Haec lucum habuisse
fertur sub monte Soracte, qui cum fortuito aliquando arsisset incendio,
& ob id transferre inde simulachrum accolae vellent, subito aiunt nemus
reuiruisse.

    Strabo author est, eos qui Feroniae numine afflabantur, nudis pedibus
ardentes prunas sine vlla laesione perambulare solitos.

HERMAPHRODITUS

R.    He was a beautiful youth, the son of Mercury and Venus, with whom
the Nymph Salmacis was in love; one day whilst he was naked, washing himself in the fountain, the nymph, who hid her self behind the
bush, leaps into the fountain, hoping thereby to have got his love, but
failing of it, prays the gods to joyn both their bodies in one, which
was effected, but the sex remained distinct; whereupon Hermaphroditus
prayed that every man who should wash there, might obtain both sexes.

    3. *Hermaphroditus,* is called the son of *Mercury,* to signifie the quality
of that star which Astronomers say is of a middle nature between *Sol*
and *Venus,* or *Luna;* for these have dominion of moisture, and therefore more passive, the radical moisture being the matter of generation,
the Sun is the active principle, and as it were the male; being the Fountain of heat, which is the active quality in generation, and introduceth
the form, but *Mercury* is partaker of both natures. 4. They that drunk
of the Fountain *Salmacis,* were said to become *Hermaphrodites,* not that
there was any such quality in that water, but because the people there-
about called *Cares,* were much given to luxury, idleness, and effeminate
pleasures. (pp. 172-73)

S.    Hermaphroditus, Mercurij & Veneris filius. . . . Hic cum vagabundus
in Caria ad limpidissimum fontem, quem Salmacis Nympha incolebat,
peruenisset, illa subito eius amore correpta (erat enim adolescens for-
mosissimus) cum neque blanditiis, neque precibus ad concubitum flectere
eum posset, simulato recessu post vepres latuit. Is autem Nympham
abiisse ratus fontem nudus intrauit: quod videns Salmacis subito ac-
currit, & abiectis vestibus arctissime eum complexa est. Sed cum ne
sic quidem obstinatum iuuenis animum exorare posset, a diis petiit, vt
ex duobus corporibus in vnum redigerentur. Quibus precibus a superis
exauditis ambo in vnum corpus coaluerunt, ita tamen vt sexus vterque
integer remaneret. Quod cum vidisset Hermaphroditus, a superis

petiisse dicitur, vt ea fonti natura maneret, vt qui vir eum intraret,
ἀνδρόγυνος, id est, vtrumque sexum habens, exiret. . . .
Hermaphroditum fingunt Mercurij & Veneris filium, eo quod stella Mercurij, ob qualitates quibus praeest mediae naturae putatur.  Nam cum
aliae stellae ab Astrologis dicantur masculinae propter maius robur
quo calorem excitant: aliae vero propter debiliores vires, & naturam
humidi cui dominantur; Mercurij stella nunc humidum abunde excitat
pro situ & motu suo.  Porro Salmacidis Nymphae fabula, non tam ad
vitium aquae quam ad inertiam & desidiosum otium, quo vires hominum
eneruantur, referenda est.  Erant enim Cares, qui eo loco habitabant,
homines desidiae & luxuriae pleni, ac foedis dediti libidinibus: vnde
& Hermaphroditi vulgo appellabantur.

### LETHE

R.   This was a river in hell, of which whosoever drank, he forgot all
forepast actions and sufferings.
2. The river *Lethe* is in *Africa* running by the City *Berenice,* which
is swallowed up by a great gulf, and runs under the ground many miles,
then breaks out not far from Berenice, which gave occasion to the
country people to think that this river sprung out of hell. (pp. 236-37)

S.   Lethe, est fluuius inferorum apud poetas, cuius aquam si quis gustasset,
omnium statim praeteritorum obliuisci eum voluerunt.
Constat autem reuera Lethen, amnem in Aphrica esse, circa extremum
Syrtium cornu, Berenicen vrbem alluentem.  Verum quoniam terrae
hiatu absorptus, & occulto meatu per aliquot lapsus millia, circa Berenicem magna aquarum copia erumpit, persuasum fuit accolis, ab inferis
eum emergere.

### LIBITINA

R.   She was the goddess of Funerals among the Romans: in her temple
were sold or lent such things as were requisite for Funerals.

### The Interpreter.

1. *Libitina* is thought by some to be *Venus,* by others *Proserpina,* the
wife of *Pluto;* who because she was the queen of Hell, was supposed
to have charge of funerals, and to be the Lady President of the dead;
but *Plutarch* will have her to be *Venus,* in whose Temple those things
were kept which were fit for Funerals. . . . 2. *Libitina* is taken for death
it self, so *Horat.* . . . (p. 238)

S.   Libitina, dea apud Romanos, in cuius templo vendebantur & locabantur
ea, quae ad sepulturam pertinebant. . . . Plut. Venerem fuisse putat...
quare Romani ea quae ad pompam funebrem spectarent, in Veneris
templo voluerint asseruari. . . . Alij malunt Proserpinam esse Plutonis
vxorem: quam, quod inferorum crederetur regina, mortuis praeesse
putabant: ideoque etiam ea, quibus morturi exonerati veluti ad inferos

deducuntur, in eius templo voluerunt asseruari. Hinc factum est, vt
Libitina poetis pro morte ipse . . . Horat. . . .

Elsewhere, as in the account of Cepheus, which is given below, Ross
seems to have glanced at two entries in the *Dictionarium*. At other times,
as with Lotis and Lycus, when one dictionary entry contained reference
to another, Ross followed the cross-reference to draw material from the
second account. When he combined two or more "histories" simply by
juxtaposition, he obviously utilized two or more of Charles Stephanus'
entries, as in the account of Scylla.[2]

### CEPHEUS

*R.* He was King of AEthiopia, Husband to Cassiope, and father of Andromeda, who for her Mothers pride in preferring her to Juno, or the
Nereids, was bound to a rock and exposed to the teeth of a Sea-monster:
but delivered by Perseus. (p. 60)

*S.* Cepheus, Aethiopum rex, Andromedae pater, quam Perseus periculo
liberatam. . . .
Cassiope . . . Cephei regis AEthiopum vxor, & Andromedes mater, quae,
quod gloriaretur Nereidibus sese corporis pulchritudine praestare, illarum indignationem incurrit. Nymphae . . . Andromeden saxo alligarunt,
cetoque deuorandum obiecerunt: quae tamen Persei virtute liberata, ei
nupsit.

### LOTIS

*R.* She was a beautiful Nymph, the daughter of Neptune, who being like
to be surprized by Priapus, called upon the gods for their assistance,
who taking pity of her, turned her into a tree of her own name, Lotis.

### The Interpreter.

*Lotis* is called also *Dryope*, that is, like an Oak, to shew the likeness
and agreement that is between the Oak and the *Lotos*, they being both
hard and firm, and not apt to putrifie: but though *Dryope* was turned
into the *Lotos*, yet I find she was another Nymph different from *Lotis*:
for *Dryope* was surprized by *Apollo*, and afterward married to *Andre-
mon*. [Note too that Ross's marginal citation of authority "Ovid. 9.
Met." agrees with that in C. Stephanus.] (pp. 239-40)

*S.* Lotis . . . vel Lotus Nympha, forma formosissima, Neptuni filia, quae
cum Priapi vim effugere non posset, inuocata deorum ope, in lotum
arborem est commutata. Ouid. nono Metam. Vide Dryope.
Dryope Oechaliae virgo ab Apolline compressa, post Andraemonis vxor,
tandem in lotum arborem conuersa est. Metam. lib. 9. Nomen a quercu
& voce factum est: fingitur autem in lotum mutata, hanc forte ob causam,
quod inter quercum & lotum aliqua sit conuenientia. . . .

LYCUS

R.     He was King of Boeotia, and husband of Antiopa, the daughter of King Nycteus: she being found with child of Jupiter, who transformed himself into a Satyr, was by Lycus put away, and Dirce became his wife: this fearing lest Antiopa might be reconciled again to her husband caused her to be kept in chains; but Iupiter pitying her, loosed the chains and sent her to the hill Cithaeron, where she was delivered of Amphion and Zethus, who afterward killed Lycus, and tied Dirce to the tail of a wild horse, which being dragged, and torn on the ground, was by the gods turned into a Fountain of her own name. (p. 245)

S.     Lycus, Boetiae rex, qui Antiopam Nyctei regis filiam vxorem duxit: quam postea, cum a Ioue in Satyrum conuerso compressam cognouisset, repudiauit, Dircemque vxorem duxit: quae verita ne Antiope cum Lyco in gratiam rediret, arctissimis eam in vinculis asseruauit: quibus Iouis miseratione dissolutis, in Cithaeronem montem profugit, vbi Amphionem & Zethum peperit: qui postea . . . eum vna cum vxori interfecerunt, vt latius docuimus supra dictionibus Amphion & Dirce.

    Dirce. . . . Verum instante iam partus tempore, Iouis miseratione vinculis soluta, in Cithaeronem montem confugit, vbi Amphionem & Zetum gemellos peperit, qui postea Lycum interfecerunt: Dircem vero candae indomiti equi alligarunt: quae diu ita per terram raptata, tandem deorum commiseratione in sui nominis fontem conuersa est. . . .

SCYLLA, AND CHARYBDIS

R.     Scylla was the Daughter of Phorcus, with whom Glaucus was in love; which Circe perceiving, infected, with poysonable herbs, the Fountain in which Scylla used to wash, by which means the lower parts of her body were turned into dogs; which when she perceived, out of impatience cast her self into the Sea, and so was turned into a Rock, not far from the white pool, or Gulf Charybdis: which had been a more rapacious woman, and had stolen away Hercules his Oxen, before she was turned into this Gulf. There was another Scylla, Daughter to Nisus King of the Megarenses; who, having betrayed to King Minos her Fathers red hair in which the Kingdoms safty consisted, she was turned into a Lark, and Nisus into a Hawk. (p. 382)

S.     Scylla, Phorci filia, quae cum mutuo Glauci amore teneretur, indignata Circe, quae Glaucum misere deperibat . . . fontem, in quo illa lauari solebat, noxiis herbis veneficisque infecit. Cuius rei illa ignara, cum lauandi gratia fontem ingressa esset, videret inferiorem corporis partem in caninos rictus esse commutatam: quam deformitatem tantopere exhortuit, vt sese statim in vicinum praecipitauerit fretum: vbi & in saxum mutata fingitur, Charybdi ex aduerso obiectum. . . .

    Charybdis, gurges vorticosus in freto Siculo. . . . [There follows a brief account of the force and fierceness of the whirlpool.] Poetae fabulantur Charybdim mulierem fuisse rapacissimam, a Ioue cum Herculis boues surripuisset fulminatam, & in voraginem hanc conuersam. . . . Scylla, filia Nisi, regis Megarensium, quae Minois paterni hostis amore capta . . . patrem purpureo capillo, in quo situm erat regni totius fatum, eumque hosti obtulit. . . . Verum cum se ab illo sperni videret, doloris impatentia in Cirem auem commutata est: Nisus autem in aliam auem sui nominis. . . .

Usually, however, particularly from the letter H, until the end of the compilation, Ross relied upon a single dictionary entry and frequently followed verbatim the account in Charles Stephanus. The following examples are typical:

### GALATAEA

*R.* She was the daughter of Nereus and Doris, whom Polyphemus the Giant did earnestly love; but being despised by her, because she loved Acis the Shepherd better; he enraged killed Acis with a great stone; whom Galataea out of Piety, converted into a Fountain of the same name. (p. 129)

*S.* Galathea, nympha marina, Nerei & Doridos filia, a Polyphema adamata: Quem cum illa sperneret, Acimque ei praeferret, indignatus Cyclops riualem saxo de rupe auulso interfecit: cuius casum miserati dij marini, in fluuium sui nominis eum commutauerunt.

### HEBE

*R.* She was the daughter of Iuno begot without a Father; only by eating of Lettice; for Iuno being invited to a Feast by Apollo into Iupiter's house, she presently conceived by feeding upon Lettice, and bare this Hebe; who for her beauty, was made Iupiter's Cup-bearer, till she disgraced her self by a fall in Iupiter's presence at a Feast, where she discovered her nakedness; by which means she lost her office, and Ganymede was chosen in her room. (p. 149)

*S.* Hebe, filia Iunonis, absque patre . . . de cuius ortu huiusmodo refertur fabula: Apollinem, cum Iunoni nouercae conuiuium, in patria sui domo parasset, inter alia lactucas agrestes ei apposuisse: quas cum Iuno auide comedisset, cum antea sterilis esset, praegnans effecta est, peperitque Heben, quam postea Iupiter ob formae elegantiam poculis suis praefecit. Verum cum Ioue apud AEthiopas coenante, Hebe pocula illi administrans, perque lubricum minus caute incidena, cecidisset, reuolutisque vestibus obscoena superis nudasset, ab officio est amota, euisque loco Ganymedes subrogatus. . . .

### HESPERIDES

*R.* These were the daughters of Hesperia, by Atlas, called therefore Hesperides, and Atlantides; they had a rich garden, wherein grew golden

Apples, which were kept by a watchful Dragon; but Hercules killed
the Dragon and carried away the Apples. (p. 174)

*S.*   Hesperides, appellatae sunt Hesperi fratris Atlantis filiae . . . quas
poetae fabulantur habuisse hortos, nemore aurifero pretiosos, a dracone
peruigili seruatos, quem Hercules dicitur interfecisse, pomaque aurea
ad vitricum Euristheum retulisse.

### HIPPOLITVS

*R.*   He was the son of Theseus and Hippolyta, the Amazon; who abhorred
the company of women, and gave himself to hunting; but in his fathers
absence, Phaedra his step-mother desired the use of his body; which
he refusing, was falsly accused by her to his father as if he had attempted to ravish her; he believing it to be true, intended to kill his
son, which Hippolytus fearing, fled away in a chariot; but as he was
on the Seashore, the Scale-fishes being affrighted at the ratling of his
Chariot, rushed suddenly into the Sea, and so affrighted the horses,
that they drag'd Hippolytus among the rocks and brambles, so that
the young man was torn in pieces, and was buried in the Wood Aricinus,
dedicated to Diana. (p. 176)

*S.*   Hippolytus, Thesei & Hippolytae Amazonis filius, qui cum coelibem
ducens vitam venatu sese exerceret, & constanti animo sperneret mulieres,
a Phaedra nouerca absente patre amatus est: cuius turpi desiderio cum
obtemperare noluisset, illa filium apud patrem detulit, tanquam de stupro
eam appellasset.   Quamobrem cum videret Hippolytus patrem nouercae
dolo persuasum de neca sua cogitare, conscenso curru fugam arripuit.
Sed dum phocae, quae tum forti in littus exierant, equorum & rotarum
strepitu perterritae, magno impetu se in mare praecipitarent, exterriti
equi frustra obluctante Hippolyto, currum per scopulos & saxa traxerunt,
iuuenemque infoelicem loris implicitum varias in partes discerpserunt,
in nemore autem Aricino Dianae sacro sepultus est. . . .

### HYACINTHVS

*R.*   This was a beautiful youth with whom both Apollo and Zephyrus were
in love at the same time: but Zephyrus perceiving that the youths love
inclined more to Apollo than to himself, grew angry, and whilst he
with Apollo were playing at the exercise called Discus, with a sudden
blast of wind turnèd the Discus or Quoit upon the youths head, and
killed him; Apollo being grieved at this loss, was comforted by Tellus,
which drank up his blood, and turned it into a flower of his own name.
(p. 179)

[Once again Ross's marginal authorities are those cited by Charles
Stephanus, with, however, the appropriate section in Comes also being
noted.]

*S.*   Hyacinthus, puer Amyclaeus, eodem tempore a Zephyro & Apolline
adamatus, Verum cum in Apollinis amorem propensior esset, aegre id

ferens Zephyrus, amorem in odium conuertit. Cum Hyacintho suis deliciis disci iactu, dum sese exerceret, Zephyrus nocendi occasionem nactus, discam ab Apolline emissum fletu suo in caput Hyacintho conuertit, puerumque interemit. Cuius mortem cum aegerrime ferret Apollo, Tellus in amatoris dei solatium, cruorem eius commutauit in florem sui nominis, Palaephatus in tractatu de Fabulosis narrationibus: paulo aliter Oui. lib 10. Metamorph.

### HYMENAEVS

*R.* He was the son of Liber and Venus, the god of marriages, born in Attica, who used to rescue Virgins that were carried away by Thieves, and restored them again to their Parents, without any violence offered to them; therefore in weddings he was wont to be called upon, as the Defender of Virginity; so Thalassius was called upon by the Romans. (p. 186)

*S.* Hymenaeus, Deus nuptiarum praeses. . . . Hic Liberi patris & Veneris . . . filius fuisse putatur. . . . Alii volunt Hymenaeum, virum Atticum fuisse, qui raptas a latronibus virgines, parentibus intactas restituit; hanc nuptialem factam apud Graecos, quemadmodum Romani in nuptiis virginalibus Thalassii nomen inuocant. . . .

### HYPSIPHILE

*R.* She was queen of Lemnus, and daughter to Thoas; when all the women of the Island had murthered their husbands, and kinsmen, she alone preserved her father alive, she fell in love with Jason, and bore him two sons but when the Islanders understood that she had preserved her father alive, she was condemned to die, but she escaped by Sea, and was taken by Pirates, and sold to Lycurgus King of Nemea, who made her Nurse to his young child; but she leaving the child a while in the meadow whilst she was showing a spring of water to the Argivi travelling towards Thebes, he was killed by a Serpent, and she condemned to die by Lycurgus, but was preserved by the Argivi. (p. 189)

*S.* Hypsiphile, Lemni regina, Thoantis filia quae cum reliquae mulieres eius insulae viros cognatosque omnes, ex communi sententia occidissent, sola patrem seruauit. Ob quam pietatem e Lemno eiecta, capta fuit a piratis, & Lycurgo Nemeae regi vendita; a quo liberaliter habita fuit, & nutriendo filio eius praeposita. Nam paulo ante fugam gemellos pepererat, quos conceperat ex Iasone, quem in Colchos nauigantem hospitio simul & lecto exceperat. Postea cum Argiuis ad Thebanam expeditionem proficiscentibus, Langiam fontem ostensura, & Archenorum alumnum humi deposuisset, ea absente adrepens serpens puerum interemit: quo nomine a Lycurgo ad supplicium quaereretur ab Adrasto, caeterisque Argiuis seruata est. . . .

IPHIGENIA

R. She was the daughter of Agamemnon and Clytemnestra: he having hurt, one day as he was hunting, Diana's Stag, she was so offended therewith, that she kept the Grecians with contrary winds in Aulis; the Oracle being consulted, it was answered that the goddess could not be appeased, but by the death of Iphigenia; Ulysses undertaking this, went and brought away Iphigenia from her mother to Aulis, under pretence that she was to be married to Achilles: being brought to the Altar, and ready to be sacrificed, Diana took pity on her, and presented a Doe in her stead, and then conveyed her away to the country Taurica, and by Thoas the King thereof she was made Priestess of all human sacrifices; her brother Orestes being mad, and coming thither, was appointed by Thoas to be sacrificed; but being known by his sister, was delivered, and they both escaped away together by sea. (p. 210)

S. Iphigenia Agamemnonis & Clytemnestrae filia: de qua fabulam huiusmodi comminiscuntur poetae. Cum Agamemnon in Aulide ceruum Dianae imprudens occidisset, Dea indignata contrariis flatibus Graecorum nauigationem est remorata. Qua de re cum vates consulerent, responsum est Agamemnonio sanguine deam esse placandam. Missus igitur Vlysses Iphigeniam astu a matre abduxit, Achilli eam nupturam simulans: cumque iam immolanda esset, Dea eius miserata, ceruam pro ea supposuit, virginem autem in Tauricam regionem transtulit, vbi a Thoante rege eius deae sacris praefecta est, quae humano sanguine fieri solebant. Quo cum postea Orestes furiis agitatus venisset, iamque esset immolandus, a sorore agnitus & liberatus est: cum qua non multo post . . . in lignorum fasce abscondito . . . quod cum in Italiam venissent, in Aricino nemore collocarunt.

JUPITER

R. He was the son of Saturn and Ops, and was born in Creta at the same birth with Juno, and was brought up on Mount Ida by the Curetes privately, for fear his father should find him, who was devouring his own children: but afterward he drove his father out of his Kingdom, and divided the world with his two brothers, Neptune, and Pluto: he took heaven for himself, the sea fell to Neptune, and hell to Pluto; he used to change himself into many shapes, and took Juno his own sister to wife. (pp. 220-21)

S. Iupiter, Opis & Saturni filius, in Creta insula eodem cum Iunone partu editus, & in Ida monte a Curetibus educatus, idque clam patre, qui ex pactione cum Titano fratre inita, filios suos omnes deuorabat . . . etiam tunc patrem vitae suae insidiam, regno eum pepulit, mundique imperium cum fratribus Neptuno & Plutone sorte diuisit: ac Ioui quidem coeli & terrae Neptuno maris, Plutoni inferorum imperium obtigit. Iunonem deinde sororum suam vxorem duxit. . . .

LEVCOTHOE

*R.*    She was the daughter of Orchamus King of Babylon, with whom Apollo being in love; transformed himself into the shape of Eurynome, her mother, having removed all her waiting maids from her, and pretending secret conference with her daughter; at last Apollo assumed his own shape, and got his desire of her; which when Clytie, who was also in love with Apollo, knew, she acquainted Orchamus the cruel King with his daughters love; he buried Leucothea alive, which Apollo took heavily: and because he could not restore her to life, transformed her into a Frankincense-tree. [Ross's marginal citation of "Ovid Met. 4" once more agrees with the authority in the dictionary entry.] (p. 234)

*S.*    Leucothea, Orchami Babyloniorum regia filia, cuius amore captus Apollo, in Eurymones [*sic*] (ea Leucothoes mater erat) figuram sese transmutauit, & tanquam secreto aliquid cum filia colloqui vellet, famulas, quibus comitata erat, secedere iussit. Deinde pristinae restitutus formae, professus quis esset post multas blanditias, non admodum inuitae vim intulit. Quod cum resciuisset Clytie, quae mutuo Apollinis amore tenebatur . . . Orchamo regi filiae amores enuntiauit: qui vt natura crudelis erat, filiam viuam defodit. Cuius mortem aegerrime ferens Apollo, cum vitae eam restituere non posset, in virgam thuream eam transformauit. Ovid. 4, Metam. . . .

LYNCUS

*R.*    Lyncus, Lynx or Lynceus, was the cruel King of Scythia, who having received Triptolemus into his house, whom Ceres sent thither to shew him the use of corn, and instruments of Husbandry, he out of ambition desirous to be thought the author of such an excellent invention, intended to murther Triptolemus in the night, whilst he was asleep, but Ceres being angry at his treachery, turned him into the beast Lynx. [The first marginal citation is "Ovid. Met. 5"] (p. 248)

*S.*    Lyncus, vt habet Ouidius: Lynceus, vt alij: Lynx vt rursus alij, rex Scythiae immanissimus, qui Triptolemum a Cerere missum, vt hominibus frugum vsum commonstraret, hospitio excepit . . . vt tam praeclari inuenti gloriam in se transferret, hospitem obtruncare constituit. Cumque iam noctu dormientem aggredi vellet, Ceres indignata in Lyncem feram eum conuertit. Ouid. 5. Metamorph. . . .

MINOS

*R.*    He was the son of Jupiter and Europa, who married with Pasiphae, the daughter of the Sun: he had great wars against the people of Megara and Athens. Megara he subdued by the treachery of Scylla, who betrayed to Minos, her fathers fatal hair; and he caused the Athenians to deliver every year seven young men to be devoured by the Minotaure, in Creta: Daedalus being entertained by him, built the Labyrinth in which Minos shut up the Minotaure; but when he understood that

Daedalus had assisted the Queen to lie with the Bull, he shut him and his son Icarus within the same Labyrinth, but they escaping were pursued in a ship by the King, who near Camerinum was slain, and so was the Minotaure by Theseus in the Labyrinth who escaped thence by the help of Ariadnes thread. (pp. 292-93)

S.     Minos, filius Iouis Europa. . . . Aristo. Polit. I Pasiphaen Solis filiam matrimonio sibi iunxit. . . . Maxima bella gessit aduersus Megarenses & Atheniensis . . . atque Megaram quidem Scillae puellae prodicione cepit, quae amore Minois capta Nissum patrem fatali capillo spoliauit: Athenienses autem eo necessitatis compulit, vt septem quotannis iuuenes in Cretam mittere cogerentur, Minotauro monstro obiiciendos. Daedalum . . . hospitio suscepit, qui cum ingenio . . . labyrinthum ei extruxit . . . cui & Minotaurum inclusit. . . . Verum cum postea didicisset, Daedalum vxori suae in tam nephando concubitu adiutorem sese praebuisse . . . ipsum quoque vna cum Icaro filio eodem labyrintho inclusit: cumque illi alis cera conglutinatis inde euolassent, classe eos in Siciliam vsque est persequutus: vbi apud Camerinum . . . occisus est. [Ross then skips to the middle portion of the entry immediately following that on Minos, which continues with the "history" of Minotaurus.] . . . Theseus . . . Minotaurum occidit, & ab Ariadne accepto filij glomere, fuga euasit. . . .

The preceding examples should be sufficient to illustrate the most noticeable aspect of the relationship between Ross's compilation and the *Dictionarium Historicum.* From the letter M until the end of the *Mystagogus Poeticus,* the following descriptions also show a comparable correspondence: "Narcissus," "Nycteus," "Oedipus," "Orestes," "Osiris," "Penelope," "Priapus," "Prometheus," "Sphinx," "Tantalus," "Theseus," "Typhoeus or Typhon," and "Vulcan." In writing the descriptive entry for each of the preceding accounts, Ross sometimes translated verbatim the shorter articles in the lexicon, sometimes—as with "Minos"—condensed a relatively long article by lifting verbatim crucial sentences from the dictionary. Similar examples other than those listed and mentioned above can be found. As a final illustration, we close this section with the account of Theseus, a "history" treated by Ross in a manner very similar to that found in his entry under "Minos":

### THESEUS

R.     He was the son of AEgeus and AEthra: his step-mother would have poison'd him in his youth: he subdued the Amazons, and of Hippolyta their Queen begot Hippolytus: he killed Creon King of the Thebans, the untamed bull in Africa, the Minotaur in the Labyrinth: and carried away the two daughters of King Minos, to wit, Ariadne and Phaedra:

he killed also Procrustes, Sciron, and Schinis, great robbers in Attica; he overcame the Centaurs and the Thebes: he went down to hell with his friend Perithous, to ravish Proserpina, where Perithous was slain, and he put in chains, but was delivered by Hercules: at last in his old age was killed by King Lycomedes. (pp. 399-400)

S. Theseus, AEgaee regis Athenarum filius, ex AEthra . . . qui adhuc adolescens, opera Medeae nouercae pene veneno periit. . . . Debellauit Amazonas, earumque reginam Hippolytem secum abduxit: ex qua & Hippolitum genuit. Creontem regem Thebanorum cadauera Argiuorum, qui Thebano in bello occiderant. . . . Oppressit & terribilem taurum in Attica. Minotaurum in Labyrintho occidit, & Ariadnam Phaedramque Minois filias clam secum abduxit. . . . Scironem, Procrustum, & Schinim latrones Atticae neci dedit: debellauit Centauros, Thebas domuit. Pirithoum praecipua coluit amicitia, quocum descendit ad inferos ad rapiendam Proserpinam: sed occiso Piritho, ipse aliquandiu in vinculis . . . fuit detentus, donec ab Hercule . . . liberaretur. Postremo iam senior . . . periit, a rege Lycomede . . . interfectus. . . .

Other material in the interpretive portions, but particularly in the descriptive entries, is greatly condensed from the corresponding accounts in the *Dictionarium Historicum,* but an occasional brief verbatim agreement clearly indicates Ross's source. Although too long for quotation here, the Latin articles of Charles Stephanus pretty clearly were the source, for example, for Ross's relatively short descriptions of Flora, Hylas, Lares and Penates, Leander, Mars, Medea, Mercury, Minerva, Orion, and Orpheus.

Two interesting examples of the way in which Ross also occasionally reworked material that he found in the lexicon are afforded by his long entries under "Musae" and "Hercules." The accounts in the dictionaries concerning the Muses have been given in full in the chapter on Spenser; the shorter account of Hercules should, therefore, serve our turn:

### HERCULES

R. [Hercules] He was the son of Jupiter and Alcmene, whom Juno persecuted out of malice; and exposed him to many dangers, which notwithstanding he overcame, and for his noble acts was deified, and placed among the stars. The chiefest of his famous acts were these. 1. He killed the two Snakes, that were sent by Juno to kill him in his cradle. 2. In one night he begot fifty sons of Thespius his fifty daughters. 3. He slew the Lion in the wood Nemaea. 4. He killed the Snake Hydra in the Lake of Lerna. 5. He overtook and killed the golden-horned Stag, on the hill Maenalus. 6. He killed Diomedes the Thracian King, and gave him to be eaten by his men-eating horses.

7. He killed the Boar in Erimanthus, a hill of Arcadia.  8. He killed
the wild Bull in Crete.  9. He slew the Birds called Stymphalides.
10. He overcame Achelous.  11. He killed Busiris the Tyrant of Egypt.
12. He slew Antaeus the Giant.  13. He killed the Dragon that kept
the Golden Apples in the Gardens of Hesperides.  14. He helped Atlas
to support the heaven.  15. He divided the Hills Calpe and Abila,
which before were united.  16. He oppressed Cacus.  17. He overcame
Geryon.  18. He killed Lacinus the great Robber.  19.  He tamed the
Centaurs.  20. He killed Eurypilus the Tyrant, with his wife & children.
21. He delivered Hesion, Laomedons daughter, from the Seamonster.
22. He slew Tyrrhenus the Tyrant of Euboea.  23. He subdued the
Amazons.  24. He went down to hell and drew up with him the dog
Cerberus.  25. He shot the Eagle that fed upon Prometheus his heart.
26. He killed Lycas the Tyrant of Thebes.  27. He brought back from
hell Alcestes.  28. He overcame Cygnus the son of Mars.  29. He
killed Thoedamus, and brought away his son Hylas with him.  30. He
sacked Pylus, and killed the King Neleus with his family except Nestor.
31. He killed Zetis and Calais, the sons of Boreas.  32. He travelled
through the torrid Zone, and sands of Lybia.  33. He overcame the
Apish people Cercopes.  34. He purged Augaeus his stable.  35. He
passed on foot over Lybian Syrtes, having lost his ship.  36. He erected
two pillars in Spain and Africa.  37. He killed Eurytus the Tyrant of
Oechalia, whose daughter Iole he carried away and married her; at
which Deianira being displeased, sent him a cloak dipt in the bloud of
the Centaur Nessus, thinking thereby to have reclaimed him; but it
put him into such a madness, that he burned himself.

S.        Hercules, Iouis & Alcmenae filius. . . . [There follows a discussion ab-
stracting material in Cicero's *De Natura Deorum,* wherein six Hercules are differentiated, etc.] Hercules autem Alcmenes filium maxime
nobilitauit implacabile Iunonis odium, quae, quod ex pellice natus esset,
perdere illum cupiens, nouis semper monstris obiecit: quae res expecta-
tionem eius maxime fefellit.    Ille enim semper victoriam referens,
immortale sibi decus peperit, adeo vt illa prius iubendo, quam hic
laborando defatigaretur. . . . [There follows a brief general discussion about Hercules' heroic virtue.] Primo itaque cum adhuc in cuna-
bulis iaceret, geminos angues a Iunone immissos elisit.    II. Thespij
filias numero quinquaginta adhuc puer . . . vna nocte compressit, sus-
cepitque quinquaginta filios. . . . III. iam adultus hydram colubris &
capitibus pullulantem, face & ferro in Lerna palude oppressit.    IIII.
Ceruam aëripedem, aureaque habentem cornua, in Maenalo monte cursu
comprehendit atque interfecit.    V. in Nemaea sylua . . . leonem iugu-
lauit. . . . VI. Diomedem Thraciae regem, qui equos suos hospitum
carnibus & sanguine pascebat, deuicit, victumque ipsius equis in pabu-
lum dedit.    VII. in Erymantho Arcadiae monte terribilem aprum . . .

cepit, eumque viuum ad Eurystheum attulit. VIII. Stymphalides aues...
interfecit. . . . IX. Taurum, insulam Cretam fere totam deuastantem
domuit, eumque vinctum ad Erystheum attulit: qui postea eum Atticae
regioni immisit, cui plurimum damni intulit: sed a Theseo interfectus
fuit. . . . X. Acheloum superauit. XI. Busiridem AEgypti regem . . .
occidit. XII. Antaeum gigantem . . . suffocauit. XIIII. Aurea mala
in Hesperidum hortis, interempto prius dracone peruigili, qui ea custo-
diebat, sustulit. XV. Coelum, iam fesso & succumbente ponderi At-
lanta, humeris tulit. XVI. Geryonem . . . superauit. . . . XVII. Cacum
. . . oppressit. XVIII. Lacinum latronem extremam Italiae oram in-
festantem sustulit. . . . XIX. Albionem & Bergionem iter ipsius im-
pedientes, haud longe ab ostio Rhodani, a Ioue patre lapidum imbre
adiutus, deuicit. XX. Tyrrhenum Euboeae regem, Boeotiis bellum in-
ferentem profligauit, eumque pullis equinis alligatum in diuersas partes
discerpsit. XXI. Centauros domuit. XXII. Augiae stabulum repur-
gauit. XXIII. Hesionem Laomendontis filiam monstro marino expo-
sitam liberauit. . . . XXIIII. . . regemque Eurypylum cum vxore &
liberis trucidauit. XXV. Amazones debellavit. . . . XXVI. Ad inferos
descendit, & Cerberum . . . traxit. . . . XXVII. Alcestim Admeti regis
coniugem ab inferis ad virum reduxit. XXVIII. . . Lycum Thebarum
regem . . . interemit. XXIX. Aquilam, quae Promethei in Caucaso
relegati perpetuo renascens iecur exedebat sagittis traiecit. XXX. Cygnum Martis filium . . . vicit. XXXI. Occidit Theodamantem . . . il-
liusque filium Hylam . . . secum abduxit. XXXII. Cercopas vicit.
. . . [Under "Cercopes" Ross might read "Cercopes . . . a Ioue in simias
mutati sunt."] XXXIII. Pylum diripuit, eiusque regem Neleum, cum
tota domo praeter Nestorum trucidauit. . . . XXXIII. Zeten & Calain
alatos Boreae filios . . . interfecit. . . . XXXV. Torridam Zonam &
Lybiae aestuantes harenas incolumnis pertransiuit: Brenia & Syrtes
naue amissa pedes superauit. XXXVI. Columnae in Occidente quae
de eius nomine dictae fuerunt, erexit. XXXVII. Eurytum Oechaliae
regem occidit . . . & Iolen Euryti filiam sibi denegatam . . . vi obtinuit,
eamque secum in Euboeam abduxit. Quod cum Deianira coniunx resciuisset, maritum suum Ioles amore detineri . . . vestem illi misit Nessi
Centauri sanguine infectam, futurum rata, vt ea ratione languentem
viri amorem excitaret. . . . Cum itaque Hercules vestem sacrificaturus
induisset, in tantam rabiem versus est, vt constructa pyra seipsum com-
busserit. . . .

The verbatim agreement between Ross and Charles Stephanus is
obvious, even though Ross varies the order of Hercules' labors. In re-
working the thirty-seven tasks, for a while he follows the order of the *Dictionarium Historicum,* although his apparent haste may have caused his
entry of the fifth division in Charles Stephanus under number three, as

well as his oversight of the thirteenth division—an omission he rectifies by his number fifteen. Numbers eight and nine he had reversed. With his number nineteen, Ross seems to have varied the order consciously, going to twenty-one, twenty-four, twenty-three, etc. He never picks up Charles Stephanus' nineteen, however. The result is that he divides number thirty-five in order to round out the necessary total of thirty-seven. Although he once may have enlarged his source briefly (32 of *Dict. Hist.*), throughout he condenses the material appreciably; and at times (e.g., 7 and 9 of *Dict. Hist.*) his desire to compress the information in Charles Stephanus may have led to some errors in detail.

Ross's use of the lexicon as late as 1647 once more indicates the value of the compilation to men of letters during the period in England conventionally known as the Renaissance. The account of Hercules is characteristic. But also illustrative of Ross's vagaries in borrowing are "Icarus," "Ino," "Iphis," "Megara," "Myrrha," "Oceanus," and "Perseus."

# NOTES

1 Suidas' lexicon was first printed at Milan in 1499; other editions appeared at Venice, 1514; Basle, 1544, etc. A Latin translation was published in 1564, 1581, 1609, etc. Edited by L. Kuster, Cambridge, 1705, 3 vols.

2 For a short essay on the *Catholicon*, see Edgar Ewing Brandon's *Robert Estienne et Le Dictionnaire Français au xvi<sup>e</sup> Siècle* (Baltimore, 1904), pp. 27-28. Editions of *Catholicon:* 1460, 1473, 1487, 1495, 1506, 1514, 1520.

3 Other editions of the *Cornucopiae:* 1499, 1513, 1517, 1522, 1526-7. Cf. Brunet, *Manuel du Libraire* (Bruxelles, 1838), III, 462.

4 Among the editions of Calepine in the sixteenth and seventeenth centuries are these: 1502, 1510, 1518, 1520, 1542, 1560, 1575, 1590, 1605, 1609, etc.

5 There were editions of Robert Stephanus' *Thesaurus* in 1531, 1536, 1543, 1570, 1573, and 1740.

6 Thomas' *Dictionarium* was first printed at Cambridge in 1587. Subsequent editions appeared in 1589, 1592, 1594, 1596, 1600, 1606, 1610, 1615, 1619, 1620, 1631, 1644.

7 Gouldman's *A Copious Dictionary in Three Parts* was printed in 1664, 1669, 1674, 1678.

8 Editions of Littleton's *A Latine Dictionary in Four Parts* appeared in 1678, 1684, 1703, 1715, 1723, 1735.

9 For a concise account of Torrentinus and his work, see *Allgemeine Deutsche Biographie,* II, 245. "Grosseres Lob," the account runs in part, "erwarb er sich durch die Herausgabe eines historischen Worterbuches, *Elucidarius* . . . welches zuerst 1498 zu Deventer erschien und der erste Versuch auf diesem Gebiete war."

See also Michaud's *Biographie Universelle Ancienne et Moderne . . .* Nouvelle Édition. Paris, n.d.

10 As copies of earlier editions are not available at this time, we have used a copy printed at The Hague, 1514, with the simplified title *Elucidarius vel Vocabularius Poeticus.* This volume is in the Rare Book Collections, University of Texas, and is bound with a Latin-German dictionary of the same date, entitled *Dictionarium quod Gemma Gemmarum vocant.*

11  Ioannis Crastoni or Crestoni, a Hellenist of the fifteenth century, born at
    Plaisance; sometimes referred to under the name Ioannes Placentinus. He
    is the author of a Greek-Latin dictionary, Milan, 1478.

12  The entries are of course in Latin. We have taken the liberty of giving
    free translations of the original.

13  Deventer, 1498, 1501, 1503; Argentinae [Strassburg], 1505, 1514, 1518,
    Hagenau, 1507, 1510, 1512, 1514; Lare, 1515.

14  We write "Stephanus," the Latinized form of "Estienne," because
    "Stephanus" (Robert Stephanus, Charles Stephanus) is the form which
    appears on the title-page of the Estienne dictionaries which we refer to
    in this study.

    Editions of the *Elucidarius* as augmented by Robert and then by Charles
    Stephanus, between 1530 and 1568, are as follows: Paris, 1530, 1535, 1541,
    1550; Cologne, 1536, 1543, 1554, 1568; Antwerp, 1545, 1553.

15  The *Elucidarius* with the original title and, apparently, with little or no
    augmentation was being printed elsewhere, as in Cologne, in 1536. The
    evidence indicates that the book with the original title continued to be
    published through the greater part of the sixteenth century, sometimes in
    the original, sometimes in the translation, as in the Italian edition by Tosca-
    nella, printed at Venice in 1585.

16  A list of dates, perhaps not exhaustive, of editions printed at Paris and
    elsewhere, runs thus: 1553, 1561, 1566, 1567, 1575, 1579, 1581, 1595, 1596,
    1608, 1610, 1618, 1621, 1633, 1650, 1652, 1660, 1671, 1686, 1693. See *Cata-
    logue Général Des Livres Imprimés de La Bibliothèque Nationale*, Paris,
    1912. See also the Catalogue of the British Museum.

17  The sketch of Torrentinus in the *Biographie Universelle* (Michaud) con-
    cludes, "Cet opuscule est le premier essai que l'on connaise d'un dictionnaire
    historique contenant aussi la mythologie et la géographie ancienne. . . .
    Ainsi, malgré l'imperfection de son travail, on ne peut sans injustice re-
    fuser à Torrentinus l'honneur d'avoir donné l'idée et le modèle des dic-
    tionnaires historiques dont chaque jour fait sentir l'utilité."

18  Editions of Lempriere's *Bibliotheca* appeared in 1788, 1797, 1808, 1815,
    1818, 1822, 1828, 1833, 1838, 1843, 1888, etc.

CHAPTER II

1  John Edwin Sandys, *A History of Classical Scholarship*, 11 (Cambridge,
   University Press, 1908), 373-74; the quotation is from Olaus Borrichius'
   *Dissert. de Lexicis Latinis*.

2  *Ibid.*, II, 179.

3  See T. W. Baldwin, *William Shakspere's Small Latine and Lesse Greeke*,
   I, 191.

4  See *ibid.*, I, 187.

5  *Day-Book of John Dorn, Bookseller in Oxford, A. D. 1520*, ed. by F.
   Madan, *Collectanea: First Series*, ed. by C. R. L. Fletcher (Oxford Hist.

Soc., Clarendon Press, 1885), pp. 71-177. For Dorn's sale of Calepine, see nos. 95, 96, 783, 1022-23, 1065, 1316-17, 1585.

6 Hist. MSS. Commission, *Report on the Manuscripts of Lord Middleton Preserved at Wollaton Hall, Nottinghamshire* (London, H. M. S. O., 1911), pp. 411-13.

7 "The Library of James VI. 1573-1583. From a Manuscript in the Hand of Peter Young, his Tutor," ed. by George F. Warner, *Miscellany of the Scottish Historical Society,* I (Scottish Hist. Soc., XV, 1893), p. xlv.

8 R. B. Gardiner, *The Admission Registers of St. Paul's School* (London, George Bell & Sons, 1884), p. 452; 1578 is the earliest edition that we have so far found of a Calepine with the six languages indicated, plus Italian.

9 *Ibid.,* p. 453.

10 *Miscellany of the Maitland Club,* I (Edinburgh, 1833), 319, 327.

11 John Strype, *The Life and Acts of Matthew Parker* (London, John Wyat, 1711), p. 291. See also H. W. Saunders, *A History of Norwich Grammar School* (Norwich, Jarrold & Sons, Lt'd, 1932), p. 171.

12 Charles Hoole, *A New Discovery of the Old Art of Teaching School,* ed. E. T. Campagnac (Liverpool, 1913), pp. 201-2.

13 J. Strype, *op. cit.,* p. 291.

14 *Miscellany of the Maitland Club,* V, 323, 325.

15 Burton left his books to the Bodleian, unless they would duplicate books already there, in which case they were to go to the library at Christ Church, where his copy of a 1595 *Dictionarium historicum* appeared. "Two Lists of Burton's Books," ed. by S. Gibson and F. R. D. Needham, *Oxford Bibliographical Society, Papers and Proceedings,* I, 1922-6 (1927), 222, 245.

16 Hoole, *op. cit.,* pp. 205, xx (and 324), xxii (and 321).

17 Saunders, *op. cit.,* p. 262.

18 Gardiner, *op. cit.,* pp. 452-53.

19 *Library,* Fourth Series, XV, 459-62.

20 Rev. Frank Willcox, "The Accounts of St. Albans Grammar School," *Middlesex and Hertfordshire Notes and Queries,* I, 40. See also I, 15.

21 *Supra,* pp. 12-13, and *The Comedy of Acolastus: Translated from the Latin of Fullonius by John Palsgrave,* ed. by P. L Carver, Early English Text Soc., No. 202 (1937), p. 122, l. 27 *et passim; Miscellany of the Maitland Club,* I, 21; T. W. Baldwin, *op. cit.,* I, 715 *et passim;* Leslie Hotson, "The Library of Elizabeth's Embezzling Teller," *Studies in Bibliography: Papers of the Bibliographical Society of the University of Virginia,* II, 56, 60. Elizabeth's regard for Cooper's *Thesaurus* is well known; see, for example, the account under "Cooper" in the *DNB.* The French-Latin Stephanus dictionary may also have been in the library of Mary Queen of Scots; see *Miscellany of the Maitland Club,* I, 8, and Julian Sharman, *The Library of Mary, Queen of Scots* (London, Elliot Stock, 1889), p. 78.

22 See T. W. Baldwin, *op. cit.*, I, 173-74, based upon MS Brasenose Coll. 31; Bodleian Lib. The information concerns Alexander Nowell's notebook, which indicates what books were being used, 1535-40, at Oxford; see the list of books left with one who had lectured upon Rodolphus Agricola.

23 *The Comedy of Acolastus*, pp. lxxvii, lxxxix, xciv-xcv, and *supra*, p. 18, n. 21.

24 T. W. Baldwin, *op. cit.*, I, 715.

25 *Thesaurus* (London, 1578), sig. 4 v.

26 *Ibid.*, sig. 5 v. Translated by D. T. Starnes.

27 Hoole, *op. cit.*, p. 184; the italics are ours, except for the proper nouns.

28 Frederic H. Forshall, *Westminster School: Past and Present* (London, Wyman and Sons, 1884), p. 416.

29 *Supra*, p. 5.

30 T. W. Baldwin, *op. cit.*, I, 119, n. 4., citing information from MS o. 10.22 in the library of Trinity College, Cambridge. We suspect that Baldwin has identified the text incorrectly; it is probably the Cooper, as the Littleton quotation indicates.

31 Hoole, *op. cit.*, p. 179.

32 *Ibid.*, pp. 161-62.

33 *The Early Lives of Milton*, ed. by H. Darbishire (London, 1932), pp. 29, 71-72; see also pp. 45-46, 192, 268.

34 *Supra*, p. 18; for Chapman's use of Scapula, see Frank L. Schoell, *Étude sur L'Humanisme Continental en Angleterre* (Paris, 1926), pp. 167, 146-57.

35 E.g., T. W. Baldwin, *op. cit.*, I, 715, 718-19.

36 John Brinsley, *Ludus Literarius* (Liverpool, University Press; London, Constable; 1917), p. 76.

37 "Aut fabulam habeat, ut illud: Hercules expugnandis monstris immortalitem sibi paravit. Musae fontibus ac nemoribus unice gaudent, a fumosis urbibus abhorrent." *Desiderii Erasmi Roterdami Opera Omnia* . . . , I (Lugduni Batavorum, Petri Vander, 1703), 525. See also "De Conscribendis Epistolis," cap. IX, for counsel on the knowledge of classic myth and legend; *ibid.*, I, 353-54.

38 *Aphthonii Sophistae Progymnasmata* . . . (London, Thomas Marsh, 1583), sigs. 160r-161r. See also the suggested comparison between Priam and Dardanus, Thetis and Tethys, *ibid.*, sigs. 162v-163r.

39 For a typical *narratio, destructio* and *confirmatio*, and "Impersonation," see *ibid.*, sigs. 18r-22v; 65r-67v and 80v-86r; as well as 77r-78v; 167v-169r, 175v-176r, 179r-180r.

40 See, e.g., the divisions "ab exemplo" under "Sententia," *ibid.*, sigs. 54r, 60r, 61r. Note also the subjects listed under "Laus," e.g., "Iuno," "Mars," "Pallas," etc., sigs. 118r ff.

41 Hoole, *op. cit.*, p. 162.

42 Leslie Hotson, *op. cit.*, p. 57; *Library*, Fourth Ser., XV, 459.

43 Hoole, *op. cit.*, pp. 162-63.

44 *Supra*, p. 9; *infra*, pp. 286-87.

1 These are Agesilaus, Alexander the Great, Ambrose, Cicero, Democritus, Demosthenes, Ennius, Galen, Homer, Horace, Justinian (partly), Ovid, Pacuvius, Philip of Macedon, Phocion, Pompey, Plautus, and Theopompus.

2 Cf. Alley, *Poore Mans Librarie,* fol. 5v (Apollo), fol. 9v (Bias), fol. 10r (Argi), fol. 10v (Xenophon), fol. 12v (Cicero), fol. 34r (Cyri Regia), fol. 48v (Epicurus), etc.

3 See Douglas Bush, in *JEGP,* XXVII (1928), 162-69.

4 These are "Tereus and Progne," "Germanicus and Agrippina," "Amphiaraus and Eriphile," "Admetus and Alcest," "Minos and Pasiphae," and "Alexius." All references to the *Petite Pallace* are to the reprint by I. Gollancz (2 vols., London, 1908).

5 Bush, *op. cit.,* p. 163.

6 Cf. Suetonius, Tiberius, LIII, *et passim;* and Tacitus, *Annals,* I, 33, 69; II, 43, 73; III, 1-6, etc. Cf. also, Bush, *op. cit.,* 163. Bush cites Tacitus as a possible source.

7 The italics are ours.

8 Bush, *op. cit.,* p. 163.

9 Cooper's source is obviously Stephanus' *Dictionarium,* in the lines which run thus ". . . *primo die quo ad Thebas venit, hiatu, terrae absorptus est.* . . ."

10 Bush, *op. cit.,* p. 163.

11 The scene of the illness of Alcest, the visit of the physician and his diagnosis, etc. (I, 172-74), is adapted from the Twenty-Seventh Novel of Painter—"The Love of Antiochus with Faire Stratonica."

12 Cf. *Ars Amatoria* I, 299; 319, and "Minos and Pasiphae" in the *Petite Pallace* (ed. by Gollancz), II, 104.

13 The reference is to the Comment on Virgil, *Buc.* VI, 46, in the edition of Servius edited by Thilo and Hagen, III, 74. Cf. also, Bush, *op. cit.,* p. 163.

14 This reference is to the volume and page in *The Complete Works of George Gascoigne.* In two volumes. Ed. by John W. Cunliffe (Cambridge: at the University Press, 1910). All subsequent references to Gascoigne's *Works* are to this edition.

15 D. T. Starnes, "Literary Features of Renaissance Dictionaries," *SP* (Jan., 1940), pp. 26-50. See especially pp. 43-44.

16 C. T. Prouty, *George Gascoigne . . . ,* New York, Columbia University Press, 1942. See especially pp. 256-61.

17 University of Texas *Studies in English,* 1947, pp. 26-41.

18 See H. E. Rollins, "John Grange's *The Golden Aphroditis,*" *Harvard Studies and Notes in Philology and Literature,* XVI (1934), 177-198; and M. P. Tilley, "Borrowing in Grange's Golden *Aphroditis,*" *MLN,* LIII, 407-412. See also Rollins' Intro. to Grange's novel in Scholars' Facsimiles and Reprints, pp. vi-viii.

19 Quoted from the Scholars' Facsimiles and Reprints of the *Golden Aphro-*

*ditis* (1577), sigs. Eiiv-Eiiiir. All references to the Grange are to this text.

20 *A Treatise against Dicing, Dancing, Plays, and Interludes. With other Idle Pastimes.* With an Introduction and Notes, by J. P. Collier. Reprinted for the Shakespeare Society, 1843, p. 83. All references to *A Treatise* are to this edition.

CHAPTER IV

1 See D. T. Starnes, "Spenser and E. K.," *SP* (Apr., 1944), 181-200; also articles by Raymond Jenkins, *Shakespeare Assoc. Bul.,* XIX, 147-60; XX, 22-36, 82-94.

2 W. P. Mustard, "E. K.'s Classical Allusions," *MLN,* XXXIV (1919), 193-203. Cf. p. 196.

3 W. L. Renwick, *The Shepherd's Calendar,* edited with Commentary and Notes, The Scholartis Press, 1930. Cf. p. 189.

4 Henry Gibbons Lotspeich, *Classical Mythology in the Poetry of Edmund Spenser,* Princeton University Press, 1932.

5 Thomas Cooper, *Thesaurus Linguae Romanae & Britannicae,* 1565. Cooper's item apparently derives from Charles Stephanus' *Dictionarium Historicum, Geographicum, Poeticum,* 1561, etc. For very similar characterizations of *Flora,* compare, also, Calepine's *Dictionarium,* 1502, 1510, 1542, etc., and Polydore Vergil's *De Inventoribus Rerum* (Basiliae, 1536), p. 335. The italics in both items are ours.

6 Cooper's item on Atlas is probably based on the entries under *Atlas* in Charles Stephanus' dictionary, or on Calepine's, which is very similar. Cooper adds details, however, such as "an hill in Barbaria" not in either of the Latin sources. The added details reappear in E. K.'s gloss.

7 The italics in the two excerpts are ours.

8 The italics are ours.

9 These are found in the dictionaries of Calepine (under *Charites* and *Gratiae,* slightly different versions), Robert Stephanus, Charles Stephanus, Cooper, Huloet (1572); Mirabellius' *Polyantheae,* Textor's *Officina,* and Alciati's *Emblems* (No. 262). In the ornamented woodcut of the emblem the three Graces are represented with joined hands—one with her back toward us as if going away, the other two facing forward. This emblem is accompanied by a Latin poem of fourteen lines, explaining the relationship of the Graces to Venus, their function, their parentage, etc.

10 The italics in the quotations from E. K. and Cooper are ours. Cooper's item is a free translation of a part of the entry under *Charites* in Charles Stephanus' *Dictionarium Historicum, Geographicum, Poeticum.*

11 "Spenser and the Graces," *PQ,* XXI (July, 1942), 268-82.

12 Lotspeich, *op. cit.,* p. 45.

13 Mustard, *op. cit.,* p. 196.

14 Renwick, *op. cit.,* p. 189.

15 Lotspeich, *op. cit.,* p. 79.

16 Cf. Calepine, *Maius.*

17 The pertinent comments of Jortin, Upton, and Lotspeich are summarized in the Var. Ed. I, 236.

18 Var. Ed. I, 236.

19 Var. Ed. II, 204.

20 Lotspeich, *op. cit.,* p. 104.

21 Compare also Vincentio Cartari, *Imagines Deorum* (1581), pp. 174-76 and Erasmus' proverb "Proteo mutabilior," *Opera,* II (1703-6), 473B.

22 Var. Ed. II, 198-9.

23 For the proud and rebellious character of the giants, see also Erasmus, II, 948D, and Calepine (1609), *Gigas.*

24 "Spenser and the Muses," University of Texas *Studies in English,* 1942, pp. 31-58.

25 Cf. Milton, Elegy VI, to Charles Diodati: "Additur huic scelerisque vacans, et casta iuventus,/Et rigidi mores, et sine labe manus./Qualis veste nitens sacra, et lustralibus undis,/Surgis ad infensos augur iture Deos." (ll. 63-66).

26 Cimmerii (inquit Festus Pompeius) dicuntur Populi, qui occupatas frigoribus terras incolunt, quales fuerunt inter Baias & Cumas in regione in qua convallis jugo satis eminenti circundata est, quae neque matutino, neque vespertino sole contingitur (R. Stephanus).

27 *Thesaurus:* "Cimmerii."

28 *Adagia,* II (1703-6), 593D.

29 Under *Musa* Calepine quotes the Epigram on the Muses, ascribing it to Virgil. Compare Mustard, *op. cit.,* p. 197.

30 Renwick, *op. cit.,* p. 220.

31 Var. Ed. III, 269-270.

32 Var. Ed. III, 254-260.

33 Var. Ed. III, 201.

34 For a concise review and summary of the discussions concerning the genesis and character of Spenser's Britomart, see the Var. Ed. of *The Faerie Queene,* III, App. 2, 330-40.

35 M. Y. Hughes, *Virgil and Spenser,* pp. 348 ff.

36 *Ibid.,* p. 358.

37 These essays on the Muses are summarized in the *Var. Ed.,* I, App. IX, 506-515.

38 D. T. Starnes, "Spenser and the Muses," the University of Texas *Studies in English,* 1942, pp. 31-58.

39 See *The Teares,* 2, 57; *F. Q.,* 1.11.5; 2.10.3; 3.3.4; *Epith.,* 121.

40 See *Shepheardes Calender,* "June," 66; *Ruines of Time,* 366; *F. Q.,* 4.11.10. Cf. Lotspeich, *op. cit.,* p. 83.

41 Starnes, *op. cit.,* pp. 36-39.

42 Starnes, *op. cit.,* pp. 42-58.

43 Cf. Perottus' *Cornucopiae* (1518), the probable source of Calepine, for a more detailed treatment of Nymphs.
   The Calepine of 1609 has matter similar to that of 1542 and adds: "It. Sposa, nimpha . . . Hispan. Esposa, nimpha. Engl. A nymphe, a faire maide or virgine."

44 Latham, *The Elizabethan Fairies—The Fairies of Folklore and the Fairies of Shakespeare* (University of California Press, 1930), pp. 15, 49-53. Cf. also Spenser's *Minor Poems,* Var. Ed., II, 311-12. Latham observes that the *Bibliotheca Eliotae,* 1532 (1548?) makes "elfes or fayries" the English equivalent of *nymphae, naides, dryades,* and *hamadryades.*

45 The comments of Jortin and Church are summarized in the *Var. Ed.,* III, 265.


CHAPTER V

1 See F. S. Boas, "Aspects of Classical Legend and History in Shakespeare," *Proceedings of the British Academy* (1943), XXIX, 107-32.

2 Cf. T. W. Baldwin's *William Shakspere's Small Latine and Lesse Greeke,* I, 490.

3 Robert Kilburn Root, *Classical Mythology in Shakespeare* (New York, 1903), p. 40.

4 *Shakspere's Small Latine,* II, 428-30.

5 Charles Stephanus' *Dictionarium,* the source of Cooper's entry, refers to Absyrtus as *paruulum fratrem.* Comes' *Mythologiae,* 6.7., one of the sources of Stephanus, does not refer to Absyrtus as small or young.

6 Root, *op. cit.,* p. 34.

7 Stephanus, *s. v. Agamemnon,* a source of Cooper, uses no term corresponding to "magnanimous."

8 Stephanus refers to Agamemnon as "qui omnium Graecorum consensu imperator delectus ad expeditionem Troianam profectus est."

9 Root, *op. cit.,* p. 36.

10 Boas (*op. cit.,* p. 14) quotes these lines and other allusions to Hercules in the plays. He notes the deviation from the classical legend in the reference to the Hesperides as gardens, but he does not suggest the source of Shakespeare's information.

11 *S.v. Centauri* and *Pirithous,* Stephanus tells that at the wedding of Pirithous, the Centaurs were driven off, some put to death, by Theseus and the Lapithae. Under *Hippodamia,* however, Stephanus says that the Centaurs were driven away by Theseus and Hercules.

12 Cooper's source for this passage and that on *Centauri,* quoted above, is Stephanus' *Dictionarium.*

13 *Opera* (1703-06), I, 356 F, cited by Baldwin, *Shakspere's Small Latine,* II, 245-46.

14 Translated by Baldwin, *idem.*

15 Cooper's sketch of Lucius Tarquinius is a free translation of the following entry in Charles Stephanus' *Dictionarium, Historicum, Geographicum, Poeticum,* Cooper's addition being the epithet "noble and chaste matrone," and the final *Vide Lucretia:*

"Tarquinius superbus, septimus et vltimus Romanorum rex, à moribus cognomen adeptus. Tulliam Seruij Tullij filiam vxorem duxerat, prae feroci ingenio mulierem, cuius consilio socerum interfecit, regnumque scelestè occupauit. . . . Demum cùm Sextus eius filius, Lucretiae per vim stuprum intulisset, cum vniuersa familia in exilium actus, ad Porsenam Hetruriae regem se contulit: qui pro eius restitutione ne quicquam Romanis bellum intulit. Liu. Plutarch."

16 In the account of Lucretia Cooper translates, with frequent interpolations from other sources, the following entry from C. Stephanus' *Dictionarium:*

"Lucretia, Romanae pudicitiae praecipuum lumen, filia Lucretij Tricipitini praefecti vrbis, vxor Tarquinij Collatini: quam Sextus Tarquinius, cum precibus exorare non posset, vi oppressit. Stricto enim gladio in cubiculum irruens, mortem minabatur, ni voluntati suae obsequeretur: addebátque, se cum mortua iugulatum seruum positurum vt in sordido adulterio necata diceretur. Quibus minis illa perterrita, vt infamiae suspicionem effugeret, expugnari sese passa est. Postridie verò conuocatis patre, marito, caeterisque amicis, obortis repente lachrymis, tyranni flagitium detexit, & educto cultro, quem sub veste occultum, habebat, sese statim confodit. Qua re moti pater cum marito & caeteris amicis, populo ad arma concitato reges expulerunt. Liu. ad finem lib. 1. ab vrbe."

The interpolations or expansions by Cooper are these: (1) "both to hir tyme, and to all ages following," (2) "being intertayned for kindreds sake in hir house," (3) for *seruum,* "one of hir servaunts," (4) "shamefull reproch," (5) "rather than for dreade of death," (6) omission of father *(patre)* of Stephanus, (7) "desiring them earnestly to seeke revengement of the same," (8) "affirming that the example of Lucrece shoulde never be a cloke for light women to excuse the unfaythfull breache of wedlocke." These interpolations or changes by Cooper are of special interest in this study because the interpolated passages are definitely echoed in Shakespeare's *Lucrece,* indicating that he had read Cooper's summary. This inference does not rule out the possibility that the poet had also read the Latin summaries in Stephanus, including one on Tarquinius Collatinus, not here quoted.

17 Baldwin, *Literary Genetics* (p. 108) cites this parallel, which we had noted before seeing his book. Baldwin thinks that Shakespeare is the author of The Argument and that he was summing up the facts "from Livy and Ovid as they had been integrated by Marsus in his notes to the passage on Ovid." Baldwin does not explain, however, why Shakespeare did not make his Argument consistent with the story in the poem proper.

18 See James M. Tolbert, "The Argument of Shakespeare's *Lucrece:* Its

Sources and Authorship," University of Texas *Studies in English,* XXIX
(1950), 77-90. Tolbert questions Shakespeare's authorship.

19 Compare *Lucrece* (l. 7): "Of Collatine's love, Lucrece the chaste."

20 Baldwin quotes

> "Haply that name of 'chaste' unhappily set
> This bateless edge on his keen appetite."
>                              (ll. 8-9)

Baldwin suggests that "chastity" derives from the notes in the Basle
variorum edition of Ovid's *Fasti* (1550). He quotes Constantius as using
*castitas* and Marsus as employing *pudicitia.* "So the text of Ovid in the
variorum would have thrust the word *castitas* upon Shakespeare's attention; the text of Livy would not have done so" (p. 100). Compare, however, the first sentence in Cooper's sketch of Lucretia: "A noble woman of
Rome, wife to Tarquinius Collatinus, and a singular paterne of chastitie,
both to hir tyme and to all ages following." Would Shakespeare have
needed more of a "thrust" than this?

21 Cf. also "the noble and chaste matrone Lucrece," in Cooper's sketch of
Lucius Tarquinius.

22 Cf. *Lucrece:* Tarquin "With shining falchion in my chamber came."
(l. 1626)

23 Cf. also *Lucrece,* ll. 514-18; 670-72. Alike in essentials though differing
slightly in details, these three accounts of the same episode might indicate
hasty composition, or revision which was not thoroughgoing. Baldwin
(p. 129), notes only ll. 670-72, and suggests Paulus Marsus' quotation of
Dionysius in Ovid's *Fasti* (1550) as the source.

24 See also C. Stephanus' *Dictionarium (Lucretia):* "ni voluntati suae obsequeretur." This is Cooper's source.

25 Stephanus has *infamiae,* but no words corresponding to "shamefull reproch."

26 See ll. 239, 672, 832, 1189.

27 For other instances of "reproach" in *Lucrece,* see ll. 504, 612, 824, 829.

28 See *Lucrece,* ll. 504, 539, 636, 794, 1025, 1055, 1173, 1638.

29 It is also used *(infamiae)* in C. Stephanus' *Dictionarium.*

30 Though The Argument affords some details of the general story not found
in Cooper's summary (under *Lucretia*), Cooper's sketch is in fact a more
appropriate general outline for the poem than is The Argument. It seems
probable indeed that The Argument was hastily prefixed to the poem without much attempt to harmonize the two accounts. This circumstance would
explain the inconsistencies between Argument and poem.

31 These have been noted and analyzed by James M. Tolbert in his unpublished doctoral dissertation on *Lucrece,* University of Texas, 1950.

32 Compare Livy: "Ego me, etsi peccato absolvo, supplicio non libero; nec
ulla deinde impudica exemplo Lucretiae vivet." Compare also Painter:
"As for my part, though I clear my selfe of the offence, my body shall

feel the punishment, for no unchaste or ill woman shall hereafter impute no dishonest act to Lucrece."

Baldwin (*On the Literary Genetics,* p. 148) quotes Marsus' notes on Ovid's *Fasti* (Basle, 1550, p. 149), concluding "Nec ulla deinde impudica Lucretiae exemplo uiuet."

33 In a summary statement of "The Literary Genetics of Lucrece," Baldwin writes, "He [Shakespere] has used a copy of Ovid with the notes of Marsus, who had correlated most of the Latin sources, especially Livy, and along with it Painter's version. He had of course used also Cooper's *Thesaurus* for a dictionary" (*ibid.,* p. 153). Apparently, Shakespeare consulted the Historic and Poetic section of Cooper more extensively than Baldwin has indicated.

34 See, for example, a portion of the Appendix on the Fates, *infra,* pp. 373-74.

35 Cooper's *Thesaurus* has been emphasized, but compare as well the material sketched by Root with the appropriate entries in Charles Stephanus' *Dictionarium.*

CHAPTER VI

1 "Conversations with Drummond," *Ben Jonson,* I, 138, 223-25.

2 We use the form Jonson would probably have preferred; *Ben Jonson,* IV, 4.

3 *Ben Jonson,* I, 253-58.

4 *The Odysseus of Homer* (London, John Russell Smith, 1857) I, 216-17, ll. 585-89.

5 Charles Francis Wheeler, *Classical Mythology in the Plays, Masques, and Poems of Ben Jonson* (Princeton University Press, 1938), p. 39.

6 Simpson sees a veiled contemporary allusion in the lines which include this reference (*Ben Jonson,* IX, 551). The passage cited as grounds for this belief, however, expresses a quite different purpose and idea. The matter is of no great importance.

7 Simpson follows H. S. Mallory (in the Yale edition of the play; cf. *infra*), and explains the phrase by referring to the father of Ganymede, i.e. Tros, King of Phrygia (*Ben Jonson,* IX, 567).

8 Ben Jonson, *Poetaster,* ed. by H. S. Mallory, Yale Studies in English, XXVII (1905), xli-viii.

9 *Ibid.,* pp. xlviii-liii. In his citation of such matter, believed to be pertinent, Simpson does not follow the Yale editor, though from his notes one judges that he relied heavily upon the American scholar (*Ben Jonson,* IX, 536).

10 See also Appendix on the Fates.

11 *Masque of Queens,* gloss *p* on l. 132.

12 *Hymenæi,* ll. 7-19; see also, E. W. Talbert, "The Interpretation of Jonson's Courtly Spectacles," *PMLA,* LXI (1946), 454-73.

13 See, e.g., Allan H. Gilbert, *The Symbolic Persons in the Masques of Ben Jonson* (Duke University Press, 1948), *passim,* as well as the articles by D. J. Gordon which are noted in n. 27 below.

14 *Justinus Trogi Pompei Historiarum Philippicarum Epitoma,* ed. by J. Jeep (Leipzig, Teubner, 1876), p. 17.

15 *Diodorus of Sicily,* tr. by C. H. Oldfather, II (Loeb Classical Library, 1935), 89-91.

16 Cited variously in different editions, e.g., 1543: "Propert. lib. 3. eleg. 11. 3."

17 See *infra,* pp. 205-6; *Ben Jonson,* I, 265.

18 *Dio's Roman History,* tr. by E. Cary, VI (*Loeb Classical Libr.,* 1917), 293-95: *e.g.,* "About this same time the Ethiopians, who dwell beyond Egypt, advanced as far as the city called Elephantine, with Candace as their leader, ravaging everything they encountered. At Elephantine, however, learning that Gaius Petronius, the governor of Egypt, was approaching, they hastily retreated before he arrived, hoping to make good their escape. But being overtaken on the road, they were defeated and thus drew him after them into their own country. Then, too, he fought successfully with them, and took Napata, their capital, among other cities. This place was razed to the ground, and a garrison left at another point; for Petronius, finding himself unable either to advance farther, on account of the sand and the heat, or advantageously to remain where he was with his entire army, withdrew, taking the greater part of it with him. Thereupon the Ethiopians attacked the garrisons, but he again proceeded against them, rescued his own men, and compelled Candace to make terms with him."

19 *C. Plini Secundi Naturalis Historiae,* ed. by L. Janus (Leipzig, Teubner, 1870), I, 253, ll. 186-87.

20 *Ben Jonson,* X, 506.

21 *Hygini Astronomica,* ed. by B. Bunte (Leipzig, Teubner, 1875), p. 67.

22 With Catullus' *novo viro,* "Invisente novo proelia torva viro," l. 20, compare Jonson's "new-wedded Lord"; see also the dictionaries' *"nec multis diebus post."*

23 For the passage in Comes, see *infra,* n. 26. That Linus might possibly have been the son of Apollo and Terpsichore is mentioned by Gyraldus, VII, under "Musae," passage beginning "Virgines etiam. . . ."

24 Wheeler, *op. cit.,* p. 164.

25 E.g., *Ben Jonson,* VII, 639, textual note, gloss h.

26 *Myth.,* IV, x.

27 The relationship of these three masques to the more specialized treatises has been effectively and amply demonstrated by D. J. Gordon in "The Imagery of Ben Jonson's *The Masque of Blacknesse* and *The Masque of Beautie,"* and *"Hymenæi:* Ben Jonson's Masque of Union," *Journ. of Warburg and Courtauld Institutes,* VI (1943), 122-41; VIII (1945), 107-45.

28 *Infra,* Appendix on the Fates.

29 A note in this masque, the *Haddington Masque,* well illustrates Jonson's use of the more specialized treatises and the relationship between them and the lexicons (p. 257, l. 249):

"The ancient *Poets,* whensoeuer they would intend any thing to be done, with great *Masterie,* or excellent Art, made *Vulcan* the artificer, as *Hom. Iliad. Σ.* in the forging of Achilles his armour: and *Virg.* for *Aeneas, Aenei.* 8. He is also said to be the god of *fire,* and *light.* Sometime taken for the purest *beame:* and by *Orph. in Hym.* celebrated for the *Sunne* and *Moone.* But more specially, by *Eurip.* in *Troad.* he is made *Facifer in nuptijs,* which present office we giue him here, as being *calor naturae,* and *praeses luminis.* See *Plato in Cratyl.* For his description, read *Pausa. in Elia."*

Cartari refers to Pausanias in his description of Vulcan: e.g., "Ainsi le raconte Pausanias, touchant les fables des Grecs, et dit qu'entre les autres peintures, que les Athenians auoient, se trouuoit celle de Bacchus: car Vulcan demeuroit au ciel, à deslier Iunon, et que les Lacedemoniens, au temple de Minerue, auoyent pareillement Vulcan, qui deslioit sa mere." Cartari then says that the gods went to Vulcan for their armour: ". . . ainsi que Thetis y fust, pour les armes d'Achilles son fils. . . . Venus eut pareillement de luy les armes, qu'elle bailla depuis à Enee. Et quand les Poëtes veulent descripre quelque grande chose, faicte auec grand artifice et industrie, ils dient que Vulcan la faicte, ou les Cyclopes, à la forge de Vulcan." *Les Images des Dieux des Anciens* (Lyons, 1581), pp. 462-63.

In writing the preceding gloss, moreover, Jonson was indebted to Comes: e.g., "Atque Orpheus in hymnis Vulcanum, Solem, & Lunam, & astra, & lumen purissimum, atque aethera ipsum nominauit, vt est in his. . . ." *Myth.,* II, vi (p. 76). Note likewise Comes' "Atque illud primum, quod è sola qui φάεος ἰςωρέςὶν siue luminis praeses fieri omnino non potest. . . ." (p. 78) Earlier Comes had written "Hunc Deum facem ferre in nuptijs inquit Euripides in Troadibus, cum faces accensae ad nuptias afferri solerent, vt patet ex his. . . ." (p. 75)

Compare also the corresponding article in the *Dictionarium.* It begins with the statement that "Vulcanus, deus ignis praeses" and ends "Artis fabrilis praestantia omnes creditur superasse: quo sit, vt quicquid artificiose ex mettala vnguam fuit fabricatum, ad Vulcanum referatur authorem: quo in genere sunt . . . Achilles & AEneae arma . . . Vulcani allegoriam prolixe admodum descriptem habes apud N Comitem, mythologiae libro 2. cap. 6."

30 For the pertinent passages in Gyraldus and Ripa, see D. J. Gordon, *"Hymenæi,"* *Journ. of Warburg and Court. Inst.,* VIII, 134-35, n. 3. We do not believe that Gordon would object to our conclusion as phrased here.

31 Wheeler, *op. cit.,* p. 124.

32 D. J. Gordon calls attention to the passages in both Ripa and Comes, *Journ. of Warburg and Court. Inst.,* VIII, 143 (concerning p. 216, gloss *o* of *Hymenæi*).

33 *Pomponii Mela de Situ Orbis Libri Tres,* ed. by J. Reinold (Eton, E. Williams, 1826), p. 42. The italics are ours.

34 *Journ. of Warburg and Court. Inst.,* VIII, 107-45.

35 Wheeler, *op. cit.,* p. 168.

36 *Love's Labour's Lost,* 4.3. 351.

37 Wheeler, *op. cit.,* pp. 172-73.

38 *Thesaurus:* "Anticyra, An Ile ouer agaynst the mountayne, where the herbe Elleborus groweth, which pourgeth melancholy. . . . Whereof grewe this prouerbe, spoken to men in their melancholy. Nauiga ad Anticeras, Go sayle to Anticyra, as who sayth, pourge your melancholy."

39 The Greek appears in the 1573 edition, but not in that of 1543. The article on "Fortunatae insulae" in Charles Stephanus is not greatly different.

40 Wheeler, *op. cit.,* p. 97.

41 The item appears after one on "Macarius"; the bracketed material appears in the 1573, but not in the 1543, edition.

42 Cf. Wheeler, *op. cit.,* pp. 180-1; the lines cited here from Seneca seem more appropriate than those given by Wheeler. The subsequent quotation is from *L. Annaeis Senecae Tragoediae,* ed. R. Peiper, G. Richter (*Bibl. Script. Graec. et Rom. Teubneriana,* 1902), p. 206.

43 *Apollodorus, the Library,* tr. by J. G. Frazer, I (*Loeb Classical Lib.,* 1921), 346-7.

44 Cf. *Andreae Alciati V. C. Emblemata, cum Claudii Minois ad eadem Commentariis et Notis Posterioribus* (Lyon, 1600), pp. 646, 648-9.

45 Wheeler, *op. cit.,* p. 83.

46 We cite the 1573 ed.

47 The dictionaries do not agree. C. Stephanus has (1) "Iouis et Latonae filia" under which appears the reference to Virgil and (2) "Filia fuit Persae, filij Solis, et fratris AEtae." R. Stephanus, not in the 1543, but in the 1573 edition, has (1) "ponitur pro Diana sive Luna sive Proserpina," then "Perseide vocat, hoc est, Persae filiam, sive ille Solis filius, et AEstae frater fuit," and (2) "Hecate altera, ex Asteria Latone sorore Perseo Titane nata, cui Jupiter . . . ," citing the *AEneid,* IV, 609.

48 *Myth.,* III, xv; X, "De Hecate."

49 *Supra,* pp. 151-52.

50 Gordon corrected a few errors in the work cited above, i.e., *Journ. Warburg and Court. Inst.,* VI, 122-41, when reprinting his study in *England and the Mediterranean* (Oxford, University Press, 1945); this last work is the one we refer to hereafter; *q.v.,* pp. 105, 120.

51 *Ibid., passim;* see also Don Cameron Allen, "Ben Jonson and the Hieroglyphics," *PQ,* XVIII (1939), 290-300 and Allan H. Gilbert, *op. cit., passim.*

52 In the 1543 ed. of the *Thesaurus Linguae Latinae,* the entry under *Nilus* is identical except for the reading "Niger" instead of "Nigris" and except for the last sentence, which in Robert Stephanus is as follows: "Denique multis ostiis fertur in mare AEgyptium. . . ."

53 The list of twelve names (ll. 287-90), as Gordon points out, can also be found in Gyraldus.

54 Gordon, *op. cit.*, p. 105, calls attention to the following passage in Gyraldus: "Aethiopia Diana cognominata, teste Stephano, qui et eius uarias opiniones recenset. Quidam enim sic appellatam putant à regiuncula quadam Lydia αἰθιόποον nomine, ubi coleretur. alij, quòd cùm apud Aethiopas uersaretur, eam Apollo abduxerit. nonulli παρὰ τὸ αἰθειν, ab ardore uidelicet, quòd Luna sit, ut Callimachus ait. quidam, quòd ea Hecate sit, quae facibus uti putabatur, ut Erastothenes prodidit." Although Gyraldus and the *Dictionarium Historicum* are almost identical, we believe that the material cited here and below from the lexicon among the *AEth's* justifies our emphasis upon Charles Stephanus.

55 *Diodorus of Sicily*, tr. by C. H. Oldfather, II (*Loeb Classical Library*, 1935), 89-91.

56 *Supra*, n. 54.

57 *Hygini Fabulae*, ed. M. Schmidt (Jena, H. Dufft, 1872), p. 36.

58 "The Rape of Proserpine," ll. 88-91; see also, ll. 71-100. *Claudian*, tr. by M. Platnauer, II (*Loeb Classical Library*, 1922), 324. On Jonson's indebtedness here to Claudian, see Gifford's notes, *The Works of Ben Jonson*, III (London, Chatto & Windus, 1910), 118; portions of Claudian are, of course, quoted by Simpson, *Ben Jonson*, X, 572.

59 Wheeler, *op. cit.*, pp. 65-66.

60 His conception likewise is in accord with the neo-Platonic doctrine mentioned above, which is also apparent in this masque, though worked out in a much less intricate manner. Although we are aware of no discussion of this feature of Jonson's entertainment, neither space nor the unity of the chapter allows for its development here. For his allotment of time to the Parcae, see the Appendix on the Fates.

61 Cartari's treatment of the Hours is too long to reproduce here, although the entire discussion is particularly apt. See also Comes' discussion with its illustration (IV, xvi) as well as the account in Gyraldus. Also of interest is *Themis Dea, sive de Lege Divina, Stephani Pighii Campensis* (Antwerp, 1568), pp. 109-36.

62 Cartari's compilation was sometimes so advertised on the title-page.

63 The texts we have used of the works not heretofore cited are as follows: *Johannis Rosini Antiquitatum Romanorum Corpus Absolutissimum cum Notis . . . Thomae Dempsteri J. C. . . . .* (Leyden, 1663)—nothing is quoted from this edition, however, that did not also appear in the 1583 text—; *Commentarius de Praecipuis Divinationum Generibus . . . ab Authore Ipso Casparo Peucer . . . .* (Frankfurt, 1593).

64 *Supra*, pp. 146-47.

65 *Lactantii Placidi qvi dicitur Commentarios in Statii Thebaida*, ed. R. Jahnke (*Bibl. Script. Graec. et Rom. Teub.*, 1898), pp. 168-69, 388-89.

66 Wheeler, *op. cit.*, p. 158.

67 Wheeler, *ibid.*, pp. 119-20, points out that Asterie is named in Pherecydes' *Fragments, 70*; yet in Comes, as well as in the dictionaries, Jonson could have found Idmon's genealogy. The *Mythologiae* does not give the citation of Valerius Flaccus, however.

68 C. Stephanus, and Comes, IV, x. Robert Stephanus writes "Apollo, inis. . . . Cui (vt Macrobius inquit) variae fuerunt potestates. Nam fuit author carminis, praeses vaticinii, sagittandi peritiam habuit, artem medicinae percalluit, et chordae vocalis."

69 The conclusion to be drawn from the passages cited here has been grossly misunderstood by Professor Simpson, *Ben Jonson*, X, 640. The material assembled in this chapter and elsewhere must be viewed *in toto*, in its context, and in its explicit sense—with "inferences" we are not concerned. We are, above all, concerned with the total picture presented in this chapter and elsewhere.

70 Under "Medico," etc. ("Medicus, a medicina dictus") and "Musica," etc.

71 For the edition known to have been in Jonson's library, see *Ben Jonson*, I, 266.

72 C. H. Herford and Percy Simpson emphasize what they consider to be an abrupt shift between Main Masque and Induction (*Ben Jonson*, II, 317). T. M. Parrott, however, considers the dance of pilgrims to be a "transition" to the main masque ("Comedy in the Court Masque: A Study of Ben Jonson's Contribution," *PQ* ("Renaissance Studies in Honor of Hardin Craig," 1941), XX, 437. See also Enid Welsford, *The Court Masque* (Cambridge, 1927), p. 184. We consider the masque to be much more effectively unified than has hitherto been pointed out.

73 See *infra*, Appendix I, for a discussion of this masque and the omnipotence of Jove or of the Fates.

74 Of the "erudite" particulars in Jonson's mythology not so far discussed, gloss *y* on Jove's omnipotence (1. 443): *"Vide Orpheum in hymn. de omnip. Jovis,"* could have been supplied by Comes' discussion, as could gloss *z* on Jove's nod (1. 463): *"Mos Jovis, annuendo votis et firmandis om[i]nibus, Apud Homer,* &c." The content of this last gloss is decidedly commonplace. For Jonson's reference to the owl and the "Hernshaw" as Minerva's birds, see *infra*, n. 84. This detail was also a mythographer's commonplace; e.g., *Les Images des Dievx des Anciens . . . par le Seigneur Vincent Cartari . . . traduites en François & augmentées par Antoine Dv Verdier. . . .* (Lyons, 1581), pp. 436-37, and the print on p. 430.

75 *Ben Jonson*, I, 251-52 (for the use of the *Antiquitates*); the pertinent passage in Rosinus is as follows: "Sed sufficiant ista hoc loco. Plura ex veterum monumentis magna cura et diligentia conquisivit . . . *Gasparus* [*sic*] *Peucer* in suis doctissimis Commentariis, de Divinationum generibus. . . ." *Op. cit.*, p. 208.

76 Peucer, *op. cit.*, p. 379; Rosinus, *op. cit.*, p. 205.

77 Peucer, p. 379; Rosinus, p. 206.

78 Peucer, pp. 378-79; Rosinus, p. 205. Details in Jonson that are not in the passage from Peucer quoted above can be found elsewhere in the *Commentarius*, pp. 375, 77. The italics are ours.

79 Rosinus, *op. cit.*, p. 200.

80 *Ibid.*, p. 206. See also gloss *n*, discussed in the footnote immediately following.

81 Gloss *m* elucidates line 327; the material Jonson summarizes, too long for quotation here, is in Peucer, pp. 376-77, and Rosinus, pp. 200-1. A sample is given in the text, while the citations of authority in gloss *m* are discussed *infra*, p. 186.

Gloss *q* elucidates "The Signes are luckie all, and right" (l. 368) by explaining the difference between Greek practice, followed in l. 368, and Roman practice. As the passage quoted *supra*, p. 184, shows, only Peucer notes that "Homerus Orientem dextrum, Occidentem fecit sinistrum." Peucer, p. 379; Rosinus, p. 205.

Gloss *n* elucidates line 334. Down to the citations of authority, which are discussed *infra*, pp. 186-87 and nn. 88 and 89, the gloss summarizes very briefly material in Rosinus' discussion of the Salii, pp. 223, 262.

82 For the remainder of gloss *p*, see n. 84 *infra;* the italics are ours.

83 The only particular that fits neither in this discussion of Rosinus and Peucer nor in the discussion that immediately follows is a portion of gloss *x* on "princely Augur" (l. 422): *"Romulus augur fuit, & Numa, & reliqui reges Romani, sicut ante eos Turnus, Rhamnetes, & alij. Lacedemonij suis regibus Augurem Assessorem dabant. Cilices, Lycij, Cares, Arabes, in summa veneratione habuerunt Auguria."* For the passage "sicut . . . Auguria," we have found as yet no close parallel; cf., however, Peucer, pp. 376-7; Rosinus, pp. 200-1; and *supra*, n. 79.

84 With the exception of *anser* and *nycticorax*, from the discussions in Peucer and Rosinus plus the discussion of the swan in the article on Apollo in Comes' *Mythologia*, p. 188, Jonson could have found the nature of the birds included in that portion of gloss *p* not discussed above, p. 185, and in the lines that the long gloss elucidates (ll. 349-359). *Anser* Jonson could have found in Livy (see *infra*, p. 186) and *nycticorax* might easily be padding, resulting from the other types of owls he and his sources had been concerned with.

Gloss *s* reads *"Ardea, & Ardeola, rerum arduarum auspicium. Minervæ sacra. Apud Homer. Iliad. K.* δεξιὸς ἐρωδιὸς.*"* The lines it elucidates are

> Minerva's *Hernshaw, and her Owle,*
> *Doe both proclaime, thou shalt controle*
> *The course of things,*
>                                        Idmon.
>                         *As now they be,*
> *With tumult carried.* . . .
>
>                                        (ll. 379-84)

Both are possibly explained by the following note in the *Thesaurus:* "Ardea. . . . Avis est, sic dicta quasi Ardua, inquit Servius; quae quum altius volauerit, significat tempestatem. Virg. 1. Georg. 73 [364]. Atque altam supra volat ardea nubem. Graece dicitur ἐρωδιὸς. *Ardeola,* pen. corr. diminutiuum, vt ait Sipontius." See *supra,* n. 74.

85 " 'And whence, pray, did you augurs derive that staff, which is the most conspicuous mark of your priestly office? It is the very one, indeed, with which Romulus marked out the quarter for taking observations when he founded the city.' " " 'It was placed in the temple of the Salii on the Palatine hill, and, though the temple was burned, the staff was found uninjured.' " *Cicero . . . De Divinatione,* tr. W. A. Falconer (*Loeb Classical Library,* 1923), p. 259. Cf. Varro, V, 85. The following passage in Comes' article on Apollo (p. 190) also supplies a possible connection: "Quamuis duo fuerunt Pæanum genera, quorum vsus erat etiam in bellis: nam horum alterum genus Marti ante bellum erat dicatum, alterum Apollini post victoriam."

86 *Supra,* p. 183.

87 See *supra,* p. 183.

88 See Herford and Simpson, I, 265. The edition also included the poems of Tibullus and Propertius.

89 At least two editions with commentary on the texts of Catullus, Tibullus, and Propertius were printed at Paris in 1608, the place and year of Jonson's edition. One was by J. Passeratius; the other was a reissue from the office of M. Orry of the 1604 text. The title of the Orry text corresponds to the title in Jonson's library, *Opera omnia quae exstant* (Herford & Simpson, I, 265). The fullest commentary on the "Ad Coloniam" in the *Opera omnia quae exstant* is taken from Julius Caesar Scaliger (pp. 53-54), who quotes the line from Pacuvius, as does Muretus in his commentary (p. 52), gives the line from Virgil, and notes, *i.a.,* that "Itaque recte ὑμνωδὼς Salius veritur a vetere Glossario vnde Virgilius dixit salios ad cantum. . . ." The other pertinent passage from Scaliger runs as follows ". . . autem ludij Martis dicuntur Salij, & Mars ipse Salisubsulus, Pacuuius: *Pro imperio sic salisubsulus vostro* [sic] *excubet.* Quod procul dubio est ex fine Prologi cuiusdam, ut illud Plautinum. *Vt vos item alias, pariter nunc vos Mars adiuuet."* The line from Pacuvius is thought to be from the *Armorum Iudicium;* with a reference to the ancient use of the word *salisubsulus,* it apparently was introduced into commentaries on Catullus by Guarinus (1521) in a form slightly different from that which Jonson quotes. Apparently Muretus in his edition of 1554 first gave the form Jonson uses. The commentary in the 1608 text by J. Passeratius is much briefer than that in the other edition, and there is no reference to Pacuvius.

90 *Sexti Pompei Festi de Verborum Significatu quae Supersunt cum Pauli*

*Epitome*, ed. by W. M. Lindsay (*Bibl. Script. Graec. et Rom. Teub.*, 1933), p. 2.

91 *Servii Grammatici qvi Fervntvr in Vergilii Æneidos Libros I-III Commentarii*, ed. by G. Thilo (Leipzig, 1878), p. 132.

92 See a short portion of gloss *x* (*supra*, n. 83) ; possibly a few details in gloss *s* (*supra*, n. 84). To these should be added the last statement about the dove in gloss *r:* "Nuntiæ pacis"—apparently Jonson's addition. See also, *supra*, p. 182, on Apollo's offspring.

93 Herford and Simpson, I, 393-94 and *supra*, p. 135; on the importance of the audience for an interpretation of masque and entertainment, see E. W. Talbert, "The Interpretation of Jonson's Courtly Spectacles," *PMLA*, LXI (1946), 454-73.

94 See W. D. Briggs, *Flügel Memorial Volume* (Stanford, Stanford University Press, 1916), 59-60; Herford and Simpson, IX, 498; C. B. Hilberry, *Ben Jonson's Ethics in Relation to Stoic and Humanistic Thought* (Chicago, University of Chicago Press, 1933), pp. 8-10, 18-20, *et passim*.

95 See A. H. Gilbert, "The Function of the Masques in *Cynthia's Revels*," *PQ*, XXII (1943), pp. 216-17.

96 For the Folio additions, see Herford and Simpson, IV, 17-22.

97 When he looses his arrows at the dancing courtiers, Cupid remarks to Mercury that "it makes no matter which of the couples. Phantaste, and Amorphus, at you" (V, x, 25-6). Thus this particular couple are representative of the other fatuous dancers; and their subsequent speeches, while showing the ineffectiveness of the arrows on self-love, also demonstrate the courtiers' audacity in considering themselves better than Cynthia.

98 Briggs, *op. cit.*, pp. 62, 64-66; Herford and Simpson, IX, 508; Simpson in his notes, however, pays singularly little attention to this study, published in 1916, by an American scholar.

99 See A. H. Gilbert, *PQ*, XXI, 216-30.

100 For the relationship between courtly entertainment and treatises *de regimine principum*, see E. W. Talbert, *PMLA*, LXI (1946), 454-73.

101 See the studies by D. J. Gordon noted above.

102 The translation we have used in that by L. Williams, *The Heroic Enthusiasts . . . by Giordano Bruno*, II (London, Quaritch, 1889), pp. 52, 68-69 (II, ii). The passages from which the preceding quotations are taken appear in the Italian (Parigi, 1585; i.e., London, J. Charlewood) as follows: "Diana splendor di specei intelligibili" (sig. M2r.) ; "Vede l'amphitrite, il fonte de tutti numeri, de tutti specie, de tutte raggioni, che é la Monade, vera essenza de l'essere de tutti: et se non la vede in sua essenza, in absoluta luce; la uede nella sua genitura che gl'é simile, che é la sua imagine: per che dalla monade che é la diuinitade, procede questa monade che é la natura, l'uniuerso, il mondo; doue si contempla et specchia come il sole nella luna, mediante la quale ne illumina trauandosi egli nell'emisphero del le sustanze intellettuali. Questa é la Diana, quello

uno che é l'istesso ente, quello ente che é l'istesso uero, quello uero che é la natura comprensibile, in cui influisce il sole et il splendor della natura superiore secondo che la vnitá é destintá nella generata, et generante, ó producente et prodotta"; ". . . onde il furioso si uanta d'esser preda della Diana . . . che inuidiar possa ad altro huomo che non ne può hauer ch'altre tanto, ó ad altro diuo che ne haue in tal specie quale é impossibile d'essere ottenuta da natura inferiore, et per consequenza non é conueniente d'essere desiata . . ." (sigs. M8v-N).

103 Sears Raynolds Jayne, *Marsilio Ficino's Commentary on Plato's Symposium* (University of Missouri Studies, XIX, no. 1), p. 160.

104 In, for example, his *De Triplici Vita, passim.*

105 That Cynthia thanks the masquers, who are fatuous vices disguised as virtues, need not be taken too seriously or literally. Soon after her words the characters unmask at her command, since she wishes to see whom she is rewarding, and the goddess immediately recognizes them for what they are. The situation is almost one of dramatic exigency, providing the "surprise" expected in the last act; and when the final maxim of Cynthia is read in the light of the entire speech, the "catastrophe" amounts to a courtly bid for royal support of "poesy" and of such a judicious man as Crites, who perceives and aids in correcting the abuses of the age. For a different point of view, see A. H. Gilbert's comments on Cynthia, *PQ, XXII,* pp. 225-26, 230.

106 See nos. 109, 110 of Alciati's emblems, *op. cit.;* notice likewise Cartari's treatment of Plato's doctrine of love, with the appropriate illustration (end of text, French translation).

107 Boccaccio, VII, lix.

108 *Metamorphoses Ovidiana Moraliter a Magistro Thoma Waleys . . . Explanata* (Paris, 1515), sigs. xxviii$^b$-xxxix$^a$ (III, xii).

109 *Fabvlarum Ovidii Interpretatio, Ethica, Physica, et Historica, tradita in Academia Regiomontana a Georgio Sabino, et in unam collecta et edita studio et industria T. T.* (Cambridge, Thomas Thomas, 1584), p. 119. For the pertinence of Sabinus, see *infra,* pp. 344-45.

110 Alciati, *op. cit.,* no. 69; Geffrey Whitney, *A Choice of Emblemes, and Other Devises* (Leyden, 1586), p. 149 (no. 41 of pt. ii).

111 Berchorius, *op. cit.,* sig. xxxviii (III, xi).

112 *Fabvlarum Ovidii Interpretatio,* pp. 119-20.

113 See, e.g., Boccaccio, V, xxx, and XII, ii; Comes, VI, xiii.

114 As in *Met.* III, 141-42, 175.

115 E.g., *Ben Jonson,* I, 393-96; IX, 529-30.

116 See, e.g., Douglas Bush, *Mythology and the Renaissance Tradition in English Poetry* (Minneapolis, 1932), p. 71 and n. 11.

117 The italics are ours.

118 See Appendix I.

119 As the quotation from Comes indicates (*supra,* p. 207), the interpretation

undoubtedly developed from Fulgentius' moralization about Actaeon's dogs; consequently if the moralization were strictly applied, Actaeon would have had to represent a lustful and curious presumption and at the same time be the victim of ingratitude. See *Fabii Planciadis Fulgentii V. C. Opera,* ed. R. Helm (*Bibl. Script. Graec. et Rom. Teub.,* 1898), pp. 62-63. Boccaccio preserves Fulgentius' interpretation; while Legouais (I, 574-603), Berchorius (sig. xxxvi^a), and Alciati (p. 60), for example, interpret the dogs respectively as the indolent, the ungrateful, and the rogues who attach themselves to the powerful or the rich.

120 See, e.g., Herford and Simpson, I, 397-98, 411.

121 *A Study of Ben Jonson* (London, 1889), pp. 20-21; cf., W. Gifford, *The Works of Ben Jonson,* I (London, 1912), 205; M. Castelaine, *Ben Jonson* (Paris, 1907), p. 267; F. E. Schelling, *The Complete Plays of Ben Jonson,* I (Everyman's Library, 1910), xv; *CHEL,* VI (N. Y., 1910), 13.

### CHAPTER VII

1 The quotations from *Earth and Age* and other works of Heywood are from *The Dramatic Works of Thomas Heywood. Now First Collected with Illustrative Notes and a Memoir of the Author.* Six Volumes . . . London . . . 1874. As the lines are not numbered in the text, our citations will be to volume and page, as in (6. 148), meaning Volume 6, page 148.

The dictionary references are to Thomas Cooper, *Thesaurus Linguae Romanae et Britannicae,* 1565, and Charles Stephanus, *Dictionarium Historicum, Geographicum, Poeticum,* Geneva, 1638.

2 Calepine has a similar entry for *Sibyllae,* but he includes *Phrygia* and other words not found in Heywood and Stephanus.

3 In his annotation (6. 150 (k)) Heywood uses the term "black flagge" and "sable flagge" instead of "black sayle"; but he employs "cast himselfe... into the Sea," as in Cooper. C. Stephanus' *Dictionarium,* the basis of Cooper's item, has Theseus jump from a high tower, not a rock, as in Cooper and Heywood.

4 Stephanus does not have the idea which might be a basis for Heywood's "And being man, the shape of woman bore." This seems to be an echo of Cooper's "by nature framed a man, in conditions to be a verie woman."

### CHAPTER VIII, PART I

1 *The Works of John Milton* (gen. ed., F. A. Patterson), XVIII (New York, 1938), 327; cf. also 287, 318, 323, 326.

2 *The Early Lives of Milton,* ed. by H. Darbishire (London, 1932), p. 29.

3 *Ibid.,* pp. 71-72; cf. also pp. 45-46, 192, 268.

4 *Dictionarium Historicum, Geographicum, Poeticum* (1638). This edition is cited throughout, unless otherwise specified.

5 Cf. Ez. 8:14—"Then he brought me to the door of the gate of the Lord's

438 NOTES, PAGES 230-265

house [i.e., 'in the sacred porch'] which was toward the north; and, behold, there sat women weeping for Tammuz."

6 Charles Grosvenor Osgood, *The Classical Mythology of Milton's English Poems* (New York, 1900), p. 43.

7 M. Y. Hughes, *John Milton: Paradise Regained, The Minor Poems, and Samson Agonistes* (New York, 1937), p. 290.

8 Walter MacKellar, *The Latin Poems of John Milton*, Cornell Studies in English, XV (Yale University Press, 1930), pp. 255-56.

9 Hughes, *Paradise Regained*, p. 51.

10 *Ibid.*

11 George W. Whiting, *Milton's Literary Milieu* (University of North Carolina Press, 1939), pp. 66-68.

12 Osgood, *op. cit.*, p. 8. ·

13 *Poetical Works of John Milton*, ed. by David Masson, III (London, 1903), 310.

14 Hughes, *Paradise Regained*, pp. 44-45.

15 Osgood, *op. cit.*, p. 14.

16 Whiting, *op. cit.*, pp. 84-85.

17 Osgood, *op. cit.*, pp. 16-17.

18 Masson, *op. cit.*, p. 334.

19 *The Complete Poetical Works of John Milton*, p. 395.

20 Osgood, *op. cit.*, p. 17.

21 *The Complete Poetical Works of John Milton*, ed. by Harris Fletcher (New York, 1941), p. 159.

22 Osgood, *op. cit.*, pp. 17-18.

23 *Ibid.*, p. 18.

24 Hughes, *Paradise Regained*, p. 548.

25 *Ibid.*, p. 524.

26 Osgood, *op. cit.*, p. 25.

27 Hughes, *Paradise Regained*, p. 35.

28 Davis P. Harding, *Milton and the Renaissance Ovid*, University of Illinois Studies in Language and Literature, XXX (1946), 50-53.

29 E. C. Knowlton, "The Allegorical Figure Genius," *Class. Phil.*, XV, 380 ff.; "Genius as an Allegorical Figure," *MLN*, XXXIX, 89-95; "The Genii of Spenser," *SP*, XXV, 439-56.

30 A. W. Verity, *Paradise Lost*, II, 468.

31 Osgood, *op. cit.*, p. 46.

32 MacKellar, *op. cit.*, p. 253.

33 Hughes, *Paradise Regained*, p. 50.

34 MacKellar, *op. cit.*, p. 220.

35 "Ovid and Milton." Unpublished doctoral dissertation, Cornell University, 1935. App., p. 35.

36 Harding, *Milton and the Renaissance Ovid*, pp. 45-47.

37 George C. Taylor, *Milton's Use of Du Bartas* (Cambridge, 1934).

38 Whiting, *op. cit.*, pp. 50-51; 55-56.
39 M. Y. Hughes, *Paradise Lost* (New York, 1935), p. 390.
40 *Ibid.*, p. 120.
41 *Ibid.*, p. 333.
42 Harding, *Milton and the Renaissance Ovid*, pp. 86-87.

CHAPTER VIII, PART II

1 *Geographical Review*, VII (1919), 322-38.
2 Hughes, *Paradise Lost*, p. 16.
3 Osgood, *op. cit.*, p. 5.
4 Allan H. Gilbert, *A Geographical Dictionary of Milton* (Yale University Press, 1919), p. 23.
5 Whiting, *op. cit.*, pp. 104-5.
6 Gilbert, *A Geographical Dictionary*, p. 29.
7 *Ibid.*, p. 31.
8 Hughes, *Paradise Lost*, p. 335.
9 Gilbert, *A Geographical Dictionary*, p. 39.
10 *Ibid.*, p. 164.
11 Thomas Keightley, *The Poems of John Milton with Notes*, I (London, 1859), 194.
12 Cf. MacKellar, *op. cit.*, p. 249; Gilbert, *A Geographical Dictionary*, p. 80.
13 *Ibid.*, p. 82.
14 Hughes, *Paradise Regained*, p. 500.
15 Compare Osgood, *op. cit.*, p. 10; Gilbert, *A Geographical Dictionary*, p. 103.
16 *A Geographical Dictionary*, p. 106.
17 *The Complete Works of John Milton*, ed. by Harris Fletcher (Boston, 1941).
18 Hughes, *Paradise Lost*, p. 23.
19 Compare Masson, III, 299; MacKellar, p. 209; Hughes, *PR*, p. 84.
20 Gilbert, *A Geographical Dictionary*, p. 191.
21 *Paradise Lost*, II (Cambridge University Press, 1929), 368.
22 Hughes, *Paradise Lost*, p. 115.

APPENDIX I

1 *Miscellany Scottish Hist. Soc.*, I, xlvii; Leslie Hotson, *op. cit.*, 57; *Library*, Fourth Series, XV, 459; see also Hoole, *op. cit.*, p. xx.
2 *Supra*, pp. 25-26.
3 "Satire II," "Quaedam sunt et non videntur," ll. 22-30. *Works of John Marston*, ed. by A. H. Bullen, III (London, J. C. Nimmo, 1887), 269-70.
4 Hoole, *op. cit.*, p. xx. The possibility that Marston refers to Albricius' *Imagines Deorum* is remote. Although cited by Jonson, Browne, and Burton, this work was much less widely known than the compilation by Cartari. See A. H. Gilbert, *The Symbolic Persons in the Masques of Ben Jonson* (Duke University Press, 1948), p. 10, n. 25.

5 We use the Venice edition of 1572.

6 The work is so described on the title page of, e.g., the Padua, 1608 edition.

7 *La Sepmaine ov Creation dv Monde, de Gvillavme De Salvste. . . . En laquelle esté adioustez argument general, amples sommaires . . . annotations . . . et explications . . . par S[imon] G[oulart de] Senlis* (Geneva ?, 1593), pp. 116-17 (note 48 of the Second Day).

8 Editions have been cited in previous notes.

9 *The Boke named the Governour*, ed. by H. H. S. Croft, I (London, 1880), 67-68, 28, and 123 ff.

10 See T. W. Baldwin, *op. cit.*, I, 355, 338-41, 426-28, as well as Appendix A of D. C. Allen, *Frances Meres's Treatise "Poetrie,"* Univ. Illinois Studies Lang. & Lit., XVI (1933), pp. 85-90.

11 Pico della Mirandola in a letter to Ermolao Barbaro, dated Florence, 1485, quoted by John Addington Symonds, *The Renaissance in Italy*, II, *The Revival of Learning* (London, John Murray, 1929), 242.

12 *Wilson's Arte of Rhetorique, 1560*, ed. by G. H. Mair (Oxford, Clarendon, 1909), p. 195.

13 "Defence of Poetry," *Elizabethan Critical Essays*, ed. by G. G. Smith, I (Oxford, 1904), p. 65.

14 *The Works of Francis Bacon*, ed. by J. Spedding, R. L. Ellis, D. D. Heath, VI (London, 1878), pp. 696, 698-99.

15 Hoole, *op. cit.*, p. 162; the italics are ours.

16 *Fabvlarum Ovidii Interpretatio, Ethica, Physica, et Historica, tradita in Academia Regiomontana a Georgio Sabino, et in vnum collecta et edita studio et industria T. T.* (Cambridge, Thomas Thomas, 1584), pp. 85-86. See, e.g.: "Sed nos omissis labyrinthis disputationum de Necessitate, dicimus fatum significare prouidentiam diuinam, quae bona conseruat, gubernat, et adiuuat, mala reprimit ac tollit: et alio modo agit in motibus coeli et elementorum, alio modo in hominum gubernatione, quibus non eripitur libertas voluntatis, sed iusto iudicio adiuuat Deus iustos, et deserit sontes, vt eos puniat."

17 *Library*, Fourth Series, XV, 466, where it is described as "Publij Ovidij Nasonis Operum To: ij cum notis vario*rum* Franc. 1601." See *infra*, Appendix II.

18 *Pub. Ovidii Nasonis Svlmonensis Poetae Operum* (Frankfort, 1601), I, 188-89; II, "Tristia," 99, col. a, F; III, 46, col. a, A, and 161, col. a, E.

19 The titles for both editions are *Ambrosii Calepini Dictionarium*.

20 Giovanni Boccaccio, *Genealogiae Deorum*, I, v: "Seneca uero has in epistolis ad Lucillum fata uocat: dato Cleantis dictum dicens. Ducunt uolentem fata: nolentem trahunt. Circa quod non solum eorum describit officium: eas s. sorores omnia ducere: sed etiam trahere: non aliter quam si de necessitate contingant omnia: quod longe apertius sentire uidetur in tragoediis Seneca poeta tragicus: et in ea potissime cui titulus est Œdipus: ubi dicit. Fatis agimur credite fatis. non sollicitae possunt curae mutare

rati stamina fusi. Quicquid patimur mortale genus. Quicquid facimus uenit ex alto. Seruatque sua decreta colus Lachesis dura reuoluta manu." For the passage in Seneca, see *infra.*

21 ". . . haec illis condicio; et nominum eiusdem proprietate contingit, ut sit Atropos praeteriti temporis fatum, quod ne deus quidem faciet infectum; futuri temporis Lachesis a fine cognominata, quod etiam illis, quae futura sunt, finem suum deus dederit. Clotho praesentis temporis habet curam, ut ipsis actionibus suadeat, ne cura sollers rebus omnibus desit. deum vero ire per omnes." *Liber de Mundo*, XXXVIII. *Apulei Opera Quae Supersunt*, ed. P. Thomas, III (*Bibl. Script. Graec. et Rom. Tevbneriana*, 1921), 174.

22 I.e., according to the 1572 Venice edition, which is typical.

23 Comes lists some fourteen authors or works, citing some twenty-two passages; Cartari lists some eleven authors, citing some fourteen passages. The editions used for these figures and for the preceding figures from Gyraldus are as follows: *Natalis Comitis Mythologiae sive Explicationis Fabvlarum Libri Decem* (Patavii, 1637); *Les Images des Dievx des Anciens . . . par le Seigneur Vincent Cartari . . . traduit . . . et augmentées par Antoine Dv Verdier* (Lyon, 1581); and the *De Deis Gentium* (Basileae, 1560).

24 The discussion here is descriptive and not meant to indicate borrowing or inter-borrowing.

25 The 1587 Venice edition, e.g., reads ". . . teneua una, Cloto, la piu giouane, la conocchia, e tiraua il filo; l'altra Lachesis di maggior età l'auolgeua intorno al fuso, e la terza Atrapo già vecchio lo tagliauo."

26 I.e., "Clotho, colum baiulat: Lachesis, net: Atropos, filum frangit," see *supra*, p. 349.

27 *Op. cit.*, IV. 2. 47.

28 See also *infra*, pp. 358-59, and the passage in Comes on the Fates and Pan.

29 Compare Gyraldus; after the conventional etymology of *Clotho*, the passage runs ". . . Lachesis uerò sors nuncupatur, Atropos quoque sine ordine dicitur: hoc uidelicet sentire uolentes, quòd prima, sit natiuitatis euocatio: secunda, uitæ sors, quemadmodum quis uiuere possit: tertia, mortis conditio, quæ sine lege uenit."

30 The authority for Martia is phrased by Gyraldus as follows: "Marcil. Ficinus in Platonem, et Socinus Bentius medicus et Philosophus, in eo qui est de Felicitate. . . ."

31 The pertinent passage in the *Hieroglyphica* occurs in "Liber XXXII," "Quadrifrons." Giovanni Pierio Valeriano, *Hieroglyphica* (Basle, 1556), p. 299.

32 Lib. V, vi.

33 Under "Jupiter," (Lib. II, i) some typical passages are as follows. "Qui Iouem aethera; aut aliquid praedictorum esse crediderunt, illum Parcis inferioriam putarunt. at Hesiodus in Operibus et diebus cum de tranquilitatem maris loqueretur, Iouem fatum esse arbitratus in haec verba prorupit.

. . ." "Nam quidam ipsum esse Iouem existimarunt . . . fatum scilicet ventis elementis imperans. At omnium fatum esse sensit Homerus in lib. 1 Odyss." "Ea de causa efficitur vt Euripides in Supplicibus vanam esse sapientiam mortalium existimerit, cum omnia humana fato et ineuitabili quadam necessitate traherentur, quam vim Iouem in his appellauit. . . ."

34 *Infra*, pp. 375, 366-67.

35 *Supra*, pp. 344-45.

36 *Infra*, pp. 364-65, n. 39.

37 Lib. xlviii, "De Colv et Fvso": "Mors."

38 See Lib. xliv, "De Stella": "Fatum."

39 This quotation is preceded by a typical discussion connected with the lines quoted above from Juvenal: "Dictae sunt Parcae stamina de colo nascentibus detrahere, quibus vniversa vitae fortuna contineretur: quia pro primo aeris temperamento, quem nascentes infantes imbiberunt, crediti sunt a philosophis et mores, et fortunam, et actiones, et vim etiam vitalem habere et haurire: quarum omnium rerum euentum ac finem Fatum siue Parcam appellarunt illud ita esse testatus est Iuuenalis Satyra septima in his:

> *—distat enim, quae*
> *Sydera te excipiant modo primos incipientem*
> *Edere vagitus, et adhuc a matre rubentem."*

The discussion after the other passage quoted above from Juvenal continues with the general topic: "Illud sane non negauerim plurimum posse in nobis aeris vim, quo nascentes primum imbuimur, tum ad vires corporis, ad temperamentum, et ad fortunas benignitatem, quam imprimit in nobis occulta vis siderum, tum etiam ad morum bonitatem, et animi magnitudinem: quod etiam expressimus ita in nostro libello de Venationibus:

> *Scilicet et multum refert ad corpora, vires,*
> *Et mores, genitale solum quae sydera spectant."*

40 The passage in Cicero occurs in the context of Carneades' argument against Stoic theology, specifically when he was concerned with demonstrating the impossibility of maintaining a hard and fast line between the divine and the human: e.g., if Jupiter and Neptune are gods, so is their father Saturn and his father Caelus, and his parents, Aether and Day, and all their brothers and sisters "whom the ancient genealogists name Love, Guile, Fear, Toil, Envy, Fate, Old Age, Death, Darkness, Misery, Lamentation, Favour, Fraud, Obstinacy, the Parcae, the Daughters of Hesperus, the Dreams: all of these are fabled to be the children of Erebus and Night." *De Divinatio*, Loeb Classics (1938), p. 329. Cf. *infra*, p. 375.

41 *Op. cit.*, VI, 695.

42 The line in Latin—probably much more familiar to school-boys and users of Comes in general than the Greek cited in the *Mythologiae*—runs as follows:

> "ille deinde
> Cuncta feret, quae Fata dabunt, Parcaeque seuera
> Nascentis neuere parens quando edidit ipsum."

43 *Infra*, p. 371.

44 The pertinent passage in Fraunce runs as follows: "He that is but of a meane conceit, hath a pleasant and plausible narration, concerning the famous exploites of renowned Heroes, set forth in most sweete and delightsome verse, to feede his rurall humor. They, whose capacitie is such, as that they can reach somewhat further then the external discourse and history, shall finde a morall sence included therein, extolling vertue, condemning vice, euery way profitable for the institution of a practicall and commonwealth man. The rest, that are better borne and of a more noble spirit, shall meete with hidden mysteries of naturall, astrologicall, or diuine and metaphysicall philosophie, to entertaine their heauenly speculation." Abraham Fraunce, *The Third part of the Countesse of Pembrokes Yueychurch: Entituled, Amintas Dale* (London, Thomas Woodcocke, 1592), sig. B2r.

45 Herford and Simpson, I, 253-54, 266.

46 See *Merchant of Venice*, 2.2. 62-9; *2 Henry IV*, 2.4. 212-3; *Midsummer's Night's Dream*, 5.1. 348.

47 See the appropriate entry, e.g., in H. G. Lotspeich, *Classical Mythology in the Poetry of Edmund Spenser*, Princeton Studies in English, No. 9 (1932). Lotspeich does not quote the passage from Comes, *supra*, p. 356; in the editions we have used of the *Genealogiae Deorum*, the interpretation of Clotho's name is ascribed to Fulgentius, *supra*, pp. 357-58.

48 *Supra*, p. 349, and n. 20.

49 The concluding remarks of the epistle (CVII) counsel addressing Jupiter as Cleanthes did. Seneca translates the Greek of Cleanthes, expressing unfaltering obedience to the ruler of the heights of heaven, and apparently adds the last line. Thus fate will always find us ready and thus the great soul is distinguished from the puny one:

> *Duc me parens, celsique dominator poli*
> *Quocumque placuit. nulla parendi mora est.*
> *Assum impiger. fac nolle. comitabor gemens:*
> *Malusque patior, quod pati licuit bono*
> *Ducunt volentem fata, nolentem trahunt.*

Sic vivamus, sic loquamur, paratos nos inveniat atque impigros fatum. His est magnus animus, qui se Deo tradidit: at contra ille pusillus ac degener, qui obluctatur, et de ordine mundi male existimat, et emendare mavult deos quam se." *L. Annaei Senecae Operum.* II (Amsteldami, D. Elsevirium, 1672), 528-9.

50 Lotspeich, *loc. cit.*

51 *Cataline*, 5. 600.

52 *1 Tamburlaine the Great*, 1.2 174.

53 *Supra*, p. 360.

54 Aeschylus' *Prometheus*, e.g., is cited by C. G. Osgood, *The Classical Mythology of Milton's English Poems*, Yale Studies in English, No. 8 (1900), p. 34.

55 See *The Masque of Beautie*, ll. 282-5:
    When Loue, at first, did mooue
    From out of *Chaos,* brightned
    So was the world, and lightned,
    As now!
The gloss runs as follows: "So is he faind by *Orpheus,* to haue appear'd
first of all the *Gods:* awakened by *Clotho:* and is therefore call'd *Phanes,*
both by him, and *Lactantius."* The "awakened by Clotho" is, as has been
pointed out, a mythological commonplace; the remainder of the gloss is
very close to the words of Gyraldus: "Phanes etiam dictus est Amor, quòd
ex Chao primus apparuerit, quod Orph. et Lactantius aiunt."
56 *An Entertainment,* 36-41; *Lovers Made Men,* 88-104.
57 For the following comparison, cf. *supra,* pp. 369-71.
58 Tr. by Paul Shorey, *op. cit.,* II, 505, 517 (617D, 620E).

### APPENDIX II

1 See, e.g., Harding, *Milton and the Renaissance Ovid, passim;* and *supra,*
pp. 25-6.
2 *Ovid's Metamorphoses Englished Mythologiz'd and Represented in figures*
*by G. S.* (Oxford, John Lichfield, 1632); the Regius-Micyllus quotations
are drawn from *Pub. Ovidii Nasonis Svlmonensis Poetae Operum,* III
(Francofurti, Typis Wechelianis apud Claudium Marnium et haeredes
Joannis Aubrii, 1601). Pagination from the commentary is given only
when the pertinent passage might not be found easily by reference to the
comparable material in Sandys.
3 The Lactantius commentary is included, most conveniently, in the Frankfort, 1601, edition. Sandys' Comments are italicized; we use italics for
convenience in reference.
4 The italics are ours; for the reason, see the summarizing paragraph below.
5 This generalization holds true also for any relationship between Sandy's
account and entries in Comes under "Jason" (VI, viii, p. 316) and
"Boreas" (VIII, ii, p. 453). Under this last entry, e.g., one might find
the names and information about the sons of Boreas. The wealth of detail
in a portion of this last passage, is typical: "Fabulantur Chionem praeterea
et Zetem et Calaim natos fuisse ex Orithyia, qui una cum ceteris Argonautis in Colchos nauigarunt, de quibus ita meminit Apollonius lib. 1.
. . . Suscepit Boreas praeterea ex Orithyia Cleopatram, quae postea Phineo
nupta Cramben et Orythum et Hemum illi peperit, vel, vt alii maluerint
Thyrum et Maryandinum, quam Arplicem, at non Cleopatram vocarunt. . . ."

### APPENDIX III

1 Charles William Lemmi, *The Classic Deities in Bacon* (Baltimore, 1933),
*passim;* see also *supra,* pp. 25-6.
2 The parallel passages concerning Minos, in the next group of illustrative
examples might be included here. "Minos," however, is immediately followed by "Minotaurus," and the two entries might well be considered, for
all practical purposes, as one "history."

# INDEX

Thammuz and Hammon, 237-38

——, *Paradise Lost,* composition of, 227; problem of reference works in, 24

——, proper-names in:

Ades, and Orcus, compared with C. Stephanus, 228-29

Adonis, compared with Calepine and C. and R. Stephanus, 229-30; suggested sources of, 229

Aetna, compared with Calepine and C. Stephanus, 289-90; suggested source, 289

Alcairo, another name for Memphis, 288

Ammon, compared with C. and R. Stephanus, 236-37

Arimaspian, compared with C. and R. Stephanus, 239-40

Arnon, compared with C. Stephanus, 293; suggested sources, 293

Aroer, compared with C. Stephanus, 293-94; suggested location of, 294

Ashdod, compared with C. Stephanus, 288

Asphaltus, compared with C. Stephanus, 294-95; suggested source, 294-95

Astarte, compared with Calepine and C. Stephanus, 240

Azotus, compared with C. Stephanus, 288, 297-98

Babel, building of, compared with C. Stephanus, 267

Bellerophon, compared with Calepine, Comes, and C. Stephanus, 240-41

Bosporus, compared with C. Stephanus, 298; suggested sources, 298

Briareos, compared with Calepine, Cooper, and C. and R. Stephanus, 242-43; confusion of Giants and Titans in, 242-43; with Typhon, note on in Cambridge edition, 242

Cadmus, and Hermione, compared with C. Stephanus, 243-44

Carmel, compared with C. Stephanus, 298-99; suggested source, 298

Chersonese, compared with C. Stephanus, 300-301; suggested sources, 300

Cleombrotus, compared with Calepine, Cooper, and C. and R. Stephanus, 246; suggested sources, 246

Crete, compared with C. Stephanus, 305

Cusco, compared with C. Stephanus, 306; possibly based on Purchas, 306

Deucalion, compared with Comes and C. Stephanus, 248-49; suggested sources, 248

Dodona, compared with C. Stephanus, 307-308; suggested source, 308

Empedocles, compared with C. Stephanus, 250; possible sources, 250

Erebus, compared with C. Stephanus, 250-51; with Nox and Chaos, suggested sources, 251

Gehenna, compared with Cooper and C. Stephanus, 317-18; suggested sources, 317

Graces and Hours, association of, 258-59

Hermon, compared with C. Stephanus, 320

Hesebon, compared with C. Stephanus, 320; Scriptural basis of, 320

Horoniam, compared with C. Stephanus, 320

Iapetus, identified with Japhet, son of Noah, 260; parentage of, compared with C. Stephanus, 259-60

Ida, Mount, in Crete, allusion to, 321; Trojan, association with judgment of Paris, 321; compared with C. Stephanus, 321

Imaus, compared with C. Stephanus, 321-22; debt to Ortelius, 322

Japhet, and Javan, compared with C. Stephanus, 259-60; suggested sources of, 260

Javan, suggested sources of, 260

Jordan, compared with Calepine and C. Stephanus, 323; suggested sources of, 323

Joshua, compared with C. Stephanus, 260-61; suggested sources of, 260-61

Lethe, compared with Comes and C. Stephanus, 336

Melibaean, compared with C. Stephanus, 337

Memphis, compared with C. Stephanus, 324-25

Mexico, compared with C. Stephanus, 326; suggested source, 326

Mulciber, compared with C. Stephanus, 284; suggested source, 284

Nimrod, based on Genesis, 264-65; compared with C. Stephanus, 265-68; · example of Milton's synthesis